Additional Acclaim for *Marianne in Chains*

"A searching inquiry . . . Provocative—and timely."
—*Kirkus Reviews* (starred)

"Robert Gildea's remarkable book is based on massive archival research and probing interviews. The result is the most humane and nuanced account of wartime France to date. If there is one book on Vichy that people should read then this is surely it."
—Michael Burleigh, author of *The Third Reich*

"A daring and completely original account of the German occupation of France between 1940 and 1945 . . . Full of the telling anecdote, written at a fast pace, *Marianne in Chains* is both readable and scholarly, provocative and convincing."
—Ruth Harris, author of *Lourdes: Body and Spirit in the Secular Age*

"The strength of this book lies in the author's appreciation of the complexity of people's behavior under pressure. Delving behind postwar stereotypes, Gildea reveals the myriad paths ordinary French citizens took to survive the occupation."
—*Publishers Weekly*

"As engaging as it is innovative."
—*Booklist*

"*Marianne in Chains* has a powerful immediacy and a powerful sense of place. Robert Gildea's readers come to grips with the awful choices facing the people of the Loire Valley, especially those in authority, after 1940."
—Robert O. Paxton, author of *Vichy France: Old Guard and New Order*

MARIANNE IN CHAINS

*Daily Life in the Heart of France
During the German Occupation*

ROBERT GILDEA

PICADOR
A METROPOLITAN BOOK
HENRY HOLT AND COMPANY
NEW YORK

www.picadorusa.com

Picador® is a U.S. registered trademark and is used by Henry Holt and Company under license from Pan Books Limited.

For information on Picador Reading Group Guides, as well as ordering, please contact the Trade Marketing department at St. Martin's Press.
Phone: 1-800-221-7945 extension 763
Fax: 212-677-7456
E-mail: trademarketing@stmartins.com

Design by Paula Russell Szafranski

Library of Congress Cataloging-in-Publication Data

    Marianne in chains : daily life in the heart of France during the German occupation / Robert Gildea.
      p. cm.
   ISBN 0-312-42359-4
   EAN 978-0312-42359-9
   1. World War, 1939–1945—France. 2. France—History—German occupation, 1940–1945.

D802.F8M2616 2003
940.53'44—dc21   2002045503

First published in the UK by Macmillan, London

First published in the United States by Metropolitan Books, an imprint of Henry Holt and Company

First Picador Edition: June 2004

D 10 9 8 7 6 5 4 3

To the memory of
Richard Cobb
(1917–1996)

CONTENTS

CONTENTS

MAPS

Occupied France, 1940-45

Legend:

- — - — International border
- ——— Demarcation line
- ——— Military regions Ⓐ Ⓑ Ⓒ
- Study area
- Area annexed by Germany
- Governed from Brussels
- Occupied by Italy

200 kilometres

LUXEMBOURG

Metz

Strasbourg

GERMANY

ont

SWITZERLAND

Chambery

Grenoble

ITALY

Digne

Nice

Aix-en-Provence

CORSICA

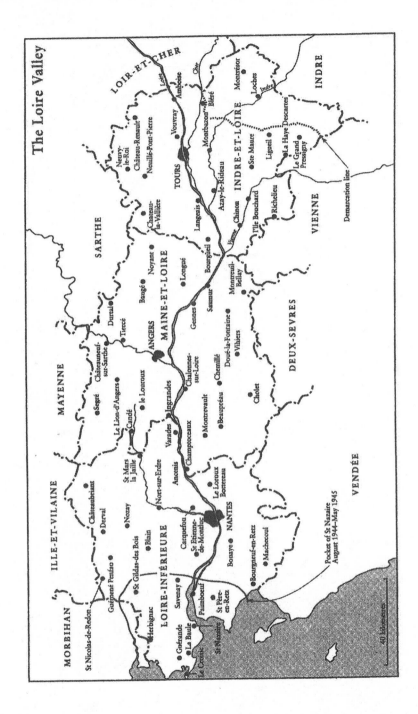

The Loire Valley

MORBIHAN
ILLE-ET-VILAINE
MAYENNE
SARTHE
LOIR-ET-CHER
INDRE
INDRE-ET-LOIRE
VIENNE
DEUX-SÈVRES
MAINE-ET-LOIRE
LOIRE-INFÉRIEURE
VENDÉE

St Nicolas-de-Redon
Guémené-Penfao
Châteaubriant
Derval
Nozay
St Gildas-des-Bois
Blain
Herbignac
Savenay
Carquefou
St Étienne-de-Montluc
Guérande
La Baule
Le Croisic
St Nazaire
Paimboeuf
St Père-en-Retz
Bouaye
Bourgneuf-en-Retz
Machecoul
NANTES
Le Loroux Bottereau
Nort-sur-Erdre
Ancenis
St Mars la Jaille
Candé
Le Lion-d'Angers
Segré
Châteauneuf-sur-Sarthe
Tiercé
Durtal
ANGERS
Le Louroux
Varades
Ingrandes
Champtoceaux
Montrevault
Beaupréau
Chemillé
Chalonnes-sur-Loire
Cholet
Vihiers
Doué-la-Fontaine
Gennes
Saumur
Montreuil-Bellay
Bourgueil
Longué
Noyant
Baugé
Château-la-Vallière
Langeais
TOURS
Neuillé-Pont-Pierre
Château-Renault
Neuvy-le-Roi
Vouvray
Amboise
Blére
Cher
Montbazon
Azay-le-Rideau
Chinon
l'Île Bouchard
Richelieu
Le Bouchard
Ste Maur
Ligueil
Loches
Montrésor
Indre
La Haye Descartes
Le Grand Pressigny
Demarcation line

Pocket of St Nazaire
August 1944–May 1945

Loir
Cher
Indre
Vienne

40 kilometres

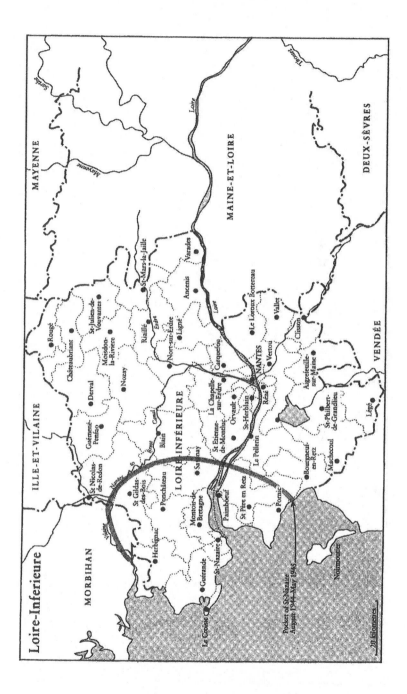

Loire-Inférieure

MAYENNE

SARthe

Sarthe

Mayenne

Loire

MAINE-ET-LOIRE

DEUX-SÈVRES

Thouet

ILLE-ET-VILAINE

Rougé

Châteaubriant

St-Julien-de-Vouvantes

Moisdon-la-Rivière

Derval

Noozay

Guémené-Penfao

Canal

Blain

Brut

St Nicolas-de-Redon

Vilaine

St Gildas-des-Bois

Ponchâteau

Herbignac

Montoir-de-Bretagne

Savenay

Mère

St-Nazaire

Guérande

Le Croisic

MORBIHAN

LOIRE-INFÉRIEURE

St-Mars-la-Jaille

Varades

Ancenis

Erdre

Naillé

Nort-sur-Erdre

Ligné

Loire

Carquefou

La Chapelle-sur-Erdre

Orvault

St-Herblain

St-Étienne-de-Montluc

Rézé

NANTES

Le Pellerin

Paimbœuf

St Père en Retz

Bourgneuf-en-Retz

Machecoul

Pornic

Le Loroux Bottereau

Vallet

Clisson

Verrou

Aigrefeuille-sur-Maine

St-Philibert-de-Grandlieu

Legé

VENDÉE

Noirmoutier

Pocket of St-Nazaire
August 1944–May 1945

20 Kilometres

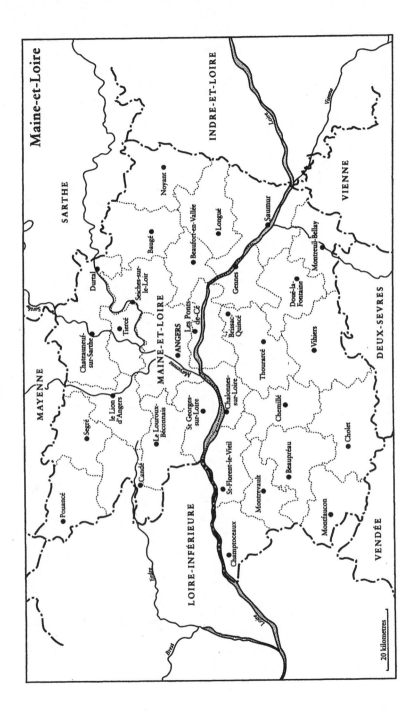

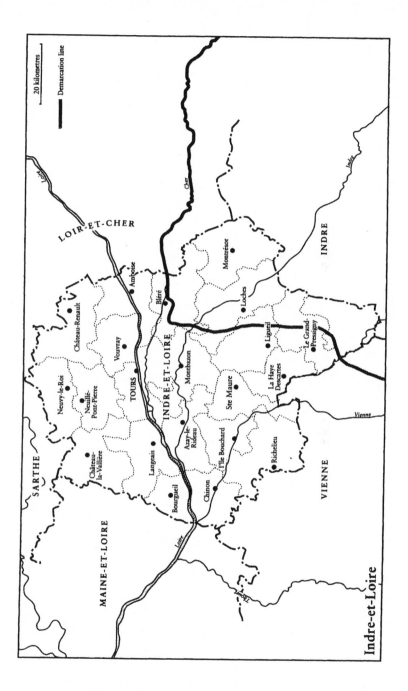

Indre-et-Loire

MARIANNE
IN CHAINS

Introduction

The rules of the Academy of Tours forbid the audience from asking the speaker questions but not, it appears, from causing a riot. In 1997 I was invited to present a paper to this society of local notables and antiquaries by its president, a Jewish doctor, professor, writer, and former member of the Resistance. Having undertaken a certain amount of oral history in the region, I entitled my talk "What the French of the Loire Valley Think in 1997 of the German Occupation." The gist of the presentation was that under the four years of Occupation more complex relationships than those of brutal oppression had developed between Germans and French and that far from always going hungry the French had managed to keep themselves fed and even to enjoy themselves. The president, who had recently suffered a bereavement, was unable to attend and the secretary, chairing the meeting in his place, had difficulty keeping order. At one point a man got to his feet and shouted, "What about the 230 people who were shot in Tours during the Occupation?" At another moment, when I cited a country dweller who said that her family had never wanted for food under the

Occupation, there was a wave of murmuring and shaking of white heads in the room. Although two teachers whom I knew approached me after the talk to endorse what I had said, I was left with the feeling that I had defaced the tablets of stone on which the official history of the Occupation and Resistance had been written.

The officers of the academy, now rejoined by the president, wined and dined me in style and the secretary invited me to submit my paper for publication in the proceedings of the academy. Having read it, however, he returned it to me saying that "while each of the examples rings true, your audience, myself included, failed to find in it the precise reflection of our collective memory of the German Occupation." The Occupation, during which he had taught at the lycée of Orléans, he said, was characterized by four things: cold, hunger, the absence of freedom, and, above all, fear. "At any moment," he explained, "you could be arrested for a subversive remark, a contravention of the curfew, a violation of German legislation, a little transaction on the black market, or for listening to the BBC."[1] After criticizing me for giving too much space to the "small minority of petty Angevin and Vendean nobles" from farther down the Loire who clearly sympathized with the Vichy regime, he invited me to return to Tours to interview a Freemason who represented the more progressive opinions of Touraine.

The following summer I duly returned to Tours to record the interview, fully prepared to revise many of my previous opinions. What I heard, however, was the exact opposite of what I had expected. While the interviewee's father had indeed been a Freemason, he himself had steered well clear of an organization that was anathema to the Vichy regime, membership of which would have jeopardized his career. As a middle-ranking official in the prefecture of Tours, he had also avoided the Resistance. Since he was in charge of the local distribution of industrial products, he was obliged to negotiate with the Germans and initially, he said, tried to resist their demands. But the Germans told him bluntly, "If that is how you feel, Monsieur, you will be in Germany tomorrow morning." At the trial of the secretary-general of the prefecture of Bordeaux, Maurice Papon, earlier that year, he added, it had been suggested that it was possible for French officials to resist the Gestapo. "That is simply not true," he asserted. To reinforce his point he told the story of two fellow officials and a friend who had annoyed the Germans or become involved in resistance and whose imprudence or stupidity had been rewarded by arrest, deportation, or death. As for the Jews, he said, actually shedding a tear, "The Gestapo were arresting everybody. And to think that it happened in our country. We helped them to escape when we could, but we couldn't always."[2]

To the lunch that followed the interview were invited the president and secretary of the Academy of Tours and the secretary's wife. Each took a radically different view of the Occupation. The secretary, who had returned my paper to me with the clear signal that it would not be published in the proceedings of the academy, reiterated his theme of the extreme severity of the Occupation. He cited a French school inspector who told him not to assign his pupils Latin texts from Tacitus, lest the Germans view them as encouraging resistance. His wife, Camille, sweetly contradicted him, suggesting that the Occupation posed no difficulties for those who went about their ordinary business. The prefecture official, in a jovial mood, now boasted of what he called "the first act defying the enemy." He recalled that, returning from the army after the defeat in 1940 to his home village, where, on an isolated road a pine-log barrier signaled the demarcation line between the zone occupied by the Germans and the unoccupied zone, he amused the locals by painting the tail of the grocer's dog red, white, and blue and sending the dog under the barrier into the occupied zone. Meanwhile, on his arrival at the lunch, the Jewish resister had quietly slipped me a clipping from a local paper from the time of the Papon trial entitled "Was There a Papon in Touraine?" The article argued that the prefectoral corps in Touraine, which included our host, had been "good servants of Vichy."[3] At lunch the resister questioned the patriotism of most French people under the Occupation, citing French officers in his POW camp in 1940 who, with German officers, had toasted the death of "the whore" (*la gueuse*), as the Republic was known to its enemies. After we left the house, he referred to the long lines of French people eager to see the anti-Semitic Nazi propaganda film *The Jew Süss*. He himself had forfeited both his professorship at the hospital and his medical practice as a result of Vichy's anti-Semitic legislation, been threatened with arrest after a German soldier was shot in Tours in 1942, and had fled for his life to the unoccupied zone, where he joined the Resistance.

The most striking thing about these incidents is that in ordinary homes more than fifty years after the event, the German Occupation is still a subject of heated debate, and a debate that is far from being resolved. This is explained in part by the shame and guilt felt by French people about the Occupation. Shame that a country that prided itself on its greatness was brought to its knees after a six-week war and was occupied, bullied, and plundered by the hereditary enemy. Guilt that the country that defined itself from the French Revolution on as the cradle of liberty should hand over power to an authoritarian regime that was a puppet of the Third Reich, try to suppress all dissent, and hand over to the Germans for deportation to Auschwitz Jews who had sought asylum in France as well as Jews who were fully French citizens. The explanation of the debate, however, also lies in the fact that the French have never faced up to their wartime past in any sustained and systematic way.[4] Unlike in South Africa, no Truth and Reconciliation Commission was ever set up to allow the French openly to express their anger and remorse. After the first wave of purges for collaboration, which were rapidly wound up in the interest of national unity, several decades passed before the recent spate of trials for crimes against humanity—of the Gestapo chief in Lyon, Klaus Barbie (1987), of the Militia leader Paul Touvier (1994), and of the secretary-general of the prefecture of the Gironde, Maurice Papon (1997–98)—and arguably the waters of perception are now even muddier than before. Obstacles in the way of establishing an agreed version of the truth are not only intellectual. Much is at stake ideologically and politically in the interpretation of the Occupation period, and rival views are propagated and defended by interest groups that are constantly vigilant lest their orthodoxy be challenged.

The conversation at Tours suggested that there were three competing interpretations of what conditions were like in France under the German Occupation. The first was that resistance was the highest form of honorable conduct. For want of something grander, small gestures of resistance, such as sending a dog with a tricolor tail into the occupied zone, were magnified to assert the patriotic credentials of the "good French," but it is interesting that the president of the academy, who had resisted most, said least about it. The second view, on which the president concentrated, was that the Occupation was characterized less by the oppression of the Germans than by the cowardice and treachery of the French. Many, far from resisting, welcomed the demise of the Republic to further their ambitions and were happy to persecute Freemasons, communists, and Jews, whom Vichy blamed for France's decline and defeat. This was the story of the "bad French" about whom subsequent generations felt such shame and guilt. The third view, that of the official in private and of the secretary in conversation, was that in what amounted to a Nazi dictatorship or SS state it was almost impossible to resist. The best option was to keep one's head down and focus on more important things like finding enough food to eat and fuel to keep warm. There was, to complicate matters, even a fourth view, expressed almost inaudibly by the secretary's wife and plainly contradicting what her husband had said. This was that in some respects the German occupation had been benign, that the Germans had not been vicious toward those who minded their own business, and that some sort of accommodation between French and Germans had been possible. Like the contributions of the Dormouse at the Mad Hatter's tea party, however, this view was dismissed as irrelevant and shelved without discussion.

This local conversation would be of little consequence if it did not echo debates that have long gone on at a national level in France. Despite the argument that Nazi tyranny was so pervasive that all resistance was impossible, it was important for the French to recover a sense of honor and dignity by asserting that after their armies had been defeated they began actively to resist the German Occupation, as civilians, as best as they could. Those who emerged from hiding, returned from German camps, and came to power after the Liberation were in a position to write the history of the "good French" who had resisted and to claim through their virtuous actions the authority to rule France. The account of the Resistance that they elaborated effectively became a religion, with a number of articles of faith. The first was that it began on 18 June 1940 when General de Gaulle, speaking on the BBC, called on the French not to give up the struggle. In this way he became the repository of French legitimacy, coming into his inheritance on 25 August 1944 when he marched down the Champs-Élysées in liberated Paris. The second was that it was a pure and heroic movement, with a long roll call of martyrs who died in the struggle to drive out the occupying forces. The third was that, however diverse the origins and opinions of the participants, the Resistance expressed a common commitment to such eternal French values as the rights of man and a one and indivisible France. The fourth was that, though active resistants were a small minority, the Resistance was approved and supported by the vast mass of the French people, who emerged from the Occupation with their pride intact, since only a handful of traitors had collaborated with the enemy. The fifth article of the credo was that the Resistance, which continued the struggle where the French army had left off, had an indisputable military significance and alongside the Allies contributed significantly to the liberation of France.[5]

The dominance of this story of the "good French," however, was countered by the story of the "bad French" who had not resisted but had collaborated actively with the German occupiers. In his study of Vichy France published in 1972, the American historian Robert Paxton argued that at least until 1943 most French people had supported the Vichy regime, which had declared for a policy of "collaboration" with Germany. He also calculated that those who resisted the Germans had numbered no more than 2 percent of the adult population—or a maximum of 10 percent if one counts those willing to read clandestine material put out by the Resistance.[6] This interpretation was supported by Marcel Ophuls's 1970 film, *The Sorrow and the Pity* (*Le Chagrin et la Pitié*), subtitled *Chronicle of a French Town under the Occupation*, which depicted the French as far from heroic and indeed self-seeking, cowardly, deceitful, and self-deceiving. So emphatically did it challenge the official view of the "good French" that it was not shown on French television for ten years.[7] More recently still, resistance heroes who had enjoyed a virtual cult of personality, such as Jean Moulin, who was tortured to death by Klaus Barbie in 1943, or Raymond and Lucie Aubrac, who worked with him and survived, have had their reputations challenged. It has been suggested, for instance, that Moulin, de Gaulle's emissary to unite the squabbling resistance movements in France, was in fact a Soviet agent, while Raymond Aubrac, who fell into Gestapo hands in 1943 and was then released, had been turned into an agent of Klaus Barbie and betrayed Moulin.[8]

The story of the "bad French" began to bite with the documentation of Vichy France's involvement in the Holocaust by Robert Paxton and Michael Marrus in 1981 and by Serge Klarsfeld in 1983.[9] On 16 July 1992 Jewish organizations marked with maximum publicity the commemoration of the fiftieth anniversary of the roundup of 12,000 Jews by the French police under René Bousquet, working hand in glove with the SS. President Mitterrand attended the ceremony but refused to accept responsibility, on the grounds that the crime had been committed not by the Republic, which had been abolished in 1940, but by the Vichy state. The following year René Bousquet, who was a friend of Mitterrand and thought to be protected from justice by him, was shot dead by a lone gunman. At the roundup commemoration in 1995, the new president of the Republic, Jacques Chirac, called the deportation a "collective offense" for which the French must take responsibility.[10] This admission marked a breakthrough in the French's coming to terms with their past instead of heaping all blame for the past onto a regime that was long gone and had been declared "null and void" by General de Gaulle. Not everyone agreed that the French should be so repentant. The Gaullist politician Philippe Séguin, whose father had died fighting for the Resistance, denounced the "climate of permanent collective expiation and self-flagellation of which a certain number of French people are becoming sick and tired."[11] Some historians, too, pointed out that the current debate had become so "Judeo-centric" that the German Occupation and Vichy had been reduced to a detail of the Holocaust.[12]

The story of the "good French" was increasingly tarnished but it was far too uncomfortable for French national identity simply to replace it with a story of the "bad French." One way out was to make a distinction between the Vichy regime, which was admittedly bad, and the French people, who were basically good. Vichy may have deported Jews, it was said, but many more were saved than perished because ordinary French people fed, hid, or otherwise helped them in their distress. Former president Valéry Giscard d'Estaing, whose family had weathered the Occupation in the Auvergne, argued at the time of the Papon trial that the French people may have welcomed the new head of state, Marshal Pétain, in 1940 but soon parted company with his government. Moreover, he asserted, "between 90 and 95 percent of French people did not even speak to a German during the five years of the Occupation. I am telling the French youth of today so that they do not have cause to be ashamed of their grandparents."[13] The theme of a major international conference organized by Jean-Pierre Azéma and François Bédarida in Paris in 1990 was *Vichy and the French*, suggesting that the two were now considered distinct entities.[14] From the tension between the "good French" and the "bad French" emerged the "poor French," who were portrayed, like the Jews, as victims and martyrs who had suffered intolerably under the Occupation from cold, hunger, and fear. Dominique Veillon's work on the survival of the French argues that, "for the majority of the population, daily life was reduced to the obsession with food and cold. In the towns the average French person spent a good deal of his time looking for something to put in the pot."[15] The term *les années noires*—the dark years—first popularized in the title of a diary published in 1947, was resurrected in the 1990s by Azéma, Bédarida, and Henry Rousso and also adopted by Julian Jackson to characterize his 2001 survey of Vichy France.[16]

Was it possible, I wondered, to find out what *really* happened in France under the German Occupation? An admirer of Richard Cobb—who after the war revealed to British and French historians alike the richness of France's archives, in this case for the period of the French Revolution—I was convinced that the secrets of life under the Occupation lay in the departmental, municipal, and church archives of provincial France. The archives of the wartime period were closed for several decades after the Liberation but a law of 3 January 1979 liberalized access by laying down a thirty-year rule. Exceptions were made for files "containing information likely to harm private individuals or concerning state security or national defense," which were closed for sixty years, and judicial documents, including purge trials, which were closed for a hundred. Special dispensation might be granted to the bona fide historian, file by file, subject to the consent of the branch of the administration, police, or judiciary that had deposited the files in the archives. Cautious officials, however, concerned less about state security than about the good standing of the administration, may be reluctant to grant access to documentation that might show that administration—of Vichy or otherwise—in a bad light. Over half the files consulted for this study were formally closed, and special dispensation was kindly granted. But some areas were more reluctant than others: in one department the archivist had to negotiate on my behalf with the prefecture for several months before access was permitted to a single classified file relating to the Occupation's short-term, medium-term, and long-term legacies. French archives were supplemented by the archives of the German military administration, some of whose files were captured at Tours, some of which are kept in Paris, but most of which are preserved in the Bundesarchiv-Militärarchiv in Freiburg-im-Breisgau. There was, interestingly, no problem of access to the German archives in Freiburg, perhaps because the German state ceased to exist for some years after the war and its workings were exposed by the Allies. Typically, however, access to a short run of photocopies from the Freiburg archives relating to the assassination of the military governor of Nantes in 1941 and deposited in Nantes by a local historian has been assumed by the mayor of Nantes as if they originated from the municipal administration.

Even once access is granted there is no guarantee that the files have not been weeded to remove compromising documents. In 1946, for instance, the prefect of Maine-et-Loire sent round to his services a circular headed "Destruction of documents concerning racial distinctions between French people," in which he explained that under the law of 9 August 1944, which reestablished republican legality, "all traces of the exceptional legislation passed under the Occupation must be eradicated and all documents relating to Jewish identity must be destroyed." The telltale copy of this circular discovered in the archives of the arrondissement of Cholet was annotated in pencil at the subprefecture: "Do we have any here? If so, destroy them. Notify police captain, captain of gendarmerie, mayors." The police captain of Cholet duly reported a week later that "the police station of Cholet no longer has any files or indexes concerning Israelites who were resident in this district."[17]

Censorship can be exercised informally as well as formally. One local historian, who told me that he had received a number of threatening telephone calls during his publishing career, showed me a document only on condition that I would not publish it. It was a letter written in 1982 by the widow of General Kurt Feldt, who had headed the German military administration in Angers in the latter part of the Occupation, recalling that her husband had been welcome in the château of one of the leading notables of the city and that because of the gas shortage he had regularly given to the man's mother a lift to the city center. The practitioner of this perfect example of "cohabitation" could not be revealed without risk of a lawsuit because the habitual narrative of events would immediately present it as a form of collaboration.

Rich as the administrative records are, one of their shortcomings is that things are seen through the filter of the official mind. Of course, it is possible to gain some impression of private lives and private opinions from reports written by the police or gendarmes, from the interviews undertaken by investigating magistrates, or simply from letters of complaint or denunciation sent in to the administration. More eloquent were the diaries and written recollections I managed to trace, the jewel among which was the unpublished wartime diary of the bishop of Nantes, which the diocesan archivist was initially unwilling to let me see because the events were still too close. Organizations specializing in collecting data from the Occupation period, such as the Comité d'Histoire de la Deuxième Guerre Mondiale, have also amassed an archive of recollections, but these are relatively patchy and may not answer the questions that interest the modern historian.[18] For these reasons about fifty interviews were undertaken between 1996 and 1999 with survivors of the period and some of their close relations.

There is a school of thought that dismisses oral history as unreliable evidence, as the ranting of old men and women.[19] My own experience, however, shows that with the passage of time those who witnessed the Occupation are willing to talk about it candidly, as never before. To find interviewees I had myself interviewed by a local paper under the headline "Angevins, Tell Me about Your Life under the Occupation."[20] The day the article appeared, the phone did not stop ringing. Contacts established in this way quickly led to others and to neighboring departments. Only one individual I approached flatly refused to speak to me. Initially, I went to interviews equipped with a list of questions, but I soon discovered that it was pointless to try to corroborate the details of events that were external to people's lives and that occurred over fifty years ago. It became clear that the best approach was to have the interviewee simply tell the story of his or her experience and then to probe more at specific points. There is no doubt that many who lived through the Occupation are still marked by events that transformed their lives: the death of a friend in an aerial attack, the arrest and execution of a loved one, or even a bungled operation for appendicitis and what seemed like an eternal diet of beans.[21] These events are etched in the memory and often provide the subjects around which interviewees will construct a narrative.

Naturally, an individual's story is never wholly personal but is shaped by the collective memories and accounts that have dominated discussion of the Occupation over the intervening years. Interviewees often adopt a particular discourse, seeking to align their own lives with the model of the Resistance, like the official who sent the tricolor dog into the occupied zone or the former printer who told me that, when the Germans arrived in his town in 1940 and threw cigarettes to the crowd, he solemnly crushed with his foot the one that fell close to him and then spat on it.[22] Others, by contrast, expound a "Pétainist" version of events that is effectively taboo in public discourse but often voiced very forcefully in private by individuals who clearly believe that their view has not been given credence. They will argue, for example, that most French people supported Marshal Pétain as the only alternative to the direct rule of a gauleiter, that the Resistance was composed of "bandits," "terrorists," or communist subversives whose folly provoked German reprisals against innocent civilians, and that the Resistance had no significant role in the liberation of France, which was achieved by Allied armies.

There are occasionally moments in an interview, however, when an account that has been carefully constructed hits an obstacle and something that has been hidden breaks the surface. If the dominant line is that the Vichy regime collaborated with the Germans but ordinary French people bore no responsibility for this, an individual such as our printer might construct a story to show that he never had any dealings with Germans, until he lets slip that Germans did talk to him in his office and that occasionally he drank with them. Sometimes the interviewee rehearses a familiar script while the tape recorder is playing and says what he or she really means after it has stopped. Thus the mayor of a village that narrowly escaped German reprisals in 1944 as a result of resistance activity in the area confided as I was about to leave, "In any case, I am against the Resistance." This moment has been called a "rupture in the narrative" or "boundary crossing," when the "hidden transcript" beneath the rehearsed narrative suddenly begins to play.[23] The interviewer gets a glimpse of an alternative reading of events, such as the more or less amicable "cohabitation" of French and German attitudes to the Resistance.

The interviewer has to listen sympathetically and build enough trust for the interviewee to feel safe delivering an account that may well be difficult to relate. Perhaps the British historian, who is not readily identified with a particular camp, is able to elicit more confidences. The danger arises, however, that the interviewer may become persuaded, even seduced, by a point of view that is deeply felt but by its nature one-sided.[24] Survivors of a massacre in Touraine in 1944 provoked by a resistance attack on a German convoy were reluctant to criticize the Resistance when I met them in 1997 but demonstrated by their tears in the graveyard what they really felt. Returning home, I, too, burst into tears. I had clearly been won over to a viewpoint that was critical of the recklessness of much resistance activity, but I also needed to distance myself and recover objectivity. The next issue was how to write about the experience. Could the account of the survivors be integrated into the overall story as anything other than "opinion," "voice," or "memory"? Should it be weighed differently from the official documentation, which was just as likely to be have been produced from a particular angle and with the object of persuading superiors?

With few exceptions, the interviews undertaken were with ordinary French people who could offer an account of what the German Occupation was like in the small towns and villages of France. Enough had been written about the major politicians and statesmen, the leading resisters and collaborators.[25] My own work concentrates on workers and peasants, manufacturers and landowners, women and children, Catholics and Jews, notables and officials up to the rank of prefect. The fine work of Philippe Burrin has explored how French and Germans found ways of "accommodating" to each other in occupied France but moves in the exalted sphere of high politics, big business, and leading intellectuals rather than in that of ordinary people.[26] Pierre Laborie has investigated the attitudes of ordinary people as "public opinion," using the data thrown up by Vichy's secret mailopening service. It takes the pulse of changing popular views of Vichy but treats the French people as a bloc and opinion as something that can be traced on a graph.[27] My own approach is to locate ordinary people in the communities to which they belonged. This might be a neighborhood, village, town, or *pays*, an area with a distinct geographical or historical identity, usually a small town and its hinterland.[28] What matters about the community is less a given area than the unwritten rules that govern its members and do not apply to outsiders.[29] The perspective of the local community makes it possible to reassess the complex relations between French and Germans, between Vichy and the French, and between the French themselves, not according to some higher code of "good" and "bad" actions that was handed down at the Liberation but according to what the community thought was good or bad for it under the Occupation.

This is a study of ordinary communities and ordinary people in what is sometimes called *la France profonde*. An attempt to study the whole of France would eliminate local color and human interest so my focus is on the Loire Valley, a typical region of occupied France in so far as any region may be deemed typical in the rapidly changing French landscape of these years. Although the Loire and its tributaries provide a unity, what emerges is that even in this limited area the Occupation was experienced very differently: from large seaports with a substantial German presence to isolated hamlets where Germans were rarely seen, from cathedral towns that endorsed the reactionary philosophy of the Vichy regime to villages where stones were thrown at religious processions, and from communist strongholds in railway suburbs to the fiefs of nobles still perfumed by the ancien régime. What the area offers, however, is a cross section of communities in which the challenges of the Occupation can be explored: displacement and absence, work and play, physical and spiritual needs, and concentric circles of conflicting loyalties.

The lightning German offensive of May–June 1940 defeated the French armies, toppled the government, and cut the country in two. The northern two-thirds of the country was placed under German military rule and the so-called Free Zone in the south was governed by a new regime based in the Massif Central spa town of Vichy.[30] Under the armistice concluded between the French and German governments, the occupation of northern France was provisional until the end of the war and Vichy remained formally sovereign in the Occupied Zone as well as in the south. In practice, however, the French administration in the Occupied Zone continued to administer, but virtually out of contact with Vichy. The French civil administration was therefore obliged to do business daily with the German military administration, and soon each mirrored the other at the local, departmental, and regional levels. The Germans were happy to let the French administration continue to administer under a system of indirect rule, so long as it delivered public order and a flow of resources for the needs of the Wehrmacht. They drew a distinction between the western provinces of German-occupied Europe, where effective local government ensured the delivery of order and resources, and the eastern provinces, such as Poland and the Balkans, where the indigenous government scarcely existed and the German military found itself from the start fighting a guerilla war with local populations. For its part, the French administration, isolated from Vichy, found that the confidence of the Germans could even increase its authority over its charges. Moreover, the brutal relationship of occupier and occupied was tempered by the sharing of a common set of military, cultural, and even religious values that made it easier to reach agreement. The German occupation meant in many ways less dictatorship and more negotiation between two (admittedly unequal) bureaucracies to contain discontent and defuse crises before they erupted into open violence.

The presence of the Germans affected ordinary people and communities as well as the military. Their arrival in 1940 was preceded by rumors of atrocities they had committed en route, including rape, robbery, and other violence. Many of these reports, however, were recycled from the Great War, and this time the Germans were keen to make a good impression in order to facilitate Franco-German cooperation.[31] Units marched through French towns and villages, occupied public buildings and hotels, and were sometimes billeted in the private homes of families for weeks or months. French people were taken on by the Germans as cleaners, cooks, and laundry women, relationships of service that frequently led to sex. Vehicles, horses, and foodstuffs were requisitioned, but many businesses were offered contracts to supply the German military, and informal opportunities to trade with Germans on the black market multiplied. The influential image of the French as passive victims of the Occupation has to be set against ample opportunities for profit and pleasure that many were only too ready to take. Some, of course, simply pursued self-interest; but just as administrations tried to define what was legal in terms of private relations between French and Germans, so French communities fixed the bounds of what was morally acceptable and what was not. How morality was defined collectively by the French under the Occupation, as opposed to how it was defined after the Liberation, is an important theme that will be explored.

Relations between the French in the Occupied Zone and the Vichy government are also explored from the viewpoint of the community. Having dissolved parliament and the *conseils généraux*—the French equivalent of county councils—Vichy was in theory more authoritarian than any regime since the First Empire of Napoleon I. It was also seen to be reactionary, taking revenge on the politicians of the Third Republic who were held responsible for France's decline and the defeat of 1940, and abolishing the Republic. Marianne, symbol of the Republic, was henceforth in chains. And yet, isolated in the Free Zone, Vichy was unable to provide much support for the French administration in the Occupied Zone, which therefore became dependent for the cultivation of consent on local notables. These were the most prominent figures in the towns and villages because of their wealth, professions, or family connections; they served as mayors and local councillors—the lowest layer of local administration that could not be dissolved.[32] Some mayors and councillors were purged, on the grounds that they were not reliable rather than for the ideological reason that they belonged to the dominant parties of the Third Republic, the Radical and the Socialist. What mattered for Vichy was "rallying" to the new regime, and plenty of radicals and socialists had voted full powers to Marshal Pétain on 10 July 1940 when parliament convened for the last time in the casino of Vichy. Pierre Laval, who intensified the collaboration between Vichy and the Third Reich when he became head of the government in 1942, realized that the politicians of the Third Republic were also local notables with great influence in their constituencies and were needed to embed the administration more firmly. He thus restored the *conseils généraux* in all but name. Local notables essentially mediated between Vichy, the Germans, and the community, delivering order and resources for the first two but protecting the autonomy and interests of the latter. They had performed such a function since 1940, when many mayors opened the doors of their towns and cities to the advancing Germans for fear that resistance would provoke bombardment and massacre. Such feats of local if not national patriotism wonderfully increased their authority for the course of the Occupation. Whether as the pressure grew they were successful in defending the interests of all members of the city equally is open to question. In the long run, arguably, peasants and workers were better served than Jews.

Another buffer between the French population and the German authorities was the Catholic Church. The Catholic hierarchy was undeniably loyal to Marshal Pétain and was doubtless more assiduous in its concern for absent prisoners of war and conscripted workers than in its concern for persecuted Jews. As an institution, however, it limited the influence of Nazism, and it also played a key role in providing hope for those struck by pain and grief. In the chaotic world of occupied France, it interceded for them with the saints and the Virgin Mary, which for many years seemed a more hopeful source of deliverance than the Allied invasion that never seemed to come.

The French people, of course, suffered terrible hardships under the Occupation, but they were more than traumatized souls lining up for the next loaf of bread or dodging bombs. As a result of defeat and occupation, French society was in a state of shock: normal patterns of life were disrupted, moral certitudes were undermined, raw nerves were exposed. And yet, far from being atomized and cowed, the French formed new relationships, built new networks, and discovered new forms of solidarity to deal with the challenges and crises inflicted by the Occupation. What is most striking about the French under the Occupation is not how heroic or villainous they were but how imaginative, creative, and resourceful they were in pursuit of a better life.

Solidarity did not, in the course of things, mean solidarity with just anybody. One of the most marked consequences of the Occupation was the narrowing of horizons. Frightened by the unfamiliarity and unpredictability of the new order, people fell back on their families, their churches, their trades, their villages, towns, and *pays*. Communities also divided against themselves. Old tensions erupted under stress, and some individuals whose loyalties to Vichy or the Germans were suspect risked becoming the objects of denunciation and persecution. The witch-hunt was a corollary of communities' falling back on themselves. The denunciation of suspects, which was deemed highly unpatriotic after the Liberation, was welcomed under the Occupation as a patriotic gesture.[33]

The moral universe of occupied France was notoriously murky. What was right and what was wrong, what patriotic and what unpatriotic, may have been clear in 1944, but not before. Much of the confusion may be explained by conflicts of loyalty within a succession of concentric circles. Just as individuals were retreating to the village, town, or *pays*, so, ironically, the Vichy regime demanded greater sacrifices for the benefit of a France that had almost ceased to exist. Should a farmer, for instance, hand over his harvest to the Vichy agency to supply urban markets at fixed prices, or should he keep some back to feed his family, his regular clients, whom he would supply at a fair price, or Parisians or Germans, from whom he could make a killing? Was hoarding unpatriotic, or was it patriotic to refuse to supply the Vichy agency on the grounds that it might pass on the stocks to the Germans?

Matters were complicated by the fact that there was not one *patrie*: there were two or three. People might be loyal to Vichy as the established or legitimate government. They might, however, feel loyal to de Gaulle and the Free French in London, later to become the provisional government of the Republic in Algiers, on the grounds that they considered Pétain a usurper and traitor. They might even have a first loyalty to Moscow, because after 1941 the Soviet Union alone resisted Hitler militarily and alone preserved the hope for delivery of Europe. If the object of patriotism was contested, so was the manner of its expression. It could be expressed by "moral force," peacefully, by laying a wreath at a statue of Joan of Arc or coming out onto the streets at a time appointed by the BBC. Rebuilding a patriotic community symbolically was enough for many, but for others it did nothing to loosen the grip of the occupier or stir up insurrection. This minority believed in "physical force" patriotism, including the assassination of members of the army of occupation. Such actions might be considered the height of patriotism by the Communist Party but were decried by the local community in which the assassination took place, some of whose members were executed as a collective punishment because the culprit himself could not be found. Here loyalty and even sacrifice to the ideal of a fighting France was diametrically opposed to loyalty to the interests of a town or city that simply wanted to see out the Occupation with as little grief as possible.

The outbreak of war between Germany and the Soviet Union in June 1941 fundamentally changed the balance of forces and the tempo of the Occupation in France. Not only did it cause communists in France to open a "home front" against the Germans in the hope of provoking a domestic uprising; it also caused the Germans to step up the war against the enemy within—notably communists and Jews—and massively to increase their resources and labor for what was now a Total War. From this moment, the negotiated period of the Occupation may be said to have ended. As armed resistance increased, the Germans no longer trusted the French authorities to deliver the public order and resources they required. Collaboration as a system of indirect rule, involving cooperation between French and Germans authorities, gave way to collaboration as the imposition of terms on the French administration and police and to a shift of influence from the German military to the German secret police. Hostage taking ended but was replaced by systematic terror against communists, the deportation of foreign and many French Jews, and the conscription of French labor for the armaments factories of the Reich.

German repression and the labor draft provoked more resistance, but each new resistance organization was liable to be denounced and discovered, and its members executed or deported. Just as significant was the alienation of local communities whose reserves and manpower were now under attack. Squeezed in between the increasingly greedy and brutal German authorities and the increasingly angry and frightened local populations were French officials and local authorities. They were placed in an impossible predicament: forced to affect loyalty to Vichy and the Germans if they were to keep their jobs but risking rejection by local populations if they failed in their duty of protection. Increasingly they resorted to dissembling and the double game, becoming a less and less reliable link in the chain of command.

At the same time, incessant Allied bombing raids on German installations in France paralyzed the German war economy. Even before the Allied landings of June 1944, the German military machine had virtually ground to a halt. The fear of a resistance dominated by the communists was a powerful incentive to prevent revolution as the Germans left, ensure the continuity of the French state, and guarantee, too, that the Liberation was less a power struggle between Gaullists and Vichy than an orderly transfer of power between Vichy officials and the officials-in-waiting of the new Republic. The doctrine of republican legitimacy required that all those who had voted full powers to Marshal Pétain or been appointed by him should be removed. Loyalty to one's town or *pays* was no longer sufficient in 1944, and some indication had to be given of sincere commitment to the Resistance and the general over the water. Against this, however, the need for efficacy and continuity in government meant that, especially at the local level, notables were carried over and wielded their influence much as before. In this area, as in others, the Liberation was a moment of dashed hopes and unfulfilled dreams.

At this point we return from our search for the Occupation in the archives to the memories of the Occupation that were being constructed even as the Liberation took place. As soon as he returned to Paris, General de Gaulle brought down the tablets of the Resistance for the admiration of the crowd. Over the next few decades, locally as well as nationally, the story of the heroic resistance of the French people was rehearsed and commemorated. The "bad French" were marginalized and the "poor French" were recast as extras supporting the "good French." Discordant voices wishing to tell other stories were drowned out. And yet those other voices continued to make themselves heard, in their own small theaters rather than on the national stage, in public with their own shrines and monuments or in private among like-minded disciples and anyone who might care to listen. The final part of this book attempts to give space to this multiplicity of accounts, not only out of a sense of historical fairness but because these stories, as much as the records of the archives, offer new clues and new insights to the historian in search of occupied France.

1

Encounter

On 18 June 1940, as the recently formed government of Marshal Pétain sued for an armistice, General de Gaulle, broadcasting on the BBC, famously told the French people that though the battle of France was lost, the war—a world war—was not over: "Crushed by superior mechanical force today, we can conquer in the future by virtue of a superior mechanical force. There lies the destiny of the world. . . . Whatever happens, the flame of French resistance must not be extinguished and will not be extinguished."[1] On that fine Tuesday the French were unlikely to be tuning in to the BBC or even to be paying much heed to de Gaulle's message if they happened to hear it. The German army had swept all before it in a lightning campaign since 5 June. The government abandoned Paris on 10 June and declared it an "open city" that would not be defended against the oncoming Germans, who entered it on the fourteenth. The roads were clogged by a jumble of retreating soldiers and civilians fleeing for fear of atrocities the Germans might commit, as they had on previous invasions in 1870 and 1914. The prefect of Loire-Inférieure reported a "veritable wave of refugees" driven before the German armies, confident that if they could cross the Loire they would somehow be safe.[2] By the middle of June there were over 250,000 refugees in his department—Belgians, followed by inhabitants of the Nord/Pas-de-Calais, the Ardennes, and Alsace-Lorraine. Marinette Rameau, a young bourgeoise of Angers, noted in her diary on 17 June that "the spectacle on the roads is lamentable: routed soldiers in twos and threes, refugees pulling the most heterogeneous vehicles with difficulty. . . . Exhausted, they are walking like automatons toward a single vague goal: the south." Her parents gave a lift to a mother and son who were bound for Bordeaux; the woman, who was wearing all her jewelry, hoped in the midst of all the chaos that the boy would still be able to take his *baccalauréat*.[3] As the Germans approached inexorably, families in threatened towns had to decide whether to stay or go. While the Rameaus quickly returned home, another bourgeois family of Angers, hearing bombs falling on the local airfield, decided to leave the city for the island of Noirmoutier, off Nantes, where they had a second home and were convinced they would be safe. By the end of the month, however, 4,000 Germans had occupied the island, taking over the summer cottages and swimming in the sea each morning.[4]

As the German forces drove south, the French high command tried one last throw of the dice: to hold up the Germans on the Loire by blowing up the bridges across it and defending the towns along it, allowing the retreating army as much time as possible to keep ahead of the invaders. The decision to defend the Loire and the towns along it struck panic in the hearts of local citizens, municipal authorities, and refugees. A wedge was driven between the military commanders and civilians who understood that any defense of their town would expose it to aerial and artillery bombardment and a potential massacre in the streets. Since the rumors of atrocities committed by German soldiers were turning out to be groundless (and it later transpired that the Germans were under strict instructions to act with discipline and courtesy), civilians became much more fearful of the consequences of resisting than of the consequences of surrender.

In the annals of the French military one operation stood out as worthy of its glorious past. Saumur, overlooked by its chocolate-box castle, was the home of the French cavalry school, from which many of the military elite graduated. For three days, from 19 to 21 June 1940, the cadets of the school undertook a heroic defense of the Loire over a wide front in order to protect the retreat of the French army. When further resistance became impossible, a small unit gathered to bear away the standard of the school, lest it fall into German hands. Almost immediately the cadets of Saumur acquired a mythic status, which will be examined later.[5] In June 1940, however, in Saumur as elsewhere, soldiers and civilians were at each other's throats over the question of resistance or surrender. The mayor of Saumur, a vigorous radical-socialist called Robert Amy, whose son would be killed in action that month, was desperate to prevent his town from being turned into a battlefield. According to the government, towns of over 20,000 inhabitants were to be declared open cities and would not be defended, but Saumur was not big enough to fall into that category. Meanwhile the commander of the cavalry school, Colonel Michon, was adamant that his orders were to defend Saumur and the Loire and that he counted on the mayor's patriotism to support his efforts. The general commanding the sector, whom Amy reached by telephone, refused to change his orders and equally refused to order the evacuation of the town. On 19 June the Germans began to shell Saumur and the population either hid in cellars or limestone caves in the cliffs or fled. On 20 March the Germans entered the town, seized the elderly *procureur de la République* (leading magistrate), Louis Ancelin, as a hostage, and took him by sidecar to military headquarters at Chinon. There the German general threatened reprisals against Saumur for the killing by French fire of a German sent to parley under a white flag. Ancelin replied that he knew nothing of the incident and was not a soldier but a magistrate, although he had been wounded four times in the Great War as an officer and held the Legion of Honor. At this the German general saluted him, saying that "we respect the combatants of the last war, who defeated us, but we despise the little rabbits of this one." Ancelin was released and driven back by Major Wahrenburg, a portly Prussian who was to take command at Saumur and, as a magistrate in civilian life, looked forward to sorting out with Ancelin differences between French and German law thrown up by the Occupation.[6]

For mayors and magistrates the overriding concern in June 1940 was not resistance but avoiding military confrontation that could inflict terrible damage on the civilian population. Mayors summoned emergency meetings of town councillors and other notables, including bishops, who had not been welcome in town halls for the seventy-year duration of the anticlerical Third Republic, in order to construct a lobby for cease-fire. Frantic telephone conversations took place between mayors and the government, now evacuated to Bordeaux, about whether their towns were to be treated as open cities, between military commanders and mayors who asked them to leave rather than defend their towns, and ultimately directly between mayors and German military commanders about the surrender of the towns. They were not operating in a vacuum but under pressure from the local population and passing refugees, who were so averse to combat that they were prepared to disarm French soldiers who were too keen to have a go at the Boche.

Tours had been the capital of France for two days, 12–13 June 1940, after the French government, as in 1870, abandoned Paris in the face of the approaching Germans. While the ministers set up base in the château of Cangé, a few miles to the east on the outskirts of the Amboise forest, Churchill and his staff arrived in a Hurricane squadron for a meeting of the Supreme Allied War Council at the prefecture of Tours. The airfield had already been cratered by German bombs, no one came to meet them, and a café owner who claimed he was closed had his arm twisted to provide lunch for the British prime minister. At the prefecture Churchill found Interior Minister Georges Mandel, Clemenceau's former secretary, shouting orders into two telephones at once and inspiring hope "like a ray of sunshine." Unfortunately, though, Mandel was not a member of the Supreme War Council, which convened at 3:30 P.M. with eight Britons and two Frenchmen—the dithering premier, Paul Reynaud, and the silken secretary of the French war cabinet, Paul Baudouin. Reynaud asked, on behalf of his government, what Britain's attitude would be if the French, notwithstanding the Franco-British agreement of 28 March not to conclude a separate peace with Germany, did so. Churchill replied that the British government could not agree to release the French from their obligations but said that it would not descend to reproaches or recriminations if they sued for an armistice nevertheless.[7] It was no doubt a mistake that Churchill was not invited to address the French ministers at Cangé, to stiffen their resolve, for their meeting at 5:00 P.M. was dominated by the "defeatists" under Marshal Pétain, who now made a formal proposition that the government seek an armistice with Germany as "the necessary condition of the survival of eternal France."[8] As the ministers headed off for Bordeaux, the population of Tours unwittingly made clear that their sympathies lay more with Pétain than with Churchill: the fighting had to stop. The Germans resumed their bombardment of the airfield and the city and arrived on the banks of the Loire on 18 June.

That day, as de Gaulle in London appealed to the French to continue the fight, a delegation of the inhabitants of a neighborhood to the east of the railway tracks marched to the Tours city hall and told the mayor that if the city was defended they would not hesitate to throw themselves in front of the cannon of the French artillery.[9] The mayor, Ferdinand Morin, himself of working-class origin, a practical socialist rather than an ideologue and from the pacifist wing of the party, convened a meeting with the prefect and archbishop of Tours, Monsignor Gaillard, and made desperate calls to Bordeaux to have the city confirmed as open. But he was confronted by a military commander who claimed to have orders to hold up the Germans on the Loire for forty-eight hours. At 11:00 P.M. on 18 June, the bridges over the Loire to the north of the city center were blown up and a motley collection of troops, many of them North African, took up positions in such places as the municipal library. The next morning they opened up on the Germans from the library with machine guns, and the Germans riposted by shelling the city. The wind whipped up a fire that burned for three days, killing about a hundred people, destroying many ancient buildings, and leaving 9,000 homeless.[10] The librarian reported that the pages of burning books were carried as far as Azay-le-Rideau and Chinon.[11] On 20 June the Germans demanded the surrender of the city, and in an extraordinary scene of biblical symbolism, the mayor, prefect, and (according to some accounts) the archbishop set off in the mayor's own fishing boat across the Loire to where the Germans awaited them.[12] Hoping against hope that the military had done their duty and that the civilians would remain disciplined, Morin promised on his honor and his life that there would be no resistance if a truce were granted, and the Germans entered Tours at dawn the next day.

Whereas after the return of de Gaulle in 1944 some act of resistance was required for honor, in 1940, as the French state collapsed, loyalties shrank very sharply from the *patrie* to one's own town or village. The duty of a mayor in these circumstances was to show personal bravery by staying at his post but, as father of his community, not to expose his charges to unnecessary dangers. In July, while Morin was away in Vichy voting full powers to Marshal Pétain to restore the French state, the municipal council of Tours unanimously endorsed a motion that, by going to meet the Germans and offering his honor and life as a guarantee, he had "deserved well of the city" by averting its "total ruin."[13] To underline the point, Morin was presented the following year with an embossed presentation volume the size of a pavement slab, signed by literally thousands of Tourangeaux, "workers and intellectuals, shopkeepers and civil servants, whatever their divergences of opinion or diversity of condition in the past," according to the assistant mayor, who wished to thank Morin for saving the city and sparing hundreds of innocent lives.[14]

In Chinon, thirty miles to the west, the pattern was the same. As German forces approached on 19 June 1940, frantic negotiations took place between the mayor and the French military commander in the vicinity. The military commander was under instructions to defend the bridges over the Loire and the Vienne to ensure an orderly retreat for the French army, but the mayor was fearful that any defense of the town would provoke artillery bombardment and Stuka attacks, leaving much of it in ruins, like Tours. Eventually the French commander saw reason, and as the population hid in their cellars in the early hours of 21 June, Mayor Henri Mattraits stood alone on the quai as without incident the German troops entered the town. He later explained to the municipal council that Chinon—"open to everyone, . . . proud to be able to show its natural beauty and artistic riches to tourists the world over"—had been fortunate not to suffer the same fate as Tours. One of the assistant mayors then thanked the mayor "on behalf of the decent and hardworking population of Chinon" for remaining at his post, day and night, inspiring confidence in the citizens by his sangfroid, and duly announced that he had "deserved well of the town."[15]

Farther west still, beyond Saumur, at Angers, the same battle between soldiers and civilians was fought. The Germans began to bomb the railway station, and though it had been announced on the radio that towns of over 20,000 inhabitants would be declared open cities, on 18 June French soldiers began to set up machine guns on the banks of the Maine in front of the medieval château. The inhabitants of the neighborhood implored them not to fire on the Germans, for fear of the consequences.[16] The local military commander was insistent that Angers should be defended, but the mayor, Victor Bernier, a tight-lipped and sharp-featured pharmacist, called an emergency council meeting, which resolved that Angers was not in a position to stand a siege and did not want to see bridges blown up or women, children, or the elderly evacuated.[17] The deadlock was broken the next day by a phone call from a French-speaking Captain Stein of the approaching German forces, who claimed to be with a division and threatened to reduce Angers to ashes with heavy artillery and Stukas if the slightest resistance was shown. The French commander was persuaded not to defend the bridges over the Maine that led to the city center, although he did not exclude a defense of the Loire, to the south of the city. Mayor Bernier traveled by car with the prefect and a French officer to meet the Germans some miles north of the city and, like Morin, offered himself as a guarantee that there would be no resistance.[18] On 20 June the local press carried an announcement that "all resistance and all armed opposition is formally prohibited and will be severely punished by the French authorities. The prefect and mayor appeal for calm, coolness and discipline on the part of the population."[19] As one Angers merchant wrote to a colleague who had left the city with his family, "Our good city gave itself up like a flower."[20] No discredit however was done to the mayor. On the contrary, Victor Bernier was warmly thanked by the municipal council for "sparing the inhabitants a certain and useless massacre," and remained in office until the last year of the Occupation.[21]

In Nantes, the largest city in the region, the process of Occupation went more smoothly in the short term, but the mayor did not distinguish himself either by a bravura performance as the Germans approached the city or by tactful and disciplined conduct subsequently. The idea of a "Breton redoubt" or a bridgehead in Brittany permitting the British to support a last stand of the French army, which Churchill had tried to sell to Reynaud in the early part of June, quickly evaporated.[22] There was no issue of Nantes being declared an open city; there were no frantic telephone calls or dangerous missions by car or boat. The Germans simply streamed in on trucks and motorcycles, while the Nantais crowded the pavements to gape at them. "Civilians surrounded the soldiers and tried to question them, showing no animosity, while the Germans took photos of them," a schoolmaster wrote disapprovingly in his diary. "Similarly, as the the troops crossed the place Royale, the German soldiers waved at the children, inviting them to wave back, while other soldiers filmed the scene for propaganda purposes."[23] The curé of Sainte-Croix noted that the Nantais were hanging out their windows to look at the Germans, while in the evening the German soldiers invaded the shops and markets, "mass-buying jewelry, silk stockings, and binoculars, etc."[24] There seemed to be an atmosphere of festivity rather than of mourning.

Nantes, however, was a busy seaport with a large population of seamen, dockers, factory workers, and prostitutes and a tradition of left-wing politics, a simmering urban pot in a calm rural hinterland over which nobility and clergy still exercised influence almost unchallenged. Brothels were temporarily closed, but German soldiers shot the doors down and lined up four or five to a bedroom in the seedy hotels to which the prostitutes had repaired. On the second night of the Occupation a German sentry, jostled by a passing black man, riddled him with bullets and tossed him into the Loire.[25] The Feldkommandant, or German military governor, in Nantes was concerned about his troops' lack of discipline but even more about the threat of resistance from the local population. Resuming a practice that had operated in occupied parts of France in 1870 and 1914–18, he required the municipality to draw up a list of hostages, preferably of notables with influence, twenty of whom a day would be kept at a hotel to guarantee order among the population. The municipality convened the town's main authorities and organizations and a list of 300 potential hostages was drawn up.[26] The bishop, Monsignor Villepelet, offered himself for the first watch in the Hôtel Vendée and provided a list of thirty clergy. After a week the hostages were simply required to stay the night and the curé of Sainte-Croix noted that he had dined soberly with an architect, a museum conservator, and an industrialist next to Germans who were loudly quaffing champagne.[27] Early in July the Feldkommandant ruled that, given the "loyal and peaceful attitude of the population up to now," hostages had no longer to sleep at the hotel but simply to remain in town.[28] The system was still operating a year later when the president of the Commercial Court, designated a hostage for the third of fourth time, complained that it should be democratized and all electors included.[29] Democratized it was a month later, with terrible results.

At the end of the day it was the mayor rather than a roster of hostages who answered for the good behavior of the population. From the late summer of 1940, things in Nantes started to get worse, not better, and it soon transpired that the mayor was not part of a solution but part of the problem. For mayors to survive politically it was necessary for them to tread a difficult path between being fathers of their citizens, protecting them against German aggression, and maintaining cordial relations with the German military authorities, insulating them from popular violence. Auguste Pageot, an emotional and somewhat tactless socialist, failed on both counts and did not last in office until the first Christmas. One of the most common acts of resistance was to cut the communications cables laid by the German military for the effective functioning of their machine. Unable to find the culprits, the Germans responded by imposing massive fines on the local community, a collective punishment that was strictly forbidden under the Hague Convention of 1907. After one telephone cable was cut at Nantes on 8 August 1940 the Feldkommandantur imposed a collective fine of two million francs, followed by a second fine of five million francs when a second cable was cut on 8 September. Mayor Pageot, who claimed that he was unable to demand a further sacrifice from his towns-folk, was already in trouble because of another incident. During the night of 30–31 August, the war memorial in honor of the dead of 1870, which depicted a nude hero of antiquity slaying a dragon, was overturned by chains attached to a truck. The Germans wanted the municipality to remove the prone statue, which was attracting crowds and becoming a threat to public order, and telephoned the town hall three times to have something done. Mayor Pageot wanted to make patriotic capital out of the incident, however, and proposed to lead the muncipal council in a body to lay a wreath on the ruin. He stormed into the Feldkommandantur, where the Feldkommandant and the prefect had just agreed that the statue must be removed and that French and German police would conduct parallel investigations into who was responsible: one theory was that the culprits were fairground people. Pageot interrupted them to protest what he called a premeditated provocation by the Germans that "wounded our most worthy patriotic sentiments to the depths of our hearts"; he was ordering the work to remove the statue to cease, he said, so that the people of Nantes could meditate more deeply on the brutality of the Occupation. The next day the municipal council met to consider Pageot's motion to lay a wreath as a body but was split; accordingly, the mayor went alone before lunch to lay a wreath with a tricolor ribbon inscribed from the "town of Nantes."[30]

As a result of this incident and others, the exasperated Feldkommandant realized that he could no longer work with Pageot, who was arrested on 10 October and thrown in prison. When the municipal council voted their solidarity with Pageot, the Feldkommandant thought of having them arrested too, but decided against it. He himself was treading a narrow path between insisting on the cooperation of the French authorities and averting any measure that would needlessly provoke the Nantais. He hesitated between court-martialing the mayor and releasing him on condition that he resign, but this Pageot refused to do until just before Christmas. Pageot was released from prison and exiled to the Free Zone to prevent his stirring up more trouble in Nantes.[31] The striking thing about the episode is that the prefecture at Nantes supported the Feldkommandant against a mayor who was less patriotic than irascible and rude and that the Nantais did not rise up—as the Feldkommandant feared they might—to protest the dismissal of their mayor. Franco-German accommodation was an art that had to be learned in the interest of all parties, and most parties managed it extremely well.

The settlement of this issue involved German authorities not only in Nantes but also in Angers and Paris and set in motion the institutional framework of the military administration that the Germans imposed on occupied France. It resembled a colonial administration with the difference that it was exercised over a highly civilized Western European country. At the pinnacle was the Militärbefehlshaber in Frankreich (MBF), or military commander in France, based in Paris at the Hôtel Majestic on the avenue Kléber. The two generals who occupied this post were cousins who sprang from the Prussian military aristocracy, Otto von Stülpnagel until the spring of 1942, then Carl-Heinrich von Stülpnagel.[32] Born respectively in 1878 and 1886, they were representatives of German military might from the imperial age and far from Hitlerian. Otto, as we shall see, disagreed with his superiors over the ruthless reprisals implemented by the army high command in 1941, while Heinrich struggled against the tightening grip of the secret police and was executed as a traitor after the bomb plot of 20 July 1944 against Hitler. Under the military command for the whole of France were the four regional military administrations. District B, based in Angers, was the so-called Southwestern Region. The first regional commander, General Karl-Ulrich Neumann-Neurode, born in Silesia in 1876, was a shadowy figure of whom little is known except that he loved animals.[33] In July 1942 he was replaced by General Kurt Feldt, a West Prussian of the Twenty-fourth Panzer Division who was ten years younger. Subordinate to the regional commander were the Feldkommandants, one for each department, whose opposite numbers were the French prefects. In April 1941 the Vichy government gave some of its prefects new responsibility as regional prefects, supervising a group of departments and hoping to operate with more clout vis-à-vis the German military. The crucial interface of Feldkommandant and prefect, however, was scarcely changed. At the base of the German military administration were the Kreiskommandants, one for each arrondissement, whose opposite numbers were the French subprefects. This was the link that operated, for example, in the small town of Chinon.[34]

The organization of the various authorities reflects little, of course, of the reality of arrangements between French and German officials, which were more than simply a brutal relationship between occupiers and occupied. Negotiations had to be entered into, and negotiations were facilitated by good personal relations and a common cultural framework of military honor, European civilization, and Christian religion. The defusing of the Pageot affair in Nantes, for example, was made possible by the good working relationship between the Feldkommandant, the prefect's interpreter, and the ruling notables of Nantes. The Feldkommandant, Lietenant-Colonel Karl Hotz, was no stranger when he arrived as military governor in 1940. Born in 1877 in Wertheim-am-Main, he had learned French while serving in the garrison of Metz, which in 1871–1918 was part of imperial Germany. Attached to the Bavarian general staff during the First World War, he then went into industry and came to Nantes in 1930–33 as manager of Brandt of Düsseldorf, which, with funds from the Dawes Plan, was diverting the waters of a tributary of the Loire into an underground canal system through the city center. Highly musical, he bought the latest popular songs from Les Trois Rossignols and played the piano in the salons of the bourgeoisie and nobility of Nantes.[35] After he returned to Nantes he was invited to play the trumpet at the château of the Marquise Yolaine de Sesmaisons outside Nantes. Her husband, Olivier de Sesmaisons, belonged to a family of military nobility that traced its ancestry back to the time of Saint Louis; as a large landowner, he was an influential local politician.[36] According to their sons, whom I interviewed in 1998, the French and German military castes were drawn together by "a sense of honor, courtesy, and the chivalric spirit" that transcended national boundaries.[37] The German officers of the military administration were usually in their sixties, men who had trained in the Second Reich and were veterans of the First War, during which they had learned to respect their opposite numbers in the French military.

National boundaries were also transcended by a sense of belonging to a common European civilization. Hotz's link with the prefecture was Edmond Duméril, a German teacher at the Lycée Clemenceau who served as interpreter at the prefecture. Duméril expected to meet a large, brutal Prussian at the Feldkommandantur but instead found "an old man, dry, short, dressed in an artillery officer's uniform," with a "broad smile and kindly expression." He discovered that they had studied, ten years apart, under the same professors at the University of Tübingen. The ages of these individuals were as important culturally as they were militarily. Duméril regarded Hotz, age sixty-three, as a representative of the old, civilized Germany, quite different from the young Nazi Schuster who was his immediate subordinate. While Schuster listened to Hitler's every word on the radio, Hotz hid a history book under his papers and in conversation applauded Duméril's citation of Goethe's words on the death of Schiller.[38]

A third factor that brought French and German elites together was organized religion. Most Germans, admittedly, were Protestants, and Monsignor Villepelet, bishop of Nantes, used the excuse that his cathedral was Catholic to deny the German authorities the right to use it.[39] Relations with Hotz's successor, Baron von und zu Bodman, were much better, because he was a Bavarian Catholic. "He is so distinguished and well educated," mused the bishop when they met in December 1941, "one can sense that he is of noble race." They spoke of the baron's origins in Munich, and the bishop asked him if he knew Cardinal Falhauber. "Not only do I know him," replied the baron, raising the stakes, "but I also know the pope, whom

I often saw at Munich when he was nuncio. I even went to his coronation." Moving on to royalty, he spoke of Queen Elizabeth of the Belgians, the widow of King Albert and herself a Bavarian princess; of the young King Leopold, who had recently remarried; and of the royal children.[40] Monsignor Villepelet, a doctor's son but a prince of the Church, felt much more at ease with this ambassador of the German Reich than he ever had with the French republican officials elected or appointed under the Popular Front.

In the Angers region the key relationship was between the French prefect (later regional prefect), Jean Roussillon, and the Feldkommandant, Colonel Kloss. Kloss was clear that the French administration must bend to German will and expressed pleasure at the intention of the prefect and his subordinates "to work loyally with the Germans." He was clear also that German authority and the German military must be accorded respect. But he realized that if the French were to consent in any way to German rule it would be necessary to maintain at least the illusion that they were still being governed by French administrators who enjoyed some independence. For his part, Roussillon needed to extract as many concessions as possible from the German authorities to make the Occupation tolerable for the French. On the other hand, given the lack of communication with the French government in Vichy, in the nonoccupied part of France, Roussillon came to learn that the support of the German military regime actually gave him an authority and effectiveness vis-à-vis the French population that he could not otherwise have contemplated. The relationship between Feldkommandant and prefect was therefore much more complex than a simple one of command and obey, reproducing as it did the system of "indirect rule" between colonizers and indigenous elites as developed in the British Empire by Frederick Lugard, former governor-general of Nigeria.[41]

A good working partnership was built up between Roussillon and Kloss, the former reporting that relations were "more than courteous: they are almost trusting and based on a reciprocal loyalty. They could quite easily become cordial." Thanks to this "spirit of comprehension with Kloss," he clarified, "the measures ordered by the military high command [in Paris] are applied with moderation and flexibility in Maine-et-Loire."[42] Unfortunately, the buildup of confidence on a local level was all too often interrupted by the redirection of officials in accordance with the wider needs of the military or civil bureaucracies. In April 1941 Colonel Kloss moved from Angers to Tours, from where he was to run both Indre-et-Loire and Maine-et-Loire as a single large Feldkommandantur. Roussillon regretted the departure of Kloss, who, he said, had kept the German military on a tight leash, preventing them from abusing the French population. Now, he said, "we are confronted by subaltern officers who do not care to shoulder too much responsibility and do not have the same authority or influence over the troops." He took solace from Kloss's promise to visit Angers once a week, a promise that, given his busy schedule, he was not able to keep. Roussillon's opposite number from this point was less the regional commander General Neumann-Neurode, whom he nevertheless found "considerate" and "courteous" when they did meet, than General Dr. Medicus, chief of the administrative section of District B. After a couple of months Roussillon was heaping the same praises on Medicus as he had heaped on Kloss, saying that Medicus's influence had grown rapidly in the district, that his "pro-French sympathies, which he demonstrated at every possible opportunity," had made the confident relationship that he himself had enjoyed with Kloss even stronger and had even served to reinforce the authority of the French administration. After Medicus returned to Angers following a brief posting to Greece in the summer of 1941 Roussillon was even more outrageous in his superlatives, praising the German's "perfect propriety and remarkable understanding of the French mentality."[43]

Meanwhile the French authorities in Tours were in their turn discovering the advantages of having Colonel Kloss at the Feldkommandantur. His predecessor, Captain Marloh, had been particularly harsh and unyielding, and no tears were shed when he and his team were sent off to Belorussia. Jean Chaigneau, the prefect of Indre-et-Loire, said that he was "delighted by the ease and courtesy of my relationship with the German authorities, which are due in large measure to the understanding of Colonel Kloss."[44] The German authorities were similarly impressed by Chaigneau, not least because he had had a distinguished career in the 1914–18 war. "He works well and conscientiously with the German administration," noted one confidential report. "His reputation as a clever and energetic administrative civil servant goes before him." A comparison with the number two in the prefecture of Tours, secretary-general René Feld, confirms that the German ideal of a good French official was one who was brisk, straight-dealing, and even courageous. Feld, the Germans observed, always worked hard to meet German demands fully but was "soft of character."[45] His shifty conduct may have been explained by the need to conceal his Romanian-Jewish origins with overzealousness in the German cause. The French saw only the overzealousness, and in some circles in Tours his reputation was crisply summed up by his nickname: Feld-kommandant.[46]

Relations between French and German officials took place not only within a system of personal contacts and common cultural assumptions but also within a legal framework defined both by the armistice convention and by international law. When the Germans arrived in Nantes, notices immediately went out to the civil authorities instructing them to "use all their energy to ensure that no individual undertakes any act of hostility against the German army or the German military command." Once French armies had laid down their arms it was understood that all resistance would cease, and yet the Germans were worried in the early days that the Occupation would encounter massive popular opposition. The Kommandantur of Nantes told the town hall that "any passive resistance, act of violence, sabotage, or work stoppage must be prevented with the utmost rigor, and the guilty parties arrested and punished." It went on to list the crimes that were subject to martial law: "1. assistance given to non-German soldiers in occupied territory, 2. transmission of information to the detriment of the German army and Reich, 3. assistance to French POWs, 4. offenses against the German army and its commanders." It added a further list of punishable offenses: street gatherings, distribution of leaflets, public meetings and demonstrations, and any other activity hostile to Germany."[47]

This may have seemed like law by *Diktat* but in fact the Germans were operating within the terms drafted by the great powers at The Hague in 1907 and added to by France and Germany in the armistice convention of 1940. The armistice was not a peace treaty and made provisions for a situation that was by definition temporary, before any peace treaty was signed. Military occupation, moreover, did not abolish French sovereignty, which extended formally into occupied France, but balanced it against the security needs of the occupying forces. The French government was free to make laws but always within the requirements of German military security. In pursuit of that security, the German authorities could make their own laws and, if necessary, overrule French laws that conflicted with them. The French people were guaranteed protection of their lives, property, and religion so long as they admitted defeat, obeyed the occupying authorities, and offered no resistance. Resistance by noncombatants was not the same as war by soldiers: it was regarded as violating the laws of war and was punished under martial law. Under military occupation, resources might be requisitioned for the needs of the army of occupation, but only in so far as the country could bear the burden and on issue of receipts that would later be honored. One basic principle laid down was that communities could not be considered collectively responsible for acts committed by individuals. Collective punishments, such as hostage taking or collective fines, were thus prohibited.[48]

Despite the legal attempt to reconcile French sovereignty and German security, in practice they tended to conflict. When French rights came up against German military security, which was to give way? There was no international tribunal to which appeal could be made. Communications between French authorities in the Occupied Zone and Vichy were deliberately frustrated by the Germans and had to be carried on indirectly through the delegate-general of the French Government in the Occupied Territories (DGGFTO), who from January 1941 was Fernand de Brinon, together with a delegate of the Ministry of the Interior, the rather faceless Jean-Pierre Ingrand of the Conseil d'État, both resident in Paris. Ingrand effectively had the powers of a "minister *in partibus*" while the delegate-general had the status of ambassador and in effect was serving in a foreign country under German rule.[49] It did not help that de Brinon was highly devious and manipulative, intent on ingratiating himself with the Germans as a counterweight to Vichy rather than on defending French interests, a path that led to his being shot as a collaborator after the war. In the event, the French administration in the Occupied Zone was very much isolated from Vichy and left to fend for itself. The extent of French sovereignty depended on daily negotiations between French and German authorities in the regions and departments. As well as the declarations of cordiality and trust we have witnessed, there were veritable wars of nerves, feinting and fencing, threats and blandishments, bluff and counterbluff, claims to more power or resources than were actually to hand.

One issue over which French and German authorities struggled for the upper hand was the appointment and dismissal of mayors. Vichy legislation on local government was applicable in all parts of France, and at the end of 1941 the German authorities renounced the right to have a say in the appointment of mayors as a result of talks in the Franco-German commission overseeing the terms of the armistice.[50] In practice, the German authorities were happy to respect the local administration in place, so long as it effectively carried out the task of maintaining order—that is, of insulating the army of occupation from any popular discontent. Towns like Nantes and Saint-Nazaire, large ports with a tradition of labor militancy, were regarded as particularly sensitive. The warm relationship between Feldkommandant Hotz and the prefecture of Loire-Inférieure did not prevent him, as we have seen, from arresting the clumsily patriotic socialist mayor, Pageot, forcing him to resign, and exiling him to the Free Zone. Hotz's successor in Nantes, Baron von and zu Bodman, may have been emollience itself in his dealings with the bishop of Nantes, but when it came to Ferdinand Blancho, the socialist mayor of Saint-Nazaire, who resigned in opposition to Vichy but remained the hero and possible demagogic leader of the dockers, he brooked no compromise. During heated debates in February 1942, regional prefect Roussillon argued that Blancho was under police surveillance and that tougher action would only provoke the dockers. Bodman insisted that it was precisely Blancho's influence over the dockers that made his departure necessary, and Blancho was duly put on a train for Paris, whence he traveled south and joined the Resistance.[51]

The rules of the Occupation thus evolved according to case law rather than legal principle. This was the situation as much in the judicial system as in the administration. In order to protect the security of the military, the Germans established a network of military courts to administer martial law. Any action deemed to threaten German military security was brought before the military court, although other cases were left to the French system of civil and criminal courts. The German military courts were tough but not arbitrary, and they worked according to set procedures. The accused was entitled to a defense provided by a French lawyer, although the pleading had to be in German. In Nantes, the defense was generally provided by Maître Guineaudeau, with Duméril on hand to translate. "Until the death of Hotz," Guineaudeau reported after the war, "we obtained a good deal from the staff of the German justice system. I would say that they had a sort of professional conscience to which we could appeal. The judges did not think in the same way as the police. Often we were able to save heads."[52]

One of the tasks of the French defense was to convince the German judges that opposition to the Occupation was often ritual or comic rather than a threat to security. The twenty-three-year-old son of a magistrate who amused himself and German soldiers by drawing caricatures of them in the Grand Café on the place de la Bourse in Nantes, for example, found himself in hot water when he drew a caricature of the Führer that they found insulting. He was sentenced to two months in prison by the military court until French lawyers persuaded the Germans to have a better sense of humor and he was released. Similarly, a country priest who let the children in his Sunday school group laugh at a scarecrow wearing a German helmet was threatened with three months in prison until the French defense convinced the court that "to laugh while passing by but without stopping was not an offense." Trickier was the case of Arthur Martineau, a sixty-five-year-old cement merchant of Sainte-Marie-de-la-Mer who had an obsessive desire to cut German telephone wires. On the first occasion, his death penalty was lifted after a French medical witness convinced the court that he had suffered brain damage as a result of a cerebral hemorrhage. After his release, unfortunately, he repeated the offense and was promptly shot.[53]

The German system of military justice was neither as severe as might be imagined, at least in the early years of the Occupation, nor as pervasive. When the German military administration of District B tried to take cognizance of the case of two traders illegally selling above the fixed price and prefect Roussillon resisted, he was supported by de Brinon in Paris, who argued that under the Hague Convention occupying powers were authorized to act to ensure public order but that while price hikes might in theory affect public order there was no reason for them not to be dealt with by the French courts. Sometimes the German military courts themselves did not wish to become involved in exclusively French matters.[54] When a man in Touraine tried to bring a defamation suit against two brothers who had called him a "bandit" and a "Boche," the German military court promptly returned the dossiers to the French court, saying that the case was "a quarrel between two French people."[55] This is not to say that any case that went before the French courts was handled leniently and with due process. The

Vichy government invented its own system of exceptional courts, the so-called Sections spéciales, to deal with the Communist threat. Immortalized by the 1975 Costa-Gavras film *Special Section*, they were found not just in Paris but wherever a regional appeals court could mutate into one of them. They effectively spared the Germans the business of repression and made a specialty of arbitrariness. The Section spéciale of Angers sat for the first time in September 1941 and was particularly fond of handing out heavy sentences to anyone who so much as sang the "Internationale." One young man received three years for singing it in a café, while a tax official received five years for teaching it to a band of peasants in a farm courtyard and conducting them.[56]

Negotiating the Occupation involved not only individuals but communities. Any critical moment, such as the death of a French or German in confused circumstances, might suddenly bring an otherwise uneventful community into a matrix that involved the occupation forces, the Feldgendarmerie and French police, mayors and their councils, the subprefect and Kreiskommandant, the prefect and Feldkommandant, and possibly higher authorities too. Everything here was at stake, from finding the guilty party to calming local troops and the local community and preserving the reputation and honor of the French and German authorities. Three deaths in two communities within the space of a couple of months may be used to investigate French and German nerves at their rawest and negotiating skills at their highest premium.

After the heroic fighting by the military cadets of Saumur in June 1940, the school was turned into a temporary POW camp, before evacuation to camps in Germany was organized. On Christmas Eve 1940, three French soldiers escaped from the camp and took refuge in a laborer's cottage. They were tracked down by German soldiers and one of the Frenchmen was shot as he hid under a bed. The funeral was attended by the subprefect, Robert Milliat, who was writing a book on the epic of the cadets of Saumur, by notables of the town, by veterans' associations; and also, in a spirit of reconciliation, by an escort of German soldiers and two German officers representing the camp commander.[57] Good relations in the town seemed to weather this incident, but two months later they were threatened when a roofer named Frank Le Cosquer was killed by a German patrol doing its rounds in Saumur. The version of the Feldgendarmerie was that Le Cosquer, arrested for being without papers, proceeded to kick and punch his captors and was shot while trying to escape. Milliat told the Kreiskommandant, Major von Wahrenburg, that such trigger-happiness was regrettable and that it would be better if German soldiers used their weapons only when their lives were in danger. He underlined his point by attending the funeral, at which 1,500 citizens turned out, in full uniform and at the head of the municipal council. Wahrenburg felt that this demonstration had been instigated by the prefect, and Kloss wrote angrily to Roussillon to protest this challenge to the Wehrmacht's honor. Roussillon replied that Le Cosquer had been an "honest worker who gave no trouble" and that he had acted both to "appease the painful emotions that had gripped the community" and to "restore a climate indispensable to a good understanding between the army of occupation and the civilian population." Kloss refused to give way, saying that if the prefect had been apprised of the full facts he would not have turned the funeral into a demonstration.[58]

The stubbornness of both parties left the tension in Saumur unresolved. Relations were not helped by another killing, a day before, in the usually quiet town of Cholet. Though an industrial center, Cholet was an outpost of the Vendée and firmly under the control of the paternalistic employers and the Catholic Church. There was great confusion and bewilderment, therefore, when a German soldier, a Corporal Müller, was shot late at night by a civilian with a revolver who then escaped into the darkness. Suspecting an act of resistance, Colonel Kloss immediately had the mayor arrested, decreed an 8:00 P.M. curfew, closed all cafés and restaurants, and imposed a fine of one million francs on the townspeople. This time the funeral was staged as a German military occasion, with band playing and volley of rifles, to impress the locals with the honor attributed to an ordinary German soldier. The mayor, Alphonse Darmaillacq, a textile factory owner, later wrote that he was forced to follow the cortege. Kloss, who came to Cholet, claimed that a thousand townsfolk attended, the men bareheaded "in the French custom," that the mayor, subprefect, and police commissioner expressed their sympathy personally to him, and that the mayor offered a substantial reward to anyone helping with the arrest of the culprit.

All was not clear in Cholet, however, and doubts about the identity of the murderer accumulated. The Kreiskommandant of Cholet, Major von

Trotha, persuaded Kloss to reopen the case. No serious crime had been committed in Cholet for seventeen years and relations between the Choletais and the Germans had been good. The murderer was said to have spoken in German before he pulled the trigger. Müller had become separated from his companions between the café-restaurant Tamisier and the café Coeffard, a house of ill repute, because he went to meet a stranger at the Hôtel de France and was shot as he crossed the main square. It emerged that German soldiers often went out in civilian clothes at night, particularly when they were visiting brothels, so that the evidence increasingly pointed to the fact that Müller was shot by a German soldier in civvies. It was a question not just of righting a wrong but of mollifying French public opinion. The German war effort was demanding more and more industrial labor and French workers had to be attracted onto projects such as building the Atlantic war in Brittany. To alienate a usually quiet industrial town like Cholet by levying a massive fine to punish a crime that might not even have been committed by a Frenchman was simply counterproductive. On 28 April 1941, Kloss therefore made the unprecedented gesture of *refunding* the million-franc fine to the citizens of Cholet.[59]

The German authorities came to realize that the efficient functioning of the Occupation involved a trade-off between maintaining order by sticks and maintaining goodwill by carrots. In the case of Saumur, Kloss refused to cede—on the grounds that a common worker dealt with harshly was the price paid for order and any apology would impugn the honor of the army—whatever resentment was felt by the community. In the case of Cholet, the honor of the army had already been secured by a magnificent funeral, and the collective fine imposed on a community that was probably not responsible did not make order more secure. On the contrary, true Vendeans that they were, the Choletais were taking refuge in a sullen opposition that could eventually undermine the German war effort. Harsh and yet rational, the German military authorities understood that the tacit consent of the French people was indispensable to the success of the Occupation.

2

Cohabitation

In one of the great classics of the Occupation, Vercors's *Le Silence de la mer*, finished in October 1941 and published by an underground press in Paris early in 1942, a German officer, Werner von Ebrennac, is billeted on a French family comprising the narrator and a young woman, his niece. Each evening, after his work at the local Kommandantur, the officer tries to make conversation, saying how much he has always loved France, how much French literature complements German music, how they should unite as wife and husband, and how, as in *Beauty and the Beast*, the love of beautiful France will liberate the German from his beastly imprisonment and reveal the handsome prince within. The niece, to whom these words are subliminally directed, never raises her eyes from her sewing and never speaks, the narrator continues to smoke his pipe, and the officer, confronted by an unyielding silence, never sits down and soon withdraws with the words, "*Je vous souhaite une bonne nuit.*" The story hinges on his visit to Paris, where his friends are preparing the "wonderful union of our two peoples." He returns, having met soldiers who experienced the horrors of the Russian front and who have a totally different perspective on the Franco-German relationship. He confides to the narrator and his niece that the soldiers laughed at his naïveté given the worldwide struggle for power, pointing out that the real plan was not to seduce France but to destroy it, body and soul, and ensure that she could never rise again. "*Adieu*," he declares and is gone the next morning, when silence descends on the narrator and his niece also.[1]

Fifty-five years later I visited Marinette Rameau in her oak-beamed family home in the Angevin countryside close to the Loire. Born in 1909, she might be the same age as the niece in *Le Silence de la mer*. She is a tall, elegant, and still beautiful woman who not only kept a diary of her wartime experiences but is happy to talk about them freely. She never married and it is as if some of the most significant emotional moments of her life occurred under the Occupation. This, for Marinette Rameau, meant a succession of German officers billeted on the family's town house in Angers on the promenade facing the château across the Maine. The most memorable of these officers was Captain Wilhelm Koester, who arrived on 21 July 1940. Whereas Werner von Ebrennac, asked by the narrator whether he is descended from a French Protestant driven out by Louis XIV, regrets that he is not, Wilhelm Koester declared, "I love to speak French. . . . I admire your culture; my wife is of southern origin, her ancestors from Vignolles [Charente] came to Germany after the revocation of the Edict of Nantes, but we are now Catholics." Marinette's mother proposed to serve the officer in the study, but he insisted, "Madame, you do not understand. I wish to eat at your table. Choose: do you prefer to have a civilized officer or four soldiers who will be much less so?" Far from freezing him out, the Rameau family acceded to Koester's request. Marinette, whose eyes were for handsome men rather than for sewing, was delighted. She discovered that Koester, aged forty-seven, was a sculptor and director of the Fine Art School at Trier. "I have to admit," she wrote, "he is very distinguished and perfectly educated." His orderly, Willi Gehendges, turned out to be his pupil at Trier. Marinette noted that he spoke little French but played the violin "like a virtuoso, and by heart: Beethoven, Schubert, Mozart, Strauss, Neapolitan romances, and modern tunes."[2] Her only regret was that the captain and his orderly stayed for less than a month, and when I interviewed her in 1996 she told me the whole story again, rhapsodizing about the virtues of "le capitaine."[3]

Marinette Rameau's appreciation of the cultivation of the German military was reinforced in May 1944 when "a French Apollo" turned up at the house with an accommodation slip issued by the Kommandantur. Her mother tried to turn him away, saying that her rooms were reserved for Germans, but the Apollo was a leader of the French counterinsurgent Milice (militia) and would not take no for an answer. A month later, returning from the family retreat on the Loire, Marinette found vomit in the garden, cigarette ends trodden into the stair carpet, wineglass stains on the pedestal table, bullet holes in the bedroom walls, and two Milice fighters still in bed. She complained to the Milice headquarters and then reprimanded the uninvited lodgers. "I have to tell you, *Messieurs*," she scolded, "that we have had Germans throughout the war in the rooms that you occupy. They were always clean and polite and would never have done what I have just seen in the garden or left the doors wide open. It is painful to me to observe that this is the behavior of French people. You ought to be ashamed of yourselves."[4]

These stories of German officers billeted on French homes could scarcely be more different. The difference lies not in the portrayal of the officers, who are equally refined and civilized, but in the reaction of their French hosts. The first was greeted by a persistent and glacial silence, the second, if Marinette Rameau was as loquacious then as she is now, was probably carried away on a torrent of words. One explanation may simply be that not all families responded in the same way to their guests, but it must be remembered that *Le Silence de la mer* is a political parable, a lesson in patriotic behavior for the occupied French written as the initial goodwill between French and Germans began to turn sour. It is a warning not to trust to appearances, to beware of the mailed fist in the glove. Marinette Rameau's story may be the romantic daydreams of a thirty-one-year-old spinster, but it is significant that her judgment was confirmed as the war continued, as a result of the bad behavior not of the Germans but of the French. Moreover, despite the official postwar orthodoxy that contact with Germans was reprehensible, fifty years on she is still captivated by the memory of Captain Koester. This is not to say that Vercors's account is fiction and Rameau's reality, but that relations between French and Germans under the Occupation cannot be reduced to German oppression confronted by French patriotism. Despite the obvious inequality of power between the parties, interactions between the two were multifaceted, subtle, and complex. From Marinette Rameau's account we understand that the Germany of Goethe and Beethoven was never quite eclipsed for many French people by the Germany of Hitler, that the clash of Latin and Teuton was disturbed by Germans fluent in French and by Germans descended from French stock, and finally that the German officer, cultivated and honorable as well as virile, exercised a magnetic attraction, particularly over French women.

The experience of Marinette Rameau of a succession of Germans billeted on the family home was not necessarily typical. The German Occupation did not mean that the country was constantly teeming with troops looking for accommodation. True, in the autumn of 1940 the German military authorities required the French administration to undertake a sort of Domesday Book of every village, to ascertain how many officers, NCOs, troops, and horses could be accommodated in each commune, firstly under ordinary billeting (one bed per soldier) and secondly under heavy billeting, with the troops sleeping on straw. For Ligueil, a village of 2,028 near the demarcation line in Touraine, for example, ordinary billeting meant 35 officers, 71 NCOs, 905 troops, and 247 horses, while heavy billeting meant the same number of officers and NCOs but 2,258 troops and 428 horses.[5] In the event, fears of occupation on this scale were not realized. Unless they were part of the military administration in larger centers, German troops were generally on the move and never stayed long in one place. Most small towns and villages were troubled for a few days or weeks at the beginning and end of the Occupation and sometimes a little in between, but rarely more. A historical survey undertaken on a commune-to-commune basis in Maine-et-Loire (Anjou) in 1948 makes possible a fine calibration of the German presence. In the Mauges, the village of Andrezé was occupied between 21 and 23 June 1940 and 8 August and 8 November 1942, when the troops moved into the unoccupied zone; no damage was reported. The nearby village of Le Fuilet was occupied from 21 to 29 June and 14 to 25 July 1940. The mayor reported that the German forces occupied the town hall, broke chairs, made holes in the wall, and removed flags and his scarf of office; when they returned in 1944, headlong in retreat, they stole twenty bicycles. An analysis of over 200 reports received reveals that only 10 percent of communes in Anjou said that they were occupied throughout the war, 15 percent were never occupied at all, and in between 26 percent were occupied once, 29 percent twice, and 20 percent more than twice.[6]

Clearly, the impact of the German Occupation was very uneven. Cities, ports, suburbs close to airfields, and administrative and communication centers saw more Germans than out-of-the-way villages. For security reasons, Germans were reluctant to stay in isolated farmsteads outside the *bourg*, or village nucleus. Rural dwellings were not attractive because only one room was generally heated, serving as both kitchen and living room for the family. The mining village of Nyoiseau in rural north Anjou was inspected three times as possible accommodation for German troops and each time rejected as unsatisfactory. On the last occasion, early in 1944, the secretary of the town hall told the German officer that "this is a mining area and if your soldiers start drinking with them, it could turn nasty."[7] Given the choice, German officers preferred elegant châteaux and seaside villas. Well-connected politicians, industrialists, and generals were often able to pull strings to avoid their properties being taken over. General Huntziger, who had lost the battle of Sedan in June 1940 and now represented France at the commission to oversee the armistice at Wiesbaden, was able to keep his villa at the fashionable resort of La Baule out of German hands.[8] But the ancient duke of Blacas, mayor of the pious and picturesque town of Beaupréau in the Mauges, who had no such connections, had to suffer three invasions of his château by German officers between June and September 1940. Not only did he receive no notice, he complained, and have to provide beds, sheets, washbasins, tables, chairs, a typewriter, and a radio, but the Germans used up fifteen tons of his pure Welsh anthracite, which would be impossible to replace for the winter, given the British blockade.[9] Maybe the cold finished him off, for he died the following year.

In the towns, the Germans requisitioned public buildings such as barracks, convents, schools, and halls and also took over the hotels. Busy seagoing and trading cities like Nantes had giant hotels with up to 200 rooms, but the hotels in less commercial, more military and administrative centers like Angers were much more modest, with between 30 and 50 rooms on average. This caused problems when Angers was chosen by the Germans as the capital of its military administration for the whole of southwest France. In the summer of 1940 there were 8,000 German soldiers in the city, out of a total of 10,000 in the department. Although there were four barracks that could house over 5,000 men, and convents and schools could accommodate another 1,000—at least until the term began in September—while châteaux for the general staff were plentiful in the noble-ridden countryside, many officers and men still had to be billeted *"chez l'habitant,"* as the French said.[10] This meant not only large town houses like that of the Rameau family but much more basic housing too, of both middle- and working-class families.

Some German lodgers, of course, were better than others. The Rameau family's first two lodgers had ugly dueling scars and drank Pommery champagne by the case into the early hours. Marinette's mother, who had the room beneath them, was greatly relieved when they left after four days.[11] Colonel de Sauvebeuf, who ran the charitable Secours National in Angers, had four German soldiers billeted on his house near the château in August 1940. On the sixth night they brought home some "women of loose morals" and made so much noise that he had to ask them to be quiet. It should not be imagined, however, that the French had to suffer in silence. Regularly they complained to the Feldkommandantur and were often obliged. Sauvebeuf asked the Feldkommandantur to inform the soldiers that he kept a "respectable house" and that they should behave with more decorum.[12] Odette Goxe, whose middle-class family lived frugally in the predominantly working-class neighborhood of Saint-Michel, received a mixed bag of lodgers. The first officer, she recalls, looked like a pimp and spied in cafés. She went to the Feldkommandantur to complain, and they removed him. The second officer came back drunk and burst into the children's bedroom by mistake. As she left for the Kommandantur, the terrified officer asked her not to say that he had had women back, or he would be sent to the Russian front. The third officer, she subsequently learned, was the director of the military prison at Angers and had a ferocious reputation. At home, however, he was open and friendly, and asked her permission to take her children to the fair, where he spoiled them. On their return the youngest child was triumphant. "You see," he proudly proclaimed, "he didn't kill me!"[13]

It may be that to seek redress successfully from the occupying authorities was unusual, but the Germans, while keeping the French on a tight leash, were keen initially not to alienate them unnecessarily. The harmonious coexistence was facilitated by the attitude of Germans posted to France. Many came as sexual and gastronomic tourists as much as soldiers. The *douceur* of France and of parts of France like the Loire Valley in particular was something to cherish. After the Russian front was opened up, the alternative of service in France seemed like a dream, and even in comparison with Germany, as the war progressed, France was seen as a land of plenty. "*Leben wie Gott in Frankreich*" was a phrase much used by German soldiers to sum up the ease of life in France.[14] Lieutenant Helmut Voss, before the war a municipal employee and a member of the Social Democratic Party, now in charge of one of the Angers barracks, told of a soldier who had shot himself rather than go to Russia and of the joy of troops who learned that they were being posted back to France, especially after the cold winter of 1941–42.[15] Helmut Radssat came to Angers from the Sudetenland early in 1944 and remained for five years, first in active service, then as a POW. "France was the country for which many German soldiers were nostalgic," he recalled, "particularly those who had fought on the Russian front." They had a special affection for the canteen of the Verneau barracks in Angers. "The precious aroma of wine and brandy was quite new to me. In Germany such luxuries were becoming more and more scarce. It was in those barracks that I learned to know and appreciate good wines. We could also buy toiletries, lingerie for women, and so on. Things that we had not been able to obtain in Germany for a long time, particularly of that quality."[15]

Although the formal relationship between Germans and French was that of occupier and occupied, there were other ways of defining the relationship. Since the armistice Germans and French were no longer at war, but the war continued around them and in one sense made them both its victims. This was particularly true after the Russian campaign began to take its toll. In addition, not all Germans in occupied France were soldiers. Some were civilians, for example, builders and building workers employed by the Todt Organization in defense work. One of the projects on the outskirts of Angers was the conversion of the château de Pignerolles into a bunker-bound command center for naval activity in the Atlantic. The lodger in the Rameau household in the autumn of 1942 was a Rhinelander named Josef Liesenhof, a civilian whose Cologne building firm was working on the château. Marinette Rameau noted in her diary that he was not chauvinistic and asked her repeatedly, "*Warum der Krieg?* I have nothing against you, so why should we be enemies?" And she replied, "*Ja, warum?* I ask myself the same question."[16] Two German workers involved in the same project lodged for five or six months in the Leterme household, of which the father was a quantity surveyor, using the bedroom of a daughter who had just married and moved out. Michel Leterme, then aged twelve, remembers that they were ordinary, decent men who drank coffee in the kitchen and shared their cigarettes. In their rudimentary French their constant refrain was "*La guerre, grosse malheur.*"[17]

Michel Leterme's father was a veteran of the 1914–18 war who, like many graduates of the trenches, kept his helmet hanging up at home as a badge of that confraternity. The confraternity, interestingly, existed not only between French or Allied veterans but also between French and German soldiers who, though they were supposed to be hereditary enemies, had endured the same unspeakable experiences. Jacques Hervé, whose family lived in Tours and went to Germany under the Service du Travail Obligatoire (STO) in 1943, recalls that a café owner next door escaped deportation to Germany after the intervention of a German soldier who had been held a prisoner in Tours in 1918 and was eager to do a favor for a fellow veteran.[18] Bonds formed by military honor, which were stronger than national animosity, went back a long way. Léon Mousseau, a country doctor in Saint-Mathurin on the Loire, sent his wife and children to his mother-in-law's house in the Vendée for safety. When a German officer was billeted there, an old aunt took him to see the portraits and war decorations of ancestors going back to the First Empire. The officer clicked his heels and said, "Madame, I pay homage to our unfortunate adversaries!"[19]

It is true that German respect for French military honor was severely dented in 1940. The French soldiers of 1940 had not shown the same valor as their fathers of 1914 and duly forfeited the esteem the German military showed for their equals. In the blitzkrieg of June 1940 the Germans were astounded by the absence of French resistance. "Where is the enemy?" wrote a member of the Swabian division approaching the Loire. "On the right a couple of men disappeared into the bushes. But of the enemy nothing is to be seen. Where are the *poilus?*"[20] We have already seen how the German general who accepted the surrender of Saumur told the *procureur* Louis Ancelin that the Germans respected the combatants of the last war, who defeated them, but despised the little rabbits of 1940, who ran away.[21] Helmut Voss observed that just as French men failed to do their duty so French women now showed their mettle. For him French women were holding the country together, making their houses spotless in the morning, but then doing themselves up in the afternoon to take a walk with their children and husbands, who themselves seemed to do little other than hang about on street corners and prop up the bar in cafés. The women, he said, were defined by "intelligence, elegance of appearance and speech. After the shock of the defeat they showed strength of will and energy and were able to cope much more quickly than the men."[22]

For the German military this was not just a question of an appreciation of French manners. They took the view that, by failing to defend their homeland, French men had also forfeited the right to their womenfolk. It was not that the conquerors assumed the right to rape the women of the defeated nation, but the power to seduce was one of the fruits of victory. French women, for their part, were equally fascinated by the *Übermenschen* who had taken control of their country. A million and a half Frenchmen were in German POW camps, leaving their women alone to fend for themselves. German soldiers, by contrast, were surrounded by the aura of victory, had the benefit of an artificially strong currency that enabled them to offer French women stockings, jewelry, and drinks, and, according to one woman from Touraine, "They were the best-looking men I have ever seen."[23]

The Occupation opened up many possibilities for relations between French women and German men but this did not mean that there were no rules. The German authorities forbade marriage between German soldiers and the women of defeated nations, and Slavs working in Germany who had sex with German women could be punished by death. The Germans were also obsessed with the threat to their troops of venereal disease and demanded that the French authorities keep prostitution under control.

On the other hand, they regarded any interference by those authorities in relations between German soldiers and French women as a slight to their honor. The French had their own rules about what was proper in relations between French women and German soldiers. To have sex was a challenge to the French family, community, and country, but the rules that applied at the Liberation, when "horizontal collaboration" was punished by head shaving and possibly prosecution for intelligence with the enemy, were not necessarily the same under the Occupation, when single women were coming up against Germans in their employment and in social situations. The 1940 catechism of the socialist Jean Texcier, *Conseils à l'occupé*, which recommended that the French be "correct" with the Germans but not friendly, said nevertheless that French men should not refuse Germans a light or interfere with a French girl negotiating business with a German soldier, who would get "only what he paid for."[24]

Some relationships between German soldiers and French women were entirely bound by the codes of courtly love. Helmut Voss, for example, fell in love with the French secretary of the German captain who was in charge of the city of Angers. She was "a delightful young woman with sparkling blue eyes, always beautifully dressed," who, when he found an excuse to go to her office each Saturday, greeted him with the words "Here comes Mr. Faithful." Once he ran into her at the theater, where she had gone with a girlfriend, and was smitten by her "perfect manners, charm, friendliness, and yet distance," for obviously she did not want the relationship to develop. Other relationships were less discreet and transgressed the boundaries of the licit. Marinette Rameau tells of a German officer called Hubert who used to visit the dentist's wife in a white convertible, bringing her all sorts of delicacies, such as game. The dentist's surgery was on the second floor of a block in Angers in which her father had the office of his veterinary supply business. One day, coming out of the office where she was typing, Marinette bumped into the dentist's wife, "wearing white satin pajamas and red shoes," in the arms of the German. Later, she said, the dentist's wife had a child who was "very blond" and was generally assumed to be Hubert's.[25] Berthe Vaillant, wife of an official at the prefecture of the Creuse, came to Ligueil, near the demarcation line, with her daughter Denise in 1940 to look after her ninety-year-old mother. A few months later the German customs service established an office at Ligueil, and Denise, aged thirty-five, met a customs officer named Müller, who began to come around to the house, singing in German as Berthe played the piano. Then the recitals became parties and the parties feasts; German officers started to come from as far as Tours and Châtellerault and the postmistress and other local women joined in the celebrations, dancing with the officers. Clearly they enjoyed spending time with well-bred officers who drove up in large cars. Sometimes the officers stayed the night; as Berthe said, "I never refused the Germans a room." Caught by the Forces Françaises de l'Intérieur (FFI) at the Liberation, Denise admitted having sex with Germans and said she had fled the town for fear of having her head shaved. Making merry with Germans was not well regarded in a small community, and getting up too close was likely to attract accusations of treachery. The postman and the doctor were among those who claimed that the dancing women were all Gestapo informers and that the house was an "information bureau" for the Germans. Berthe and Denise Vaillant went before the Cour de Justice at Tours in December 1944. The charge of denunciation was not proven, but Denise was sentenced to five years in prison for "relations with the enemy." What was regarded as a challenge to the integrity of the community under the Occupation was seen as much more serious by the courts at the Liberation, although rumor and gossip alone were not enough to convict.[26]

Receiving Germans at home was frowned on more than meeting them in bars, cafés, and restaurants. Relationships developed easily between waitresses, barmaids, proprietresses, and Germans, who were often regular customers, tended to drink a good deal, and tipped generously. Marie-Louise Coiscault, who served in her parents' bar, L'Artichaut, in the river-crossing town of Chalonnes-sur-Loire, was nineteen when the Germans arrived in 1940. Among the daily customers, she became friendly with Corporal Müller, from the Saarland. There is a photograph of her, her friend Jeanne, and Müller in a meadow close to the town, smiling at the camera, arms linked. After Müller left Chalonnes, Marie-Louise sent him food packages and supplied his German comrades who remained with eggs, meat, and potatoes in return for soap and pâté. She wished to marry him after the war and wrote to his family. Instead she was taken to court, where she protested that she had not had relations with other German soldiers, although naturally she had been obliged to serve them and talk to them when they came into the café. In spite of this, she was deprived of her civic rights for five years and required to live outside Chalonnes for a year.[27]

Sometimes during the Occupation itself members of the community complained that relations between French women and German soldiers were going too far. In March 1941 a group of French women were seen waving good-bye to a contingent of German soldiers leaving the railway station of the seaside town of Le Croisic. The next day a notice went up on the wall of the auction house listing the women who had "come to bid fond farewells to the occupying troops." They included the nineteen-year-old daughter of the owner of the Au Bon Vin Nantais café, the proprietress of the Café de Paris, and her barmaid, also nineteen. The local subprefect who investigated the incident was more concerned with the act of denunciation than with the leave-taking; and suspicion fell on a former railway employee of Le Croisic station who was thought to bear a personal grudge. The inquiry was inconclusive but suggests that in 1941 informing was regarded as a greater threat to the fabric of the community than waving good-bye to Germans.[28]

Denunciation, from one perspective, was a patriotic act, bringing to the attention of the authorities illegalities, disloyalties, and threats to the state that might otherwise remain hidden. But it also represented a betrayal of the secrets of the community, which were perhaps best kept from the prying of the French state, let alone of the German authorities. Its magic was that it gave extraordinary powers to the weaker members of the community, in particular women, but its poison bitterly divided communities against themselves. The peaceful town of Chinon was almost torn apart under the Occupation by Madeleine Longuépée, a former dressmaker from a less fashionable provincial town, middle-aged, childless, and divorced. Kept by Adalbert Chevalier, the owner of the Café des Terrasses, who put up a photograph of Hitler and a notice welcoming "our German friends," she became involved in his sideline of procuring French girls for the delight of German officers who repaired to the café after a hard day giving orders at the Kommandantur. One of these girls, Simone Peltier, aged fifteen, who had sex with Germans both in the bar and on a sofa in a cellar opposite, had a quarrel with Chevalier and complained to the French gendarmerie. An inquiry into "the incitation of minors to debauchery" was launched by the examining magistrate, Leopold Florens, and the *procureur de la République* at Chinon, M. Ponset, but it did not get far. Ponset and Florens were summoned to the Feldkommandantur in Tours in November 1940, told that France had been defeated, and ordered to hand over all files concerning immoral acts. Ponset affected to rule Chinon like a robed noble of the eighteenth century and had declared, "I have the Kreiskommandant [of Chinon] entirely in my hands, I can do with him exactly as I want, I will continue to enforce French laws and ignore German ones and no one will notice." These words were relayed by Chevalier to the Germans, who promptly arrested Ponset. For his part Ponset was convinced that Chevalier was only doing as instructed by his mistress, Mme Longuépée, "the inspirer of his deeds," who had gone to pull strings with the German authorities in Paris to ensure that Ponset was brought low.

The Kreiskommandant of Chinon made clear that he had quite a different notion of where power lay. He told Florens, who was also questioned, that "we are the victors! You have been beaten! The women, even the children of your country, are no longer yours! Our soldiers have the right to have fun, and if you do anything to slight the honor of the German army you will be arrested like M. Ponset. Chevalier and others are there to keep an eye on you." But Chevalier was putty in the hands of Mme Longuépée. A year later he confessed to Florens that "all the evil comes from that woman Longuépée. The woman is a tyrant. She subjugates me. Listen, *Monsieur le juge*, it was she who had M. Ponset arrested. She went to Paris to fix it." Florens told the magistrate preparing Mme Longuépée's trial after the Liberation that he had never interviewed the woman, "but she had the reputation of a shrew at Chinon, extremely dangerous for the Resistance because of the contacts with the German milieux. Not because of her charm but because of her diabolical intelligence and spirit of evil."[29]

Mme Longuépée's malice was not exhausted by the arrest of Ponset, who was in fact released by the Germans after three weeks on condition that he move to a post in unoccupied France. Around that time she was in Mme Gauthier's grocery shop in Chinon when M. Bagarie, the postman, came in. When Mme Gauthier asked for news of his son, Bagarie said that the boy was delighted to be in the unoccupied zone, away from the Boches. Mme Longuépée commented that the Germans were going to win the war, to which Bagarie replied that those who served them deserved to be shot one day. Bagarie was far from being a resistant: he was a former gendarme who sent his children to church school and sold large numbers of photographs of Marshal Pétain to raise money for the charitable Secours National. But Mme Longuépée was determined to lure him into her trap. She returned to the attack, defending Marshal Pétain's policy of collaboration with Germany. At this, Bagarie allegedly took a photograph of the marshal and, making an appropriate gesture, announced that it was fit only for toilet paper. His actions promptly reported by Mmes Longuépée and Gauthier to the Feldkommandantur of Tours, Bagarie was hauled before a German military court and sentenced to ten months in prison for insulting both the German army and Marshal Pétain.

When the post office investigated the case, they found that there was more to it than a vendetta between Mme Longuépée and Bagarie. Bagarie was a school friend of Ponset's and Mme Longuépée, having got rid of Ponset, wanted to get rid of his friends and allies as well. She was able to enlist Mme Gauthier, the grocer, by blackmailing her. She knew that Mme Gauthier had had an affair with a French officer in Saumur while her husband had been away at the front in 1940 and that she had given birth to a stillborn child. Mme Gauthier, for her part, was keen to have Bagarie out of the way because her husband, who had a temporary job with the post office, coveted Bagarie's permanent one. The Germans were quite happy to release Bagarie so long as Gauthier was given his job. But this violation of administrative propriety was unacceptable to the French postal service. As far as it was concerned, Bagarie was a good employee whose southern temperament had got the better of him, while Gauthier was a bad one. More importantly, to let two women of "deplorable morals" dictate who was to be employed in the post office was out of the question.[30]

After a third incident in the space of five months, the French authorities endeavored to recover control of the situation. Mme Josseaux, wife of the bank manager of the Chinon branch of the Crédit Lyonnais, went into a grocer's shop in Chinon (we are not told if it was Mme Gauthier's) and met the cook of the Kreiskommandantur, who was buying fruit for her German employers. "You can give them the pits," observed Mme Josseaux wryly. "That is good enough for them." Mme Josseaux was duly denounced and arrested, but at this point the subprefect, Paul Cay, had had enough. He warned his opposite number, the Kreiskommandant, of the "deplorable effect that these arrests—based for the most part on the accounts of people of the most dubious conduct and morality—may have on the population." He told the prefect more explicitly that the arrests were made after denunciations by people accredited with the Kreiskommandantur. "Whether it is Mme Longuépée of Porte du Château, Mme Gauthier of rue Jean-Jacques Rousseau, Mlle Crosnier of place Jeanne d'Arc, Mme Pichon and her daughter of rue Marceau, Mme Albertini and her daughter of rue Voltaire, Mlle Meunier of rue Marceau, Mlle Simone Peltier of les Closeaux, Mme Mireille Beury of les Grésillons, both in Chinon commune, Mme Galle at Beaumont, Mme Delory of the rue du Mûrier, their bearing betrays without a doubt the mission that they are accomplishing."[31] This litany conveys a fear that although it was men who held public office, the town was effectively being run by a mafia of women who exercised an insidious influence at the Kreiskommandantur. The French authorities tried to persuade the Germans, in the interest of orderly and hierarchical administration, not to listen to women who through menial employment or sex had come into contact with them. The Germans' own concern with order and hierarchy, it was hoped, would induce them to see eye to eye with the French and terminate the reign of these females.

After her break with Chevalier and Longuépée, Simone Peltier went to live in a nearby hamlet with a member of the collaborationist Milice named Crosnier and then terrorized the local inhabitants by threatening to have anyone who crossed her arrested by the Germans. After the Liberation Crosnier was found in a wood with his hands tied behind his back and two bullets in the head in what turned out to be a settling of scores within the Milice.[32] Chevalier, Longuépée, and Peltier were arrested, interned, and sent for trial. Two peasants and a grocer testified against Simone Peltier as an immoral person addicted to the easy life and easy money, and she was sentenced to three years for denunciation. At their own trials Chevalier and Longuépée accused Peltier of lying about the scenes of debauchery with Germans alleged to have gone on at the café. Longuépée admitted that she had reported Bagarie for wiping his bottom with a photo of Marshal Pétain but she denied that she had denounced people to the Germans and argued that, on the contrary, she had used her contacts with the Germans to save young men from being sent on forced labor service to the Reich. Meanwhile Chevalier claimed that he had hidden three

Jewish doctors who had been entrusted to him by his son-in-law in a flat he owned in Paris. The Cour de Justice was not convinced: Peltier was sentenced to three years in prison, Longuépée to five, and Chevalier to ten.[33]

The view of the Germans that as victorious soldiers they had first claim on French women did not go unchallenged by French men, especially in the rough and tumble of Saturday nights, when drink flowed freely. There were particular hot spots like the port districts of Nantes and Saint-Nazaire, teeming with German soldiers and sailors whom French youths in gangs were willing to take on. One fight in Nantes in September 1941, for example, led to the wounding of two German soldiers and the arrest of two Frenchmen, with both the French and German police involved. For the French police chief this was not a question of the rights and wrongs of sleeping with Germans but a matter of public order. In the little cafés of the quai de la Fosse, where musicians played, and the square in front of the Bourse, where a fair was often set up, "all the young people, male and female, and soldiers, too, get together every night and particularly on Saturdays, Sundays, and holidays," he observed. "Incidents often happen in these places because of the mingling of males and females and above all because of the abuse of alcohol."[34]

Between flirting, picking up girls, buying rounds, and paying for casual sex, the lines were extremely fuzzy. Both French and German authorities attempted to isolate prostitution from other relationships and regulate it under well-established procedures for reasons of public health and public order. But to control a range of sexual activity through regulations designed for a well-defined category of prostitutes who were registered, kept in brothels, and subjected to medical examination was extremely difficult. Scarcely three weeks after the arrival of the Germans in Angers, the Kommandantur instructed the local police chief to clamp down on what he called the "covert prostitution" going on in hotels, cafés, bars, and even private houses, where there were many "debauched women." Inverting the conventional balance of menace between occupiers and occupied, he insisted that "these women who practice covert prostitution represent a very great danger for German soldiers.... They are a veritable plague." Suspects, he said, should be arrested, medically examined, sent to the dispensary if they were found to be infected, and properly registered if they admitted to being prostitutes; establishments that allowed such women to ply their trade should be closed down. A sweep by the French police in Angers discovered thirty-seven women in brothels, twenty-five registered prostitutes working privately, and forty-one covert prostitutes, of whom twelve were found to be contagious. Separate brothels were established for Frenchmen and German soldiers, with an elite brothel for German officers. Notices were posted in all brothels and in the homes of women working privately to the effect that women were not allowed to attract clients from windows or on the street and had to take at least one bath a week and that German soldiers should use condoms and be issued cards with the name and address of a contact who could be traced if they developed VD. The clampdown did little, however, to minimize the problem: the number of prostitutes discovered in Angers rose in the weeks before Christmas 1940 to sixty in brothels and sixty registered individuals, with ten covert workers, and the number of covert workers suddenly rose again to thirty in February 1941.[35]

One problem with the regulation of prostitution was that the message the Germans put out was ambivalent. They demanded action by the French police to guard against the scourge of VD, but as a point of honor they were reluctant to allow interference in the amorous pursuits of German soldiers. In 1943, for example, an incident flared up in Cholet when Mlle Denise Lacomme was officially registered as a prostitute by the French police. This provoked her suitor, Karl Speyer, who oversaw the shoe industry in the west of France for the purposes of the German war economy, to burst into the police station to announce that her registration was "an offense to the German army" and that he was going to "shoot all her lovers, have all the officers who contributed to her registration imprisoned as Gaullists, and put a bullet in the police inspector too." The SS chief in Angers, Hans-Dietrich Ernst, told regional prefect Roussillon to dismiss the inspector in question for "anti-German activities." The inspector was summoned to the Feldkommandantur at Angers and told that Mlle Lacomme would not undergo a medical examination. He expressed surprise, since he had orders from the Feldkommandantur to clamp down on clandestine prostitutes like Mlle Lacomme, an unemployed hairdresser who plied her trade from the terrace of the Hôtel Blanchard, opposite the railway station. He had no idea why Speyer was so angry, given that he was "only one number on a long list." For the French authorities it was intolerable that such a woman could make their police look ridiculous. The regional prefect stood firm and refused to dismiss the inspector. On his side, Ernst realized that the German authorities also stood to look ridiculous by hitching their honor to a such a dubious woman, and he withdrew the dismissal order.[36]

As the Occupation wore on, it became more and more difficult to deal with prostitution and the public-order issues associated with it. German troops returning from the Russian front looked to have a good time in France and did not take no for an answer. In the sleepy town of Ancenis, on the banks of the Loire, soldiers who had done twenty-two months on the eastern front had a particular fondness for the Au Bon Muscadet café, where they were "attracted more by the charms of Madame Dubillot [the proprietress] than by the drinks." Finding the café closed one evening, they started firing their pistols. Two weeks later, finding the Stella brothel in the town closed, they fired off more shots, wounding a fisherman in his boat. The distraught mayor tried to convince the Kreiskommandant and prefect to set up mixed patrols of French and German gendarmes to keep a watch on such brothels, but even the Kreiskommandant had little authority over troops who didn't stay long in the area. Meanwhile a local doctor who tended the wounded fisherman was concerned that the presence of the Germans was driving up prostitution at an alarming rate: "minors, wives of POWs, mothers of small children are causing a veritable scandal that is having a disastrous effect on the morality of our young people."[37]

It was not only prostitution that blurred the lines of casual sex. The Occupation created a multitude of menial jobs for women—as cleaners, laundrywomen, bar staff, and waitresses in the Soldatenheime, or officers' casinos—that often led to sexual relationships. In seaside resorts such as La Baule, Pornichet, and Le Croisic, where many of the military and naval forces working at Saint-Nazaire were housed in holiday villas, local girls taken on formally as maids in the villas were willing to provide more generous service.[38] Slightly above the ruck, Simone Deflandre, a divorcée in her early thirties who had been a nurse and masseuse, ran the Bar de la Plage and supervised the maids who worked in the villas at La Baule; she went out with a Captain Piel, a dental surgeon in civilian life who not only wined and dined her in restaurants but also looked after her teeth.[39]

Cohabitation between French and Germans was as much about money as about sex. Obviously the Germans were in a position to plunder and exploit the French economically. But just as personal encounters between French and Germans were not just about rape but about patterns and codes of love and sex, so also economic relations were constructed according to certain norms and were not always to the disadvantage of the French. Requisition was not the same as theft: a note was issued to the provider that was redeemable, at least in theory, from the French or German authorities. Neither did the Germans only take: leading sectors of the French economy boomed under the Occupation because of German orders, while Germans were always ready to pay handsomely on the black market for scarce items or luxuries.

Inevitably things were not always as ordered as this. Less than three months after the armistice, the curé of Le Loroux, near the demarcation line, sent an anguished letter to Marshal Pétain saying that since 24 June the commune had been occupied by 210 Germans and 80 horses. The German soldiers had taken over the schoolhouse, billeted themselves on the inhabitants and in some cases driven them out, removed furniture from houses, taken hay and straw for their horses and wood and groceries for themselves, and performed military exercises in the beet fields. "Observe the terms of the armistice?" he asked. "Permit German forces to respect nothing, to take what families require for their own needs without the permission of the French authorities, to steal whatever they want without a requisition order, for the disgusting pleasure of reducing people to the greatest misery?" An agricultural official from Tours went to the village to see and reported back that there were now only eighty soldiers, that Germans taking wood and coal was nothing unusual although perhaps they might now gather hay and straw from other communes as well. He said that nothing had in fact been taken without a requisition receipt's being issued, that "relations between the population and the troops were correct," and that for his part the mayor had not complained.[40]

Similar abuses went on in Nantes, where the Germans, having ruled that all goods that had entered the port since 3 September 1939 were legitimate war booty, confiscated stocks of tea, coffee, sugar, chocolate, rice, and vegetable oil. Ordinary troops were more interested in consumer goods and, waving blank requisition slips or indeed no slips at all, piled into the city's department stores and, according to the perfect, took "radios, refrigerators, champagne, flowers, expensive antique or modern furniture, carpets, drapes, luxurious dinner services, watches, chandeliers, bicycles, cars, and even pleasure boats."[41] He complained to Feldkommandant Karl Hotz, and Hotz was prepared to rein in his subordinates if they went too far. When a Luftwaffe officer took the car of the head of the women's teacher training college in Nantes on the grounds that "she did not like Germans," issuing a requisition note and then taking it back because it compromised him, then dragging her to the Feldkommandantur and keeping her waiting for two hours, Hotz "became crimson, as if he were going to fly into a violent temper." He declared that to take a car without issuing a requisition note was theft and that no innocent person should be held in the Kommandantur without his orders.[42]

The French, who prided themselves on their Gallic cunning, found many ways to get around the threat of requisition. Periodically, farmers were required to take their horses to town so that the Germans could make a selection. Odile Talon, a farmer's daughter from outside Angers who regularly went out with Germans and had influence with them, was able to get some peasants who came to her exempted.[43] Alternatively, tricking the Germans served peasant self-interest and was later presented as patriotism. René Bretault, from the Angevin village of La Pommeraye, recalls that he took a twenty-five-year-old before the German commission and was told, "Rauss!"[44] Sometimes the trade in horses went in favor of the locals. When the Germans arrived in Loire-Inférieure they noted that horses were in short supply because in the previous year the *French* army had requisitioned 8,800 of them, 50 percent more than the Germans would have. Since they had an interest in getting the crops, not least to ensure fodder, they actually lent their own military horses to French farmers for the duration of the harvest.[45]

The Germans in general regarded France as a rich country but a backward and unproductive one whose resources needed to be developed rationally if exploitation on a long-term basis was to be a success. Helmuth Voss, in Angers, compared France to "a beautiful older woman." "The houses, fields, and gardens," he said, "are somewhat neglected, the whole seems unplanned and disconnected, the technology is thirty years out of date and makes us smile, the looks are seductive only from a certain distance."[46]

Shortly after he arrived in Angers, Feldkommandant Kloss called a meeting of the prefect, his economic advisers, and a number of mayors and leading producers to impress on them the need to increase productivity, in particular, he made clear, the yield of the wheat harvest had to be increased the following year by 25 percent. He emphasized that the proposed cooperation was in deliberate contrast to the way the French had treated the Rhineland when they occupied it in 1923. "The French authorities and economic leaders," he duly reported, "are quite ready to work according to the directives of the military administration and to take and follow through the necessary measures."[47]

One obsession of the German authorities was the amount of agricultural land that lay fallow or abandoned. The French argued that productivity was limited by the number of farmers held by the Germans as POWs, but the Germans would not accept this explanation.[48] On one occasion they demanded the dismissal of the director of agricultural services of Indre-et-Loire, whom they saw as the tool of "the Jew Aaron," former president of the Chamber of Agriculture of Indre-et-Loire, for sabotaging their drive to increase the wheat harvest.[49] Another obsession was the plague of Colorado beetles that infested the potato crops. Each June the Germans issued instructions for the peasants to spray their crops and for children to be taken out of school three days a week to collect and destroy the pests. In July 1941 the Feldkommandantur of Loire-Inférieure complained that the potato fields were still infested and demanded another campaign in August, but the rural mayors replied that the children were on vacation and their teachers gone and that the farmers did not want children in their fields anyway.[50] A final obsession of the Germans was the infestation of rats in slaughterhouses, tanneries, butcher shops, dairies, and even restaurants. The chief veterinary officer in Tours, a Dr. Herbig, told the prefect that the vermin were destroying food and fodder, propagating disease, and undermining buildings; he ordered a program of destruction by traps and poison in the summer of 1941. Unhappy with the result, he ordered a second attempt in the fall.[51] The Germans remained frustrated by the incompetence of the French and suspected that their foot-dragging was deliberate.[52]

The German authorities were concerned primarily with the economic contribution the French could make but were also seduced by their artistic treasures. Of course the financial value of the treasures was important, but there is evidence that the Germans could be better conservators than the French. In the autumn of 1940, for example, Count Metterich, the head of the army's artistic conservation unit, visited Touraine with a delegation of about twenty German museum directors and conservators to inspect its historic buildings.[53] He saw to it that the treasures of Versailles, which had been moved for protection to the depository of Brissac, outside Angers, received adequate supplies of scarce coal to ensure adequate heat.[54] A list was drawn up of châteaux that for artistic reasons were not to be occupied by German forces, including the châteaux of Chenonceaux, Villandry, Ussé, Azay-le-Rideau, Langeais, Brissac, and Saumur.[55] After a visit to the châteaux of Saumur, the subprefect complained to the mayor, much to the amusement of the Kreiskommandant, that the windows were broken, the collection was scattered, and the caretaker refused to show them around because he said it was his day off.[56]

Even when military needs took precedence over art, the German authorities were prepared to listen to arguments from the Ministry for Industrial Production as to why certain statues of historic significance should be preserved. Statues of Joan of Arc were generally protected, but the statue of Rabelais at Chinon, whose ironic and subversive message did not sit well with the conservative, moralistic tones of Vichy's National Revolution, was at risk. The statue was duly earmarked for removal early in 1942 and Chinon was forced to present Rabelais in a new light in order to hold on to him. The municipal council petitioned Marshal Pétain on behalf of "the father of the French language . . . born in this region that he loved so much and that inspired most of his works." The minister for industrial production decided to recommend to the German authorities that Rabelais be permitted to stay on his pedestal.[57] The statues of the nineteenth-century sculptor David d'Angers in Angers and the statue of Balzac in Tours, however, were among those considered more useful as German bullets than as monuments to French artistic pride.[58]

The contribution that France could make to the German war effort was of course central, and it is clear that German production orders lifted the French economy out of the recession into which it had been plunged after the defeat of 1940. War industries no longer had any purpose, the British imposed a blockade that caused severe shortages of coal and thus of electricity, and workers were laid off—first women, then men. In Loire-Inférieure, the Germans calculated in August 1940 that a third of the workforce of 85,000 were unemployed.[59] The Vichy government encouraged local chambers of commerce to reduce unemployment by developing programs to clear bomb damage, build local roads, or improve the water supply, but it was paying a vast amount to Germany as reparation and tribute under the armistice and had no funds available for Keynesian economics. Orders from the Wehrmacht, the Luftwaffe, and above all from Kriegsmarine to sustain the war effort were the obvious alternative allowing French firms to stay in business.

The experience of the small town of Cholet may serve as an example. As traditional economically as it was politically, it relied on two staple industries, textiles and shoe manufacture; in the spring of 1941 its municipal council was reduced to finding work for 150 unemployed men by enlarging the cemetery.[60] Then industries such as Radio-Électrique and the armaments firm Société Alsatienne were relocated to Cholet from Paris and German-annexed Alsace and were soon receiving German orders for ships' radios and pistols. So large was the market for supplying the armed forces that even the traditional textile industry in Cholet was inundated with orders for blackout material, carpeting, bed linens, and even handkerchiefs. Similar enterprises in nearby towns also flourished. Bessonneau of Angers employed 3,000 workers making ropes, sailcloth, and tarpaulin and later diversified into nine-man tents and camouflage netting, while Châteaubriant and Fougères produced snowshoes and army leathers for the Russian front.

The demand for finished goods soon began to outstrip the availability of labor and materials and the Germans adopted a policy of concentration, closing down smaller and less efficient firms to allow the larger units to develop. In February 1942 the Feldkommandantur of Tours presented the prefect with a list of eleven firms, including a porcelain factory, a typewriter factory, and the Mame print works, that would have to close.[61] Touraine was also the location, however, of a number of advanced precision industries that expanded by virtue of military orders, such as the Société Générale d'Optiques of Tours, Barbier-Bernard and Turenne of Amboise, which made field glasses, periscopes, and glass for headlights and searchlights, and the Compagnie des Cables, which made the cables crucial for military communication in occupied Europe.

The biggest contractors in the region were the shipyards, railway works, and aircraft factories of the Nantes/Saint-Nazaire area. In Nantes were the Chantiers de la Loire, the Chantiers de Bretagne, and the Chantiers Dubigeon; in Saint-Nazaire the massive Chantiers et Ateliers Penhoët and Chantiers de la Loire, both with over 3,000 workers. All these received orders from November 1940 on to build destroyers, tugs, torpedo boats, speedboats, U-boats, air-traffic-control boats, tankers, transport ships, whalers, and trawlers. Associated engineering works received orders for turbines and motors, steelworks for sheet metal.[62] Meanwhile in Nantes the Compagnie Générale de Construction de Locomotives (Batignolles-Chatillon) was devoting 90 percent of its output to the Reichsbahn early in 1941, while the Société Nationale de Construction Aéronautique du Sud-Ouest (SNCASO) at Nantes-Bouguenais accepted an order in April 1941 to build Heinkel 111 aircraft worth four million man-hours over two years.[63] From May 1942 there was a surge of orders not only from Heinkel of Rostock but from Junkers of Magdeburg, Focke Wulf of Bremen, and BMW aircraft motors of Munich.[64] To see that these orders were carried out efficiently, the Germans set up a separate war-economy administration, the Rüstungsinspektion, which patterned itself on the hierarchy of the military administration. In 1942 the Rüstungsinspektion B (southwest France), with responsibility for production in Maine-et-Loire, Indre-et-Loire, Sarthe, Mayenne, and Ille-et-Vilaine (but not Loire-Inférieure), was moved from Tours to Le Mans and placed under Korvettenkapitan Fock, who was directly answerable to Paris. One of its goals was to increase the number of Rüstungsbetriebe, or Rü-Betriebe, producing almost totally for the German military, and of Vorzugsbetribe, or V-Betriebe, working partly for it. By September 1942 there were forty-nine Rü-Betriebe in the Le Mans region but a year earlier there had been thirty in Loire-Inférieure alone, demonstrating its exceptional importance for the German military machine.[65] The workers in these factories generally enjoyed advantageous conditions, such as fuller rations than the average and protection from the Germans' periodic campaigns to recruit labor.

The German military machine required not only the delivery of military hardware but also enormous building projects such as the Atlantic Wall to fend off potential invasion and the construction of U-boat bases at Lorient and Saint-Nazaire from which the campaign against Allied Atlantic convoys could be launched. These projects were promoted by the Todt Organization and involved huge contracts with construction companies like the Entreprise des Travaux Publics Dodin in Nantes, which themselves often subcontracted to consortia such as the Nantes group of twenty-seven firms set up in July 1943. After the war Henri Dodin and the director of the consortium argued that initially he had refused contracts but the Germans threatened to requisition his workforce and plant.[66] But accept them they did, using labor conscripted by the Todt Organization, which was often employed under atrocious conditions. One man sent to build the submarine base at Saint-Nazaire said that everything was geared to obtaining the quickest possible results: the men worked from 7:00 A.M. to 7:00 P.M. alongside Spaniards, Portuguese, Italians, Czechs, Poles, Russians, and Arabs and continued through air-raid warnings (for which no shelters were provided anyway). The food was plentiful but bad, they slept on thin mattresses, and hygiene was nonexistent. The workers were like civilian prisoners with unspecified release dates, he said.[67] Meanwhile the Entreprises Dodin made a profit of between fifty and eighty million francs working on German defenses.[68]

There has been much debate as to how free employers were to work for the Reich and whether "economic collaboration" should be considered in the same way as other forms of collaboration. What employers said after the war about having their arms twisted is difficult to weigh. In 1943, according to the Rüstungskommando of Le Mans, the owner of a foundry at Sainte-Jammes-sur-Sarthe initially refused an order to make 50,000 15.5 cm shells, but mainly because he thought his factory would promptly be bombed by the Allies; he was soon induced to change his mind.[69] The term *survival collaboration* has been invented by historians to define working for the Germans on pain of seeing one's plant and/or labor requisitioned, but these same historians argue that German orders were "the driving force of the French economy" under the Occupation, accounting for up to 70 percent and even 90 percent of firms' orders.[70] The temptations, moreover, were not confined to shipyards, engineering plants, and building enterprises. The German war machine created a vast market not only for military hardware and buildings but for food, drink, scrap metal, and luxuries. It imposed price restrictions and legislated against hoarding, but goods were in such short supply and demand was so intense that even the Germans were unable to prevent the flourishing of a black market and were even instrumental in developing it. The French, meanwhile, were only too delighted to procure wanted goods and sell them to the Germans at exorbitant prices.[71]

Those who profited included not only hardened speculators but ordinary individuals with an eye for a good deal. Among the first, Roger Flamant was well known in the La Baule area. Before the war he had had a large textile dye works at Anor in the Nord, which he sold, taking off for Morocco to make another fortune. During the war he became a property developer in the resorts of La Baule and Le Pouliguen, buying up large villas and dividing them into apartments for a postwar vacation business. He was well connected with the German authorities, who sold him materials from buildings they had demolished and even lent him trucks to transport them.[72] At the other end of the spectrum was Raymond Couturier, a mechanic and foreman at the SNCASO works at Château-Bougon, who also ran a café called L'Envol. When the Germans arrived he gave up his job at the aircraft factory to concentrate on his café, then made a fortune hiring out horses and carts for the German air base at Château-Bougon and supplying the Germans with black-market goods in the bargain.[73]

Some speculators had their fingers in a number of pies. M. Maud, for example, had a clandestine abattoir at Montreuil-Bellay in Anjou and delivered meat to the Germans billeted at the cavalry school of Saumur. He also had a secret distillery that sold liquor to the Germans at 500 francs per liter; he exported the rest by rail to Nancy. With his profits he obtained supplies of sugar, copper, and bronze, which he sold to the Germans, and did a trade in bicycles new and secondhand, hunting rifles that had been left at the cavalry school, and small arms that had been abandoned by British soldiers in 1940.[74] Other speculators were more specialized and more organized. George Besson, a commercial traveler, was the head of a trafficking ring that bought up wine from Touraine winegrowers for between eight and fifteen francs a bottle and sold it to German clients in Paris for fifty-five francs. Equipped with passes issued by corrupt Germans, the ring was able to send truckloads to the capital without being stopped by French or German authorities, and the five ringleaders were said to have made 1.5 million francs in three months.[75]

Occupied France was full of rags-to-riches stories along the lines of Jean Dutourd's *Au Bon Beurre*. In the little village of Coueron, outside Nantes, Joseph Aubineau was a laborer in 1940. He worked for the Germans as a carpenter, then bought a cart, then a truck, and became a road hauler. He was said to have been involved in an "intense black-market trade with the Germans, supplying them with wine, pork, poultry, eggs, etc.... He was reputed to be the biggest trafficker in the region."[76] In many ways it was impossible to cohabit with the Germans and not make money off them. Those who got into trouble at the Liberation were seen to have gone too far, in particular to have preferred German clients to local customers, or to have combined profit with sex. Mme Laurence Morandeau, who ran a café in the same village of Coueron, was accused of saying that she preferred one German customer to twenty French ones and of indulging with her daughter Suzanne in "veritable orgies" with Germans while her husband took pictures of them with a camera stolen from work. She denied the orgies as "pure invention" and stated baldly, "I did like all traders, I served Germans in my café because I had to, but I never collaborated with them."[77] One is inclined to believe her, and the thousands like her who simply did business with the Germans because they were good customers with money to spend. Some, like the Morandeau family, ended up in court, but most got away with it and went on to make money out of the next wave of foreigners. As one peasant joked, "During the Occupation I worked for the Germans and now I am going to work for the Americans."[78]

The sullen rejection of the Germans represented by Vercors in *Le Silence de la mer* has to be set against a more nuanced analysis of cohabitation between French and Germans that held good at least for the first two years of the Occupation. The image evoked by the historian Philippe Burrin of the "blind town" refusing to make eye contact with the Germans was more patriotic ideal than reality.[79] Beyond the power relations of French and German authorities there were manifold private relations between French and Germans that tended to revolve around money and sex. These relations were not arbitrary but governed by rules negotiated between French and Germans and among French people themselves. To receive Germans at home, for example, unless they were billeted, was felt to be different from mingling with them in a public place under the public gaze. To accept German production orders openly was not the same thing as trafficking with Germans on the black market. Very often the measure of what was acceptable was its impact on the community: production orders might keep the local economy afloat and people in work, whereas trafficking deprived the locality of scarce resources. The impact of the Germans was not wholly negative; naturally, they wished to exploit France's resources to the full but this sometimes entailed observing traditional practices and eliminating vermin and pests. It has also been calculated that Germans did their bit to tackle France's demographic deficit by fathering between 50,000 and 70,000 children.[80] Perspectives also changed with time, so that practices tolerated by communities weakened by evacuation and the absence of POWs in 1940 were judged harshly in 1944 when communities were seeking to rebuild themselves after the Liberation. Sexual misdemeanors were punished more harshly than economic collaboration, partly because they might be linked to intelligence of the enemy and the denunciation of compatriots, partly because the threat to family, community, and male honor was felt to be much greater. The perspective of 1944 should not, however, prevent us from remembering that in many respects occupied France was another country where they did things differently.

3

Separation

At the end of June 1940, Odette Goxe returned to Angers from the island of Noirmoutier, off the Brittany coast, where she had fled with her mother, Ninette Bordereau, and young children, in an attempt to find her father, who had been taken prisoner by the Germans. French forces, which had collapsed and fled west and south before the German advance, had been rounded up in the tens of thousands and herded into makeshift prisoner-of-war camps. She discovered that he was with his whole regiment in a camp of 30,000 men near Le Mans, but when she arrived the Germans had suspended all visits because women were rioting outside the camp. Back in Angers on 2 July she witnessed another column of prisoners being marched through the town on their way to the Le Mans camp. There was a "surge of solidarity that could not have been predicted at that time of food restrictions," recalls Odette Goxe. "From all the windows and door-ways people brought the captured soldiers everything they had: sugar, bread, wine. The order was given for the column to stop so that this unprecedented gesture could be completed in safety." Odette returned to

Noirmoutier "completely shattered by all these emotions and in real need of rest." Meanwhile her mother, though in no doubt about the "calvary" her husband was having to endure, took solace from the firm belief that he would be home soon.[1]

This story sheds light on the predicament both of refugees and of POWs in the turbulent summer of 1940. The Bordereau/Goxe family did not have to travel far and their return to Angers was relatively unimpeded, but other refugees were less fortunate. Early in July the Germans decided that because of military operations all refugees would have to stay south of the Loire and Cher Rivers, so that those who had fled before the advancing German armies were now unable to return home.[2] The Germans were keen that the refugees should not remain idle but should help bring in the harvest where possible.[3] Later in the month they divided the Occupied Zone into five subzones, with different rules applying to each. Those who had fled from the Paris region or from between the Seine and the Loire were allowed to return; those who had come from between the Seine and the Somme could return only if they were farmers or employed in the public services; while those who had come from north of the Somme, essentially the departments of the Nord, Pas-de-Calais, Aisne, and Somme, were not allowed to return at all. Belgians and Dutch were obliged to go home, and pressure was put on those who had left Alsace and Lorraine, now annexed by Germany, to go back. The German authorities ordered a census of all Alsatians and Lorrainers, allegedly for statistical purposes, but rumors began to spread that those who did not go back would have their property confiscated. Elizabeth Walter, who had come to Nantes from Strasbourg in September 1939 and was now employed at the prefecture, wrote to her employers on behalf of a number of her compatriots who wanted to stay in Nantes.[4] The last official repatriation train for Alsatians and Lorrainers had in fact left Nantes at the end of October, one of many that furrowed the country in the late summer and autumn of 1940, taking refugees back to their place of origin, free of charge if they could not pay. Numbers in the Loire Valley declined from 250,000 in the Loire-Inférieure in June to only 18,000 in October and from 100,000 to under 10,000 in Maine-et-Loire.[5]

While the refugees were going home, the POWs were behind barbed wire in camps, often in the most atrocious conditions. Some buildings that the Germans took over, such as the Cavalry School of Saumur, provided reasonable accommodation, but Brittany became a veritable gulag of encampments in the open fields: 20,000 at Savenay, 30,000 at Château-briant. Until barbed-wire fences were in place the German sentries kept their human flocks together simply by promising that they would soon be liberated.[6] The water was suspect, there was little food, no sanitation, no shelter, and in the pouring rain the ground turned to mud under-foot. The local hygiene inspector's worries about an outbreak of typhus or dysentery were exacerbated by the presence of African prisoners.[7] The bishop of Nantes, who visited the camps early in July, was more concerned about the prisoners' souls and about ensuring that soldier-priests who had also been captured were provided with portable altars.[8] The Marquise de Sesmaisons, whose husband was a prisoner of war and who worked for the Red Cross, harassed the German authorities to obtain permission for prisoners to work outside the camps or even be released. She was "providence itself," said one local mayor, "counting neither time, nor effort, nor expense."[9] In Nantes, Léon Jost, a busi-nessman who had lost a leg in the First World War and received the Legion of Honor, set up a committee with two other veterans, Alexan-dre Fourny and Fernand Ridel, to provide food to the camps. Under cover of this charity, the committee organized escapes to the nonoccu-pied zone for over 2,000 POWs. For their pains, seven members of the committee and its female secretary were arrested in January 1941 and sentenced by a German military court to three years in prison.[10]

The shadow of the 1.5 million POWs hung like a pall over occupied France. From the three departments under review here, there were 45,000 POWs at the end of 1942, 10 percent of the active population.[11] With as many soldiers imprisoned as there were soldiers killed in the 1914–18 war, most families in France were without a husband, father, brother, or son. The separations caused both material hardship and mental anxiety, for no one knew when the loved one would return and fervent hopes were repeat-edly disappointed.[12] For all the antifeminist rhetoric of the Vichy regime, which preferred women to stay at home and bring up children, women were increasingly called on to assume new responsibilities and new roles—they were "liberated" in fact if not in law.[13] The response of French com-munities to the POW tragedy was powerful and imaginative. The "surge of solidarity" evoked by Odette Goxe continued throughout the Occupation in the form of committees to raise funds and send packages to loved ones hundreds of miles away in German stalags and oflags. The fate of the prisoners was a major concern of the government, which managed to get some prisoners brought home, and also of the Church, which promoted national days of prayer as well as aid. And yet the picture was not all rosy. The whole issue of POWs revealed schisms as well as solidarities in French society: power struggles between and within organizations involved in supporting the prisoners, tensions between local communities or businesses wishing to care for *their* prisoners and representatives of central organizations wanting them to take a wider view, political conflicts between those involved in what was supposed to be charity, and even corruption and crime festering under the cover of altruism.

In the early months of the Occupation French women unable to trace their husbands laid siege to the authorities. Mme Bonin, a mother of three from a working-class suburb of Angers, told the prefect that she had had no news of her husband for months. "I am very anxious about what has happened to him and why he has not come home," she said. "Life is very hard and I only have my military benefit to live on."[14] When POWs were found and logged, prefects were lobbied from all sides—municipalities, government departments, magistrates, politicians, bishops, and private firms—requesting that they intercede with the German authorities for the release of members of their staffs. The archbishop of Tours wrote both to the Feldkommandant, urging the release of priests and schoolmasters in holy orders who had borne arms, and to the Red Cross on behalf of priests who had been military chaplains or stretcher bearers and thus, under the Geneva Convention, should not be held.[15]

The German authorities were not inclined to be generous. They entertained requests only in respect of certain categories, such as farmers, workers in vital industries, and civil servants who were indispensable. Feldkommandant Marloh of Tours decided in August 1940 to consider no more than five or ten applications a week, while Feldkommandant Kloss of Angers ruled in September that requests would have to be drawn up in French and German and sent not to him but to the Prisoner-of-War Information Bureau in Paris.[16] For the Germans, the French POW population represented an immense resource of hostages, the promise of whose return home could be used to exert pressure on the French to behave well. Later in the war the POWs were used as a bargaining counter, exchanged (on very unequal terms) for French workers needed in Germany to turn the wheels of the Reich's economy. But, as we have seen, the Germans also had an interest in the functioning of the French economy, required to sustain the army of Occupation and the German war machine itself. So, for example, they were prepared to allow French POWs to leave their camps in the summer of 1940 to help bring in the harvest. The fact that nearly a third of French POWs were from agricultural backgrounds (and 60 percent of Angevin POWs) made this policy economically sensible.

Letting POWs work in the fields was of course a security risk, whether they were under German or French guard. In Touraine, which was bifurcated by the demarcation line, the first escape was registered in mid-August 1940. In September there were few, but in October there was a rash of escapes, as POWs pretended to go for walks on Sunday or claimed they were going to bathe in the Vienne. Sometimes they escaped not just in ones or twos but in groups of six or eight from the same farm, and in March 1941 fifteen North African prisoners escaped from their rural accommodation by piercing the wall at the back of a cupboard.[17] Escapes also took place from legitimate POW camps. Three prisoners escaped from the cavalry school of Saumur on Christmas Eve 1940; they took refuge in a laborer's cottage in Saumur and one was shot dead while hiding under a bed.[18] After such incidents the German authorities decided that the time had come to move French POWs en masse to Germany. The first contingent of 1,000 from Saumur left on 6 January, followed by 1,200 ten days later. After that the escape stories were mainly those of French African troops whom the Germans were not keen to import. In February thirty-four escaped and Kreiskommandant Baron von Gall threatened to impose a collective fine on the town. Subprefect Robert Milliat called a meeting of the police, gendarmerie, and Catholic and Protestant church leaders to put pressure on individuals, notably in the Red Cross, who were suspected of helping escapees.[19] It seems that the meeting was something of a charade. In March over a hundred African soldiers escaped from the cavalry school and Feldkommandant Kloss duly imposed a fine of 500,000 francs, which was advanced from municipal funds and recouped by an extraordinary tax on the townspeople. When another group of Africans escaped in

April, an irate von Gall summoned Milliat and threatened another fine of 500,000 francs. Milliat replied judiciously that he would do his best to find them but "my honor as a Frenchman would forbid me from handing them over if they were discovered."[20] This patriotic commitment by a local official toward Africans who, though black, were soldiers in the French army contrasts eloquently with the treatment meted out to Jews, many of whom were French, a year or so later.

From time to time small groups of prisoners returned to France, either for good or for a period of leave. First there were the sick, then fathers of large families such as the Marquis de Sesmaisons, with his eight children, who returned on 27 December 1940. In the spring of 1941 a number of farmers returned, then in the summer veterans of the 1914–18 war, for whom the Germans had a particular respect, such as Colonel Canon Panaget. The trickle of homecomings encouraged speculation about more returns. Contradictory rumors spread in the Mauges in the spring of 1941 to the effect that mayors were going to be able to select one POW in their commune who could come home or, alternatively, that peasants with more than twenty hectares would be released.[21] Such were the rumors of an imminent "massive" release of prisoners that Feldkommandant Kloss and prefect Roussillon had to act in concert to scotch them lest disappointment fuel social unrest.[22] It took more than a press communiqué to silence the speculation, however, and in July 1941, just after the German invasion of Russia, it was being whispered that *all* French prisoners would be home before the end of the year, to make room for the torrent of Russian POWs.[23]

For the vast majority of POWs, the trip to Germany was the beginning of a term that ended only in the spring or summer of 1945. To overcome the pain of separated families, communities and churches invented a multitude of ways to stay in touch, and their efforts were often reciprocated by the soldiers in the camps. Indeed, it would be fair to say that fundraising and support activities on behalf of the POWs were among the greatest stimulants of sociability under the Occupation, drawing divided families out of their isolation, rallying the wider community around households in difficulty, and mobilizing the faithful to look after the spiritual health of the needy.

Support for the POWs was generated locally, but it was also vigorously promoted by the government. For the Vichy regime, encouraging concern for the prisoners was a way of stressing the message that France had been punished for past errors of self-indulgence, was in a period of mourning, and must seek regeneration through altruism and solidarity. A committee to support the POWs was set up in virtually every commune in France, and communes that were slow to respond were sharply criticized. To reply, as did the mayor of a small commune near Saumur, that the locals were too selfish and difficult and that at the age of seventy-two he no longer had the energy to dragoon them into action, was not good enough.[24]

In fact, the enthusiasm with which most communities set about raising funds to send food packages to the POWs was remarkable. At a time when all public gatherings had to be authorized by the German authorities and when the French authorities showed marked disapproval of merrymaking, POW events provided an excellent excuse for combining duty and pleasure. Fund-raising became the rationale for boule competitions, for football matches between neighboring communes, for concerts and amateur dramatics that played fast and loose with the Germans' keenness to spot political content in plays. Tombolas and lotteries were particularly popular, although the Secours National, the national charity, took a cut of all funds raised. The annual *kermesse*, or patronal festival, usually held in the summer or early autumn, was also geared to helping the POWs. In September 1942, for example, a commune near Saumur held a fair complete with a bar, a pastry booth, a greasy pole, ringtoss, weight-throwing and jumping competitions, a theatrical show, and children's games.[25] A year later another Angevin commune organized a fund-raising event at which it was demonstrated that the packages the local people had sent, if piled on top of each other, would be 2.5 times as high as the Eiffel Tower and that the string used would reach around the commune nine times.[26]

The Secours National, which ran successive campaigns for a variety of good causes, devoted a week in November 1941 to mobilizing the country's youth to collect funds for the POWs. The effort was promoted not only as a money raiser but as a way to promote solidarity between young people who had not yet reached military age and those who had served their country and paid a price. "Solidarity shares" worth fifty centimes each were sold in schools by the pupils, in workshops and businesses by apprentices and trainees, and on the streets by all of them.[27] In Angers, a variety of events put on by children and teenagers and attended by the regional prefect were accompanied by a live broadcast by Marshal Pétain.[28] An event organized by the popular-education secretariat and patronized by local Catholic and conservative notables raised funds to send books to the POWs. It was promoted as "the only way for them to escape from moral isolation" and made much of the fact that, with paper in short supply, books were now comparatively rare and expensive.[29]

In all these fund-raising and networking activities a key role was played by the Catholic Church. Its most obvious contribution was to organize national days of prayer for the POWs and to earmark collections for them. These activities offered an opportunity for church and state, which had not enjoyed good relations under the Third Republic, to draw together and for men, who had traditionally left the business of worship mainly to women, to return to the fold. On one of the prayer days, 29 November 1942, Monsignor Villepelet, bishop of Nantes, noted: "At 3:00 P.M. I led a procession of prisoners' wives, mothers, daughters, and sisters to Notre-Dame de Miséricorde, and at 5:00 P.M. in the cathedral there was a wonderful turnout of men, with the prefect and mayor in the front row. Great crowds in both churches, with sermons given by the Abbé Lordonné and Father Marboeuf, both freed prisoners."[30] Collections that day went to the Chaplaincy for Prisoners of War in Paris, which sent portable altars, altar linens, vestments, Bibles, service books, and Communion wine and wafers to the Catholic priests who had themselves been taken prisoner and were authorized to serve as chaplains in the camps.[31] Locally a system of spiritual adoption was developed whereby each diocese took a particular interest in camps where soldiers from that area were concentrated: Stalag IA for the diocese of Angers, Stalag IXB for that of Nantes, and Stalag IVC for that of Tours. At Stalag IA the chaplain organized a day of prayers to coincide with one held in Angers, and a prisoner who was subsequently liberated reported "how comforting it was for all of us to know that at the same moment we were united in fervent prayer for our dear France."[32]

This points to another of the links forged between France and Germany, the intense correspondence exchanged between bishops and the clergy of their diocese imprisoned in the camps. Some of the clergy tried to remain in good spirits, such as the Angevin curé René Sallé. "Abbé Vergnaud, curate of Vern, and Abbé Gohier, seminarist from Challan, as well as the Salesian Abbé Hardy are here with me," he wrote to the bishop of Angers, Monsignor Costes, "and there are a few Angevins, good types, good Christians, with whom we have prayer meetings from time to time." More pessimistic was Michel Guéry, who had been working on a large German farm. "It is so hard. For two years I didn't meet either a priest or a seminarist." Now he was part of a work team attached to the camp hospital and was able to help with religious services there. "In spite of that," he confessed, "my thoughts rarely leave my dear diocese. I dream of my parish, of the young people above all. . . . It is hard to be deprived of all that at an age when one should be throwing oneself into it. May our suffering be offered up for the future harvest."[33] The relationship between young cleric in exile and bishop was summed up by a priest from the diocese of Nantes who, after relating how teary-eyed POWs in a camp in the Tyrol pinned pictures sent by their children to their bunk beds, asked: "Are you not, after all, the father of the great sacerdotal family of the diocese and are not the priest-prisoners, exiled for nearly four years, a little more your children because they are more unfortunate?"[34]

In all this correspondence about fathers and children what is missing is the wife and mother. Yet the imprisonment of husbands and fathers in German camps affected no one more than French women, who were left with the burden of raising children and keeping their families fed, clothed, and housed. For the Vichy regime, moving close to the Catholic Church, the duty of women was to return home to have children and, as pious and virtuous mothers, to educate them. Men had failed to defend the nation but to regenerate it was the task of women. Mothers, proclaimed the archbishop of Tours for Mother's Day in 1941, were "a factor of first importance in the work of moral and social restoration that we all want to see for our country," and sermons must exalt "the maternal virtues: the spirit of faith, the spirit of sacrifice, sleepless vigilance, and constant self-abnegation."[35] "France will be what mothers have made it," echoed the mayor of the small town of Baugé on Mother's Day 1942. Mothers had "simply obeyed this double imperative of Genesis: 'Be ye fruitful, and multiply' and 'In sorrow thou shalt bring forth children.' Always smiling and resigned, they have agreed to be this mission and the holocaust of this redemption." Reluctantly, he conceded that the wife would have to substitute for the husband if he was mobilized or taken prisoner or if he died for the *patrie*, all the while "remaining the mother, the good mother, the *maman*."[36]

The law of 11 October 1940 excluded married women from employment in the public sector, except where the husband's income was insufficient for the household.[37] Mme Talbot, who had been hired as a philosophy teacher at Cholet's girls' school in 1939–40, was told in 1941 that the position was no longer available. She would have to make way for a woman in her twenties who would pursue a career in teaching—and besides, some male teachers being moved from the lycée of Brest because of the danger of air attacks now needed jobs in Cholet.[38] Married women were given incentives to stay at home, such as the priority card that allowed women with small children the right to go to the head of the food line or a special ration card if they were pregnant or breast-feeding. They were encouraged to have big families by the award of medals each Mother's Day—bronze for five children (legitimate ones, of course), silver for eight, gold for ten. The fifteenth child had the honor of having Marshal Pétain himself as a godfather. When, for example, the Huteau family of Nantes, described by the local priest as honest working-class, had their fifteenth child, they received a silver thimble, a large check, and a photograph of the marshal. The delighted father declared that the photograph would be "framed and given a place of honor in our little home, so that my children will grow up under his gaze."[39] How the mother responded we do not know.

This laudable ideal of the wife and mother did not correspond to the reality of life under the Occupation. Life was hard for all women, not least for the wives of POWs. In the first place, how were women whose husbands were in POW camps supposed to have legitimate children? The allowance they received from the authorities was meager, the whole fundraising business seemingly a fraud. In June 1942, on the second anniversary of the armistice, with the soldiers still behind barbed wire, a chain of handwritten letters was passed from hand to hand in Nantes, calling on the wives of POWs to protest. Fine speeches had been made, they said, but nothing had been done. In particular, huge amounts of money had been collected for the prisoners and given to the Red Cross to ensure a free package for each prisoner, but the cost of the goods was then charged to the families. A demonstration took place outside the gates of the prefecture, and the prefect agreed to receive a delegation of women who demanded two packages a month for their husbands, not one, and then complained that their allowances as wives of POWs were laughable. He dismissed the incident as inspired by communists but conceded in private that further demoralization of the families of prisoners might result in social unrest.[40]

Bread riots were a traditional activity for women who (even with husbands present) assumed responsibility for feeding the family.[41] Female labor was also traditional, at least among the working classes. Many women who would not necessarily have sought work were driven onto the market under the Occupation. Some took jobs as seamstresses, laundry women, or cleaners, if need be with the Germans. Others took over the farm or business, sometimes employing a significant number of workers. Despite its scorn for women working, the Vichy regime eventually had to repeal the law against the employment of married women because of growing labor shortages and came around to recognizing that the contribution of the wives of farmers or artisans who were POWs was crucial to the survival of the enterprise. Pétain himself wanted to award medals to forty such women in each department on Labor Day 1943. Among those decorated at Angers were Georgette Brunet, who left her prewar job to run her husband's leather business, and Hélène Boisteau, who ran her husband's roofing business with eight workers. Unfortunately, the authorities did not reckon with the pressures on working women: Mme Hubert of Allonnes, who had three children and ran her husband's charcuterie on her own, sent her apologies for not attending the ceremony on Sunday, 2 May, in Angers; her meat arrived on Saturdays, she explained, and there were no trains on Sundays.[42]

It was all very well for the Church and regime to preach the virtues of motherhood and family life, but the long absence of husbands in German POW camps put relationships under enormous strain. As the years passed, some women inevitably looked for support, protection, and love elsewhere. In small communities this did not pass unnoticed. The mayor of a wine-growing village near Saumur reported "the behavior, or rather *misbehavior*, of two wives of prisoners in my commune, scandalizing the inhabitants and threatening the upright young men." The prefect replied that under the law of 23 December 1942 to "protect the dignity of the family home from which the husband is absent owing to the circumstances of war," a man might be fined for living with the wife of a POW, but only if the husband lodged a complaint. The mayor, furious, argued that the husbands were in a German camp and one who had been burned in an Allied air raid was nearly blind; he insinuated that the women were prostitutes and that the vice squad should be brought in. "It is not with such examples that the young people of France will revive our poor country." The wife of the injured POW later divorced, sold the farm, and moved to Saumur, where she ran a café.[43]

Sometimes husbands complained from POW camp and tried to begin divorce proceedings, but if Vichy was clear about one thing, it was that divorce should be more difficult. The law of 2 April 1942 prohibited divorce within three years of marriage and did not consider adultery cause enough. So when POW Paul Urien, on hearing of his wife's behavior, told prefect Dupard, "I have only disgust for that woman, who is not worthy to bear my name. . . . I never want to see her again," the prefect replied that divorce was now difficult and slow and there was no special provision for POWs.[44] In any case, the husband was often just as much to blame for the breakdown of a marriage. Albert Loiseau, a POW from the working-class suburb of Saint-Pierre-des-Corps, asked for a divorce and for his two children to be entrusted to his mother. A social worker told the prefect that his wife was "without morality and shamelessly admitted she was pregnant for the second time since her husband was taken prisoner" but that "they got on very badly before the war. There were often rows when M. Loiseau came home drunk and beat his wife." She saw no reason Mme Loiseau should forfeit either the children, since she looked after them well, or the allowance due to her as the wife of a POW since she had nothing else to live on. The prefect concurred.[45]

In the final analysis, the campaign of Vichy against immorality and the regime's desire to protect the family were often at cross-purposes. This contradiction, however, allowed women in an impossible situation to begin a new life while retaining custody of their children or, in some cases, abandoning them. The wife of a POW could not be divorced simply because she was sleeping or cohabiting with someone else, and children were rarely taken away because there was nowhere else for them to go. Mme Vétault of Jumelles, whose husband was a POW in Saxony, eventually stopped writing to him and moved in with a butcher named Eugène Chaudronnier. She had already been prosecuted for an abortion and found not guilty, was now pregnant again by Chaudronnier, and had put her four-year-old daughter by Vétault into an orphanage in Saumur. The French authorities took away her military allowance and decided to cut the family benefit she received for her daughter and give it and the daughter to Vétault's seventy-four-year old father, but he wanted nothing to do with the idea. They also decided to prosecute Chaudronnier under the law of 23 December 1943 but there is no record of the outcome.[46] Mme Vétault, despite her perceived immorality, secured the family arrangement she wanted.

The position of POWs improved a little after the summer of 1942, when Prime Minister Pierre Laval negotiated with the Germans an exchange of French workers who would go to the Reich in return for POWs who would be reunited with their families in France.[47] This process, known as the Relève, was trumpeted by the Vichy government as a triumph of hard bargaining, but the small print revealed that only one POW would return for each *skilled* worker sent to Germany. The return of prisoners was thus modest: only 100,000 for France as a whole and 1,000 of the 14,400 POWs of Maine-et-Loire in the year after August 1942. In April 1943 prisoners who contracted to return to Germany as "free workers" were allowed home briefly on leave, but their numbers amounted to no more than a thousand for France as a whole. Eight were given a reception by the mayor of Nantes, but in the end three did not return to Germany: one was too sick and two went missing for family reasons.[48] In the summer of 1943, after the introduction of the Service du Travail Obligatoire (STO) made life extremely difficult for many families, Laval managed to negotiate the return of 2,000 POWs nationally as an exceptional measure. This provoked a hectic scramble to demonstrate need and revealed extraordinary circumstances such as that of the Piron family near Saumur. The parents, aged sixty-nine and fifty-nine, were farming eighteen hectares with two daughters aged twenty-two and eighteen. A third daughter was married, and of their eight sons three were POWs, one had been requisitioned for the Todt Organization, one was requisitioned for the STO, two were married with children, and one was a boy of twelve.[49] Theirs was an extreme example of the disruption of family life by the German occupation.

The return of POWs, however slow, added a new dimension to the solidarity required of the French. It was a case now not only of caring for POWs in German camps by sending packages but also of caring for the returning POWs. A new organization, the Maison du Prisonnier, was set up in the summer of 1942 to coordinate the different services that already existed and to cater to developing needs. The general rule was one Maison per department, at Tours, Angers, and Nantes, but Saumur acquired one early in 1943 and then Cholet, claiming it had more POWs to cope with than Saumur, set one up. The Maisons dealt with questions of benefits, employment, and even relationships. When a POW returned, the military allowance that had been paid to his wife was canceled, but he became entitled to a range of benefits such as free public transportation, free movie admission, and a free fishing permit. These implied that he would simply sit around relaxing, but clearly there were pressures to return to work as soon as possible. For those in agriculture or related work—about 43 percent of POWs in Loire-Inférieure, 52 percent in Indre-et-Loire, and 63 percent in Maine-et-Loire—the demand was only too intense.[50] Neither did industrial workers find difficulty recovering their old jobs or finding new ones, even without training, at a time when the Germans were stepping up labor recruitment for the Reich.[51] The biggest problems seem to have been experienced by the self-employed, such as M. Tijou of Saint-Pierre-des-Corps, who complained that his painting and decorating business had been squeezed out by businesses that had secured all the public works contracts, or the shoemaker M. Madelin, who fell foul of the regulations governing the allocation of raw materials and received no leather or rubber because he had no registered customers.[52] Some ex-POWs made such a mess of things that they were soon on the road back to Germany. One man from Saint-Nazaire quarreled so violently with his wife that he went back to Germany voluntarily, leaving his child and his butcher's business to his mother-in-law. Another man, from Nantes, arrested for stealing sugar, and not having proof that he was a former POW, was put on a train against his will with a contingent of workers destined for the Reich only a few days before the city was liberated by the Americans.[53]

For all the energy that went into helping prisoners of war and their families, the conflict and corruption endemic in occupied France could not but infiltrate the very organizations that were supposed to demonstrate the solidarity of the French people in their hour of need. Some of the conflicts arose from political differences, others from tensions between local communities and more centralized authorities or within local communities themselves. The collection of large quantities of money and goods in the midst of scarcity, moreover, was an invitation to some French people, who perhaps felt themselves no better off than the POWs, to cheat and pilfer. In some respects they were right. As the Atlantic ports were subjected to Allied aerial attack, culminating in the massive bombardment of Nantes on 16 September 1943, the balance between needy and provided for subtly shifted, so that in a curious reversal of charity, at the end of the Occupation, POWs were sending the product of their collections to the bomb victims of their hometowns.

Tensions within organizations set up to assist POWs were apparent from the summer of 1940. The committee set up in Loire-Inférieure by veterans headed by Léon Jost both to supply the makeshift prison camps in the department and to orchestrate escapes was not allowed to function without interference. Catholic and conservative institutions such as the Association Catholique des Chefs de Famille, which claimed 80,000 members in the department, muscled in under the leadership of the Marquis de la Ferronnays, president of the *conseil général*, and lobbied the prefect to become involved. A departmental committee to assist POWs was duly formed, within which the veterans' escape committee continued to function covertly, vulnerable, however, to the prying of the Catholic conservatives. A fight broke out between the veterans and the conservatives, as a result of which, it was alleged, one of the conservatives, a M. Roger, denounced the veterans, who were arrested and court-martialed by the Germans. Sentenced to three years in prison in July 1941, they were to suffer a much worse fate following the assassination of the Feldkommandant of Nantes the following October.[54]

The departmental committee to assist the POWs in Loire-Inférieure came under further pressure because of differences in policy with the city of Nantes. The mayor of Nantes, Gaëtan Rondeau, took the view (as did the wives of the 5,500 POWs of Nantes) that the departmental committee handed out so few goods to prisoners' families that they had to fall back on their own rations to make up the packages. A separate Nantes committee was set up in February 1942 under a local barrister, Alexander Vincent, who was to become prefect of Loire-Inférieure at the Liberation. This local committee undertook to provide a second, free package each month to the families of POWs, to supplement the one provided, at cost, by the departmental committee. It was to be financed by a grand raffle and to include cans of meat and vegetables supplied by local canning firms. The wives of POWs who demonstrated in June 1942 were pressing in the same direction as the Nantes committee and against the departmental committee, which as a result of the Nantes initiative reduced its allocation to Nantes.[55]

Local patriotism was always the order of the day when it came to collecting for POWs, and committees set up in each commune to support POWs had the prisoners of that commune particularly in mind. This focus clashed with the national overview of organizations like the Secours National, which wanted to spread the funds more widely. In the winter of 1940–41, for example, the Secours National ran a campaign to collect money for blankets, clothes, and linens for POWS, relying on the generosity of communes, schools, and businesses. When the money was forwarded, businesses and communes often asked that a proportion of it be devoted to their particular prisoners, emphasizing that the success of the collection was accounted for by locals who understood themselves to be giving to their own, but the Secours National was reluctant to accede to such requests.[56] In 1942 bureaucracy became even tighter, and local fundraising events were required not only to give 50 percent of their receipts to the Secours National but to apportion another 20 percent to a departmental commission that vetted all fund-raising events for POWs. Promoters such as M. Vanneyre, president of the prisoners' committee of the Madeleine district of Angers, protested. Told that he had not handed over enough money, he replied that donors had given directly to the Red Cross for packages and for local families of POWs in difficulty. "Why try to replace us?" he asked. If people knew that 70 percent of their donations were being spirited off elsewhere they would stop giving, "and who would have the right to blame them?"[57]

The struggle of local community against central authority was not the only fault line to appear in the commitment to POWs. Even local communities that were supposed to have a common purpose and identity could be divided against themselves, and the prisoners' support committee simply became a forum in which local antagonisms were played out. Saint-Brévin-les-Pins was a commune at the mouth of the Loire opposite Saint-Nazaire, looking out over the Atlantic. About as far as one could get from the

German border, it tended to attract a number of exotic outsiders who did not necessarily fit in with the locals. The prisoners' committee set up by Mayor Guillou in 1940 functioned without incident until the summer of 1942, when Auguste Herault, a war-wounded shoemaker, Freemason, and member of the League of Rights of Man, accused his political rival, Raoul Marchand, a shopkeeper and right-wing municipal councillor, of stealing chocolate from the packages destined for POWs and selling it on the black market. The mayor called the committee to thrash out the matter, and after a struggle Herault resigned. Guillou then filled up the committee with POWs who had been liberated, including Captain Amédée Modena, an Italian who had fought in the French Foreign Legion in 1914 and 1940 and recently become a French citizen. But Herault did not give up the fight and allied with another outsider, a retired captain named Victor-Antoine Mas, who had come to Saint-Brévin as a refugee in 1940. Mas revived the accusations of chocolate theft against Marchand in the press in September 1943, and Modena came to Marchand's aid. Herault then laid into Modena, accusing him of being a transalpine ruffian, a communist, and a Jew—and running the risk of drawing him to the attention of the Germans. After the Liberation Herault tried to rally the new prefect to his version of events, while Modena argued that he had joined the Resistance and that Herault and Mas were anti-Semites and collaborationists. A fight that started over chocolate bars for POWs thus exposed the divisions within a seaside village: left against right, natives against newcomers, self-styled resisters against supposed collaborators. The only compensation was that the exchanges of abuse took the form of a local quarrel rather than of denunciation to the Germans, which would have led to deportation and tragedy.[58]

Tensions between collaborationists and resisters in fact penetrated POW organizations at the highest level. Most subversive was the collaborationist Mouvement du Prisonnier, which recruited the wives and mothers of POWs by claiming to be able to bring about the liberation of their husbands and sons and recruited newly repatriated POWs by claiming to have been responsible for their liberation. When the Maisons du Prisonnier were set up, it tried to ensure that its supporters were appointed to key positions. This led to a series of conflicts, exposures, resignations, and dismissals that seriously undermined the Maisons and made them much less effective than they might have been. Jean Roussillon, regional prefect of Angers, was alerted to the danger early on and became extremely concerned by the Mouvement's plentiful resources, propaganda, and contacts.[59] When the departmental delegate of the Mouvement, M. Oger, was appointed the director of the Maison du Prisonnier in Angers, Roussillon collected a dossier documenting his incompetence and tried to replace him with his own candidate, the hero of the pro-Vichy Catholics, Canon Panaget. Roussillon managed to have Oger's appointment canceled in June 1943, but the Maison remained under the influence of M. Duchange, the secretary in charge of employing ex-POWs, who wore the uniform of the collaborationist Rassemblement Nationale Populaire (RNP) and was said to be in close touch with the Gestapo.[60] Meanwhile Roussillon did not last the course himself, dismissed under German pressure in July 1943. In Touraine, similarly, the departmental delegate of the Mouvement, a schoolteacher named Philipon, acted as a veritable kingmaker in appointments to the Maison du Prisonnier. He unseated the first director, Landry, in August 1943, vetoed the proposed replacement, and finally sanctioned Georges Renault, a former notary's clerk and apartment manager.[61] By the end of 1943 it was fairly clear that the Maisons du Prisonnier of Angers and Tours were in the pocket of the Mouvement du Prisonnier.

The POW support movement was undermined from within not only by political conflict but by corruption and crime. Fund-raising events that sold foodstuffs in short supply became a front for black-market operations, while the promotion of entertainment attracted "impresarios" interested only in fleecing the organizers and the public. Laval tried to clamp down on such "commercial enterprises" by setting up departmental commissions to approve all fund-raising events for POWs and by banning from them buffets, lunches, dinners, or public auctions of foodstuffs.[62] These measures did not, of course, manage to eliminate corruption, which went to the heart of the Maisons du Prisonnier themselves. M. Lardy, director of the Maison of Tours, surprised one of his aides, Colonel de Busnel, siphoning off for the benefit of the staff the twenty liters of milk that arrived every Sunday for the teas organized for the children of POWs.[63] In Angers one of the staff of the Maison used his contacts with freed prisoners who were winegrowers in the region to organize a vast black-market operation in wine. He held court in the cafés around the Maison du Prisonnier, struck up friendships with German army truck drivers to ensure transportation, and resold the wines under the table to Angers retailers.[64] The final antisocial act at the expense of the POWs was theft of or from the packages addressed to the prisoners in Germany. Here the best placed for crime were railway employees and warehousemen. If caught, they faced stiff sentences from the exceptional courts, or Sections spéciales, set up by Vichy. Two railwaymen in Angers received terms of four and five years, and a ring of twelve individuals headed by a retired major who was in charge of the distribution center for POWs in Angers and including warehousemen, an accountant, and even a woman driver for the Red Cross were given sentences of between three and seven years.[65]

As the Occupation continued, it seemed that the altruism of the French began to wear thin and that the tremendous solidarity that greeted the first initiatives on behalf of the POWs gave way to self-seeking and corruption. At the same time, paradoxically, examples multiplied of POWs organizing their own fund-raising networks to support loved ones at home, who were becoming the collateral victims of Allied air attacks on the submarine bases, naval shipyards, and armaments factories of Lorient, Saint-Nazaire, and Nantes. From 1941, the POWs of Stalag VIIIC set up departmental committees to strengthen ties between prisoners and their native *pays*. After the air attacks of April 1943, those from the five Breton departments, including Loire-Inférieure, formed a special regional group and raised 5,600 Reichmarks, or 11,200 francs, for those left hurt or homeless in the Breton coastal towns. This was echoed by the Brittany group of Stalag IIIA, which sent 870 Reichmarks for the Breton ports, specifying in particular Saint-Nazaire.[66] The bombing of Nantes on 16 September 1943 destroyed, among other things, its Maison du Prisonnier, killing fifteen of the staff and visitors. This tragedy provoked a wave of sympathy and support among POWs, who wrote to the mayor expressing the wish to adopt children who had been orphaned. Thus, for example, the POWs of Kommando 106 at Borna, near Leipzig, adopted Françoise, whose father had been a POW since 1940, whose mother had been killed on 16 September, and whose grandmother, looking after her, was injured and left homeless.[67] The support of POWs was offered in prayers as well as in money. Sergeant Louis Nouais, a priest-prisoner at Stammlager IVF, told the bishop of Nantes how shocked he was to hear of the death of Canon Boisellier, a stalwart of the diocese, on 16 September: "The great suffering of the people of Nantes has been carried as far as IVF; I had to inform several comrades of the death of a wife or child, sometimes of several loved ones. Mass was celebrated on 3 October for the victims of the disaster."[68] The wheel had come full circle, and whether inspired by Christian charity or a love of the *petite patrie*, those in exile who should have been helped were in their turn helping those at home, who, for once, had greater need than they.

The case of POWs illustrates both the disruption of families and communities by defeat and occupation and the energetic attempts of those who had been separated to rebuild networks of solidarity. Communities rallied to send food and messages to the POWs, and later, when the war engulfed civilian populations in France, the POWs replied in kind with help to bomb victims. Churches were filled as many turned to prayer for the release of their loved ones. Left to fend for themselves, many women rose to the challenge of running farms or businesses as well as families. On the debit side, stresses and strains inevitably undermined much of the work of solidarity. Some families broke up as women sought support and affection elsewhere. Fund-raising and charity sometimes provided opportunities for corruption and theft. Collective enterprises might be damaged by faction and politics. Tensions were evident between those who felt solidarity with POWs in their community and organizations seeking a broader national approach to the relief of suffering. As in so many other respects, the Occupation drove people to narrow their horizons and give priority to family and community over national loyalties.

4

Bread

During the first winter of the Occupation, Georges Mazeaud, a glovemaker in the Saint-Lazare district of Paris, took up his pen and wrote "with some shame" to a country cousin he scarcely knew. "We are hungry, my children, grandchildren, my wife, and I. I never thought that at the age of sixty-six I could write that, but there it is. The food supply in Paris is entirely inadequate, and many are undernourished." Like most other Parisians, Mazeaud had roots in the provinces. He had left the village of Concourson-sur-Layon, near Saumur, as a baby in 1875 when his father sought a better life as a draftsman in the capital, but now that cold and hunger gripped Paris the balance of advantage seemed to have shifted in favor of his rustic relatives. His correspondent, Gaston Grenouilleau, was a forty-three-year-old winegrower and cooper in Concourson-sur-Layon, reputed for its soft Côteaux du Layon wines. Mazeaud asked whether Gaston could send any spare food he might have by registered mail, declaring it as a trade sample, up to the permitted weight of three kilos. "Bacon, cheese, butter, pasta, in fact anything you can eat" would do.[1]

Ten days later Mazeaud wrote again to say that he had just paid eighty francs for a skinny chicken: could Gaston please send poultry, beans, "rillettes like Aunt Léontine's?" "I said to my wife, as I wrote," he added, "that life is a like a play: I was born in Concourson, I drank its milk, and now in my old age it is Concourson that will perhaps continue to keep me alive." Now that the family connection was reestablished and the shame diminished a little, Mazeaud also asked whether Gaston could also send parcels to his son Roger, thirty-six, who had been demobilized in July and was a sales representative for a chemicals firm, Roger's wife, Suzanne, and their four-year-old daughter, Françoise; to his daughter Madeleine, whose husband was a POW, and their twelve-year-old son, Bernard; and to his eldest daughter, Lucienne, whose husband was also a POW and who was out of touch with her two teenage children in the non–Occupied Zone. A week later he wrote to thank Gaston for the first package, which had arrived that day, saying, "The rillettes are wonderful and have the taste of Concourson." On 30 January 1941 he acknowledged receipt of a joint of lamb, the first they had eaten since May 1940.[2]

Mazeaud was a proud man and kept scrupulous accounts of what he owed Gaston. He also initiated a two-way traffic, taking orders for gloves and sending them to Concourson. Gaston was to use them to offset the debt. For while the countryside was awash with food, manufactured goods were generally hard to come by. In April 1942, for example, Mazeaud sent twenty-nine pairs of gloves, having taken off the prices and telling Gaston that he could easily charge five francs more than the eighteen to thirty francs they normally sold for. His daughter Lucienne asked whether Gaston could send some bottles of white wine for her son's wedding and later sent a check for 200 francs to pay for the seventeen bottles that had been "le roi de la fête," enjoyed by twenty guests. Another of Mazeaud's sons, Paul, who was in the clothing business, was supplied with food from the countryside by his own clients but offered to send two smocks for the children, two shirts, a blouse for Gaston's wife, Sidonie, and a pair of work trousers worth 805 francs in return for some wine, which was retailing for between 100 and 130 francs a bottle in Paris. Whether the wine was for personal consumption or a little private trade is uncertain.[3]

Meanwhile Mazeaud's requests for food continued—pork, mutton, beef, rabbit, duck, chicken, rillettes, sausages, butter, but not rutabagas, he joked, "with which we are saturated." The void seemed impossible to fill. "Soon we will become vegetarians out of necessity," he complained, "and perhaps even have to do without bread. The women in particular spend half their time lining up for one thing or another." Come the summer, however, he was requesting vegetables and lamenting, "I should have stayed in Concourson instead of coming to Paris when I was fifteen months old. Perhaps I would have some fields and some vines too. But I was young!" The following spring Mazeaud reflected, "The most important thing in the world is to eat. We are almost reduced to the level of beasts." In the spring of 1943 he told Gaston that they were becoming "skeletons," that his weight was down to fifty-four kilos, and that he had spent some time in the hospital with anthrax. There were often glitches in the transport system—chickens dying in the summer heat, packages sent by train getting stolen—and the Liberation did not suddenly bring plenty. On his seventieth birthday in February 1945, Mazeaud reflected wryly that "the Allies helped us to victory but did not bring abundance or even basic necessities." He himself survived the war but his daughter Madeleine, though "radiant" when her POW husband returned in 1945, had nevertheless been seriously weakened and died the following year. "The war killed her little by little," Mazeaud wrote.[4]

Georges Mazeaud never met Gaston Grenouilleau, either during the war or afterwards. But their correspondence, squeezed into a biscuit tin by Gaston's son Paul, suggests a great deal about survival during the Occupation. People went hungry, especially in large cities and above all in Paris. Those in the country, however, despite the pressure from the French and German authorities to hand over their produce, kept enough back for a parallel market, supplying friends and relations and in return acquiring the clothing and other manufactured goods they needed. Severe shortages and high prices set the French against one another in the struggle for survival, and yet their inventiveness in getting by—the famous "Système de Débrouillage" or "Système D"—actually required them to establish new networks and to cooperate as never before. Survival was not only about lines and scratching out a meager existence but about developing family, neighborhood, and business contacts in order to make life possible.

Inventiveness and solidarity were at a premium because although the

Vichy government put systems in place to deal with shortages and price rises they were neither effective nor popular. In each department it appointed a director-general of supply (Ravitaillement), who was supposed to ensure that markets were provided with agricultural produce, a price control commission to make sure that price levels fixed by the administration to protect consumers were adhered to by businesses, and groups that brought producers and traders together to ensure that each trader obtained a fair supply of the goods available. Customers had to register with particular traders for the operation of rationing, which was introduced from September 1940. Children under six were entitled to three-quarters of a liter of milk a day and children between six and twelve to half a liter. Adults between twenty-one and seventy were entitled to 350 grams of bread per day, at least at the beginning of the Occupation, 300 grams of meat and 50 grams of cheese a week, and 500 grams of sugar, 200 grams of butter, 200 grams of margarine, and 50 grams of rice a month. Manual workers and farm workers were entitled to more food than white-collar workers. Rations in France were actually higher than those fixed in Great Britain in January 1940, when an adult was entitled to only 4 ounces (113 grams) of butter and 12 ounces (340 grams) of sugar, but rations were always limited by what was available and generally declined over the period of the war.[5]

Despite the energy spent on constructing and enforcing the official economy, the results were meager. To be fair, many problems were beyond the control of the Vichy administrators. The British imposed a blockade on trade with France as they had during the Napoleonic wars, and British coal, on which much industry in the west of France depended, dried up. The Germans confiscated as war booty imported stocks of tea, coffee, sugar, rice, chocolate, and Algerian wine they found in ports such as Nantes and Saint-Nazaire.[6] Integrating France into their war economy meant the systematic requisition of agricultural as well as industrial goods, and here the question of how far the Vichy administration acted as a "shield" against the Germans became an issue. At times it seemed that the French Ravitaillement services acted less to protect French markets from German plundering than to abet German greed. Colonel Constant Rouleau, director-general of supply for the five departments of the Angers region, was also responsible for supplying meat to the Germans in the twelve departments of Bezirk B and was accused after the war of doing nothing to temper German demands for oats, potatoes, and other produce. Rigid and authoritarian, he was said to have admired German discipline, put on his uniform to present his respects to German officers on New Year's Day, enthusiastically showed visitors a revolver and a hunting rifle they had given him, and gone hunting with them on more than one occasion.[7]

In many ways the Angers region, known as the garden of France, was less at risk from shortages than, for example, the Mediterranean coast, with its wine monoculture and paucity of wheat or livestock.[8] In the spring of 1941 the prefect of Maine-et-Loire reported that "the food supply problem has become particularly serious in this department, which until now had been in a privileged position because of its agricultural resources." Fortunately, "apart from a few insignificant incidents in long lines in front of butchers or other food shops, the population has endured this test with courage and dignity."[9] Eighteen months later, in the winter of 1942–43, the assessment was more pessimistic:

> Housewives are complaining bitterly about the absence of butter, milk, and cheese. They are saying that no oil has been available since November. . . . Eggs have not been distributed in any rational way. Shopkeepers are complaining that they have not received the quantities corresponding to the number of clients registered with them, of which the Ravitaillement has been informed, so that they are completely unable to satisfy their customers. It is not uncommon to hear criticisms, even among shopkeepers, of the "incompetence" of the services concerned.[10]

The large seaports of Nantes and Saint-Nazaire, cut off from their overseas trade and less well served by the hinterland, were even worse off. In the winter of 1941–42 there were no vegetables on the market, and only an emergency convoy of 655 tons of potatoes sent to Nantes in February 1943 saved the situation. Just before Christmas 1943 women planned to demonstrate in front of the prefecture, to demand an increase in the bread ration; and only a last-minute deal prevented them from going ahead.[11]

The failure of the Vichy administration to keep markets adequately supplied was explained not only by objective shortages but by its counterproductive policy of forcing producers to supply markets at fixed prices. The policy gave rise to parallel circuits of supply and demand that offered goods at higher prices than the official rates and therefore might be seen to exploit consumers but that were also more efficient in that the supply was generally kept up. In November 1940 a group of Angevin women sent a semiliterate letter to the prefect protesting the unscrupulous profiteering of a number of traders. Stockings bought for 25 francs in Marseille were being sold in Angers for 125 francs. Cloth imported from Lyon was being sold at similarly ridiculous prices: "Madame Grégoire in the rue Corneille thinks Angevin women are stupid," they continued, "saying that even cuts of 300 francs a meter were going like hot cakes. . . . Meanwhile blouse sellers can't believe how much their bank accounts have grown since the war."[12] Clearly, officials had to answer such complaints and be seen to do so, but there were dangers in being too heavy-handed. The stall holders in the Lafayette market in Angers complained the following summer that the police had come around ordering them to sell beans for less than the maximum price of twelve francs per kilo, because coarser beans had been mixed with the fine ones, and to sell sour cherries for ten francs a kilo instead of thirteen, for which only the Montmorency variety qualified. Murmuring that they would not be back the following Wednesday, the stall holders packed up their wares. The losers, said their spokesman, would be the inhabitants of the *quartier*, for producers could always remain on their farms and sell to wholesalers for prices that were every bit as good as, if not above, the maximum. He suggested that if the police were more diplomatic the interests of everyone might be better served.[13]

Increasingly, producers and wholesalers boycotted the official market, preferring to sell to retailers or middlemen on the black market at prices way above the maximum. This arrangement had obvious benefits for them but risked antagonizing those who were left out of the loop. In Tours, where vegetables seemed to disappear from the market stalls, it was discovered that wholesale market gardeners were selling to greengrocers at prices exceeding the maximum while providing them with fictitious legal invoices. The overpriced stocks were then kept at the back of the shop to be sold under the counter to customers willing to pay a premium.[14] A hard-pressed woman from Amboise argued that

> there are two categories of consumers, the rich who eat and those who line up for an hour only to be told that there is nothing left. In the butcher shops, favored customers place their orders and have them delivered to their houses; they are sure to eat. At the poultry merchant Leclerc, the blind is hermetically closed but favored customers are invited in at the side entrance, where they are sold rabbit and other produce under the counter. It is shameful. Likewise in grocers' shops when you ask for some tins or chocolate to make a package to send to our dear prisoners in Germany, you are told that there is nothing left. Not content with starving the workers, these unscrupulous traders even refuse help for our prisoners.[15]

The market gardeners' syndicate of Cholet, finally, saw no reason to supply cauliflowers to the local market, where it was subject to price controls, if they could send them to Paris, where they would fetch much higher prices from the restaurants, the rich, and the Germans. "It is unacceptable for some citizens to accumulate fortunes in a matter of months through the misery of others," complained an employee of a Cholet firm when he found not a single cauliflower on the market that morning. "These bad French people should be punished. Tough measures should be passed, including prison and the confiscation of their goods for organizers of famine."[16]

The black market that developed in parallel to the official market may have been criticized as a Darwinian jungle of ruthless profiteering and exploitation but it was more complicated than that. The black market was not a single market but a system of concentric circles. The wider and more impersonal the market, the more exploitative it was likely to be. The widest circle involved selling to distant clients in Paris or other large cities. In the summer of 1942 vacationers descended on the region from Paris, buying up potatoes and beans at inflated prices from a delighted peasantry, leaving those living on fixed incomes, like pensioners, small *rentiers*, workers, and white-collar employees, with little.[17] By the following summer the gap between those having difficulty feeding and clothing their families and those making "scandalous fortunes" in a manner "dangerous for social order" had become a matter of concern to the authorities.[18] Charles Graeve, a dentist from Lille who had set up in Chinon after the outbreak of war, bought local wines (the 1941 and 1942 vintages were excellent) for 60–80 francs a liter to sell in the Paris region for 450–500 francs. Involved with him were his twenty-three-year-old son, Étienne, who was about to be appointed an official of the Peasant Corporation set up by Vichy to run agriculture, and his thirty-year-old daughter Elisabeth, who was employed by the Vichy Youth Administration. The subprefect tried to warn the local press off publishing the story, because the Graeve family was well connected within the Vichy administration, but investigations revealed "a vast black-market organization with ramifications throughout France." It did not do for those with responsible posts in the Vichy regime to preach the rhetoric of work, family, and fatherland, to the extent of appearing in their official functions at Mother's Day celebrations, while publicly flaunting the millions of francs they had made on the black market. Eventually Étienne was interned administratively by the prefect and Elisabeth forced to resign, but the affair demonstrated extraordinary corruption and hypocrisy at the heart of the Vichy system.[19]

The smallest circle, like that of Georges Mazeaud and Gaston Grenouilleau, was purely familial. Working people living in large cities suddenly discovered or rediscovered lost country cousins who, previously forgotten and even despised, now became of the greatest value. Sending food parcels from the country was often no more than gift-giving or part of a barter system. Money scarcely came into it except as a tally of debt and credit, although it played a greater role if the exchange network extended beyond the family to other members of the community or if Parisian relatives saw the opportunity for a little profit selling family wine in an inflated market.

Between these two circles was an intermediate one that included friends, neighbors, and customers. It was larger than the family circle but operated on the basis of personal, face-to-face contact. Based on monetary exchange, it set a fair price that offered a privileged supply to the customer and a decent return for the supplier. For this reason it has sometimes been called a gray market rather than a black one. The ultimate sanction of this moral economy was denunciation of a too-greedy supplier to the French or

German authorities. This served to limit the extent of the market, for suppliers were unwilling to do business with customers they did not know or trust.

The typical relationship of this kind evolved when the producer or stall holder no longer saw the benefit of selling on the official market but was willing to do deals with regular customers who came out to the farm. Michel Leterme, a boy during the Occupation, remembers cycling with his father thirty-two kilometers each way from Angers to Champigné to buy food from a farm. Of course, there were farms closer by, but the farmer's wife was known to them, as she used to have a stall in the market in Angers.[20] Given the small and diminishing bread ration, millers were particularly in demand. Christian Beugnet of Chinon recalled cycling ten or fifteen kilometers to see M. Peraud, a miller, who he says was "in our sector" and "an honest fellow who tried to satisfy everyone except when the economic inspectors were around. Then he said, 'Not today.'" His recollection implies a clientage between townsmen and farmers who knew and trusted each other, evading the sparsely provided official market for their mutual benefit. Under the Occupation, added his wife, Léonie, "people knew each other better."[21]

Personal contact between suppliers and customers was one factor that kept prices fair; the other was the risk of denunciation, which in turn had an effect on the extent of the market. Andrée Trudeau, who worked in the ration-ticket office of Saumur, lived on her father's farm just above the château where wheat, wine, and potatoes were grown. Her father had some wheat milled privately for his own consumption and found himself accosted by townspeople coming to his door keen to buy flour and potatoes. Andrée admits that such trade was illegal but denies that it was clandestine since "everyone knew about it." She points out that "honest and conscientious as he was" he did not overcharge them, arguing that he provided a fair and valued service. The great fear was being denounced, and on one occasion her father was. Fortunately, the fraud officers did not find his stocks of flour, but the lesson was clear: deal with those you know, not with outsiders.[22] André Treulier, a winegrower in Le Thoureil, downstream along the Loire, talked to me in a cellar that was an Aladdin's cave of vintages going back before the war. As we sipped wine from the Occupation period, he described an autarkic economy of the narrowest dimensions. "There was not much to eat," he said, and people had to "piously conserve" what stocks they had in case of shortage. There was no black market, simply because they had "nothing to sell." Later he conceded that he did not want to sell to people he did not know, because they might have been "spies" and have had him sent to jail as a "public enemy." He remembered hiding in the house while some unknown townspeople laid siege to his farm in order to buy from him. Prices, he said, rose fast, and people thought that they might make a lot of money, but unfortunately there was nothing to buy so they simply saved. After the war he bought the vineyards he had been working, together with the manor house, from the two old ladies who owned it and turned himself into a seigneur of the Domaine de Norgevault. With his flat cap and blue overalls, he looked like the peasant described by Tocqueville in *L'Ancien Régime*, who appears poor to avoid paying too much tax.[23]

Farmers and winegrowers generally did well under the Occupation. As a result, marriage between a bourgeois and a peasant was no longer beyond the realm of possibility. In a memoir, Dr. Léon Mousseau of Saint-Mathurin describes how the daughter of one of his patients, the widow of a magistrate, married a farmer who courted her by offering her chops and rillettes whenever he killed a pig.[24] The good fortune of shopkeepers is admirably portrayed in Jean Dutourd's 1952 novel, *Au Bon Beurre*. A more provincial version of the Parisian dairy merchants might be the Cohu-Denis family, the petit bourgeois aristocrats of Trélazé, a working-class suburb of Angers. Like the farmers, shopkeepers who made a good living under the Occupation also seem to feel the need to deny that they engaged in the black market or made huge profits. They underline that they provided a good service, compensating for the failings of the official market, and demanded no more than a fair price. Lucienne Cohu, who with her husband had a charcuterie business in Trélazé, recalls that there was "a big traffic in meat, but not within the trade. Masons and roofers began to kill animals and people bought from them, but the meat was cut up anyhow, it was sheer waste." As supplies of pork from the authorities dried up, charcutiers had to fall back on beef. M. Cohu went out to farms in his gas-powered van to "stock up secretly," purely to satisfy their customers. As for prices, Mme Cohu says, "we didn't take a lot of money. We were long established in the commune. We didn't want to exploit the German presence." "We never sold at higher than the fixed price," echo her daughter and son-in-law, Jacqueline and Louis Denis, who were bakers in Trélazé during the Occupation. Of course, some people sold at four or five times that price, but not the professionals. Later Jacqueline Denis takes out a collection of "little notes" she received from customers at the time, one of them from an angry working-class woman. It reads:

> Do you want to drive people to steal? Don't complain if after all this the workers take everything they can from you. We want to stay honest but we are driven to do wrong. I told you that if I hadn't found myself pregnant against my will I would not lower myself again to ask for credit. I would rather put my children into care than continue to suffer for being honest.

"People had moments of wickedness," explains Mme Cohu, "if you had three children and no bread."[25]

There is no doubt that the working classes did not do well during the Occupation. The high point of their success had been in 1936, when the election of the Popular Front government had been greeted by a national wave of strikes that forced a raft of concessions, including wage hikes, a forty-hour week, paid vacations, and collective bargaining.[26] Labor flexed its muscles, both in federations and in unions that met in Bourses du Travail subsidized by the local municipalities. The Socialist and Communist Parties enjoyed unprecedented influence, the first in government, the second by putting pressure on the government from parliament, the unions, and the street. The downturn came after the Munich agreement of 1938, when the government of Daladier turned to the right, ended the Popular Front, abolished the forty-hour week, and defeated the striking unions, and then after the Nazi-Soviet pact, when the government dissolved the Communist Party.[27] This repression was only confirmed under the German occupation and Vichy.

The burning issue for the working classes under the Occupation was the cost of living. The price of foodstuffs soared and wages simply failed to keep pace. It should not be imagined, however, that the workers were totally cowed under the Occupation. Strike action was limited and often only symbolic, but they resorted to it nevertheless. Although the famous miners' strike in the Nord in May 1941 has attracted much attention, it was not the only example of industrial action in occupied France.[28] The industrial area of Nantes and Saint-Nazaire was also highly volatile. Moreover, although strikes were few, the fact that they occurred in plants harnessed to the German war machine raised the stakes sharply. Vichy and French employers were put under intense pressure by the Germans to settle disputes immediately, which weakened rather than strengthened their hand. And while Vichy was keen to deal ruthlessly with communists, it did not wish to alienate the mass of workers, whose hard work and political loyalty it wished to develop.

In March 1941 Marcel Blanchard, secretary of the CGT engineers union of Saint-Nazaire since 1936, when he had been a driving force behind the strikes and factory occupations, urged a meeting of 600 shipyard and aviation workers in Saint-Nazaire to rejoin the union and pursue a campaign for wage hikes. In response, on 2 May, the riveters of the Ateliers et Chantiers de la Loire in Saint-Nazaire led a slowdown and forced management to make concessions. This was followed in August 1941 by a strike of dockers in Nantes, who refused to unload a shipment from Dakar until their wage demands had been met.[29] In October quarriers employed by the Entreprise de Travaux Publics de l'Ouest, or Entreprises Dodin, which worked for the Todt Organization, went on strike and also turned out workers at a neighboring quarry. The Todt Organization twisted the arm of the local Dodin manager to get the men to return to work, which they did after a day, but the subprefect of Saint-Nazaire discouraged punishment, declaring that the strike was a response to the rising cost of living in the countryside, not to communist ideas.[30] By contrast, when the aviation workers of SNCASO in Nantes-Bouguenais went on strike in June 1942, the police took the view that they had been stirred up by a sixty-year-old militant named René Daniel, a shop steward who had been fired from the Batignolles locomotive factory in 1938 for communist propaganda. They advised the prefect of Loire-Inférieure to jail him, although if possible without magnifying the incident, for fear of stirring up trouble in neighboring factories where tempers were running high.[31]

How effective workers were in achieving their goals was determined by their industrial muscle as well as by the circumstances of the Occupation. At first glance, their organization seemed rather fragile. Trade union membership had slumped since the strikes of 1938 and the clampdown on labor militancy that followed. The advent of Vichy was seen by many in business and the administration as an opportunity to have done with organized labor for good. Many employers ceased all negotiation with trade unions, and some municipalities now decided to refuse unions access to the Bourses they subsidized.

In fact, local officials and employers often acted prematurely, for it was the intention of neither the Germans nor Vichy to extinguish trade union activity. A German ordinance of 28 August 1940 that governed the formation of associations specifically allowed for the meeting of organizations that had a purely economic or occupational function, so long as the local Kommandanturs were informed in advance. Moreover, Vichy's minister of labor, the former trade unionist René Belin, spelled out to prefects that the law of 16 August 1940, which set up Comités d'Organisation (COs) to run each industry, dissolved only *national* organizations of employers and workers, such as the CGT and CGPF, leaving intact departmental and local unions meeting in the Bourses du Travail. Prefect Roussillon was obliged to remind mayors that any bans on trade unions entering Bourses du Travail were improper and provocative and that "the minister has clarified that workers are to be treated on the same terms as employers, so that they do not feel in any way marginalized from the work of national regeneration being pursued by the head of state."[32] Admittedly, the Vichy government was not united, but the Labor Ministry and Marshal Pétain were explicit that regeneration meant social peace rather than industrial confrontation, and weaning the working class away from communism rather than eroding the benefits won by organized labor.

One area where labor and Vichy could agree was on raising very low wages. For the unions it was a question of defending workers against the escalating cost of living while for the government it was one of inoculating them against communism and stanching the flow of labor to factories working for the Germans, where wages were up to twice as high. The law of 23 May 1941 permitted the authorities to increase "abnormally low" wages but this required implementation at the local level. The animating force for labor in the Angers region was Raymond Déaud, leader of the tramway workers and secretary of the Maine-et-Loire union of unions. He presided over resolutions for a minimum wage from labor leaders at both a regional conference for the west of France in Rennes in July 1941 and a departmental conference in Angers the following November, which persuaded prefect Roussillon to agree to a minimum wage of 1,000 francs per month or 5.75 francs per hour for Nantes, though less for smaller towns in the region and for women.[33]

The flexibility of the Vichy government on wages was a carrot to entice "healthier" elements of the labor movement into accepting its Labor Charter, which was published on 4 October 1941.[34] The fight against communism would continue unabated, announced Interior Minister Pierre Pucheu, but officials were to try to end misunderstandings that had arisen between workers and employers and workers and the government, and to "avoid all propaganda that might depict the marshal's government as reactionary and retrograde."[35] The labor law, like most other corporatist projects, was a massively ambitious redesigning of the architecture of industrial relations with the aim of eliminating both class war and rivalry between different trade union federations, notably the CGT and Catholic organizations. Its main provision was to establish a single trade union for each "occupational family," merging employers, managers, white-collar workers, foremen, and workers locally, regionally, and nationally. As such an enterprise would take some time to set up, the collaboration of all these strata was to be launched at each factory level in social committees that would deal not with running the business but with working conditions and welfare. The failure of Vichy in the long run to persuade workers of the benefits of the Labor Charter bears eloquent witness both to the weakness of a regime that was more authoritarian in theory than in practice and to the vitality of the labor movement under the Occupation, which has hitherto been seriously underestimated.

The Labor Charter was a powerful challenge to organized labor. A minority of labor leaders saw it as a framework that they could either grasp in order to save the unions or reject and risk annihilation. Foremost among the partisans of the charter was Déaud, who from his base at the Bourse du Travail of Angers effectively served as the intermediary between René Belin and CGT leaders in the west of France.[36] For the 1941 conference of the Maine-et-Loire union of unions he brought in Marcel Roy, national secretary of the engineers' union, an anticommunist unionist close to Belin himself, to put the case for the charter and "a policy of involvement rather than of abstention." Déaud had a vision of a syndicalist state in which trade unionists would be free not only to build their labor empires but also to participate in the political decision making that had been the privilege of parliamentarians before 1940 and was now monopolized by bureaucrats. He challenged the 1943 conference of the Maine-et-Loire union of unions by asking, "If tomorrow the trade union movement had the opportunity to send its representatives to the various assemblies responsible for running the country—without the trickery of political parties—would it not be well advised to seize it?"

Most trade unionists, however, were suspicious of the charter. They saw it as a trick by which all the gains they had made since 1936 could be rolled back. Catholic labor leaders feared that their separate organizations would be eliminated by the single union system. CGT leaders thought that it threatened the autonomy of trade unions consecrated by their own Charter of Amiens of 1906 and that it left no place for the local and departmental union of unions based in the Bourses du Travail. The importance of local solidarity in the labor movement is underlined by the response of various industrial communities to the charter. Saint-Nazaire, for example, responded quite differently from Nantes. This was mainly because of the stance of Marcel Blanchard, the former militant of 1936, and of his mentor, François Blancho, former socialist deputy and still mayor of Saint-Nazaire. Blancho attempted to negotiate a place for labor and working-class communities within the Vichy system, at least until his resignation as mayor in May 1941 and even until he was required by Vichy, under pressure from the Germans, to move to the non–Occupied Zone in March 1942. Blanchard was singled out by more progressive elements in Vichy as a labor leader who had the confidence of the workers of Saint-Nazaire and, though a socialist, had helped prevent those workers from falling prey to communism. The third member of the Saint-Nazaire team was Emmanuel Jouvance, secretary of the local union of unions and municipal councillor under Blancho, who was convinced that the labor movement was destined either to flourish within the framework of the charter or to die outside it. They paved the way for a high-profile visit to Saint-Nazaire by regional prefect Roussillon on 26 February 1942 at which representatives of employers, engineers, technicians, and trade unions signed a solemn declaration repudiating class struggle and committing themselves to "the implementation of the Labor Charter at Saint-Nazaire in the spirit of union, loyalty, and justice defined in the preamble to the law of 4 October 1941."[37]

The labor movement of Nantes, by contrast, was hostile to the charter. Communism was stronger there, thriving on the climate of fear and hatred caused by the execution of forty-eight hostages in Nantes and Saint-Nazaire on 22 November 1941. Trade unionism was weak, with perhaps only 1,200 out of a possible 10,000 members, and the labor leaders saw opposition to the charter as one way to build support. Blanchard and Jouvance were unable to convince Auguste Péneau, secretary of the union of unions of Loire-Inférieure, that the charter was the way forward. Péneau, nicknamed The Fortress by Jouvance, was sixty-four, a generation older than the charter enthusiasts (Jouvance was fifty-three, but Blanchard was forty, Roy thirty-nine, and Déaud thirty-four), and wedded to the principles of the Charter of Amiens. Péneau scoffed:

> You make me laugh when you say that there will be no trade union activity when the charter is implemented if we don't adopt its machinery. I have already told you I would not give my little finger for it. Yesterday's trade unionism is sufficient unto itself. The workers must reject all collaboration with employers, as required in the law. The role of shop stewards drawn from the union will be just as strong and sustained, indeed more so, when they operate independently as when they have to take account of the opinions of engineers, technicians, managers, and even white-collar workers. I want to stay faithful to the trade unionism that has been our raison d'être and to which the workers are attached. In the future the workers will remember those who stuck to this system

and did not seek for whatever reason to place trade unionism
under government control. They will reject those who in any
way forfeited their independence.[38]

For Jouvance, Péneau was a representative of old labor who was simply not
alert to the requirements of the new order. In fact, Péneau had a fine sense
that the dogged attachment of the working classes to their old organizations and their deep suspicion of politics made the charter's chances of
success extremely small. Perhaps, farsighted in his wisdom, he was also
grooming himself for the end of the Occupation, when he would be elected
president of the Liberation Committee of Loire-Inférieure, the local parliament of Resistance organizations.

Whether in Nantes or in Saint-Nazaire, despite the hard work of Blanchard and his team, the charter remained a dead issue. The large shipyards
and factories like SNCASO had still not set up social committees by the
spring of 1944 and were reprimanded by Raymond Déaud in his capacity
as emissary of the Social Committees Office.[39] One large plant where the
social committee was given a fair trial was the main employer of the railway
suburb of Saint-Pierre-des-Corps, the Compagnie Industrielle de Matériel
de Transport (CIMT), which made rolling stock. The committee diluted
shop stewards with representatives of fathers of large families, war veterans,
young workers, female workers—categories that were suggested by the
Vichy motto of Work, Family, and Fatherland. When the social committee
actually met in the spring of 1943, the shop stewards complained that their
grievances had been rejected and that the director had told them that "he
would do what he liked and that if they didn't like that it would make no
difference."[40] As a result, when a new social committee was elected, CGT
unionists boycotted it and 80 percent of the ballots were returned blank.
The prefect of Indre-et-Loire concluded that "the majority of workers in
this important engineering works have made clear that they have no interest
in the implementation of the Labor Charter."[41]

The magnificent architecture of the single union scarcely ever got
beyond the paper stage. Far from being "single," the new unions never
managed to overcome the traditional divisions between different localities,
between Catholics and non-Catholics, between employers and workers.
Joseph Le Scelliour, leader of the Catholic union of Trélazé, refused to

join the "single union" of miners on the grounds that it would be taken over by the CGT, if not by communist elements dedicated to class struggle.[42] Under the charter the single union was subdivided for each industry into four distinct unions of employers, engineers and managers, white-collar employees and foremen, and manual workers. In Nantes and Saint-Nazaire it was reported that attempts to set up these unions were undermined by the "resistance" of white- and blue-collar unions.[43] Each union in the hierarchy had to draw up its own statutes, which were officially endorsed and published in the *Journal officiel*. Since these publications appeared right down to July 1944, it seems clear that few of them were functioning in any real way.[44] In the end, even the administration seemed to lose interest in the charter. Whereas early in 1942 regional prefect Roussillon had been on a tour of major industrial firms to urge support for it, two years later the prefect of Loire-Inférieure, Georges Gaudard, had more important things to do than attend the launch of the new unions. Invited to participate in the inauguration of the single union of hairdressers on May Day 1944, he declined, and though the hairdressers postponed the occasion until 22 May he still sent his apologies.[45]

Securing the loyalty of the French peasantry was in theory a good deal easier for the Vichy government than winning that of the workers. The peasants were regularly praised by Vichy as the backbone of economic life, defenders of the patriarchal family, and guardians of traditional values against the decadence and corruption of the cities.[46] Unemployed city youths were encouraged to return to the land both to relieve the shortage of labor suffered in the countryside because of the absence of POWS and to undergo moral regeneration. The underlying assumption was that in the work of national regeneration the peasantry, salt of the earth, led the way. There was, however, a lesser-known Vichy discourse on the peasantry that expressed its exasperation with the peasants' reluctance to supply official markets with their produce and preference for either an autarkic economy providing for their own families and communities or lucrative black-market activities. Regional prefect Roussillon dug deep into the rhetoric of the French Revolution when he described them as *affameurs*, deliberately starving the industrial workers and small artisans of the towns, placing their private interest before the general interest. They were driven by a "spirit of lucre," making "undreamed-of profits" and "golden fortunes. . . . Once the disinherited class," he continued, "the peasantry is now suffering the present hardships less than anyone else."[47] Jean Chaigneau, prefect of Indre-et-Loire, went even further. He asserted that the peasants were deliberately taking revenge on the urban population for the red peril of 1936 and the brief ascendancy of the urban workforce. Their "engrained individualism" must now be replaced by "the spirit of solidarity and mutual aid on a national scale."[48]

The Vichy regime did not confine itself to criticizing the peasantry but developed a battery of officials and measures to bend it to the requirements of the national interest. Under Director-General of Supply Rouleau was a corps of Ravitaillement officials to ensure that delivery quotas were met, a hierarchy of officials to enforce price controls and bring proceedings against those reaping illicit profits, and a gendarmerie that became increasingly involved in checking suspicious vehicles and raiding isolated farms in pursuit of black-market activity in the countryside. One strategy adopted to fight the black market was to centralize the slaughter of livestock and the manufacture of dairy products in large abattoirs and commercial dairies and to ban butter making and slaughtering on farms. Another was to harness the support of the administration, the Church, and the media for the "battle of wheat," to ensure that stocks of grain were delivered to bridge the so-called *soudure*, or gap, between one harvest year and the next. In the Loire-Inférieure, where the German presence was particularly dense and temptations to farmers correspondingly great, the subprefects of Saint-Nazaire and Châteaubriant toured the communes of their arrondissements in the spring of 1942 to urge the peasants to deliver their grain, and the new secretary of state for Ravitaillement, who had a reputation for tough talking, came in person to Nantes to exert further pressure.[49] Improved relations between church and state under Vichy were used to persuade local bishops to exhort farmers via the diocesan weekly and the pulpit to hand over what remained of their grain stocks in the name of Christian charity.[50] Official communiqués appeared regularly in the press, farmers who had not met their quotas were named and shamed, and when articles critical of the government's punitive and incompetent supply policy appeared anonymously in the local press, the authors were tracked down and punished.

In the case of *L'Echo de Paimboeuf*, the writer turned out to be a prominent defender of rural interests, Dutertre de la Coudre, a former deputy, mayor, and councillor-general of Machecoul, but he was nevertheless reprimanded by the prefect of Loire-Inférieure and required to publish a recantation declaring his total loyalty to Marshal Pétain.[51]

Obviously the government had no alternative to adopting a tough stance against rural black-market activities, but it is also clear that its policies did not cow the peasantry and if anything made them more hostile, not to Marshal Pétain himself but to the administration in general and to the Ravitaillement in particular. After prefect Chaigneau told the mayors of Indre-et-Loire that peasants must in future not kill pigs without informing the *mairie*, on pain of heavy punishment, he received a blast from someone who described himself as "a true peasant":

> If the peasants are harassed this much one thing is clear, that in future they won't even bother to raise pigs. There is no law that can force someone to work if they don't want to so why should our wives squelch in manure if they are not allowed to send a lump of bacon to a son who is a POW or a married daughter who has left home and needs the extra to feed her family? If peasants were free to do as they wished things would be a lot better than they are at present, when we can't sell an egg or a rabbit without risking a prison sentence and the only freedom people have is to die of hunger. If the gendarmes start to raid farms to see what is going on we haven't got guns anymore but we have got forks. If you want peasants to do their duty, then do yours first. . . . Back the peasants, don't bully them.[52]

The anger of the peasantry placed rural mayors in a difficult position. On the one hand, they were supposed to be the agents of the government in the locality, no longer elected but appointed. On the other hand, they were responsible to their local communities and that meant protecting the peasantry. The Marquis de Sesmaisons, mayor of La Chapelle-sur-Erdre, outside Nantes, and a leading figure in the agricultural organizations of Loire-Inférieure, told the prefect that he spoke for all the rural mayors in the department when he said that the rations and sanctions applied to farmers were ridiculous. In order to work the farmer should be allowed to "eat as much as he wanted," not be limited to a mere 350 grams of bread, which was half of what he needed. In addition he should be allowed some autonomy in trading; while the Ravitaillement and price controls should come down on "flagrant and unjustified irregularities," the authorities were otherwise advised to act with tact and discretion. Greater freedom, he suggested, would mean a more responsible and responsive attitude to the market on the part of peasants, not more autarky and black marketeering.[53]

The principal response of rural communities faced by repeated demands for meat, milk, eggs, potatoes, wheat, and oats was a sulky noncooperation. Mayors generally put themselves at the head of their discontented constituents and used the threat of resignation to devastating effect. Comte Henri de Champagny, a brilliant former soldier, the flamboyant mayor and councillor-general of Somloire in Anjou, who in the end was deported by the Germans, simply slashed the butter quota required from his commune from 375 to 50 kilos.[54] Jacques de la Grandière, mayor of Grez-Neuville and member of Vichy's Conseil National, said that the quota required of his commune was totally unjust. Why should it provide 75,000 eggs a year when a neighboring commune of the same size was asked for only 9,000? "That's it!" he told the director of Ravitaillement. "I shall tell my constituents not to declare a single hen at the October census." The Marquis du Puy, a keen hunter and the mayor of Courléon, argued that the unfair size of his cattle quota compared with that of other communes made his position untenable, and he threatened resignation if it was not reduced.[55] Other, less eloquent or well-connected mayors took refuge in stubborn silence. "When he does not just refuse to execute orders," the district Ravitaillement officer complained of one mayor, "he indulges in passive resistance by giving the impression that he knows nothing and can do nothing, a very easy way to slough off the duties of his office and refuse all responsibility."[56]

The idea of "passive resistance" to requisitions was much vaunted after the Liberation as a patriotic gesture. Since much Vichy requisitioning took place to meet German needs, farmers and farming communities were well placed to argue that autarky was patriotic. In Maine-et-Loire farmers refused to surrender their milk to the Maggi dairy company on the grounds that the butter made in the Maggi dairies was being used to grease the axles of German cars and trucks. Such silly rumors, the company told the prefect, were costing it 150 tons of butter a month, enough to feed 600,000 people.[57] There were in fact cases of the German authorities imposing collective fines on communes for nonfulfillment of quotas, and nonpayment of these could equally be presented as patriotic. Gennes, near Saumur, was dealt a fine of 225,000 francs in 1943 for nondelivery of oats, which was shared between twenty-eight farmers, but by March 1944 only eight farmers had paid a total of 20,000 francs and the mayor was trying to obtain credit from the state.[58] Patriotic the French peasants may have been, but in general they were acting on behalf of the *petite patrie*, that of their community or *pays*, rather than of the wider French *patrie*. It is significant that one of the regions most reluctant to deliver was the Mauges, around Cholet. In 1793 the demand for conscripts for the revolutionary armies had triggered the Vendean revolt there, and 150 years later the same autarkic hostility was capable of driving the local peasantry to acts of violence against French officials in defense of their autonomy. The police noted that "in the countryside, especially in the Cholet region, traditionally more refractory [than others], there was a marked particularist sentiment that could provoke a will to resist government decisions."[59] In the autumn of 1943 the authorities were complaining of "a raising of shields" in the Mauges and a refusal to meet quotas of meat, milk, and potatoes.[60] Early in 1944 there was a dramatic outbreak of violence in the Mauges commune of La Pommeraye, when two Ravitaillement officials who went to investigate a clandestine abattoir were accosted, accused of working for the Germans, and threatened with reprisals after the war by an angry crowd of fifty people headed by the Catholic schoolteacher, a father of nine, and a winegrower who was the son of the mayor. As the officials left, the father was heard shouting at the crowd to puncture the tires of their car. Intendant Ganot, head of Ravitaillement in Maine-et-Loire, asked the prefect for an exemplary punishment, against both the man who ran the clandestine slaughter business and the leaders of the riot. "The more difficulties Ravitaillement officials have to contend with," he urged, "the more authority they need to be given."[61]

In fact, the more authoritarian the Vichy government became, the more rural communities resorted to isolationism and the black market. Fortunately, Vichy had another instrument in play, the Peasant Corporation. Just as the Labor Charter was supposed to harness the working class to the higher goals of the national community, so the Peasant Corporation would restructure rural unions to bend farmers to the needs of the economy as a whole.[62] Committees were set up at the national, regional, and departmental levels to organize one corporative agricultural union in every commune, each under the direction of a syndic, and then to marshal these unions into regional (in effect, departmental) and national corporative unions, under their own regional and national syndics.

Unlike the Labor Charter, where the structures were implemented only to a limited extent, the hierarchy of the Peasant Corporation materialized quite successfully. The main question was whether it did the task set for it or not. At the annual meeting of 500 syndics from Indre-et-Loire at Tours in December 1943, the national syndic, M. Pointier, with regional prefect Charles Donati at his shoulder, told his audience that the corporation must be "the voluntary auxiliary of the Ravitaillement service." "It is up to us," he continued, "to make sure that quotas are delivered on time and not to leave this to the gendarmerie or the price-control bodies, which have their own duties. The corporation has one immediate interest: to ensure that an unbridgeable gulf does not open up between the urban and peasant populations."[63]

The peasantry, however, had other ideas for the corporation. In the first place, farmers used it to seize control of the agricultural unions, which had flourished since the end of the nineteenth century, from the large landowners. Henri de Champagny was a key figure in the Union Agricole de Maine-et-Loire and second in command of the regional corporative organization committee launched in September 1941 to develop the structures of the corporation, but when the regional syndic of the corporation came to be elected in Maine-et-Loire in 1942, he was defeated by Henri Dèze, a peasant who had won his activist spurs in the Parti Agraire of Henri Dorgères in the 1930s. His deputy, Eugène Forget, who was also close to Dorgères and had been a Parti Agraire candidate in Maine-et-Loire, reflected that "this was the first time a peasant farming his own land had been elected to a position of departmental responsibility in an agricultural union. The least one can say about the corporation in Maine-et-Loire was that it was decreed from on high but was the manifestation of free peasant opinion."[64] Having taken over the corporation, the peasantry made sure that it functioned less as an auxiliary of the Ravitaillement services than as a drag on their efforts. Henri Dèze lost no time arguing for an end to the requisitioning of farmyard products such as eggs and poultry.[65] When intendant Ganot stepped up fines for farmers who did not meet their quotas, Dèze conveyed to regional prefect Donati "the anger rising among the rural population."[66]

For all the threats, blandishments, and restructuring of the Vichy government, the French peasantry was able to preserve much of its autarky and black-market dealings. Punishments remained minimal, and of course applied only to the minority who were caught. In Maine-et-Loire a third of proceedings brought for price infringements were dropped, and only 15 percent resulted in fines.[67] Fines for illegal slaughtering of livestock imposed on farmers, farm laborers, and others (cattle breeders, butchers, charcutiers, carpenters, and even a postman) in Loire-Inférieure ranged from 1,000 to 2,400 francs, that is, very small amounts.[68] There is plenty of evidence that fines such as those imposed by the Ravitaillement for nondelivery of quotas were not paid, "covering with ridicule," said prefect Tracou of Indre-et-Loire, "both those who pay their fines and the administration."[69] This was not only a question of inefficiency or incompetence on the part of the authorities. A balance had to be struck between the toughness urged by intendant Ganot to ensure the authority of the public services and the discrimination and flexibility recommended by the Marquis de Sesmaisons to retain the cooperation of the peasantry. Commenting on a demonstration provoked by the arrest of three people accused of clandestine slaughtering for domestic consumption, not for the black market, the police chief of Tours argued against the "excessive zeal" of some Ravitaillement officials, which risked provoking serious incidents intended to "put [the officials] in their place."[70] The district chiefs of the Ravitaillement in Maine-et-Loire were advised by the prefect to "reconcile the imperious needs of the Ravitaillement with the susceptibility of the mayors and their constituents." They were to use persuasion, reminding the peasants of the hunger suffered by townspeople, and only then brandish the threat of judicial proceedings. In a word, they should be "both forceful and subtle."[71]

There was one other reason the black market was never stamped out. The authorities, while mainly doing their duty to the best of their ability, were also caught up in the loop of corruption and crime. This seems to have been increasingly the case toward the end of the Occupation. When Frédéric Brémond, a baker in Chalonnes-sur-Loire, was investigated by the local gendarmerie for black-market acquisitions of wheat, one of the gendarmes pointed out that he was a valuable informer and that it would be best if the authorities treated him leniently.[72] The Atlantic coast was even more like the Wild West. M. Hery, the district Ravitaillement chief of Guérande on the Breton coast, went native on the issue of clandestine slaughtering. He took the simple view that rations were not enough and that people should eat, not least those doing hard work for the Germans. He was said to have regularly given verbal permission to slaughter animals, assumed "the air of a benefactor of the local population, and simply made up his own policy."[73] Nearby at La Baule it was reported that a gendarme and two inspectors of the economic control service were frequently seen having free drinks at the bar of the Café Ramet, where they were on excellent terms with the proprietor and where the waitresses were involved in a substantial black-market trade in cigarettes. Further inquiries suggested that economic service officials regularly ate with the tradespeople they were supposed to be inspecting in Nantes and Saint-Nazaire and that the private gains available to those in authority far outweighed the benefits of doing things by the rules.[74]

At the end of the day, the Vichy was never as authoritarian as it pretended to be, both because it had to come to terms with vested interests and because it was riddled with corruption. In addition, its attempt to control the economy in the national interest failed because it was unable to fulfill the task it set for itself to supply markets and because it was seen by too many sectors to be unjust. Parallel circuits of supply sprang up that the government attacked as selfish black marketeering. In fact, these circuits had distinct advantages: they balanced the supply of distant markets at a profit with the supply of local markets at a fair price, and they kept resources out of the hands of the Germans unless the Germans were prepared to offer black-market prices. This defense of local and trade interests was reflected also in Vichy's attempts to set up corporative economic organizations in the national interest. Though a few trade unionists saw the Labor Charter as the blueprint of a syndicalist state, most saw it as a threat to trade union organizations that survived under the Occupation and Vichy and that they were not prepared to jeopardize. By contrast, the majority of the peasantry went along with the Peasant Corporation but only because they managed to bend it to their own local and professional interests.

5

Circuses

André Roussel is a dapper man with swept-back gray hair and a clipped mustache, more suggestive of a barber than a rock star. Still living in Bléré, the small town near the demarcation line where he grew up, he reminisces about what young people like himself did under the Occupation. He left school at the age of fourteen in 1940 and worked in his father's grocery six days a week. His contemporaries, he says, also started work young and wanted, come Sunday, "to have a bit of a good time." There were not many distractions. The Pagoda cinema, open only on weekends, was for family entertainment, and children went with their parents. There were billiards at the Café du Chalet and Ping-Pong at the Café du Commerce, but the Café de la Ville was full of aging cardplayers. The youth of the little town divided into age groups, each with its own meeting place, where they ate and played records on weekends. The older ones met at the old mill, the middle ones (of whom he was one) in a barn, the younger ones somewhere else. Sunday night was dance night for the older and middle ones, who each had their separate dances. André played the accordion for the middle ones, in a small band that had no name but whose drummer was called Quick. Generally they danced in a large cabin in the forest of Amboise; otherwise they found a barn belonging to one family or another. They were a tight-knit group, eight boys and eight girls who all knew one another and had nothing to do with outsiders.

The most significant thing about the dances is that they were illegal. The Vichy government took the view that France was in mourning after her defeat and that, so long as families were deprived of their loved ones in POW camps, merrymaking was to be banned. Dances took place in secret and news of an event was passed by word of mouth, not unlike the contemporary rave, says André Roussel, although on a smaller scale. "We were more afraid of the French gendarmes than of the German customs officers" who patrolled the demarcation line, he points out. The Germans were concerned only with security and "couldn't care less, seeing that we weren't terrorists," whereas "the gendarmes would have caught us had they been able to." They had lookouts posted on the road, and "when there was the slightest alert we turned everything off, just like in the Indochina war [where he fought after 1945]; we pretended not to know one another and dispersed." Defiance of the authorities, however, had nothing to do with the Resistance for André. He was, he says, completely apolitical. "As a shopkeeper," he explains, "my father belonged to no party and neither did I. That is the best way. A shopkeeper must only ever listen to his customers' family news and nothing else, if he wishes to keep his clientele." Moreover, the world of the young people and that of those he repeatedly calls "the partisans" were completely divorced. Once, just before the Liberation, the young people decided to hold a dance in the street in the village of La Touche, but the partisans arrived and started firing, so they scattered. "I didn't know any partisans," he asserts. "I never went around with them, never associated with that lot." He was, he repeats, "only eighteen and the only thing that interested me was going out with girls and playing the accordion."[1]

At the time, it is clear, the Vichy establishment was far more concerned about the morality of young people than about their politics. One veteran of two wars wrote to the prefect of Indre-et-Loire to complain of young people smoking on the streets of Tours. "German officers have told me how surprised they are to see the practice tolerated, and I share their opinion entirely." He also complained that schoolchildren of both sexes were cutting classes and going to the movies on weekday afternoons, "their books and papers under their arms." The head of education in the department (who incidentally would become prefect at the Liberation) agreed that something had to be done about young people's idleness and the "harmful refuge" they found in the back rows of cinemas.[2] Prefect Chaigneau responded by banning youth under eighteen from cinemas on weekday afternoons, but he clearly believed that more would have to be done to discipline their behavior. "The mentality of young people is still a cause for anxiety," he reflected a few months later. "They have a critical, skeptical, and intolerant attitude that is fairly typical of that age, together with a serious lack of moral sense and civic spirit. They let themselves go both physically and intellectually and are suspicious or scornful of the few among them who display energy and faith."[3] Some of those few, who were involved in Catholic and lay youth movements, were told by the delegate of the Ministry of Youth in Touraine that the vices of young people included not only watching unsuitable films but drinking too many apertifs—in defiance of the prefect's edict, prohibiting the underage from frequenting cafés without their parents—and reading pornographic magazines, which were still on sale in the kiosks of Tours despite a ban that the police seemed to have no interest in enforcing.[4]

One question that needs to be asked is what kind of associative life functioned under the Occupation. According to the account of André Roussel, there were few distractions and young people were obliged to fall back on entertaining themselves. To some extent, he is correct. A youth club in Bléré run by former members of the Jeunesse Ouvrière Chrétienne (JOC), called the Artistic Cricket, was authorized by the French authorities in 1942, but another one, called Arts and Youth, was turned down the following year on the grounds that one such society existed already.[5] In Amboise, less than ten kilometers away, in the autumn of 1940, there was l'Étoile, a popular education and sports society open to children over twelve, a Ping-Pong club at the Café du Château for boys over fourteen, and a cycling club based at the Café Belle Vue for boys over sixteen. Youth clubs, or *patronages*, the main function of which was to keep young people off the streets, were attached to the schools, both the municipal lay *patron-*

age and the Association Saint-Denis for church school pupils, both over 200 strong. For those interested in music there was the Amboise Municipal Band (thirty-six men, one woman, and nineteen children) and the Amboise Philharmonic Society (eighteen men and eight women). Mutual aid societies that flourished in the years before the welfare state included the Amicable Association of Military Medal Holders, the Amboise Solidarity, based at the Café Desmazeau (men only), and the Amboise Amicable Association of State and Department Civil Servants, which was mixed. There were charitable organizations like the Association of Notre-Dame of Perpetual Grace, which numbered 110 women, and the Amboise Association for Free Assistance to the Poor Sick, run by fifteen men. Finally, there was a gardening, or allotment, club, the Petit Jardinage Amboisien, whose type became extremely popular under the Occupation as hobby converged with the benefits of an additional source of food.[6]

The pattern of associations, dedicated to sport, games, gardening, music, mutual aid, and charity, was repeated with variations across all the towns of the region. In the railway suburb of Saint-Pierre-des-Corps, up the line from Amboise and Bléré, the biggest association was the mutual aid organization of the CIMT railway workshops, with 745 men and 28 women members. The CIMT also had a fishing club with 446 members, all male. There were a number of sporting clubs aimed at young people, from the Étoile Sportive Notre-Dame, for over nines, and the Étoiles de la Médaille, for over thirteens, to the Étoile Cycliste, based at the Café de l'Univers, with 120 members over fifteen. The Églantine football club, for youths over fifteen, seems to have acted as a cover for communist activity. One peculiarity of the town, which reflected the influx of immigrant labor into the railway workshops, was the presence of cultural associations for foreigners—the Masaryk Association for Czechs, about which the Feldkommandantur wanted to know more, and the Prosvita Ukrainian Association, which was closed down by the prefecture.

In Saumur, the only association for outsiders was the Cloucado del Soulel, founded in 1926 for French southerners, though the Protestant minority also had their own benevolent society run by Protestant society ladies. The literary pretensions of the town were indicated by its Society of Letters, Sciences, and Arts, founded in 1910, aping that founded in

Cholet in 1880, and the Society of Agriculture, Sciences, and Arts of Angers, which claimed to date back to 1685. There was more diversity among the sporting clubs than in Amboise, with a Saumuroise Athletic Union, started in 1903, for gymnastics, shooting, and military training (now banned), a women's gymnastic club, a tennis club founded in the 1920s, and three cycling clubs, a rowing club, a rugby club, a road-walking club, and an aeronautical club, all set up in the 1930s. Alongside these rather English and elitist clubs were more popular clubs devoted to "boules, billiards, and cards," with a particular enthusiasm for the Angevin version of *boules de fort*, or crown bowls. One club where Saumur blazed a trail in 1929 was the Rallye Cor, or hunting horn society, for which the members dressed in hunting pink. It was copied by the elite of Cholet three years later, blending with the horse-racing society, presided over by industrialist and mayor Alphonse Darmaillacq, and the Rural Hippomobile Society, formed to counteract the pernicious influence of the car. What otherwise characterized Cholet was the rash of associations set up to defend Catholic education, including the influential Catholic Association of Family Heads under the presidency of industrialist Bernard Pellaumail, and the various veterans associations differentiated by rank, class of recruitment, or theater of action. Though dominated by industrialists, Cholet was firmly committed to Catholic and military values in society.[7]

Such a survey, combined with what we know about trade-union activity and agricultural organizations, suggests that the French did not spend the Occupation cowering in their homes or feeling too suspicious of their neighbors to cooperate socially. Civil society flourished, independently of any commitment to Resistance activity or otherwise. Of course, not all these associations were fully active in the autumn of 1940: many were undermined by the absence of their activists, who were mobilized for the war and often then removed to POW camps. They also functioned under rules laid down by the French and German authorities, which were highly bureaucratic if not restrictive. But the Germans and the Vichy government did not have the same objectives, and the clash of those objectives often opened spaces in which associative life could blossom more than it might otherwise have done.

The obsession of the Germans was military security. No organization or movement that threatened the Wehrmacht could be allowed to stand.

The German ordinance of 28 August 1940, which governed French associative life, prohibited the wearing of any uniforms or insignia, as a way of eliminating paramilitary as well as military organizations. All processions were banned, and that included the traditional rag procession with floats of the *gadz'arts*, the students of the technical École d'Arts et Métiers in Angers.[8] Sporting organizations were permitted so long as they were registered with Vichy's Commission for Physical Education and Sport, but sporting events charging entry required permission from the German authorities. Cultural organizations had to be registered, and in 1941 the Feldkommandantur of Tours was concerned about one called the Future of the Proletariat, which advertised a meeting at the Café de la Concorde in the local press. The panic did not die down until the police made clear that the society was "essentially philanthropic and humanitarian" and did not discuss politics.[9] Theatrical and musical events also required permission from the German authorities, and the text of any play, song, or libretto to be performed had to be submitted for censorship to the Propagandastaffel. Public libraries were ordered to remove any anti-German works and report action taken to the military administration. For some reason, the Bibliothèque Saint-Michel in Angers saw fit to take *Mein Kampf* off the shelves.[10] The curfew was used to ensure that no threat could be posed to the army under cover of darkness and restricted social life in cafés, restaurants, and cinemas and at dances and weddings. Where there were any security incidents, the curfew was moved up for a matter of days or weeks.

The concerns of the Vichy government were somewhat different. Security was not so important except against the threat of communist activity, which was aimed as much against the Vichy regime as against the Germans. Vichy was convinced, for example, that the Églantine football club of Saint-Pierre-des-Corps and the Nantes branch of Amis de la Nature, to promote camping for workers, were communist fronts.[11] The overriding program of Vichy, however, was the moral regeneration of the French nation, by means of the National Revolution, to cure the ills that had led to defeat in 1940 and to pave the slow way to recovery. France had dropped out of the war. It was allowed an armistice army of 100,000 men, the same as the French had allowed the Germans after 1918, but after the Germans invaded the Free Zone in November 1942 even this was dissolved. Regeneration was thus to be not military but moral. Selfishness was to be replaced by dutifulness, decadence by discipline, individualism by community spirit, division by unity.

One of the main instruments of national regeneration for Vichy was the Légion Française des Combattants.[12] It was an alternative to a fascist party considered far too revolutionary for the Vichy old guard and brought together and replaced rival organizations of veterans in the name of new-found union. As a movement of veterans with banners, berets, and uniforms, it was considered a military threat by the Germans, who banned it in the Occupied Zone. In our three departments, the only place where it functioned was the unoccupied southeast sector of Indre-et-Loire centerd on Loches. There it was founded by Dr. Abribat, vice president of the Touraine Poilus, and on 4 May 1941 the 1,300 legionnaires, drawn up on the place Verdun in Loches, in the presence of the mayor and his council, the Thirty-first Infantry Regiment, the Compagnons de France, scouts, schoolchildren, and *patronages*, received their colors from General Auguste Laure, inspector-general of the legion, and took the oath of loyalty to Marshal Pétain.[13] Though the German authorities banned the legion in the Occupied Zone, they infuriated the Vichy regime by recognizing the four main veterans' movements that Vichy had dissolved in favor of the legion, so long as they held no meetings, avoided politics, and set up no military or sporting organizations.[14] In Saumur, the local branch of the National Union of Disabled, Discharged, and Former Servicemen (UNMRAC) tried to exploit this loophole by coming a thousand strong to lay wreaths at the war memorial on Armistice Day 1940. The fight that ensued was not with the Germans but with the Vichy regime, which argued that the veterans' organization was defunct under French legislation.[15] Interestingly enough, when nearly three years later Canon Colonel Panaget, the president of the Anjou section of the National Union of Combatants (UNC), just back from a POW camp, wished to set up a Maison du Combatant in Angers along the lines of the Maison du Prisonnier, regional prefect Donati raised no objection because of the great prestige enjoyed by Panaget as a veteran of two wars and the worthiness of his ambition to link the men of 1939–40 with those of 1914–18.[16]

Two other militaristic organizations that the Germans refused to countenance in the Occupied Zone were the Chantiers de Jeunesse, which were camps for twenty-year-olds who would normally be doing military service, and the Compagnons de France, who were volunteers under twenty participating in land reclamation, forestry, harvesting, and building sports fields.[17] The rather paltry equivalents promoted in Occupied France by the General Secretariat for Youth were rural youth centers set up in a few requisitioned châteaux to put delinquent youths from Paris to work on agricultural projects in the hope that some might remain on the land. So sensitive was the German military administration that it ordered the closure of two of these camps, one of which was near the Breton coast, as security risks, before being persuaded that no possible threat existed.[18] But neither did the centers do much in the way of moralizing French delinquents or promoting the return to the land. Youths sent there thought only of how to escape. André Garnier, aged seventeen, was recaptured twice by the gendarmerie of Baugé after he got away from the center of La Roussière in attempts to return home to his mother in Angers. André Célarié was luckier, managing to escape from the same center after two weeks and making it to the Free Zone.[19] As for local farmers, they were predictably extremely reluctant to accept assistance from urban delinquents at the centers, which became prey to other Vichy agencies keen to turn them into farm schools for the sons of peasant families who were already committed to the land.[20]

For the National Revolution to succeed, the motivation had to come spontaneously from existing organizations. Scouting was one of those paramilitary movements banned in the Occupied Zone, not least because the Germans suspected it of having English connections.[21] The fact was that nine-tenths of scouts were under the wing of the Catholic Church. If scouts were good at one thing, however, it was secrecy. The Chinon scouts deftly renamed themselves the Open-Air Chinon Youth and were duly authorized by the Feldkommandantur at Tours. Elsewhere they camouflaged their summer camps as vacation colonies, hoisting the tricolor flag and lighting campfires when Germans were at a safe distance. When the British and Americans began to bomb French ports and cities, they metamorphosed into *équipes nationales*, which served as one of the emergency services, responsible for pulling victims from the rubble of buildings and administering first aid. In one sense too they had the last laugh. The Third Angers troop under Pierre-Yves Labbe founded a sea-scout group that had itself authorized as a sailing club. Then, in August 1944, as the Americans approached Angers, Labbe sent his lieutenant Louis Bordier to meet them over the small, ill-defended Pont des Pruniers to take the Germans in the rear.[22]

The largest and most influential instrument of national regeneration was without doubt the Secours National. Although not founded by Vichy—it was set up in 1915 and was revived by the Republic at the outbreak of war in 1939—it was given new powers under a law of 4 October 1940 to coordinate all agencies "helping civilians afflicted by the war and its consequences." Most important, it was granted "exclusive authority to engage in and permit public fund-raising," which gave it immense resources and the power effectively to dictate to all charitable organizations. The Secours National was a vast charity monopoly that launched waves of fund-raising, such as its winter campaigns each November to collect food and clothing for evacuees, bomb victims, wives of POWs, and the unemployed and low-paid. "Solidarity coupons" were on sale everywhere, in theaters, concert halls, cafés, restaurants, wine shops, schools, and on the street. The Secours National was also a highly effective instrument of propaganda, less perhaps for the Vichy regime than for Marshal Pétain himself. It labored under his "high patronage," and sales of postcards of Pétain both raised money and stimulated the cult of personality. The target for sales in Indre-et-Loire in the winter of 1940–41 was 300,000, hardly less than the population of the department, and a year later the bishop of Angers claimed that each of his 100,000 church attendees had a card.[23]

For the Secours National, fund-raising and propaganda were important in themselves but always in the service of a wider aim, to restructure French society around the principle of solidarity. A reserve army captain, the manager of a business in Niort, was scandalized one cold February morning in 1941 to witness the "selfishness" exhibited at the market on the place Lafayette in Angers. "There was complete panic around the stall of a charcutier," he told the prefect, "with customers fearful that they would not be served." To offset this kind of attitude he proposed a "kindness week" that would weave together the bonds of social solidarity torn asunder by the struggle for survival. On the first day women and girls would take fruit and puddings to the sick in the hospital, on the second men would take wine to gentlemen in old age homes, on the third and fourth young people would take up a collection for orphans and children would bring them sweets, and on the fifth and sixth days all Angevins would raise money for municipal charities.[24] Far from being treated as far-fetched, the suggestion was accepted by the prefect, who initially called for a "kindness week" in March, then simplified it to three days: a day for children, a day for families, and an old people's day. The main headache was not the appeal but obtaining lists of families who were hard up but not normally in receipt of charity. This involved close cooperation with the Catholic Church, which was far more knowledgeable about this sort of thing than the prefecture.

Fortunately, the Secours National was run not by prefects but by departmental delegates assisted by action committees of representatives of the Church, charitable organizations, education, industry, and agriculture. There were also Secours National delegates in each arrondissement, canton, and even commune. The departmental delegate in Maine-et-Loire was Colonel François de Sauvebeuf, a Kiplingesque figure who had been educated by Jesuits in Tours, trained at the cavalry school of Saumur, and after he retired from the army in 1920 tried his hand variously at running a peat farm and a stud farm and working for an oil company. His undistinguished professional career was amply compensated by his accumulation of honors in Anjou. By 1940, at the age of sixty, he was vice president of the National Union of Combatants (UNC) under Colonel Panaget, secretary of one of the three Red Cross societies, that of the military wounded, and vice president of the Society of Agriculture, Sciences, and Arts of Angers. More controversially, he had joined the Croix de Feu of Colonel de La Roque, a paramilitary organization of decorated soldiers of the Great War that was highly critical of the parliamentary Third Republic, and became president of the local Parti Social Français, the reactionary if not fascist party that replaced it after 1936. There is no doubt that Sauvebeuf was a vigorous and effective head of the Secours National in Maine-et-Loire, but his political activity was to prove his Achilles' heel.[25]

The activities of the Secours National were rich and diverse. It collected, sorted, mended, and distributed large amounts of old clothes—over 80,000 articles of clothing in Maine-et-Loire in 1941. It took over the supervision of the Mutual Aid Kitchens of Angers, a network of nearly a dozen food counters and cheap restaurants usually run by nuns, from the night shelter in the old Doutre quarter and the Brisepotière refectory for industrial workers from outside Angers who could not get home for lunch, to the Foyer de l'Ouvrière in the rue Pasteur, which was intended as a safe haven for female salespeople, office workers, and students. Some people could pay, while others had free or half-price vouchers. Many of the restaurants also served as school canteens, the poorer children receiving free lunches paid for by the municipality. Nearly 5,000 meals were served per day in November 1941 and the number was rising. In the winter of 1941–42 many more middle-class people, experiencing difficulties finding food themselves, turned to the kitchens.[26] For children, the Secours National supplied vitamin-enriched biscuits and sweets to schools, forty-one tons of them in Maine-et-Loire alone in the winter of 1941–42. For working families it developed allotments that were in extremely short supply and distributed seeds and seedlings for vegetable growing. Last but not least, it helped organize summer camps and Christmas parties for children and Mother's Day celebrations to reward women who were doing their patriotic duty by raising large families. "In a word," concluded Colonel de Sauvebeuf, "we want to found a school of generosity that will bring together as pupils all French people and happily replace the monstrous school of selfishness in which they have been educated for so many years."[27]

The Secours National was a veritable engine of social solidarity, one of the most successful institutions of Vichy, although its hegemony did not go unchallenged. It had a reputation for being Catholic, bourgeois, and right-wing. Colonel de Sauvebeuf's first office had been in the house of the cathedral canon who had preceded him before his death in 1940, and stalwarts of the Angevin organization included such Catholic notables as Pierre Poisson, a commercial lawyer, and his cousin Francis Poisson, vice president of the Saumur chamber of commerce, and Joseph Le Sciellour, leader of the Catholic trade unions in Angers. Sauvebeuf tried to remedy this situation, seeking, for example, to add a representative from a "left-wing union," but this never happened and the "clerical complexion" of the organization was criticized even by Vichy government officials, from Interior Minister François Darlan on down, who feared an anticlerical backlash.[28] Indeed, opponents of Vichy reaction were able to exploit hostility toward the Secours National. In Maine-et-Loire, for example, rumors spread that the vitamin-enriched biscuits distributed to schools by the Secours National were contaminated with the tuberculosis bacillus, and parents began to stop their children from accepting them. The rumors were whipped up by *Le Petit Courrier*, which was ostensibly the official organ of the prefecture, and prefect Roussillon was forced to publish communiqués dismissing them as unfounded.[29] The damage done to the authority of the Secours National was nevertheless considerable. Sauvebeuf himself was highly vulnerable as the local leader of the Parti Social Français, which became suspect to the Gestapo as anti-German. Arrested in March 1943 and deported to Germany, he died in Flossenburg in October 1944. After his disappearance the Secours National of Anjou never really recovered its direction.

One of the dilemmas faced by the Secours National was what constituency to target. Its brief, to attend to the totality of the civilian population hit by the war, was impossible to fulfill. It did its share of good deeds for the traditional poor but increasingly became obsessed with the new middle-class poor. A delegate in Touraine drew the attention of his superiors to "the critical and profoundly sad situation of people living on small private incomes" from property or stock that had lost value since the First World War, let alone since the beginning of the Second. He said that to offer help to these people was "extremely delicate since they were accustomed to living comfortably and had never begged." One case thrown up was that of a commercial traveler with nine children who lost his job when the firm employing him collapsed in 1940 but who, as a home owner, was not entitled to benefits when he became ill; the Secours National gave him 5,000 francs to cover his tax arrears.[30] In Angers concern was expressed that "female white-collar workers of irreproachable morals and excellent appearance" had been driven out of the Foyer de l'Ouvrière restaurant by workers and tramps and that a new restaurant should be set up to serve them.[31] A preference was developed for helping the genteel poor back to independence and respectability rather than encouraging dependency among the traditional poor, who were rarely grateful anyway for what they were given. When Marie-Louise Poirier of Cholet complained of the "swindle" by which she had been asked to pay fifty francs and ten textile points from her ration book for what she called "rags" from the Secours National, she was told that her attitude revealed "a mean ingratitude and a marked hostility toward an organization of national solidarity" and that any further defamation would trigger judicial proceedings against her.[32] This patronizing attitude only confirmed to the underclass that they were not the first concern of the Secours National.

Although it could not possibly meet all its commitments, the Secours National antagonized other charitable organizations by rigidly defending its monopoly status. At meetings of the commission set up in Loire-Inférieure to approve all fund-raising events for POWs, the delegate of the Secours National voted against all requests to organize fund-raising events; the idea of delegating this role to other charities was never considered.[33] Other charitable and even public bodies, however, missed no opportunity to assert their autonomy. For Christmas 1943 the Secours National of Touraine planned a single big party for all the children of evacuees, POWs, and workers sent to Germany. But POW organizations, the employers of *La Dépêche du Centre* newspaper, and the mayors of numerous communes insisted on having their own private parties and the principle of unity was shattered. Not surprisingly, Secours National fund-raising plans to help those hit by Allied bombing and evacuated to less-exposed regions met with concerted resistance. Not content to solicit charitable donations, the Secours National went over to a system of thinly disguised taxation. Traders in Touraine, asked to contribute a fifth of the value of the patent tax they paid to the government, coughed up only 6 percent of what was demanded, many arguing that peasants, starting with the wealthiest winegrowers of Touraine, were now much better off than they were. These farmers were also asked for a sou (five centimes) for each hectare, but despite letters to the rich winegrowers underlining "the imperious duty of solidarity toward your co-citizens afflicted by the war," not one in twenty of them paid up.[34] Of course, Touraine was a predominantly Radical area on which the grip of Vichy was limited, but such opposition revealed significant fault lines in the edifice of social solidarity.

Solidarity required from above was one thing; solidarity promoted spontaneously from below was another. The French needed no encouragement to get together for sport, culture, or entertainment, where necessary in defiance of the rules imposed by Vichy and the German authorities. They were also able to exploit the contradictions between the Germans' priority of military security and Vichy's concern with moralization.

One of the great passions of French country life was hunting. A privilege confined to the nobility on horseback during the ancien régime, the practice had been democratized since the Revolution and every Frenchman with a permit duly delivered by the *mairie* was entitled to stride out with his gun and shoot game. For security reasons, the Germans could not tolerate this license: orders were given that all firearms were to be handed in at the local *mairie* on pain of the severest penalties. Some guns were wrapped up in cloth or leather, hidden, buried, or sunk to the bottom of ponds, but hiding a gun made an individual vulnerable to denunciation by a resentful neighbor or even spouse and was not undertaken lightly. In the autumn of 1941 the Germans realized that to turn town halls into arms dumps was risky, and they henceforth required mayors to hand over their stocks to safe sites like the Caserne Blucher at Tours, where 11,000 weapons ended up. While they were at it they ordered any remaining firearms to be handed in, and the mayor of Bléré reported that he had received eight hunting rifles, five revolvers, and fifty-two cartridges.[35] Earlier on, the Germans showed no concern for weapons merely of historic interest such as muskets and blunderbusses, but in the spring of 1942 they demanded even these, together with swords, sabers, and bayonets.[36] Such were their doubts that all weapons had been handed in that in August 1943 they declared an amnesty for any firearms still to be declared, and one mayor reported that he had taken to the Blucher barracks "(1) a rifle without a butt, (2) an old pistol in poor repair, and (3) an old musket."[37]

Without their guns the French were unable to hunt and the privilege reverted to the German military, which was only too happy to indulge its taste for sport on its own terms. Touraine, with the forests of Amboise and Chinon teeming with the wild boar and deer the French were not allowed to touch, was particularly attractive, and Dr. Herbig in Tours served as the Germans' hunting officer. Herbig in fact met with the president of the Hunting Federation of Indre-et-Loire, the Baron de Champchevrier, and its secretary-treasurer, Louis Théret, an accomplished gamekeeper with indispensable knowledge of local game. The result was that the Germans issued licenses to a few dozen individuals, such as the Baron de Champchevrier and the Comte de Blacas of Rigny-Ussé, effectively restoring the hunting privileges of the nobility abolished 150 years before. At the same time, they allowed the gamekeepers of these land-owners to carry guns to combat poaching. Some hunts involved Germans and Frenchmen together, a form of collaboration that Frenchmen were reluctant to admit after the Occupation.[38] But in 1942 the mayor of Chênehutte-les-Tuffeaux complained that not enough Frenchmen with guns were permitted to go on a Franco-German boar hunt: only one had a gun whereas what was really needed was "25 or 30 good hunters" who knew the paths and were armed.[39] It should be added that the German military applied their own hierarchical rules to their own men, issuing permits to select officers and NCOs but never to ordinary soldiers.[40]

While this return to privilege was fine for French nobles and German officers, it led to the same complaints from peasants as before 1789; their fields, they said, were being overrun and their crops spoiled by rampaging boar and plagues of rabbits. One concession won was that farmers were allowed to catch rabbits with ferrets, dogs, or traps, but the Germans tended to view French stories of plagues of wild animals as much exaggerated.[41] Even the Germans, however, could not put a stop to poaching, which for the French had become a question less of sport than of survival. When the carcass of a deer was found in the forest of La Ferrière in Anjou, the Germans threatened to impose a fine of a million francs on the village, until the subprefect of Segré persuaded them that the animal had been shot by ordinary German soldiers who had run off. Years after the Occupation it transpired that the deer had indeed been killed by Frenchmen, but from outside the commune.[42] Elsewhere hunting—or poaching, as it was now called—went on more or less unimpeded. In La Pommeraye, where the Ravitaillement officials were to be accosted in 1944, there were "nocturnal safaris" with the aid of guns hidden or provided by an obliging gendarme from Montjean. One night the hunters returned at 4:00 A.M. with a bag of eighteen hares.[43]

While hunting was formally under strict control, fishing was less so, except during the spawning season between mid-April and mid-June. Like hunting, fishing became a necessity as well as a sport, as the number of workers in fishing clubs like that of the CIMT at Saint-Pierre-des-Corps demonstrates. The problem with fishing, however, was that there was a shortage of stock. In 1941, responding to pressure from the local fishing organization to allow fishing on Sundays and public holidays during the spawning season to supplement meager rations, prefect Roussillon issued an order permitting it so long as the catch was used only for family consumption and not sold. But he was immediately overruled by the Ministry of Agriculture, which took the long-term view that fish stocks had to be preserved, however hungry people were, and he was forced to withdraw his instructions.[44] The German authorities were also concerned about stock shortages, not least because they allowed ordinary soldiers to fish, and the issue of security came into play too. Notwithstanding the decrees of the French Ministry of Agriculture, in 1942 the Feldkommandant of Angers required the prefect to issue a regulation prohibiting night fishing from or near bridges, saying that the prefect of Indre-et-Loire had already obliged.[45] Such restrictions did not apply to German soldiers, who did not care for the traditional art of rod and line but blew the fish out of the water from motorboats with grenades. One veteran of the French occupation of the Palatinate after 1918 said that French soldiers doing the same thing there had been punished by their commanding officers and that this "vandalism" and "piracy" must stop. Prefect Roussillon wrote to the Feldkommandant to protest but received no answer.[46]

To sporting activities that involved no possible security risk the Germans had no objection, whereas the Vichy authorities might be more difficult. Horse racing continued as a sporting and social event, a high point being a race organized in Chinon in July 1943 to raise funds for the POWs. Prizes were offered by the local demobilized soldiers, veterans, repatriated prisoners, the prisoner support committee, the municipality, the Commercial and Industrial Union, and the Peasant Corporation. The seriousness of the fund-raising did not detract from the splendor of the occasion, with the press reporting that "the racegoers milled about in the thousands at the weigh-in and in the paddock. Elegant outfits brightened up the stands, giving the appearance of a multicolored garden."[47] Every spring and summer saw a rash of local cycle races: three times around Angers on 2 March 1941, sponsored by *Le Petit Courrier*; Angers to Saumur and back on 22 May 1941, organized by the Angevin Pedal Club; and the Grand Saint-Léonard Prize on 1 June, awarded to the winner of seven circuits of the village of the same name. New kinds of transportation called for new kinds of races, such as the twenty-five-kilometer trailer race held in Chinon in May 1941 to make a competitive sport of monotonous trips with trailers into the country in search of food. The race finished at the municipal stadium, where Mayor Henri Mattraits blew the whistle to start the final of the departmental football championship sponsored by *Le Petit Courrier* and won 4–0 by the Chinon team.[48]

The only thing that stood between the French and their enjoyment of football was occasional German crassness. The ironmonger who ran the Saint-Pierre *patronage* in Nantes complained that its first championship match against an Angers team had to be called off because the Germans has requisitioned the football field.[49] But the Parc des Sports at the Malakoff Stadium in Nantes seems to have been a veritable mecca of sport. On 7 December 1941 a rugby match between the Stade Nantais UC and the Paris Post Office workers was followed by an amateur football match between the Western League and the Southwest League, both events attended by the prefect. In July 1943 a festival of gymnastics and physical education was held at the stadium, organized by the Anjou committee of the Gymnastic and Sporting Union of French Youth Clubs.[50] Meanwhile at the Bessonneau Stadium of Angers on 27 June 1942, in front of the prefect delegate, police intendant, head of education, and a crowd of 6,000, 1,500 athletes from all over Maine-et-Loire took the "oath of the athlete" to Marshal Pétain.[51] Sport, and in particular athletics and gymnastics, corresponded to the Vichy ideal of a healthy mind in a healthy body and to the virtues of fitness, individual prowess, and teamwork.[52]

The Vichy regime put a great deal of time and effort into providing structures for young people that would educate them in morality, duty, and patriotism. Just as each department had a delegate of the Secours National, so each had one from the General Secretariat of Youth, who was supposed to coordinate and promote initiatives for young people. The delegates faced an uphill struggle. Teachers, clergy, Catholic youth organizers, and even municipalities resented the encroachment of these newcomers on their turf, the more so because they suspected a hidden agenda of forging a single national youth movement along vaguely fascist lines. H. Biessy, Vichy's departmental delegate in Touraine, accused all these groups of variously trying to sabotage his efforts. He tried to put in place a network of correspondents in each canton, a team of clean and energetic youth leaders on whom he could rely, but even where these were up to the task they resigned or were drafted for labor service in Germany. The only organization that offered support, he said, was the small Francist movement, which drew young men of fascist inclinations, but Biessy was the first to confess that "it is difficult to argue in favor of the educational value of such a movement when all [its members] ever do is write on walls."[53]

The most difficult problem the delegates faced nevertheless was the alternative entertainment open to young people. One of the manias of the Occupation was theater going and some of the plays put on raised the eyebrows of Vichy traditionalists. M. Goupil de Bouillé, a member of the administrative commission of Indre-et-Loire, objected to a play called *We Are Not Married*, by the Charles Baret theater company, put on in Bourgueil at the invitation of the lay youth club. Much of it took place in an artist's studio where a scantily clad model disported herself; he saw the whole thing as an apology for free love. "Allow me to point this out in my capacity as departmental delegate of the rural family and president of the cantonal committee of family organizations," he wrote to the prefect. "I am certain that you will not allow the marshal's moralizing program to be flouted in this way."[54] The teacher responsible for allowing the play was duly reprimanded. On the positive side, the best way to promote moral and uplifting fare was to sponsor classic theater. A touring company called The Revival clearly spotted a gap in the market. Its director, Christian Casadeus, secured the patronage of Ferdinand de Brinon, Vichy's ambassador in the Occupied Zone, and finance from the Education Ministry to bring the plays of Molière and Dumas to a string of provincial towns. He dreamed of reaching all audiences, with matinees for young people and private performances for workers organized by firms' social committees, but he still had to reckon with the fact that some municipalities were interested only in commercial productions that would maximize returns.[55]

Meanwhile plays were produced on a vast scale by schools, youth clubs, Catholic youth movements, sports clubs, and factory social committees, partly as entertainment, partly to raise funds either for their own activities or for good causes like the support of POWs. Most of the plays, playlets, and songs were comic, sentimental, or harmless, but their contents still had to be approved by the German authorities, which after mid-1942 meant the Sicherheitspolizei, or security police. The formality of the German police created a rod for its own back: between August and December 1942 the police processed 284 requests to perform plays and concerts in Indre-et-Loire alone.[56] Most of the hard work, to be fair, was passed on to the Propagandastaffel, which must have all but died of boredom. In a large file of plays, songs, and libretti that passed through its hands at Tours, the sole red pencil mark crossed out the phrase "American chic" from a song about a mustache.[57] The Germans blew hot and cold when French flags were draped on the stage for a performance of the unavoidably patriotic *La Fille du Régiment* at the municipal theater of Angers in 1942, but other political references eluded them altogether. The Jesuit Collège de Saint-Grégoire put on Charles Péguy's *Jeanne d'Arc* at the municipal theater of Tours in May of the same year. When Joan reached the phrase "We must boot the enemy out of France," it is said that the audience rose to clap while the Germans present sat bemused.[58]

More sensitive than theaters from the German point of view were cinemas.[59] In this golden age of the movies there were five cinemas with 4,500 seats in Angers, six with 4,300 seats in Tours, and nineteen with 11,500 seats in Nantes.[60] The largest cinemas had 1,000 seats and, teeming with young people on a Saturday night, could be a security risk. The German authorities required cinemas to register but they did not care what films were shown. Trouble tended to occur during the projection of newsreels, which were basically German, Italian, or Vichy propaganda. In the darkness the audience could express its opinion anonymously by catcalls, stamping, coughing, applause, and even shouting. The German authorities insisted that the French come down heavily on miscreants. They regularly closed or threatened to close cinemas where incidents had taken place, and when they prosecuted individuals the sentences were generally tough. For example, André Tallourd, a young carpenter arrested in October 1940 for a disturbance during a German newsreel at the Athénée cinema in Saint-Nazaire, was prosecuted by the French authorities only for drunkenness, whereas Roger Morel, a young optician from Le Mans, was sentenced by a German military court to two years in prison for applauding the bombing of a German hospital by the RAF.[61] After the outbreak of hostilities with the Soviet Union, the Germans became even tenser. The Feldkommandant of Tours ordered newsreels to be shown in half-lit houses in order to expose demonstrators, and stern warnings were issued to audiences about the consequences of subversive behavior. In March 1943, after the audience at the 1,000-seat Majestic in Tours had coughed all the way through footage of Pierre Laval making a speech in support of French workers going to Germany and laughed at a shot of a German soldier removing a No Entry sign on the demarcation line, the German police arrested seventy young people and closed the city's cinemas for a week.[62]

Obviously the Vichy authorities could not sanction criticism of Laval, but the main concern of the Vichy establishment was not anti-German sentiment but immorality. Not all cinemas were at risk. In Loire-Inférieure, where the Church and the Catholic family movement were strong, 60 percent of cinemas were parish-based, owned by the Catholic *patronages*, or youth clubs, and generally called the Familia. The clergy leased their premises to traveling projectionists and retained complete control over what was shown.[63] Influencing what went on in commercial cinemas was more difficult. Jean Briand, president of the Jeunesse Ouvrière Chrétienne in Loire-Inférieure, complained in July 1941 that seven out of the ten films currently being shown in Nantes undermined the virtues of hard work, family dignity, female modesty, or masculine pride. He had recently passed a suburban cinema on a Thursday afternoon, when schools were closed, and witnessed the supervisor of an after-school club taking nine-year old girls to see *The Maltese House*, "a film as immoral as you can get, sadistic, humiliating to women, ridiculing marriage, preaching free love, and ending in suicide."[64] On a few occasions the Catholic lobby was able to influence the authorities. In 1942 Dr. Yves Bureau, the president of the family associations in Loire-Inférieure and a frequent lobbyist, prevailed on the mayor of Nantes to ban those under twenty-one from one particular film. He was concerned that when the film opened children as young as twelve had been to see it, and he quoted a survey that said that working-class youths under sixteen liked violence and those over sixteen sex. "The cinema unhinges young people," he observed. "They spend a restless night after the film. The next day they do nothing but dream and talk about what they have seen. Some of them imitate gangsters and finish up before the juvenile court."[65]

One of the points made by Dr. Bureau was that censorship in the Occupied Zone was, paradoxically, far laxer than that in the Free Zone. Over 200 films banned in the latter continued to be shown in the former. This was because the German authorities had the upper hand, wanted no meddling in their censorship, and were disturbed more by catcalls in cinemas than by sex. When the French courts fined a cinema owner in Maine-et-Loire 6,000 francs for not having a permit, the German authorities said that the man was registered with the Propagandastaffel and ordered proceedings to be dropped.[66] The same contrast between the German and Vichy authorities was clear when it came to dancing.[67] The Germans imposed a curfew for military reasons and from time to time gave permission to hotels or restaurants to stay open late for a wedding. But in June 1941 they formally ceded responsibility to supervise dancing to the French authorities, who were more than keen to exercise that power. When the Kreiskommandant of Cholet issued a spate of licenses to hoteliers and café owners, allowing weddings and other family parties to continue beyond the curfew, he received a rap on the knuckles from the subprefect, who made clear that the business of the Germans was only closing times, while permission to allow the dance attached to French sovereignty.[68] French policy, introduced during the war of May–June 1940 and developed by Vichy, was that so long as France was in mourning for its defeat and the absence of its loved ones in German POW camps, concentration camps, or German factories, modesty and decency should be cultivated and dancing banned.

There was a brief window after the armistice when it was assumed that dancing would be allowed to revive. Owners of cafés, restaurants, and hotels were eager to reopen their dance floors and boost their clientele. The Vichy authorities, however, reiterated that public dancing was prohibited. In Touraine there was a wave of petitions—from "a young woman who loves dancing," protesting that balls were not "places of debauchery but somewhere one can have fun gaily and freely, without another thought"; from a group of "young people who want to make the most of being twenty"; and from fifty youths who, taking the altruistic tack, said, "We are working with all our heart and with all our strength for the speedy recovery of our country. We hope that you will understand us and reward our labors by allowing the dance floors to reopen very soon."[69]

For a while the Vichy authorities were prepared to allow private dances. In April 1941 prefect Chaigneau of Indre-et-Loire was giving permission for dances at weddings on the grounds that "if a dance takes place at a private house it is impossible to prohibit it." But two months later, after a so-called private dance in the village of Reugny was crashed by 300 people, he told the mayor that no more dances at all would be allowed.[70] Prefect Roussillon of Maine-et-Loire was moving in the same direction. In September he told Mireille Gense of Coutures, who requested permission for a dance at her wedding, which would be "entirely a family occasion and no more than the little bop [*sauterie*] usual on such occasions," that both public and private dances were formally prohibited "for reasons of decency that you will readily understand."[71] The following July Roussillon clarified his policy for the region:

> Given the grave circumstances, which require a dignified and reserved attitude from all French people and render it impossible to tolerate public behavior that is misplaced merrymaking and flouts the country's state of mourning, it is decreed that in the territory of the five departments of the Angers region all public and private dances, noisy or rag processions, singing or licentious behavior on the public highway, all music that can be heard outside, whether by loudspeaker, jazz band, gramophone, or radio, are and remain forbidden.[72]

The effect of these regulations was simply to drive dancing underground. The craze got bigger, and the authorities noted a veritable explosion of dancing in the summer of 1943. Prefect delegate Daguerre of Maine-et-Loire was obliged to reissue the ban and told his mayors that even Marshal Pétain was concerned about "the upsurge of clandestine dances, especially in the countryside." He himself had observed the many dances organized by café owners, hoteliers, and private individuals "in isolated houses, barns, and even in the main squares of certain villages or hamlets." He would not dwell, he added, "on the shocking character of such merrymaking at a time when hardship afflicts so many families. Only too often women whose husbands are in POW camps are persuaded to dance, a scandalous state of affairs that demoralizes the prisoners who get wind of it."[73]

The amount of clandestine dancing that went on is a fair indication of the limits of Vichy's National Revolution. Since it was clandestine it is impossible to quantify with any accuracy. Dances were raided by the gendarmes, who tried to make arrests and submitted reports. The gendarmerie of Vernantes on the Touraine border of Maine-et-Loire, for example, unearthed four clandestine dances involving up to eighty people there and in the neighboring commune in the Christmas–New Year period of 1943–44 alone.[74] But what they discovered represented only the tip of the iceberg. A well-dressed young man picked up on the road at Chanceaux, just north of Tours, early one morning in June 1943 turned out to be an agricultural laborer who had just slept over at a dance and had been to one the previous Thursday and another the Sunday before that. "They take place nearly every Sunday," he said, reeling off the names of the farms, "either at La Boulas, or at La Hardinière, or at Les Rentries."[75] As for André Roussel of Bléré, he and his friends were never caught by the gendarmerie, he says. Undeniably, there was a complete subculture of clandestine dancing that has left little trace in the records.

This dancing was foremost an expression of youth culture. Of course, it may be seen as a political statement, in that it was banned by the Vichy authorities, but breaking the curfew can scarcely be called resistance. The Occupation nourished political awakening, but it also stimulated political indifference, escapism, and hedonism. The young people born in the aftermath of the Great War were not prepared to see their youth ruined by another war. Opportunities for amusement in the countryside were limited. "Just when the return to the land is being preached," two young men told the prefect of Indre-et-Loire, "all entertainment is being totally abolished. Can peasants go to the cinema? Do they play boules or cards at their age? Of course not. That is why we are asking you to permit dancing at least for a few hours on Sunday afternoons."[76] At its most basic, dancing was the obvious release for young people who worked in the fields, shops, or workshops six days a week. Sometimes it was part of the ritual observed by twenty-year-olds about to leave for military service or, when that was suspended under the Occupation, about to go to Germany as labor conscripts under the STO or to celebrate their return. The frenzy of dancing increased at Christmas and New Year's but also around 14 July, which was traditionally marked by dancing in the streets yet was a commemoration heavily discouraged by Vichy. Although dancing and the sale of food were strictly banned at parish patronal festivals or kermesses, they were generally tolerated by mayors, and the laughable level of fines made the gendarmerie virtually powerless.[77]

Dancing, food, drink, and money went easily together. André Roussel argues that drinking did not take place at clandestine dances, although afterwards the dancers sometimes retired to drink in an isolated limestone cave, and once he had to bring a legless friend home in a wheelbarrow. If dances took place in barns or farmhouses, the parents or uncles of the dancers were generally involved and often took the opportunity to earn some money. Dancing was a good cover for black-market activity. As the gendarmerie of Longué, near Saumur, surprised a clandestine dance in a barn, over a hundred young people scattered, leaving a table groaning under bottles of wine and a fifty-liter barrel, drunk to the last few liters. The owner, Auguste Josselin, aged seventy, confessed that he had organized the dance with his thirty-one-year-old son, Maurice, charging the boys twenty francs and the girls ten francs and selling wine for forty francs a bottle. The gendarmes were delighted to book him not only for organizing a prohibited dance but for selling liquor without a license.[78]

One representative of the Vichy regime thought that clandestine dances, put on with the consent of parents, was just another example of how spoiled the young farmers were in Touraine. On the one hand, he said, were the disinherited class of agricultural laborers, woodcutters, and carters; on the other, the sons of winegrowers and farmers, who were often only children destined to inherit a very profitable concern. "The child has no respect for old age, infirmity, or suffering," he argued. "Religion and Country are for him vague notions that disappear under the weight of egoism and the increasing desire for comfort. From children who are never denied anything we get a youth that thinks only of pleasure and of every pleasure: new clothes and clandestine dances more numerous than ever."[79]

Let the last word be left to the curé of Nouzilly, ten kilometers north of Saint-Pierre-des-Corps. One night in April 1944, as the Allies bombed the railway yards as part of their campaign to destroy the German military infrastructure before a seaborne invasion, his parishioners were dancing at a wedding that gradually sucked in more guests and went on all night. Did they rush to join the emergency services? Were they encouraged to join the Resistance? They came out of the dance to watch the fireworks in the night sky and then went back to dance until dawn. "While unfortunate victims were dying under the bombs," bemoaned the curé, "these ignoble people continued their insanity. Where is this mentality going to lead us? To certain perdition."[80]

Associative life and civil society thus flourished under the German Occupation more than has often been imagined. Sometimes it was encouraged by Vichy, through the Secours National or its various attempts to organize, educate, and moralize young people. Just as often, however, it was an expression of youth subculture that challenged the boy-scout morality of the regime. Sometimes, as with hunting, handpicked Frenchmen and Germans enjoyed themselves together, but hunting for ordinary people was illegal and no different from poaching. Theater and cinema newsreels could be used as vehicles for anti-German statements, but much sport and entertainment went on that did not have a political spin. The range and variety of camaraderie and merrymaking demonstrated eloquently that much of ordinary French life continued under the Occupation.

6

Demonstrators

Liberation came early to Loches in southern Touraine. On 12 July 1940, to be precise. The German troops who had occupied it three weeks before left, and there was a riot as people tried to get their hands on gasoline stocks left behind before the French gendarmes arrived. By the afternoon everything was ready for the theatricals, and the inhabitants hung tricolor flags from their windows as General Mouton led the Thirty-second Infantry Regiment of the armistice army into the town. The soldiers were drawn up in the main square, the French flag was run up, medals were awarded, and a wreath was laid at the war memorial. "Loches is no longer occupied!" ran the headline in the local paper.[1]

The reason for the liberation was not armed struggle but diplomacy. It was discovered in the fine print of the armistice that Loches should be in the Free Zone, and after consultation at the Armistice Commission in Wiesbaden, German forces withdrew. This incident betrayed some of the confusion of the early days of the Occupation, but it was a confusion that did not last long. People, goods, and even letters were not allowed to cross the demarcation line without permission from the Germans, although the flow could be turned on or off like a tap, in order to put pressure on the government in Vichy. In the early days, when the German military was in control of the border, things were often quite relaxed. La Haye Descartes, right on the line, became a kind of frontier town. French and Germans mingled in the cafés. On one occasion the French stood up to sing the "Marseillaise," took the Germans' revolvers, and would not return them until the Germans, too, had stood up to sing, fists in the air. On another the barn of a saddler named Théo caught fire, but it was on the wrong side of the line and the Germans would not let him through without a pass. Théo was so abusive that they gave in, and French and Germans put out the fire together. Then Théo opened a barrel of wine on the pavement, and the local vet remembers seeing "French and Germans returning arm in arm to La Haye, singing with the saddler, who was still abusing the Germans, reminding them of Verdun, where he had fought, and of their defeat in 1918."[2]

In February 1941 things were tightened up. The military on the line were replaced by professional customs men who had dogs and motor bicycles and took their job extremely seriously. One person was shot that month, but the usual penalty for anyone caught crossing the line was a month's prison in Tours.[3] Many who crossed the line were making a bid for freedom: men who managed to escape from POW camps when they were still located in France, others who wanted to continue the fight by joining the armistice army in North Africa, or Jewish families who were fleeing persecution. In January 1941, when Franco-German relations were going through a bad patch, a rumor spread that the Germans were about to conduct a census of all men between the ages of eighteen and forty-five, with a view to holding them hostage, and there was a rush for the line before the idiocy of the rumor was exposed.[4] It should not be forgotten, however, that just as many people wished to cross the line the other way, *into* Occupied France. There were refugees who had fled before the German armies in 1940 and were not allowed back into the so-called Forbidden Zone of northeastern France.[5] There were soldiers who had been demobbed in the southern zone and wanted to get back to their families. There were young men whose applications to join the armistice army had failed and who turned up penniless in Tours, treating the prefecture as a kind of consulate.[6] Finally, there were businessmen who wanted to visit the Paris Trade Fair in September but did not want then to find themselves stranded. These came, not walking long-distance from Marseille, but in buses from Châteauroux, which made regular trips right up to the line.[7]

In theory, most of them could make the journey legally with a pass, or *Ausweis*. But passes were difficult to obtain from the German authorities and deliberately rationed. *Frontaliers* living on the line found it easier to obtain passes, as did professionals such as priests, doctors, midwives, and vets. This explains the extraordinary activity of André Goupille, the vet of La Haye Descartes, who had a reputation among the line-crossing fraternity as a reliable contact and who received a large mailbag of letters from satisfied clients. One father from the Pas-de-Calais who sent money to his daughter in Toulouse via Goupille told the vet and his wife "how sweet it is in our distress to find sympathetic hearts that beat not only in time to ours but above all in a Christian way, which is much rarer at the present time."[8] But for every angel like Goupille there were a dozen con men like Roger Audebert, a mechanic from Tours who gave up his regular job for the more lucrative one of *passeur*, asking 200 or 400 francs per person (Goupille said the standard rate was 50 francs per head) and then not even taking his clients to the line but dropping them off short of it so that many had to turn back. Whereas Goupille was arrested by the Germans in January 1942 for passing letters and spent five weeks in prison, Audebert was arrested as a swindler two months earlier by the French police in Loches and interned.[9] Goupille was always quick to thank the farmers near the line who kept him informed about the position of customs men. But his task and the chances of his clients were not helped by the odd black sheep like Sidonie Bichet, a farmer's wife from Courçay who was said by other farmers in the village to have swept the demarcation line from the top of her house with German binoculars, shouting if she saw anyone suspicious to her daughter, who would then cycle to the nearest customs post. Her husband was a POW in Germany and she even took one of the customs officers, Herr Walter, nicknamed "Fil de Fer," as a lover.[10]

The vast majority of French people who fell under the Occupation stayed put. Family ties, jobs, studies, friendship, or community networks gave them no alternative. The Occupation, as we have seen, contracted the horizons of most people and rooted them even more firmly in their localities. Survival and sociability, bread and circuses, became their main obsessions. That said, they had to habituate themselves to the presence of the Germans, in their streets, in their places of entertainment, even billeted in their homes. Some worked for the Germans, traded with them, flirted with, slept with, or informed them; others made sure that they had as little to do with them as possible. The vast majority of course resented their presence but were powerless to do anything about it.

Some angry and fearless young people, in the immediate aftermath of the Occupation, refused to see it as definitive and, perhaps taking de Gaulle's appeal of 18 June at face value, dreamed of resistance. In the autumn of 1940 the eldest son of Louis Ancelin, the magistrate of Saumur who had "saved" the town in tense negotiations with the Germans, led a group of youths between the ages of sixteen and nineteen who met in secret in the surrounding countryside to set up a "clandestine militia." They had found some weapons abandoned by the retreating French army and planned to attack the Germans in the rear when they themselves retreated, which the youths imagined would be fairly soon. When subprefect Robert Milliat got wind of this escapade, he summoned *procureur* Ancelin to his office. The magistrate was "extremely annoyed" and promised to "admonish his son severely." Milliat then called in young Ancelin and his group and warned them that their activities were not only useless but dangerous, exposing their families and the populations of the Saumurois to "terrible reprisals" from the Germans. While young Ancelin was sent away to board at a college in Cholet, Milliat reported to the prefect that he feared the youths were being manipulated by English agents. The prefect, for his part, veered between verdicts of childish behavior and a foreign plot before settling on the reasonable theory that "we are looking at impetuous young people who are irritated by the oppressive atmosphere of the Occupation."[11]

Young people soon learned that any kind of military resistance was out of the question. Not only was the balance of force totally stacked against them, but the German strategy of massive reprisals was a powerful disincentive. One alternative was to draw on the battery of commemorations and festivals around which the identity of the Republic and nation was constructed: 14 July, Armistice Day, or Joan of Arc Day. The Germans, exercised by the needs of military security, banned processions, parades, badges, and tricolor flags in the Occupied Zone. They also held the Vichy authorities responsible for maintaining order as a condition of involving them in indirect rule. Some kind of symbolic gesture on these key anniversaries, however, was a way for French people to reach for a moment beyond their narrow communities or material concerns and re-create the identity of the Republic or nation. On some of these occasions the Vichy authorities would be holding their own ceremonies, within the limits of the German law, in order to broadcast the regime's values of work, family, and fatherland. The strategy of protesters was thus to defy German bans as far as they dared and to subvert or reclaim official ceremonies for an alternative set of values, Gaullist or communist. At the end of the day it took very little to make a patriotic statement: a tricolor buttonhole, a slogan or sign chalked on a wall, a wreath laid with a message. Such gestures were a nod and a wink to every other patriot, weaving the gossamer of the French Republic or nation together in a virtually invisible way. Similarly, only a minimum of imagination was required to jolt the leaden message of Vichy ceremonies and put a more playful one in its place. The battle for hearts and minds took place in a world of codes and symbols. But the symbols were supercharged and the stakes were high. By the end of the Occupation it was as easy to be arrested for a buttonhole as for a bullet.[12]

Traumatized by defeat, and four days after parliament voted full powers to Marshal Pétain, who promptly abolished the Republic, few French people were in a mood to mark 14 July, that celebration of the republican nation. Even in the Free Zone, in Loches, there was only a "sad" little ceremony at the cemetery, where the mayor and municipal council laid a wreath in honor of the dead of two wars.[13] In the Occupied Zone the German high command prohibited the flying of the national flag or the singing of the "Marseillaise," and in Loire-Inférieure the prefect decided that although there would be a public holiday no ceremonies would take place.[14]

By Armistice Day on 11 November some of the shock had worn off and the French were beginning to chafe under five months of occupation. Edmond Duméril, interpreter at the prefecture of Loire-Inférieure, noted that the Germans had "an extraordinary fear of demonstrations," and the twenty-second commemoration of their own defeat in 1918 was more than they could stomach.[15] No ceremonies, not even religious services, were allowed; neither was the laying of wreaths at war memorials, even by isolated individuals. Even more than the generation that had fought the war, it was the young people who wished to express their outrage. In Paris, students openly defied the ban by marching down the Champs-Élysées, where German military paraded daily. Many arrests were made, and students sent before courts-martial received prison sentences.[16] The movement also spread to the provinces. In Chinon, posters appeared on the walls announcing ironically, "French people! Listen to this appeal to the population: male and female workers are required to narrow the English Channel." The local military commander, the Kreiskommandant, summoned his French opposite number, the young subprefect Paul Cay, and warned that if such posters or graffiti appeared again severe punishment would be meted out to the townspeople. The subprefect summoned the mayor of Chinon, Dr. Henri Mattraits, and the head of the college, Auguste Correch. The two of them had been educated together and had served together in the trenches of Flanders. They were patriots but they could see no sense in gratuitous provocation, particularly as they were held personally responsible by the German authorities for keeping order in the town. Correch agreed to lecture his students, and the mayor said he would have words with their families to ensure that youthful high spirits did not get out of control again.[17]

In Nantes, university students made common cause with students at the Lycée Clemenceau and the Lycée de Jeunes Filles and tried to organize a school strike on what was to be a Monday. Attempts were made to lay wreaths at the imposing war memorial close to the prefecture, but the way was barred by French municipal police and the Feldgendarmerie. Scuffles broke out on the steps of the Théâtre Graslin, where some students started to chant the "Marseillaise." They had their identity cards confiscated and had to go to the Kommandantur to retrieve them.[18] Most spectacularly, the previous night a university student, Michel Dabat, and a sixteen-year-old schoolboy, Christian de Mondragon, climbed the tower of the cathedral and tied a tricolor flag to the lightning rod. The next morning huge crowds gathered to gape and comment as firemen struggled to find a way to bring the flag down; news of the exploit spread "like a powder trail," in Mondragon's words, all over Brittany and was even greeted as an act of resistance by the BBC.[19]

The Feldkommandant of Nantes promptly called for the Lycée Clemenceau to be closed down. Prefect Dupard had a difficult task to persuade him to change his mind and then summoned the headmaster to impress on him the need to restore discipline and combat Gaullist propaganda. On the positive side, he told the interior minister, the students were the only group susceptible to Gaullist propaganda, and "everywhere I have been able to satisfy myself that the immense majority of the population venerates Marshal Pétain, approves his decisions, and is infinitely grateful for his efforts."[20] Even the students were not uniformly Gaullist. Mondragon recalls that, when he asked among his friends for a flag, some offered help, others immediately made themselves scarce, and still others asked him what he wanted it for. He says he expected the whole town to be decked with tricolors and only wanted his to be the highest.

The protesting students may have been a small minority, but they certainly unsettled both the German and the Vichy authorities. The absence of a commemorative excuse did not deter them. Early in 1941 a graffiti campaign of anti-German slogans began in Angers, targeting buildings occupied by the Germans. Under pressure from the Feldkommandantur, prefect Roussillon published an "appeal to the population," especially young people, saying that if the graffiti did not stop "there would be regrettable consequences for the population at large, notably, collective reprisals."[21] On the night of 13 March, however, a new campaign began—the V sign for victory, often accompanied by the cross of Lorraine, which had become dear to Lorrainers after their annexation in 1871. The Feldkommandant of Angers immediately saw this as Gaullist propaganda and ordered the owners of buildings where the signs had been drawn to remove them at once; Roussillon was instructed that the French police must work closely with the German police to track down the culprits.[22] But the campaign spread. The police commissioner of Saumur reported that 150 V signs had had to be erased in his district. Meanwhile the craze spread to Nantes, where V signs and Lorraine crosses appeared beginning 23 March, first in chalk, then in paint. The speed with which they appeared, said the police chief, was explained "not only by the ease with which they can be drawn but by the rebellious attitude [*l'esprit frondeur*] of young people who are convinced that they will not be caught." The police doubled their surveillance, arresting three students painting graffiti on the prefecture and charging them for defacing a public monument, then catching three adolescents drawing a V on a shop front and sending them home with a warning.[23] The night of 29 March, however, was particularly bad. Feldkommandant Hotz told prefect Dupard that V signs had appeared all over occupied France the previous night, "clearly in response to a single order from the enemy. This anti-German propaganda," he insisted, "cannot be tolerated in any way." He held the prefect responsible for removing all the signs within forty-eight hours, on pain of severe reprisals. Prefect Dupard duly sent orders to subprefects, the police, and the gendarmerie to complete the cleanup operation by 2 April at noon. He told the mayor of Nantes to mobilize teams of the unemployed with buckets, the head of education to instruct head teachers to lay down the law in their schools, and other mayors that "such goings-on are nothing to do either with courage or with patriotism. It is not by drawing on buildings that the French will contribute to national recovery."[24]

Prefect Dupard's circular admirably illustrates the gulf of understanding between the Vichy regime and the young patriots. For Vichy the National Revolution was intended to restore a moral order that would wash away the sins that had brought about the catastrophe of 1940, including the disobedience and hedonism of youth, but renewing the war against Germany was not part of the agenda. For some young people the restoration of national dignity could come about only through a patriotic upsurge, brushing aside the old elites who were themselves to be blamed for the failure of 1940. This divergence of approaches was clearly evident in the commemorations of May Day and Joan of Arc Day in 1941.

May Day, since the 1890s, had been the day on which the labor movement flexed its muscles, demonstrated proletarian solidarity, and stated its demands.[25] Now the Communist Party had been dissolved, the labor movement was losing members, and class conflict was to be replaced by class harmony. The Germans took no chances, banning all meetings and processions, but the Vichy government was also worried that the Communist Party would try to stage a comeback, spreading tracts, sabotaging industry, organizing demonstrations, and even launching a general strike. To combat this, security was tightened and Marshal Pétain was to broadcast reassuringly to factory workers at 5:00 P.M. Not only was work the first element of "work, family, and fatherland," but 1 May also happened to be St. Philip's Day. There were some incidents. When May Day dawned in Nantes, a red flag decorated with the hammer and sickle was discovered flying from the flagpole at the war memorial.[26] A communist tract denounced attempts to appropriate May Day by "Philippe Pétain, that senile old man and pretender to the throne," but was no more complimentary to de Gaulle, who was accused of wanting to drag the French into "an imperialist war for the benefit of Anglo-Saxon capitalists."[27] Leaflets and bills called for a general strike but work continued as normal: prefect Dupard was with the workers of the Ateliers et Chantiers de la Loire to hear Pétain's speech, while the subprefect of Saint-Nazaire visited the SNCASO aeronautics firm.[28]

In Angers, the Employers Federation of Anjou organized a "Festival of Work and Social Concord," the high point of which was a mass in the cathedral presided over by the bishop and attended by all the town's dignitaries. In his address, Canon Pinier of the Catholic University of Angers reminded the congregation that "the maxim of social concord, which is so necessary to build a harmonious city, is also a law of the gospel."[29] In the afternoon there was a large sporting event at the stadium, and the police were delighted that the "extreme left-wing" Églantine sports club of Trélazé had attended and that there had been no incident.[30] What became clear, however, was that the Gaullists, too, tried to appropriate May Day. The order from the BBC was that at 6:30 P.M. people should make their way into the town hall in silence, wearing tricolor ribbons or rosettes if they so wished. Eye contact alone would carry the message of mutual recognition and hope. Moving singly or in groups of two or three, the townspeople staged a demonstration that was not a demonstration. In Nantes, those on the move were young people and women taking advantage of the closure of shops and schools, so that the scene looked "exactly like what happens during rush hour in the city center. Nothing was said, there were no shouts," reported the prefect, with the result that neither the French nor the German police intervened.[31] In Angers also, it was remarked that the crowd was made up of young people, mostly students, four of whom, wearing tricolor ribbons, were taken to the police station to check that they were not communists. It soon became clear, confessed the police chief, "that these young students belonged to Catholic families and were in no way communists. They told me that they were royalists and that they had come to the demonstration that was due to take place before the town hall for purely patriotic reasons." Not communists, not even really demonstrators, certainly smarter than the police, they were released.[32]

Maybe the Vichy authorities cursed the plethora of public holidays in May, for within ten days they had to deal with Joan of Arc Day. No doubt Joan of Arc was easier to handle than the festival of labor: canonized in 1920, declared a national heroine in 1921, she was the official as well as the Catholic patron saint.[33] The only danger was that she would be portrayed as a military heroine who had expelled the enemy from French soil. Wary of this, the German authorities banned all processions, although they permitted the laying of wreaths at the foot of statues of Joan of Arc, which were part of the public furniture of most French towns. At church services attended by Vichy officials and notables, Joan was presented as an inspiration to moral rearmament rather than to military glory. In Angers cathedral, Monsignor Costes underlined Joan's "superhuman energy" and "incomparable purity" and invited the faithful "through the intercession of Joan of Arc, to pray for the courageous energy and austere practice of purity that are necessary to rebuild our dear country."[34] In Chinon, the Church's control of the cult kept radical-socialist Mayor Mattraits away in 1941 but he duly attended in 1943, when the sermon was given by Canon Panaget from Angers, a hero of two wars. The commemoration of Joan of Arc in fact brought civic and ecclesiastic authorities together in a town usually split between clericals and anticlericals.[35]

The authorized version of bishops, mayors, and prefects did not, however, go unchallenged. At Bléré, on the demarcation line, a swastika flag was removed and a tricolor bearing a Lorraine cross hoisted to the top of a poplar tree during the night preceding Joan of Arc Day. The Feldkommandant was clear that the perpetrators must be young Gaullists, although the mayor argued that the culprits must have come from outside the commune, probably from the Free Zone.[36] During the afternoon following the official wreath laying in Angers, many private individuals discreetly laid wreaths with messages such as "Protect France," "Ever faithful to Saint

Joan, the country's liberator," and "Kick them out."[37] A secret Gaullist organization in Nantes called the Sons of France left the first wreath by the statue of Joan of Arc, a huge one with patriotic banderole, which officials with their smaller wreaths tried in vain to cover up.[38] Crowds also carried wreaths to the graves of six British airmen who had been buried the day before in the cemetery of La Gaudinière, outside Nantes. The Feldkommandantur considered this anti-German provocation and told the prefect as much. The cemetery was closed, but a crowd of fifty young women, arriving with their wreaths at 6:00 P.M. to find the gates shut, began to shout, "Long live de Gaulle! Down with the Boches!" until French police moved them on.[39]

It was becoming clear by the summer of 1941 that the dissident network included not only male students from the universities and secondary schools but female students and women from outside the education system. The female admirers of British airmen who made their mark at the cemetery of Nantes were not an isolated example. Gisèle Neau, a girl of eighteen from the outskirts of Saumur, was prosecuted for her part in the V sign and Lorraine cross campaign and fined ten francs, although her father was held civilly responsible as she was a minor. A thirty-seven-year-old housewife of Saumur, Jeanne Barbault, was sent before the public prosecutor for distributing tracts written in pencil attacking Marshal Pétain and Prime Minister Darlan, as was a widow, Jeanne Brouiel, who had been to a photographer in Saumur to order a hundred prints of General de Gaulle.[40] The opposition movement was also spreading from towns to villages and from middle-class secondary school students to working-class students of the *écoles primaires supérieures* (EPS). After V signs appeared on French and German road signs, the road itself, and the embankment wall of the riverside village of Les Rosiers-sur-Loire, near Saumur, during the night of 17–18 June 1941, the first anniversary of de Gaulle's appeal, the trail led to three local youths aged fifteen, sixteen, and twenty-one, "all belonging to honorable families, the fathers of two of them wounded and decorated in the 1914–18 war." Meanwhile, at the EPS Chevrollier in Angers, pupils were using the official portraits of Marshal Pétain for target practice, firing erasers, chalk, and balls of papier-mâché at them.[41]

The German invasion of the Soviet Union and the consequent launch of a campaign of terror by French communists dramatically raised the stakes as far as demonstrations were concerned. For a long time they had been considered by the authorities to be little more than schoolboy pranks, rebellious but good-natured and not a major security risk. In March 1941 the Feldkommandant of Tours reported that he did not think any more sinister organization stood behind the Gaullist supporters, who were just "small groups of young intellectuals without particular significance."[42] On 20 October 1941, however, the Feldkommandant of Nantes was assassinated by a hit squad that was thought to be either Gaullist or communist, and the Germans responded swiftly and brutally with mass executions. From this moment, demonstrations were much more difficult to organize and much more risky to take part in.

For 11 November 1941 the German authorities prohibited all meetings and demonstrations, allowing only religious services and wreath layings. Particular attention was paid to student activity, given what had happened the previous year. In Angers, a wreath with the dedication "To those executed by firing squad at Nantes and Bordeaux" was found by the police at the foot of the war memorial at 10:30 P.M. on 10 November and quickly removed. Also strewn around were small bills reading, "May all our glorious dead of the 1914–18 and 1939–40 wars protect our allies. A group of 38 young women of France." Regional prefect Roussillon was satisfied that the clampdown had worked, reporting that "the greatest calm prevailed that day and the orders given by the Communist Party had no effect whatsoever."[43]

The extent to which both French and German authorities were prepared to go to head off unrest was well illustrated by the events of 1 May 1942. The attempt by employers and the Church to hijack May Day continued, with the bishop of Angers telling a congregation of employers, managers, foremen, and workers that the Labor Charter was the embodiment of social justice, to which religion brought the "indispensable support" of "a restoration of moral values" in the workplace.[44] Marshal Pétain again spoke to the workforce on 1 May (a Friday) at 5:00 P.M., and two firms in Tours were reprimanded by the prefect when it was discovered that they had not broadcast the marshal's words, on the grounds that they had no radio set.[45] Much more serious was the punishment meted out to three young communist militants who were picked up by French police in Tours while painting graffiti the night preceding 1 May. A demonstration calling for their release was hastily called outside the town hall of Tours at 6:00 P.M. on 1 May, but to no effect. This time the culprits were not just exuberant students but protesters linked to a wider movement, and the French police used torture to expose the trail that led to two young communist leaders. Instead of acting autonomously, the French police handed the five young communists over to the Gestapo.

Despite or even because of harsher repression, sacred commemorative moments for France and the Republic continued to be a focus for opposition to the Germans and to the Vichy authorities, who were increasingly seen to be their collaborators rather than a "shield" to protect the French people. Pierre Laval's government was extremely concerned that 14 July 1942 would become the occasion of mass demonstrations by Gaullists and communists and demanded tight security and brutal discipline if necessary. In Trélazé, the slate-quarrying suburb of Angers, tracts were found denouncing the concentration camps as new Bastilles and the persecution of the Jews as a revival of the wars of religion. They further condemned the execution of patriots and the subjection of peasants to the *taille* (poll tax) and *corvée* (forced labor) of prerevolutionary days; the Vichy government, it was said, were robbing them of their produce for the benefit of the German troops, "that new race of seigneurs." In Saumur, in M. Boiron's café, the orchestra suddenly struck up the "Marseillaise" at four in the afternoon, and people inside and out sang with a will, despite the presence of three or four German soldiers, until the police intervened and Boiron lost his license for the weekend.[46] In Loire-Inférieure, the prefect reported that the attitude of the population was "very dignified," although three communists had been arrested distributing tracts at Trignac, which led the police to a communist cell in Saint-Nazaire, where three more arrests were made.[47]

Unlike in the Free Zone, where 14 July 1942 was the occasion for an outburst of criticism of the regime, in the Occupied Zone the machinery of repression made demonstrations extremely risky. After the relative failure of the protests that day, Prime Minister Laval fully expected the communists to try to redeem themselves by promoting demonstrations on 20 September 1942, the 150th anniversary of the battle of Valmy.[48] This was the day the citizen-soldiers of France routed the Prussians, who had invaded to put the French king back on the throne, and prompted the Convention parliament to depose the king and proclaim a republic. There was certainly a good deal of communist propaganda in evidence. In Nantes, the police found hundreds of tracts in the days leading up to the anniversary and bills inviting people to demonstrate on Sunday, 20 September, at 6:30 P.M. on the place du Commerce: "Let us show the enemy that we are prepared to fight to liberate the country's soil. Out with the Boches. Death to Hitler the murderer. Death to the traitors. Down with Pétain. We will have another Valmy. Bread and weapons." A tract produced by the communist-run Popular Women's Committees appealed to women working for famine wages for the German war machine to join "housewives, wives of POWs, and Catholic women" in the same demonstration, "as at Valmy the people rose up against the coalition of kings."[49] At Segré, in Maine-et-Loire, a tract of the communist youth movement was found instructing young people to parade in front of their town halls, to lay wreaths at war memorials, and to wear red, white, and blue. "On 20 September the soldiers of the Revolution crushed Brunswick's Prussian hordes at Valmy," it read. "On 20 September 1942 the young people of Maine-et-Loire will join the young people of France to demonstrate their invincible spirit of struggle and their will to free the country from Hitler's hordes."[50]

There is little evidence that the communist propaganda barrage gave rise to much actual demonstration, but revolutionary and patriotic symbols summoned up sentiments of solidarity and widened the gulf between government and people. Very little was needed in this universe of historical signs to express commitment one way or the other. Students loyal to Marshal Pétain wore the *francisque*, the tricolor axe and fasces that were the symbol of the Vichy regime. Though the German authorities formally banned all badges in their ordinance of 28 August 1940, in practice they did nothing to punish wearing the *francisque*, and regional prefect Donati was all in favor of it.[51] In the spring of 1943, however, a craze spread among opposition students and from them to young workers of wearing badges made from fifty-centime, one-franc, or two-franc coins, in which the head of Marianne, symbol of the Republic in Phrygian cap, was etched. The prefect of Loire-Inférieure ordered the police to clamp down and two apprentices, a plumber and a butcher aged sixteen or seventeen, were stopped by the police in Nantes.[52] More sensational, Benjamin Decure, an apprentice mason of sixteen, was set upon on 1 May 1943 by two collaborationist Francists who tore the Marianne badge out of his buttonhole. Calling for reinforcements, they then went to his home armed with clubs, beat up the apprentice and his father, and slapped his mother.[53] As divisions within the French population intensified, badge wearing, at once discreet and provocative, was defining the loyalties of the young people of Nantes.

Demonstrations in 1943 and 1944 showed that the authorities were failing to make the art of commemoration work for them and consequently losing the affections of the people. Labor Day was moved to the nearest Sunday in order to avoid any disruption of work. In Tours, the municipal theater was already booked for some other event on 2 May 1943, so the ceremony was moved to the Majestic cinema. The awarding of medals to deserving artisans or wives of artisans who had taken over from their POW husbands was undermined by the omission of representatives from artisans' organizations from the guest list, by the failure of the medals to arrive from Marshal Pétain's private office, and by the inability of four of the prize-winners to turn up because of bad weather or transportation problems.[54] When Labor Day came around in 1944, there were fears that the Communist Party would try to launch a general strike and factory occupations, as in 1936, with the backing of workers' militias. Orators were instructed to take an aggressive line, echoing the sentiments of the national-socialist minister of labor, Marcel Déat, to be broadcast from the Palais Chaillot in Paris.[55] In Tours, the event in the Majestic cinema was interrupted by an air-raid warning that emptied the audience of the many attached to the civil defense corps. The few who were left included the presidents of the Chamber of Commerce and Chamber of Trades, who were shocked by the rabid speech of one of Déat's emissaries in support of the New European Order and the counterinsurgent Milice.[56] Of the working classes all that can be said is that they were a long way from strike action but thoroughly alienated by Vichy's desperate line.

With Labor Day the Vichy regime still thought in terms of appropriation, but there was no sense in which the commemoration of 14 July could be made to work for the regime and it was therefore met only with repression. The Laval government was almost in a state of panic about the way in which the day might be exploited by communists. In the event, all that was apparent was dissident gestures but no outright resistance. In 1943 Laval told regional prefects that all demonstrations were banned, that anyone planning "an antinational action" should be interned, and that if necessary order should be maintained by declaring a state of siege under a law of 1849. The word from the communist-led Front National was that people should come onto the streets at 7:45 P.M., a later time than usual, to merge with those going out for the evening to the theater or cinema, walking alone and not in any organized way. In Angers, it seemed only that the evening crowd was larger than usual, some wearing a little tricolor ribbon or bouquet.[57] In Nantes, about 3,000 people "processed" in the town center, and at 8:30 P.M. about 150 of them struck up the "Marseillaise." These were dispersed by the police, and only one man, a drunk, was arrested.[58] For 14 July 1944 the discrepancy between what the government feared and what actually transpired was even greater. Laval warned of a possible insurrection and told prefects and police chiefs that if demonstrations looked like they were turning into uprisings they should not hesitate to open fire. What actually happened was that the dog did not bark. For five or six weeks since the Normandy landings, the real action had been elsewhere. A flower seller in Joué-lès-Tours doing a trade in red, white, and blue flowers was told to pack up his wares and go home. In the afternoon in Tours, young women with tricolor ribbons and young men with tricolor buttonholes were asked to remove them. In Châteaurenault, a tricolor flag flew all day from the town hall.[59] In Angers, there was even less activity. "Instructions issued by dissident forces," reported the police chief, "have had no effect on the Angevins, who besides have a horror of all violence."[60]

These demonstrations may be either dismissed as childish pranks of little consequence or given the status of a kind of "pre-resistance" that led on to more decisive acts. Jacques Maurice, recalling the V signs and tricolors that were painted in Azay-le-Rideau on 14 July 1941, claims that "by such demonstrations we learned to fear our German masters less and toughened ourselves for the future. Many future *maquisards* started this way."[61] Such claims, made in retrospect, may be somewhat extravagant. Symbolic gestures contributed little to the downfall of the German

Occupation. Their importance was elsewhere, as subtle and imaginative ways by which the French were able to recognize one another in the construction of a patriotic universe. Sometimes the demonstrators were caught and punished but the object of the exercise was not to break the laws laid down by the German authorities or Vichy but to tease and subvert official legitimacy. The efforts at protest were a manifestation of the strategies resorted to by French people to preserve their dignity and express their faith in the future.

7

Trimmers

Early in 1942 a group of teachers at the Medical School of Tours sent a long report to the prefect of Indre-et-Loire to complain about their director, Dr. Paul Guillaume-Louis. They accused him of "directorial autocracy," corruption, and favoritism. Since taking over the school in 1928, they said, he had flooded it with Romanian, Yugoslav, Armenian, and Greek students, most of whom were Jews. On the strength of this expansion, they alleged, he had obtained a decree from his "great friend" Camille Chautemps, the Radical Party boss of Touraine, upgrading the school to full degree-giving status in 1938. This led to his being promoted to commander of the Legion of Honor and having a self-congratulatory bust of himself placed in the school when the new buildings were opened in 1938 by the Jewish minister of education, Jean Zay. The expansion of the school created a plethora of jobs, which, they argued, he had given to his "comrades," such as Émile Aron, Freemason, socialist, and Jew, appointed professor of physiology in 1936. When the Vichy regime deprived Aron of his chair, Guillaume-Louis gave him a job in the teaching hospital, of which he was an administrator, until this trick was exposed by the collaborationist paper *Je suis partout.* "The presence of Dr. Guillaume-Louis as director of the Medical School of Tours," it concluded, "is a sure guarantee of the reign of favoritism, arbitrariness, immorality, and cronyism, for the benefit of a certain mafia most of whom belong to the demophiles' Masonic lodge. We request the immediate dismissal of this extremely dangerous person who embodies opposition to the principles of the National Revolution."[1]

This attack on Guillaume-Louis found favor with the Vichy regime because it highlighted vices that were identified with the Third Republic, which had led France to defeat in 1940. The Third Republic was seen as the "Republic of comrades," a radical and socialist mafia linked by Freemasonry, and Protestant, Jewish, or anticlerical rather than Catholic, looking after its own and excluding others from the honeypot of jobs, privileges, and honors. It was a mafia that had acquired a tentacular grasp on power, colonizing the administration, controlling the press, and using both to manipulate elections and dominate representative institutions. Guillaume-Louis himself was not only the medical eminence in Indre-et-Loire who had examined the brain of the writer Anatole France after his death for physical manifestations of genius but also mayor and *conseiller général* of the small town of Montbazon, south of Tours. This mafia's grasp on power made it extremely difficult to shift, even by the authoritarian Vichy regime. Moreover, so long as a politician was willing to "rally" to the new regime and put aside regrets for the "ancien régime" of the Third Republic, Vichy saw the advantage of keeping him on, because his influence over those who had elected him had been demonstrated and he was probably the best person to bring them into line. Thus Guillaume-Louis had been confirmed as mayor of Montbazon in 1941 and, when the elected *conseils généraux* were replaced by small, appointed administrative commissions to advise prefects, he was included on that of Indre-et-Loire.

Given the changeability of the international situation and the difficulty of forecasting which regime would be in power a year or so down the road, however, it was better not to cozy up too closely to Vichy. The dismissal of Guillaume-Louis from the medical school, following the hostile petition of the teachers, was a blessing in disguise. Had he continued to take part in Vichy's institutions much longer, it is likely that he would have been purged from the *conseil général* when it was revived in 1944, sharing the fate of Mayor Mattraits of Chinon. A short period in opposition was enough to give a gloss of "resistance" to a notable who had, to begin with, been endorsed by Vichy. In the event, Guillaume-Louis not only was included on the 1944 *conseil général* but also triumphed in the elections of 1945, when other radicals were routed in Touraine, and became president of the new assembly.[2]

Navigating the treacherous reefs of occupied France it was generally less advisable to embrace the Resistance wholeheartedly than to trim one's sails to the erratic gusts of wind. The case of Guillaume-Louis illustrates, more-over, that political survivors were just as common as political casualties. This may be explained in part by the chameleon skills of France's trimmers and the way in which they spun webs of power and influence that were difficult to dismantle. It may also be explained by the contradictions of a regime that, while hammering the reactionary and moralizing ideology of the National Revolution for all it was worth, did not have the clout to carry through a root-and-branch purge of the political class.

The reform of institutions in a formal sense was decisive. Days after Marshal Pétain was voted full executive, legislative, and constitutional pow-ers on 10 July 1940, he suspended parliament indefinitely. Then on 12 October the *conseils généraux* were abolished. These measures did away with the elective assemblies that had been conquered by the left since 1936. Parliamentary elections due to be held in 1940 and postponed because of the war, however, would undoubtedly have given victory to the right. A deeper reason for these radical measures was therefore the abolition of representative institutions that were seen to have weakened France at a time when its international competitors were going over to tougher, more authoritarian regimes and to have led it down the slippery slope to defeat. The National Revolution planned by Vichy was to be driven from above, by bureaucrats and technocrats who would not have to be answerable to meddling and self-serving politicians.

Politicians were sent back to their constituencies to graze. They were deprived of access to ministers and prefects, which under the Third Repub-lic had enabled them to obtain subsidies, contracts, favors, exemptions, and honors for their constituents, either individually or collectively, in order to sweeten their voter base with a view to the next elections. No longer did they have what was called *le bras long*, that ability to influence those in power that made them invaluable to their own supporters. And yet the Vichy regime was unable to drive away the politicians of the Third Republic simply by shutting off their access to the central government. These politicians were figures of national significance only because of their local power bases. They were not career politicians who lived "off" politics but notables who lived "for" politics, wielding influence in the local community by virtue of their family, wealth, profession, and connections.[3] Before they became deputies or senators, they followed a *cursus honorum*, starting as mayors of their communes, then becoming *conseillers généraux* of their cantons, positions that served both as a political apprenticeship and as a means of making important contacts and alliances. The ownership of a local newspaper was also indispensable. This was less a business enterprise than a political mouthpiece for the local politician, a public-relations exercise, and an electoral tool.[4]

In some urban pockets, of course, socialist or communist politicians emerged on the back of the labor movement and mass parties. Nantes, as we have seen, was controlled by a Socialist Party machine under Deputy Mayor Pageot, while in Tours the socialist Ferdinand Morin, deputy since 1914, took the town from the radical Camille Chautemps in 1925 and made it his fief through municipal socialism. The railway suburb of Tours, Saint-Pierre-des-Corps, went communist in 1920 when a railway strike was abandoned by the moderate CGT national leadership, leading to 2,500 dismissals, and communists split from socialists at the Congress of Tours. Since then the town was run by the aptly named Robespierre Henault, a railwayman who had lost an arm in an industrial accident, and by a council of young workers of the Paris-Orléans Railway Company who were often foreign to the town.[5] Otherwise there were two basic models with which politicians in the Loire Valley tended to identify.

East of Angers, in the Saumurois and Touraine, radical politicians such as Léon Courson, mayor of Noyant and deputy of Chinon, or Paul Bernier, mayor of Mouzay and also a deputy, held sway. They were landed, involved in the liberal professions or commerce: Courson was a pig merchant. They were often connected by membership in Masonic lodges, which were nonreligious if not antireligious, and by affiliation with organizations such as the League of Rights of Man, founded during the Dreyfus Affair, and the

Education League, whose mission was to undermine the Catholic Church's control of the school system and entrust it to the secular state.[6]

West of Angers, in the Mauges and Loire-Inférieure, politics were run by noble, landowning families who, far from having been swept away by the French Revolution, extended their influence over their local constituents in the modern age through agricultural organizations, the defense of the Catholic Church and church schools, and cultivation of the memory of the Vendean uprising against the French Revolution. Deputies of Loire-Inférieure like Marquis Henri de La Ferronnays and Jean Le Cour Grandmaison pursued careers in the army or navy before virtually inheriting their fathers' seats (in 1907 and 1919, respectively) and promoting agricultural unionism as a tool of conservative hegemony. The senators tended to have more professional or academic credentials: Louis Linyer was a brilliant barrister in Nantes, François de Saint-Maur was professor at the Angers Law Faculty, while Gustave Gautherot was professor at the Catholic Institute in Paris. As conservatives they dominated the *conseil général*, of which Henri de La Ferronnays was president from 1931. The binding force and mass base was provided by the Catholic Association of Family Heads of the Diocese of Nantes, under the auspices of the bishop, with sections in every parish and a membership of 20,000 in the 1930s. It was linked to the National Catholic Federation of General de Castelnau, set up after the right lost power to the radicals in 1924 to fight what was seen as a Masonic conspiracy to de-Christianize France. Henri de La Ferronnays acquired a martyr's crown and boosted the movement in 1925 when he demanded that Édouard Herriot, the radical prime minister, withdraw his denunciation of an alliance between the Catholic Church and bankers, for which the marquis was himself expelled from the Chamber of Deputies.[7]

Before it could settle its score with politicians, the Vichy administration had to put its own house in order. Unreliable prefects were purged in the hot summer of 1940. Fernand Leroy of Loire-Inférieure was dismissed because he was deemed ineffectual, because he had been appointed by the Popular Front, and because he was rumored to be a Jew, which he was not, although he was married to one.[8] The new model Vichy prefect was to be altogether more decisive. "You have been functionaries," the interior minister told them. "Now you will be leaders."[9] Philippe Dupard, a man of huge presence who took over as prefect of Loire-Inférieure, quickly got rid of Leroy's *chef de cabinet* and secretary-general, the top two posts in the prefecture, removed the police chief of Nantes on the grounds that he had once been a Freemason, and dismissed the subprefect of Saint-Nazaire for being in the pocket of the socialist municipality.[10] Jean Roussillon, who took over as prefect of Angers, was dynamic, ambitious, outspoken, but also difficult, moody, and irascible. He was seduced by the idea of "direct administration," whereby the prefect would relate directly to those he was responsible for instead of finding local politicians in his way, and planned monthly meetings with mayors in each arrondissement.[11] He was determined to break the back of the politicians of the Third Republic and carve out his own empire. But he would soon find that the ancien régime, as he called it, would not lie down so easily.

Some deputies, as it happened, gave little trouble. Roussillon described Émile Pérein, radical-socialist deputy of Angers, as a "colorless figure" who had still not made contact with him six months after his appointment. Robert de Grandmaison, center-right deputy for Saumur, was "by far the most intelligent parliamentarian in the department, and also by far the most keen to meddle in his constituency." Grandmaison was said to have burst into the office of the mayor of Saumur before a council meeting and attacked Marshal Pétain as "an old man . . . old, very old," and "entirely in the hands of the Germans."[12] Gaston Moreau, deputy mayor of Baugé after defeating a radical-socialist against the swing in 1936, was described as a "curious person who would have interested Balzac. He is unstoppably talkative, which creates the illusion of hyperactivity. Dreams of playing a role in the Baugeois." In pursuit of this role, he held weekly meetings of the mayors in his canton to examine the prefect's circulars and listen to their grievances. Roussillon was concerned that his circulars were being "discussed and interpreted" by lowly mayors and that Moreau was still behaving as a deputy, finding a new way to weave local contacts and create debts that would be recalled if ever elections returned.[13]

These were only pinpricks compared with the real thorn in Roussillon's flesh, Anatole Manceau. Manceau was senator for Cholet, a liberal who had been elected in 1925 against Léon Daudet of the dynamic royalist movement Action Française, who attempted to parachute into the seat from Paris.[14] Now that the Senate was suspended, Manceau returned from

Vichy to his local power base. He was president of the Chamber of Commerce of Cholet, which, in the absence of the *conseil général*, took on more importance as a tribune. Above all he was the owner of *Le Petit Courrier*, the biggest newspaper in the department. Relations between Roussillon and Manceau began well. In November 1940 Roussillon visited Cholet, where a new subprefect was taking over, and met the mayors of the arrondissements. He was welcomed by Manceau, who told him of the magnificent activity of the local textile and shoe industry. Roussillon adopted *Le Petit Courrier* as the official newspaper of the prefecture, in which important public announcements would appear. But there the cooperation stopped. Manceau was keen that in return for his "official" status he should have privileged access to the prefecture and a certain influence there. For Roussillon this went against the new doctrine of Vichy, that former parliamentarians should expect "a courteous reception, but no more." The old days when prefects were at the beck and call of local deputies and senators in order to distribute jobs and favors and "make" elections were finished. Manceau felt left out in the cold and took his revenge by reprinting in *Le Petit Courrier* an editorial published by a hostile Paris journalist, Jean Luchaire, in *Les Nouveaux Temps*. Roussillon riposted by suspending *Le Petit Courrier* for twenty-four hours on 1 December 1940. Manceau replied by proxy with an article in *Les Nouveaux Temps* arguing that France was collapsing into "so many fiefs, ruled at the whim of prefects. This was the desire neither of parliament nor of the marshal." Meanwhile Roussillon was given a rap on the knuckles by Feldkommandant Kloss, who told him that he had no right to censor a newspaper without consulting the German authorities.[15]

Roussillon did everything he could to undermine Manceau's power base. He tried to abolish the Cholet Chamber of Commerce on the grounds that one such institution per department was enough (Maine-et-Loire had three), but Manceau saved it. Manceau was included as a member of the new municipal council of Cholet in April 1941 but was undoubtedly behind the pantomime of 24 June, when the council passed a unanimous vote of confidence in Marshal Pétain but divided evenly on a following vote of confidence in the autocratic prime minister, Admiral Darlan. Roussillon stormed down to Cholet and reconvened the municipal council in the prefecture, where he lectured its members and forced them to take a new vote, on pain of collective dismissal. The only councillor to be dismissed was, predictably, Manceau, for insulting Admiral Darlan. Roussillon complained that even if Manceau "had lost his mass appeal he was still in touch with what remains of his old electoral organization, through personal and often friendly contacts with mayors and other local figures, and is only too often an agent of demoralization and antigovernment propaganda." In exasperation, he took the extraordinary step of replacing Manceau on the municipal council by a cleric, the Abbé Douillard, archdeacon of Notre-Dame de Cholet, on the grounds that Cholet had been the capital of the Vendean rising against the French Revolution in defense of Church and King in 1793, and it was good to keep the Church sweet.[16]

Manceau had no mind to let Roussillon off the hook. In the Cholet Chamber of Commerce and at private dinners, he continued to criticize the prefect and Darlan and now began to suggest that the aging Marshal Pétain was losing his memory, was no longer capable of governing France, and had even fallen prey to the Action Française to the extent of declaring the royal pretender, the Comte de Paris, his successor.[17] *Le Petit Courrier* published pieces giving credence to the rumors circulating that the vitamin-enriched biscuits distributed to schoolchildren by the Secours National had been contaminated with the tuberculosis bacillus.[18] The prefecture demanded that the paper publish a communiqué dismissing the rumors and accused the paper of an "antinational campaign and an attitude contrary to the public good." Manceau refused and instead published parts of his angry correspondence with Roussillon, which showed the prefect in a very bad light. Roussillon then refused to send any of his communiqués to *Le Petit Courrier* for a fortnight, hoping to bring it to heel, but Manceau blocked him, using his influence with the Propagandastaffel to persuade them to ban all other local papers from publishing the prefect's communiqués, so that the prefect was reduced to writing directly to hundreds of mayors. To complete the victory, Manceau hired the local branch of the collaborationist Mouvement Social Révolutionnaire to step up their attacks on Roussillon as an incompetent prefect who was incapable of checking Gaullist propaganda or the black market and whose own civil servants were involved in it. In the end, Roussillon was summoned by General Matthaei of the military administration of Bezirk B in Angers, to give an account of himself.[19]

The dogfight between prefect and politician demonstrated that the Vichy regime did not have it all its own way. It abolished parliament and the *conseils généraux*, and its officials were advised to adopt an authoritarian style and haughty attitude toward politicians who returned to their constituencies. This, however, was to reckon without the surviving local power base of politicians and their skill in manipulating a political system that the German presence had made more complicated. Even if the Senate no longer existed, Manceau was able to use his prestige as a senator and the political connections that had put him there. The presidency of the Chamber of Commerce of Cholet gave him authority over the industrialists who ran the town and the ability to persuade the municipal council to vote in large numbers against Admiral Darlan. Above all, as a press baron he was able to hold the prefecture, which had no official mouthpiece apart from his own *Petit Courrier*, for ransom. Throughout he played a double game, protesting his loyalty but constantly sniping. Loyal to Pétain he might have been, but he had no time for Darlan and even while acknowledging this vote he was spinning webs around the German authorities and collaborationists of the worst odor to bring down the prefect who had snubbed him. A year or so later it was Roussillon who left the scene, not Manceau.

It became clear that to drive through the National Revolution Vichy would have to pay as much attention to power in the localities as to power in the center. Municipal councils and mayors had been elected in 1935, on the same wave that had brought the Popular Front into government in 1936. Municipal elections due in 1941 would, like national elections, have registered a shift to the right, but that was beside the point. Vichy wanted to gain full control of local government, abolishing the local democracy that had finally been consecrated by the Republic in 1884. Some authoritarian measures had already been taken before 1940. The communist municipality of Saint-Pierre-des-Corps was dissolved in October 1939 as part of the clampdown on communists after the Nazi-Soviet pact and replaced by an appointed "special delegation," while a Vichy prefect interned Robespierre Henault, the former mayor, early in 1941.[20] A law of 16 November 1940 allowed the interior minister and the prefect between them to appoint mayors and municipal councillors in towns, defined as having a population of over 2,000. Villages (under 2,000) were not expected to give any trouble and would remain under the regime of 1884, although no elections would be held during the war and existing mayors and councillors would simply be carried over.

This catchall law gave Vichy the opportunity to go through local government with a fine-tooth comb and purge its political enemies. Some difficult left-wing mayors were unceremoniously removed. Mayor Pageot of Nantes, who exasperated the Germans as well as the French administration with his bombastic and misplaced patriotism, was replaced by Gaëtan Rondeau, a sixty-eight-year-old former lawyer and top municipal administrator of Nantes described as "very courteous, intelligent, and cultivated, upright and honest, with a perfect understanding of the cogs of the municipal machine." His right-hand man (*adjoint*), Abel Durand, sixty-two, was a professor at the Law School of Nantes, a practicing Catholic, and a departmental delegate of the Secours National, "combining intellectual qualities of the first order with great energy in the community, which he devoted to agencies of social relief."[21] The other nuisance in the region was Robert Amy, radical-socialist mayor of Saumur. He was seen as having been insufficiently bold when the Germans arrived—all the credit going to *procureur* Ancelin—and was generally considered the prime mover of radicalism and Freemasonry in the Saumurois. He and his council were replaced by an appointed special delegation under a lawyer, Maître Baudry, until subprefect Milliat judged that he had not sufficiently changed his spots. Baudry, he reported, "has remained a man of the left, if not *the* man of the left, and I use these words in the old-fashioned sense, given that at the present time we are not supposed to remove those who have rallied to the marshal's policies."[22] Baudry was duly replaced by a barrister, the acting police chief, René Drouart, who seemed the perfect choice until he was caught up in a sex scandal.

The subprefect's comments showed that he had fully imbibed the instructions of the Ministry of the Interior. Clearly 1940 was a new chance for the right, displaced in 1936 and arguably on the ropes from as long ago as 1877. For Charles Maurras, leader of the royalist Action Française, 1940 was a "divine surprise" that would simply ring out the left and ring in the right. For other Vichy ministers, however, things were more complex. Civil strife had to be replaced by national unity, which meant winning over former political enemies to the new project. In his long circular to prefects in January 1941, Interior Minister Marcel Peyrouton therefore said that the object of the combing of municipalities was not a "massive replacement" of mayors and councillors but only the removal of those who were demonstrably hostile to the regime. Old political rivals should be forgiven "if their rallying to the new politics is complete and sincere and gives no sign of *arrière-pensée*." New appointees should not just be "reactionaries": "the new order is not supposed to be a sort of *moral order* [his italics, referring to a period of reaction in the 1870s] or revenge for the events of 1936." Those required were "people of indisputable morality in both their public and their private lives and of absolute devotion to the policies of the marshal's government."[23]

One of the striking features of municipal politics under Vichy was thus the survival of some left-wing mayors. It indicates that what mattered was open endorsement of the regime and tested authority over the local population. In Tours, Ferdinand Morin, endeared to the townspeople by his courage as the Germans began to bombard the city in June 1940 and to the regime by his vote as deputy of full powers to Marshal Pétain in Vichy, was confirmed as mayor in March 1941. At the ceremony prefect Chaigneau said that "the choice made by Marshal Pétain summoning you to head the municipal administration has had the most gratifying repercussions among the population, if I trust to the flattering commentaries that followed the appointment."[24] He had already told the minister that "in Touraine, which is very calm and balanced and people have a solid common sense, the replacement of M. Morin at the town hall of Tours by somebody else would not be understood. In the present climate his dismissal would be considered a psychological error which I simply could not commit."[25] Although elections had been abolished, it was as if a phantom plebiscite had been held and had delivered a resounding verdict: Morin must stay.

Even more surprising, at the other end of the region in the port of Saint-Nazaire, the socialist François Blancho was confirmed as mayor. Orphaned, a worker from the age of thirteen in the Penhouët shipyard, trade unionist, socialist, mayor, and deputy of the port by the age of thirty-five in 1928, undersecretary of state for the navy between 1936 and 1938, and as such the boss of Darlan, then commander in chief of the French navy, he was superficially the very politician who was anathema to Vichy. When he was reappointed mayor in March 1941, the departmental Taxpayers Federation expressed outrage to Marshal Pétain that one of "the demagogues 'who did us so much harm,' to use your own expression" was still in business, not least because Blancho was also "one of the great artisans of the disorganization of the naval arsenals who preached holidays and disarmament while the Germans were rearming relentlessly."[26] On the positive side, however, Blancho had voted full powers to Marshal Pétain and was the acknowledged leader of the working class in an essentially working-class town, who had kept Saint-Nazaire a socialist fief in the face of the communist challenge and had played a moderating influence in labor disputes.[27] Rather than being dismissed, he resigned in May 1941 in protest at Admiral Darlan's uncompromising attacks on the record of the Third Republic. "Orphan from a very young age," he said at the Liberation, "I owe everything to the working class, whose sufferings and hopes I have shared. . . . I cannot accept that our fellow workers might have to be ashamed of the man who was for so long their spokesman."[28]

The resignation of Blancho, followed by that of the socialist councillors, highlighted the difficulties Vichy faced in running a town in which class divisions were so clear. The unenviable task of the subprefect of Saint-Nazaire, in his own words, was to "find a man who was not branded politically but who was converted to ideas of social progress and who, even without the support of the socialists, could win over some workers to serve. He should unite under his leadership all men of goodwill belonging to all classes of the population and representative of all the currents that are loyal to the government."[29] For the new mayor he hit upon Pierre Toscer, a man the same age as Blancho who had started work as a fitter in the Ateliers et Chantiers de la Loire. There, however, their paths diverged as Toscer had obtained a technical training at the Arts et Métiers, become an *ingénieur*, inspector of technical education, in Loire-Inférieure, and then manager of the Chantiers Loire Saint-Denis. He was seen to be the candidate of the shipyard employers, but as a self-made man he was respected by the workers and had qualities that transcended the lines of class struggle: a local man, a veteran of 1914–18 with the Croix de Guerre, a father of four, a practicing Catholic (with one brother a priest and a sister a nun), significant in what was, after all, a Breton port. No doubt in the light of this appointment the interior minister, Pierre Pucheu, a technocrat rather than a reactionary, told prefects that, if mayors and municipal councils were to be replaced, the new council should "correspond as much as possible to the general physiognomy of the town." In former socialist or communist towns it was "a particularly bad idea to hand over the control of municipal business to elements that were the very opposite of the previous party," and especially to those who had previously been defeated in local elections. This would be interpreted as a "provocation that would alienate the population from the new administrative setup, . . . a revenge of past struggles and a disregard of public opinion." In working-class towns, notables should be avoided and the ideal choice would be a worker who had the respect of his comrades, whether in the trade-union movement or not, "who seems to you to have consciously rallied to government policy."[30] Unfortunately, the Vichy regime would discover that these "rallied workers," worth their weight in gold, were an increasingly rare commodity, and "pseudo-workers" like Toscer found it difficult to maintain the stance of class neutrality when demands for labor for the Reich began to bite in 1942.

Of course, working-class towns such as Saint-Nazaire were atypical in western France. The main problem faced by the Vichy regime was not bridging the class divide but being sure that mayors and councils that had ostensibly "rallied" to the government were not in fact playing a double game and actually resisting the new order. The occasional mayor, such as M. Chatelain of La Gâvre, was silly enough to be arrested by the Germans after they raided his house and discovered a photo of General de Gaulle and extracts from his broadcasts. Chatelain went to prison for seven months, after which he was persuaded to resign by the Vichy authorities.[31] Most mayors, however, were more discreet and criticisms of them were often no more than hearsay. Of François Servant, a lawyer and mayor and *conseiller général* of La Haye Descartes on the demarcation line, it was said that though his family was religious he belonged to Masonic lodges in Chinon and Châtellerault, that he was an active radical-socialist who had supported strike action in 1936, and that his loyalty to Marshal Pétain was "wholly superficial": he was an Anglophile, hostile to Franco-German collaboration.[32] Yet it was often difficult to remove these local notables, partly because their influence was entrenched and valuable, partly because they gave the administration just as much loyalty as was necessary while otherwise buying time and keeping their options open.

Even in Indre-et-Loire, that bastion of radical-socialism and anticlericalism, only 36 percent of mayors were replaced by Vichy.[33] One good example of survival was Dr. Tardif, mayor and *conseiller général* of Longué, near Saumur, who had run against Manceau and Daudet in the senatorial elections of 1925. A hard-bitten radical-socialist and anticlerical, the quintessence of the Third Republic, he was precisely the sort of subprefect Milliat would have been delighted to dismiss or persuade to resign. But Tardif refused to resign, "preferring to be replaced in a way he could glorify later and present himself as a martyr of the ancien régime." While "there are doubts about the genuineness of his current commitment to the marshal's ideas," Milliat reported, Tardif had moderated his extreme views and was now proposing to name a street off "our beautiful Verdun Square" in honor of Marshal Pétain. "Either this man is sincere," wrote Milliat, "or he is a fine Jesuit. . . . Even at his ripe age the old radical fighter is diabolically intelligent."[34] A year later the prefect delegate described Tardif as "an old fox, an old boar, unshakably attached to the past," but just as unshakable, it seemed, in his *mairie*.[35]

Just as important as political loyalties in the evaluation of mayors, as the circular of the interior minister made clear, was public and private morality. This proved the downfall of René Drouart, the head of the special delegation of Saumur, which replaced the elected council. The trouble started early in 1943 when, in his capacity as a barrister, he defended a gypsy girl accused of stealing money from the old lady who employed her, in the course of which he impugned the integrity of the police. Since he had until recently been in charge of the municipal police force, his words upset the local police and magistrates. He was then accused of having a mistress, a dressmaker whose seventeen-year-old son was employed at the town hall, and he stepped down provisionally as mayor to bring a libel suit against his accuser. On the night of 5–6 April 1943, a handwritten poster was plastered on the walls of Saumur. It read, "Your mayor M. Drouart is dismissed. Why? Because of a public scandal of concubinage. And this man has the nerve to judge and preach morality. Drouart, you are just a bastard."

Drouart had his supporters, such as the author of an anonymous letter to the prefect that claimed to unveil the hypocrisy of the town fathers:

> Is our captain of the gendarmerie, who is constantly with his girlfriend in the rue Beaurepaire, dismissed for this much?

And our engineer M. Bouvy, who is busier with M. Gouin's wife than with what ought to be his own business, is he placed on the Index? As for the president of the Chamber of Commerce, M. Pichard, commonly regarded as God, his mistress is real enough for him; he had the house she lives in built for her. This liaison is public knowledge in Saumur and goes back a long way before the events [of 1940]. Have these grand seigneurs got rights while everyone else has duties? As for the curé of Saint-Nicolas, he prefers men to women. His mistress is called M. Bernon and lives not so far from you.

The point about Drouart, however, was not that his immorality was exceptional but that he had lost the confidence of those who mattered in Saumur. His four deputies (*adjoints*) at the town hall, who included a retired major and a retired captain, together with a number of other councillors, threatened to resign collectively if the prefect did not dismiss him within a fortnight. The decision was one that came not from a sanctimonious administration but from an outraged corps of notables. They obliged Drouart to write a letter of resignation that the prefect then accepted. Vichy could not dictate or fail to act in the teeth of local opinion, and the conduct of local affairs was always a matter of negotiation between the two.[36]

The influence of local notables was felt not only in the towns but also at the regional level. It made its mark during the great debate of the spring of 1941 about whether Vichy was going to continue running France as a centralized state, which had been the model since the Revolution and Napoleon, or whether it would relax the viselike grip of the center and devolve more power to the provinces or regions. The argument in favor of decentralization was that centralization had repeatedly allowed revolutionaries who seized power in Paris to impose revolution on the rest of the country; to decentralize would insulate the provinces against revolution. It would also undermine small movements in parts of France that believed themselves to be ethnically or historically distinct—such as Brittany or Flanders—and wanted even greater autonomy. The argument against decentralization was that to resurrect the provinces was to resurrect the influence of the prerevolutionary elites with their local power bases and to run the risk of the disintegration of the state. After all, if the revolutionaries and Napoleon had fashioned the centralized state, the restored monarchy had seen no reason to melt it down. The Vichy regime was indeed torn two ways, between an urge to decentralize so as to break the power of left-wing governments that had cynically used the state machine to impose their ideology and a fear that with the weakening of the French state under the German Occupation this was scarcely the moment to weaken what state power existed.[37]

In the absence of a parliament, Vichy set up the Conseil National, a consultative body of notables to advise on constitutional matters.[38] One of its commissions—which Jean Le Cour Grandmaison, former deputy of Loire-Inférieure and vice president of the Fédération Nationale Catholique, sat on—examined the issue of administrative decentralization and proposed a network of governors who, above the heads of the prefects, would superintend a grand strategy for the regions and be advised by regional councils in which not only territorial but also economic and spiritual interests would be represented. In some sense they would build on the economic regions established in France after 1917 but would bring in notables involved in family, social, or religious issues. The Conseil National marked a step down the road away from representative democracy and toward the corporative state in which, under the aegis of the government, not abstract individuals but the concrete interests of "real France" would be represented.

Decentralization was not simply decreed from on high but was the subject of a great deal of local jockeying. As early as August 1940 the bishop of Nantes received a visit from Hervé Budes de Guébriant, president of the Chamber of Agriculture of Finistère, who told him of Vichy's plans to set up a province of Brittany in order to undermine the Breton nationalists who had just set up a Breton national council at Pontivy and announced the creation of a separate Breton state. Guébriant thought that he was the firm favorite to be governor of Brittany and wondered whether the bishop saw a place for Nantes within it.[39] Whether Nantes and Loire-Inférieure were a part of Brittany was a matter of long and heated debate. The Archaeological and Historical Society of Nantes and Loire-Inférieure, 600-strong, reminded the prefect that Anne of Brittany, whose marriage to Louis XII in 1499 had marked the union of Brittany and France, had been born in the ducal château of Nantes and that Nantes was the capital of Brittany, never to be separated from it.[40] Meanwhile a movement of collaborationist Breton nationalists called the National Socialist Youth targeted Loire-Inférieure with their propaganda. In December 1940 tracts called for the destruction of a French state indebted to authoritarian prefects and Masonic politicians, and in February 1941 graffiti such as "Free Brittany" and "Neither Albion nor Mariâne. A Breton government" appeared, while "Down with Rondeau" was scrawled on the town hall in May.[41]

The debate over the future of Brittany showed that in the city of Nantes there was far from a consensus. Paul Brossier, president of the Chamber of Commerce of Nantes, and Abel Durand, professor of political economy at the law school, *adjoint* to Mayor Rondeau, and an expert on regional questions, advanced the counterargument that to reconstitute the five departments of Brittany would be a backward-looking revival of an ancien régime province, an unforced concession to the autonomists, and a disaster from the economic point of view. The capital of historic Brittany would inevitably be Rennes, not Nantes. Brossier and Durand proposed a region whose "spinal column" would be the departments of south Brittany (Finistère, Morbihan, Loire-Inférieure) and the Vendée, which had been linked since 1919 in an economic region that basically federated a number of chambers of commerce, and served as an agricultural hinterland for Nantes.[42] The two north Breton departments of Ille-et-Vilaine and the Côtes-du-Nord might be added, but to check autonomism Brittany would then be submerged in a larger "Armorican region" including the Mayenne, Sarthe, and Maine-et-Loire. The capital of this region would necessarily be Nantes, with its seaport, communications, and population of 200,000, twice the size of Rennes. Prefect Dupard was won over to this school of thought, met Admiral Darlan in March 1941, and put pressure on Jean Le Cour Grandmaison, sitting on the key commission.[43]

While Nantes was fighting the pretensions of Rennes, Angers was fighting those of Nantes. Competition between regions generally articulated competition between major cities whose status as a regional capital was at stake. In May 1941 a delegation went to Vichy from Angers, led by two splendid aristocrats, Viscount Jacques de la Grandière, another member of the Conseil National, and Count Joachim du Plessis de Grenadan, dean of the Law Faculty of the Catholic University of Angers, whose name, said prefect Roussillon, was "synonymous with chivalric impartiality and generosity as well as with fidelity to the national and religious principles to which he has devoted his life."[44] They argued that Anjou had nothing in common with Nantes, "whose political influence stops virtually at its suburbs and which has only the usual, anonymous force of attraction of any large port." Nantes represented evil: urban anonymity, trade, and socialism. Against it Anjou must seek an alternative alliance with Maine, now the Mayenne and Sarthe departments. They had similar economies based on grain, cattle, textiles, and shoes and had a natural capital in Angers, whose magnificent royal house had ruled at various times England, Provence, Naples and Sicily, Poland, and Hungary. With its cathedral, Catholic university, and appeals court, it was "the Athens of the West." Implicit was the argument that Anjou-Maine would be a bastion against the modern world, dominated by the landed nobility, the Church, and the liberal professions, still in the ancien régime in spirit if not in fact.[45]

Neither Angevins nor Nantais had much to say about the Tourangeaux, who did not figure in their regional plans, and the Tourangeaux repaid the compliment by planning to split Anjou and annex half of it. Ironically, there were strong economic links provided by the fifth economic region, which grouped the chambers of commerce of Lorient, Nantes, Angers, Saumur, Tours, and Le Mans, while the Assembly of Chambers of Commerce of the Loire basin included those of Saint-Nazaire, Nantes, Angers, Saumur, Tours, Blois, and Orléans. Both met fairly regularly, at least in the early part of the Occupation, essentially to lobby government to make the Loire navigable and improve rail communications from the Loire Valley to Lyon.[46] These links, however, did not seem to feed into political thinking when it came to the debate on regions. The Chamber of Commerce of Tours produced a glossy brochure entitled *Tours, Provincial Capital*, in which it was argued that Tours was a turntable of communications, an archbishopric, the historic center from which Louis XI had created the unity of France, and the seat of national government when Paris was evacuated in 1870 and 1940. The extent of the province was not clear, but the aim was to take a chunk of Maine-et-Loire on the grounds that that department was not a unity. Within Maine-et-Loire, the brochure argued, the Saumurois was really an extension of Touraine and ought to be absorbed by it, while the department west of Angers was more feudal and had more in common with Loire-Inférieure. "Nothing in the government plan," the brochure concluded, "requires that a department has to belong as a whole to one of the regions being created."[47]

As it happened, there was nothing in the government plan either that required any of the lobbies of provincial notables to be satisfied. Vichy's law of 19 April 1941 ignored the recommendations of the Conseil National and set up not provincial governors but regional prefects. These were to be drawn from the existing corps of prefects, and in the department where a regional prefect was created, his departmental responsibilities would be carried out by a so-called prefect delegate. The purpose of the reform was not decentralization to please regionalists but the concentration of administrative power at a regional level to deal more effectively with the challenge of the German military administration and the problems of communicating with Vichy. Prefect Roussillon reported from Angers that since 1940 "the prefects in the Occupied Zone had been completely cut off from the government and thrown back upon themselves, without advice or instructions, able to correspond to Vichy only via the tenuous and theoretical link of the Délégation Générale." This had resulted in "an incoherent autarky of each department and different interpretations of government orders from prefect to prefect."[48] A regional prefect, he said, would be able to impose a certain order and consistency on a group of neighboring departments. Meanwhile the location of the regional prefectures took account of the design of the German military administration, and since Angers was the base of Bezirk B, which controlled Southwest France, it was clearly logical to make Angers the capital of a region. The exact contours of the regions were published in July 1941: that of Angers included Maine-et-Loire, Loire-Inférieure, Indre-et-Loire, Mayenne, and Sarthe. Roussillon, predictably, was promoted to regional prefect for Angers and given Pierre Daguerre, formerly subprefect in Dieppe, as his prefect delegate for Maine-et-Loire.

Immediately there was an outburst over the configuration of the regions. The Nantais, in particular, were aghast to have been upstaged both by Rennes, which became the regional capital of a Brittany that excluded Loire-Inférieure, and by Angers, the regional capital to which they were now beholden. Mayor Rondeau exploded in the press and Brossier's protest, endorsed by the Chamber of Commerce, at this slight to "the uncontestable and uncontested metropolis of the West" was forward to Vichy. Students from the law, medical, and commercial schools, together with the Arts Faculty of Nantes, staged a one-day strike. At a reception in honor of the regional prefect of Angers, one Breton mayor refused to drink the toast, saying, "Here, *Monsieur le préfet*, Muscadet and Anjou wine are not drunk from the same glass."[49] A year later, when steps were being taken to set up a Breton consultative committee at Rennes, which would draft a charter for Brittany, rumors circulated that Loire-Inférieure would become part of the regenerated Breton region, under Rennes. This might have satisfied some regionalists but not the city fathers of Nantes. Immediately Brossier and Rondeau wrote to Laval demanding that Nantes be made either the capital of the vast Armorican region envisaged in 1940 or the capital of a little region including Loire-Inférieure and the Vendée, currently attached to the Poitiers region, or a free city. On no account, however, would they accept subordination to Rennes.[50]

The notables' noses were also put out of joint by the administrative concentration that put more power in the hands of prefects and gave back none of the influence that notables had wielded in the *conseils généraux*. The *conseils généraux*, which under the Third Republic had become representative assemblies of between thirty and fifty, with which the prefect was bound to reckon, were replaced by truncated administrative commissions of between seven and nine. As far as the commissions' social composition went, however, prefects generally understood that it made sense to include the most influential members of the *conseils généraux* rather than indulge in social engineering. Prefect Roussillon, for example, pointed out that the *conseil général* of Maine-et-Loire "was always patriotic in spirit, hardly prey to political agitation or demagogic excess." Out of thirty-four councillors there were only eight radicals or radical-socialists and no socialists at all; 55 percent were large landowners, 45 percent nobles, and 47 percent over sixty years old, and Roussillon proposed to take seven of the nine new commissioners from the old *conseil général*. Here, however, he came into conflict with the Interior Ministry, which, as with mayors, was not content to hand the baton to reactionaries but determined to widen the field from which councillors were drawn. Prefects must include representatives of other groups, including fathers of large families, skilled workers, and younger men. Roussillon was forced to drop several aging nobles, to include two industrialists, both thirty-eight and respectively fathers of six and ten children, and to bring in Daniel Cadeau, a worker from the Bessonneau factory in Angers, who was described by the local press as "kind, simple, paternal, in his modest dwelling that was yet clean and as if perfumed by family virtue."[51]

Despite the standoff between central and local government over the administrative commissions, the notables in place survived quite well. Victor Bernier, mayor of Angers, president of the *conseil général* of Maine-et-Loire in 1940, became leader of the department's administrative commission in 1941. Marquis Henri de La Ferronnays, president of the *conseil général* of Loire-Inférieure in 1940, was there to reply to the speech of prefect Dupard at the opening session of the administrative commission, pledging loyalty to Marshal Pétain and to "the three notions at the foundation of the new state: work, family, country."[52] As for Indre-et-Loire, councillors who were also deputies, such as Léon Courson and Ferdinand Morin, were not carried over, but the radical-socialist councillors-general were still there in the shape of Paul Guillaume-Louis and François Servant, mayor of La Haye Descartes, whose "rallying" was still under scrutiny.[53] Henri Mattraits, medical doctor and mayor of Chinon, elected to the *conseil général* in 1929 to succeed radical-socialist boss Camille Chautemps, was preferred over his rival, Pierre Labussière, also a medical doctor and a radical-socialist; Labussière had defeated him in the *conseil général* elections of 1937 but was considered too Rabelaisian a figure in his closeness to folkways, his appetite for the bottle, his oaths and obscenities, and his general violation of the conventions of bourgeois taste.[54]

In the long run, who survived politically was less important than where the power lay. The administrative commissions met monthly in Indre-et-Loire, on a Saturday afternoon in the prefecture, and three times a year in Loire-Inférieure for no more than a day. Chaired by the prefect, they were far from lively. In Tours, the three former councillors-general—Guillaume-Louis, Servant, and André Gouin, a banker and the mayor of the Tours suburb Fondettes—became slightly more vociferous under the new prefect, Jean Tracou, a former naval man, but Jean Goujon, a garagist and member of the Chamber of Trades, said nothing in two years. It may be that all references to politics were excised from the minutes: the business the commissions dealt with—subsidies, scholarships, school buildings, church towers, doctors' fees, local roads, railway schedules, sewerage—was essentially routine and parochial. There is a strong sense of the First or Second Empires, when for most of the time liberal democracy was heavily censored.[55]

This was a reflection of a concerted drive by the Vichy regime to have done with the corrupt and self-serving reign of the politicians and to increase the authority and prestige of public officials. All French prefects were summoned to Vichy on 19 February 1942 to take a solemn oath to Marshal Pétain and to demonstrate that national unity overrode the division between Occupied and Free Zones. Interior Minister Pierre Pucheu, who orchestrated the ceremony, announced that with the suspension of France's decadent political institutions prefects were now "the political guides of opinion, the intellectual and moral leaders of those they administer; they have the duty, in a word, to aspire to the role of real spiritual chiefs." He was, he said, continuing the work of his friend and predecessor at the ministry, Admiral Darlan. "Your government no longer wants to know parties or partisans of the past," he concluded. "It sees in France only French people," all of whom had to follow the marshal on the path he had traced.[56]

All this was music to the ears of Jean Roussillon, who now had a reason to assert his authority over the other prefects of his region in his mission to destroy the ancien régime of parliamentary intrigue. Pierre Daguerre, prefect delegate of Maine-et-Loire, noted that Moreau, the deputy mayor of Baugé, with his eye on future elections, was having his photograph included in packages sent to POWs, while Robert Grandmaison, "obsessed by his electoral fief" in the Saumurois, was "worried about a diminution of his rights of suzerainty." "It is vital," he reported, "that the prefectoral administration replaces parliamentary activity, which is seeking to survive."[57] The Baugeois and Saumurois were to some extent an extension of Touraine, which was the real problem. The new prefect, Jean Tracou, a naval man who had headed Admiral Darlan's office, shared all the political prejudices of his master, Roussillon, who was well pleased with him. He warned of the *attentisme* of the supporters of the old politics. They do not believe that "the Pétain experiment" will last or succeed. They laugh at the label of "*ralliés*" that has sometimes been given to them too generously and allowed them to keep their positions of command. Confidently they await the return of the old system. From the beginning of the century the department has been the finest example of a "rotten borough" of left-wing parties that the parliamentary regime has produced. As before, it is richly larded with Freemasons, sympathizers of Freemasonry, creatures of the Chautemps dynasty, and supporters of the Popular Front. A timid purge has affected only the small fry, those without importance. The bosses are still in place. In no way have they rallied to the marshal's government. Quite simply, they are prudent and waiting.

The cancer, said Tracou, went as far as the administrative commission, which was controlled in his opinion by Dr. Guillaume-Louis, "the grand elector, liegeman, and close friend of Camille Chautemps," and François Servant, "the rural grand elector, client of deputy Bernier, and himself the declared enemy of the government." Meanwhile Ferdinand Morin, mayor of Tours, despite his courage in 1940, was "one of the most remarkable representatives of the previous regime," antimilitarist, antireligious, a "mediocre administrator" whose only concern was to cultivate his electorate.[58]

To confront the issue Roussillon went to Tours and made a major speech at the prefecture to the heads of administrative departments, notables, and the press. He underlined the goals of the National Revolution and made clear "the intention of the new administration to no longer tolerate the failings of the past and to complete the break with unassimilable elements of the ancien régime." How easy it was to uproot this regime was another question, and Roussillon told Pucheu that "the department of Indre-et-Loire is one of those where, in the past, under the influence of the likes of Chautemps, Bernier, and Morin, radicalism and Freemasonry have thrust their deepest roots and larded the public services with their clients."[59] Some "improvements" were made. As we have seen, Guillaume-Louis was denounced by a faction of his own staff, lost his directorship of the medical school, and dropped from the political scene. Laval's police chief, René Bousquet was keen to intern a few leading "Gaullists" in each department to "encourage the others." Prefect Tracou suggested Robert Chautemps, a forty-eight-year-old lawyer and cousin of Camille Chautemps who was regarded as amoral and dissolute. "Too clever to express his opinions openly, he acts deceitfully and by denigration in private, an ironic and sarcastic mind that uses every opportunity to criticize the marshal and M. Laval." Another suggestion was Charles Dubourg, a printer and former *adjoint* of Morin on the municipal council of Tours. Though he claimed to be a friend of Laval, he was "constantly in the cafés of the market quarter, stirring up discontent among café owners and traders."[60] His arrest, moreover, helped bring down Morin, who was prevailed on to step aside as mayor of Tours in December 1942.

The idea that the notables of the Third Republic could simply be purged, however, remained a dream. The tentacles of their clientage system spread too far, as the Vichy prefects in their more lucid moments appreciated. More important was the fact that they *were* the notables, and without their cooperation no regime could function. The Vichy model of direct administration, with prefects and subprefects cutting out the political middleman and making regular tours to meet rural mayors, was impossible to sustain in practice. Besides, the invisible hand of the local politicians, grand electors who had built their careers on cultivating mayors, schoolteachers, shopkeepers, café owners, and the like, was always there, and in the last resort Vichy simply had to negotiate. Vichy was caught in a hopeless contradiction, wanting to make government more autonomous and destroy the remnants of parliamentarianism but needing to find a broad popular base that even in a democratic system was mediated by notables.

This contradiction soon became obvious in the functioning of the administrative commissions. Interior Minister Pucheu, so keen to energize and even politicize the prefectoral corps, also realized that the truncated and powerless commissions sitting beside them occasionally had no purchase on the country at large. In December 1941 he therefore declared that "the moment has come to associate the representatives of the *pays réel* closely to the work of the government." The commissions were to be enlarged from seven or nine to fifteen or twenty-five individuals, "not resembling assemblies of notables but corresponding to the social composition of the department, representatives of the liberal professions, of rural populations, of the working class, and of the economic interests of the region." For the administrative commission of Loire-Inférieure prefect, Dupard proposed a shoemaker who also taught for the Chamber of Trades, a fitter and a boilermaker who were shop stewards at the Chantiers Dubigeon and were also on the Nantes municipal council, and a turner at the Chantiers de Penhouët at Saint-Nazaire who was secretary of the Catholic engineers union. He also however proposed Pierre Toscer, mayor of Saint-Nazaire, the director of the Chantiers de Bretagne, and Yves Bureau, professor at the Medical School of Nantes, father of eight, and lobbyist on family issues.[61] On the administrative commission of Indre-et-Loire the silent worker Goujon was joined by André Garantie, secretary of the Bourse du Travail of Tours, municipal councillor, and supporter of the Labor Charter, by Émile Oudin, a Catholic railway unionist and president of the Catholic unions in the department, and by Charles Vavasseur, member of the Conseil National, mayor of Vouvray, and producer of the local sparkling wine.[62]

The enlarged administrative commissions had not met, however, before the government of Pierre Laval planned an even more radical reform. While adopting a new collaborationist and authoritarian line, turning France into much more of a police state, he also realized as a veteran politician of the Third Republic that if bridges were not built to the political class the regime was doomed. "Deprived of all decision-making powers and all right of initiative," wrote one Interior Ministry official, "the administrative commissions give the prefect only a platonic and ineffectual support."[63] The answer, extraordinarily, was found in the return of the *conseils généraux*, or something very close to them, called departmental councils. At a meeting of regional prefects of the Occupied Zone in May 1942, Laval's acolytes Georges Hilaire of the Interior Ministry and police chief René Bousquet explained Laval's view that the departmental councils would be made up of one councillor per canton, as were the *conseils généraux*, except that they would be appointed, not elected. Obviously, councillors would have to have "rallied" to Marshal Pétain and his government but, stated Hilaire, "only those who belong to condemned milieux—Gaullists, communists, warmongers—would be excluded. Socialists who had rallied would not be left out." The "idea of social representation" used in appointments to the administrative commissions would be a factor but what really mattered was an individual's "influence over opinion" and "the maximum authority in the local environment." A reliable gauge of this influence and authority was having been elected mayor or councillor-general, and this meant in effect a return to the rule of notables. The typical candidate would be the mayor of the main town in the canton. Inevitably this would prejudice the chances of workers' representatives who had been accommodated on the commissions, but Bousquet pointed out that "the aim was *the constitution of a political assembly* [my italics], to be recruited according to political, not occupational, criteria. It was quite different from the representation of the Corporation Paysanne and the Charter of Labor, which was done on an occupational basis."[64]

And so it came to pass that under the law of August 1942 all notions of corporative representation were brushed aside. When the furriers' organization in Indre-et-Loire argued that each occupational family under the Charter of Labor should be represented, it was told that being a municipal councillor was a minimum qualification.[65] Labor representatives were now considered much less attractive. Jean Goujon, the garagist who had sat silently on the administrative commission in Tours, was not included on the grounds that he "had no credit with the working class. A decent fellow, who represents nothing." On the political front, the opportunity was taken to weed out those who, though mayors of the main towns in the canton, failed the fidelity test. Out finally in Indre-et-Loire were Ferdinand Morin, whose days as mayor of Tours were numbered; François Servant, described as being "at the forefront of prewar electoral struggles," and Paul Guillaume-Louis, "considered the standard-bearer of Masonic, Gaullist, and anticlerical sectarian elements in the department."[66] On the other hand, Henri Mattraits, the solid and respectable mayor of Chinon, was chosen over the *conseiller général* of Chinon, Pierre Labussière, since a confidential report warned that Labussière's loyalty to Pétain was doubtful, that he "passed for an Anglophile," and that though he wielded influence among his rural clientele "his demagogy and his slovenliness gave him an unsavory popularity."[67]

There was, however, no automatic blacklisting of parliamentarians, according to the early rhetoric of Vichy. In his proposals to the Interior

Ministry, prefect Tracou of Indre-et-Loire took into account "the political situation of the department, as it appears from the legislative elections of 1936 and cantonal elections [to the *conseil général*] of 1937, in which radicals and socialists had done well." Although the new councillors were not elected, the understanding was that the "dosage" should reflect the balance of political opinion. Robert de Grandmaison was finally admitted to the council in Maine-et-Loire, on the grounds that he was the dominant radical figure in the Saumurois. He was delighted to return to house-to-house campaigning, only to discover, reported prefect Daguerre with some ironic pleasure, "that he did not find the support he hoped for. In fact he even had some rather scathing rejections."[68] René Tardif was considered since, "although he was very attached to his political ideas, he seemed to have rallied to the government. . . . His former colleagues of the *conseil général* appreciate his strong and lively intelligence."[69] In the end, however, he was thought too unreliable and dropped. Gaston Moreau, mayor and former deputy of Baugé, was kept out initially because he had attended a meeting of the collaborationist Jacques Doriot in Angers and was suspected of being Doriot's candidate for prefect in the event of an extreme-right-wing coup. But he was also thought to be too subtle a politician to commit himself irrevocably to the fascists and had to be included when the first choice for the canton died.[70] In Loire-Inférieure, finally, the socialist deputies Pageot and Blancho, who had demonstrated their unreliability and had in any case moved to the Free Zone, were excluded, and Jean Le Cour Grandmaison, also in the Free Zone, was left out, but otherwise the cohort of aristocrats and their academic allies were back: the Marquis de La Ferronnays, Hubert de Montaigu, Gustave Gautherot, and Louis Linyer.

In many respects the departmental councils were the *conseils généraux* resuscitated, and contemporaries were only too aware of this when they finally met in the spring of 1943. At the opening of the departmental council of Loire-Inférieure, prefect Dupard praised the old *conseil général*, which had "always preserved the ancestral traditions that are the basis of French greatness," and paid especial homage to its last president, the Marquis de La Ferronnays. Taking up the theme, the new president of the departmental council, Ricordeau, mayor of Saffré and barrister at the Nantes bar, said that the council was "a continuation of age-old institutions": the provincial assembly of the ancien régime (pre-1789 style), the departmental councils of the Revolution, and the *conseils-généraux*, which were variously appointed or elected.[71] In Maine-et-Loire, at the opening of the council, Jean Roussillon announced likewise that "the new assembly is, in essence, only a reproduction of the old one," even to the extent that Mayor Victor Bernier of Angers, president of one, was also president of the other.[72] For one local paper the ancien régime comparison was full of revolutionary foreboding. The list of councillors, it scorned, "gives us a taste of the past: that of Louis XV and [his wife] Marie Leczynska. . . . Everywhere names with handles, conservatives, monarchists, national republicans. . . . The new Parliament is born. The registers of grievances will follow."[73]

The continuity between *conseil général* and departmental council was greatest where the traditional elites still held sway in 1940. In Indre-et-Loire, for example, the "rotten borough" of radicalism, only five of the twenty-four seats (21 percent) were filled by former councillors-general. In Loire-Inférieure, split between conservatives and socialists, the proportion was seventeen out of forty-six (37 percent). In Maine-et-Loire, which apart from the Saumurois was dominated by the right, twenty-one of the thirty-two members of the new departmental council (62 percent) were carried over from the old *conseil général*, offering clear proof of the adaptability of the local notables to the pressures of the Occupation.

Just as significant, however, were the limits set to the bridge building between the new departmental councils and the public at large. As the Occupation wore on and the fortunes of war changed, adaptability came less to mean changing one's spots to fit in with the new regime than to mean holding back as the odds against the durability of the "Pétain experiment" shortened. *Attentisme* may have been a dirty word invented by Vichy but it corresponded to a calculation that it would pay not to be too compromised by association with the regime the day the Americans landed. This reluctance to serve was already apparent in the failure to fill all the places on the departmental councils. That of Maine-et-Loire was complete, but there had been great difficulty finding candidates to sit for the radical Saumurois. Six cantons out of twenty-four were without representation in Indre-et-Loire, including the bases of Guillaume-Louis and Servant, although numbers were made up by two workers—Garantie and Oudin—carried over from the administrative commission. Most worrying, ten of the forty-six seats on the departmental council of Loire-Inférieure were empty. The gaps multiplied as a result of resignations as the fortunes of Vichy faltered. Garantie, sensing rather late that the labor movement had long been moving in the opposite direction, resigned from the departmental council and from the municipal council of Tours in January 1944. Absenteeism increased as many who remained formally members stayed away. At the second session of the council of Indre-et-Loire there were four absentees, while in June 1944 only six of the nineteen councillors turned up and, for want of a quorum, the meeting was postponed until 8 July. On that day Charles Vavasseur, the president, spoke of the suffering into which the country had been plunged and the council bravely adopted a motion appealing "to all French people to gather around Marshal Pétain and work together for the uplifting of our dear country."[74] Loyal this minority was, but it was a small group of notables who had now lost all influence and authority and were twisting in the wind.

Many if not most of the members of the departmental councils were mayors, who were experiencing their own conflicts of loyalties. At the beginning of the Occupation Vichy enjoyed a certain luxury as to whom to confirm and whom to remove, particularly in the large towns, while expecting that rural communes would look after themselves. Increasingly, however, rural communes began to present problems. Even in the conservative, Catholic Mauges, the subprefect had to investigate Comte Hubert d'Anthenaise, accused in *Je suis partout* of "leading a ceaseless and perfidious campaign against the marshal's government" and of telling people that the population of Anjou was going to be deported to Upper Silesia.[75] This turned out to be a libel by a rival in Action Française, but in Montfaucon-sur-Moine the problem was real enough. The mayor resigned in 1941, the municipal council was dissolved, and a special delegation was appointed under a former mayor to look after the commune. But the commune remained totally divided between factions, the leader of one of which was placed under house arrest in the summer of 1944.[76]

Incidents such as these obliged the government to extend the powers it had to replace elected mayors, *adjoints*, or municipal councils by appointed special delegations. But as with representation higher up, the government was torn between taking a tough line to ensure loyalty to Pétain and the

Vichy government and not alienating support that was increasingly difficult to count on. When Pierre Laval returned to power he ordered all busts of Marianne removed from town halls and schools but also advised prefects to use their powers to interfere in municipal politics sparingly. There was the danger that local councils would "become discouraged or lose their authority," and if new delegations were appointed care needed to be taken to represent the local population as broadly as possible.[77] The obvious way out of the contradiction was to work closely with local government and energetically rally support. Prefect Daguerre told the mayors of Maine-et-Loire that they must "think in common, act in common, obey in common" because, according to the best teaching of Vichy, a house divided against itself could not stand. After his third tour of the department in March 1943, he said that he had criticized those who had fled the country and asserted that "those who have stayed at their posts with some risk since the Occupation have no lessons in patriotism to take from those who ran away."[78]

Many prefects and subprefects were as diligent as they could be in their meetings with groups of local mayors. More seductive was the ritual of an introduction to Marshal Pétain himself. In October 1943 eight mayors from each department in the Angers region were selected to make the trip to Vichy. They included mayors of large towns—Nantes, Saint-Nazaire, Angers, Cholet, Saumur, and Tours—but also of smaller communes. Dr. Guillaume-Louis, mayor of Montbazon, was rather surprisingly invited but replied that, while "very touched," he was unable to accept because of "pressing professional obligations in Tours." Since he was no longer director of the medical school we may conclude that he felt that at this stage of the Occupation it would be unwise to have his picture taken shaking hands with Marshal Pétain. The Touraine delegation went bearing gifts: an 1884 magnum of Vouvray, two bottles of Bourgueil and two of Montlouis (communes of two of the mayors), some leather from the tanning factory of Jacques Hervé, mayor of Châteaurenault, some fruit from Athée-sur-Cher, where Rémy Poitevin was farmer and mayor, and some books from the publisher Mame of Tours. At the ceremony the eighty-seven-year-old marshal showed that he had lost none of the art of conversation. He spoke to the mayor of Tours about his visit to the city in October 1940 after meeting

Hitler at Montoire; to the Comte de Tristan, mayor of Chambon, who had only recently been released from a POW camp, about life in Germany; to Mayor Hervé about leather; to Mayor Boutet of Bossée, a farmer, about milk and butter; and to Mayor Reneuve of Montlouis, a pig farmer, about pig killing.[79]

It is significant that the mayors from Touraine included none of the familiar radical bosses. These were already thinking of rallying according to their own rules, reviving the Association of Mayors of Indre-et-Loire. Founded in 1919, it had been in eclipse since 1939 but Emile Gounin, a rich shoe manufacturer and the radical-socialist mayor of Amboise, was keen to relaunch it. The problem for the administration was that it was a fief of radical mayors and that, though Gounin was "by a long way the most active and intelligent member," it would be unwise to put him at the head of it. Anticlerical, possibly a Freemason, and pro–Popular Front, he was ostensibly loyal to Vichy but "the sincerity of his conversion is questioned by many of his adversaries and his spirit of intrigue makes him quite redoutable." As a compromise, prefect Tracou suggested resurrecting the association under Charles Vavasseur of Vouvray, a good Pétainist who was due to be president of the departmental council. But regional prefect Roussillon would have nothing to do with the association at all, arguing that it was a subversive vehicle of radical mayors of the Third Republic. This was not the moment, he asserted, "to recycle people who only recently had a fierce part in local electoral struggles on the political circuit and to reestablish an organization that would be at best a useless intermediary and at worst a screen between the administration and the people."[80]

With or without such associations, however, mayors were in the nature of things intermediaries between the administration and the people. They could choose to act as transmission belts relaying official instructions or as screens or buffers to protect local people from official pressures. As the Occupation progressed, those pressures intensified. Mayors were responsible for delivering quotas of grain, milk, butter, or livestock; they were responsible for delivering quotas of labor for Germany. They had on their backs not only the Vichy administration but the Germans, and the more demands were made, the more angrily local populations reacted, making the position of the mayors almost untenable. In November 1942, with the implementation of the Relève to exchange workers for POWs, a rash of mayors resigned in the Châteaubriant area. They had been insulted and molested and had even received death threats from workers who had been chosen to go to Germany or because their own sons had mysteriously not been chosen.[81] Jacques Hedouin, the Vichy-appointed mayor of Vernoil-le-Fourrier on the Anjou-Touraine border, refused to hand over wheat that had been requisitioned, on the grounds that he needed it to feed the local population before the new harvest came in. Accused of "communal autarky," he argued that he had always "defended his commune without any ill will" and promptly resigned.[82] Of 282 mayors in Indre-et-Loire, 37 resigned in 1942 and 27 in 1943, the typical mayor being a farmer over sixty.[83] Defending the interests of one's commune might win the loyalty of the locals but it infuriated the Germans, who as their situation deteriorated demanded ever more foodstuffs, labor for Germany, and labor for local defenses. In the first two months of 1944 alone, they arrested twenty mayors or their secretaries in Touraine. Squeezed between Vichy and the Germans on the one hand and an increasingly frightened and hostile population on the other, mayors were increasingly siding with the local population. The loss of mayoral support compounded the loss of support on the departmental councils. The notables finally turned their backs on Vichy, and without the notables Vichy could not survive.

The vigor of local government, set alongside the flourishing of trade unions, peasant organizations, charities, and cultural associations, confirms that civil society, despite the difficulties it faced, was in no sense eclipsed under the German Occupation. It also demonstrates that the authoritarianism of the Vichy regime was limited by its reliance on the influence of the local notables who, by virtue of their family connections, professional status, or private wealth, ran the municipal and departmental councils. Vichy was unable to purge local government of its ideological enemies even if it had wanted to. Despite the subsequent brutal reputations of Interior Minister Pucheu and Premier Laval, it was Pucheu who advised that local government must reflect the political makeup of the locality while Laval wanted to bring back the political class as a whole through a revival in all but name of the *conseils généraux*. What was required of local notables, independent of their political affiliation (unless they were communists), was that they express loyalty to the Vichy regime. Some were happy to do so emphatically, others paid only lip service while waiting for times to change. These were the trimmers who, as we shall see, ensured a peaceful transition to the new republic in 1944. Their pivotal role between Vichy and the people calls into question the distinction that has gained some authority between the Vichy regime on the one hand and the French on the other. The most one can say is that the task of mediation became more and more difficult as pressure from the Germans for labor and resources increased and that, increasingly, local administrators were either siding with the local population against the authorities, passively if not actively, or using resignation as the obvious exit from their dilemma. By 1944 the Vichy regime in occupied France had lost its anchor in the local community.

8

Saints

Early in the evening of 2 June 1944, four days before the Allied landings in Normandy, a large crowd waited on the outskirts of Ancenis, a market town on the Loire at the gateway between Anjou and Brittany. At the head of the crowd were the bishop of Nantes, the mayor of Ancenis, and his council.

There were thousands of people, reciting the rosary, singing familiar anthems, offering to heaven the supplications of the *Parce Domine*. Children from the schools and catechism classes, pupils from the Institution Saint-Joseph, the Petit Séminaire of Guérande, the Enfants-Nantais Day School, and the Joliverie who had been evacuated [from the coast] to the Ancenis area, young men and women of Action Catholique, nuns of every order and every habit were drawn up in the beautiful green setting of the hospital courtyard. Then behind the surplices of the choristers and priests appeared the white vision of the Madonna. What a moving moment it was finally to behold the Virgin, who had already traveled halfway across France and was now here to spread her blessings among us.

The statue of Our Lady of Boulogne, carried in her boat, was welcomed by Monsignor Villepelet, who warned her nevertheless that she would travel "the path of suffering" across the diocese, greeted by the families of prisoners of war, by evacuees and disaster victims, by the ruins of Nantes and Saint-Nazaire. Taking words from the mouth of Joan of Arc, he said that

> there always was great distress [*grande pitié*] in the diocese of Nantes. Has this beautiful jewel of Christianity been cast into the crucible of suffering in order to throw up ever brighter flames? We accept the will of your Son. But we ask you to bind our wounds and dry our tears. You, whose eyes have cried so much, understand us. Bring the comfort of your maternal tenderness to our unspeakable grief. Share with us our way of the cross, and as you advance bring forth under your feet joyful days, dawns that herald peace. *Prospere procede et regna!* In your splendor and majesty, proceed and reign.[1]

This rapturous welcome for a statue of the Virgin Mary was replicated in a thousand towns and villages all over toward the end of the Occupation. To make this possible, four identical statues had been made and sent off on their own itineraries, assuaging the hungry faithful. The reception of Our Lady of Boulogne suggests a piety and fervor that might be thought uncommon in the mid–twentieth century, which was, after all, supposed to be a period of secularization.[2] People were only too willing to accept the Catholic version of events, that war, defeat, and Occupation had been visited on the French for their sins—their materialism, selfishness, pleasure seeking, and turning away from God. Salvation would come only through prayer, repentance, a return to the paths of righteousness. God would offer his protection again, but the Almighty could be approached by mere humans only through the intercession of the saints and above all of the Virgin Mary.

For the bishop of Nantes and his flock, appeals to Providence were the traditional and obvious way of responding to catastrophe. Four years earlier, in May 1940, as German forces swept into France, Monsignor Villepelet promised that, like his predecessor, who during the German invasion of 1870 promised to build a new church to bear witness to the protection of Nantes by the Sacred Heart, he too would build a new church dedicated to Mary the Mediator should the city of Nantes be saved. Saved it was from the bombardment suffered by Tours, Saumur, Angers, Rennes, and Bordeaux, but his prayers for the protection of France had not been answered, and the causes for this had to be sought.[3] Speaking on 16 June 1940 to the Federation of Young Christian Women of Nantes as the Germans advanced toward the city, he was in no doubt what the causes were. France had been defeated not by military inferiority nor even by social strife but by de-Christianization and sin. "France has driven Christ from the law courts and schools," he proclaimed. "She has expelled the religious congregations. She has systematically and deliberately destroyed all faith in the souls of too many of her children. She has tolerated vice, immorality, and wrong. She has undermined the family by divorce and suppressed the birth rate."[4] The remedy to this disaster was also plain. The French must return to the ways of God, by prayer, repentance, reparation, even sacrifice. All those with the power to intercede—angels, saints, the Virgin Mary—must be mobilized. Eventually God would be placated and would restore the hand of protection to France.

In one way the defeat was already a start. It had cleared from power the republican politicians, manipulated by Freemasons and Jews, who for seventy years had pursued their work of de-Christianization. The new regime under Marshal Pétain was thus to be welcomed. Following a meeting of the cardinals and archbishops of the Occupied Zone on 28 August 1940, all dioceses recommended three rules of conduct to the clergy and faithful, which were published in October: "(1) Absolute loyalty to the legitimate power in France; (2) The greatest spirit of order and exact discipline in relations with the Occupation authorities; (3) The greatest discretion in things said, either in public or in private." One of those archbishops, Monsignor Gaillard of Tours, immediately had the occasion to put those rules into effect on 25 October 1940, when, following his meeting with Hitler at Montoire, just to the north of the diocese, Marshal Pétain, accompanied by prefect Vernet and Mayor Morin, visited him in his palace. Pétain praised the bishop's conduct during the bombardment of the city by the Germans, and in reply Monsignor Gaillard "guaranteed the confident admiration and perfect loyalty of the whole diocese, clergy and faithful, with respect to the marshal and his government, as well as the constant prayers that would rise from Touraine to call down heavenly assistance for him." Evidently moved by his experience, in January 1941 Monsignor Gaillard told the faithful that "French citizens are not only the friends but the subjects of Marshal Pétain," who was no less than "God's representative." Within days, however, the assembly of cardinals and archbishops of the Occupied Zone, meeting in Paris, were in fact moderating their language, replacing loyalty to the "legitimate power" with loyalty to the "established power" (15 January 1941). Obedience was still required, but already (except perhaps for starstruck Monsignor Gaillard) Vichy had lost a little of its aura.[5]

No particular ideological revolution was required here. The Church always rendered unto Caesar what was Caesar's. But the Vichy regime made it easy by reversing much of the anticlerical legislation that had been passed since 1870. Religious instruction could be given in state schools for the first time since 1882. State subsidies could be made to private Catholic schools for the first time since 1886. Religious congregations that had been driven out of France under legislation of 1901 and 1904 were allowed to return.[6] The Masonic lodges, which were seen by Catholics to be at the origin of this anticlerical offensive, were dissolved.[7] Relations between Church and state, which had been virtually nonexistent under the Third Republic, were rebuilt. "How times have changed!" exclaimed Monsignor Villepelet as prefect Leroy and his Jewish wife were replaced by prefect Dupard, who asked him to confirm his twins and invited him to dinner at the prefecture and, two years later, organized a huge wedding for his daughter in the cathedral.[8] Monsignor Gaillard instructed his parish clergy to meet the "temporal authorities"—mayors, schoolteachers, tax collectors, delegates of the Secours National, Youth, and Sports—and reserve them places in church, so that when he appeared on a pastoral visit or for Joan of Arc Day or Mother's Day, he might be introduced by name.[9]

The Church did not have it all its own way. Vichy was not a clerical regime and ministers changed so fast that the promises made by one were rarely kept by the next. Rector Vincent of the Catholic University of Angers lobbied hard to obtain official recognition, state subsidies, and degree-giving powers for the "Catho," only to find, as he put it, that the Education Ministry was still staffed by "militant secularists, if not Freemasons," who frustrated him at every turn.[10] In spite of such setbacks the Catholic Church remained an extremely powerful institution and was becoming even more powerful. Given that, under German military administration and cut off from Vichy, the state was a shadow of its former self, it could be argued that the Catholic Church, rather on the Irish or Polish model, was the strongest French institution in occupied France.

Included in the Church was not only the hierarchy of bishops and priests but the religious congregations, especially those of women, who had weathered the anticlerical onslaught of the turn of the century and had a powerful role in hospitals, charities, and church schools. In 1943 there were fourteen female religious congregations in Angers—from the Carmelites to the Little Sisters of the Poor—sixteen in Tours, and seventeen in Nantes.[11] Most parishes had a *patronage*, or youth club, the object of which was to provide wholesome recreation for young people, and the Catholic Scout movement was far more developed than its secular rival, the Éclaireurs. The interwar period saw the development of Action Catholique, which, under the control of the clergy, developed different branches to colonize different constituencies: Jeunesse Étudiante Chrétienne (JEC), the Jeunesse Agricole Chrétienne (JAC), and the Jeunesse Ouvrière Chrétienne (JOC), which was said to be expanding in Tours as fast as the Communist Youth was declining.[12] Mobilized against a new threat of anticlericalism from the Cartel des Gauches government of 1924–26 was the National Catholic Federation of General de Castelnau and its affiliated branches, which included the Catholic Association of Family Heads of the Diocese of Nantes and the Catholic League of Anjou, under Viscount Palamède de la Grandière.[13] For both, the baptism by fire was a demonstration in March 1925 against Freemasonry, attended in Angers by an estimated 50,000 people.[14] Inevitably, there were women's organizations that paralleled those dominated by men, such as the Patriotic League of French Women in the diocese of

Nantes, headed by the Marquise de La Ferronnays. Far from being out of touch, the Church was always quick to put the latest technology to use. The Catholic press included a weekly diocesan magazine and parish magazines for most parishes, the Association of Family Heads of the diocese of Nantes promoted local Catholic radio, while 60 percent of cinemas in Loire-Inférieure were controlled by Catholic *patronages*.[15] Admittedly, the influence of the Church was not equal in all parts of the region, as measured by the rough indicator of what proportion of the adult population attended mass on a Sunday. West of Angers, at the turn of the century, the proportion was over 90 percent in the diocese of Nantes and the arrondissements of Cholet and Segré. East of Angers, by contrast, the figure was 58 percent in the arrondissement of Baugé and 48 percent in that of Saumur at the turn of the century and 18 percent in the diocese of Tours in 1936–39, falling to 11 percent in the canton of Bléré and 8 percent in that of Château-la-Vallière. In what was historically the Vendée, the grip of the Church was thus immovable, whereas east of the river Layon the challenge of anticlericalism and religious indifference was far stronger.[16]

Despite its stronger position vis-à-vis the Vichy state, however, the Catholic Church had much to fear from Nazi persecution. Having liquidated all opposition parties, the Third Reich began to attack the press, schools, and youth movements of the Catholic Church in Germany on the grounds that what was formally religious practice concealed political opposition to the regime.[17] In France the main concern of the German military authorities was with anything that might be construed as a threat to the army. Their initial position on occupying France was nervy and intolerant. It soon emerged, however, that German regulations concerning the Church were confused and unevenly applied and that a headstrong bishop could on occasion force his adversaries to back down.

When the Germans arrived in Nantes they forbade bell ringing, lest it be used as a call to arms. After a month, however, they relaxed the ban, in time for the bells to ring for the feast of St. Anne, patron saint of Brittany.[18] German officers went to the printer of *La Semaine religieuse* of Nantes, having heard a story that the bishop had written a fiercely patriotic pastoral letter, and the Kommandantur asked the bishop to stop "all attacks on the

German army and all propaganda agitation by the clergy among the population by spoken or written word." It required *La Semaine religieuse* to be submitted for censorship prior to publication and tried to stop "politics" from infiltrating the magazine in the shape of prayers for POWs and letters from priests in POW camps.[19] Purely religious processions were generally permitted, but there was some confusion over what "purely religious" meant. Funerals were sometimes used as an excuse for draping a tricolor flag over the coffin, and that was banned. Traditional processions to cemeteries and graveside speeches on All Saints' Day, 1 November, were prohibited throughout occupied France because since the Great War it had become a prelude to Armistice Day, which commemorated victory over Germany in 1918 and was very popular with veterans. Only prefects and mayors were allowed to lay wreaths on behalf of the French people. But while the Feldkommandant of Nantes enforced the ban rigidly, that of Angers permitted processions that were "purely religious." Such was the confusion that some mayors in Loire-Inférieure formally dissociated themselves from processions led by the parish priest lest they get into trouble, while in Nueil-sur-Layon, in Anjou, the priest and the mayor were both arrested by the local gendarmerie on the grounds that they were violating the ban.[20]

Other targets of German repression were Catholic youth movements such as the JAC and JOC, which fell under the ban of 28 August 1940 prohibiting all uniformed movements. In Nantes, a Jocist (that is, a JOC member) wearing the movement's badge was arrested and interrogated at the Kommandantur.[21] In Angers, Feldkommandant Kloss complained that "a large number of young people, accompanied by clergy, have recently been going on trips to the country, either by bicycle or on foot. These trips are more than purely religious and thus cannot be allowed." General Neumann-Neurode reported that the surveillance of banned Catholic youth organizations was extremely difficult. The clergy were trying everything to regroup the Catholic youth in sports clubs. In the spring of 1941 there was a regionwide scare that the JAC was continuing to function illegally, and prefects were put under pressure by the German authorities to instruct prefects that all meetings that were not "purely religious" were prohibited. This stipulation was incomprehensible to some local clergy. The curé of Champtoceaux, for example, said that young people had been meeting for the last few months but "do not belong to any organization. The meetings are to instruct them in agriculture and religion. There has never been any question of talking politics, and we are totally committed to obeying the orders of the marshal." A French cleric, used to a tradition where many associations were required to eschew politics, could not see the thrust of a ban that was determined by reasons of military security.[22]

One of the reasons the Germans had difficulty enforcing their restrictions was the stubbornness of the French clergy. True, some clergy were easier to intimidate than others. Monsignor Costes had labored in the shadow of the previous bishop of Angers, who was ninety when he eventually died in 1940, so that Costes was somewhat fragile when he took over at the age of sixty-seven. The adjective most frequently used of him was *good.* "He never tired of being good," his funeral orator declared. In August 1940 he told his clergy never to comment from the pulpit on current affairs and to deal only with religious and moral issues. "Repentance, courage, dignity in the face of adversity, conscientious work, prayer, trust in Providence, confidence in the inexhaustible goodness of God, effort to the point of sacrifice, limitless love of those who are wounded in their body or soul," all these were what they should aim to preach. So timorous was he that he canceled the main Mother's Day service in Angers 1941 because he thought—owing to a mistranslation— that the Germans had banned it; subsequently he had to apologize shamefacedly to his flock.[23]

Monsignor Villepelet, bishop of Nantes, was made of sterner stuff. Ten days after the Germans arrived in Nantes he received a telephone call from the town hall to say that the Kommandantur had requested the use of the cathedral the following Sunday for a service. For Villepelet, the holding of a Protesatnt service in the cathedral was a "scandal" that must be prevented at all costs. When the German Protestant pastor turned up to make the request in person, Villepelet flatly refused, saying that "it is not a question of nationality but a religious issue." But when the German Catholic chaplain, whose superior—the bishop of Paderborn—he happened to know, asked a month later to use the cathedral for Catholic services that had already taken place, he said, in Angers, Villepelet played for time by replying that he would have to consult the papal nuncio. The climax came at Christmas 1940, by which time it was clear that the cathedrals of Tours and Bourges had been used for Protestant services, a swastika flag hanging from the pulpit. Villepelet was visited by the ordinance officer of Feldkommandant Hotz, who demanded use of the cathedral for Christmas Eve. Villepelet again refused, at which the colonel, "cold and impassive," threatened to requisition it. Villepelet reiterated that "the cathedral is the personal church of the bishop; I cannot allow a Protestant service to take place there, under my eyes." He offered the Germans the Church of St. Donatian as an alternative, but the colonel protested that the German military would regard this as a slight. The next day, however, the colonel returned with a Protestant pastor and conceded that St. Donatian, with its twin towers, had a cathedral-like facade, so honor was saved. The cathedral was preserved for the diocese, and Christmas Eve saw a gathering of the Catholic faithful as never before, with people clinging to every possible perch, the doors open onto the crowds left outside, and nearly 3,000 Communion wafers consumed long before everyone was satisfied.[24]

With time the German military became a little more discerning about the kinds of activities that constituted a security risk. In April 1941 they decreed that traditional religious processions would be able to take place without permission, so long as they were informed in good time. This meant that the Fête-Dieu or Corpus Christi processions of June 1941 were staged with especial splendor. "This year," declared Monsignor Villepelet, "because of the situation we are going through, our prayers will be still more plentiful and more fervent. You will pray for France, for your dear war dead, for your prisoners, for the peace of the world." The procession through the streets of Nantes of the Holy Sacrament under its dais of velvet embroidered with gold, brought together Church and state in a public display of solidarity. Led by the curés, choir school, and seminarists, the Host was followed by Monsignor Villepelet; his vicars-general, archpriests, and canons; notables such as Jean Le Cour Grandmaison of the Conseil National and Paul Brossier, president of the Chamber of Commerce; the municipal council and members of the former *conseil général*; girls who had taken First Communion in their tulle veils, carrying lilies, roses, and gladioli; children from the church schools; and parishioners with their banners.[25] Purely religious, and for that reason the only kind of procession the German military were prepared to tolerate, the stylized expression of ecclesiastical magnificence nevertheless had a resonance in the community that was more than simply religious.

The art under the Occupation was to sustain the widest variety of Catholic activity, beyond traditional religious services and processions. In the diocese of Nantes, the Catholic Association of Heads of Families remained active, with annual retreats each January; indeed taking advantage of the Vichy law of December 1942 that set up family associations in each commune, it seized control of them. Its new president in 1941 was Dr. Yves Bureau of the family movement, who used it as an additional platform for his campaign against immoral plays, films, and dancing.[26] More delicate were the maneuverings of the JOC, which was officially banned but, like the Scouts, continued to meet clandestinely or in other guises. Père Salmon, chaplain of the Touraine JOC, recalled that "we met in places that were carefully blacked out and as the hour of curfew drew close we stopped the study group so that no one was arrested on the way home by German patrols. For retreats we went to Cormery in small groups so as not to attract attention, since the demarcation line was close by." He remembers the dramatic meeting in 1943 when the executive had to decide what line to take over the Service du Travail Obligatoire (STO), the requisition of young men for labor service in Germany. In the end they decided to leave the decision as to whether to refuse to go to the conscience of those involved. Those who went would give spiritual support to young French workers but their ambitions would not stop there. "If we meet young German workers over there," they resolved, "we will make them into Jocists and plant the Jocist cross in place of the swastika."[27]

Refusing to go to work in Germany was often seen as a token of resistance, but the notion of resistance in the case of the Catholic Church has to be put in context. The defense of the Catholic Church as an institution was in itself a "politics of presence" that offered a guarantee against the Nazification of France and the French.[28] There were clergy who became more involved in Resistance activities, reaching out to those in overlapping institutions, such as the armed forces, or simply to their brothers, Christian or otherwise. Canon Robin, dean of St. Martin's cathedral in Tours, had served as an army chaplain and briefly been a POW in France in the summer of 1940. He would regularly shelter escaping POWs, employing them in the gardens or cellars of the cathedral for a few days, before passing them to other contacts: Captain Morel of the Tours gendarmerie and a cluster of agents along the demarcation line, including Abbé Lacour, curé of Athée; Abbé Lhermitte, curé of Esvres-sur-Loire; Abbé Péan, curé of Draché; Abbé Roussel and André Goupille, respectively curé and vet of La Haye Descartes. Those they helped ranged from POWs to Resistance workers and Jews. The casualty rate of these agents was extremely high. Canon Robin survived to become bishop of Blois but Captain Morel was deported and executed in Cologne in 1943, Abbé Lacour and Abbé Lhermitte were deported in 1944 and never returned, Abbé Péan was arrested after saying mass in February 1944 and was tortured to death by the Gestapo in Tours.[29] Some clergy belonged to established Resistance networks. In May 1942 Père de La Perraudière and Père de Solages of the Jesuit Collège de Saint-Grégoire of Tours both put on Péguy's controversial *Jeanne d'Arc* in the college, as we have seen, and said a private mass in the Carmelite convent for the five young communists who had been executed by the Germans outside the city on 16 May.[30] They were members of Ceux de la Libération, which was closely linked to Libération-Nord, a larger network that grouped both Christian democrats such as Anne-Marie Marteau of the Modern Girls College in Tours and socialists such as the former deputy of Tours, Jean Meunier. Père de La Perraudière was arrested when the Gestapo decimated Libération-Nord in September 1943, and he died in Dachau in April 1945, while Père Solages fled south and became chaplain to the Maquis in the Tarn.

To a large extent these clergy took their cue from those around them. The German authorities in Cholet reported that, "with few exceptions, the clergy articulate the mood of the people against us." One priest had told a meeting of young people that the air attacks on industrial targets in Paris, of which Vichy made such intense anti-British propaganda, were not necessarily the work of the British. Another told peasants from the pulpit that they did not have to obey the bishop's orders to deliver grain, because it would only be passed on to the Germans.[31] For the Vendean population of the Mauges, who had risen up against the French Revolution in 1793 and experienced triumph, defeat, and savage repression, the local

Resistance hero was Dom Sortais, abbot of the Trappist monastery of Bellefontaine. A veteran and former POW, he was said to have hidden British airmen and STO dodgers in the monastery, and he frequently declared from the pulpit that the French owed nothing to the Germans, not even obedience.[32] He incarnated a Catholic and conservative resistance to oppression that was the very essence of the Vendée.

These clergy, with their roots in local communities, did not act with the approval of the hierarchy. Bishops, as we have seen, cooperated with the state authorities to urge peasants to deliver their quotas of milk and grain. Archbishop Gaillard of Tours wrote severe and disapproving letters to Abbé Péan, nicknamed "Péan le fou."[33] Monsignor Villepelet agreed to hold a solemn funeral in his cathedral for M. Le Bras, a Nantes judge involved in the business of repression, who had been shot dead by three "terrorists," as Villepelet called them, who walked into his office.[34] For the upper clergy, communism, which fired so much of the Resistance, was just as bad as Nazism, if not worse. To assess the contribution of the Catholic Church to resistance or collaboration, however, is largely to miss the point. For the Church, salvation would come not by force of arms but by divine intervention. The way forward, according to this worldview, was to return to the way of God. Defeat and Occupation had been sent as a punishment for the sins of the French people; liberation and peace would come from Providence, once the French had shown themselves worthy again of his protection. The main business of the Church under the Occupation was therefore to step up prayer, repentance, and renewal, to call on the Virgin Mary and the saints to intercede with God. This was in no sense just spiritual abstraction. Through saint cults and pilgrimages the Church used its spiritual leverage to offer protection and hope to local populations who traditionally dedicated their prayers to specific saints and their local shrines.

Religious devotion in the diocese of Tours centered on the cult of Saint Martin, bishop of Tours in the fourth century who famously gave his cloak to a beggar and was beheaded in 397. His head was placed in a separate reliquary in 1323 and was exhibited every first of December until the Revolution.[35] Moribund since then, the ceremony of exhibiting the head of Saint Martin was revived by the archbishop of Tours under Vichy. On 30

November 1941, a procession of choirboys, seminarists, students of the Jesuit Collège de Saint-Grégoire, schoolchildren, nuns and other women, the archbishop and his vicars-general, notables such as René Feld, secretary-general of the prefecture, and André Gouin, banker and leading conservative politician, bore the holy relic to the cathedral, where 3,000 people were seated. The following year Monsignor Gaillard decided that in view of renewed enthusiasm for the cult of Saint Martin, the date of his ordination, 4 July 370, would be marked by a great procession of his relics along the banks of the Loire to the monastery of Marmoutier. "We are not asking Saint Martin for the miracle that will save us with no effort from ourselves," the archbishop announced at the monastery. "We are rather asking for the faith of former times—religious faith to begin with and then its constant companion, patriotic faith—and with that faith the disciplined energy that will make us the true artisans of our salvation."[36]

In the diocese of Angers, the greatest enthusiasm was for the Marian cult, which had taken off after the defeat of 1870 under the great bishop of Angers, Monsignor Freppel. Each 8 September, the date of the Nativity of the Virgin Mary, no fewer than three pilgrimages to Marian shrines took place. The first was to Our Lady of Béhuard, a shrine on a small island in the Loire below Angers, where a chapel had been built and the Virgin solemnly crowned in 1923. The second was Our Lady of Marillais, farther down the Loire near Ancenis. The third was Our Lady of Gardes, a high point of the Mauges, whose chapel was serviced by the Trappist monks of Bellefontaine. Of the pilgrimage to Béhuard of 8 September 1942, presided over by Monsignor Costes, a reporter noted that "many good people whom we met on the island had come impressive distances on foot. While the humble faithful recited their rosary as they walked, more educated people found themselves remembering the fine prayers Louis Veuillot [an influential nineteenth-century Catholic journalist] said on the road to Our Lady of Lorette or those of Charles Péguy as he made his pilgrimage from Paris to Chartres." So great was the crush to take Communion that young people arriving on foot were still lining up for it at 2:00 P.M.[37]

The Angevins, particularly those of the Mauges, also defined their Catholicism by reference to the Vendée, when the west rose in defense of Church and King against the persecutions of the French Revolution and experienced triumph, defeat, and savage repression. The year 1943 was remembered as the 150th anniversary of the rising, not least by the Church, which seized the opportunity to extend its influence. In March 1943 Monsignor Costes said a solemn mass in honor of the statue at Le Pin-en-Mauges of Cathelineau, one of the great leaders of the Vendean rising of 1793, known as "the saint of Anjou." The statue had been pulled down after the Revolution of 1830 but was now ceremonially restored to its plinth. The following June the nearby commune of Bourgneuf-en-Mauges was dedicated to the Sacred Heart of Jesus, the symbol under which the Vendean army had fought, "to beg forgiveness for all the faults committed by France . . . and to ask him to continue his protection of the commune in the trying times we are living through." In February 1944 Monsignor Costes said mass in Le Loroux Béconnais, north of the Loire, in honor of the local curé, Noël Pinot, who was guillotined for his beliefs 150 years previously and was locally considered a martyr. Finally, on 16 April 1944, Monsignor Costes was at the so-called Field of Martyrs outside Angers, remembering the 2,000 women and children who were shot there by revolutionary forces between 12 January and 16 April 1794, asking the assembled faithful to pray to hasten the process of their beatification at Rome.[38]

In the diocese of Nantes, suffering was not history but actuality. One of the great shrines of the city was Our Lady of Bon Secours, revered since about 1450 for protecting sailors from the sandbanks of the Loire; the statue and sanctuary were in the Église de la Sainte-Croix. Monsignor Villepelet took refuge with other clergy and nuns in the cellars of the Catholic college during the Allied air raid of 23 September 1943 and remembered emerging to see "an immense brazier throwing gigantic flames skywards, a scene from the Apocalypse." Miraculously, the statue was saved from the burning church of Sainte-Croix and, moved to the cathedral sacristy, became the focus of nine days of pilgrimage and thanksgiving the following November.[39] Other shrines beloved by the Bretons were dedicated to Saint Anne, mother of the Virgin Mary and patron saint of Brittany, whose feast day was celebrated on 26 July. Each year a *pardon*, or religious festival, was held in Nantes for Breton-speaking emigrants to the big city. At that of 1941 Monsignor Villepelet prayed to Saint Anne for "the end of our present sadness and the dawn of better days." There was another shrine to her at Vue, south of Nantes, although the main celebrations took place at Sainte-Anne-d'Auray, in the Morbihan, and were traditionally attended by the five Breton bishops of Rennes, Quimper, Saint-Brieuc, Vannes, and Nantes.

While the clergy spoke of repentance and reform, some young people began to use pilgrimages as a cover for political demonstration. At the pilgrimage to Vue on 26 July 1942, for example, it was discovered by the Feldkommandantur that hundreds in the procession of 5,000 young people were wearing "Gaullist" insignia in red, white, and blue, sporting the cross of Lorraine.[40] In such ways "purely religious" ceremonies could be infiltrated or subverted in order to convey a political message.

All these pilgrimages, however, were but a foretaste of the great event of the spring and summer of 1944, the Return of Our Lady of Boulogne. Said to have entered the port of Boulogne miraculously in 636, in a ship sailed by angels, the statue and the three copies made of it were the centerpiece of a Marial congress held in Boulogne in 1938 to mark the 300th anniversary of the dedication to the Virgin Mary of the Kingdom of France by Louis XIII on learning that he had an heir. The statues were taken secretly over the demarcation line to Le Puy, where another Marial congress was held on 15 August 1942, and thence to Lourdes. In the meantime the French bishops endorsed the papal consecration of humanity to the Immaculate Heart of Mary, and a Grand Return for the four statues was planned to start in March 1943. Of the four routes from south to north, one went from Bordeaux to Angers and Nantes and a second from Lourdes to Poitiers and Tours. As the processions made their way from town to town and village to village, streets were decked out in garlands, and the faithful came forward to confess to the missionaries who accompanied the statues. The Grand Return to Boulogne was supposed to signal the Grand Return of the French people to God, which in turn would bring salvation. The redemption of France was not a military question but a spiritual one. As the *Semaine religieuse* of Nantes said, "to obtain an end to the fighting we must first establish our peace with God."[41]

One of the statues entered southern Touraine from Poitou on 17 May 1944, received by Archbishop Gaillard and 150 of the faithful. Particular enthusiasm was manifested at Richelieu, where the procession grew to 2,500 strong, 500 took Communion, and 37 of the sick lay in the church to receive grace.[42] The statue moved on to Loches and Chinon before reaching Tours on 24 June, and on into the less Catholic north and east of the department in July. Abbé Jacques Ménard, who had just graduated from the seminary of Tours to his first cure of souls in Athée, following the arrest of Abbé Lacour, said it was "a *pays* given to the devil." As the cortège crossed the nearby village of Dierre, "the little Kremlin," he recalls, stones were thrown at it.[43]

The statue that progressed through the dioceses of Angers and Nantes received quite a different reception. It entered the diocese of Angers on 12 March 1944 from the Vendée, to be greeted by Bishop Costes and an array of churchmen, the local mayor in bare feet, carrying a cross, "a huge meditative crowd," and "kilometer upon kilometer of garlands, flowers, and triumphal arches." A ceremony was held at a column erected in honor of the Chouans, who had fought the battles of the Vendée. On 16 March the procession was met at the outskirts of Cholet by Mayor Darmaillacq at the very spot where four years earlier he had negotiated with the Germans to spare the town. This time he was there with the municipal council and a crowd of 15,000: "The whole town was there," reported the *Semaine religieuse*.[44] On 14 April Our Lady reached Angers, the float dragged by young militants of Action Catholique, barefoot, met by regional prefect Donati and municipal councillors such as Charles Poisson who fell to their knees. The statue was installed in the cathedral, where 20,000 of the faithful came to pay their respects—first children, then women, then in turn pupils, young ladies, and men, in elaborately choreographed order.[45]

The liberation of France did not take place miraculously, and ironically the passage of Our Lady of Boulogne coincided with some of the worst Allied bombing of the war. Angers suffered its first attack on the night of Whit Sunday, 28 May 1944. Bombs aimed at the station killed many Angevins who took refuge in the church of St. Laud and destroyed the bishop's palace. Monsignor Costes would undoubtedly have been killed had he been there and not at Béhuard, where the statue was resting that night. On 15 June Nantes suffered an air attack that seriously damaged the cathedral and killed an archpriest. The miraculous statue of Our Lady of Bon Secours was feared destroyed, but firemen pulled it from the ruins six days later, its face intact, and restoration seemed possible.[46] Even before the attack, the prefecture had forbidden children from taking part in the procession, lest it was machine-gunned from the air. Monsignor Villepelet decided that Our Lady of Boulogne could not be housed in the cathedral, or even in another city church, and it was hurried through the streets, gathering a thin crowd of two or three thousand, and taken to the grotto of Our Lady of Lourdes at Le Pont-du-Cens. There a crowd of 20,000 did gather for an evening service in the open air, described as a "veritable apotheosis" by the *Semaine religieuse.* Mayor Orrion of Nantes was there, carrying a crucifix, as was Ricordeau, president of the departmental council. "You yourself have wanted to be the Great Missionary of France," Monsignor Villepelet told Our Lady of Boulogne, "at a moment when the return of peace is linked to the return of souls toward God." And there the Grand Return ground to something of a halt, as the bishop of Vannes thought his diocese "too disturbed by terrorism and the Maquis," as well as vulnerable to air attacks. "People are not in the right frame of mind," he said, to welcome the statue, which therefore remained for the time in the diocese of Nantes, cared for by the Sisters of St. Gilda's.[47]

The story of the Grand Return of Our Lady of Boulogne seems like a medieval epic that has wandered into the secular age of the twentieth century. It seems incredible that people were praying for the deliverance of France to four plaster statues of the Virgin Mary when the future of Europe was being settled by arsenals of modern technology. And yet this was an understandable response precisely because ordinary people had no control over the battles being fought around them, inflicting mounting casualties of French citizens. Collective prayer to the Virgin Mary and other saints and martyrs served the purpose of bringing down divine protection to local communities that felt deprived of more immediate sources of defense. This devotion, mediated by the Catholic Church, was also part of the Church's strategy to ward off foes whose cohorts seemed to be multiplying: Nazi paganism was in retreat, only to be replaced by Anglo-Saxon materialism and Soviet communism. The Church had successfully safeguarded its interests under Vichy and during the German Occupation; now it needed to meet the challenges of liberated France. Some clergy, as we have seen, distinguished themselves by Resistance activities and earned themselves a role in the Liberation Committees that sprang up in the summer of 1944. Dom Sortais, as we shall see, was recruited to the local Liberation Committee at Cholet, while the Jesuit Père de La Perraudière, though a deportee who was never to return, was included on the Departmental Liberation Committee of Indre-et-Loire, which had a strong contingent of Christian democrats such as the Tours schoolteacher Anne-Marie Marteau. Such people were able to continue the defense of the Church's interests either through traditional conservative politics or through a renascent Christian Democracy that was one of the outstanding features of the Liberation.

9

Sinners

Just before the arrival of the Germans in 1940, stories circulated in the small town of Bléré that lights had been seen flashing on and off in the château of a Hungarian landowner in the commune. The local wisdom had it that this was a signaling system set up to send information to the enemy. The mayor of Bléré and the gendarmerie visited the château and reported that the flashing lights were no more than the light on a staircase being switched on and off. After the Occupation, however, the demarcation line ran right through the estate, which only served to fuel local rumor and keep up the stream of anonymous letters to the prefecture. The Hungarian, named Strausz, was a former agricultural chemist and theater producer who had married a French woman of a highly respected family, Mlle de Berly, in 1934 and called himself Strausz de Berly. He moved into the château of Fossambault in 1937 and farmed the property. He spoke German, which enabled him to persuade the Kommandantur to grant special passes to the local inhabitants because they needed to cross the demarcation line on a daily basis. But far from endearing him to the locals, his contacts with the

Germans rendered him even more suspect. In December 1940 he was publicly accused of spying by his cleaning lady and summoned to appear before the justice of the peace of Bléré. The cleaning lady admitted that she had lied and the police inspector investigating the case said that Strausz had been slandered, "because his wife is deeply patriotic and would never have allowed her husband to become involved in spying." Shortly afterwards the demarcation was moved slightly north, so that the whole of Strausz's property was located in the Free Zone, and no more was heard of the case.[1]

What is suggested by this spy mania is an intense suspicion of foreigners that war, defeat, and occupation only served to heighten. The war saw an obsession with "fifth columnists" who were infiltrating and passing secrets to the enemy, and anyone who was marginal or different was a likely suspect. Although married to a French woman of good family, farming the land and playing the seigneur, the Hungarian was regarded as an interloper and traitor. How much more difficult for those without local ties to rise above the suspicion and fear of local communities, for whom the weapon of denunciation was always to hand. In this instance, the notables and authorities, who no doubt moved in the same circles as Strausz and his wife, did not give credence to the gossip of the community. Had they done so, as both Vichy and the German authorities did in other cases, the outcome would doubtless have been very different.

War and occupation saw the progressive exclusion from the local and national community of travelers, foreigners, Jews, communists, and Freemasons. On the eve of the German offensive, in April 1940, the French republican government prohibited what it called "nomads," defined as those "without home, or country, or proper occupation," from traveling the country. These gypsies were seen to be a risk to "national defense and the protection of secrets" and were to be interned. The French government distinguished them from "forains," defined as traveling traders and artisans, who "for the most part had honorable reputations." The German military, however, made no such distinction and in November 1940 banned traveling traders, too.[2]

Any foreigners, as the case of the Hungarian Strausz shows, were liable to persecution in wartime. Most vulnerable were foreign Jews, who accounted for 70 percent of the Jewish population of 300,000 in France before the war. In the Gentile imagination they already suffered from being nomadic and immigrant, to which all the traditional prejudices heaped on Jews had to be added. They had come in waves: Russian, Romanian, and Polish Jews after pogroms in the 1880s, Baltic, Hungarian, and more Romanian and Polish Jews after the formation of the new national states of Eastern Europe following the collapse of the Russian and Austro-Hungarian empires in 1917–18, and German Jews after the triumph of the Nazi party in 1933.[3] Among the German Jewish refugees were the interlocking families of Abraham, Rothschild, Grumbacher, and Meier, who fled to France in 1934. Rather than live in the town, they bought the abandoned estate of Sainte-Radegonde in the village of Chênehutte-les-Tuffeaux, near Saumur, and began to farm it. Though they were hardworking and discreet, they stood out as an exotic little colony in the garden of France and were repeatedly denounced to the authorities for spying. In 1939, with the outbreak of war, the four fathers were rounded up and interned as a security risk, leaving only the patriarch Albert Abraham and his wife, Lina, both seventy-three, their three daughters—Selma Rothschild, Fanny Grumbacher, and Martha Meier—and their daughter-in-law, Erny Abraham, and nine children, aged twelve to nineteen.[4] Other Jews who left Germany later, in 1939, wanted only to get out of Europe. Over 500 German Jews armed with visas for the United States left Saint-Nazaire in May 1939 on the *Flandre*, only to be turned back from Havana and forced to return to Saint-Nazaire. There the neediest were looked after by the Jews of Nantes, through their Refugee Assistance Committee.[5]

In October 1940, after the Germans ordered a census of all Jews in the Occupied Zone, there were 736 Jews in Loire-Atlantique, overwhelmingly in Nantes and Saint-Nazaire, 314 (43 percent) of them foreign, particularly Poles (93), Germans or Austrians (73), Romanians (30), Turks (27), and Russians (24). In Maine-et-Loire, there were many fewer Jews, 231 French and 57 foreign. These included the Sternchuss family of Angers, for example, composed of two Polish grandparents, their son David, born in Warsaw in 1893, and his young wife, Regina, born in Budapest in 1913—both described as of "indeterminate" nationality—and their five children, born in Angers between 1931 and 1940.[6] In Indre-et-Loire, there were 372 French Jews, 46 children of foreign Jews registered as French, and 185 foreign Jews, half of whom were Polish.[7] This number, however, was soon to be increased. Many foreign Jews who had settled in the main cities of eastern France—Nancy, Metz, and Strasbourg—were advised by the French government to evacuate to Bordeaux when fighting broke out in May 1940. When the Germans occupied the Atlantic coast, however, they decided that the foreigners crowded there constituted a security risk. Alsace-Lorraine had been annexed by Germany, and foreigners were forbidden to return there, so in December 1940 a group of 300 foreigners "of all social conditions, nationalities, and religions, mingling priests, nuns, intellectuals, workers, prostitutes, and about 120 gypsies," were processed and divided into foreign Jews and Polish Catholics, who were sent to the relatively open camp of La Lande, at Monts, south of Tours, and gypsies and other travelers put behind barbed wire in the camp of La Morellerie, at Avrillé-les-Ponceaux, near Langeais.[8]

In the demonology of occupied France, communists were second only to Jews. For the Germans, "Judaeo-Bolshevik" was often run together as the compound most dangerously opposed to the Third Reich. In France, communists were seen as a fifth column, controlled by Moscow, now building the Popular Front to drag France into a disastrous war with Germany, now allying cynically with Germany under the Nazi-Soviet Pact to leave France totally exposed to Hitler. The French government replied by dissolving the French Communist Party in September 1939 but the communists continued to be feared as a clandestine movement that could strike at any time. The Nantes police chief reported in October 1940:

> It is certain that the ex-communists have not disarmed but are continuing their disastrous propaganda under the cloak. At the moment I am having the Café d'Alsace in the rue Jamin watched. It is run by an Abel Detée, whose clientele consists of a certain number of individuals who belonged to the former Communist Party or who subscribe to extreme views. Five or six of them meet frequently to discuss politics, sometimes for several hours. One of them is Paul Gautier, a boilermaker, living at 6, rue de Bourgneuf, who is suspected of having distributed copies of a tract called *Workers and Ordinary People of France*.[9]

A month or so later, with no letup in the leaflet campaign aimed at factories in the Nantes–Saint-Nazaire area, the police launched a series of raids and interned thirteen communists. This only provoked a graffiti campaign in January 1941, with "Power to Thorez!," "Soviets everywhere!," and "The USSR will win!" daubed in red paint, particularly in the Barbin district of the city, which was worrying the police. More raids in Nantes followed, but with the German invasion of Russia in June 1941 things threatened to get out of hand. To cut off the slogans movement, thirty-four communist militants were arrested and interned in the camp of Choisel near Châteaubriant, once used for POWs but now given over to holding communists from all over France.[10]

The police had their favorite communist suspects from before the war, but the picture was changing quickly as young people became involved and new tactics were tried. When copies of a tract called *L'Avant-Garde* began to inundate letter boxes in Tours and Saint-Pierre-des-Corps, the prefect reported that "we are faced by a new occult organization, difficult to catch at work because of the blackout in the streets and the speed of the operation. It nevertheless appears that these tracts have been brought from Paris by railway workers." Brought they may have been by railway workers, but they were distributed by youths such as the two boys of Tours Higher Primary School, one of whom carried a revolver. The prefect realized that the French Communist Party in Touraine was being revamped with "very young people unknown to the police," "young fanatics pushed forward by former militants who organize them while remaining in the shadows."[11]

Another feature of the secret communist movement in the region that exercised the authorities was the fact that it was not confined to urban or industrial areas but appeared in a few rural pockets, too. In Maine-et-Loire, the slate quarries of Trélazé, outside Angers, were a center of communist agitation, but so was the village of Turquant, near Saumur. Bléré and the surrounding villages in the valley of the Cher, down the tracks from Saint-Pierre-des-Corps and close to the demarcation line, such as Dierre, nourished communist activity, as did the Loches area in the unoccupied part of Touraine. The communist schoolteacher of Dierre, M. Delanoe, was moved to another village, but the post of secretary of the *mairie* was then taken by Gabriel Bouffault, who found his twenty-one-year-old son, Robert, a job in the *mairie* of Bléré, even though both had been expelled from the Orléans area for communist activity. Gabriel was particularly friendly with Henri Berthelot, the rural policeman of Dierre, from whom he managed to get a demarcation line pass for locals. The police were concerned that the three of them could "pass at will from one zone to the other, serving as liaison agents between the communist and antigovernmental elements of both zones."[12] Meanwhile, in the Free Zone, the Loches area was a hive of communist activity. Secretaries of *mairies* such as Georges Moreau, seventy-five, of Montrésor, and Marceau Begasset of Saint-Senoch, whose wife, the postmistress, was just as dangerous, were joined by postman Alexandre Buret of Le Petit-Pressigny and artisans such as shoemaker Camille Pingault of Le Grand-Pressigny and Raymond Gabillet, a blacksmith of Perrusson. It was not industrial workers but state employees and artisans who were the prime movers of communism in the Loches area and, though few, they enjoyed wide support among the population.[13]

Jewry and communism were suspected as occult and tentacular organizations that were working insidiously and indefatigably against Vichy and the Germans. One other organization was regarded in the same way: Freemasonry. It was seen as a secret network of radical republicanism that had insinuated its members into positions of power and influence in the Third Republic, primed anticlerical attacks on the Catholic Church and its school system, opposed militarism and greatness, and generally led France down the slippery slope to defeat. Under laws of 13 August 1940 and 11 August 1941, Masonic lodges were banned and Masonic officers discovered in high places were ruthlessly "outed," having their names exposed in the *Journal Officiel* and the press. *La Dépêche* of Tours and *Le Petit Courrier* described as "highly instructive" a long list of Masonic dignitaries that appeared in the *Journal Officiel* of 15 August 1941. There were seventeen Blochs, eleven Cohens, and various Blums, Blumenthals, and Blumenfelds, a tempting convergence of Freemasonry and Judaism. Also named was Camille Chautemps, radical boss of Touraine and former prime minister. "French people will be stupefied to see this long list that brilliantly demonstrates the network that Masonry has woven in all branches of national activity in order to secure its disastrous domination of the country."[14] The corollary of this exposure was that any Freemason employed in the public service would immediately be dismissed. In this respect, declared Interior Minister

Pucheu, "Masonic dignitaries are assimilated to Jews." Freemasons holding any of the offices listed in article 2 of Statut des Juifs of 2 June 1941 would lose their jobs.[15] In the new Vichy order neither Masons nor Jews could hold any position of influence or authority. Whether after this they would be treated the same remained to be seen.

All these groups—gypsies and travelers, foreigners and Jews, communists and Freemasons—were excluded from national life as the price of national redemption. National unity as it was conceived by Vichy was founded on the persecution of such elements, whose sins were held to be responsible for France's ills and had to be purged so that France could be whole once again.[16] All were punished, some brutally, some with more discretion. Of course, the extermination of the Jews after 1942 was in a class apart. But until 1942 it is interesting to examine the process of marginalization and exclusion in a broad context, in order to search for similarities as well as differences. Were some kinds of punishment saved for one group rather than another, and were they meted out with equal efficiency and effectiveness?

The first stage of the purge was to dismiss Freemasons and Jews from positions of power and influence. Neither were permitted to remain as public servants, and salaried public servants were required to sign declarations—on pain of dismissal and loss of pension rights—that they were not Freemasons or Jews. A public official found to be a communist would certainly be dismissed, and that would be the least of his troubles. The same went for elected as for appointed officials. Robespierre Henault, the communist mayor of Saint-Pierre-des-Corps, was not only dismissed as early as 1939 but suffered a period of internment in 1941.[17] Camille Aron, mayor and councillor-general of Le Boulay in Touraine, was a winegrower and great supporter of farming: founder and president of two local mutual aid associations to insure cattle and protect against fire damage, member of the Chamber of Agriculture of Indre-et-Loire, and secretary-treasurer of the regional Crédit Agricole. He was also president of the League of Rights of Man in the department and Jewish. As a result, he was required to resign as mayor and councillor-general, and though the municipal council asked the government to make an exception given his twenty-eight years of service as mayor to the commune, to agriculture, and to the poor, its request was in vain.[18]

The punishment of Freemasons seems to have been less systematic than that of communists and Jews. True, the lay public-school system, which was fairly well riddled with Freemasons, especially in radical and anticlerical areas like Touraine and the Saumurois, was dealt a heavy blow. André Moreau of Vernoil-le-Fourrier, on the Saumurois-Touraine border, was dismissed as a Freemason from his teaching position in October 1941. The prefect then discovered that as secretary of the *mairie* he was "the effective mayor of the commune, which did nothing without consulting him and was even proposing to petition against the disciplinary measure I have just ordered."[19] Moreau was duly removed as secretary of the *mairie* as well. Two members of the municipal council of Tours—one of them an *adjoint* to Fernand Morin, a civil engineer, president of the building employers federation, and chevalier of the Legion of Honor—were also exposed as Freemasons and dismissed. But other Freemasons were harder to shift, generally for the very reason Vichy disliked them—namely, their influence and connections in the Third Republic. Some mayors in Touraine who were reputed to be Freemasons, such as Émile Gounin of Amboise and François Servant of La Haye Descartes, managed to hold on to their *mairies*. M. Déré, director of the hospital and hospice of Saumur and officer of the "Perseverence" Grand Orient lodge in the town, remained in his position because by some accident it was not one of those that Freemasons were not allowed to hold under the law of 11 August 1941. It was said that he had "*le bras long*, that he knows too many secrets and can't be touched." Though the lodge was officially dissolved, he gave it a phantom existence by continuing to hold meetings of up to seventeen members, including former mayor Robert Amy, at the hospital. When the concierge reported Déré to the police, Déré demonstrated his influence by having her taken to court and evicted. She was left to meditate on the conundrum "I have always done my duty but have to bow to M. Déré, who was an official of the Perseverence lodge of Saumur."[20] Even more telling as an example of influence was the case of Michel Legeron, a police chief who was transferred from Bordeaux to Angers in 1940. When he was exposed as a Freemason in 1942, prefect Roussillon dismissed him forthwith, only to receive a scalding riposte from secretary-general of police René Bousquet, who said that the administration of the national police service was his responsibility and the prefect's order was thus null and void.[21] This champion of a Masonic policeman was of course the same Bousquet who four months previously, in conjunction with the SS, had organized the mass roundup of foreign Jews in Paris.

The occasional communist functionary seems to have been able to hold on to his position. The mayors of Dierre and Bléré were summoned by prefect Tracou to be instructed to dismiss Gabriel and Robert Bouffault, respectively the secretary of the *mairie* of Dierre and an employee of the *mairie* of Bléré. The mayor of Dierre said he would dismiss Bouffault *père* when he had found a replacement; the mayor of Bléré simply failed to attend the meeting.²² Other communists were less fortunate. Marceau Begasset lost his job as secretary of the *mairie* of Saint-Denoch, near Loches, and his wife was dismissed as postmistress. He was then reported by the police for frequenting café owner Abraham Crespin, who was known as a former communist, and for ceaselessly criticizing the mayor. The prefect of Indre, who was in charge of the nonoccupied part of Indre-et-Loire, duly ordered his internment.²³

At the other extreme was the case of Claude Millot, an employee of the Indirect Tax Office in Nantes. Investigated as a suspected communist late in 1940, he was said by his boss to have once been the secretary of the Chantenay cell in the industrial suburbs but to be no longer active. Regional prefect Roussillon was not convinced and ordered the Sûreté to reopen the dossier. This time the Sûreté confirmed that he was politically retired, but it was still decided that he would be transferred to Le Havre. At this point Millot went underground and he was arrested by the Sûreté in August 1942. Now it was argued that he was the "intellectual" behind the terrorist wing of the Communist Party in the Nantes region. He was handed over to the Germans, who tried forty-one other suspected members of the terrorist wing by court-martial in January 1943, and was one of the thirty-seven then shot.²⁴

Communists in the public service were considered a security risk by both the French and the German authorities and thus liable to the most extreme sanctions. Jews were considered, at least at the beginning of the war, less as a security risk than as an evil cancer that explained France's present predicament. While the Germans wanted above all to exclude them from economic life, the French wanted to exclude them from public life and influence. Vichy's Statut des Juifs of 3 October 1940, developed by that of 2 June 1941, removed Jews from employment in the public services and the media and subjected them to strict quotas in the liberal professions. Just as significant as the substance of the measures, however, was the way they were implemented. The law was applied suddenly and brutally to individuals who had been excellent public servants and were fully integrated into the French national community. Of the 2,000 employees of the municipality of Nantes, only three individuals declared that they were Jewish: Eva Dreyfus, who had been an army nurse in 1918, Marie Faigenbaum, who was only eighteen, and Jean Sofer, a naturalized Romanian in the police service. Sofer visited the head of personnel to say that he was "on good terms with the Occupation forces and counted on the goodwill of the administration not to throw him onto the street." "Unfortunately," added the head of personnel in his report, "the law is the law," and the acting mayor of Nantes, a socialist named Prieur, noted in the margin, "Alas, yes."[25] All three were dismissed as the administration took refuge behind the black and white of the regulations.

If the law had been applied according to clear bureaucratic rules, that would have been at least a step in the right direction. Only too often, however, French and German authorities cynically ignored the rules they had invented for themselves. The rules defining Jewishness were admittedly contradictory. Built into the legislation was a tension between Judaism as a religion and Jewishness as a question of race. The German ordinance of 27 September 1940, which imposed a census of all Jews in France, defined a Jew as someone who belonged to the Jewish religion or had at least three Jewish grandparents. The Statut des Juifs said nothing about religion and defined a Jew as someone with three Jewish grandparents or, alternatively, two Jewish grandparents, if his or her spouse was Jewish.[26] Many Jews in France did not practice their religion or had converted to Roman Catholicism but this made no difference in practice as far as the German authorities were concerned. The Feldkommandant of Tours told the prefect that he must issue identity cards stamped with the word *Juif* or *Juive* to Jews who had been at some point baptized in the Catholic faith. "Baptism," he declared, "has no effect."[27]

Neither did such niceties make much difference to Vichy officials. When twenty-year-old Pierre Terrier, an interpreter at the Saumur town hall, was dismissed on instruction of the German authorities, who had learned of his Jewish background, inquiries began into the Jewishness of his mother, Marcelle Terrier née Geissmann, who had a haberdashery and hosiery shop in Saumur. Mme Terrier told the Saumur police that she was not Jewish, because neither she nor her parents had ever practiced the Jewish religion; "she persisted with this simplistic solution," said the police chief, "and with the impossibility of proving her ancestry" because her parents had been born in Mulhouse, Alsace, which had now been annexed by the Germans. Subprefect Milliat asked the Kreiskommandantur in Saumur whether they could look up her racial origins in Mulhouse, but the Germans replied roundly that it was up to Mme Terrier to provide proof of her non-Jewishness—and within three weeks. Prefect Roussillon told subprefect Milliat that "whether an individual practices or does not practice the Jewish religion need not be taken into account," and Milliat later came around to the view that Mme Terrier was Jewish. The only evidence she had offered to the contrary was the testimony of several rabbis who said that her parents did not practice the Jewish religion, "which obviously has nothing to do with the question of race", said Milliat, just as the fact that "recently she has been ostensibly going to mass" was completely irrelevant.[28]

Since the Revolution, French citizenship had been based on the idea that membership in the French national community was an act of will, underpinned by a readiness to assimilate French language and culture and to fight and shed blood for the *patrie* if necessary. Religion was regarded as a private matter and ethnic origin was not considered a definition of Frenchness. The emancipation of the Jews at the Revolution meant that they could acquire full citizenship, become educated and assimilated, practice their religion or not as they liked, and defend the home of the Rights of Man on the battlefield. The Statut des Juifs gave some grudging recognition to this. Exceptions could be made, allowing Jews to remain in the public service or professions, if they had been decorated in the 1914–18 or 1939–40 wars, had received the Legion of Honor for military reasons, or had made a significant contribution to the French state in the fields of science, arts, or letters. Whether or not these exceptions were granted in practice, however, was another matter.

René Ross was dismissed under the Statut des Juifs from his teaching position at the École Pratique, or technical college, of Saint-Nazaire in the autumn of 1940. His family came from Alsace and both his grandfathers had been wounded in the war of 1870. When Alsace was annexed by Germany in 1870, his grandfathers opted for French citizenship and moved to France. René was born in Béziers in 1891, was educated at the École Supérieure d'Électricité, and published papers on electricity and ballistics. He had a glorious military record, winning the Croix de Guerre and the Croix du Combattant in both 1914–18 and 1939–40 and the Legion of Honor for military services. He joined the Socialist Party (SFIO) in 1914 but was a moderate. He disapproved of the factory occupations in Saint-Nazaire in 1936 and left the SFIO for the Radical Party, for which he was a regional delegate. Though Jewish, he converted to Protestantism in 1938. He qualified for exemption under the Statut des Juifs because he met not just one criterion but all four of the military and scientific criteria. And as he wrote to Marshal Pétain, "I had the honor and pride to serve under your orders at Verdun. . . . I appeal to your exalted sense of justice." Ross gained the support not only of the director of the École Pratique but also of the head of education in Loire-Inférieure and even prefect Dupard, who was no soft touch. To no avail. The Conseil d'État ruled that, although his scientific publications were "remarkable," they did not have the necessary brilliance to merit exemption, whatever that meant. His military honors evoked no patriotic recognition and his conversion to Protestantism was simply not considered. In December 1941 Ross appeared on a list of Jewish hostages against whom reprisals would be taken if terrorist attacks continued. He wrote angrily to the prefect protesting at any suggestion that he might be the accomplice of murderers who shot German soldiers in the back. He had fought the Germans for six years, he said, but always "face to face"; he was "as French as anyone else." But definitions were shifting. To be a citizen, totally assimilated, and a patriot was now not enough to qualify as French. Jewish blood disqualified one, and the exceptions written into the Statut des Juifs to give weight to services rendered in patriotic blood were not worth the paper they were written on. On 18 January 1942 Ross was arrested by the Germans.[29]

Losing their employment in the public sector was only one part of the persecution meted out to Jews. Their private businesses and other property were also confiscated. While the French authorities were more interested in eliminating Jews from positions of power and influence, the Germans wanted to destroy their place in the economy. The German ordinance of

27 September 1940 that imposed the census also required all Jewish businesses to put up a yellow sign in the window saying, *Jüdisches Geschäft/Entreprise juive*. A second ordinance, on 18 October 1940, defined a Jewish business as having one Jewish associate or partner or, if it was a limited-liability company, a third of its directors or shareholders. These businesses were to be placed under the management of an Aryan administrator and to display a red notice. To close even more loopholes, a third ordinance, on 26 April 1941, stated that no one in a senior position in a business or in contact with the public, such as a shop assistant or an artisan who sold his goods in his shop, could be Jewish.[30]

There were many equivalents of René Ross in business who obediently put up their yellow sign but appended to it some remark that they were war veterans and had been wounded or decorated. The German authorities were incensed by this practice and ordered it stopped. Prefect Dupard, meanwhile, was anxious that such signs would be a provocation to anti-Semites and provoke a wave of window breaking; he instructed the police to keep a close watch on Jewish businesses.[31] The Germans were also impatient to see all the signs put up by the deadline of 1 November and keen to sniff out businesses that were Jewish but had not declared themselves as such. Again Dupard tried to offer some protection to the businessmen of Nantes, telling Dr. Rheinfels of the Feldkommandantur, for example, that Petrus and Einar Mosesson were not Jews but Swedish Protestants, while the forebears of Raoul Leclerc, a manufacturer of car radiators, were "pure Aryans, belonging to old French and Catholic stock from the west of France."[32]

It may seem surprising that when it came to the "Aryanization" of Jewish businesses, the French public could be a good deal more anti-Semitic and mercenary than the French administration. The labor inspector of Maine-et-Loire, Lehlmann, refused to organize a census of Jewish employees in private firms with a view to dismissing them, saying that his job was to protect workers.[33] By contrast, Édouard Laraia, who owned the Café de la Ville in Saumur, saw the opportunity to deal with a rival by complaining to the subprefect that "the Jew Lazare Schnerb" had not yet put up a yellow sign on his Hotel-Bar Budan. Asked by the police what proof he had that Schnerb was Jewish, Laraia could only reply that when he had called him a "dirty Jew" Schnerb had not replied. The police reported that it would be necessary to ask Schnerb directly whether he was Jewish but that he was currently in Pau.[34]

In larger firms, which ran the risk of being Aryanized if they had a Jewish partner, non-Jewish partners regularly turned on their Jewish colleagues and forced them out. In Nantes, the Société Parisienne de Confection was 92 percent owned by the Galeries Lafayette, itself Jewish, and three of its directors—Bernheim, Blum, and Meyer—were also Jewish. Bernheim and Meyer resigned and Blum, who refused to go, was dismissed by an extraordinary meeting in October 1940. Meanwhile nearly 60 percent of the shares were bought by the Crédit Commercial de France. Instead of waiting to be Aryanized, businesses promptly Aryanized themselves in order to avoid complications.[35]

Aryanization involved the appointment of non-Jewish provisional administrators to manage and ultimately sell Jewish businesses. Those who participated gave a clear and material sign that they were prepared to make themselves rich on the backs of the Jews. The Chamber of Commerce of Saumur proposed the notary Louis Raimbault to manage the few Jewish businesses in the town; the chambers of commerce of Angers and Cholet were reluctant to become involved, but mainly because they saw that the best option from their point of view was to give the Jews a little more time to liquidate their businesses and release scarce stocks onto the market.[36] Some of the fine flower of the Catholic elite did not hesitate to seek or recommend appointment. In Angers, for example, Viscount Palamède de la Grandière, senator and stalwart of the Catholic League of Anjou, wrote to his "dear friend" Xavier Vallat, head of the Commissariat Générale aux Questions Juives (CGQJ), to recommend a client as an administrator (unsuccessfully, as it happened). The task of administering Jewish businesses in Angers essentially fell to the very Catholic Charles Poisson, appropriately enough a bankruptcy lawyer, who took over four firms— mainly in ladies' fashions—in the spring of 1942, and his cousin Pierre Poisson, who was in charge of seven.[37] When it came to selling off the businesses there was no shortage of takers crowding like vultures for easy pickings. The prefect of Loire-Inférieure had a very full mailbox. The Federation of Furriers wrote asking to dismantle the fur trade in Loire-Inférieure and shift the stock to Paris. The Organization Committee of the Leather Industry wanted to take over all the tanneries and shoe and leather-goods factories. Individuals also wrote in. Marcel Bourguignon of Brest wanted a shoe, fine leather, shirt, or souvenir shop. Eugène Hue of Paris wanted only a shirt business. M. Hincelin of Drancy wanted an electrical business while Mme Richard of Paris was looking for any hotel, boardinghouse, or shop in the Nantes–Saint-Nazaire area. She was put in touch with Gabriel Hervouet, the provisional administrator in Saint-Nazaire, for hotels were still up for grabs. Most inquirers, however, were disappointed: the businesses had already been sold.[38] The details of the process of Aryanization provide hard evidence of the anti-Semitism of at least a portion of French people, including the wealthy and privileged, a conclusion that goes against the grain of some recent writing that tends to blame the Vichy regime while exculpating the people.[39]

The relentless persecution, which gradually closed down opportunities for Jews to make an honest living, drove them into poverty, clandestine activity, and despair. After the German ordinance of 26 April 1941, only artisans and workers who had no contact with the public were allowed to continue. On the estate of Sainte-Radégonde in Chênehutte-les-Tuffeaux, Marion Abraham and Sédi Grumbacher were permitted in June 1941 by the German authorities to continue as seamstresses working for a Mme Drais in Saumur, while Ernest Meier was authorized to work for his parents as a farmhand. In Angers, however, David Sternschuss, an artisan tailor with five children, was told to finish his current orders by the end of August 1941 and to accept no new ones.[40] Some Jewish entrepreneurs tried to find ways around the throttling restrictions. M. Katz of Angers, whose jewelry business had been sold in March 1941, continued to work from home, until he was found out and told by the secretary-general of the prefecture that if he continued to work "he would risk punishment, including internment in a concentration camp."[41] The clandestine economy worked best when non-Jews were economically dependent on Jews rather than rivals. Adrien Geismar was a Jew who had taken over the running of the shoe factory of Francis Chené in Saint-Florent-le-Viel in the Mauges in 1936, when it was on the verge of bankruptcy, and totally rebuilt it. In June 1941 Chené told the authorities that Geismar was a "commercial technician specializing in the receipt, inspection, and use of raw materials necessary to the factory" who had no contact with the public. Prefect Roussillon accepted this formula but the Paris-based police who dealt with Jewish questions reported that "Francis Chené is always present but the business is run financially and commercially by Geismar," who was even trying to take over a shoe factory in a neighboring village.[42]

Systematically and ruthlessly, the German and French authorities expelled Jews from the economy and, when they resorted to the black market, clamped down on them as criminals. In April 1941 Vichy asked prefects to intern a number of foreign Jews "known for their antinational attitude, who had entered the country illegally, particularly after 1 September 1939, and whose absence of resources makes them a burden on the national economy." No reason was given, and it can only be assumed that it was to intensify the climate of fear. Prefect Dupard reviewed a number of victims in his bailiwick. He passed over the Horowitz family, who had come from Berlin in 1939 and were living off their own resources while waiting for a U.S. visa so they could join their daughter in Cleveland. Likewise he passed over Dina Garber, a Russian Jew who was living with her son on a small pension after her business was closed down. In the end he decided to intern a Portuguese Jew named Michael Fresco and a Constantinople Jew, Isaac Hodara, former vanilla traders who now sat around in the cafés of Nantes "exchanging large sums of money the origin of which is unknown given that they have no occupation, so to speak." To make up numbers he also interned the Lithuanian Jew Mordacheff Gruseka, who since the closure of his business was living with his mistress, Mme Augureau. No bad reports had been received about him, although he had recently been fined a paltry fifty francs for complicity in the receipt of stolen goods.[43]

"France was not a gulag," asserted Abbé François Jammoneau, who was secretary to the bishop of Nantes under the Occupation, when I met him in 1997.[44] For those excluded for their sins from the national community, however, internment in a camp was a fact of life. In December 1940, as we saw earlier, the gypsies and travelers put on trains from Bordeaux to Tours were interned at La Morellerie, near Langeais, while the foreign Jews and Polish Catholics were sent to the La Lande camp in Monts, outside Tours, which had originally been built to house Vietnamese workers at the Ripault munitions factory. There the regime, organized by the prefecture, was initially fairly liberal. Some inmates were even allowed to live outside the camp, in the village of Monts or in Tours, so long as they reported once a week to the Kommandantur. They bathed in the Indre and went on walks and bicycle rides in the countryside, not least to collect supplies from farms to augment their meager diet. Between the Catholic Poles and Polish Jews there was no love lost. The Catholic Poles who worked at the Ripault factory protested that they were treated unfairly, given that there were nearly 500,000 Poles living free in France while they had the misfortune of being refugees. "We are not political detainees," they said, "and never have anything to do with the Jews."[45] The Jews fell back on their own devices, receiving gifts from Jewish communities in Bordeaux, Angoulême, and Poitiers and medical aid from a Jewish charity in Paris. A school and a nursery were opened, the children had dancing lessons, the adolescents courted, and some marriages were celebrated.[46] Jérôme Scorin, a young inmate of the camp, recalls that the Jews did terracing work inside and outside the camp and helped neighboring farmers thresh wheat in the summer of 1941. Prefect Chaigneau, on the other hand, reported that the Jews alone did not take part in horticultural work, "demonstrating once again that if the Jew excels in commerce, with very few exceptions he does not want to do manual work" and prefers the black market.[47]

All this changed in October 1941. The German authorities decided to reorganize their camp system. Foreign Jews were to be moved to the camps of Pithiviers and Beaune-la-Rolande in the Loiret, which were already filling up with foreign (mainly Polish) Jews arrested in Paris, while La Lande would be used to hold 500 communists from the Paris region. In the event, it was decided that only adult males would be sent to Pithiviers, a "stupefying decision" that would break families up. On the day the buses came, panic swept La Lande as the men were marched out. There were heart attacks and a miscarriage. A doctor certified thirty-eight men as unfit to travel and forty-five (including Jérôme Scorin) escaped. The German authorities were furious, pointing out that the bid for freedom of "these individuals from international nomadic tribes" should have been predicted and suggesting that "the mass escape had been tacitly and silently tolerated by the French authorities." They demanded the punishment of those responsible and the erection of barbed-wire fencing around the camp. The barbed wire was obtained from the La Morellerie camp, which was dismantled, and the gypsies and travelers moved to a new camp at Montreuil-Bellay, inside Maine-et-Loire. It had been used before the war to house Spanish republican refugees working at a local munitions factory and after the war was lost as a POW camp for French soldiers. By April 1942 there were over a thousand gypsies and travelers at Montreuil-Bellay, brought in from all over the west of France. Once the barbed wire had gone up around La Lande, meanwhile, it was decided to bring the men back from Pithiviers. "Knocking down the gates, jostling the gendarmes, who this time allowed themselves to be totally overwhelmed, great throngs of women and children threw themselves at the doors of the coach. That December, when even the sun wanted to play a part," wrote prefect Tracou with some emotion, "was and will remain for many, I am convinced, the finest day at the camp of La Lande."[48] The rejoicing was brief, however, because for the 300 foreign Jews held at La Lande the camp turned out to be an antechamber of Auschwitz.

Foreign Jews were interned merely because they were foreign Jews. They had sinned collectively against France and indeed Christendom, and there was no sense that they should undergo due process of law to establish individual guilt. With the communists there was still the notion that they had sinned individually, although the legal process that offered protection became more and more arbitrary. When Raymond Gabillet, the blacksmith of Perrusson, was arrested in October 1941, General Mouton, who commanded French forces in the Indre and unoccupied part of Indre-et-Loire, told the prefect in Tours that he preferred internment to trial because he regarded the *procureur* of the Republic in Loches as "feeble" and that, if Gabillet was acquitted by the courts, people in Loches would think that Vichy was not serious in its anticommunism.[49] The wobbliness of the ordinary courts was one reason Vichy invented "special sections" of its appeals courts to deal promptly with communists. These were perfectly capable of meting out harsher punishments than German military tribunals. The student from the Higher Primary School of Tours who was caught distributing tracts and possessing a revolver, for instance, was given one year in prison by the German military court but five years' forced labor by the Section spéciale of Orléans, with six months for his friend.[50] The Section spéciale of Angers sentenced Pierre Brocheteau, a thirty-five-year-old tax clerk, to five years in prison for leading a group of peasants of the Baugeois in a farmyard rendering of the "Internationale."[51] Désiré Gauchais, a blacksmith from Turquant, near Saumur, and a communist, was found to be storing piles of subversive tracts; first interned in Fontevrault prison, he was sentenced to five years' imprisonment by the Section spéciale of Angers.[52] Others were simply interned without further ado. The magic of the internment was that it was an administrative decision, not a judicial one, taken by a prefect, not by a court. Increasingly, communists, like Jews, became the victims of internment decisions, without further legal process.

Over a period of three weeks in May 1941, more than 200 communists arrived at the camp of Choisel, outside Châteaubriant. They came from both small local centers like Le Croisic on the Breton coast and Laval and large centers such as the former abbey of Clairvaux, Poissy, or La Santé prison in Paris. The population of Châteaubriant was curious but in no way sympathetic. While traders relished the idea that business would expand with the size of the camp, ordinary citzens feared that there would be additional pressure on scarce foodstuffs. It was not that the camp had previously lain empty. Until January 1941 it had been a POW camp under German control, from which a stream of escapes had been organized by the prisoners support committee of Nantes.[53] Since then it had been used to house over 300 gypsies and travelers, together with a few score "undesirables," or common-law criminals, from Nantes or Paris: gangsters, pimps, and black marketeers. The undesirables tried to make overtures to the communists but were cold-shouldered. The communists considered themselves "a class apart, a caste that could revolutionize society." Although surrounded by barbed wire, the camp was not totally secure. On 19 June 1941 escapes were made by four gypsies, four undesirables, and five communists, including Fernand Grenier, deputy of the Parisian suburb of Saint-Denis, Eugène Hénaff, secretary of the CGT union of unions of the Paris region, and Léon Mauvais, a member of the Central Committee. Security was tightened, the number of gendarmes increased to sixty-five, and the barbed-wire fence raised higher. The gypsies and travelers were removed to a camp in Moisdon-la Rivière and replaced by communists, who numbered 564 in September 1941. Internal discipline was increased, with roll calls, unannounced searches, a curfew, and censorship of correspondence. It was impossible, however, to isolate the camp totally. News of the German invasion of the Soviet Union filtered through at 7:00 A.M. on 22 June 1941 from the radio of someone living near the camp. "The first reaction was stupor," reported the camp governor, "the second delirious joy, but since then there has been anxiety because the internees learn only of German victories."[54] The internees would have much more to be anxious about in the coming months. The entry of the Soviet Union into the war triggered a campaign of communist attacks on the Occupation forces in France, and the Occupation forces responded with a strategy of massive collective reprisals. Under this strategy, it was announced in September 1941, all communists interned by the French authorities, for whatever offense or none, were designated hostages who could be taken out and shot if reprisals were ordered.

Whereas in many ways, as we have seen, the Occupation drew communities together in a common enterprise of survival, it is also clear that the need to blame someone for the ills that had befallen France defined communities narrowly against outsiders. Mysterious international movements or groups were singled out for blame as fifth columnists and traitors. Freemasons, communists, and Jews were liable to lose their jobs and, in the case of Jews, their businesses. Communists and Jews who had become uprooted from their homes were liable to be interned. Influence counted for more than the rule of law. Thus Freemasons who should have been drummed out of office often managed to cling on by virtue of their connections, but Jews who might have retained their employment even under the laws Vichy made for itself were dismissed. Most serious of all, there is much evidence, particularly from the process of Aryanization, that Gentiles were quick to dump Jewish partners and only too happy to take over their businesses. Anti-Semitism, the evidence firmly shows, was not confined to the Vichy regime.

10

Murder

It *was still* dark in Nantes at 7:30 A.M. on Monday, 20 October 1941, when two German officers, having taken coffee at the Café du Nord, crossed the cathedral square on their way to work. As they entered the rue du Roi Albert, leading off the square, two young men emerged from the shadows and quickened their pace behind them. Two shots rang out. One of the officers exclaimed: "*Die Shuften!*" (The bastards!) and fell forward onto his face. As the second officer crouched over him, shouting for a doctor and a telephone, the two men dashed into the maze of narrow, ill-lit streets that surrounded the cathedral, jumped onto a streetcar that kindly slowed down for them on the rue de Strasbourg, and disappeared.[1]

Fifty years later, one of the assassins argued that his deed was "an act of war" that "unleashed armed resistance in the west of France."[2] The local population, one would imagine, was delighted to be rid of a member of the army of Occupation, the more so because the victim, as it turned out, was Lieutenant Colonel Karl Hotz, the Feldkommandant of Nantes. And yet this was far from the case. The immediate fear of the French authorities and citizens alike was that the Germans would inflict savage reprisals on the population, which they did. The authorities particularly regretted the assassination because the mayor and prefect had a good working relationship with the Feldkommandant. Hotz was especially appreciated by Edmond Duméril, interpreter at the prefecture, who noted in his diary, "I have lost a sure support with the Germans. He was a just, intelligent man who was in no sense a Hitlerian, a friend of the French and particularly considerate toward me, linked to him almost daily for over fifteen months as I was. Will the Nazis replace him with some odious Prussian saber rattler?"[3]

The immediate concern of the French authorities in Nantes was how to limit the wrath of the German military. The mayor, Gaëtan Rondeau, went to the Feldkommandantur at once to present his condolences, particularly to Captain Wilhelm Sieger, who had been walking with Hotz when he was shot. Hotz had been "just and good" to the Nantais, Rondeau declared, assuring the Germans that the assassin could not possibly have been French. He added that as mayor and head of the municipal police, he was at the disposal of the German authorities as a hostage. He got an icy reception and was told that the matter was far too serious to be resolved locally; decisions would be made in Paris and Berlin. At 10:00 A.M. the prefect, the corpulent M. Dupard, arrived to present his own condolences and returned at midday to present those of Vichy's ambassador in occupied Paris, Fernand de Brinon. Dupard's position as guarantor of the security of the Occupation forces was even more delicate. At 6:00 P.M. he was arrested by the Geheime Feldpolizei, or secret military police, and held overnight in the Lafayette prison while his offices were searched.

The message of the French authorities to the people of Nantes, alerted by poster, was was that the killing was a heinous act and that the culprits must be found. Everyone understood the desperate situation that would otherwise arise. The prefect's appeal paid homage to the "intelligent understanding" of Colonel Hotz and urged the people to "maintain the unity of the fatherland in loyalty, order, and dignity" by finding the guilty men. The appeal issued by the mayor and municipal council, which met in emergency session at 5:00 P.M., was even more explicit. They called the colonel "just, good, and welcoming," expressed their indignation at the "cowardly assassination," and urged the Nantais to demonstrate their own condemnation of the "odious crime" by helping to uncover the assassins.[4]

The citizens of Nantes reacted as they were supposed to, sending messages to the town hall and prefecture that were generally forwarded to the Feldkommandantur as evidence of their goodwill. One anonymous message on 21 October said that "under the circumstances there is no longer victor and vanquished but a defenseless foreigner who has been the victim of a cowardly attack within the walls of the city of Nantes. No Frenchman worthy of the name can remain indifferent to such a savage act, the honor and reputation of France itself being at stake." Similar condemnations of the murder came from the 350 members of the Union of Retailers, the Employers Associations of Loire-Inférieure, and the coordinating committee of the War Invalids of Loire-Inférieure.[5] The principal newspaper of the city, *Le Phare*, mixed its condemnation with clarification as to who the culprits might be:

> All good French people, all those who have a sense of honor, are outraged and have poured scorn on the criminals who acted under cover of darkness, shot from behind, and ran away. THE ASSASSINS MUST BE FOUND. . . . They belong to the small but fiercely active clan of agents paid by London and Moscow who, to cite General von Stülpnagel [military commander in France] himself, "have only one goal: to sew discord between the occupying power and the French population." He who shoots in the back German soldiers who are only doing their duty here is not a patriot but a cowardly murderer and the enemy of all respectable people. . . . Lieutenant Colonel Hotz was a great soldier with a magnificent past. Since his arrival in Nantes he always demonstrated qualities of tact, fairness, and generosity in his difficult task. We bow before his body, expressing here the sentiment of all French people worthy of the name.[6]

Le Phare was on the right path when it surmised that the assassins of Colonel Hotz were in the pay of London or Moscow. Communists in France, who had been disoriented by the Nazi-Soviet Pact in 1939, found their revolutionary and patriotic instincts once more coming together after the German invasion of the Soviet Union in June 1941. They sought to exploit the massive transfer of German soldiers to the eastern front by launching an armed struggle against the occupying forces in France. On 21 August 1941 a young Alsatian living in Paris, Gilbert Brustlein, was at the Métro station Barbès-Rocheouart, when Pierre Georges, alias Fabien, a veteran of the International Brigades, shot the naval adjutant Alfons Moser. The Germans demanded the execution of six hostages by way of reprisal, and to keep control of the situation the Vichy government agreed to set up a special court, which duly condemned six communist leaders to death. The cycle of attack and repression intensified, so that by the end of September fifty-eight hostages had been guillotined or shot. At this point the communist leadership decided to switch the campaign to the provinces, and commando groups were sent to Bordeaux, Rouen, and Nantes.[7] The Nantes commando team consisted of Gilbert Brustlein (twenty-two), Marcel Bourdarias (seventeen), and another former member of the International Brigades, Spartaco Guisco (thirty-one). Brustlein and Bourdarias took the train to Nantes on 16 October, independently of Spartaco, and dined regularly over the next few days at the Boîte à Sardines restaurant on the rue Paul Bellamy. In the early hours of 20 October, the three set explosive charges on the railway line at the western exit from Nantes, hoping to catch a trainload of German soldiers, then Brustlein and Spartaco walked into the center of town in search of their prey. In the attack Brustlein fired two shots at Hotz but Spartaco's revolver, aimed at Captain Sieger, jammed. As the Germans sealed off the town and began extensive searches, Brustlein and Spartaco left by the north and then separated. Brustlein walked north and slept in a haystack before boarding the train from Rennes to Paris.

The assassination of the Feldkommandant of Nantes may have been intended to trigger armed resistance but in the short term it set in train a strategy of repression that had been devised in advance by the highest German military authorities. On their arrival in France the Germans had instituted a hostage policy, keeping notables in a hotel overnight on a rotation basis as a guarantee against misbehavior. What was now planned was something completely different. On 16 September 1941 Field Marshal Wilhelm Keitel, chief of the Wehrmacht high command (OKW), issued a circular to the effect that communist insurgency constituted a danger to the German war effort and that the Führer had ordered that the severest measures be taken to crush it in the shortest time. Accordingly the assassination of one German soldier was to be answered by the execution of fifty to a hundred communists and "the manner of the execution was to increase the deterrent effect (*die abschreckende Wirkung*)." In response, General Otto von Stülpnagel, military commander in France, issued orders that all those held by the French authorities for communist or anarchist activities were now considered German hostages and could not be released without his consent. The head of each German military region was to draw up a list of 150 communist hostages, rising to 300–400 in greater Paris.[8] When the news of the assassination of Hotz reached the Führer's headquarters at 10:30 A.M. on 20 October, Keitel proposed that 100–150 hostages be shot and a reward offered of one million gold francs leading to the capture of the killer, so that the French would plead with London (he made no mention of Moscow) to refrain from future assassination orders. Stülpnagel was keen to retain some control of the crisis, to take national and local circumstances into account. He accepted 100 executions but fought for three days' grace to allow time for the murderer to be found. Hitler ruled at 2:00 P.M. that fifty hostages were to be shot at once and another fifty in forty-eight hours, should the criminal not be found.[9]

If communist hostages alone had been executed, local opinion in Nantes might have found the reprisals less difficult to bear. These were essentially outsiders, 564 of them held in the Choisel camp at Châteaubriant, forty miles away. But there was a tension among the German military occupying France between those who wished to punish communists alone and those who wished to enforce good behavior by executing a far wider spectrum of the French population. The thinking of this latter group placed at risk a local stock of noncommunists, namely, the veterans of a prisoner support committee who had organized the escape of scores of POWs from makeshift camps, including that of Châteaubriant, before POWs had been sent to Germany.[10] The ringleaders—including Léon Jost, decorated with the Legion of Honor, lawyers Alexandre Fourny and Fernand Ridel, a grade-crossing supervisor named Marin Poirier, and a secretary, Marcelle Litoux—were arrested in January 1941 and sent for trial by a German court-martial the following July, with Edmond Duméril pleading for the defense, which had to be in German. The Germans were torn between a strict application of martial law, echoing the treatment of Edith Cavell in the First World War, and the need to placate French opinion to ensure the success of the policy of collaboration. Six of the ringleaders, including Jost, Fourny, and Ridel, were sentenced to 3 years in prison for intelligence with the enemy, while Poirier got 4¹/₂ years. The defense appealed but in August the communist campaign of assassination took off. Poirier was again defended before the German court-martial by Duméril but was sentenced to death explicitly to intimidate (*abschrecken*) the French population. Despite pressure applied by Duméril and French magistrates on Hotz, the colonel was unable to prevent the execution of Poirier on 30 August but asked Duméril to send his condolences to the widow.[11] Jost, Fourny, and Ridel, in a Nantes prison, were now sitting targets.

On 21 October 1941 Otto von Stülpnagel announced the German decision on bloodred posters pasted all over the Occupied Zone:

> Cowardly criminals in the pay of London and Moscow shot the Feldkommandant of Nantes (Loire-Inférieure) on the morning of 20 October 1941. To date, the murderers have not been arrested. To expiate this crime I have ordered that fifty hostages will be shot in the first instance. In view of the gravity of the crime, fifty more hostages will be shot if the guilty parties are not arrested before 23 October at midnight. I am offering a reward totaling fifteen million francs to inhabitants who contribute to the arrest of the culprits.[12]

Controversy has centered in the question of the hostages on the extent to which the Vichy government was the powerless victim of events and how far it was actively involved in the repression. Certainly, national and local government were eager to catch the perpetrators. The city of Nantes offered a reward of 200,000 francs and the French government another 500,000 francs for information leading to the arrest. As for the choice of hostages, the French Ministry of the Interior, headed by Pierre Pucheu, had been involved from the announcement of the hostage policy in nudging the Germans toward placing particularly dangerous communists at the front of the firing line. One of Pucheu's envoys, Chassagne, made several visits to the Châteaubriant camp to inspect the register of internees and prepare lists. When, on 20 October, immediately after the assassination, the Kreiskommandant of Châteaubriant, the Pomeranian Captain Kristukat, demanded the register of internees from the French camp commandant, Pucheu and Chassagne immediately went into action in conjunction with the subprefect of Châteaubriant, Bernard Lecornu. After frantic telephoning they drew up a shortlist of sixty names, copies of which Lecornu took to Kristukat and Pucheu to Stülpnagel. The final decision was made at the regional level by the Abwehr, or military counterespionage, of Angers. It was concerned that the executions be a lesson not just for the communist party but for Nantes and the west of France as well. The twenty-seven names from the Châteaubriant camp were all communists, including a parliamentary deputy and Guy Môquet, the seventeen-year-old son of a second deputy, three local politicians, three trade union leaders, and five teachers. Three of the eighteen on the Nantes list were also communists but the majority was accounted for by the six veterans' leaders, including Jost, Fourny, and Ridel; two young resistants linked to London, Jean-Pierre Glou and Jean Grolleau; Michel Dabat, who had raised the tricolor on the cathedral on Armistice Day 1940; and a farmer who had been sentenced to death for not handing in his hunting rifle. Six names were added from Nantais held at the Fort de Romainville in Paris.[13]

Much was at stake at this tense moment of the Occupation when so many lives were in the balance. The policy of collaboration followed until then presupposed that the German military would allow French authorities some autonomy in decision making, so long as they guaranteed the security of the Wehrmacht. The beginning of armed resistance called all this into question. The practice of indirect rule that had functioned effectively for eighteen months seemed on the point of breakdown. A struggle took place between the supporters of direct confrontation, namely, the communist commandos and the staff of Hitler's headquarters behind the eastern front, and the supporters of accommodation and compromise, that is, the German military in France and the local and national French authorities. The former were reluctant to make decisions in a purely military light but paid attention to the wider political context. The latter held on to the shred of hope that their claim to deliver local loyalty still counted for something and that they might yet be able to influence German decisions.

There was some desperate last-minute negotiation when the names of the hostages became known to French officials on 22 October. Subprefect Lecornu tried to persuade Kristukat to remove Guy Le Môquet and two others who were due to be released, but Kristukat would agree only if Lecornu provided three substitutes, so he abandoned the bid. In Nantes, Duméril dashed between the Abwehr, Gestapo, and Feldkommandantur and managed to have Ridel and one other person removed from the list of hostages. Stülpnagel, for his part, was prepared to see the list reduced to forty-eight hostages without the substitution of new names.[14] At 3:00 P.M. prefect Dupard and Mayor Rondeau joined forces with the bishop of Nantes, Monsignor Villepelet, to send an address to Marshal Pétain to ask the Germans for clemency, but by that time the executions were under way.[15]

Toward noon on 22 October, Catholic priests were summoned to the prisons of Lafayette and Les Rochettes in Nantes to inform the hostages of their fate, giving them two hours to write to their families. As the hours passed, a reprieve seemed possible, but at 4:00 P.M. German soldiers arrived to take the sixteen hostages to the firing range of Le Bêle, outside Nantes, where they shot them in groups of three or four. At Châteaubriant, the French gendarmerie were brought inside the wire and ordered to fire without warning on any internee who refused orders. At 11:30 A.M. Kreiskommandant Kristukat arrived with eight Feldgendarmes carrying automatic weapons and asked for the twenty-seven designated hostages to be handed over. They were led to an empty hut, where subprefect Lecornu announced their fate. The curé of Saint Nicholas church refused to minister to atheists so another priest had to be found. The hostages told him that the Communist Party was to have its martyrs like the early Christian Church and that they were happy to die to make France a better place. At 2:30 P.M. the SS arrived in a truck and drove the hostages away. They were taken through the center of Châteaubriant, singing the "Marseillaise," much to the distress of the townspeople, on their way to the quarry, where stakes had been erected. They were shot in three batches of nine, shouting, "Vive la France!" before each volley.

No Frenchman was present at the executions. Neither were the names of the victims known until they were published in the papers on 23 October. The father of one of the Nantes victims, Michel Dabat, choked on his morning coffee when he learned that his son had been shot. The brother

Refugees in the Loire area, June 1940 (AD M-et-L)

Tours after the bombardment of June 1940 (AD I-et-L)
The price of military resisitance in French towns was bombardment by advancing German forces. For this reason, mayors were keen to have their towns recognized as "open towns" that would not be defended.

War Memorial of Nantes, destroyed 30–31 August 1940 (AD L-A)

Lieutenant Colonel Hotz reviews his troops in Nantes. (AM Nantes)
The German military dramatized its superiority in regular reviews such as this.

Feldkommandantur 588 in Tours (AD I-et-L)
Feldkommandanturen, units of the German military administration, were regularly moved from one part of the Reich to another. FK 588 remained in Tours for about eighteen months.

Heroes' Memorial Day celebration
in an Angers ceremony (BAMA)

Marinette Rameau (collection of Mlle Rameau)
This young woman appreciated the culture and manners of the German officers billeted on her family home.

Angevin POWs in Pomerania (AD M-et-L)
The absence of one and a half million French soldiers held in German POW camps divided many families.

Tobacco line, Touraine (AD I-et-L)
The difficulty of obtaining necessities through regular channels was the main reason for the flourishing black market.

Requisition of horses, Cholet (AD M-et-L)
French peasants claimed that Gallic cunning and passive resistance frustrated the regular requisitioning of horses.

Bronze statues at Angers station awaiting transport for meltdown (AD M-et-L)
For some aesthetes the removal of many manifestations of the "statue mania" of the Third Republic was a good idea, but for most it was a humiliating blow to national pride.

André Roussel's clandestine band, Bléré (collection of M. Rousel, pictured on right)
The young people of occupied France agreed on one thing: nothing was going to stop them from enjoying themselves.

Dr. Paul Guillaume-Louis (collection of Émile Aron)
Director of the Tours Medical School and radical politician

The Marquis de la Ferronnays
(commune of Saint-Mars-la-Jaille)
Uncrowned king of the Catholic royalists in southern Brittany, the marquis became a bastion of the local Vichy establishment but had the misfortune to be later designated a collaborator.

Senator Anatole Manceau, by Richard Reimans, 1943 (Société des Sciences, Lettres, et Arts de Cholet et de Sa Région)
Senator, president of the Cholet Chamber of Commerce, and press baron, this notable had numerous run-ins with the Vichy authorities but was unable to convince the Liberation authorities that he had resisted in any way.

Marshal Pétain receives a delegation of mayors from Touraine in Vichy, October 1943 (AD I-et-L)
This ritual cultivation of community leaders by the national leader came at a time when local communities were increasingly thrown back on their own resources in their dealings with the German authorities.

Unveiling the statue of Vendean hero Jacques Cathelineau, Le Pin en Mauges, March 1943 (commune of Le Pin-en-Mauges)
The collapse of the anticlerical Third Republic gave Catholic conservatives the opportunity to renew the cult of local heroes who had opposed the French Revolution.

Our Lady of Boulogne in Saint-Florent-le-Viel, Anjou, May 1944 (collection of
Michel Lemesle)
*The tour of France by three different statues of Our Lady of Boulogne resonated
with the sense of guilt and desire for redemption of the Catholic faithful.*

The camp of La Lande in Monts, outside Tours (collection of Jérôme Scorin, pictured
third from right)
*Conditions in internment camps were intially not too harsh, but before long they
were closed by barbed wire and became antechambers of Auschwitz.*

Body of the Feldkommandant of Nantes, Lieutenant Colonel Hotz, October 1941 (AM Nantes)
The killing led to the execution of forty-eight hostages; desperate negotiations averted the execution of a second batch of victims.

Funeral of German soldier shot in rue du Hallebardier, Tours, February 1942 (AD I-et-L)
The death of this ordinary German soldier led to reprisals as well, though the Germans targeted Jews and communists to minimize the alienation of local communities.

Rue du Calvaire, Nantes, after the Allied air raids of September 1943 (AM Nantes)
Allied bombing of military installations was some-times inaccurate, and Vichy made considerable propaganda capital out of civilian casualties.

Monsignor Costes and regional prefect Donati comfort mourners after the
Whitsun air raid on Angers, 1944 (AD M-et-L)
*The rapprochement of Church and state under Vichy is admirably captured by
this poignant scene following an Allied air raid that hit a church close to the
railway yards of Angers.*

Maillé (Touraine) after the massacre of 25 August 1944
*German reprisals became much more arbitrary in the summer of 1944, as ill-
disciplined units wreaked vengeance on communities suspected of harboring
"terrorists."*

Michel Debré as *commissaire de la République*, Angers, August 1944 (AD M-et-L)
*De Gaulle's representative (and the future prime minister) at his desk in the
prefecture of Angers. Debré consciously embodied the new legitimacy although,
like many other officials at the Liberation, he had also served Vichy.*

Liberation of Angers, 11 August 1944. Debré is no. 1, Mayor Bernier no. 4.
(AD M-et-L)
*The wizened mayor of Angers, who had "saved" the town by concluding a
truce with the Germans in June 1940, welcomed the Americans four years later.*

Liberation of Tours, 1 September 1944. Jean Meunier and Robert Vivier climb
the steps of the Hôtel de Ville. *(La Nouvelle République)*

Le Coz and his Maquis *(La Nouvelle République)*
The forgettable face of the Resistance: Le Coz, whose Maquis band controlled the Loches area of Touraine, was subsequently shot as a common criminal.

Jacques Chombart de Lauwe/Colonel Félix (collection of Isabelle de Paysac)
The divided face of the Resistance: while Colonel Félix commanded Resistance forces in the Saint-Nazaire area, his alter ego, Chombart de Lauwe, orchestrated the transition of the right in southern Brittany from Vichy to the Fourth Republic.

Country children near Angers sing the "Marseillaise", 6 June 1944 (Violette Lemasson)
The Normandy landings were eagerly greeted, although Violette Lemasson, one of the girls pictured here, said the Occupation in her small village had not brought undue hardship.

Surrender of the German forces of the pocket of Saint-Nazaire at Bouvron, 11 May 1945

General de Gaulle lays a wreath at the monument to the
Marquis of Saffré, June 1950. (collection of Pierre Hervé)
*The unveiling of monuments in the years after the war
was central to the construction of the story of the Resistance.*

Gilbert Brustlein, seventy-two, revisits
the rue du Roi-Albert, Nantes.
(collection of Louis Oury)
*Brustlein, who fired the shot that
killed Feldkommandant Hotz on 20
October 1941, returned to the scene
fifty years on. He received a hostile
reception from the citizens of Nantes,
who considered him an outsider who
had brought them little but grief.*

General Leclerc greeted by the curé and mayor of Grugé l'Hôpital and the
subprefect of Segré (Anjou), September 1946
*General Leclerc returned as a local hero to the small commune in Anjou where
in 1940 he had been issued a pass to the Free Zone.*

Unveiling of statue of General Leclerc in Grugé l'Hôpital, 1980
*By erecting this statue of General Leclerc, the village, which had an uncommonly
quiet Occupation, solidified its association with a hero of the Free French.*

Unveiling a new plaque at the camp of La Lande, December 1995 (Collége de Monts)
The original plaque marking the internment camp made no mention of the Jews held there; it took three years' of campaigning to rectify this omission. Serge Klarsfeld is on the prefect's left.

Students from the College of Monts at La Lande, December 1995 (Collége de Monts)
According to some Resistance leaders, the Resistance has now been replaced by the Holocaust as the dominant memory of the Occupation period, especially among young people.

of another victim, Jean Grolleau, could not refrain from calling two Germans traveling on the same streetcar "bastards" and was promptly arrested.[16] The ambivalence of the public was pinpointed by one police report, which said, "The population openly condemns the act of the assassin [of Hotz] and hopes that the search is successful. But the punishments inflicted by the German authorities have sown consternation everywhere. No one accepts that the act of a criminal on the run should be paid for by such a large number of human lives."[17]

Immediately, battle was joined to obtain a reprieve for the fifty more hostages who were destined to be executed if the killers of Hotz were not found by midnight on the twenty-third. A number of fresh arrests had been made, including that of the socialist former deputy mayor of Saint-Nazaire, François Blancho, who had resigned over his disagreement with the government of Admiral Darlan. Marshal Pétain drafted a message to Hitler saying that he was ready to go to the demarcation line and surrender to the Germans as the one and only hostage, but he was dissuaded by his ministers, led by Pucheu. Instead he made a broadcast to remind the French people that the armistice by which they had laid down their arms still held and that they had no right to shoot Germans in the back. Only continued collaboration with the Germans could make the Occupation tolerable, he said; the foreigners who had ordered the killing of Hotz wanted only to hurt France and had no concern for the grief it caused "our widows, our orphans, our prisoners." "Frenchmen," he said, "your duty is to stop the slaughter. . . . I appeal to you with a broken voice: 'Do not allow any more harm to be done to France.' "[18]

Marshal Pétain was not the only person to offer himself as a sacrificial lamb. Mlle Paulette Benoîte, a teacher at the Nantes Conservatory, said that she "belonged to a milieu in which young women, even at the age of thirty-eight, have no experience of public life." She asked to be taken to the Kreiskommandant of Nantes to offer herself, for no other reason than "my private veneration of the marshal and the simple calculation that my life is less useful than that of fifty men." She spoke for some time with the Kreiskommandant, Major von Hasselbach, who deplored the execution of the veterans and believed that those in high places had no inkling of their status, but her offer was politely refused.[19] The trio of prefect, mayor, and bishop of Nantes made a personal call on the Feldkommandantur in the afternoon of 23 October. They were received by Lieutenant Colonel Baron von und zu Bodman, the Kreiskommandant from Saint-Nazaire, who was standing in for Hotz. The bishop warmed to him as a "kindly man, Catholic and royalist," after his own heart. "I will do everything I can," said the baron, "and I am sure that there will be a measure of clemency. But it is not up to me."[20]

Clearly, the ultimate decision would be made in Paris or in Berlin, not in Nantes. Mayor Rondeau duly sent a delegation to Paris consisting of the assistant mayor, Abel Durand, and the head of the Nantes bar, Maître Guinaudeau, who had been involved in the defense of the veterans' leaders in July. Their mission was to visit Vichy's ambassador in Paris, Fernand de Brinon. In his letter, Mayor Rondeau warned of "the unanimous movement of indignation at yesterday's horrible execution, which mixed together communist militants with the glorious combatants of the Great War. . . . It has plunged our town into a painful stupor, a sort of moral darkness from which there is no telling what unstoppable emotions may arise if the volleys of a second execution ring out tomorrow."[21]

Rondeau also used a connection dating back to his involvement in the Franco-German Committee in the 1930s. One of his associates on that committee was the president of the Groupe Collaboration and editor of the collaborationist *Gerbe* newspaper, Alphonse de Châteaubriant. He urged Châteaubriant "in the name of our fraternal friendship and of our common efforts in the past to prevent a Franco-German war" to intercede with Otto Abetz, the head of the German embassy in Paris and a former activist in their movement.[22]

The main strategy of the French authorities was to express their goodwill toward the Germans and their continuing commitment to the policy of collaboration. They were also keen to show that the breakdown of order that had resulted in the assassination of Hotz would not be allowed to recur. Hotz's funeral, scheduled for Friday, 24 October, offered an invaluable opportunity to demonstrate that the practice of indirect rule was still working. The Germans made clear that the French police were expected to provide security at the funeral, and their effectiveness would be on trial. Over 1,000 police and 500 gendarmes were drafted for the occasion from neighboring departments and Paris, for a crowd that in the end numbered 3,000. In his keynote speech the military commander of southwest France,

General Neumann-Neurode, announced that "starting from the principle that understanding between peoples and close cooperation between them is the first requirement in the new Europe, [Hotz] carried out his responsibilities in close collaboration with the French authorities." Baron von und zu Bodman, now officially promoted Feldkommandant of Nantes, went even further, suggesting that it was precisely because of Hotz's championship of Franco-German understanding that he had been assassinated by English agents.[23] The French authorities were careful to endorse these sentiments, and the funeral cortège was followed by regional prefect Roussillon, departmental prefect Dupard, and Mayor Rondeau, as well as by a number of French delegations, including the Groupe Collaboration and the fascist Parti Populaire Français (PPF). Wreaths were laid by the prefect, the mayor and municipal council, the civil servants of the department, and the PPF.[24] The only notable absentee, watching from his window, was Monsignor Villepelet. He adopted the convenient position that the service was a Protestant one and that to attend the funeral was in some sense to endorse the execution of the hostages so closely linked to it. His absence did not go unnoticed, with one Nantais arguing that he should have tolled a mourning bell and said a requiem mass.[25]

The bishop of Nantes had his own agenda. The following day he sent a telegram to the archbishop of Paris, Cardinal Suhard, urging him to make personal contact with Hitler. Suhard later confirmed that he had received the bishop's telegram "with some emotion" on Saturday, the twenty-fifth, and himself sent a telegram directly to Hitler that same evening. On Monday Monsignor Villepelet went to the town hall to urge the mayor and council to pray to the Virgin Mary to intercede, only to be met by a courteous refusal in the name of the religious neutrality of French politics. The bishop went on alone to the church of Sainte-Croix, where he took a vow before the statue of the patron saint of the city, Notre Dame du Bon Secours, that if the second batch of hostages was spared he and his successors would light a candle to her every year for fifty years.[26] The members of the Breton military nobility were also active. Identifying with the Prussian or Bavarian military nobility, they maintained social contacts with them from early in the Occupation that were put to political use at a time of crisis. Thus the Marquise de Sesmaisons sent a wreath to Hotz's funeral, intervened to ensure that her friend Maître Ridel was not executed along with the other veterans on 22 October, and then persuaded the commander of a local Luftwaffe base and SS Brigadier General Ernst to telephone Hitler's headquarters to insist that Franco-German collaboration would be sorely undermined by a second wave of executions.[27]

Most poignant of all the intercessions, however, was the petition submitted by thirteen of the twenty grieving families of the Nantes hostages. Organized by the father of nineteen-year-old Jean-Pierre Glou, it "accepted with courage and resignation the cruel loss that afflicts them" and expressed confidence in the Germans' "feelings of humanity" to call off more executions. Mayor Rondeau called it "a heroic gesture of French solidarity [that] honors the city of Nantes." It was taken to the Feldkommandatur, where Captain Sieger described it as "precious to influence the higher authorities." Baron von und zu Bodman announced that there was hope of a favorable outcome and actually missed his Sunday lunch to take the petition to General Neumann-Neurode in Angers for forwarding to Paris and Berlin.[28]

It is of course impossible to weigh the relative importance of these intercessions. From what is known about the responsiveness of the Third Reich to public opinion it may be surmised that they counted for little. Yet there was clearly a disagreement between the highest military authorities in Berlin and the military authorities in France. The closer to the local situation the German military were, the less happy they were with the policy of mass executions. In this equation the attitude of Otto von Stülpnagel, the head of the occupying forces in France, was central. He was in touch with the French prime minister, Admiral Darlan, and was himself a shrewd assessor of Germany's best interests. As we have seen, he was keen in the immediate aftermath of the assassination to allow more time to catch the killers. In the afternoon following Hotz's funeral he sent a telegram to Hitler's headquarters warning of the dangers of applying savage "Polish methods" to France:

> I have stated my opinion that the great mass of the French population is foreign to these assassinations, which are much more likely to have been carried out by small groups of terrorists in the pay of England. I have clearly come to the view that because of the particular situation in France I am

opposed to the mass execution of hostages. This must inevitably provoke increasing bitterness in the population and make future political rapprochement extraordinarily difficult, if not impossible. Admiral Darlan said to me in my conversations with him that as a soldier he fully understood the harsh measures taken but he has persuaded me that the mass executions are doing exactly what England wants, stirring up the French against us and putting an end absolutely to a reconciliation of the two peoples (on the radio England is already gloating over the executions). Darlan's policy of collaboration would be compromised if it ceased to be understood by the French people.

I have myself warned enough against the use of Polish methods in France. I have acted with moderation and staked my ideas and myself on this. The measures taken in Nantes were imposed on me from above. I was placed under the most intense pressure. I now wish to have a clear statement of intent from the Führer as to whether he wishes to inflict these draconian measures in the circumstances I have described and put up with the political consequences I have outlined, which will undoubtedly follow. I must stress again most emphatically that in the long run these measures are not appropriate.[29]

Corroboration of von Stülpnagel's views comes from Ernst Jünger, a man of letters, socialite, and similarly humane member of the German army in Paris. He observed that the mass execution policy had "unnerved and profoundly shaken" von Stülpnagel. The general also saw that the contribution of French industry to the German war effort meant that relations with the French people must be as positive as possible and that, given the lengthening campaign on the eastern front, "it was important that German influence in Europe continued beyond the period when it was based on bayonets alone." Finally, he feared that collective reprisals played straight into the hands of the Resistance and that the cycle of terrorist attack, reprisals, and resistance had to be broken.[30]

In the short term, however, Otto von Stülpnagel's telegram may have had some influence. Hitler made the final decision about the second batch of hostages in two stages. On Friday, 24 October, he decided to grant a seventy-two-hour stay of execution, until 27 October at midnight. Then, on Tuesday, 28 October, the execution was postponed indefinitely. France was seen to be an area where occupation went smoothly and resistance was minimal. In areas invaded more recently by the Germans, where their authority was more fragile, such as the Balkans and the Ukraine, the punishment of acts of resistance was much more savage. Thus the ambush of a German column near the Serbian town of Kragujevac provoked the execution on 21 October of 2,300 Jews and communists, while a series of bomb explosions in the city of Kiev, in immediate response to its occupation by German forces on 19 September 1941, led to the massacre on 29–30 September of 33,771 Jews at the ravine of Babi Yar.[31]

Though the French had been granted a reprieve, the menace had not been lifted irrevocably. Hitler ruled that the French would have to demonstrate not only in word but in deed that their commitment to the policy of collaboration with Germany was genuine. In the event, the cycle of terrorist attacks and mass reprisals began again in December, but this time outside Nantes. While the Nantais breathed a sigh of relief, Otto von Stülpnagel resigned in February 1942 in opposition to the continuing policy of mass executions. This was less because of humanitarianism than because he took a long-term view of the conditions needed to ensure Franco-German collaboration and because he felt that, though closer to the theater of events than Hitler's immediate staff, he was denied any flexibility in decision making. He was replaced by his cousin, Carl-Heinrich von Stülpnagel, a former member of the Armistice Commission, who would have his own reasons for falling out with Hitler two years later.

How far the assassination of Hotz and the collective reprisals that followed contributed to French resistance can be examined in some detail in the case of Nantes. Although the incident was later presented by militants as the trigger behind the Resistance in the west of France, for the local population it served only to illustrate the madness of armed resistance and the benefits of avoiding reasons to upset the Germans. This was not collaboration in the later sense of supporting the German mission ideologically but collaboration in the original sense of maintaining good relations between French and Germans, whether at the public or private levels, in order to benefit all concerned.

The Germans, it will be remembered, offered a reward for information leading to the arrest of the assassins, and this reward was added to by the French government and the municipality of Nantes. Patriotic solidarity might have kept clues about the perpetrators from the French and German authorities, but for some, patriotism ordained that they should reveal what they knew, to avert mass executions and to underpin public order, and the size of the reward could not be sniffed at. Mme Marie-Louise Huau, the fifty-three-year-old owner of the Boîte à Sardines restaurant in Nantes, noticed that the two young men who had eaten there in the days leading up to 20 October had not returned since. She reported this absence to the French police on 22 October and was interviewed by the Gestapo on 26 October. She recognized Gilbert Brustlein from a photograph shown to her and the French police had a lead on him by 4 November at the latest.[32] Mme Huau claimed her reward and eventually obtained 500,000 francs from the Germans, 100,000 francs from the prefecture, and 80,000 francs from the town of Nantes. Spartaco and Bourdarias were executed by the Germans on 17 April 1942, although their involvement in the assassination of Hotz was not known; Brustlein was never captured. Arrested and questioned after the Liberation, Mme Huau declared that she intended to give the money to a charity for POWs when the war ended. She did not know that the men she had denounced were patriots and was indeed convinced that she had saved the lives of the other fifty hostages. An alternative view, put by a local fishwife, was that Mme Huau boasted of the money she had earned by denouncing Hotz's killers and struck fear into the inhabitants of the neighborhood, who thought she might denounce them as Gaullists.[33]

It is possible that Mme Huau was the sole collaborator in a town full of Gaullists, but the way in which the city reacted to Gaullist propaganda after the hostage affair suggests otherwise. The reprieve of the second fifty hostages was interpreted locally as a victory for the policy of collaboration in which the citizens of Nantes demonstrated that their good conduct since the assassination of Hotz had paid dividends. Mayor Rondeau announced that "the attitude of the population of Nantes and that of the families of the victims, emotional as it was, weighed heavily in the recent decision of the German authorities."[34] From London, General de Gaulle insisted that no one should shoot Germans until he gave the order, given the certainty of reprisals, but ordered a "gigantic standing to attention" or "French national strike" between 4:00 and 4:05 P.M. on 31 October, a wonderful expression of fraternity and a warning to the Germans of the threat surrounding them.[35] The German authorities made it clear that any such demonstration would be regarded as overt support for the assassins of Hotz. Prefect Dupard called his subprefects, service chiefs, and other notables together on 30 October to "ensure the failure of the demonstration called by the English radio," while Mayor Rondeau warned all municipal employees that any following of "instructions given by foreigners" would entail severe punishment, even dismissal.[36] Some 70 percent of the workforce in the biggest factory in Nantes stopped work for five minutes, and four people who halted on the highway in Nantes were asked to move on, but otherwise there was no response.[37] Most Nantais understood that to demonstrate was to provoke the Germans for no good reason.

The other key test of Gaullist opinion in Nantes was the response to the general's award of the Croix de la Liberation to the city on Armistice Day, 11 November 1941. This honor, intended for individuals and communities contributing to the liberation of France and its empire, hailed Nantes as "a heroic city that, since the capitulation, has mounted a fierce resistance to all forms of collaboration with the enemy. . . . By the blood of its martyred children it has just borne witness before the whole world of the French will to national liberation."[38] Fearing that to accept such an honor would antagonize the German authorities, Mayor Rondeau and his council decided not to acknowledge it. For his part, de Gaulle interpreted this gesture as a snub for which he would make the city pay in the future. Though the old municipality was dissolved at the Liberation, the new mayor and council were unable to prevail on de Gaulle to visit the city and make the award in person until January 1945, and even then he declined to stop at the town hall. Under the Occupation the population was scarcely converted to the gospel from London, seeing as they did the virtues of patient negotiation within the framework of the German presence. Public opinion in the department, the prefect reported in December 1941, had been transformed over the previous month. "The painful events of Nantes and the excesses of the English radio have caused many people to ponder," he said. "Not only have a large number of those who had remained hostile to the policy of Marshal Pétain seen the necessity for all French people to rally round the head of state, but even those who were privately champions of the marshal but did not dare refute pro-English arguments are no longer afraid to speak out and denounce the activities of those who persist in criticizing everything the authorities do."³⁹ Only the communists begged to differ. A clandestine paper attacked "Pétain the Defeated, Darlan, and, in our department, Dupard and Rondeau the Boche, partisans of total 'Kollaboration'" for using the death of Hotz as a pretext to massacre true patriots and of raising the hue and cry against his killer to cover up their own shameful involvement in the black market and prostitution.⁴⁰

Although the assassination of Hotz and the mass executions that followed were not necessarily the trigger that launched the Resistance in the west of France, they were clearly a turning point in Franco-German relations. Although the crisis in Nantes and Châteaubriant had partially been resolved by desperate negotiations, relations in the future would be increasingly strained. On the first anniversary of the execution of the forty-eight hostages, Edmond Duméril reflected that the brutality had "killed eighteen months of our efforts to bring about the collaboration of the two peoples, in the opinion even of Kommandants von Hasselbach and von und zu Bodman."⁴¹ Military leaders who recognized the need for the tacit consent of the French population were brushed aside. The Germans now feared that terrorists were hidden in the otherwise peaceable population and were no longer persuaded that the French authorities could guarantee the Wehrmacht against attack. The model of "indirect rule" by which the Germans allowed the French authorities substantial discretion in return for maintaining public order was called into question. A new form of collaboration was introduced, based less on negotiation between Germans and French than on *Diktat*, the imposition of terms. The whip hand on the German side passed from the military authorities, who were tough but fair, to the secret police, who were interested only in repression. This might have led to a head-on collision between Nazi dictatorship and French Resistance, and certainly there were now militants who believed that only violence would teach the Germans a lesson. On the other hand, peaceable local communities feared that violence they did not sanction and over which they had no control would only provoke savage reprisals against them. Thus, violence drove a wedge not only between French and Germans but between resisters and communities.

11

Terror

May Day was traditionally a moment when the labor movement made a show of strength, but under the German Occupation extreme caution was required. Unfortunately, on the night of 30 April–1 May 1942 three young Frenchmen—Robert Guilbault (twenty-one), André Anguille (twenty-two), and Robert Couillaud (twenty-six) were caught red-handed by two French police officers as they painted anti-German slogans on the walls of Tours. The municipal police had received instructions from Commissioner Moracchini to clamp down on "antinational propaganda" and to make an example of any offenders. There had been a spate of terrorist incidents in Tours since the beginning of the year, and although painting graffiti or distributing tracts was fairly anodyne, the first May Day since the entry of the Soviet Union into the war was bound to be a moment for the Communist Party to raise its profile and an opportunity for the authorities to capture its militants. The trio arrested were rather innocent communist sympathizers, but once they were in police hands the trail led to bigger fish: Maxime Bourdon (twenty-five), the organizer of Communist Youth in Indre-et-Loire, arrested on 4 May, and André Foussier (twenty-two), the leader of the Front National (essentially communist) students, arrested on 7 May.

Although the young men had been arrested by the French police, they soon found themselves in the hands of the Gestapo. How this happened was the subject of conflicting accounts. The young men told their parents that they were beaten by two officers of the Sûreté, Euzenat and Bernard, on orders of Commissioner André Maurice, who then telephoned the Gestapo and handed them over. The father of André Foussier made his own inquiries and came to the same conclusions about the responsibility of Maurice. The guilt of Maurice was substantiated after the Liberation by another police officer, who said, however, that he could not bring allegations against Moracchini, who was his "hierarchical superior."[1] Interviewed in October 1944, Maurice, since then promoted to head of the Sûreté Nationale in Paris, said first that he had absolutely no memory of how the young men had been interrogated and how the Gestapo had got hold of them, then recalled that they had "no traces of violence" on their bodies when he had interviewed them and blamed a subordinate officer for alerting the Gestapo. Moracchini, interviewed in December 1944, by which time he was secretary-general of police for the Angers region, said that "the unfortunate victims were not handed over willingly but snatched by force according to procedures dear to the oppressor." This clashed somewhat with the memory of another officer, who recalled on the night in question seeing Maurice "swinging an enormous club as long as a walking stick" in front of three young men in handcuffs and Moracchini "sitting in his armchair while a very merry German officer was patting his stomach and saying, 'Good collaboration'; on the desk was a bottle and five or six glasses of white wine, filled to the brim."[2]

The consequences of being handed over to the Gestapo were lethal. Had the five young men remained in the hands of the French police they would have gone before the *procureur de la République* and probably been interned; in the hands of the Gestapo they were brought before the military court of the Feldkommandantur of Tours on 14 May 1942 and sentenced to death. Prefect Tracou went to see Feldkommandant Kloss, who gave him a fair interview, and made urgent representations in Paris, but the appeal for clemency was rejected and the five young men were taken to the

Ruchard military camp outside Tours on 16 May and shot. Although their execution was carried out in secret, rumors began to spread and with them shock and disbelief. "Many people refuse to believe that the sentence has been carried out," Moracchini told Tracou. "There is a great deal of hostility in the working-class milieu and even those without ideological commitments are appalled." Tracou relayed to the regional prefect news of an "intense reaction of amazement that has still not calmed down."[3] Unable to cope with the grief, André Foussier's mother committed suicide three months later. A huge crowd turned out for her funeral on 25 August. Returning home after the funeral, Foussier's father, too, killed himself. His burial three days later was, according to the account of communist militants who had escaped the net, "a formidable and silent patriotic demonstration."[4]

For the Tourangeaux, the execution of five young men whose crime was scarcely more than vandalism was incomprehensible. What made it outrageous was that the French police had at best caved in to the Gestapo, at worst actively collaborated. For many French people these youths were patriots who happened to be inspired by the force that was putting up the staunchest resistance to the Nazis on the eastern front. As far as the Vichy regime was concerned, communists were as much their enemy as that of the Germans and their activities "antinational" as well as anti-German. What mattered for Vichy was to retain enough influence to negotiate with the German authorities on fair if not equal terms. Even over the hostage crisis in Nantes-Châteaubriant they had managed to persuade the Germans to spare a second batch of victims, and General von Stülpnagel argued successfully with his superiors that further terror would be against German interests. Unfortunately, the bargaining position of the French authorities was becoming steadily weaker, negotiation more difficult, and compromise more unlikely. One reason was that as the campaign against the Soviet Union became bogged down, as communist resistance in Europe grew bolder, and as the Allies, too, began to inflict damage in the west, German reactions grew angrier and more unpredictable. Another reason was that military administrators who favored a more moderate approach were gradually moved on, and the German military administration itself became displaced in the spring and summer of 1942 by the secret police.

The tragedy of 16 May 1942 was not an isolated incident but followed a number of attacks on German installations and personnel. For a time, in Tours, the French and German authorities managed to limit the extent of collective reprisals, but their task was becoming harder and harder. On the night of 12–13 January 1942 a German train was derailed on the Paris-Bordeaux line near Tours and a bomb was thrown into the Café La Paix, a Tours nightspot frequented by German officers. It did not go off. Feldkommandant Kloss was inclined to impose a collective fine of a million francs on the town, but prefect Tracou managed to persuade him that the culprits were not locals at all but the Brustlein gang and Kloss contented himself with ordering an 8:00 P.M. curfew for a fortnight. As he told Tracou, "I do not see myself as a conqueror here; I want only to work in full agreement with you and to facilitate your mission as Marshal Pétain's representative."[5]

This understanding was severely threatened when a German sentry by the name of Kropiunik was shot outside a gasoline dump in the rue du Hallebardier in Tours on the night of 5 February 1942 and died a few days later. The German authorities arrested fifty hostages—ten communists and forty Jews—both foreign and French. For the first time in the region, Jews entered into the German equation of collective punishment. Émile Aron, a doctor in Tours, was warned by his maid that the Feldgendarmerie were on their way to his house, and he managed to escape from a rear entrance, making his way over the demarcation line and thence to Switzerland.[6] Prefect Tracou, arguing that the death was probably the result of a brawl between Germans, managed to persuade the German authorities to release two teachers, on the grounds that they could not possibly have been guilty, along with two communists and eleven Jews on health grounds. Feldkommandant Kloss was convinced that the deed had been done not by a local but by a terrorist from outside and tried to avoid any executions. His superiors were prepared to show a little flexibility in the interests of Franco-German relations, but at the same time the penalty for killing even the humblest sentry needed to be made clear.[7] In accordance with German policy on reprisals, General von Stülpnagel might have ordered the execution of fifteen hostages, but he satisfied himself with ten. To avoid the violent community response provoked by the shooting of high-profile veterans and local youths in Nantes, those selected were six communists sentenced to long prison terms—five by French courts and one by a German court, who were held some way off in the former abbey of Fontevrault, where the execution took place on 21 February—and four Jews who had been interned by the French authorities.[8] The thinking now was that Jews as well as communists were beyond the pale of the local community, which would be less exercised by their execution than by that of someone more integrated into it.

While this repression in Touraine was finely calibrated politically, at the other end of the region Allied involvement in an incident provoked a much more violent and arbitrary German response that pointed the way to what might happen in the future. On the night of 27–28 March 1942 a small British flotilla of commando launches escorted the torpedo boat *Campbelltown* unnoticed up to the port of Saint-Nazaire for the purpose of destroying the floodgate of the immense dry dock that was due to receive the battleship *Tirpitz* for repairs and, if possible, damaging the U-boat base as well. The *Campbelltown* jammed itself up against the floodgate and blew itself up with a delayed charge while the forces leaped ashore. In the fighting 59 British commandos and 85 sailors were killed, while 109 commandos and 106 sailors were taken prisoner by the Germans, but that still left 252 of the crew unaccounted for. The Germans were convinced that they were being sheltered by the inhabitants of Saint-Nazaire and distributed a poster to the effect that a further attack on the German army would result in the execution of a tenth of the population in the district where the attack occurred. During the night of 30 March a second delayed explosion rocked the port, and the Germans ran amok, shooting through doors and windows, throwing grenades into apartments, breaking into houses to force the population onto the streets, and continuing to shoot at them. In the carnage eighteen were killed and twenty-six seriously wounded. Twelve hundred people from the port district were then taken "like a common herd," in the words of the bishop of Nantes, to the former POW camp at Savenay, twenty miles away, where they were held under the orders of a colonel sent from Angers because the local Kreiskommandant, Major von Trotha, was deemed to have forfeited too much authority. Fearing that savage reprisals might be taken, Mayor Tosca and subprefect Lecornu of Saint-Nazaire raced to the camp by car and tried the unorthodox tactic of thanking the colonel for haved saved the inhabitants of the port district from further risks and offering to evacuate them to Le Croisic. Lecornu agreed to the colonel's condition that all papers should be checked, in order to flush out any British or Canadian servicemen in disguise, and was able to agree to the release of the civilians.[9] The incident demonstrated that the German authorities were not always in control of their subordinates in extreme situations and that negotiations, while they continued, hung by a thread.

Meanwhile the Germans experienced in the practice of Franco-German cohabitation since the beginning of the Occupation were leaving the scene. In July von Trotha was promoted from Saint-Nazaire to Nantes to replace Baron von und zu Bodman, the distinguished Bavarian Catholic who had so impressed the bishop of Nantes, while Colonel Kloss, whose flexibility had been much appreciated by the French authorities in Angers and then in Tours, left the region. Over the next two years there were five different Feldkommandants in Tours, making it impossible to develop a working relationship. Even before then Otto von Stülpnagel had resigned and the new Militärbefehlshaber, his cousin Carl-Heinrich, informed Ambassador de Brinon that from 1 June on a high commander of the SS and German police would be in position in occupied France and that all police matters that had previously been dealt with by the German military administration would be taken over by the high commander, Carl-Albrecht Oberg, who was Reinhard Heydrich's man in occupied France for the integrated services of the state security police (Sicherheitspolizei, commonly known as the Gestapo) and the security service of the SS (Sicherheitsdienst, or SD).

By this time Hitler had grown exasperated with the ineffectiveness of the Darlan government, and German pressure was applied to Pétain to drop Darlan and bring back Laval, this time as head of government, in April 1942. As a guarantee of more serious collaboration, Laval appointed the thirty-three-year-old technocrat René Bousquet secretary-general of police. Bousquet held a series of meetings with Oberg and endorsed the principle of collaboration of the French and German police against the common enemy—anarchists, communists, and terrorists—in return for having the German policy of reprisals against hostages ended and a certain autonomy granted the French police. He realized that communists interned by the French authorities for their own security reasons had been used for target practice by the Germans with disastrous results for Franco-German collaboration. He also realized that the numbers of Feldgendarmes and

Gestapo that the German police could deploy in France was limited and that some conditions might be attached to the collaboration of the French police. He was concerned above all to define a sphere in which French citizens arrested for crimes that did not constitute a threat to the army of occupation would be dealt with by the French police and the French judicial system, under French law. For Oberg, there were few gestures of opposition and resistance in occupied France that did not threaten the army of occupation, and as far as he was concerned the function of the French police was simply to act as executive agents of the Gestapo. The so-called Bousquet-Oberg agreement of July 1942 outlining the parameters of Franco-German police collaboration was in fact the subject of very different interpretations on each side. At a meeting of regional prefects and regional Sicherheitspolizei/SD commanders on 8 August, Oberg praised the international police collaboration promoted by his late colleague Heydrich, recently assassinated by Czech partisans, and emphasized what the French police could do for German security. In his letter to prefects of 13 August enclosing the definitive text, however, Bousquet emphasized that the French police would not have to choose hostages and that French citizens accused of crimes that did not threaten the army of occupation would be dealt with by the French system.[10]

How much autonomy the French police preserved would depend very much on the outcome of power struggles in the locality. The regional police chief in Angers, SS Hauptsturmführer Dr. Hans-Dietrich Ernst, made clear from the start that he would tolerate no lapses in collaboration. Early in July he informed regional prefect Roussillon that Moïse Ossant, a police inspector in Saumur, had been sent before the military court of the Feldkommandantur of Angers for "anti-German activity." Asked to provide French staff for the Saumur *Soldatenheim*, he had proposed a team totally unfit for service. "Of eleven women," complained Ernst, "three were visibly sick, one was pregnant, one was syphilitic, and three others seemed to be prostitutes; only three could be employed." The military court ordered preventive detention, a sentence that Ernst quashed—if only to demonstrate that even German military justice had to bow to the Gestapo—on condition that Ossant be transferred from Saumur.[11] A week later he produced his own version of the Bousquet-Oberg agreement, leaving precious little autonomy to the French police. He told Roussillon that he expected a daily report to be submitted to him, in German, on "all incidents and phenomena liable to trouble public tranquillity, security, and order," as well as "isolated incidents out of the normal course of things." He was to be informed of what inquiries were taking place, and by whom, by a specially designated police chief. Special reports were required on any sabotage of German installations or any attacks on members of the German army. Incidents in each department were to be reported to the local SS. Given that this reporting system totally cut out the French police hierarchy, Roussillon made representations to Ernst. But the furthest he got was that incidents would be reported to the police intendant in Angers for forwarding to the regional Sicherheitspolizei/SD.[12]

Some idea of the character of the departmental SS commanders may be gained from the case of Georg Brückle, head of the Sicherheitspolizei/SD in Tours. In his early thirties, Brückle was a native of Prague and spoke German with a Slavic accent. He had a low opinion of the French police, except for the crack Anti-Communist Police Section (SPAC), but had a good working relationship with Joseph Boucherie, a commissioner whom he regarded as someone "who may be trusted absolutely from a political point of view." He managed to get Boucherie promoted to police commissioner at Tours, a position left vacant after the departure of Moracchini, calling him the right man in the right place "to guarantee an irreproachable and productive collaboration with the French police here." This collaboration did not include French police arresting women servicing Germans as clandestine prostitutes, which sent him into a fury. Brückle himself, a regular at the Casanova nightclub, was reputed to have had 200 mistresses in Tours and environs. One French woman with whom he lived for a year, Colette Wetter, bore him a child and disappeared a few months later, no doubt for her own safety. The employees of the Tours Gestapo had much in common with Brückle. Of the thirty-two—twenty-nine men and three women—seven were born outside the 1937 frontiers of Germany: three were Alsatians, two Sudenten Germans, and two Romanians. One in three of the men had a French mistress, and most were corrupt. The most feared was probably an Alsatian woman in her late twenties, Klara Knecht, who had been a secretary and interpreter at the Feldkommandantur before graduating to the Gestapo. Relations between the Gestapo and the French people were not only sexual; plenty of informers gravitated around the

Gestapo for money or revenge. Among them were Antoine Devraud of Tours, a railway employee, and Phang Bang, the Vietnamese domestic of Mme Hélène Jobineau, whose Resistance network based at her château south of Tours he betrayed.[13]

The picture that begins to emerge is that while French authorities were able to argue with and even to frustrate to some extent the demands of the German military administration, dealing with the Gestapo was an entirely different matter. In August 1942, for example, the Feldkommandantur of Angers asked the prefect to send him a list of all the mayors, municipal councillors, curés, and primary school teachers in the department within four days; the prefect replied that this went against clear French government policy and asked, no doubt rather naïvely, for a "formal guarantee that the list you request will not be used to select hostages."[14] The following October the Kreiskommandant of Nantes, who was keen to monitor POWs who had returned on leave and even those who had been released definitively, wished to mobilize the French gendarmerie to undertake the task. This provoked protests from prefect Dupard and from the local gendarmerie commander, who smelled a whiff of hostage taking.[15] With the Gestapo, however, orders were rarely disobeyed. When Dr. Ernst became convinced that Catholic priests in the Mauges were stirring up anti-German feeling, he asked for them to be moved to different parishes. Admittedly, Canon Douillard, archdeacon of Cholet, was first arrested to make the point, but neither regional prefect Roussillon nor Monsignor Costes, bishop of Angers, put up any fight; indeed, Roussillon urged Costes to accept a "benign punishment," for fear of provoking anything worse.[16]

The purpose of police collaboration, of course, was to facilitate the campaign against the common enemy, the communists. Bousquet's idea was that the more the French police demonstrated their effectiveness, the more autonomy they would achieve. This led them sometimes not to wait for orders but to take the initiative. In a massive operation in Nantes on 27 August 1942, for example, the Anti-Communist Police Section and the Nantes Sûreté rounded up 143 communists, 42 of them Spanish republicans and 101 French. Of these, 41 were identified as the authors of twenty terrorist attacks in the Nantes area. The most notable of this group was Raymond Hervé, who, since he joined the Special Terrorist Organization (OS) of the Communist Party in March, had sabotaged the Batignolles locomotive factory, killed a suspected collaborator, thrown a bomb into a luxury hotel in Nantes used by the Germans, and stolen ration cards and money from various town halls and châteaux. Hervé was being interrogated by examining magistrate Le Bras in Nantes on 9 September when an armed group of his communists burst in, shot the magistrate dead, and escaped.[17] This incident led to a massive roundup of suspects over the following two days, but without success. Then, on 15 September, the Spanish leader of the Nantes OS, Alfredo Gomez-Ollero, was arrested in Saint-Nazaire, and his trail led to the arrest of more Spanish and French communists, including Marcel Viaud, a Châteaubriant schoolteacher and member of the Party since 1934, accused of hiding terrorists on the run.[18]

The French administration was delighted by this campaign, which effectively destroyed the Nantes OS. Prefect Dupard noted that Fourcade, head of the Sûreté, "had particularly excelled since June in the investigation [sic] of the Communist Party and its terrorist organization in Nantes. I request that M. Fourcade be promoted to principal commissaire as soon as possible. . . . From the national point of view, his attitude cannot be faulted in the least." Whether the success of the French police in the long run increased their autonomy was another question. At first, things seemed to be going that way. Yves Bayet, secretary-general of the Nantes prefecture, reported that "the anticommunist operation allowed the French police and administration to make direct contact with the SS. I was very happy to observe that they not only collaborated closely with us to help us but also handed over to us a certain number of communists whom they had arrested previously, so that we could interrogate them and hand them over to the French courts." Dr. Ernst, visiting Nantes, personally thanked the prefect for the "excellent work undertaken by the French police." After the assassination of examining magistrate Le Bras and the subsequent arrests, Oberg, the SS police chief, made it clear that, while members of the communist youth group and ordinary members of the PCF would be tried by French courts, members of the terrorist OS would be tried by a German military court.[19]

In the end the French police and administration, imagining that they were acting independently, in fact simply did the dirty work of the SS and then found matters taken out of their hands. The French judicial system was entirely sidelined, except insofar as the assize court of Loire-Inférieure, decked out in swastika flags, was used as a stage for the court-martial of Feldkommandantur 518. No fewer than forty-two defendants were brought before military judge Dr. Gottlob on 6 January 1943, for crimes running the gamut from assassination, sabotage, and illegal bearing of arms to small offenses such as hiding stocks of ration cards. Edmond Duméril, who helped the defense because the trial was conducted entirely in German, noted that "the Germans intended to conclude this trial by an apotheosis of justice in the shadow of the swastika. They were therefore without pity." Such terror would be struck into the hearts and minds of the French population that they would in future neither engage in violence nor protect those who did. The verdict divided the defendants into "assassins," "guerillas" (*francs-tireurs*, or *Freischärlelei*), and "accomplices" but took the view that the will to commit a crime amounted to the crime itself and that "this harsh period of war requires the harsh punishment of those who attack the German army or commit crimes in occupied territory. Those who do so risk their heads and must be eliminated." Dr. Gottlob acquitted two, sent three to prison, and condemned the other thirty-seven to death. The judges left the courtroom hurriedly as the oldest defendant, a retired railway worker named Henri Adam, led the singing of the "Marseillaise." In the days that followed, the prefect, mayor, and bishop of Nantes made representations for mercy on behalf of the condemned, but prefect Dupard was so pessimistic that he requested a pardon for only ten of them. The time when negotiation might bear fruit was past. Nine of the condemned were shot on 29 January 1943, twenty-five more on 13 February, and the last three, tortured in order to extract information about other comrades, were finally executed on 7 May.[20]

Collaboration between the French and German police and administration now meant that the former were used and abused, and greater collaboration between police forces meant the decreasing enthusiasm of the French public for collaboration in a wider sense. The collaborationist *Phare de Nantes* toed the German line, denouncing as "outlaws" and "terrorists" those who "call themselves patriots but in fact serve the interests of quite another country" and "are ready at any moment to sacrifice the property and lives of French people."[21] In his report to the Interior Minister, however, prefect Dupard noted that "these severe sentences have made a deep impression on public opinion, which tends to consider the perpetrators of crimes such as the murder of examining magistrate Le Bras, the theft of ration tickets, arson attacks on crops and buildings, or sabotage as guerillas and patriots." He regretted that the accused had not been tried by a French court, which would have handed down lesser sentences. But now that the German police had the upper hand the only solution was "good anticommunist propaganda," which would impress on public opinion that terrorist attacks were "the work of brigands and criminals, not that of patriots, partisans, or guerillas."[22] Even René Bousquet realized that the balance of police collaboration and autonomy agreed on with Oberg the previous August was not working. At a meeting of regional prefects and chiefs of the Sicherheitspolizei in April 1943, he protested that even when German military personnel and installations were not directly threatened, and where the culprits had been arrested by the French police, the Germans were citing the principle of the security of their army to take custody of the arrested individuals and send them before German military courts. Although Oberg reiterated that the division of responsibility as agreed in August 1942 would continue, clearly the Germans were now saying one thing but doing another.[23]

The negotiations between Oberg and Bousquet that led to the collaboration of French and German police against the communists in the late summer of 1942 had precedent in the treatment of Jews. Comparing the persecution of communists and the persecution of Jews sheds a great deal of light on the attitudes of the French police and administration on the one hand and on the attitude of the French population on the other. Bousquet's concerns about the autonomy of the French police were not voiced at all in relation to the deportation of the Jews, and much of the detailed negotiations with the German authorities early in July 1942 were carried out by his deputy Leguay and the head of the Commissariat Général aux Questions Juives (CGQJ), Louis Darquier de Pellepoix. The French police tried to safeguard French Jews while letting foreign ones go but were otherwise enthusiastic stooges of the German police and keener than the Germans to have Jewish children deported with their parents. The initial reaction of the French population was one of indifference. Since the deportation was supposed to concern not French Jews but only foreign ones, there was little hostility to the removal of those who were regarded as unwelcome immigrants. Only when Jewish children began to be separated from their families and French Jews began to be caught up in the net did any kind of hostile reaction take place.

On 30 June 1942 de Brinon sent a circular to all prefects in the Occupied Zone informing them that Oberg had published an ordinance the previous day declaring that all French Jews over the age of six were to wear a yellow star, on pain of a fine, prison, or transfer to a "camp for Jews." This discrimination, which had applied to Polish Jews from 1939 and German Jews from 1941, was intended to divide Jews from the rest of the national community and to establish whether non-Jews would show solidarity or simply look to their own survival. Many French Jews could not believe that this measure applied to them and asked the French authorities to obtain an exemption, but the authorities demonstrated impatience or indifference. Mayor Rondeau of Nantes wrote to prefect Dupard to request an exemption for Raoul Jacob, seventy-six, who in 1919 had apparently saved Aristide Briand, the prime minister and foreign minister who in the 1920s had promoted Franco-German rapprochement, from a communist plot to kill him. Dupard forwarded the request to de Brinon, only to be told that it was not in de Brinon's power to grant dispensations and that he should address himself to Obersturmführer Marnitz, the SS chief in Nantes.[24] Georges Salomon, a salesman who said he did not practice his religion and was married to a Catholic, asked the prefect of Maine-et-Loire whether, as "the son and grandson of French citizens" from Alsace and a veteran of two wars wounded in 1917, he really had to wear the yellow star. Prefect delegate Pierre Daguerre, who was alleged to have protected Freemasons in his previous position as subprefect of Dieppe, clearly had little time for Jews. He told the mayor of Salomon's commune that "if he did not wear the star from 7 June I will have to report him to the Feldkommandantur with a view to having him interned in a concentration camp."[25] Subsequently he secured confirmation from the CGQJ that the French definition of a Jew, which included Jews who did not practice any religion, was to be observed in preference to the German definition of a Jew as one who had two Jewish grandparents *and* belonged to the Jewish faith.[26] Some Jews, bowing to the law, chose to wear their stars with pride. In Saumur, Rabbi Henri Lévy, a former army chaplain, wore his with his Croix de Guerre and Légion d'Honneur, and as the traditional Fête-Dieu procession passed through the streets a priest left it to step onto the pavement and shake his hand. Such gestures of solidarity were magnificent but did not do anything to alter the course of events: on 18 July Lévy was arrested and deported.[27]

The roundup of Jews in Paris on 16–17 July 1942, commonly known as the *rafles du Vel d'Hiv* because over 13,000 Jews were arrested and crammed into the Velodrôme d'Hiver cycling stadium, is well documented, as are the roundups of Jews in the Free Zone the following month. Much less well known are the roundups in the Occupied Zone outside Paris on 15–16 July 1942, which some books simply fail to mention.[28] No doubt the number of Jews there was relatively small—in June 1942 there were 387 (240 French, 95 foreign, and 52 "evacuated from the coast") in Maine-et-Loire and 304 (105 French, 199 foreign) in Loire-Inférieure. Numbers in Loire-Inférieure had more than halved from 736 (422 French, 314 foreign) in October 1940, largely because of escapes to the Free Zone, although they had risen in Maine-et-Loire from 288 (231 French, 57 foreign) since then. And yet this region had its own concentration camp for foreign Jews at La Lande, near the village of Monts, outside Tours, together with a work camp for foreign Jews, mainly deported from Paris, at Clefs, in woodland north of Angers, while resorts like La Baule on the Atlantic coast west of Nantes were notorious congregating grounds of Jews on the move. Most deportations to concentration and extermination camps in the east left via Drancy, an unfinished housing estate north of Paris. It was from Angers, however, that the only convoy to journey directly from the French provinces to Auschwitz left on 20 July 1942 with a cargo of 824 Jews.

Debate has raged as to whether the Nazis or Vichy bore more responsibility. The French police were perfectly candid about their role in the deportation, which in the first instance was limited to foreign Jews aged sixteen to fifty, men and women, except those women who were pregnant or breast-feeding. A police official of Loire-Inférieure reported that "gendarmes assigned to the German security police on 15 July accompanied German soldiers of the Feldgendarmerie who were organizing the arrest of Jews." Subprefect Bernard Lecornu reported that "following instructions received from the prefecture and at the request of M. Einfeld, the SS chief, the police commissioner of Saint-Nazaire provided three officers to guard the Jews," fifty-four of whom had been arrested.[29] On the night of

15 July between eight and midnight and the next morning at five, reported the police commissioner of Angers, "my staff helped the German SD in the operations against the Jews."[30] "A detachment of gendarmerie alerted on 15 July at 4:50 P.M.," said adjutant Barreau of the Gennes brigade, near Saumur, "helped two German gendarmes guard and transport the persons arrested, without becoming involved in the details of the arrest."[31] Among those arrested were the German Jewish clan who owned the Sainte-Radégonde estate in Chênehutte-les-Tuffeaux, with the exception of the grandparents Abraham, in their seventies, and their daughter-in-law, Erny. The arrested Jews were taken to the Grand Séminaire in Angers, where they were joined by other groups of Jews transported from as far away as Le Mans and Poitiers. A contingent of 133 "healthy" Jews out of a total of 291 left the La Lande camp for Angers on 16 July, making room for 200 Jews rounded up in Tours on 15 July. Having been confined fifteen to a cell in the Grand Séminaire of Angers for several days, the whole contingent of 824 Jews was loaded onto a train and sent off in the direction of Auschwitz.

While the responsibility of Vichy is now well established, there is still controversy about how ordinary French people reacted to these terrible scenes. Did they care? Were they shocked? Or did they simply close their doors and shutters and thank God that it was not them? Abbé Henri Richer, who came from an extremely Pétainist family and was a seminarist in Angers at the time, remembers seeing a German soldier tease a Jewish girl with a piece of cheese in the courtyard of the Grand Séminaire and, though he knew that the Jews were crowded fifteen to a cell, feeling more sympathy for the German soldiers because of the heat.[32] "Until now," reported the police commissioner of Angers on 16 July, "the vast majority of the public has remained fairly indifferent to the Jewish question and continues to show reserve. Today, however, many are not hiding their sympathy for those who appear to be victims of persecution."[33] Writing shortly after the 824 Jews held in the Grand Séminaire had been taken away and "certain particularly painful details about the roundup had emerged," the prefecture of Maine-et-Loire noted that "there is some concern that a current of pity may be provoked in favor of the Jewish race, now seen to be martyrs, even among those who fully approved the protective measures taken by the government such as that restricting their access to public office."[34] The subprefect of Cholet was less agitated, suggesting a discrepancy between private sentiments and public attitudes. "Though the measure has been sharply criticized by people under their breath and troubles the conscience of most French citizens," he reported, "it has not provoked any manifestation of collective sympathy. The arrests have left the population rather indifferent and have not caused any unrest."[35]

The French were generally shocked more by the manner of the deportation than by the deportation itself because the story that the Jews were being taken to labor camps in Eastern Europe was widely accepted. In Angers, Jews were seen being loaded onto cattle trucks, the doors of which were then locked; parents and children had been separated.[36] Though Laval and Bousquet had insisted that children be deported with their parents precisely to avoid this kind of scene, the Germans at this point wanted to remove only healthy adults to keep alive the fiction of labor camps in the east and decided that the children would stay. In Tours, as a consequence, prefect Tracou reported "a violent hostility to the way the occupying authorities were going about things, especially with regard to small children abandoned to the most complete destitution."[37] After the adults fit to travel were removed from the La Lande camp, their sixty-five children were entrusted to other families in the camp and were joined the next day by thirty-two more children, for whom families had not been found after the roundup in Tours.[38] But the predicament of the children gave non-Jews a concrete opportunity to show solidarity. The subprefect of Saumur was summoned by the Feldgendarmerie on the evening of 15 July, the day before the roundup, and told with the utmost discretion to find premises where children could be accommodated for two or three days. The custody of nuns or priests was to be avoided, he was told, the understanding being that they were overly sympathetic or might have escape networks. Since the holidays had begun, the subprefect hit on the girls' secondary school.[39] In Angers, seventeen children had to be dealt with; two were housed with other Jewish families, three disappeared, and the rest were taken in by non-Jewish families. The five Sternchuss children of Angers—Nathan (eleven), Mina (nine), Lola (six), Simone (four), and Odette (two)—were entrusted to a family friend, Mlle Frouin, in Château-Gontier, while their traumatized mother was interned in the lunatic asylum of Gennes.[40] The sympathy shown by non-Jews angered Gestapo chief Ernst, who ruled on 24 August that Jewish children were no longer to be looked after by "French families." "I will decide in all cases," he added, "where Jewish children stay."[41] Some non-Jews continued to show solidarity. Mme Lévy, who came from Lorraine and was allowed to remain in Beaupréau with her one-year-old and five-year-old so long as she reported daily to the gendarmerie, failed to show up on 24 September and was last seen pushing her baby carriage toward Saint-Florent. It was assumed that she had been given a lift to the station in Varades or Ancenis and would try to join her husband in the Free Zone.[42] Other French people were less sympathetic, not least because the deportation left Jewish assets as ripe fruit for acquisition. Within two days of the roundup of 16 July, Dr. Georges Barrault of Les Ponts-de-Cé, outside Angers, approached the German authorities to take over the practice that a Polish Jew, Dr. Gurwicz, had been managing for the widow of a local practitioner. Barrault pointed out that under the Statut des Juifs Gurwicz was "ethnically unqualified" to run the practice and that he had refused to wear the yellow star; in any case, Barrault was impatient to acquire the business as soon as possible to develop a "maison de cure."[43]

Assistance from Gentiles made it possible for some Jews to elude the roundups. While thirty-six Jews were arrested in Angers on 15–16 July, nineteen French Jews and fifteen foreign ones managed to escape.[44] It is quite clear, however, that the condition laid down by Laval and Bousquet—which by and large was observed in the Paris region—namely, that only foreign Jews would be deported, simply did not stick in the Loire Valley. Of the thirty-six Jews arrested in Angers on 15–16 July 1942, for example, no fewer than fifteen were of French nationality. Of the 824 Jews finally deported from the Grand Séminaire of Angers on 20 July, 337 were Poles, 286 were other foreign nationals, and 201 were French.[45] The statistics on the Atlantic coast were even more telling. Of the sixty-five Jews arrested on 15 July 1942 in the arrondissement of Saint-Nazaire, for example, fifty-two were French. These included Armand Lévy of Saint-Nazaire, his wife, and their eleven-year-old daughter. When his father-in-law, Lucien Bernheim, eighty, also a French citizen, heard of their arrest he wrote to the prefect assuming it was an "error" and requesting that they be released.[46] We do not have the reply of prefect Dupard but subprefect Lecornu later told him that *all* the French Jews in his arrondissement had been arrested in July but that this was not a problem for the French administration. "It is my opinion," he announced, "that the question of principle concerning the arrest of French Jews should be put to the German authorities."[47]

The position of the French administration seems to have been that, regrettable though it was and irrespective of the fact that French police had been openly involved in the roundups and arrests, responsibility lay entirely with the Germans. A barrister of Tours wrote to prefect Tracou on behalf of his client Mme Estelle Isakow, a local shopkeeper, and her daughter, Paulette, who were both naturalized French but had been arrested and sent to La Lande. Tracou replied bluntly, "I regret to have to tell you that since these measures have not been taken by the French authorities, I have no means of improving their lot," and he referred the barrister to the Sicherheitspolizei, 118 boulevard Béranger.[48] After an article appeared in *Le Pilori* about the number of French Jews arrested in Touraine and regional prefect Roussillon asked Tracou to comment, Tracou answered rather disingenuously that "the French police have not arrested any Jews, let alone French Jews. Everything has been carried out by the German services." He conceded that about sixty of the arrests had been of French Jews, but these were Jews who had been brought to the attention of the German police for other reasons and were therefore suspect.[49]

By this time the Union Générale des Israélites de France had started to put pressure on the prefecture of Angers to do something about the arrest of French Jews, in particular to order the release of those being held in the camp of La Lande. It observed that the exemption of French Jews had been scrupulously observed in Paris and the department of the Seine and demanded to know why the administration in the Loire area was so careless. Prefect delegate Daguerre took the official line that "these police operations were carried out on the instructions of the SS and according to information that it alone possesses." But he forwarded the complaint to SS chief Ernst and wrote also to Pierre Laval to say that his information indicated that a large number of French Jews had indeed been arrested in his area. The prefect representing the Ministry of the Interior in Paris simply told him to sort the problem out with the local German authorities. Dr. Ernst replied that "the French Jews arrested during the operation against the stateless Jews had all rendered themselves guilty. For that reason they have been transported to labor camps in the east."[50] Daguerre forwarded this reply to the Ministry of the Interior in Paris, saying that he now considered the matter closed. Again, it appears that agreements made with the Germans were not worth the paper they were written on. But it also seems that, faced with a clear violation of the agreement, the French administration did not challenge the Germans' high-handedness or question the emerging logic that all Jews were "guilty" simply by dint of being Jews. Whether, as the reply of prefect Tracou to Roussillon suggests, they were imbibing the German ideology or whether they simply did not have the will to stand up to the Gestapo, the result was the same: in this part of the Occupied Zone at least, the distinction between French and foreign Jews amounted to nothing.

The deportations thus progressed unimpeded, in sharp contrast to the attempts to deport French labor under the Relève and the STO.[51] On 4 September, 422 Jews—145 men, 277 women and children—left the camp of La Lande for Drancy. The only ones left were seventy-eight children, seven pregnant women, ten very sick patients, four elderly people, and a Jewish doctor and a student to provide some sort of service. By the end of October all the Jews had gone and La Lande took on a new function, as an internment camp for over 250 female communists.[52] On 7 October French police and gendarmerie chiefs were summoned to see Gestapo chief Ernst in Angers and told that, following orders from Hitler and Göring, all remaining foreign Jews, including children, the old, and the sick, were to be rounded up "without pity" on Friday, 9 October, at 7:00 A.M. and deported. They would be allowed to take two blankets, two pairs of shoes, underwear, and washing things but would have to hand over identity papers, ration cards, money, valuables, and even keys to the SS. The operation would take place under the direction of the SS but, said Ernst, the SS were too busy themselves to make the arrests and manage the deportation, which would be up to the French police and gendarmerie. Naturally, said Ernst, French Jews would not be included.[53]

The arrests, prefect Daguerre later confirmed, almost with pride, were undertaken "*uniquely*" by the French police."[54] Thirteen people were arrested in Angers, including the five Sternchuss children and their grandmother Rebecca, thirty-four were arrested elsewhere in the department, and sixty-nine were brought from Tours. All 116, as in July, were housed in the

Grand Séminaire of Angers until, on 16 October, they were taken in three buses to Angers station, where they were put on a train to Drancy, escorted by twenty-two French gendarmes and two Feldgendarmes. Not only were the French police happy to play the leading role, they did not seem concerned that, as usual, French Jews were caught in the net. Of the 116 Jews deported, forty were French, according to the official lists, and the number was probably forty-seven because some, like the Sternchuss family, were now cited as Polish whereas previously they had been recorded as French.[55] Among those in the contingent from Tours were some extremely eminent French Jews, now all in their seventies, such as Albert Lipman, former first president of the appeals court of Tours, and his wife, Berthe, from Lorraine; merchants David and Benjamin Aron, who originated from Dole in the Jura; and David's wife, Alice, born in Constantine, Algeria, and active in the Croix Rouge.[56] Alice and David Aron were in fact moved from Drancy to the Rothschild Hospital in Paris and wrote to the prefect of Indre-et-Loire asking that since they were third-generation French, had lived in Tours for fifty-seven years, and were "highly respected in commerce," they be allowed to return to Tours. The prefect replied that the German police prohibited their return, and David Aron died in the Rothschild Hospital the following month.[57]

While the French police and administration seemed to be hardened to the deportations, public reaction was becoming less ambivalent. Too much significance should perhaps not be attached to the gesture of M. Dupré, manager of the café opposite the Grand Séminaire of Angers, who submitted a bill for 12,220 francs for meals provided to the inmates between 13 and 16 October, since he had a living to make. Prefect Daguerre detected a growing concern among local people, not least because with the arrest of French Jews as well as foreign Jews the line between who was liable for persecution and who was safe was becoming blurred. "There have been harsh criticisms of the deportation of women and small children brought together in Angers from several departments," he wrote. "The population has not been indifferent to the removal of whole families, taken in trucks across the town to the railway station. People are saying everywhere, 'Today, it's the Jews, tomorrow it will be the others.' "[58] Gradually, it seems, the pressure of public opinion was beginning to have an effect on the attitude of the French authorities. True, there were scarcely any more

Jews in the region. After the roundup of thirty-eight Jews in his department on 9 October, prefect Dupard reported that "there are now no Jews, whether French or foreign, on the coastal stretch of Loire-Inférieure," which is the only place they had ever been anyway.[59] In June 1943 the Renseignements Généraux section of the police reported that there were no Jews left in Maine-et-Loire.[60] In fact, there were still sixty-four mainly Polish, Russian, and Turkish Jews at the isolated work camp of Clefs, north of Angers, but they were rounded up by the Sicherheitsdienst on 22 November 1943 and arrived at Drancy two days later.[61]

The persecution of the Jews was now virtually of academic interest, reduced to tracking down Jews on the run from Paris and elsewhere and exposing Jews lying low under false identities. These were the concerns not of the prefectoral administration, the police, or the gendarmerie, but of the professional anti-Semites of the 'CGQJ. This outfit, sinister though it sounded, was isolated and extremely ineffective. Its regional delegate in Angers from September 1942, Georges Gasseau, was a smooth talker but a fraud who had no staff, failed to pay his office phone bills, plundered the properties of deported Jews, and was finally dismissed in the spring of 1943. The CGQJ had a file on 200 to 300 Jews in the region, but most of the bogus Aryans it tried to uncover were in fact genuine. It needed a network of paid informers but did not have the funds and discovered that public opinion was against it.[62] The police and prefectoral administration found it obsessed and interfering. For nine months, for example, it was determined to nail a certain Jacques Cohen or Coen, an antiques dealer of Nantes, as a Greek Jew, black marketeer, and Gaullist spy. The Nantes police, supported by the prefecture, insisted that the name was Coen and that he had a baptism certificate and had been married in a Catholic church. The regional delegate of the CGQJ replied that it had medical evidence of Co(h)en's circumcision and that "his baptism in the Catholic religion in no way changes his racial identity." In the end the matter was decided by the Germans, who arrested him in April 1944.[63]

The deportation of the Jews ceased to interest the general public for one very simple reason: the heavy hand of the Gestapo was now descending not only on Jews and communists but on ordinary French citizens. The limited comfort brought by the sense that only the traditional Judeo-

Bolshevik demons were at risk was undermined by the fact that anyone suspected of opposition, let alone resistance, was liable to arrest and deportation. Among those who fell under suspicion were soldiers, notables, politicians, teachers, students, and eventually even bureaucrats and the police. The Gestapo terror also exposed division and treachery among French people. Just as in Germany the Gestapo was thin on the ground and relied on German citizens' denouncing one another, so also in France, as we saw in Chinon, the French were only too happy to turn one another in.[64] Moreover, after the show trial of communists in Nantes in January 1943, trial even by the military court of the Feldkommandantur was a luxury of the past. The Gestapo acted secretly and those they arrested simply disappeared—first tortured to reveal their accomplices, then quietly shot on a nearby firing range or deported to Germany. The model of deportation without trial introduced for the Jews, who, after all, had committed no crime, became standard practice for all other victims.

On 11 November 1942 German forces marched into the Free Zone, and the armistice army, 100,000 strong, was disbanded. Some of the cadres of the armistice army formed the Organisation de la Résistance Armée (ORA), which after two years' obedience to Marshal Pétain tended to be loyal less to de Gaulle than to his even more right-wing rival for leadership of the Free French, General Giraud. Giraudist opinion, it seems, was particularly strong in the region of Loches, the small town in the south of Touraine "liberated" in July 1940 when the demarcation line was redrawn but now once more occupied.[65] The Thirty-second Infantry Regiment, which had liberated Loches, immediately fell under suspicion. In January 1943 three members of the Gestapo, on orders from Brückle in Tours and apparently with the approval of Bousquet in Paris, called on the police chief of Loches to enlist his cooperation. They then arrested the recently demobilized commander of the regiment, Robert Martin, and two other officers.[66]

Less than two months later a knot of influential individuals in the Angers region were arrested. One, oddly enough, was the regional propaganda chief, Michel Favre. Regional prefect Roussillon was unable to extract the reason for his arrest from Gestapo chief Ernst but told Laval that "it seemed to be connected to the arrest of several people belonging to the PSF [Parti Social Français] and royalist circles in Angers."[67] He was able to secure the release of Favre but not of the head of the Secours National, Colonel François de Sauvebeuf. Sauvebeuf was also president of the Anjou federation of the PSF of Colonel de La Rocque and had chaired a meeting in July 1942 when de La Rocque had attacked Gaullism and called for a "good understanding" with Germany but made clear that France would not permit any amputation of its territory—a clear reference to Alsace-Lorraine, now ruled by gauleiters.[68] More nationalist than fascist, the PSF was dissolved by SS chief Oberg in November 1943. Sauvebeuf made over the PSF office in Angers to the Secours National, then held a clandestine meeting in his house the following January. Arrested on 9 March 1943, he was sent to the transit camp of Compiègne before being deported to Germany in January 1944. He was later joined by his colleague in the Society of Agriculture, Sciences, and Arts of Angers, Henri de Champagny, mayor of Somloire, *conseiller-général* of Vihiers, a man of chivalric, royalist, Vendean, and anti-German temperament. Champagny provoked the anger of the Germans by encouraging peasants not to cooperate with the Germans' requisitioning of milk and butter, saying, "What the peasants don't hand over, the Germans can't take." The Gestapo demanded that he resign as mayor, vetoed his membership in the *conseil départemental* that had recently been established by the Vichy authorities, and then arrested him.[69] He and Sauvebeuf were sent first to Buchenwald and then to Flossenberg, where Champagny died after three weeks in March 1944 and Sauvebeuf the following October.[70]

The wave of arrests was not confined to right-wing notables but extended to teachers, who tended to be on the other side of the political spectrum. Marie Talet, headmistress of the Collège Joachim du Bellay of Angers, was arrested in February 1943, along with two of her staff, allegedly having been denounced by the headmaster of the boys' lycée. This may have been because of Talet and her colleagues' beliefs or because of the actions of their pupils, for which the Germans now held them responsible. Louis Brun, the headmaster of the Lycée Descartes in Tours, was arrested by the Gestapo after a Gaullist graffito was discovered in a pupil's desk and a half rubbed out "Vive de . . ." in the toilets.[71] The Tours police, who worked well with Gestapo chief Brückle, managed to secure the release of Brun—who was supposed to support the "policy of collaboration"—so long as he was moved to another position, but the Angers police had no such luck with Mme Talet, who was deported to Ravensbrück, where she died.

The arrest of key figures in the local community had a powerful effect on opinion. "These arrests," reported the police commissioner of Angers, "have been the subject of much conversation and create a certain fear in many circles. Increasingly, however, people no longer express their opinions, even to their friends." In the absence of hard information, rumor was rife. "This week," continued the commissioner, "people say that six people have been shot, among them someone arrested recently."[72] Prefect Daguerre noted that those arrested were very respectable and often extremely loyal to Marshal Pétain. They belonged to "the most varied social milieux: shopkeepers, peaceable bourgeois, teachers from colleges and lycées, the headmistress of the Collège de Jeunes Filles, who was universally respected. One day it's the chemist who goes to prison, the next it's a banker. Naturally these arrests are creating a special psychosis in public opinion, which makes propaganda for Franco-German understanding difficult to sell."[73] In Tours and Chinon in the spring of 1943, the Sicherheitsdienst cast its net even wider, rounding up unsuspecting Frenchmen in cafés, cinemas, stations, even on the street. "Admittedly," said prefect Tracou, "most of them were released a few days later but these operations irritate the population and create a sort of terror."[74]

Arbitrary arrests did little for the spirit of Franco-German cooperation, but the German authorities were becoming increasingly frustrated by the lack of cooperation they seemed to be getting even from French officials. On 30 June 1943 a stranded American airman named Goodman walked into the café of Jeanne Barthe, who decided that he needed equipping with identity and ration cards. Either naïvely or because she had contacts there, she took the airman round to the town hall and prefecture of Tours, where various employees and officials were willing to help, right up to the secretary-general of the prefecture, Charles Aubert. It seems that the operation was revealed to police commissioner Boucherie and Gestapo chief Brückler by Bernard Molas-Quenescourt, *chef de cabinet* at the prefecture, who was highly regarded in collaborationist circles and envious of Aubert's job. German records show that until this point Aubert had appeared honest and loyal but was now acting completely differently. Aubert and five other staff members of the prefecture and town hall were arrested on 4 July

and in September were sent before the military court of the Feldkommandantur of Tours, where Molas-Quenescourt testified against them. Aubert
was sentenced to three years' imprisonment. Tracou, impressed by "the
considerable emotion produced in the whole department by these arrests,"
went to Paris to try to secure Aubert's release, but to no avail. Aubert was
subsequently deported, and Molas-Quenescourt duly inherited his job.[75]

Increasingly, it was not just parts of the administration on which the
Germans felt they could not rely but elements of the French police. While
most of the police continued to collaborate with the Gestapo, some individuals grew disillusioned with their role and became prey to infiltration
by Resistance groups that could benefit from armed, structured, and highly
mobile organizations. Inspector Jean Vairé of Nantes, for example, headed
a group of the Sûreté of Nantes who belonged to the "Hussards of Liberty,"
orchestrated since October 1942 by a Missouri-born, French-speaking
RAF officer named Ted Wilkinson, who was an agent of the British
Special Operations Executive in the Loire area. Obliged to go underground
in August 1943, Vairé was denounced by a peasant in the Sarthe and
arrested by the Gestapo, by which time four of his colleagues in the Sûreté
had been arrested too. Condemned to death, then deported, Vairé was
repatriated in May 1945. In Angers, a young officer of the Sûreté, Henri
Robin, was arrested by the Gestapo on 31 August 1943. One colleague,
Jean Martin, fled, but another, Gaston Cousseau of the municipal police,
was tracked down. The regional prefect was informed that they had been
"forming Resistance groups and collecting weapons." Robin and Cousseau
survived Mauthausen and Neuengamme, respectively. In Saumur, finally,
Aristide Royer, a gendarmerie captain, headed a Resistance group that
included police as well as demobilized officers and NCOs of the armistice
army but that was broken by the Gestapo, with terrible consequences, in
September 1943.[76] Learning of the arrests, the normally calm people of
Anjou became anxious and fearful and started to talk about "a reign of
terror in the country like that known to exist in Germany."[77] The reign
of terror created an unbridgeable gulf between the French and Germans
but also had a second result, to unite the French and the foreigners in their
midst, who had been separated until then by Vichy's practice of divide and
rule. Henceforth everybody was at risk: they were all Jews now.

12

Conscription

On Friday, 2 October 1942, the Ministry of Information delegate for Loire-Inférieure organized a meeting at the Batignolles-Châtillon locomotive plant in Nantes to drum up support for the Relève plan by which French workers would go to work in German factories in exchange for French POWs, who would be allowed to return home. Of the workforce of 2,400, about a quarter turned out. The manager, after announcing that a quota of seventy-five workers and eight technicians had been imposed on the plant, introduced the speakers, who were a former POW and a former worker in Germany. Robert Tillaut, who had returned under the plan from two years in a German POW camp, was listened to in silence. But Lamothe, who had gone to work in Germany for six months, was greeted by shouts of "Why did you bother to come back?," "You should have stayed there!," and "Traitor!" Tillaut, who tried to mingle with groups of workers, was chased out amid whistles and catcalls, and the party of visitors left hurriedly by car. Subsequently he wrote to the Ministry of Information official to say that he could no longer help. "I went home after the Batignolles session much more depressed than I imagined. . . . I have suffered cruelly from coming up against such a lack of understanding. I addressed the workers purely so that they could hear the voice of those who are waiting behind the barbed wire. In vain. I appealed to their generosity and they were not moved. You can see how distressed I am."[1]

First thing Monday morning, 5 October, the Nantes gendarmerie picked up copies of a tract in the suburban streets signed by "the popular factory committees" and clearly communist in inspiration. Addressed to the engineering workers, the tract explained that the Relève was designed to liberate not French POWs but German workers who would then be sent to fight the Russians on the eastern front:

> The Vichy traitors and their stooges Dupard and Co. have agreed with Hitler to send men to Germany by force. You have already refused. Good. HOLD FAST. DO NOT GO. DO NOT LEAVE. Form a single bloc. Do not allow those who have been picked to leave. Tomorrow it will be your turn. Go on strike. Fight if you must to save your lives. Use every means possible to ensure that nobody goes. Show the invader and the traitors that you are not frightened, that you are decent people. Hitler will be defeated. Hasten his defeat. Don't work for him, you will only prolong the war. Stick together. NOT A SINGLE FRENCH WORKER FOR THE BOCHES.[2]

The following day, returning from lunch, the Batignolles workers were confronted by the list of those who had been selected to go to Germany. Immediately they put down their tools. The management did not report the strike but convened the shop stewards and tried to negotiate a return to work. But the news leaked out and prefect Dupard was summoned to the Feldkommandantur, where Major von Trotha threatened to arrest any workers who failed to show. As it happened, two high-ranking Vichy officials, one representing the Ministry of Information and the other Laval, had come to Nantes to investigate the incident of 2 October. They persuaded the German authorities that if they lifted the threat of arrests they would talk to the shop stewards and those selected about the duty of going to Germany. The situation was defused and the workers went back after a strike that lasted three hours in all—a gesture that was more symbolic than anything else but a courageous step taken in defiance of German orders.

The incident sheds a good deal of light on the issue of the Relève, which was negotiated with the Germans by Laval after he returned to power in April 1942 and sold to the French with the maximum of public relations spin available at the time. Fritz Sauckel, a former gauleiter, then governor of Thuringia, and now responsible for recruiting labor for German factories by fair means or foul from all over German-occupied Europe, demanded from France 350,000 workers (100,000 of them skilled engineering workers). Laval insisted that the right "psychological ground" had to be prepared and was hoping for the release of one POW for every worker recruited. Sauckel, with Hitler behind him, was difficult to impress and it took Laval eight hours on 16 June simply to get him to agree to repatriate 50,000 POWs in return for 150,000 *skilled* workers.[3] Laval announced the Relève in a radio broadcast on 22 June during which he famously said that "he hoped for the victory of Germany because without it communism will take over everywhere." Recruitment offices were opened in town centers and the authorities waited for the lines to form. They did not. By the end of July only 40,000 workers had left, only a quarter of them skilled, and a crossover of a departing train of volunteers and a returning POW train did not take place until 11 August at Compiègne, when Laval revealed for the first time the lopsided nature of the deal. It became clear to the Germans that waiting for volunteers would not begin to meet the quotas they needed and an ordinance of 22 August 1942 gave them the powers to requisition labor. Ever eager to assert the autonomous role of the Vichy government between the German authorities and their prey, Laval issued a law on 4 September requiring all male workers between eighteen and fifty and unmarried women between twenty-one to thirty-five to "undertake all work that the government sees fit in the higher interests of the nation."

Whether Vichy was acting as a brake on German demands or facilitating them is best examined in the local context. The Relève was an extremely unpopular measure that confronted head-on the interests of a French proletariat that had never been more cohesive and class-conscious. The comparison between the deportation of labor and the deportation of the Jews is instructive. The Jews, relatively few, dispersed among the local populations, and isolated from the rest of society as refugees or bearers of the yellow star, were not able to resist and elicited no more than pity when they were rounded up. The workers, concentrated in large-scale plants employing up to 2,000, firmly implanted in working-class communities, were able to show defiance and demonstrate solidarity. Moreover, whereas the French authorities acted promptly and efficiently to execute German orders to round up Jews, when it came to sending workers to Germany they were confronted by industrial action and angry public opinion and were forced to acknowledge that the Vichy regime, though nominally authoritarian, relied in reality on tacit consent.

General Kurt Feldt, who had replaced Neumann-Neurode as head of Bezirk B, summoned all four regional prefects responsible for the west of France to deliver on Sauckel's instructions. As far as Loire-Inférieure went, 6,800 workers would have to be recruited by 12 November. Any worker who refused to sign a contract or accept one signed on his behalf by the labor inspector would be treated as a saboteur. "It is not a voluntary system," reflected prefect Dupard, "but scarcely disguised requisition."[4] Torn between the formal constraints of collaboration and the anticipated wave of popular hostility, he cranked up the propaganda offensive. On 11 August 1942 *Le Phare* of Nantes published a picture of Dupard reading a speech in support of the Relève under a portrait of Marshal Pétain, his large frame seated next to the Feldkommandant of Nantes and a rather bemused and frightened young man who was being congratulated as the 5,000th worker to leave for Germany. "Bring home to the fields of peace those who left for the battlefields," Dupard urged. "It is my duty to emphasize the immense hope that the appeal of the government has inspired among our rural populations."[5] *Le Phare*, which was dedicated to the policy of Franco-German collaboration, tried to recruit other key figures for the campaign, but with little success. Monsignor Villepelet, the bishop of Nantes, told the editor that he did not comment on either political or temporal issues, and even a follow-up visit by the Propagandastaffel failed to persuade him to change his mind.[6] More serious was the attitude of Gaëtan Rondeau, the mayor of Nantes. He, too, refused to give an interview to *Le Phare* in support of the Relève and told the regional delegate of the Ministry of Information that his office required reserve and discretion in order to maintain order and calm.[7] Since the execution of the hostages almost a year earlier, Rondeau had felt squeezed between the intensifying pressure of the Germans and the increasing panic of the local population. He did not feel that he could struggle against public opinion on behalf of a policy of collaboration in which he had less and less faith. He retired to his holiday property of Tiffauges in the Vendée and opted out of the collaborationist cause. He even sent his apologies to Marshal Pétain for not being able to attend a meeting of the Association of Mayors of France in Vichy at the end of August.[8] The case of the *Phare* interview was the last straw. Regional Gestapo chief Ernst told Dupard and regional prefect Roussillon that Rondeau would have to go; the mayor had adopted a policy of "neutrality" that amounted to following public opinion away from collaboration. Dupard tried to defend Rondeau and stalled for nearly two months, but at the end of September 1942 he visited Rondeau at Tiffauges and told him that the game was up.[9] Rondeau wrote a letter of resignation on 10 October, which was read to the municipal council on 20 October, and the council in solidarity resigned en bloc.[10]

While the fate of Mayor Rondeau was being decided, opposition to the Relève was spreading among the workers of Nantes. On 9 October, 300 of the 1,100 workers at the Société de Mécanique Générale de l'Ouest engineering works, of whom half were women, went on strike in response to a notice served on a dozen young workers out of the firm's quota of sixty-two. The local SS chief arrived with three officers of the Feldkommandantur and demanded that the young men be arrested. Prefect Dupard argued that such action would "have very regrettable consequences among the workers, and his *chef de cabinet* convened the management and the Comité Social d'Entreprise to remind them of their duty. Again the crisis was defused, but three days later the Chantiers de la Loire (1,700 workers) and the Chantiers de Bretagne (2,000) went on strike when they learned of the size of their quotas. Here the issue was settled by the management, and the workers went back after half an hour. The situation that arose at the SNCASO aircraft factory in Château-Bougon on 14 October, however, was much more serious. A team of four German civilians, including a representative of the Heinkel factory in Rostock, where the enlisted workers were to be taken, arrived at the factory with ninety-five work contracts to be signed. The workers refused to sign, and the workforce of over 1,600 went on strike. The German view was that propaganda had failed and it was now "up to the authority of the Wehrmacht to overcome all resistance [*Widerstand*]." Despite the attempt of the secretary-general of the prefecture, Yves Bayet, to negotiate, the Feldkommandant ordered a military occupation the next day. The workforce was screened and twenty-four of the chosen workers were arrested and imprisoned in Nantes until they had signed. But many workers, scenting a trap, failed to turn up that day and seventy designated workers were not found. Furious, the Feldkommandant ordered the management to provide a list of a hundred new workers to replace the missing seventy, whose arrest he demanded. After hard bargaining and promises that the police were on the trail of the missing men, the prefecture managed to avoid any more arrests.[11]

The predictions of the prefecture that arrests would only serve to inflame the workforce were proved correct. On 21 October strikes broke out in the Chantiers de Bretagne and the Chantiers de la Loire, where lists of 100 and 150 workers, respectively, were posted. The prefecture was unable to calm the situation and the movement spread that afternoon to seven other shipyards and factories—including the Chantiers Dubigeon, the Compagnie Nantaise des Chargeurs de l'Ouest, the Anciens Établissements Joseph-Paris, and the Entreprises Métropolitaines et Coloniales—involving over 5,000 workers, and the following day to the Société Nantaise de Fonderies and the SNCF workshops of Nantes-Blottereau.[12] The police intendant of Angers went so far as to call it a "general strike."[13] The effect of the strike in terms of municipal politics was also considerable. The new mayor of Nantes proposed to Laval by prefect Dupard was Henri Orrion, fifty, holder of the Croix de Guerre from the 1914–18 war, president of the syndicate of wholesale druggists of the west of France, whose attitude, Dupard thought, "inspires the confidence of representatives of the German army." Unfortunately, Orrion did not inspire the labor representatives who had sat on Rondeau's council, and he was unable to find any labor leaders either within the CGT unions or outside them to serve as municipal councillors. After frantic negotiations he managed to put together a "special delegation" of ten men drawn from professional, business, and administrative circles to run the city; he would be president of the delegation, not mayor. Technocratic rather than political, it might stand for efficiency, but it did not have the support of the working-class communities that played such a vital part in the political life of the city, and it indicated that the gap between the Vichy authorities and public opinion was steadily widening.[14]

The workers who were sent to Germany made their views quite clear as special trains left Nantes at the beginning of November. One trainload of workers was immobilized when the communication cord was pulled, and agitated families on the station platform had to be dispersed by Feldgendarmes shooting into the air.[15] As they were moved off, the workers sang the "Internationale" and shouted, "Death to Laval" and "The stake for Hitler."[16] The promises of the Relève looked distinctly threadbare as, in a fortnight when a thousand workers left, only seven prisoners returned to Nantes. For all his public campaigning, prefect Dupard was forced to admit in private that "the Relève, in the original formulation conceived by the government, has indeed been a failure."[17]

The Germans, fighting for their lives on the eastern front, became increasingly impatient with the shambles of the Relève. Between 1 June and 31 December 1942, the Relève had furnished 240,000 workers for Germany, 135,000 of whom were skilled, mostly from the Occupied Zone and the industrial areas within them. Now Sauckel decided on a "second action," which would recruit 250,000 workers, of whom 150,000 would be skilled, in half the time—by 31 March—and the same again by the end of June. To ensure that French interests and sovereignty were respected, as far as they could be, Minister of Industrial Production Jean Bichelonne, another acolyte of Laval, published the law on the Service du Travail Obligatoire (STO) on 16 February 1943. This established labor service in Germany as an alternative to military service, which was clearly suspended, and was to apply in the first instance to those born in 1920, 1921, and 1922.[18] It was a powerful project but, unlike the deportation of the Jews, it failed to work.

To begin with, German demands for French labor in Germany clashed with their own demands for French labor in France, either building coastal defenses for the Todt Organization or working in factories specially assigned to production for the war effort. A German circular of 7 October 1942, for example, demanded 100,000 additional workers, especially from the building trade, to be provided by the French administration. The quota for Indre-et-Loire was 1,000, driving prefect Tracou to protest to the minister of labor that German demands were "absolutely out of proportion to the available workforce" and to remind the Feldkommandant that "a real effort is already being made to send workers to Germany."[19] Two months later the Feldkommandant told Tracou that the labor supply for Todt had been "inadequate so far and catastrophic this week" and instructed him that the full quota was to be delivered by the end of the following week. In a vain attempt to square the circle, the labor inspector admitted to Tracou that, in consultation with the employers in the construction industry, he was illicitly moving workers from protected factories to supply Todt.[20] The protected Rüstungs- or V-Betriebe, of course, also had their own claims on the French labor force, and those who worked for them could not in theory be recruited for the STO. They constituted an excellent refuge for workers who did not want to be conscripted for work in Germany, and even the German military authorities with an interest in these factories were keen to protect them from the STO recruiters. An official of the Feldkommandantur of Nantes was delighted in March 1943 that there were now eighty-eight V-Betriebe in the department, with another thirty on the way. Initially, he said, they had been able to protect their labor force but they had been "severely affected" by the second Sauckel action and recently most of the V-Betriebe had been made to surrender workers. "This double use of V-Betriebe," he concluded, "provokes a good deal of irritation and much unrest."[21] Increasingly, however, Sauckel found himself pitted against Albert Speer, the armaments minister, who believed that it would be more beneficial to keep French workers working for the German war machine in France. From the autumn of 1943, Rü-Betriebe and V-Betriebe were combined as Speer- or S-Betriebe, whose workforces would be immune to deportation. In November 1943 Oberst Keil, head of the Rüstungskommando of the Le Mans region, called meetings of French factory bosses in Le Mans, Angers, and Tours to announce that the elevation of forty-two of the seventy Rü-Betriebe to S-Betriebe would undoubtedly induce the *réfactaires* (draft dodgers) back to work.[22]

German labor demands were thus contradictory and often counterproductive. In the haste to extract quotas, they were also arbitrary, riding roughshod over categories of exemption that had been agreed on with the Vichy government. The arbitrariness, however, was at times undermined by the corruption of Germany's own officials, for cutting across the general German interest in milking the French economy was the self-interest of particular Germans who made a profit from selling individual exemptions. Since the STO was in lieu of military service, categories such as former POWs and demobilized members of the armistice army—unless they happened to be metalworkers by trade—were exempted, but the German authorities were impatient with such niceties. The labor inspector of Indre-et-Loire reported that his service could "only *strive* to obtain the respect of rules the application of which is subordinate to the interpretation of local German authorities."[23]

Arbitrariness might be efficient, but its other face was corruption. How corrupt the German administration was is difficult to ascertain, for the evidence is anecdotal, but two examples suggest that rogues were not rare. Sonderführer Hermann Brüning, the son of a Koblentz banker whose sister had married a rich Parisian, was already used to an easy life when he came to Nantes in the summer of 1942 to work for the employment service. He spent a lot of time and money at the Chez Elle bar of the Hôtel de Paris, in the company either of women or of directors of German firms who came to prospect for labor. A colleague became suspicious when an anxious Frenchman visited the office one Sunday wishing to speak to Herr Brüning and let slip that he would offer him 10,000 francs to get out of labor service in Germany. Further inquiries revealed that it was common knowledge in the cafés and bars of Nantes that Brüning took money to protect workers from labor service. He was sent before a German military court in April 1943 and sentenced to four months in prison and loss of rank.[24] Xavier Hupfer, a Lorrainer from Metz, interpreter for the economic services of the Feldkommandantur of Angers, took money for issuing certificates not only to farmers to exempt them from the STO but to industrialists who wanted their factories classified as S-Betriebe in order to protect their workforce. He was brought low by his arrogance—arguing that to avoid the STO "three-quarters of the population of France are peasants and the rest sick"—by bringing the shoe industry of Cholet to a virtual standstill by failing to process classification documents, and finally by announcing, "It's not the prefecture that's in charge but the Feldkommandantur, and the Feldkommandantur is me."[25]

One of the problems with labor service was that, even according to the rules, the burden did not fall equitably on all sectors of the population, so that those who felt penalized were more likely to put up resistance. The Relève fell solely on workers, who were supposed to take over the sacrifice of the soldier-peasants in the POW camps but who did not necessarily see it that way. The workers of the Nantes–Saint-Nazaire area resented the fact that the peasants were exempt, the more so because they were seen to be fleecing the working classes by selling their produce at inflated prices.[26] In Anjou, prefect Daguerre even spoke of a "class struggle," with the workers complaining that they alone shouldered the burden of labor service.[27] Another issue was the generation gap. Although it made sense for younger workers without attachments to leave home, in practice they often opted for a protected factory or the Todt Organization, leaving heads of families liable to be sent to Germany. Many of these inequalities were supposed to be ironed out by the STO, which imposed labor service on young men of military age, between twenty and twenty-two. Unfortunately, like universal military service, it was never quite universal. One privileged category was that of students, who were granted exemption until further notice. The workers of Nantes–Saint-Nazaire now transferred their anger at cosseted peasants to cosseted students, who, because secondary and especially higher education demanded money and leisure, were essentially middle-class. Prefect Dupard thought that the students might have been excused until 1 June, by which time they would have taken their exams and then been eligible to go. As it happened, he said, the measure looked like an additional privilege for the bourgeoisie, "which until now has not suffered much from the war and Occupation."[28] These exemptions were abolished by the summer of 1943, and prefect Tracou of Indre-et-Loire reported that this equitable measure had been welcomed by the workers, who now saw "not only their friends leaving but also peasants, students, and functionaries."[29]

Laval's strategy was always to insert the French government and administration between the German authorities and the French population, in order to preserve French sovereignty. Whether this made the burden of the Occupation lighter is open to debate. Vichy was officially committed to the policy of collaboration and thus in one sense legitimated and facilitated German rule. But the more burdens were imposed on the French people, the more popular discontent increased and the more the French

administration found itself impossibly squeezed between its German masters and a rising tide of popular anger and fear. The STO was the single
most important factor that demonstrated to the French people the perni-
ciousness of collaboration. What it meant in reality was the subject of
swelling myth and rumor. One myth was that is was "disguised deportation."[30] Just as the Jews had been told that they were being sent to labor
camps in the east, so the same story was being fed to French workers, who
were in fact being sent to "another destination."[31] Another myth was that
workers were going to service German armies at the rear on the eastern
front or even to fight alongside German soldiers against the Russians.[32]
Even if things were as people were told, and they would be working in
German factories, the Allied bombing of German cities made this
extremely hazardous. Workers who had been evacuated from Hamburg,
where their factories had been destroyed, returned to Tours in the late
summer of 1943 and reinforced fears of the holocaust being inflicted on
the cities of the Reich.[33]

The French authorities tried to steer an increasingly tricky course
between German demands and popular resentment. Prefect Dupard, summoned to a meeting at the Feldkommandantur of Nantes on 8 March
1943, was told by a representative of Sauckel that the French police were,
under instructions from Laval, "responsible for the departure of French
workers to Germany." Dupard replied that his interpretation of the STO
regulations was that the French police were responsible for arresting conscripts who failed to appear, but not for sending them to Germany.[34]
Whereas the French police seem to have acted efficiently and with alacrity
when rounding up Jews, their attitude to the STO was altogether more
relaxed. Mayor Darmaillacq's account of what happened in Cholet may
suffer a little from special pleading after the Liberation, but even if it were
only partly true it would be significant. Darmaillacq asserted that when the
young men were conscripted for the STO and many reported sick, he did
not send the police to visit them at home. When he did have to send the
police to check on certain queries, to satisfy the prefecture, he reported
that everything was in order. Some individuals were even said to have gone
to Germany, whereas in fact "they were walking quite openly around the
town." The town hall, he recounted, never became involved in choosing

who had to go, and when some failed to report to the station after a period of leave to return to Germany, he did not send the police after them.[35]

Mayors played a crucial role in issues of labor recruitment, whether for Todt or the STO. Still subject in rural areas to pressure from the Germans, they were even more vulnerable to pressure from local inhabitants, whom they knew and who looked to them to protect their interests. Mayors in Touraine, faced with a demand to find workers for the Todt Organization in February 1943, sent in such replies as "The commune is essentially agricultural and no workers live here" or simply "I am unable to choose anyone."[36] There were risks in reacting too energetically on behalf of the local population, as well as risks for not reacting strongly enough. The Marquis de Lussac, mayor of Saint-Catherine-de-Fierbois, confronted the German authorities in the presence of thirty men summoned for Todt work. When he failed to have the village baker released, he went into a tirade against the "veritable slave trade" that was being practiced. Brückle's Sicherheitspolizei were summoned from Tours and the mayor was arrested. He was sentenced to five years' imprisonment by the military court of Tours, and prefect Tracou was required to dismiss him as mayor by the German authorities in Angers.[37] M. Forest, the seventy-two-year-old mayor of Marçay and himself the father of a POW in Germany, who was alleged to have provided ration tickets to STO dodgers working illicitly on farms in his commune, was arrested on Brückle's orders and held hostage until other mayors provided Brückle with lists of STO dodgers working in the region, a crisis that the prefect was not able to resolve for nearly three months.[38] Farther west, in the arrondissement of Châteaubriant, mayors were threatened with violence if they seemed to be doing the bidding of the authorities. The mayor of Soudan received a death threat from one individual who had been selected, that of Nozay had insults painted on his house after he failed to include his son on the list of those who would go, and the subprefect complained of a "general tendency of resignations" of rural mayors who could not cope with hostility on all sides.[39]

The dilemmas caused by the STO afflicted not only local mayors but also the higher administration. Just as the Relève broke the career of Gaëtan Rondeau, mayor of Nantes, so the STO proved the undoing of the regional prefect of Angers, Jean Roussillon. The German authorities were no longer prepared to waste time negotiating or to massage French sensibilities. They now wanted their demands met in full, immediately and with no quibbling. The German authorities were impressed by Roussillon's skill and competence but began to find him secretive, opportunistic, "smooth as an eel." Although he was officially anti-British and anticommunist, he was opposed to the collaborationist parties and told the president of Groupe Collaboration that he would not publish articles in the press in favor of the STO, which he regarded as a "slave trade." He had apparently told the police not to make notes of anti-German slogans shouted by STO conscipts as their trains left and done nothing to bring anti-German officials under control. "So long as the regional prefect remains in Angers," concluded the report on Roussillon, "the work of collaboration will have no luck."[40] Roussillon was removed from office in July 1943 and was happy to pose as a victim. "The Americans will soon come and sort things out," he is alleged to have said, although he did not manage to endear himself to the Free French, who saw him as a "complete collaborator" and a man without conscience.[41]

The episcopate, as well as the civil administration, wobbled over the STO and was forced to reconsider its doctrine of blindly rendering unto Caesar. The long delay before the bishops responded to the roundup of Jews and the fact that powerful protest came from only two bishops in the Free Zone, the archbishop of Toulouse and the bishop of Montauban, has been well documented.[42] Under pressure from the Christian faithful, the episcopate responded to the STO more assertively in the former Occupied Zone, but the opportunity for bold intervention was again passed by. The first reaction of Cardinal Liénart, bishop of Lille, was, "accept it, it would be cowardly to shirk it." Within a week, in response to demands from industrial workers mediated by the Jocist movement, he announced, "To get out of it is not a sin. I am not going to advise you to go. It is a question of force."[43] The Assembly of Cardinals and Archbishops drafted an official message along these lines that was to be read out by all bishops on Easter Day. Monsignor Gaillard, archbishop of Tours, asked his bishops to come and fetch copies, which were to remain absolutely secret until then. The message claimed to discuss not the politics of the question but the religious and moral dimension, but what was central was the same ambiguity:

> We cannot, our dearest brothers, make it an obligation of conscience to submit to the requisition. Does it follow that

we are advising you to shirk it? No! We are confronted by a force that the French authorities are trying to make more humane. We ask the Christians who will be going to give the ordeal its full redemptive value for the salvation of our country and wherever they go to console, support, and comfort their comrades in work.[44]

Even this message was thought, on reflection, by Cardinal Liénart and Cardinal Suhard, archbishop of Paris, to be too outspoken. Monsignor Villepelet learned that Suhard thought the text too tragic for Easter Day, that Petain had wanted changes, and that Laval had indicated that it would undermine his negotiations with the Germans. Rather than risk exposing individual bishops to German reprisals, it was agreed that only Cardinals Suhard, Liénart, and Gerlier of Lyon would sign the text, taking full responsibility, and that it would be read on Joan of Arc Day, 9 April. Even this was an event in Nantes, where Monsignor Villepelet read the message from the pulpit in front of the mayor and prefecture officials, and the Propagandastaffel telephoned to ask for the text.[45] In Angers, reading the message was probably the bravest thing the meek Monsignor Costes did under the Occupation, although the text relayed by the regional prefect concentrated on the inhumanity of separating young people from their families and the cruel conditions they had to endure.[46]

The Church, of course, was not the only body defining a position on the STO, nor did it necessarily command the most attention. The Sicherheitspolizei of Nantes warned the prefect that they had received intelligence about a communist-inspired strike scheduled for 19 April 1943 between 11:45 A.M. and midday in the Paris region, and they demanded that all police and gendarmerie be placed on full alert.[47] Nothing happened, but on the eve of May Day communist tracts were picked up in the streets of Nantes and Tours, calling on workers variously to strike, demonstrate, refuse to go to Germany, sabotage German factories, and form groups of guerillas.[48] Demonstrations there were, as conscripts were rounded up and sent off with ever more urgency to meet the deadline of the third Sauckel action at the end of June. On 21 June, for example, a train carrying many railway employees from Nantes stopped at Angers's Saint-Laud station. The carriages had been painted with slogans such as "Vive la classe de

1942," "Vive les cheminots," "Vive la France," and "Vive de Gaulle." As the train was about to leave, a hundred or so conscripts in the front cars struck up the "Marseillaise" and everyone on the train began hurling insults at the German soldiers stationed on the platform. Fourteen young men were detained by the gendarmerie, and the train was delayed by nearly an hour.[49]

Those who actually left on the trains for Germany were only a minority of those called up, but the rate of draft dodging varied considerably from area to area. Figures for the second Sauckel action of January–March 1943 show that in Indre-et-Loire 89 percent of the quota of 2,450 reported for duty. "There is more resignation than revolt," reported prefect Tracou, putting it down to "the calm temperament of the Tourangeaux." He added, however, that they were worried that by doing their docile duty they would be considered suckers (*poires*).[50] In Maine-et-Loire, 84 percent of the quota of 2,700 reported, but there was much more recalcitrance in Loire-Inférieure, where only half the quota of 4,000 found their way to Germany. The result for the third Sauckel action in Loire-Inférieure in April–June was even worse. For a quota of 3,650 imposed on the department, only 1,324 (36 percent) actually left. Since 400 young men were in fact transferred from the Todt Organization, the real total was 924 (25 percent). The number of draft dodgers was calculated as 1,130. Curiously, the highest rate of refusal was not in the arrondissement of Nantes, where the strikes against the Relève had concentrated (40 percent), or even in that of Saint-Nazaire (60 percent) but in the arrondissement of Châteaubriant, in the deep Breton interior, where it was 80 percent. The main enemies of the STO were the peasants, who in the summer of 1942, when the "class of '42" was conscripted, were effectively summoned for the first time. In this region of isolated farms and *bocage* it was easy to find illicit agricultural work and be fed without the need for tickets. The local farmers were delighted to find a new source of labor and were extremely sullen and obstructive when the gendarmerie made inquiries, which was rarely.[51]

For many historians, and even for Laval in his negotiations with Sauckel, the STO dodgers fed directly into the Resistance. This is a myth that dies hard. For the vast majority of *réfractaires*, however, the purpose of dodging the STO was to increase their chances of survival, and joining the Maquis was only one of their options. In the Mauges commune of La

Pommeraye, a dozen young men went on the STO but two tried (unsuccessfully) to flee to the Spanish frontier and many simply went to ground locally, one emerging at the Liberation to hoist the tricolor onto the church spire. The collective history of the village makes no mention of the Maquis.[52] Near Segré, the son of the stationmaster of La Ferrière-de-Flée hid most of the time in a concealed room above the station, receiving his ration tickets from the daughter of the *secrétaire de mairie* and having lunch regularly with his family.[53] If there was a political dimension to opposition to the STO in this part of western France, it was a rerun of the Vendean uprising of 1793, when Catholics and royalists resisted being conscripted into the armies of the Republic so as to fight on the eastern frontier for a cause they did not believe in. This equivalence is reinforced by the fact that the most anti-STO area of Anjou was the Mauges, the Angevin Vendée. As early as 1942 the German commander in Cholet reported that the local people were "particularly attached to their family and home [*Heimat*] and can be taken from them only with great difficulty."[54] On 28 June 1943, at the high point of the deportation of the class of '42, when 428 youth left Angers station, 335 of them peasants, the song of the Jeunesse Agricole Chrétienne was heard more than the "Internationale," and the slogans painted on the carriages included "Vendée, cabbage eaters" as well as "Vive de Gaulle."[55] The arrondissement of Châteaubriant, in the region most hostile to the draft, was described by the prefect as a "theater of terrorism," and in June 1944 it brought forth the Maquis of Saffré.[56] Whether its *maquisards* were always the heroes of later legend, however, was open to question. Here and in adjoining cantons of the Breton interior such as Guéméné-Penfao, Saint-Nicolas-de-Redon, and Saint-Gildas-des-Bois was a veritable Wild West in which masked and armed gangs roamed, taking ration books from *mairies*, cigarettes from tobacconists, and money, food, radios, and old weapons that had not been handed in from isolated farmhouses. On 19 May 1944 ten or eleven individuals, one of whom said he had escaped from prison in Vitré, took 33,000 francs, silver, and a radio set from the Rousseau family, who were tailors near Saint-Nicolas-de-Redon, and also shaved the wife's head. Four days later a gang speaking the local patois robbed a farmhouse in the neighboring commune. Again they took money, food, clothing, and documents and, in the absence of the husband, shaved the wife's head.[57] Of course, shaving women's heads for "horizontal collaboration" was common at the Liberation, but it is debatable whether such gestures, when accompanying armed robbery, merited the accolade of resistance.[58]

As the recruitment of labor became more and more difficult, the German authorities required, and resorted to, ever more desperate measures. One new tactic was the establishment of mixed Franco-German "combing commissions," which summoned employers to see if any more labor could be extracted from their firms. The commission in Nantes, which sat at the German recruitment office in the rue Sully, met for the first time in February 1943 but became especially active a year later, meeting four days a week. On 7 March 1944 M. Merlant of the food-processing firm Maison Amieux was summoned before the commission. He protested that his small firm had already provided five men for the Todt Organization and twelve for the STO and cited a German circular of 2 February to the effect that for obvious reasons the food industry should be protected. The commission told him that this instruction had now been overruled, and the deputy director of the Commissariat Général à la Main d'Oeuvre (CGMO), the French labor department, reported to the prefect that "employers are becoming more and more indisciplined in front of the combing commission and the proportion of employers who do not appear is now higher than that of employees."[59] It appears, however, that the director of the CGMO, Viennot, who sat on the combing commission, was playing something of a double game. General Feldt wrote to the new regional prefect, Charles Donati, to complain that the poor recruitment figures for Loire-Inférieure were made worse by Viennot's seeking to protect young workers by moving them to S-Betriebe "behind the back of the Feldkommandantur and contrary to instructions from higher authorities."[60]

One of the structural problems with the labor recruitment system was that German officials with responsibility for S-Betriebe preferred younger workers, who were thus protected from the STO, leaving older married workers to be sent off to Germany. In February regional prefect Donati visited the Hesse-Nassau area of Germany, where the bulk of STO conscripts from the region were working in towns such as Frankfurt, Darmstadt, Wiesbaden, and Mainz. His main purpose was to report back favorably on the conditions enjoyed by French workers, and he told the press on his return that they were well-housed and well-fed, each camp having a French chef. His main criticism, also delivered to the press, was that he had come across fifty-year-old Frenchmen who were war veterans and heads of families, now doing another stint of duty while too many young men, who had suffered neither the war nor the defeat, were enjoying the easy life in protected factories back home. Donati received letters not only from French wives demanding their middle-aged husbands back but from workers in Germany who disagreed with his analysis of their conditions. One of the workers in Lübeck, who told Donati that he had read his account in the *Écho de Nancy*, reported that they lived in cold huts, 150 men to a sink, worked twelve hours a day with only soup to eat, and had totally inadequate shelter from air raids. In reality, Donati was well aware of the workers' situation. "I was struck," he wrote to Laval, "by the bitterness, even the violence of their words." They felt duped and abandoned, waiting in vain for "*la relève de la Relève*" and realizing that those who had not done their duty with respect to the STO were faring very nicely. "It is a veritable army of discontented people who will return to France as soon as peace comes, to swell the ranks of the communists."[61]

Such was the pressure in the last months of the Occupation that no concessions were made to anyone, not to fathers of large families or even to women. The collaborationist Marcel Déat became minister of labor and the rumor spread that he was going to order "massive deportations" of workers.[62] A law of 1 February 1944 required the registration for labor service not only of men between sixteen and sixty but of women eighteen to forty-five. The threatened conscription of women violated a fundamental taboo and provoked a violent response from families, communities, and the Church. "Family life is still very solid and united in Anjou," reported an official of the Ministry of Information. "You will never persuade a father to accept that his daughter, even age twenty-five, will go to work a long way away, beyond his supervision and control." Given the danger of mixing women of different backgrounds and education, he predicted "a very lively resistance, not only from ordinary citizens but also from certain mayors, to the registration of women."[63] The Church's Assembly of Cardinals and Archbishops, which had previously maintained a cautious and ambiguous line on the STO, strongly condemned what it called "a serious attack on family life and the future of our country, on the dignity and moral susceptibility of women and on their providential vocation."[64] In short, their immortal souls were at risk.

The final step was to use on idle French youths the same method that had been used on the Jews: the roundup. As early as the summer of 1943 French police had raided cafés and cinemas in Nantes to check the papers of young men who might be shirking the STO, and that September the Germans simply arrested 300 SNCASO workers at the Château-Bougon airport outside Nantes, which had been bombed, and whisked them away for Todt work in Cherbourg.[65] The main season for such raids, executed by the French police on German instructions, was the following spring and summer: 16 March and 6 April 1944 in Angers and 19 May, 12, 13, 14, 18, and 21 June in Nantes. The haul rarely corresponded to the effort put in. The raid of Friday, 19 May, in Nantes involved fifty-six officers, who arrested 370 young men. Of these, sixty-six were detained, forty-two of whom were released after their papers were found to be in order. This left a total of eighteen who were selected to go to Germany and six to work for the Germans in France. The director of the CGMO (the former deputy, who had replaced the unreliable Viennot) reported that "this first operation was a great disillusion for the local German authorities, who expected a much bigger result and are especially disappointed not really to have detected the shirkers." Although the Feldkommandantur had given only six hours' notice before they went into action at 5:30 P.M., he admitted that, by no fault of his own department news, there had been "indiscretions" that rendered the operation "almost impossible."[66] If the leaks were not the fault of the labor department, they may well have been perpetrated by the police, who were clearly now operating by different rules than they had been when rounding up Jews two years earlier. The operations were becoming increasingly fruitless. During a raid on twenty-five cafés around the main railway station in Nantes on 18 June, 250 youths were checked but only three in the classes of 1940, 1941, and 1942 discovered; these were released after their situation was seen to be in order.[67] The plain fact was that young men who were eligible did not hang about cafés and cinemas in town centers on summer weekends, since the raids seemed to happen with a predictable regularity. It is also the case that it was scarcely in the interest of the French police or administration to be too tough on young people for the benefit of the Germans during those weekends in June 1944 when the Normandy landings had taken place and the Allies were on their way.

The deportation of French labor was the single most important factor that alienated the French population from the German authorities and those Vichy authorities that were seen to be relaying their demands. Strikes against recruitment for the Relève, demonstrations of STO conscripts in railway cars bound for Germany, or simply disappearing into a clandestine existence were different ways of expressing that opposition. Local authorities, squeezed between German demands and the discontent of the population, were placed in an impossible predicament. If they assisted in the business of labor recruitment they alienated their local constituencies, while if they obstructed the draft they faced dismissal as the Germans interfered increasingly in the makeup of the administration. Mayor Rondeau of Nantes and regional prefect Roussillon of Angers were removed by Vichy under pressure from the Germans for noncooperation over the Relève and the STO, respectively. The contrast in the attitude of the French administration toward the deportation of French workers on the one hand and toward the deportation of Jews on the other is nevertheless instructive. Admittedly Jews in France were often immigrants, widely scattered or already interned, making them vulnerable, whereas industrial workers and peasants, sustained by their own communities, could successfully go on strike or disappear into the countryside. The degree of opposition shown by French authorities—even the Church—to the deportation of labor, compared with their lack of action when it came to protecting Jews, suggests a double standard that throws at least some light on the question of French attitudes to the threatened Jewish population in their midst.

13

Disintegration

"*How can a* people as civilized as our former British allies be seized by such a fury of destruction, devastation, and death without in the least advancing their military cause?" asked *Le Courrier de Saint-Nazaire* after British planes bombed the port in February 1942, killing eighteen and injuring thirty-two people.[1] Following another British raid the following May, on nearby Nantes, the Kreiskommandant Major von Hasselbach prohibited military music in the soldiers' clubs and closed cinemas to German soldiers as a mark of respect for the victims. To his surprise, however, on the evening of the funeral all trace of mourning evaporated as the French crowded into the bars and cafés of Nantes and gave themselves over to loud music and laughter.[2]

These contradictory reflections shed interesting light on the predicament of French and Germans as, more than two years before the Normandy landings, the Allies began to attack the military and industrial infrastructure that underpinned the German war effort. Since most of the shipyards and factories of the Nantes–Saint-Nazaire conurbation were working for the Wehrmacht, the Luftwaffe, and above all the Kriegsmarine, they were considered legitimate targets for Allied bombers. Inevitably, and especially when American planes bombing from high altitude joined the campaign, French civilians as well as the German military suffered casualties. To some extent, this brought the French and the Germans together in common suffering. Certainly, Vichy propaganda was keen to exploit the raids to discredit perfidious Albion. Paradoxically, however, the French experienced some joy as the bombs rained down: each one was inflicting damage on the German war machine for which they were obliged to work and bringing closer the long-awaited moment of their liberation.

True, the bombing raids of early 1942 were minor compared with what was to come. The first target was Saint-Nazaire, which was attacked repeatedly in November 1942 and February 1943. Serious damage was inflicted on the Penhoët and Loire shipyards, the Saint-Nazaire foundry, the electricity works, and the nearby oil refinery of Donges.[3] On 9 November 186 people were killed, on 16–17 November 78, on 16 and 28 February 27 and 17, respectively.[4] The bombing on 28 February was described by prefect Dupard as "the most violent attack undertaken by Allied aircraft on a French town," turning Saint-Nazaire into "a huge brazier," destroying three-quarters of the town, and driving out the 12,000 people who still lived there. Such was the tragedy that the town was visited by Jean-Pierre Ingrand, representing the branch that the Vichy Ministry of the Interior was permitted to keep in Paris, and Colonel Bonhomme, aide-de-camp of Marshal Pétain and his official representative.[5]

Measures to evacuate children had been taken since the spring of 1942. Children were sent to colonies hurriedly established in châteaux and other vacant buildings along the Nantes-Angers railway line by municipalities, parishes and Catholic charities, lay school organizations, and the Comité Ouvrier de Secours Immédiat (COSI), run by Marcel Blanchard, the pro-Vichy labor leader of Saint-Nazaire.[6] Ironically, most of the children were brought back to their families in October 1942 on the grounds that the bombing had eased off; they had to be evacuated again after the attacks of November. After the inferno of February, a distinction was drawn between industrial and Todt workers, who were forced to stay despite the total inadequacy of air-raid shelters and who ceased work for this reason after a further attack on 30 March, and those tactfully deemed "useless for economic life," such as children, women, and the elderly, whose evacuation to the interior of Loire-Inférieure or to Anjou was to be organized. The evacuations of 1943, virtually unknown in comparison with the "exodus" of 1940, sheds interesting light on the relationship between very different French communities suddenly forced to live cheek by jowl with each other. "Suffering draws people together," said Monsignor Villepelet at the funeral of the victims of the Saint-Nazaire air raid of 16 February 1942, but it seems that there were limits.[7] After all, the population of Saint-Nazaire was urban, poor, and anticlerical, that of the host communities rural, prosperous, and Catholic. Anne Curet, evacuated at the age of twelve, recalls that "the peasants were generally welcoming and even generous" and that a barter economy grew up, with sewing exchanged for flour or butter, work in the fields for a meal, tobacco tickets for groceries.[8] In Rochefort-sur-Loire, on the other hand, evacuees complained that they were being ripped off by the local growers, who were asking ten francs for a kilo of potatoes normally sold for four.[9] The owners of the pink-stuccoed château de la Madeleine, overlooking the Loire at Varades, complained that the children of the COSI colony were running wild and breaking windows.[10] Villages in the Vendean Mauges, on the other side of the river, were reluctant to welcome outsiders. The mayor of Tilliers could find only one family willing to look after "a girl of five or six years old," while the mayor of Jallais told the subprefect of Cholet that he was receiving some children from the Catholic school of Le Pouliguen, seaside village next to La Baule, which was run by the same order of nuns as ran the school in Jallais.[11] By August and September 1943 the Nazarean evacuees were becoming organized and holding public meetings about their needs for food, wood, and coal, in Cholet with the subprefect and in Angers with prefect Daguerre, who claimed that as a former subprefect of Dieppe he, too, knew about air raids.[12]

By then the Allied bombers had started on the industrial suburbs of Nantes. On 23 March 1943 an air attack badly damaged the Batignolles locomotive works, which had so dramatically opposed the Relève the previous October. A huge crowd, mainly of factory workers, attended the funeral for the victims at the cathedral. Their anger was aimed at the management for not providing enough air-raid shelters rather than against the British, whose skill in targeting all twenty-four of their bombs on the factory itself they rather admired.[13] Subsequently, the works was moved away from the coast, but only as far as Cholet. On 4 July the SNCASO and Heinkel works at Château Bougon were hit, and casualties were heavy. The grief of bereaved families was compounded by the dishonesty of the undertakers of Nantes, who charged the likes of young Marcel Maringue 6,000 francs in advance to bury his father and mother-in-law, whereas the cheapest option was said to be a mere 213 francs.[14] Even more anger was directed against the Germans. Although 90 percent of the plants' capacity was restored within ten days, the Germans decided for security reasons to relocate the Heinkel factory to the Toulouse area and remove the SNCASO machine tools to Germany. The French manager of SNCASO, M. Gon, announced that he would yield only to force, so on 30 July force arrived in the the shape of a German detachment, which loaded 182 machines into thirty railway wagons.[15] Since the aircraft workers were now unemployed the German authorities ordered the French police to round them up and send them to work for the Todt Organization in Cherbourg, for a spell of six or seven weeks, it was said. On 14 September at 8:00 A.M., sixty police arrived at the airfield with twenty trucks and rounded up 220 workers, who were taken to the station and loaded onto a convoy.[16]

The most terrifying and destructive raids, however, hit the city of Nantes on 16 and 23 September 1943. On 16 September at 4:00 P.M., 160 aircraft dropped a thousand bombs on Nantes and its suburbs, only a quarter of which hit the military targets of the Chantiers de la Loire and Chantiers de Bretagne; six ships were sunk but the Chantiers Dubigeon remained unscathed. The civilian population was unprepared. There had been a vast number of alerts, many of which had been false alarms, and when raids had taken place the bombs had been accurately targeted. Many did not even bother to take shelter in their cellars. The casualties were horrendous: 812 dead and 1,785 injured. A week later, there were two raids. About sixty British planes attacked at 9:00 A.M., dropping 500 bombs. This time the civilians were ready, the targeting on the port area was more accurate, and the casualty figures were 45 dead and 110 injured. But that evening at seven there was a second raid by an American force of 150 planes striking from high altitude, many of the

650 bombs falling on shopping and residential areas. Again the Chantiers Dubigeon were spared, but 150 people were killed and 200 injured.[17] Subsequently, the figure of 1,000 dead rose to 1,300. A wave of panic swept the city and 100,000 people, or half the population, fled into the countryside. A thousand buildings had been destroyed or made uninhabitable, 20,000 people were homeless. Mail, telegraph, and telephone services went down and gas, water, and electricity supplies were gravely affected. A third of butchers, bakers, grocers, and greengrocers were out of action, and the Ravitaillement offices were hit, leaving people without ration cards for essentials for several days.[18]

The Germans had lost forty soldiers and railwaymen, a hundred German firemen helped to bring the fires under control, and Feldkommandant von Trotha attended a joint Franco-German funeral with the new prefect, Édouard Bonnefoy, on 19 October.[19] Dr. Baessler of the Feldkommandantur suggested that the mutual suffering had improved relations between the two peoples. "Perfect strangers talk to you on the street," he said, "and express their contempt for the English and Americans. People greet you politely and in a friendly way both in public and at home." On the other hand, the raids only increased the pressure on the Germans to maintain the momentum of their war production, and no concessions could be contemplated. "It is of the greatest importance to keep the workforce in Nantes," declared the Feldkommandantur the day before the second raid, but the workforce left with the rest of the population and Allied leaflets dropped on the area warning of the use of delayed-action bombs did nothing to hasten their return. "Systematic work is as good as impossible," complained the German labor office a month later, insisting that the first priority was to ensure that "workers who have left are brought back to the Rü- and V-Betriebe as quickly as possible," the current manning level having fallen to 20 percent, while the second was to force the return of food retailers. After tough negotiations with prefect Bonnefoy, it was announced that shopkeepers who did not return to the city by the end of October would lose their licenses, and workers their ration cards.[20]

The people of Nantes were in no sense eager to return. On 1 October 1943, 80,000 of them were classed as evacuees in their own department. Maine-et-Loire had 10,500 evacuees, including 5,000 from Saint-Nazaire and 2,600 from Nantes. Evacuees from Nantes were in fact supposed to go not to Maine-et-Loire but to other designated departments, such as the Vienne and Deux-Sèvres. Some workers from factories like the Batignolles were moved to Cholet, where the textile and shoe workers were generally docile, bringing with them their traditional "trade-union activity" and "political ferment."[21] Meanwhile evacuees from Lorient, a naval base farther west along the Atlantic coast and just as badly bombed as Saint-Nazaire, were detailed to go to Indre-et-Loire. Of the 11,600 evacuees there on 1 October, nearly 6,000 came from Lorient.[22] As in Maine-et-Loire, there was a balance of welcome and hostility. The ground had been prepared by the Secours National, which produced a poster headed "With Open Arms" showing a peasant leaving his pitchfork to greet a woman and two children, one in her arms, with the slogan "Any French person, anywhere in France, must feel part of a family."[23] Most of the evacuees were indeed women and children, the men having stayed in Lorient to work or returned. Among the male evacuees, masons, plasterers, and roofers were immediately snapped up for work, but many were sailors, dockers, or arsenal workers, unfit for some reason or another, reluctant to work on the land despite the demand from farmers, preferring to idle around and spend their benefits in the bars and cafés.[24] Concerns were also expressed by the gendarmerie that "some communist elements had slipped in amongst them."[25] The Lorient refugees were also prepared to fight for their rights. On 24 March 1943 they held a meeting at the Café de l'Entr'acte in Tours, convened by a wine and spirits merchant named Poulain, to demand, among other things, entitlement to an urban food ration, which they had had to surrender on arriving in a Touraine village, action against the high prices demanded by traders, and a good supply of potatoes to be transported from the Morbihan.[26] The prefecture was happy to dismiss him as a crazy megalomanic and have nothing to do with him, but it soon found that the power of the Breton press was behind the Lorientais. After the mayor of Dierre closed the soup kitchen frequented by the twenty Lorient evacuues, on the grounds that they now had their ration cards and could manage on their own, *L'Ouest-Éclair* attacked the insensitivity of the Touraine communities. This provoked prefect Tracou to defend the honor of the Tourangeaux. He asked his opposite number, the prefect of the Morbihan, to have words with the editor of *L'Ouest-Éclair*, who, he said, "by setting the population of Touraine against that of Indre-et-Loire, is creating a climate from which in the end only the unfortunate Breton refugees will suffer."[27] We have already seen that in matters of food supply rural communities tended to turn in on themselves as the pressure to share increased. The same pattern emerges with the treatment of evacuees: despite exhortations to solidarity, what predominated was suspicion and hostility.

Touraine and Anjou were lucky in that for a long time they were not the target of Allied attacks. They were both less industrialized than the Atlantic ports of Lorient, Saint-Nazaire, and Nantes and less geared into the German war machine. Even so, no part of France was without its Rüstung- and Speer-Betriebe, and in Monts, south of Tours, close to where the Jews had been interned in the camp of La Lande, the Ripault ammunition factory, which had lain fallow since the armistice, was recommissioned by the Germans in October 1942 to make torpedoes, shells, and other high explosives. A year later, however, on 18 October 1943, the factory was ripped apart by a massive blast that was heard a hundred kilometers away and shattered windows in Tours, eleven kilometers away. At the time 1,100 workers of the 2,000 employed, a high proportion of them women, were present. Of these 72 were killed, including 19 who "disappeared," 140 were seriously injured, and 500 were less seriously hurt. To begin with it was thought that the factory had been bombed or sabotaged, but it then emerged that gun cotton being unloaded was not damp enough and had ignited. The accident was a result of the pressure under which war production was operating. Despite the urgency to restart production, the factory had to be totally rebuilt and production did not begin again until March 1944.[28]

By this time Allied bombers were focusing on Tours and its railway and industrial suburb Saint-Pierre-des-Corps, which were a central part of the French communications network, linking Paris and Bordeaux. Having inflicted severe damage on German war production itself, the Allies turned next to the transportation system that supplied that machine with materials and fuel and would facilitate the movement of troops to a future Allied invasion point. On 14, 15, and 18 February 1943, the railway stations of Tours and Saint-Pierre-des-Corps, along with the CIMT railway workshops, were bombed. From the beginning of 1944 the U.S. Air Force regularly attacked the Tours airfield at Parçay-Meslay and the Liotard factory at Saint-Pierre-des-Corps, which made aircraft motors. On the night of 10–11 April the RAF returned to destroy the marshaling yards of Saint-Pierre-des-Corps with incendiary and delayed-action bombs. The station was "a mass of tangled ironmongery," said one eyewitness. "Were it not for the tunnel one might suppose that it had never existed. The warehouses where the rolling stock was kept have been completely destroyed. All that remains are a few sections of wall left standing as if by a miracle."[29] Eighteen people died, and another eleven were killed by delayed-action devices a few days later. The Rüstungskommando was relieved that the railway bridge over the Cher was still intact, but the bombers returned on 20 May to destroy that, too, snapping communications with Bordeaux and Le Mans. Unfortunately, a great deal of damage was also done to Tours itself, with 143 people killed, the archbishop presiding over their funeral in a cathedral that had itself been hit in the attack. The gossip among locals was that the English were systematically bombing the towns that Joan of Arc had passed through.[30] Ironically, the regional Rüstungskommando had moved for greater safety from Le Mans to Angers on 15 May, but on Whit Sunday, 29 May, Angers was subject to its first major attack. The Saint-Laud railway station was severely damaged, along with fifteen locomotives and a hundred wagons. Enormous damage was done to the Bessonneau factory, currently working on a German order for 670 nine-man tents.[31] Again, civilian casualties were very high, with 230 killed in the station district, many of whom had taken refuge in the local Saint-Laud church. The episcopal palace was destroyed, although as luck would have it the bishop, Monsignor Costes, was away on pilgrimage.

The destruction of rail communications threw the German military machine into chaos on what turned out to be the eve of the Normandy landings. In desperation it fell back on road transportation, which involved the sudden and brutal requisition of trucks. This time it was Touraine, at the hub of the communications network, that suffered particularly. In February 1944 the Feldkommandantur of Tours demanded 40 gasoline- or diesel-fueled trucks, which were extremely rare, and 300 charcoal-fueled ones (*gazogènes*). The new prefect of Indre-et-Loire, Ferdinand Musso, told regional prefect Donati that this amounted to over a third of the 930 trucks authorized on the department's roads and that since those of the

Rü- and S-Betriebe would be protected the full burden would fall on the domestic economy and particularly on food supply. The secretary of state for industrial production was not inclined to take a tough line, telling Donati that if any new requisition took place he could ask the German authorities not to include vehicles from "priority businesses."[32] In the Saumur area, the Germans requisitioned not only trucks but also 500 cars, carts, and horses, which were urgently needed for work in the fields.[33] Back in Tours, at the end of March, the police and gendarmerie handed all cyclists a German order to the effect that their bicycles were to be requisitioned the next day; this led to a haul of no less than 1,500 machines allegedly not needed for professional use.[34]

One of the main casualties of the breakdown of railway communications was coal supply, which fueled the electricity stations. In turn, the electricity generated powered the factories working for the German war machine. Electricity output was also reduced by direct air attacks on generating plants and the sabotage of power lines, notably those coming from the hydro-electric plants of southwest France. The failure of the electricity supply is an unsung story of the German Occupation but possibly the single most important reason the German war machine in France collapsed.[35]

In January 1944 the Rüstungskommando of Le Mans, which had responsibility for all of this region apart from Loire-Inférieure, reported that, because of coal shortages and the sabotage of pylons, supplies to the Rü-Betriebe would be reduced 25 percent if they had low-tension connections, 40 percent if they had high-tension connections, and 50 percent if they were nonmechanized. By March the current had dropped so much that only 10 percent of Rü-Betriebe were working nonstop and all of them were closed on weekends. A certain number of key factories were being privileged for supply, such as the ammunitions factory of Le Ripault, which had just gone back into production after the explosion, and the Bessonneau factory in Angers, shortly to be bombed.[36] After the begining of May, Oberst Keil of the Rüstungskommando reported, no more coal had been imported into the region and what supplies the Rü-Betriebe possessed had to be switched as a priority to the generating stations. By the end of June 1944 the electricity supply had fallen to 4.3 percent of what it had been in June 1943, and even the most important Rü-Betriebe were receiving only 2,500 kilowatt-hours a day, about 2.2 percent of their normal consumption.

At the same time the Rüstungskommando of Nantes reported that "in a few days there will be no more coal supplies left, and the electricity works will come to a complete standstill. A regular delivery of coal is *urgently* awaited." Meanwhile Keil was cutting his losses and arguing that, now that war production had collapsed in France, the most important task was to remove as much equipment as possible back to the Reich, although he was worried about how far east of Tours it would get, given the transportation problem. His report was dated 6 June 1944, which suggests that even as the Allies were landing on the beaches some German military were already thinking in terms of retreat.[37]

If one reason for the collapse of the German Occupation was the damage inflicted by the Allies on its military-industrial base, another was the growing difficulty of maintaining the policy of collaboration with the Vichy administration. The success of the Occupation had relied on collaboration between French and German officials, on both a formal and an informal basis. The isolation from Vichy of French administrators in the Occupied Zone meant that, paradoxically, they were reliant on the German military to reinforce their authority, and they had the leverage to negotiate with the German authorities and reach compromises. The German authorities, however, became increasingly dissatisfied with the ability of the French administration to deliver public order and resorted to a form of collaboration characterized by *Diktat* rather than negotiation and run by the secret police instead of the military. Pressure on the French population intensified with increasing numbers of arrests, deportations, and executions inflicted on wider and wider sections of the public, which grew more and more anxious, fearful, and alienated. The worse the war went for the Germans, and the more likely an Allied victory appeared, the more the Germans stepped up their demands and increased repression and the more local communities withdrew their cooperation and demanded protection from their leaders and administrators. French officials became squeezed in a vise, forced to choose between collaboration and resistance. One escape from an impossible choice was the *double jeu*—appearing to cooperate while in fact offering resistance. This was, however, a perilous game in which success was rare.

After the dismissal of Jean Roussillon for unsatisfactory collaboration, a new regional prefect of Angers was appointed in August 1943. Charles

Donati was a finance inspector and former director of a bank in Strasbourg whose annexation in 1940 had suggested a career in the Vichy administration. He was keen to establish good relations with local notables, who were invited in force to his installation in Angers on 9 August 1943—deputies and senators as well as members of the Conseil National and departmental councils, mayors, magistrates, generals, and churchmen.[38] Plain-speaking, he told a meeting of the Angers Chamber of Commerce that there was "at the present time a deep schism between the government and opinion." This "distrust and hostility," he continued, was undeserved because Marshal Pétain was "not a usurper but a legitimate leader" invested by parliament and "indisputably the greatest Frenchman by virtue of his military past, the glory that he evokes, his perfect success in all domains, and the heroism that he demonstrates on a daily basis, even though he is in his eighty-eighth year."[39] The German authorities liked Donati because he was a First World War veteran, who had lost his right arm in the trenches, and was an efficient, decisive administrator. They noted that he had sent his son on the STO and that if there were to be a definitive Franco-German collaboration, he would be an active participant.[40] This did not mean that he was a pushover. The Germans preferred effectiveness to supineness, and in December 1943, for instance, he sent a strongly worded letter to General Feldt, head of the military administration of Bezirk B, to demand the return of buildings in Angers requisitioned by the Germans but essential for the proper functioning of the French administration.[41]

Another decisive prefect with whom the Germans were pleased to do business was Édouard Bonnefoy, who, also in August 1943, replaced Philippe Dupard as prefect of Loire-Inférieure. Dupard, reported the Feldkommandantur of Nantes, promised much but delivered little, whereas Bonnefoy, formerly prefect of the Mayenne, was "considerably younger, more skillful, and a more diligent official. He prefers to communicate orally with mayors and others who have to execute his orders. Altogether there is now much more life in the French administration."[42] "We have a leader at last, a real leader," noted Edmond Duméril, who saw Bonnefoy as "deeply patriotic, understanding the capital importance of dialogue with the Germans." To defend French interests, it was necessary to be well informed and to negotiate. Duméril was also delighted to do business with Dr. Baessler, who was in charge of the German civil administration at the Feldkommandantur, and thought that "he could be for me what Dr. Hotz was in 1940-41." From Leipzig but of Swiss origins, he was "an intellectual, humane, considerate, in no sense a Nazi. He knows that his country is bound for disaster, he will try to moderate the draconian orders he receives and if possible temporize. He will be our firmest ally in the struggle of the French administration with the new Feldkommandant, the terrible general who came from Russia in the tragic autumn of 1943, General Reinhardt."[43] In his first month Bonnefoy took on the Gestapo, obtaining a reprieve for four of fifteen "terrorists" sentenced to death by a German military court and ensuring that twenty-seven communists arrested by the French police went before a French rather than a German court.[44] He criticized the Gestapo for giving orders directly to the French police rather than going through the prefecture.[45] When General Reinhardt, who had earned a reputation for cruelty on the eastern front, took over as Feldkommandant of Nantes from von Trotha in November, Bonnefoy opposed his demands for 2,000 peasants to help with defense work, on the grounds that conscription for military activity violated article 52 of the Hague Convention of 1907. He was prepared to argue his case publicly when Reinhardt summoned French officials to a meeting in the Château des Ducs, Nantes, just before Christmas 1943.[46] Unfortunately for the Loire-Inférieure, Bonnefoy was appointed regional prefect of Lyon at the beginning of 1944.

While Donati and Bonnefoy perfected the art of tough negotiation, other prefects were weaker in their handling of the Germans and acquired a reputation for not doing enough to protect French citizens. In January 1944 prefect Tracou of Indre-et-Loire was appointed head of Pétain's private office and secretary-general Molas-Quenescourt followed him to Vichy. He was replaced in Tours by Ferdinand Musso, formerly prefect in the Jura, who had something of a complex about his association with the Third Republic. In 1940 he had headed the office of Minister of the Interior Georges Mandel, once revered as the natural successor of Clemenceau but now reviled as a Jew who had brought France to the brink of destruction; he was shortly to be assassinated by the Milice.[47] In Tours, Musso was put under pressure by the Groupe Collaboration and the Gestapo and reacted by coming down hard on anything smacking of dissent. In February

1944, for example, local doctor and *conseiller-général* Pierre Labussière was examining sixty young men conscripted for the STO in Chinon, when he accidentally knocked a photograph of Marshal Pétain onto the floor. He was then alleged to have spat on it and torn it up, exclaiming, "Bastard," "Old fart," and "Judas." When the nurse in attendance, Mlle Rivière, voiced a protest, he responded, "And you can put it between your legs, where it belongs!" Most of the people present, knowing Labussière's excesses, took the outburst in stride. Paul Cay, the subprefect, tried to smooth things over, but prefect Musso determined to take a hard line, not least to please the Gestapo, who saw Labussière as a critic of Franco-German collaboration, liable to sabotage the recruitment of STO labor to Germany. Musso ordered the internment of Labussière, who was released in April 1944, only to be arrested by the Gestapo and deported to Germany.[48] Events finally caught up with Musso, because he was the only prefect in the region to be sent for trial after the Liberation.

It was of course possible to resist with a little too much energy, in order to maintain authority over local populations, and even to send out a signal to the Free French based in London, then Algiers, that one was a candidate for office when the German Occupation and possibly Vichy came to an end. This tactic, however, ran the risk of forfeiting the confidence of the Germans, who were increasingly intolerant of any disloyalty in the French administration. Officials who wanted to survive needed to play a double game, giving the appearance of loyalty while working in the dark to protect French interests and even open an insurance policy with the emerging Resistance. As prefect Tracou told the municipal council of Tours in December 1943 as the new mayor was invested, "Present circumstances impose on all of us a very simple rule: work hard and say nothing. If you find that too absolute, then work hard and say little."[49] What an official's objective opinions and conduct were did not really matter. German officials repeatedly confessed in their reports that they did not know what the political opinions of so and so were. Everyone wore a mask and engaged in bluff and double bluff. The danger was to be unmasked, and here collaborationist groups who genuinely believed in a Franco-German crusade against communism were a greater menace than the Gestapo.

Paul Cay was a model performer in the art of pretense. The German authorities had no reason to complain about him, noting that he worked well with them although, since they were based in Tours, they in fact saw little of him.[50] He served the Vichy regime honorably, but he was alert to the changing balance of forces and climate of opinion. After the Anglo-American landing in North Africa in November 1942, he reported to the prefect that the normally calm and indifferent population was beginning to express pro-Allied and Gaullist sentiments with some force. He admitted that "our role is very delicate," but while advising his superior that "we must enforce a more rigid discipline than ever," he was himself making secret contacts with the Resistance and taking silent steps toward the regime-in-waiting.[51] Regarded by Musso as suspect, he was ordered early in 1944 to the isolated prefecture of Villefranche-de-Rouergue in the Aveyron but went into hiding in the Loire region and resurfaced to become secretary-general of the prefecture of Indre-et-Loire at the Liberation.

Less skillful for different reasons were Marcel Saissier, who was Donati's prefect-delegate in Angers, succeeding Pierre Daguerre, and Yves Bayet, secretary-general of the prefecture at Nantes. Like Daguerre, Saissier had been subprefect of Dieppe and came to Angers with a similar reputation for protecting Masonic officials. He became the victim of a hostile campaign in the collaborationist Paris paper *Je suis partout*, which accused him of being tough on Vichy loyalists and soft on Masons, Gaullists, and communists. Although the Germans' own information suggested that he could be trusted, they could not take any risks and in the light of the collaborationist accusations ordered his arrest.[52] Meanwhile the Germans in Nantes saw secretary-general Bayet as "the most honest collaborator in the prefecture, combining with his courteous demeanor an energy and exceptional diligence in the conduct of his office." He had been an active promoter of the Relève and was said to have attended torture sessions administered by the anticommunist police squad. His fanaticism may be explained, as in Musso's case, by a past he had to live down, for his father, Albert Bayet, who had been an ardent campaigner at the turn of the century for the wrongly imprisoned Jewish army officer Alfred Dreyfus, was president of the anticlerical Ligue de l'Enseignement and had been dismissed from the Sorbonne by Vichy as the quintessence of everything it hated about the *camarades* of the Third Republic. Bayet went absent without leave around the time that prefect

Bonnefoy was appointed to Lyon. Some said that he had fled to Paris because of his links with the Resistance and his fear that he was about to be found out. Others argued that he disappeared because he had received death threats from the Resistance.[53] In the event, his insurance policy with the Resistance was not convincing enough. He failed adequately to demonstrate that his collaboration had masked a genuine commitment to the Resistance and he was sent for trial at the Liberation.

As hopes and anxieties about an Allied landing in France increased, the Germans clamped down on any sign of disloyalty. In Nantes, prefect Georges Gaudard, who moved from Besançon to replace Bonnefoy, initially made a good impression on the Feldkommandantur, although they noted that he preferred to deal with them in writing rather than, like his predecessor, face to face.[54] The report on Gaudard drafted for the Free French, however, said that he was a veteran of 1914–18 with "excellent patriotic sentiments" and was "very hostile to the Germans."[55] The Free French may have thought this because Gaudard refused German orders to offer rewards to French people to denounce "terrorists," unless, he conceded, a serious crime had been committed.[56] Though he thought he had agreed on this with Dr. Baessler at the Feldkommandantur, higher German authorities decided to take a hard line on suspect prefects. Gaudard was one of fifteen French prefects arrested on 14 May; he was about to lay a wreath at the statue of Joan of Arc. Bonnefoy was arrested in Lyon in the same offensive and was deported to Germany, where he died.[57] Gaudard was released and survived in his position for the rest of the Occupation, until the Americans appeared in Nantes. He then tried to persuade the Americans to confirm him as prefect, instead of his secretary-general, Louis Ottaviani, who had been selected to become Liberation prefect by Michel Debré, the future *commissaire de la République*. Before Debré came to Nantes in person in August 1944 it looked as though he might indeed pull off the coup. More successful in the long term was the head of Gaudard's office, René Tomasini, who was arrested by the Germans on 10 May 1944 but resurfaced at the Liberation as the head of Debré's office in Angers.[58]

Arrests were not confined to prefectoral officials. Mayors, within the local context, also had to tread the tightrope between satisfying German demands and providing as much protection as possible for local inhabitants. Again, the key to survival was to give nothing away. One example not to

follow was that of Dr. Jean Robin, mayor of Saint-Pierre-des-Corps, who
had played a crucial role in ensuring the loyalty of a predominantly communist town. In August 1943, however, during a fund-raising event for
POWs, he unveiled a commemoration stone that bore not only the names
of the war dead but also those of bomb victims and of four communists
who had been shot by the Germans. He was arrested the next day by the
Sicherheitsdienst.[59] Symbolic gestures, albeit to maintain the morale of a
local community, might be avoided whereas fighting to protect its real
interests was a necessity for a good mayor. About twenty mayors or *secré-
taires de mairie* were arrested in Touraine during the first two months of
1944 alone, mainly because the Germans regarded them as insufficiently
cooperative over the delivery of foodstuffs, livestock, labor, or vehicles.[60]
Some mayors, such as Victor Bernier of Angers, it is true, were past masters
of finding precisely the right line. Regional prefect Donati was told by the
Sicherheitsdienst soon after his arrival in Angers that the seventy-five-year-
old Bernier was "likely to exercise an influence dangerous for the occupying
forces." Donati nevertheless told Laval that the Germans had never made
a formal complaint against Bernier, who was held in high esteem by the
Angevins for his courage in June 1940, and that his dismissal would provoke a municipal crisis and "great emotion among the population." A compromise was found in March whereby Bernier continued nominally as
mayor but no longer came to the town hall to discharge business, which
would be conducted by one of his deputies.[61] This solution satisfied the
Germans while maintaining the honor of the French administration and
was, incidentally, an ideal position from which Bernier could reassert himself as mayor after the Liberation.

Such fancy footwork for a prominent mayor was rare. Local notables
found it more and more difficult to bridge the gap between increasing
German demands and brutality and the growing anger, frustration, and
fear of their communities. One by one bridges snapped as notables decided
that to keep faith with the Germans or Vichy no longer brought any advantage. This was the main reason the *conseils départementaux*, set up in the
autumn of 1943, came to very little.[62] In Loire-Inférieure, as we have seen,
only thirty-six of the forty-six seats were ever filled. Previously solid Vichy
notables lost sympathy with the Laval government and ceased to be active.
Louis Linyer, who had been injured in the air raid of 23 September and

was out of sorts with the Vichy government, went into virtual exile on his Vendean property and now lived mainly in fear of revolution. Dutertre de la Coudre, mayor of Machecoul, continued to admire Pétain but was opposed to Laval and thought that the Milice, which was trying to wipe out resistance, was far too violent. He was said to be "tired and disgusted by politics, which he now wanted to give up, both as deputy and as mayor."[63] In the arrondissement of Saumur, subprefect André Trémeaud experienced great difficulty in finding a list of local notables suitable or willing to sit on the *conseil départemental*. Gaston Moreau, for example, was regarded as too collaborationist, while Édouard Tardif, the old radical-socialist, was seen as the leader of a covert opposition in the area.[64] Ironically, subprefect Trémeaud was regarded by the Germans themselves as suspect for failing to appear at a Christmas party they organized in 1943, and he made the transition easily to the new regime in August 1944.[65] In Indre-et-Loire, no representatives for the *conseil départemental* could be found for six out of the twenty-four cantons, with obvious foot draggers being François Servant of La Haye Descartes and Dr. Paul Guillaume-Louis of Montbazon. Others did not stay for long, because they wanted to keep faith with their constituents. This was the case of the labor leader André Garantie, who had been a key figure in bringing workers over to Vichy's Labor Charter but now saw that his base was turning away from him. He resigned early in 1944 both as secretary of the *conseil départemental* and as muncipal councillor of Tours.

In Touraine, the resignation of mayors was a serious problem. There were thirty-six resignations in 1942 and twenty-seven in 1943. Two-thirds of these mayors were farmers or winegrowers and two-thirds were over sixty, which suggests that the stress of being squeezed between German demands for foodstuff and livestock and the frustration of their communities may well have been a factor. Another decisive factor was that their sons had been recruited for the STO, which destroyed what degree of loyalty they had for the regime. These "personal" reasons accounted for 15 percent of cases, political reasons for 24 percent, and health and age reasons (given rightly or wrongly) for 40 percent. Half of the 12 percent who resigned for administrative reasons were asked to resign. In 1944, as pressure from the German authorities increased, matters became even worse. "There is a certain panic in the municipalities," warned prefect Musso, "and resignations are multiplying. No one wants to remain mayor anymore, and no one agrees to become one."[67] By May Musso himself was in a state of panic, reporting that resignations were "raining down" as arrests of mayors by Germans increased and that the risk now attached to exercising the office was making it unworkable.[68] Increasingly, mayors were siding with their angry communities against the Germans and against a Vichy administration that was increasingly unable to protect them.

The pressure on mayors, as on officials, was to maintain a semblance of loyalty to Vichy and the Germans while in practice cooperating as little as possible in order to keep faith with the communities they represented. Foot dragging in the face of German demands was not the same as resistance, which was limited in the Loire region for geographical reasons as much as anything else. Some parts of the country, such as the Massif Central, the Alps, and Brittany, which had the protection of mountains and forests, sustained a Maquis more readily than the Loire Valley, which was flatter and more agricultural and had better communications. "There is no solitude in Anjou," reported the local head of the Organisation de la Résistance Armée, "no isolated shelter or defensible hiding places. A countryside divided by hedges but also crisscrossed by good roads ready-made for pursuit. . . . Such factors ensured that in this department the Resistance did not take the form of a Maquis."[69] Michel Fourré-Cormeray, who became prefect of Maine-et-Loire at the Liberation, reported that while there were few collaborators in the department, "most of the inhabitants did not join Resistance movements, were totally ignorant of what we were doing for four years, and remained fairly attached to the mystique of the marshal."[70] Michel Debré, who as *commissaire de la République* in Angers appointed him, said that the region was "defined neither by pronounced collaboration nor by resolute resistance." "The château owners," he continued, "have their sons with de Gaulle and the portrait of Pétain in their sitting rooms."[71]

Loyalty to Marshal Pétain was a powerful and durable sentiment that coexisted perfectly well both with hostility to the Laval government and with hopes placed in General de Gaulle.[72] Early in 1942 the Angers police reported that "the person of Marshal Pétain remains in general above criticism. It seems indeed that his prestige is greater than ever.

The population admires his courage and the strength of his character and seems to accord him even more confidence since it has learned that he is as far as possible defending the independence of the country."[73] It was a sentiment that permeated most classes of society. That the nobles of the west of France revered Pétain is not surprising, but a selection of twenty-four letters addressed directly from Angevins to him in 1943–44 suggests that the weakest and most vulnerable in society regarded him as an arbiter and rédresser of wrongs: three were from widows, two from wives of POWs, five from heads of large families, others from evacuees or those who had suffered bomb damage.[74] Overwhelmingly they saw him as a source of appeal when the administration had failed to address their needs. One typical entreaty was from a woman of Saumur whose request for shoes for her husband had been blocked by the bureaucracy for over a year. "Where, I beg of you, Monsieur le Maréchal, does one have to go to get shoes?"[75]

Pétain, to be sure, was increasingly a figurehead, while power concentrated in the hands of Laval, the head of government. Laval was regarded as responsible for labor conscription and other burdens inflicted on the population. Even less popular were the small groups of collaborationists who campaigned for closer relations with Germany and tougher measures against communists and Gaullists. In the summer of 1943 a number of notables of Groupe Collaboration in Nantes received packages containing little coffins in each of which were placed a miniature axe and rope. The blue-shirted Francists of Marcel Bucard, as fascist a party as France ever saw, tended to recruit young men of a thuggish disposition. At a *kermesse* organized by the municipality of Nantes in May 1943, a group of thirty of them were insulted by a man shouting, *"Aux chiottes, Bucard!"* (Dump Bucard!). The Francists replied by making a fascist salute, which provoked a riot in the crowd of about a thousand, controlled only with difficulty by the French police. Interestingly, reported the superintendent, no hostile words were directed at the German military, which did not intervene.[76] On other occasions the Francists went on the offensive, but with no happier results. Later that May six of them arrived in the small Touraine town of Saint-Maure to sell their paper. They found no takers and became involved in scuffles with local youths. Three weeks later they returned with German police in plainclothes, and after some fighting four local youths were arrested by the German police for ripping down Francist posters. The gendarmerie reported that "these incidents have disgusted the population of the region," which was "essentially agricultural and peaceful," and created "much turmoil."[77]

The fact that individuals and communities were opposed to collaborationists did not mean that they were great supporters of the Resistance. Those who wished to avoid the STO had to go into hiding: some simply lay low close to home, some found work in isolated farms or in rural industries. Most, however, needed money and ration cards and, as we have seen, took to raiding *mairies*, post offices, tax offices, tobacconists, traders, and prosperous farmsteads.[78] Vichy propaganda spared no effort to depict these groups not as patriots but as "bandits" and "terrorists," the modern version of the highway robber or the "great companies" of the Hundred Years War. Unless the capacity of Vichy for self-deception was complete, this negative image of the Maquis seems to have made some impression. "Many," prefect Tracou relayed to Laval in one of his last reports from Touraine, "see in all this signs of latent anarchy, the foretaste of civil war. Such a possibility terrifies many people and has changed what was originally sympathy for the *réfractaires* and members of 'Resistance organizations' into disapproval and fear." As a result, the articles of Jean de Corbigny in *La Dépêche du Centre*, usually unpopular because of his tough line against the Resistance, which he saw as no better than anarchy, acquired a cult following in Touraine.[79] The Nantes bourgeoisie, confronted by this approaching violence, became attentive listeners to the ferociously anticommunist broadcasts of the Vichy minister of information, Philippe Henriot.[80] The Renseignements Généraux in Angers reported in the spring of 1944 that the murder of police in Saint-Laurent by "Judeo-communist bandits" had seriously alienated the population but that the arrival in Anjou of "undesirables" of the Milice to deal with "terrorists" was no more reassuring.[81] Even after the Normandy landings the German military command in Angers took the view that the peaceable inhabitants of the region "opposed terrorism in all its forms," because they feared an eruption of the civil war much more evident south of the former line of demarcation.[82]

Whether the Resistance was regarded as patriotism or as terrorism, the least that can be said is that it was an extremely perilous exercise, not only because of the collaboration of the French and German police but because of the constant danger of denunciation or even carelessness. In June 1943 seven armed men—a schoolteacher, four teacher trainees (*normaliens*), and two farmers, a father and son—attacked a Saumur bank manager and burgled the town hall of Vern d'Anjou, north of Angers, to obtain money and ration tickets for STO dodgers in the vicinity. Stopped by three Feldgendarmes, they shot two but the third got away and raised the alarm. One of the *normaliens* abandoned his bicycle, which unfortunately had in its saddlebag a list of other teacher trainees who belonged to the communist FTPF. Fifteen *normaliens* were duly arrested by the French police and handed over to the Germans. The seven men who had taken part in the raid and one other teacher were executed at the Belle-Beille firing range outside Angers, and ten others were deported, of whom three died in camps.[83]

Undeniably courageous, but also courting great danger, was a Resistance group near Chinon led by Albert Malécot, the secretary of the *mairie* of the village of Huismes. He located a meadow in the broad valley between the Loire and the Indre that was ideal for parachute drops and small-plane landings; in March 1943 it was code-named the "Gide terrain." Malécot also recruited a small number of men from the surrounding villages of Bréhémont and Rivarennes to service any drops or landings. Unfortunately, the cover was somehow blown, and on 19 January 1944 the Gestapo raided the home of Malécot and shot him dead. On 4 March the Gestapo struck again, arresting five men from Huismes, two from Bréhémont, and two from Rivarennes. One other man managed to flee, one was never discovered, but all those arrested were deported to Germany and only one returned.[84]

Other resisters constructed wider networks, but even these were extremely vulnerable to denunciation or to exposure by a comrade captured and tortured by the Gestapo. Jean Meunier, formerly socialist deputy of Indre-et-Loire, returned from a spell as a POW in Germany to run his printing business in Tours, but through Émile Aron, the dismissed Jewish medical professor who had taken refuge in the Free Zone, he became involved in hiding agents, collecting money for the families of arrested communists, and printing false identity papers. He forged links with likeminded socialists such as Pierre Archambault and Catholics such as the schoolteacher Anne-Marie Marteau and the Jesuit Père de Solages. This group, called CND-Castille, was linked to the wider Libération-Nord movement and turned out to be the embryonic Comité Départemental de la Libération (CDL) in Touraine. But that was not before the Gestapo struck in October 1943 and through arrests, torture, and more arrests smashed the Libération-Nord movement in the area.[85] Similar blows were struck against the Resistance network centered on the gendarmerie of Saumur and Montreuil-Bellay and led by Captain Royer, which was rounded up by the Gestapo in September 1943, and against Victor Chatenay's Honneur et Patrie network, based in Angers. In Loire-Inférieure, the Armée Secrète (AS) movement, closely linked to Libération-Nord, was run by General Audibert, formerly an official of Colonel de La Rocque's Croix de Feu and in constant conflict with a communist militant named Bernier. Both Audibert and Bernier were arrested in January 1944 and deported. The organization was taken over in March 1944 by a man named Daviais, who turned the AS into a unit of the Forces Françaises de l'Intérieur (FFI), drawing heavily on STO *réfractaires*, in March 1944. Daviais was also head of the future CDL but was betrayed and arrested in April. "It was a disaster," says one historian. "They had to start again from zero."[86]

Where the paths of close-knit Resistance groups and STO *réfractaires* crossed, Maquis began to form. These were most common in Brittany, which was more isolated and forested and already, as we have seen, a lair for STO dodgers. The Maquis of Saffré was an expression of youthful enthusiasm that came into bloody contact with German forces, which became more violent the more they saw defeat staring them in the face. It traced its history to December 1943, when it was set up by Briac le Diouron, code name Yacco, and Abbé Ploquin, curate of the nearby village of Bouvron. Its sole weapon was a machine gun that was used for training purposes and shared with neighboring groups. Unstable, constantly dissolving and reforming in different places at different times, the group had no real purpose until after the Normandy landings, when it got wind of an arms drop that was to occur over the forest of Saffré on 29 June. Its amateurism was exemplary. Its members set up camp in the forest on 17 June and had a picnic 150 meters from a German sentry, who fortunately did not spot them. On that Sunday, however, they were seen by locals out for a walk in the woods, who asked them, "What are you doing there? We promise we won't tell the Boches." They decided to strike camp and returned to Bouvron, where they chatted freely in the cafés about their exploits.[87] They returned to the forest on 22 June, three or four hundred strong, but either because of their indiscretion or because of a betrayal, they were surrounded by German forces and attacked on 28 June. Twenty-three of them were killed and thirty were taken prisoner. These were taken to the château de la Bouvardière, outside Nantes, and tried by a military court the following day as illegal *francs-tireurs*, although they had precious few weapons. Twenty-seven of them—the oldest twenty-six and five of them under twenty—were shot in the park of the château between 11:00 P.M. and midnight on 29 June. According to one account, they died singing the "Marseillaise." Three *maquisards* were kept back for further interrogation and shot two weeks later; only the Abbé Ploquin was spared and deported instead. In the following repression at least sixteen other *maquisards* were tracked down and executed in the surrounding area and farms were set ablaze.[88]

Heavily outgunned, *maquisard* groups tended to avoid any direct confrontation with German forces. A more common tactic was to ambush and snipe at them as the Allies advanced and they retreated chaotically toward the east. In so doing, however, *maquisards* greatly endangered surrounding communities, which were accused by the Germans of harboring terrorists and subjected to ferocious collective reprisals. The legendary massacre in Oradour-sur-Glane on 10 June was one of many incidents that either ended in tragedy or saw tragedy narrowly avoided.

In this region the critical month was August 1944, as the Allies advanced toward the Loire and the Germans pulled out of Bordeaux and Nantes and drove for the frontier. The Germans knocked out their huge factories at Nantes, crossed the Loire to the south on 11 August, sabotaging the bridges as they went, and headed toward Cholet and the east. General Reinhardt got as far as Bourges, where his car was blown up by a mine planted by *maquisards* on 1 September and he was killed.[89] Germans began to leave Angers from 5 August, seizing bicycles from their French riders and killing if they had to. "You must be really afraid and in a hurry to leave if you have to steal our bicycles," the manager of the Rally garage in Angers told a dozen German soldiers before they shot him.[90] Farther north, in Segré, American forces arrived on 5 August but withdrew the next day, and the Germans returned. There they took sixty hostages and set fire to the town with incendiary grenades. The subprefect, mayor, and archpriest kept up a constant dialogue with the young German officer in charge, seeking to prevent a catastrophe of Oradour proportions, and the Germans eventually withdrew on 7 August.[91] Disaster was also narrowly avoided in the small village of Toutlemonde, outside Cholet, where two *maquisards* were surprised by Germans with a vanload of weapons, tortured, and shot. The young men were not local at all but worked for the Batignolles factory that had been evacuated to Cholet. Under torture they confessed that the weapons were for "*tout le monde*," and the Germans entered the village on 7 August and took the mayor, the curé, and sixty other men hostage in the schoolroom. The next morning the Gestapo arrived to interrogate the hostages and threatened to shoot twenty-one of them, including the mayor and the curé, if the "terrorists" were not handed over. Fortunately, the matter was defused by an Alsatian interpreter employed by the Batignolles works, who was able to explain in German the linguistic confusion that had brought the village to the brink of disaster.[92]

One village where disaster was not avoided, however, was that of Maillé, in Touraine. By mid-August the Allies had reached the north of the department, but the Germans still held Tours and the Loire and retreating forces were moving up into the region from Bordeaux and Poitiers. On the evening of 24 August a group of *maquisards* ambushed a retreating convoy near Maillé, provoking a German unit covering the retreat to surround the village, which they believed to be a terrorist lair. The next day they massacred the inhabitants systematically with machine guns, grenades, and bayonets, set fire to the buildings, and then bombarded the village from a distance so that the emergency services were unable to enter it until the day after. There, according to Jean Meunier, president of the CDL, they discovered

> 126 bodies, mutilated, cut to pieces or burned. . . . The body of a two-month-old baby was found, its head smashed, lying on that of its mother, who had had her throat cut and her guts torn out. A pregnant woman had been bayoneted in the bed where she lay. Another baby in a cot had been shot in the head at point-blank range. A man and a woman who had

died in the flames had embraced each other so tightly that
they looked as though they had melted together.[93]

Whole families had been killed, mainly women, children, and old men,
because most of the men had been away working in the fields. For the
Tourangeaux it was a massacre of the innocents, a typical German atrocity
that confirmed the enemy's fundamental barbarism. Of the 121 victims,
37 were under ten, 18 were between eleven and twenty, and 16 were over
sixty. Roger Confolent lost his wife and all seven of his children. Serge
Martin, staying with his grandparents that day, lost his parents and three
younger siblings, ages nine, five, and six months.

Hearing the news, prefect Musso went straight to the Feldkommandantur of Tours on 26 August to protest. Lieutenant Colonel Stenger
promised an immediate inquiry and that the guilty would be sent before a
court-martial. The guilty man turned out to be a Lieutenant Schiler or
Schleuter, who claimed that Maillé was sheltering terrorists and that he
had been acting on orders. In a difficult interview on 28 August, prefect
Musso denounced an "act of terror that no French person would ever have
committed, even under orders," and that was particularly unjustified in
Touraine, whose population had suffered four years' occupation "with the
greatest calm and perfect dignity." Feldkommandant Stenger pointed out
that three Germans had been wounded the previous night and weapons
had been found in two or three farms in Maillé but that German orders
were to punish aggressors and their accomplices, not the innocent. He
apologized to the victims and their families and said that he would happily
see the culprit shot, but the lieutenant had disappeared from the scene and
was sentenced to death in absentia by a French military court in Bordeaux
in 1952.[94] The atrocity was unpardonable, but it was the deed of an army
in panic, caught in a race against time by the advancing Allies, harried by
maquisards—an army whose units, out of contact with their superiors,
themselves behaved like terrorist bands.

Popular discontent and anxiety, fueled by labor conscription for the
German Reich, was increased by Allied bombing raids that devastated ports
and cities and drove large numbers of people into the countryside. The
German war machine was undermined not only by bomb damage to plant,
communications, and power supply but by the flight of the labor force from

targeted areas and its reluctance to return to work. Meanwhile the French administration, on which the Germans had relied to relay orders, became less and less cooperative. Unreliable officials and mayors were dismissed, but sanctions tended to produce only the semblance of cooperation rather than the real thing. Resistance networks developed among figures in key positions, and STO *réfractaires* organized Maquis here and there. These groups, of course, remained small minorities in an environment shaped by fear of anarchy and of reprisals. Most French people simply kept their heads down and waited for liberation to come from the only likely source: an Allied invasion.

14

Liberation

Early in the sunny evening of 10 August 1944, as the last German defenders abandoned Angers and the first Americans crossed the Pont de la Basse-Chaîne opposite the medieval château, Michel Debré, *maître des requêtes* at the Conseil d'État, approached the gates of the prefecture and flashed his identity card at the police on guard. Thirty-two years old, a graduate of Sciences-Po—Paris's London School of Economics—and the cavalry school of Saumur, briefly a POW in 1940, he joined Vichy's Conseil d'État at Royat, near Clermont-Ferrand, to which it had been evacuated. From 1943, however, he had a second identity, code name Jacquier, as a member of the Comité Général d'Études, which selected the prefects and *commissaires de la République* who would take power at the Liberation, preventing both a deal between Vichy and the American forces and a communist revolution. He had left Toulouse on 5 August, traveling by train and bicycle, and linked up with André Trémeaud, subprefect of Saumur, who took him in his car to Angers on 8 August. Two days later, inside the prefecture, he came face to face with regional prefect Donati and announced that he was taking over as *commissaire de la République* for the Angers region in the name of General de Gaulle. According to Donati's daughter, a girl at the time, Debré and her father exchanged a handshake, a gesture that symbolized the continuity of the French state across the Liberation.[1] Donati asked only to stay the night at the prefecture, in order to pack his bags. Debré then sat at the large desk. As he later recalled, "I had become the state."[2]

Debré sent for the new prefect, Michel Fourré-Cormeray, auditor at the Cour des Comptes, who was waiting in the café opposite. He also confirmed in office the secretary-general, Gey; the subprefect of Saumur who had acted as his chauffeur, André Trémeaud; and the subprefect of Segré, Fouet, who had saved his town from disaster a few days earlier. As head of his office he took René Tomasini, who was doing the same job in the prefecture of Loire-Inférieure and was incidentally a friend of Maurice Papon.[3] Moracchini, the Tours police commissioner, was made secretary-general of police for the Angers region. The administrative continuity between Vichy and the Liberation was thus extraordinary. What emerges from the German archives, moreover, is that the transfer of power between the retreating Germans and the French authorities was fairly amicable also. The previous day Donati had said good-bye to the German regional commander for Bezirk B, General Feldt, expressing his regrets and declaring that four years of working together with the German military administration had taught him *"that the Germans are not the enemies of the French but their friends."*[4] Despite the increasingly threadbare collaboration at the end of the Occupation, the protection of state power against communist subversion was a powerful reason for cooperation between the French and the Germans.

In about a quarter of French departments the handover of power at the Liberation lasted for less than a week, and where the departure of the Germans was followed quickly by the arrival of the Allies there was little violence.[5] Maine-et-Loire was certainly one of these departments. Rather different was the case in Indre-et-Loire, where the Americans liberated the north of the department and Debré invested a provisional prefectoral administration under Pierre Archambault at Neuillé-Pont-Pierre on 18 August, while the Germans retained the south of the department, including Tours, and maintained prefect Musso in office. The Germans blew up the bridges across the Loire on 22 August, the telephone exchange on the twenty-eighth, then the bridges over the Cher as they left on the thirty-first. In what looked very much like a revolution, on 1 September Jean Meunier, president of the CDL, went to the town hall to take over as mayor from René Guerrier and then to the prefecture to arrest Musso and install Robert Vivier as the new prefect.[6]

A closer look, however, suggests that the revolution was of the palace variety. Jean Meunier was a Third Republic socialist deputy who had been groomed to succeed the socialist deputy mayor of Tours, Ferdinand Morin: Morin had voted full powers to Pétain in 1940 and was barred from a comeback; Meunier had not and found the doors open. Paul Cay, appointed secretary-general of the prefecture, had been subprefect of Chinon until early in 1944. Prefect Vivier and Meunier were both Freemasons, which was the traditional way of making political connections under the Third Republic.[7] Vivier had in fact been *inspecteur d'académie* under Vichy until 1942; since his office had been in the prefecture he described his new appointment as simply moving downstairs. In 1977 the historian Henri Amouroux alleged in *Quarante million de Pétainistes* that as *inspecteur d'académie* Vivier held a school competition for the best essay on the life and ideas of Marshal Pétain. Vivier's son, Jack, forced Amouroux to withdraw the passage on threat of legal proceedings, and told me that his father was kept away from the visit to Tours in 1941 of Youth Minister Georges Lamirand on the grounds that he was "already suspected of hostility to the Vichy regime," and declared that his father was "a pure and absolutely honest resistant" who listened to the BBC every evening and "was a visionary like de Gaulle."[8]

Astute though the work of Debré and the other Gaullist officials was, in a sense it was an unnecessary complication in the transfer of power. It would have been even easier for the Americans simply to have endorsed the Vichy authorities in place. After all, many if not most of them were by now playing a double game, negotiating with the Germans on one side and secretly protecting the Resistance on the other. This was certainly the plot in Nantes, where Debré's chosen candidate, secretary-general Louis Ottaviani, panicked and told prefect Georges Gaudard of the plan. Gaudard won the confidence of the American colonel in charge of the city and published an appeal for calm, completely failing the local Resistance. Debré was forced to go to Nantes on 15 August to rapidly build up a power base in order to impose a prefect of his choice. The candidate he had in mind was a lawyer, Alexandre Vincent, who had worked for the Secours National and had no obvious links to the Resistance. He solicited the support of the departmental FFI leader, Colonel Félix, whose brother he had known at the cavalry school of Saumur. He lectured the American colonel on the legitimacy of de Gaulle and the fact that Vichy was now finished. He asked the Comité de Libération, which had a lively communist choir and rejected Vincent because he had once made a speech to the Groupe Collaboration, to broaden itself out and proposed the Marquis de Sesmaisons. He went to see the bishop, Monsignor Villepelet, who thought Gaullism "diabolical" and still had a portrait of Marshal Pétain hanging in his office, to assure him that the new regime wanted to collaborate with the Church and ask him to nominate a cleric to sit on the CDL, which Villepelet refused to do. Even the Marquise de Sesmaisons, sent by Debré, could not bring him around. Villepelet was prepared to render to Caesar what was Caesar's, but not a centime more. Squeezed between the Pétainist establishment, who wanted to stick with Gaudard or even have Bonnefoy back "if he were free," and the communists in the local Resistance, Debré was forced to pretend that Vincent would be only a temporary appointment.[9]

Prefects and police commissioners did not have a free hand at the Liberation but had to do business with the Comités de Libération that sprang up at the departmental, arrondissement, and local levels, mirroring the Conseil National de la Résistance. The CDLs were the assemblies both of local Resistance movements, in so far as they existed, and of political parties, trade unions, and other pressure groups emerging or reemerging after the Occupation. In some sense they acted as a "dual power," reminiscent of revolutionary situations, putting pressure on the administration to be more ruthless in the purge of collaborators, but how independent they were varied according to local circumstances.[10] Some prefects had strong personalities and were highly regarded by the committees, others less so. The influence of a CDL might be explained by its radicalism but, alternatively, radicalism might make it less representative of local opinion. Committees, in fact, had an ambivalent profile, both to articulate Resistance demands for a brave new world and to represent a broad church of opinion that was more inclined to let bygones be bygones. There was a growing sense that a fair balance had to be maintained between right and left, reflecting the political complexion of the constituency. The more that traditional parties were represented, however, the more the hard-line Resistance was swamped and the more the opinion was expressed that the Resistance had had its day and it was time to return to party politics.

At one end of the spectrum, the CDL of Indre-et-Loire had a high level of coherence, with thirteen of the twenty-two members belonging to Libération-Nord and another two to Ceux de la Libération. Politically, the complexion was both socialist and Christian democratic, but the two had worked effectively together in the Resistance. The president of the CDL, Jeun Meunier, was also the new mayor of Tours and the kingmaker in the department: prefect Vivier was his man rather than the other way around. The CDL set up and controlled the main organ of the local press, the *Dépêche du Centre*. Only in February 1945 did the communist/CGT/Front National minority (a minority of three) start to cause a nuisance. Supported by the communist *Voix du Peuple*, they attacked M. Vareilles of the CIMT, the employers' representative on the CDL, for having put pressure on his workers to do STO in Germany, and they tried to set up a local liberation committee for Tours alone. In both cases, however, Meunier used his majority in the CDL to stifle them.[11]

In Loire-Inférieure, the communist/CGT/Front National alliance was more powerful.[12] Auguste Péneau, who had led the trade unions' opposition to the Labor Charter in the department, was president of the CDL, Bernier of the Front National a vice president, while Kléber, the communist representative, was an extremely effective member.[13] The original committee of seventeen was enlarged in the autumn to include various communist front organizations, such as the Mouvement National des Prisonniers et des Déportés (MNPD) and the Union des Femmes Françaises (UFF). The main counterweight to the communists was the Marquis de Sesmaisons, mayor and *conseiller général* of La Chapelle-sur-Erdre, secretary of the Chamber of Agriculture, and one of the few representatives of the formerly hegemonic nobles in the department not compromised by collaboration. Although he was deeply conservative, his Resistance profile was guaranteed by his wife, who had battled with the Germans on numerous occasions, became president of the Comité des Oeuvres Sociales de la Résistance (COSR), and was awarded the Légion d'Honneur and the Croix de Guerre, and by his eldest son, Jean, a graduate of Saint-Cyr who had been deported.[14] This weakness of the right on the CDL undermined the position of prefect Vincent, who was considered by the communists to be a Pétainist and narrowly survived a vote of no confidence in March 1945 by eight votes to eight, with one abstention.[15]

Much more influential was the conservative and Catholic lobby in the CDL of Maine-et-Loire. Whereas in Indre-et-Loire thirteen of the twenty-two members of the CDL were affiliated with Resistance organizations and in Loire-Inférieure the proportion was six out of seventeen, in Maine-et-Loire the tally was only three out of twenty.[16] The CDL had scarcely any history before the Liberation, and the original nucleus that met on 12 August 1944, two days after the liberation of Angers, was a mere seven men. Michel Debré was keen on having the Christian democratic former deputy Albert Blanchoin elected president; in fact, the election was won by Auguste Le Tetour, a civil servant with the Vichy price-control office who was affiliated with Libération-Nord. Blanchoin, however, won the struggle to control the *Courrier de l'Ouest*, which took over from the *Petit Courrier*, discredited as the official Vichy newspaper, and at the end of August Le Tetour had to be persuaded not to resign.[17] Le Tetour himself realized that the CDL would have to broaden its membership to become more representative of Angevin opinion and commissioned René Le Bault de la Morinière, who had played the double game by accepting a Vichy nomination as mayor while joining Libération-Nord, to prospect in the Mauges. Le Bault, whose great-grandmother had been drowned by the revolutionary proconsul Carrier in the infamous *noyades de Nantes* of 1793, did not want the CDL to become like "the revolutionary committees of public safety." He swam across the Loire where the bridges were down to recruit Bernard Pellaumail, a leading Cholet industrialist; Canon Douillard, archdeacon of Cholet; and a conservative senator, Vicomte Palamède de la Grandière, one of the founders of the Catholic League of Anjou, who, Le Bault told me with a wink, would have voted full powers to Pétain in July 1940 if only he had not missed the train to Vichy.[18] He also recruited for the liberation committee of Cholet Dom Sortais, abbot of the Trappist monastery of Bellefontaine, a former POW who had preached against the Germans in the churches of the Mauges and hidden many on the run. A soldier-monk, Catholic and patriotic, he was the ideal candidate to maintain harmony in the Vendée, and his biographer claims that because of his influence no woman had her head shaved for collaboration in Cholet.[19]

The only drawback to this balancing of left and right on the CDL was that the committee became divided into two opposing factions.[20] One dispute broke out over the inclusion on the CDL of Charles Poisson, who had made money as an administrator of Jewish properties in Angers under the Aryanization laws. There was another dispute when it was discovered that Palamède de la Grandière had sat on the editorial board of a collaborationist newspaper, *Le Maine-et-Loire*.[21] The final fight erupted in March 1945 when a communist proposed that in the forthcoming municipal elections, when women were to vote for the first time, the vote be denied to cloistered nuns. This position led to the resignation of the eight-member Catholic lobby—including Le Bault de la Morinière, Palamède de la Grandière, Canon Douillard, Pellaumail, Poisson, and Blanchoin—on the grounds that even "the worst prostitutes" had the vote and that the CDL "clashes too often with the opinions of the great majority of the fellow citizens it claims to represent."[22]

The task of notables, state officials, and indeed the military at the end of the Occupation was to ensure their dominance and to keep the insurrection and anarchy surrounding the transfer of power to a bare minimum. One of the main challenges was to bring under control the FFIs that had mushroomed after the Normandy landings and especially after the Liberation less to fight the Germans than to settle accounts with collaborators. These were a conflation of the Maquis and other Resistance movements, supplemented by volunteers from the towns, led sometimes by former officers of the armistice army but just as often by amateurs with chutzpah. One idealized view of the FFIs is that they were bands of Merry Men waving machine guns and devoted to freedom and social justice.[23] A more realistic view is that they were a modern version of the historian Richard Cobb's people's armies, arresting, humiliating, and sometimes killing collaborators, informers, black marketeers, girlfriends of the Boche, and other enemies of the Resistance, little different from the bandits denounced by Vichy, except that they wore armbands to indicate their military status and sometimes left receipts for provisions, cars, and other consumer durables they requisitioned. In the four departments of Brittany adjoining Loire-

Inférieure, Luc Capdevila has calculated that in what he calls the "period of republican disorder," which climaxed in August 1944, FFIs and the like were responsible for two-thirds of the murders and summary executions of alleged collaborators and three-quarters of the head shavings of women said to have slept with Germans.[24]

Once the Germans were safely on the run, all sorts of would-be resistants joined the FFIs, many of them extremely dubious and violent men. The FFIs also turned out to be an admirable refuge for collaborators seeking to recycle themselves as patriots. To control and discipline an unwieldy irregular force it seemed obvious to appeal to men with military training, but the former armistice army was by definition staffed by Pétainists. Lieutenant Colonel Eynaud, appointed FFI chief in Maine-et-Loire, had no record of Resistance activity, made no bones about voicing Pétainist and antirepublican opinions, and said that his forces were really there to take on the communists. The CDL of Maine-et-Loire refused to recognize him in September 1944 and within a fortnight persuaded Debré to dismiss him.[25] In Indre-et-Loire, Major Balzac, who had a good Resistance record and commanded the FFIs in the liberated south of the department, was somehow displaced as commander of the FFIs in the whole department by the Viscount Major de Champmesle, a monocled graduate of Saint-Cyr, until it was discovered that he had been eliminated from the Thirty-second Infantry Regiment in 1937 for announcing in uniform at a public meeting that he would "rather see Hitler at Bourgueil than communism in Paris" and that his FFI headquarters at Bourgeuil was like an eighteenth-century salon, presided over by the Duchesse de Talleyrand-Périgord and swarming with royalists.[26]

An FFI leader who had been rejected by the Maquis of the Armée Secrète in the Loches area, run as it was by former officers of the armistice army's Thirty-second Infantry Regiment, was bound to acquire the popularity of a local hero. This was what happened to "Dr. Jean," alias Jean-Marie Scoarnec, Georges Dubosq, and Captain Le Coz, who claimed both to have been in the Foreign Legion and to have escaped from Drancy, where his wife and children had died. Rejected by the Vichy officers, he organized his own Maquis drawn from young people of a wilder disposition who in the high summer of 1944 delighted in Le Coz's passions for staying in châteaux, driving fast cars, and picking up women. But Le Coz was also a killer, who assassinated Dr. Abribat, leader of the local Légion Française des Combattants, members of the counterinsurgency Milice, and other collaborators. His Maquis liberated Loches on 16 August 1944, and in front of a crowd of 2,000 on the main square he shot the local police chief, who wanted them to go easy on purges. The Germans retook the town a week later and it required the Thirty-second Infantry Regiment to liberate it for good on 6 September. Meanwhile Le Coz pursued a veritable reign of terror in the region as it was discovered that he was no hero but a common criminal and Nazi informer who had turned to the Resistance to save his skin. "He is nothing more than a highway robber," said the Liberation prefect Vivier. "He pillages farms, demands ransoms, murders, arrests arbitrarily, tortures, and issues death threats. . . . He is an inveterate alcoholic and sadist who while pretending to fight the Germans turns his weapons against Miliciens and collaborators."[27] Vivier described Le Coz's Maquis of a hundred as "a veritable bandit business" and Le Coz himself as a "terrorist pirate, murderer, and executioner" responsible for nineteen of the thirty-one summary executions in the department.[28] Eventually, in October 1944, Le Coz was seized by an undercover police operation; a military court tried him a year later and he was shot.[29]

The problem of unruly FFIs was compounded by the fact that in the Nantes–Saint-Nazaire area the Liberation took not weeks or months but a whole year. Once the Allies had liberated Nantes they turned east, leaving 25,000 Germans in the naval and U-boat base of Saint-Nazaire, contained behind a thin line of military men and FFIs, but not hurrying to flush them out. The French authorities were indeed concerned that if the Americans took the offensive they would put at risk the lives of the 125,000 French people still under German occupation in what became known as the pocket of Saint-Nazaire. This was one of a number of pockets on the Atlantic coast, along with Lorient, La Rochelle, and Royan, where the Germans remained ensconced until the end of the war in Europe. The Americans let off their big guns at church steeples, which were being used as German lookout points, while the embattled frontier, only a few miles from Nantes, became even more of a Wild West in which FFIs roamed at will, occasionally engaging in a skirmish as the tired Germans tried to break out but often—to the despair of the local authorities—drinking, womanizing, looting farms and villages, hijacking vehicles, having fatal accidents with firearms, or selling them to racketeers behind the lines, in the luxury restaurants and brothels of Nantes.[30]

The commander of the FFIs on the Saint-Nazaire front, code name Colonel Félix, was an ambitious and authoritarian character with jet-black hair and a somewhat haughty gaze. His career sheds a great deal of light on the Liberation and how it was as much about negotiating the postwar political settlement as about recovering French territory. In particular, Felix's ascendance demonstrates how many of those who came to political prominence after the Liberation joined the Resistance extremely late, and for no other reason than to prevent any revolutionary outcome. Félix's real name was Jacques Chombart de Lauwe; an adventurer of Flemish origin, he married into a rich Franco-Irish family, the Fitzgeralds of Leinster, and with his new fortune bought an estate at Herbignac in the Parc de Brière, now within the Pocket, to suit his passion for hunting. From his estate he provided charcoal to fuel the trucks delivering the collaborationist daily of Nantes, *Le Phare*. In June 1944 he tried to get its editor and owner, René Bentz and François Portais, a son-and-father-in-law team, to hand over the paper, threatening to have his all-powerful friends close it down. In the event, *Le Phare* was closed down at the Liberation for collaboration, at which point Chombart de Lauwe tried to obtain control of its presses for a new paper he was launching, *L'Avenir de l'Ouest*.

Meanwhile, as Colonel Félix, Chombart de Lauwe succeeded in taking command of the FFIs in Loire-Inférieure, becoming involved principally in order to stop the communists from doing so. "If he hadn't been there," said his brother-in-law, Pierre de Montalembert, when I interviewed him in 1999, "completely mad FFIs would have done all the stupid things possible that you can imagine. The people of Nantes realized that they were lucky to have someone sane at the head of the Resistance in Nantes and the region. People were reassured that it wasn't run by a thug [*voyou*], which at the time was very rare."[31] Others had a different view of the methods of Colonel Félix. The CDL complained that the arrests it ordered were not being executed by Colonel Félix, who in turn argued that he recognized only the authority of the prefect.[32] Meanwhile prefect Vincent protested to Félix that his FFIs had threatened to shoot three gendarmes and had arrested seven police officers in Nantes. When a mayor declared that "several times I was marched off by the Germans between two bayonets but this is the first time I have suffered this from the French," Vincent told Félix that such incidents were discrediting the FFIs as a whole in the eyes of the local population.[33] Even Monsignor Villepelet, who knew the colonel as a member of his diocese but hated "the rule of the armband," remonstrated with him for the arbitrary arrest of one of his curés and refused him a chaplain to serve the FFIs.[34]

By October 1944 evidence of the political machinations of Colonel Félix in his capacity as Chombart de Lauwe started to come to light, posing a threat to his Resistance credentials if not to his military effectiveness. His military superior, General Hary, commander of the Fourth Military Region based in Angers, took the view that the row over the *Phare de Nantes* was a purely political matter that should be dealt with privately, that Colonel Félix had heavy military responsibilities on the Saint-Nazaire front, and that he would "forbid anything that might diminish Colonel Félix's authority."[35] This was the same general who in 1945 regretted that "too many so-called FFIs have behaved like veritable bandits and considerably discredited the Resistance."[36] Discredited or not, the Resistance of Colonel Félix endured just long enough, as we shall see, for him to secure the political legitimacy necessary to refloat the right wing in Brittany, the traditional dominant force, now compromised by its Pétainism.

One of the influential accounts of the purges at the Liberation was that they were anarchic and savage, driven through by communists in order to destroy their political opponents.[37] It is true that in some parts of France the Liberation saw a violent settling of scores by opposing factions, with lynchings, kangaroo courts, and summary executions. It was one of the priorities of the new government to bring such disorder under control, if necessary by interning those at risk from popular justice. A regular system of justice was put in place, with military courts at work in each region almost at once, then—in each department by the autumn—*cours de justice* for what were deemed criminal cases of collaboration, *chambres civiques* for cases of "unworthy conduct." Clearly, there were conflicting views about what actions perpetrated under the Occupation needed to be tried and punished and what bygones could be allowed to be bygones. As Michel Debré asked an angry meeting in Cholet early in 1945 after a prisoner was freed, "Who in this room has done nothing worthy of blame from the patriotic point of view since 1939?"[38] Justice, moreover, was not a shining sword that cut through all other circumstances. The brave new order demanded by those who had made sacrifices to the Resistance had to be set against the need to preserve public order and the authority of the state, the continuity of traditional ruling groups, and the integrity of local communities, each or all of which risked being compromised by too violent a purge. Hence at the end of the day there was just as much complaint about lack of justice, cover-ups, and the support of friends in high places as about excessive purges.[39]

The judicial cause célèbre in the Loire-Inférieure was undoubtedly that of the Marquis de La Ferronnays, mayor of Saint-Mars-la-Jaille, who controlled opinion in his fief through his local paper, *Le Journal d'Ancenis*, and who, as president of the *conseil général*, was the unchallenged leader of the right in the department. After the Liberation his arrest was requested by the Liberation Committee of Ancenis, which was astounded to see the marquise presenting a flag to the First Battalion of the FFIs at Saint-Mars and being taken up by the CDL. On the CDL the hard-liners were led by the communists Bernier and Kléber, the soft peddlers by the Marquis de Sesmaisons. The hard-liners argued that although the marquise was of Jewish descent she had been a fervent apostle of collaboration, while the marquis had effectively manipulated the prefecture of Nantes under the Occupation, helped choose the fifty hostages of Nantes and Châteaubriant, personally selected men from his village for the STO, and even had stakes knocked into his fields to prevent Allied planes from landing. De Sesmaisons rejected these allegations as totally unfounded and argued that the heroic war record of the marquis in 1914–18 alone guaranteed the uprightness of his character. Bernier retorted that plenty of veterans of 1914–18 had behaved badly under the Occupation and argued that instead of hesitating because they were dealing with someone so important they should take the view that "you cannot condemn Pétain and Laval without condemning M. de La Ferronnays."

Against the will of prefect Vincent, the CDL ordered the arrest of the marquis, which was carried out on 4 October by FFI Captain Saint-Roch. His group analyzed all the editorials of the *Journal d'Ancenis*, which contained such statements as "The victory of Germany is necessary to spare Europe the horrors of a communist invasion" (10 July 1942). The editorials were actually written by Tony Catta, who also edited the *Souvenir Vendéen*, but the Resistance argued that the marquis, as owner, had to take equal responsibility. In the pretrial period there was a clear division between, on the one hand, the CLL of Ancenis, the FFIs, and the Front National, who saw the marquis purely and simply as a collaborator, and, on the other, the veterans of his old regiment, who "considered their former colonel incapable of doing any wickedness under the Occupation," and the stalwarts of the local community at Saint-Mars, who affirmed "that he was not a collaborator but simply a supporter of Marshal Pétain."[40]

The marquis, in the end, eluded justice. A sick man of sixty-nine, he was rapidly moved from prison to a clinic run by Augustinian nuns. In February 1945 a noisy congress of local Liberation Committees in Loire-Inférieure met to demand a speeding up and toughening of the purges, which it said were being deliberately frustrated by the bureaucracy and the judicial system. It complained in particular that no important figure had yet appeared before the *cours de justice* and called for the resignation of prefect Vincent, whose appointment in any case was supposed to have been temporary.[41] At the end of March, however, the Marquis de La Ferronnays died. On the day of the funeral, celebrated by the bishop of Nantes and attended by the flower of the nobility of the west of France, Colonel Félix/Jacques Chombart de Lauwe wrote in his paper that, "though I, from June 1940, chose another path and rallied to General de Gaulle [in fact he did no such thing until June 1944], I bow respectfully to the memory of M. de La Ferronnays in the hope that everyone might have a sense of duty as strong as his." He denounced the ill treatment to which the marquis had been subjected, defended his obedience to Marshal Pétain, and argued that the motto Work, Family, and Fatherland was a good deal better than the motto that might characterize the present government: Anarchy, Vengeance, Social Decomposition.[42] In a world supposedly divided between Resistance and collaboration Chombart's intervention is puzzling at the very least. When I put this to Pierre de Montalembert, sitting in his salon in front of a shrine dedicated to his ancestor, the great nineteenth-century liberal Catholic, he smiled: La Ferronnays was no enemy of Chombart but, in the loose way in which the Bretons formulate kinship ties, his "uncle." It becomes clear that the most important thing for the likes of Chombart and de Montalembert at the Liberation was to restore the unity and dominance of the French elite, momentarily divided by the Occupation but now in need of pulling together to prevent a communist takeover.

The most famous purge trial in Maine-et-Loire was that of Anatole Manceau, senator, president of the Cholet Chamber of Commerce, and (despite his guerilla war with regional prefect Roussillon) editor of *Le Petit Courrier*, the official paper of the prefecture under the Occupation. Brought to trial in September 1945, Manceau argued that he was "a resistant of the first hour," who had kept his newspaper going, instead of closing it, to "limit German propaganda as much as possible." He said that he had been prepared to take on Vichy over its vilification of parliamentarians, had refused to let collaborationist movements dictate to his paper, and had belonged to a group of "resisting senators" who met weekly under the Occupation. Like the Marquis de La Ferronnays, he was supported by the local community and the professional institutions to which he belonged: the Cholet Chamber of Commerce, the Liberation Committee of Cholet, dominated as it was by good Catholics such as Bernard Pellaumail, Dom Sortais, and Canon Douillard, together with the new mayor. What he did not have on his side, however, was the support of the new political class. Not only was he regarded as a dinosaur of the Third Republic, but what he called the "despoilment" of the *Petit Courrier* by the Christian democrats of Angers around Albert Blanchoin and Charles Poisson had to be legitimated. Manceau was therefore sacrificed and sentenced to five months in prison, which he had already served, to the confiscation of half his assets, and to "national indignity" for life. He died a broken man in 1948.[43]

The *cours de justice* did, on occasions, act more swiftly and decisively. There was reportedly great satisfaction among the crowd that gathered outside the Palais de Justice of Tours, where the court sat on 7 November 1944, when the news emerged that Antoine Devaud, a former police officer, and Nicole Pluveau had been sentenced to death as Gestapo agents. Though Pluveau had her sentence commuted by de Gaulle to perpetual forced labor, Devaud was shot on 19 December. It soon became clear to the public, however, that, while the small fry were being dealt with severely, the big fish were not being brought to justice or were being let off lightly. In December 1944 the communist *Voix du Peuple* fired off a broadside about "the Moracchini scandal." Moracchini was the Tours police chief who had presided over the arrest, beating, and handover to the Gestapo of five young communist militants, who were shot on 16 May 1942, and had now been promoted to secretary-general of police in Angers. Meanwhile the head of Sûreté, André Maurice—who had been specifically cited by the young communists before they were shot, and by the father of one of them before he committed suicide, as the man who delivered them to the Germans—was promoted to Paris. Only the aptly named Boucherie, well known to be in cahoots with Gestapo chief Brückle, was arrested. Rather than blame the chiefs, the internal police inquiry took the easy route of blaming the subordinates, but the communist press would not lie down. "Have they protectors who are so powerful that they cannot be called to account?" demanded *La Voix du Peuple*. And when Moracchini was promoted again to divisional superintendent in Bordeaux, it proclaimed sarcastically: "To the good servants of Pétain and the Gestapo the Fourth Republic expresses its gratitude."[44]

There was also a good deal of public discontent in Tours about the immunity that seemed to be enjoyed by former members of the prefecture. Jean Tracou and secretary-general Bernard Molas-Quenescourt, who were said to have drawn up lists of communists and other dissidents for the Gestapo, were known to be enjoying their freedom in Paris. The stakes were raised by René Feld, a previous secretary-general, who had been suspended at the Liberation from his position as subprefect of Saint-Malo and was trying to save his skin by blaming his colleagues. Tracou and Molas, both with naval backgrounds, were the villains, he declared, while he, with a Jewish grandmother, had spent his time at the prefecture protecting Jews and Freemasons from the ire of Vichy.[45] Despite these attacks, the only prefecture official of Indre-et-Loire to stand trial was the last Vichy prefect, Ferdinand Musso, the spectacle moved by Michel Debré from Tours to Angers for greater security. Musso suffered a blistering attack from Paul Cay, the subprefect of Chinon whom he had fired and who reemerged at the Liberation as secretary-general of the prefecture. Musso, Cay said, was "always very docile in the face of German orders," had welcomed the collaborationist Marcel Bucard to Tours, and was fanatical about suppressing the Maquis. Regional prefect Donati tried to defend Musso, saying that of all the five prefects of the region he had been "the most 'poisoned' by the Germans and their insatiable demands."[46] Donati was shortly to give evidence at Pétain's trial, arguing that Pétain had sacrificed himself to protect France and that the marshal's maxim was, "When there are two courses open to you, take the most difficult. Then you know you are on the right path."[47] It was always possible for a Vichy prefect to claim that, while remaining in his position and even without indulging in any *double jeu*, he had defended French interests as far as was reasonably possible. Unfortunately, Musso did not even pass muster on these criteria and was sentenced to four years in prison.

Given the unedifying nature of many trials, not least as far as the French administration was concerned, the government was keen for cases liable to produce a death penalty to be processed by the *cours de justice* before 1 May 1945, so that things could get back to normal. It was precisely at this time, however, that patriots who had been deported to camps in Germany began to return to France, many of them astounded and furious that collaborators who had denounced them were still free. It also coincided with the return of workers who had gone to Germany voluntarily and, unlike STO conscripts, were considered collaborators. A man named Macret, who had returned to Loches but was being taken by the police to Tours, was dragged out of the police vehicle and lynched by a crowd of 300, including former deportees and their families. Even where individuals were convicted, an angry public might still want to get hold of them. A Vietnamese domestic servant who worked at the château of Vaux near Tours, where parachuted weapons were hidden, had, together with his friend the local grocer, denounced the châtelaine, Hélène Bruneau, and about twenty resistants involved in the enterprise.[48] The resistants were duly arrested and many of them shot, and this as late as 4 August 1944. Although condemned to death by the *cour de justice*, the two were lynched by a crowd as they emerged from the courtroom, and the Vietnamese died of his injuries.[49]

These incidents were no doubt barbaric, but they betrayed a genuine popular dissatisfaction with the effectiveness of the purges as administered by the courts. The courts, it should be stressed, were not the only instrument of the purges. Many professions were allowed to manage their own purges through their own bodies. In the case of industry, interprofessional purge committees for businesses (CIEEs) were set up in each region, presided over by a magistrate and including two representatives of the CDLs, together with representatives of workers, white-collar employees, technicians, engineers, and employers. Whom they were supposed to purge and for what, however, was a matter of debate. Workers obviously took a tougher line than employers. On 21 December 1944 the tramway workers of Nantes went on strike, first to complain that they were be driven like galley slaves and second to remove a trio of Belgian directors whom they held responsible for sending workers to Germany and for drawing the attention of the Germans to a communist worker who had been arrested and shot. The CIEE divided between Péneau, president of the CDL, who took a hard line, and the employers' representative, who wanted to go slow. The prefect was squeezed between the employers and workers of the tramway company but eventually the three Belgian managers were dismissed.[50]

The key issue with "economic collaboration" was not *whether* a firm had worked for the German war economy. The shipyards, railway workshops, and aircraft factories of the Nantes–Saint-Nazaire area, for example, had worked full out for the Wehrmacht, Luftwaffe, and above all the Kriegsmarine until they were gradually prevented from doing so by Allied bombing. The consensual view was that employers had no choice about working for the Germans and that jobs had to be preserved. What was not acceptable was doing the Germans' bidding with too much enthusiasm and putting pressure on workers to go to Germany under the Relève plan, usually by threatening to report them to the German authorities, but the penalties were mild. A manager of the Batignolles locomotive works, 90 percent of whose orders were German, got into trouble for producing for the Germans with an "excess of zeal" and for socializing with German officers, although all the CIEE did was to move him to another job.[51] At the Chantiers de Bretagne in Nantes the deputy director was accused of threatening workers with deportation to Germany if they did not work harder, but he was only suspended without pay for a year. The director, meanwhile, was said to have protected workers who resorted to slowdowns and "passive resistance" in the face of German demands and indeed was praised for his "irreproachable and entirely French attitude."[52] Elsewhere, at the Chantiers de la Loire and the Chantiers Dubigeon, the employers and managers who gained the upper hand on the CIEE practiced the usual formula of passing the buck down to lower echelons and giving their fellow employers a clean bill of health.

When the *commissaire de la République* called on Monsignor Villepelet, bishop of Nantes, on 17 August 1944, a portrait of Marshal Pétain still hung on the wall. To anchor the Liberation Committee more firmly in the department, the *commissaire* was keen to have a member of the clergy sit on it, but the bishop refused to allow one to become involved in what he called "partisan politics." "I reminded him of the position of the Church in respect of political power," said the bishop. "It recognized only one authority as legitimate until further notice but bowed to the de facto power with which it was now confronted." The bishop feared that the provisional government was not strong enough to contain the communists and that France was on the verge of a Spanish Civil War situation. At the very least the Church no longer enjoyed the influence it had under Vichy. On Armistice Day 1944, Villepelet complained that the best seats in the official stand were reserved for members of the CDL and that "had some influential people not protested I would have been relegated to the second rank." When de Gaulle visited Nantes in January 1945 and asked the bishop to celebrate a mass for him, he deferred but found the general as frosty as the snow on the ground, "a man of will rather than of feeling."[53]

There was no question of punishing bishops simply for being Pétainists; the issue was rather how to win them over to the new regime. In Angers, however, Debré was under pressure from the left wing of the CDL to send Monsignor Vincent, the rector of the Catholic University, and two of his staff before the *cour de justice* on charges of collaboration. They had, it was argued, attacked the Resistance, talked up the STO in their preaching, and recruited their students to collaborationist parties and the Milice. Debré feared that any such trial would ignite "a little war of religion" and put pressure on the hierarchy to set its house in order. Reluctantly, the bishops who acted as a board of governors of the Catholic University agreed to the dismissal of Vincent and his two colleagues, which was a triumph for secret diplomacy.[54]

The Catholic faithful were nevertheless mobilizing in anticipation of a new episode in the ongoing struggle of Church and state. The Fédération Nationale Catholique, set up to defend the Church against the Cartel des Gauches in the 1920s, was revived in 1945 as the Fédération Nationale d'Action Catholique under the presidency of Jean Le Cour Grandmaison, mayor of the *mairie* of Guenroët, former member of Vichy's Conseil

National, and future biographer of the Marquis de La Ferronnays. The diocesan branch of the FNC, the Ligue des Catholiques de l'Anjou, was revived in April 1945 as the Union des Catholiques de l'Anjou (UCA) and found a cause in the defense of state subsidies to church schools that Vichy had reintroduced after sixty years of republicanism and that the provisional government was to abolish.[55] Catholics who had initially sat on Liberation Committees and given the Liberation their blessing now resigned to fight the good fight for church schools. The Catholic choir, as we have seen, resigned from the CDL of Maine-et-Loire in March 1945. One member, Canon Douillard, then publicly accused the government of using "the sinister methods of the camps of Buchenwald and Dachau" to starve the church schools attended by two-thirds of the children in the Mauges. He was involved in a Catholic demonstration in Cholet on 2 September 1945, presided over by Monsignor Costes, that drew 30,000 and was a prelude to a demonstration of 60,000 in Angers on 7 October. Jean Le Cour Grandmaison drew a parallel with the FNC demonstration in Angers in March 1925, but the polemic was modernized to overcome the traditional association of the Church with reaction. "Catholics, like all French people," declared the leader of the UCA, "shed their blood for France in front of German tanks in 1940, endured deportation and concentration camps, resisted the enemy, and took part in the glorious liberation of the soil of the fatherland. For these reasons we refuse to be treated like pariahs, outside the national community."[56]

Over a year earlier, on 4 August 1944, American forces liberated the village of Guémené-Penfao in the northern extremity of Loire-Inférieure. A retired schoolteacher and Freemason, Mlle Rolland, and the local curate, Abbé Bersihaud, took over at the *mairie*. Mlle Marie Rolland was in fact a resistant of some experience in the region, code name Annick, but since the village was still surrounded on three sides by the Germans she asked another retired schoolteacher, André Laurens, to organize an FFI unit to defend it. Although the two were formally part of the same Liberation Committee, a power struggle broke out between them, with Annick accusing Laurens of undermining the Resistance. Laurens was initially confirmed as FFI leader in the locality by Colonel Félix's minions at Châteaubriant, then dropped, complaining that "I have been defeated by a woman of seventy-one and a discharged corporal stretcher bearer."

Annick then discovered that the CDL in Nantes had endorsed a second Liberation Committee in Guémené, under Laurens, and asked "what this farce means." Both Annick and Laurens were summoned to appear before the CDL on 5 January 1945 and Laurens was given the benefit of the doubt. Meanwhile the mayor of Guémené had been interned and a new municipal council was confirmed by the CDL, including fifteen old councillors and six new ones (not including Annick or the abbé) who had emerged from the Resistance.[57]

In the anarchic period of the Liberation such uncertainty and faction fighting were extremely common, and yet the new Republic had to ensure a rapid transition to stable local government. Resistance groups set up Liberation Committees that looked to purge discredited local councils to make room for people with Resistance credentials. On the other hand, the authorities had to be satisfied that the administration was in the hands of those who had local influence and could demonstrate competence. There was a far-reaching reorganization of municipal councils and *conseils généraux* after the Liberation, but what took place fell far short of a revolution. Criteria based on political correctness were constantly balanced against those based on effectiveness and consensus. The principles of republican legitimacy laid down in an ordinance of 21 April 1944 banned from elective office the 569 deputies and senators who had voted full powers to Marshal Pétain on 10 July 1940, and all those appointed by "the usurper" to the Conseil National, departmental councils, or municipal councils. Only notable service to the Resistance would permit such a ban to be lifted. Mayors and councillors who had "directly favored or served the interests of the enemy or the usurper" would also be dismissed. Vacancies caused by the dismissal, resignation, or death of councillors would be filled provisionally ahead of municipal or cantonal elections, due in 1945, but Resistance activity would not be the sole or even main criterion for selection. Just as important, so that the local council would be approved by local citizens, was the political profile of the commune as evidenced by the last municipal elections, held in 1935.

In Tours, there was no return as mayor for the socialist politician Ferdinand Morin, who had voted full powers to Pétain in 1940. He was said to have distrusted the Maquis as communist-inspired and "shown a certain sympathy for the Vichy government, notably for Laval, whom he knew personally." His record as protector of the city was not enough to outweigh these factors, and he did not become a municipal councillor again until 1953.[58] In Angers, the solemn Mayor Victor Bernier, not having been a deputy, was not compromised in July 1940. Instead, he was still able to play on his "saving" of the city from destruction in June 1940 and his "seriously disobeying the Occupation authorities" by going into semi-retirement at the beginning of 1944; he was welcomed back as mayor, almost as a hero. His authority was endorsed by General de Gaulle, who visited the city on 22 August 1944, twelve days after its liberation, and again on 14 January 1945. Walking with the general down the Boulevard du Maréchal Foch, the Angevin equivalent of the Champs-Élysées, gave the eternal trimmer Bernier a new dose of legitimacy.[59]

Developments in Nantes and Saint-Nazaire also strongly contrasted. Their present mayors, Henri Orrion and Pierre Toscer, both appointed by Vichy, were declared ineligible, despite Orrion's valiant attempt to dig up some "acts of resistance." Socialist mayor and deputy Auguste Pageot and Ferdinand Blancho, who had both voted full powers to Pétain in 1940, appeared before the CDL of Loire-Inférieure on 19 October 1944 in the hope of having their ineligibility quashed. Each explained that he had voted for Pétain as the least of all evils in the dire circumstances. Pageot said that he had been arrested by the Germans, forced to resign, and expelled to the Free Zone over the war-memorial affair, but thereafter he had published a few articles in a collaborationist journal. Blancho was more successful in demonstrating his Resistance credentials, as one of the second batch of fifty hostages threatened with execution after the killing of the Feldkomman-dant of Nantes, for resigning as mayor after a dispute with Darlan, and finally for being an active member of the Liberation in the Nice area. Most important, however, he had the support of the SFIO both in the depart-ment and nationally as the natural leader of the working class in Saint-Nazaire and the only politician capable of keeping the communists at bay there.[60] Blancho duly returned to Saint-Nazaire as mayor after the pocket was liberated. In Nantes, Clovis Constant, leader of the post office workers and vice president of the CDL, became mayor of a totally new muncipality at the end of August 1944, the old councillors being so faction-ridden that Debré insisted on starting with a new slate.[61] He had to wait long months, however, for an endorsement from de Gaulle, who had not forgiven the city for refusing his award of the Croix de la Libération after the execution of the fifty hostages in 1941. It was not until 14 January 1945 that the general visited the city to make the award, and then he offended Constant and the municipality by visiting the prefecture and the cathedral but not the town hall, leaving for Angers at two in the afternoon.[62] The precariousness of Constant's position was confirmed in 1947 when Henri Orrion, the Vichy mayor, swept back into power.

The "Nantes model" of a completely new council was the dream of small Liberation Committees of resisters who found themselves pitted against municipalities stuffed with Pétainists who actually enjoyed the support of the majority of the population. The Liberation Committee of Ancenis was keen to purge the local council, which took its cue from the Marquis de La Ferronnay's *Journal d'Ancenis*, and urged a new one composed of socialists, communists, radicals, Front National members, and trade unions. But prefect Vincent argued that the clean slate in Nantes was undertaken for exceptional reasons and was not a model. He saw Ancenis as a "right-wing town where radicals look like the extreme left" and proposed a more balanced "municipality of conciliation."[63] In similar towns existing mayors were toppled where charges of collaboration stuck, although they did not necessarily go quietly or forfeit local support. Alphonse Darmaillacq was confirmed as mayor of Cholet in September 1944, but then the communists, who wanted four seats on the municipal council but got two, accused him of sending a young man to Germany on the STO because he did not want the man to marry his daughter. Try as he might to paint himself as "the first resistant of Cholet," as a mayor who had risked his life six or seven times to protect the townspeople, Darmaillacq could not remove the smear and resigned as mayor and as a member of the *conseil général* at the beginning of 1945.[64] Prefect Fourré-Cormeray was reluctant to let him go but was able to replace him with another rich Catholic industrialist, Bernard Pellaumail, who commanded just as much local support and had the advantage of having sat for a time on the CDL. Other small towns, however, were in effect the pocket boroughs of certain notables and even if the administration wanted to break a habit, the shortage of candidates to take on the challenge was manifest. The mayor of Vouvray, on the Loire just east of Tours, was Charles Vavasseur, president of Vichy's *conseil départemental*, who made huge profits selling sparkling wine to the Germans, frequent visitors to his cellars, and who thought Laval was a fine diplomat and de Gaulle soft on communism.[65] Prefect Vivier reported that he was "moderate, traditionalist, 100 percent Vichyssois," but an opportunist who had celebrated the Liberation and looked like he was rallying to the new order. It was difficult to find "a citizen whose authority and republican and patriotic convictions make it possible to replace M. Vavasseur with any advantage." From this case he extrapolated the general rule that "it is very difficult to appoint a provisional municipal council that is at one and the same time republican, not polluted by Vichy, and in command of the approval of the population."[66]

The ability of mayors and municipal councillors to weather the Liberation as they weathered Vichy was thus considerable. Figures for Indre-et-Loire are incomplete but suggest that between 50 and 60 percent of mayors were confirmed in office at the Liberation. In Loire-Inférieure, where the Occupation had been more turbulent, 40 percent of mayors were confirmed, although this proportion fell to 30 percent in the arrondissement of Saint-Nazaire, which remained under Occupation until May 1945 and where purges were correspondingly greater. In Maine-et-Loire, however, which had remained cushioned from the worst of the Occupation, nearly three-quarters (73 percent) of all mayors who had been in office under Vichy were confirmed at the Liberation.[67]

Such phenomenal tenacity requires an explanation. Often there were few resisters who could provide an alternative focus and, even if there were, they found it difficult to displace notables who had controlled the *mairies* for years and whose networks of patronage were well established. Even the Liberation authorities were reluctant to remove them. The crusty radical-socialist Édouard Tardif, mayor of Longué in the Saumurois, felt compromised by his tenure under Vichy and sent in his resignation, but he had the support of the whole municipal council and three-quarters of the population. The subprefect, who persuaded him to stay on, told him, "I am surprised that an old fighter like you is thinking of abandoning a position that he has held so honorably for twenty years. More than ever the Republic needs men like you."[68] In the Mauges, where the Vendée begins, the mayor of La Jumellière belonged to the Groupe Collaboration and the PPF, and his son had been killed fighting for the LVF on the Russian front. A member of the local Liberation Committee nevertheless argued, "It would be difficult to find another mayor to set against him because he has the ear of those he administers and will be returned at the next elections. Besides, he is flexible enough to follow the new government."[69]

Even when many formal changes did take place, as in Loire-Inférieure, the reality was often rather different. Derval, near Châteaubriant, was run virtually as a seigneurial regime and the CDL was persuaded by the communist Bernier to arrest the mayor, Comte Hay de Slade, a millionaire châtelain, as a collaborator. This was in the teeth of a warning from Olivier de Sesmaisons, who said he was a great "notability" and a veteran of 1914–18 whose arrest would provoke an explosive reaction in the department.[70] The CDL sent two emissaries, who arrived with the subprefect of Châteaubriant only to find that the mayor's deputy, described as a recruiting sergeant for the Francists, had whipped up the peasants, telling them that "two communists from Nantes are here to expel the mayor. If you are good Catholics, come defend him." The emissaries were met at the town hall on 23 September by 150 angry people, most of them the mayor's farmers and laborers, shouting, "Down with communists! Down with hooligans! Down with outsiders! Long live the mayor! Locals must keep the town hall!" The emissaries were beaten up as they tried to leave. Hay de Slade congratulated his tenants, delighted that the CDL had been taught a lesson. He was dismissed as mayor but continued to open the mail and to give orders, in conjunction with the curé, as if he were still in office. A local doctor, councillor, and member of the humiliated local Liberation Committee reflected that "Cagoulards and curés are dictators in this region [*pays*]."[71]

The grip of local notables was demonstrated also by the reform of departmental assemblies in the autumn and winter of 1944–45. Vichy's appointed *conseils départementaux* were abolished and the elected *conseils généraux*, suspended in 1940, were brought back. Under the original republican legitimacy rules those who had accepted nomination to Vichy's departmental councils were not allowed to return to the *conseil général*, but this was soon felt to be too draconian, and in November 1944 it was decided members of the departmental councils would be allowed to rejoin their *conseil généraux* if they had been elected to them before 1940. As a result, the *conseils généraux* restored in 1944–45 bore a striking resemblance to those that had been abolished in 1940: 50 percent of the members (eighteen out of thirty-six, not including ten in the Saint-Nazaire pocket) of the *conseil généraux* of 1945 were carried over from 1940 in Loire-Inférieure, and 50 percent (twelve of twenty-four) in Indre-et-Loire. Again, however, continuity was highest in Maine-et-Loire, where the figure was 59 percent (twenty of thirty-four).

In terms of personalities, Indre-et-Loire saw the return of radical-socialist notables such as Gounin to Amboise and Dr. Guillaume-Louis to Montbazon. Two more radical-socialists, Jollit, mayor of Azay, and Dr. Labussière of Chinon, were included even though they had been deported to Germany; Labussière was in fact already dead. Camille Aron, unceremoniously expelled from his Château-Renault seat by Vichy as a Jew, took it up again.[72] Conservative nobles were still a powerful force on the *conseil général* of Loire-Inférieure: the Marquis de Sesmaisons in La Chapelle-sur-Erdre, the Comte de Landemont in Ancenis, François Le Cour Grandmaison in Vertou, the Comte Ferdinand de Charette in Saint-Julien-de-Vouvantes.[73] Maine-et-Loire had its quota of long-serving conservatives such as François de Polignac in Chemillé, Jean de Geoffe in Doué-la-Fontaine, Jean de Jourdan in Segré, and Jacques de la Grandière, excused from his membership in Vichy's Conseil National because his son was in de Gaulle's entourage, in Le Lion d'Angers. Henri de Champagny was kept on in Vihiers, although he was in a German concentration camp. Victor Bernier was brought back for Angers NW and recycled radical-socialists in the Saumurois included, in addition to Édouard Tardif in Longué, Jean Herard in Noyant and the veteran Robert Amy in Saumur, where he had also recovered the town hall.[74]

One of the reasons given by the Liberation administration for only a limited remodeling of municipal councils and *conseils généraux* was the conservatism of local populations, indebted as they were to the local notables who (in most cases) had protected their interests during the Occupation. What the electorate actually felt was not tested until a wave of elections in 1945: municipal elections on 29 April and 13 May, cantonal for the *conseils généraux* in September, and general elections to the Constituent Assembly in October. Many new factors came into play in these elections. Women, who had been prevented from voting in the Third Republic, not least because they were seen as electoral fodder for the Church and thus for the right, were given the vote, if only as a counterweight to the communists.

There was a general sense that some contribution to the Resistance should be a condition of seeking election, and many electoral lists were based on Resistance groupings rather than on party affiliations. On the other hand, political parties, whether old or new—such as the Christian democratic Mouvement Républicain Populaire (MRP)—were keen to restore the familiar rules of party politics and the primacy of party. Most important, there was a sense that change was needed and that the old political class, which had spent the last few years wheeling and dealing, trimming and second-guessing, was too tired and too compromised to lead the virginal Republic. This, more than anything else, explains why despite (or even because of) the near anarchy of 1944, the change in political personnel was rather limited, whereas the return to orderly democratic politics in 1945 was more dramatic. The right, however, was not displaced by the left, for one of the most impressive features of this moment was the ability of the right to rebrand itself in a world that, thanks to the Resistance, had created new rules.

In the municipal elections of April-May there were attempts in the large towns to construct joint socialist-communist lists under a Resistance banner. In Tours, the great elector was Jean Meunier, leading light in Libération-Nord and president of the CDL, as well as SFIO boss and outgoing mayor of Tours. He made a deal with Louis Salmon, briefly the communist mayor of Saint-Pierre-des-Corps at the Liberation, and secured the town hall for the socialists and communists, who acquired eleven seats.[75] In Angers, Victor Bernier was swept from power by a socialist-communist coalition, and a bearded socialist, Alphonse Allonneau, finally replaced him as mayor. In Nantes, the socialist old guard like Pageot and Prieur had been expelled from the party but Clovis Constant, a new socialist, held on. The MRP made an excellent showing overall, less in anticlerical Indre-et-Loire than farther west, where it took up the slack from Catholic conservatives compromised by Vichy and even conquered the radical fiefs of Saumur. The Radical-Socialist Party, which had been the ruling party of the Third Republic and characterized the ancien régime that Vichy wanted to destroy, was now on the defensive.

There were, of course, exceptions to this pattern. Many voters still felt loyal to Vichy, feared the communists, and trusted the local notables who had guided them through troubled times. A number of politicians who had been declared ineligible under the rules of republican legitimacy nevertheless put themselves forward for election and won, which obliged the authorities to invalidate the poll. Dutertre de la Coudre, conservative mayor and deputy of Machecoul (Loire-Inférieure), rendered ineligible by virtue of his vote for Pétain in 1940, stepped into the elections in the second round and was reelected mayor. He told the prefect that he had not engaged in any active resistance, which might have provided mitigating circumstances, "because of the heavy occupation of the coast and hinterland and because of the configuration of the landscape, flat, denuded of woods and forests and thus of any hiding place," but he had, as mayor, limited as far as possible German demands for Todt workers, STO conscripts, horses, and potatoes. The municipal council backed him up, saying that he alone, mayor for thirty-eight years, had the necessary authority and "spirit of reconciliation" and that "the population of Machecoul would feel it cruelly if the plebiscite it has just declared in favor of M. Dutertre de la Coudre were set aside."[76]

In Chinon, Mayor Mattraits told the council that he had protected the town for four years "under the German jackboot." He claimed that "one of our most glorious victories was to prevent our most cherished statue [of Rabelais] from being turned into German bullets."[77] This did not prevent the council from being dissolved and a "provisional municipal delegation" of local Resistance leaders being appointed. With splendid irony its ceremonial inauguration was presided over on behalf of the prefect by Paul Cay, who announced how delighted he was to be back in Chinon.[78] Mattraits was not finished, and in the municipal elections of 1945 Auguste Correch, the college principal and assistant mayor to Mattraits in the latter part of the Occupation, declared that Mattraits "had never been the servant of the Vichy government and, faithful to the republican tradition, he never looked for any personal profit. He did his duty entirely."[79] The slate headed by Mattraits won seventeen of the twenty-three seats on the council, and on 18 May Mattraits was duly elected mayor. The verdict of the popular vote nevertheless clashed with the rules of republican legitimacy, and despite an appeal from the council majority to de Gaulle, Mattraits was once again officially deposed. In the end the Resistance faction of the council did not benefit either. Auguste Correch was elected mayor and immediately paid homage to the devotion of Dr. Mattraits, who he said had served Chinon "with courage, probity, dignity, and disinterestedness during a difficult and dangerous period."[80] Three years later Mattraits died and was buried with great pomp after a funeral attended by the municipal council, the medical body, the hospitals, the court, the teachers and school-children, the public employees, the gendarmerie, and the population of Chinon and surrounding villages. Giving the oration, Correch reiterated Mattraits's role as the savior of his people and reminded the mourners of the plebiscite that had returned him to office in 1945. Unfortunately, he said, Mattraits had received an "odious and outrageous reward" in the form of dismissal and, despite the lobbying of powerful friends, they had "come up against a marmorean decision made by they did not know who and they did not know where." Even the local leaders of the Resistance now paid homage to Mattraits at a funeral that demonstrated eloquently that the concerns and aspirations of the local community and the concerns and aspirations of the Resistance were far from being the same.[81]

The cases of Mattraits and Dutertre de la Coudre highlight the clash between republican legitimacy and popular consent but are not necessarily typical. In general, the popular vote continued to whittle away the old political class in the cantonal elections of September 1945. Only 26 percent (twelve of forty-six) of *conseillers généraux* of 1940 survived in Loire-Inférieure, 17 percent (four of twenty-four) in Indre-et-Loire, and 12 percent (four of thirty-four) in Maine-et Loire. The game was up for compromised local notables. There was not, however, a massive shift to the left. The only communist councillor elected in the three departments was elected in Nantes, although another lost by only seventy-nine votes in Tours-Centre. The number of SFIO councillors rose from four in 1940 to six in Indre-et-Loire, from none to three in Maine-et-Loire, including Mayor Allonneau and one of his deputies, Germaine Canonne, the first woman to be elected to the *conseil général* in any of the three departments. The most significant decline was that of the radical-socialists, from six to two councillors in Maine-et-Loire and from fourteen to ten in their strong-hold of Indre-et-Loire. Though Dr. Guillaume Louis, who had broadened his appeal by joining the Front National, was elected president of the new *conseil général*, he presided over a dying empire.

The most exciting party in the region was the MRP, which took two seats in Indre-et-Loire and five in Maine-et-Loire. In Angers NW the sempiternal Victor Bernier was defeated by Jean Sauvage, a thirty-five-year-old textile manifacturer who was diocesan president of the ACJF. Though Bernier "knew everyone," Sauvage recalls, the MRP had a "new dynamism" that was disseminated through the *Courrier de l'Ouest*, which he and his friends had founded.[82] The MRP took up the baton from the traditional right, having the advantage of association with the Resistance, but the traditional right itself was by no means done for. A solid phalanx of the old guard, still influential in the countryside, weathered the return to democracy. In Maine-et-Loire, Jean de Jourdan and Jean de Geoffre still clung on, while in Beaupréau Pierre de Blacas succeeded his deceased father. In Loire-Inférieure, Olivier de Sesmaisons, Ferdinand de Charette, and Henri de Landemont were reelected to the *conseil général*, while in the liberated pocket Henri Le Cour Grandmaison was returned for Savenay. The success of the right, just as much as that of the MRP, however, was due to a new generation of conservatives who had not been blatantly compromised by association with Vichy and had even won some credit from the Resistance. In Maine-et-Loire, René Le Bault de la Morinière, who had built up the Catholic conservative choir on the CDL and the Liberation Committee of Cholet, was elected for Champtoceaux in the Mauges; later he would become the Gaullist deputy of Cholet. In Loire-Inférieure, Jacques Chombart de Lauwe, alias Colonel Félix, now mayor of Herbignac, achieved his dream of succeeding Count Hubert de Montaigu as *conseiller général* of Herbignac and now set his eyes on the Constituent Assembly.[83]

These developments were confirmed in the elections to the Constituent Assembly on 21 October 1945. These were organized on a slate system, under proportional representation, giving a good reflection of the share of the vote but making it difficult for politicians used to cultivating a local clientele. One communist was elected in Indre-et-Loire, another in Loire-Inférieure. There were two SFIO deputies in Indre-et-Loire, including Jean Meunier; two in Loire-Inférieure, including Clovis Constant; and one in Maine-et-Loire (Alphonse Allonneau). The radical-socialists, who had been prized out of the towns of Touraine in the municipal elections and clung onto the countryside in the cantonal elections, now had no deputy elected to the Constituent Assembly from Indre-et-Loire, none from Maine-et-Loire either, and only one in Loire-Inférieure. The MRP made a breakthrough in Indre-et-Loire, neck and neck with the SFIO, both winning two seats, and romped home with three of the six seats in Maine-et-Loire. "Ardently social," its leader, Charles Barangé, told the *Courrier de l'Ouest*, "it wants to offer something new while at the same time keeping its spirituality."[84] In Loire-Inférieure, however, the MRP secured only one of the eight seats, since the right held on under the guise of the National and Republican Union. This union was the brainchild of Jacques Chombart de Lauwe, a repackaged right with a list headed by a Resistance hero, General Audibert. Audibert was nevertheless a Resistance leader in the mold of the conservative west, a large landowner, head of the Clisson section of La Rocque's Parti Social Français in the 1930s, leader of the Armée Secrète in Brittany and the Loire Valley, deported to Buchenwald in 1943, repatriated to a hero's welcome in April 1945. He somewhat outrageously attacked the program of the Conseil National de la Résistance (CNR) as "neither national . . . nor resistant," drawn up, he said, by émigrés who had no mandate from anyone.[85] Meanwhile Chombart de Lauwe kept up a massive barrage in his *Avenir de l'Ouest* to clear the terrain for the right, attacking the radical-socialists as "responsible for the moral decomposition of the country between 1918 and 1939," the MRP as "intended to divide Catholics and nationalists," and the communists as stooges of Moscow, which meant "dictatorship, a dictatorship similar to Nazi dictatorship, slavery."[86] Audibert, Chombart de Lauwe, and the faithful Marquis Olivier de Sesmaisons were elected from the department to fight the good fight in the era of the Cold War.

It becomes clear that the heroic profile of the Liberation has in many instances to be revised. The Forces Françaises de l'Intérieur, often portrayed as freedom fighters, were often ill-disciplined and as likely to prey on their fellow French as on embattled Germans. Much, no doubt, is explained by the warlike context of the summer of 1944, but they proved a headache for local councils, prefects, and even the regular military itself. These elements were desperate to ensure as peaceful a transition as possible from one order to the next. At the same time, those who might have been compromised by association with Vichy or the Germans were keen to recycle themselves as good patriots. For these reasons the Liberation did not see the dramatic break in French politics and society that might be expected. Summary justice gave way to formal courts that were reluctant to try and convict more than a minority of those who might be accused of collaboration. The economy now produced for the Allied war effort rather than for the German, but above all the economy needed to turn over with as minimal disruption as possible so that business leaders suffered little from the purges. Government had to continue at the regional and local as well as at the national level. The continuity of the state at the center was reflected in the continuity of the state locally, but a local approach also reveals the tremendous continuity of local notables who carried influence in their communities. Only the elections of 1945 saw a sea change in political personnel, and even then it was not accompanied in the Loire area by a marked shift from right to left. One of the extraordinary stories of this region was the ability of the right to rebrand itself in order to prepare for the next political challenge: the defense against communism. However skillfully political continuity was managed, however, there were huge expectations of freedom and plenty among the French people, and those expectations were all too often disappointed.

15

Disappointment

It is a truth universally acknowledged that the French people danced in the streets at the Liberation. Along with French women embracing American soldiers who passed through their towns and villages, this gesture, captured in numerous images, encapsulates the sense of joy that swept the country as the yoke of German Occupation was lifted.[1] What is less appreciated was that dancing remained formally prohibited until the end of hostilities in May 1945. The Liberation merely opened the way to France's rejoining the Second World War and there was much serious fighting yet to be done. Moreover, while French territory had been liberated, there were over two million French people in German POW, labor, and concentration camps, and there was a widespread feeling that it was in very poor taste for some to make merry when so many more remained separated from and fearful for their loved ones. This induced an ambivalence and confusion that was nicely articulated by Albert Chevalier-Valin, a musician from a village just outside Saumur, where he had his instruments confiscated by three gendarmes at an illegal dance on 6 January 1945:

I would like to protest strongly about the action taken against me given that people are dancing everywhere, I repeat, EVERYWHERE. Do you need proof? The same evening that we were caught there was a big dance in the cinema of Longué and posters had even been put up. Recently dances have taken place in Fontevrault, Montsoreau, and Parnay, with the acquiescence of the gendarmerie of Fontevrault, and gendarmes even attended the dance at Turquant. . . . I have played regularly for the the *maquisards* and then the FFIs in the woods of Breille and Vernantes. . . . Here in Maine-et-Loire, which is not perhaps the same France as Paris, all requests to hold dances are systematically turned down. . . . The Fourth Republic has brought back the motto Liberty, Equality, Fraternity, but are we to believe that it is just to adorn the pediments of public buildings?[2]

It is true that this was a thorny issue and that there was an inconsistency about public policy. Dancing was not only pleasant but highly profitable, tied into the black market and an obvious way for peasants and traders to sell their food and wine at high prices. A sixty-year-old farmer, Henri Fefeu, who owned the barn in which Chevalier-Valin was playing that night, was indicted not only for organizing an illegal ball but for opening a bar without a license, for selling bread without exchanging it for ration tickets, and for clandestine pig killing to make rillette sandwiches.[3] There was massive pressure to dance not only from locals but from FFIs, regular soldiers, and passing Americans, who were less ready to take no for an answer. When the Saumur gendarmerie raided an illegal dance that had been organized by the NCOs of the cavalry school, a sergeant asked, "Why are dances allowed at Château-du-Loir [Sarthe] and not here?" and then answered his own question: "Because the prefect is an idiot [*con*] and the subprefect, too. If there is a fine, just send the bill to de Gaulle, who is my boss. No one is going to stop us from dancing."[4] Whereas under the Occupation dancers tended to scatter when gendarmerie arrived, now they were reluctant to leave and, reinforced by soldiers from the Division Leclerc, they were now in a position to win a standoff.[5] Mayors were squeezed between the requirement to enforce the law and the need to keep the local community happy, and even the gendarmes who hailed from those communities were reluctant to be tough. An anonymous burgher of Chacé complained to the subprefect of Saumur that dancing that had gone on three evenings in a row was "an insult to France's suffering and the three million prisoners and deportees who, alas, have no desire to dance. What is the point of ministerial and prefectoral bans?" Even the father of one of the Saumur gendarmes, he continued, had told the mayor not to worry about letting the dances go ahead, because the gendarmerie were in the picture.[6] The confiscation of Chevalier-Valin's instruments was part of a new clampdown that recognized that fines of 100 francs were not enough and that "the organization of clandestine dances in the region seems to be on the increase."[7] On 14 March 1945 the prefect of Maine-et-Loire renewed the ban, but the pressure on the floodgates was almost too great. Even the government came to permit exceptions to the ban, such as charity balls where money was being raised for POWs and deportees, traditional balls celebrating national or local festivals, and dances organized by Resistance groups and army units, but global permission for dancing was not finally granted until 7 May 1945.

This approach by the government may seem to have been unduly mealymouthed, but it was perfectly true that for many people the war was not over. Only two hundred kilometers from Saumur and, more to the point, only twenty kilometers from Nantes, the German Occupation continued. Bouvron, whose curate, Abbé Ploquin, had recruited a number of local youths for the Maquis of Saffré and whose villagers hoisted the tricolor on the *mairie* on 9 August, found itself reoccupied by the Germans on 12 August and on the front line of a pocket bounded by the Vilaine River in the north and then, switching southeast, by the Brest-Nantes canal. Many of the urban population of Saint-Nazaire had long since been evacuated to Touraine, but there remained 125,000 inhabitants of the town, its hinterland, and the Guérande peninsula, famous for its salt marshes, who seemed not to have been invited to the Liberation party and for whom occupation by 25,000 German soldiers would last another nine months.[8]

No doubt it was not the same proud and good-looking army that had marched into the region four years earlier. On the contrary, "it was a pathetic army," noted Abbé Verger, curé of Guenrouet, another occupied village on the canal twenty kilometers from Bouvron. "Drawn and haggard faces, limbs worn out by tiredness, bony horses, unbelievable vehicles, the remains of a routed army. Spectators nodded their heads as they watched them and said, 'We know all about that: now it's their turn!' "⁹ Now that the main theater of operations had moved elsewhere and the Germans could expect to be held responsible for any ill treatment of French citizens under international law, Franco-German relations were tolerable and not without humor. In Guenrouet, the ambition of the commander, Lieutenant Scharnhorst, was to be allowed to play the church harmonium. Since the curé would not give way, Scharnhorst's adjutant, a Viennese named Theo Damm, requisitioned a piano for him on his birthday. Damm was no saint and was even caught killing the curé's rabbits, but he was a popular figure with the locals who, with his green Luftwaffe trousers and striped top made out of tent material, was nicknamed "Peau de Grenouille." Frustration was directed toward the FFIs and the French troops, who patrolled the frontier without launching an offensive, and toward the Americans, who turned their big guns on the church towers of the region because they made excellent lookout posts for the Germans. On 18 November 1944 they destroyed the church tower of Bouvron, and on 7 December that of Guenrouet. Lieutenant Scharnhorst and Theo Damm offered their sincere condolences to the mayor and drank a glass of cognac with him, "for good times and bad."¹⁰

The pressing issue for both French and Germans was supply. Resources were limited and both sides wanted them. The farming communities near the canal were not badly off and suffered a good deal of plunder by the Germans, but the *paludiers* of the salt marshes who did not grow crops or raise cattle were going hungry. Durables such as sugar, coffee, oil, soap, wood, and matches were also scarce. Negotiations took place between the subprefect of Saint-Nazaire, Benedetti, and the German military authorities. It was agreed that the Germans would put an end to plunder and would share foodstuffs equitably so long as the French farmers handed goods over. The farmers, however, resumed their age-old ploy of hiding their produce, and the Germans now demanded the evacuation of much of the French population to allow more resources for them. This was not a direct Franco-German issue but one that divided the French military from the civil administration. The prefect and subprefect took the Germans' point about the welfare of the population, but the French military had no wish to make the lot of the Germans easier. Neither did the local population want to move, for fear of having their empty properties and farms pillaged. A compromise was worked out whereby 10,000 people would be evacuated if they so wished, and a supply train would go to the pocket once a month. A first batch of evacuees from the hard-pressed Guérande peninsula arrived in Nantes on 23 October, and a first supply train went to the pocket on 30 December, returning with a load of salt. Far from being sympathetic, the Nantais overwhelmingly felt that their fellow citizens in the pocket should sort themselves out (*qu'ils se débrouillent*), and farmers were reluctant to provide dairy products that might still go to feed the Germans. It was even rumored that the salt train was to supply black marketeers in the west of France.[11]

The management of the pocket was a good episode in Franco-German cohabitation and a good example of negotiation in time of war. Liberation came eventually on 11 May 1945 when, in the middle of a poppy field in Bouvron, General Junck handed over his pistol to General Kraemer of the U.S. army, flanked by General Cholmel of the French, and formally surrendered. Now the local inhabitants could experience the joy their fellows had savored months before, although the liberation of the pocket brought credit neither to French FFIs and soldiers nor to the local population. FFIs forced German soldiers to drag them in carriages around Saint-Nazaire, while the local inhabitants threw stones at the Germans as open trucks ferried them away to POW camps.[12] General Cholmel's army of liberation in fact behaved no differently from any other army of occupation, moving into the holiday villas on the coast at La Baule and loading furniture and kitchen equipment into military trucks for their own use. Even a herd of cows at La Baule airfield, requisitioned by the Germans, was seized by the French military as booty instead of being returned to farmers. The prefecture noted sadly that "pillaging is even worse than when the Germans were here."[13]

The partial evacuation of the pocket of Saint-Nazaire in 1944–45 was only another episode in the drama of evacuation that had started with the bombings of Lorient, Nantes, and Saint-Nazaire in 1942–43 and continued with the Normandy landings of June 1944. For the Allied landings and bombardment of Norman towns drove columns of refugees away from the coast, many of them crossing Anjou and Loire-Inférieure on their way south. The mayors of Baugé and Noyant complained at the beginning of August that "a wave of 600 to 800 homeless per day is exhausting local resources, using about 40 percent of the horses that are currently needed for the harvest, and leaving a local population that has plenty of goodwill completely overwrought."[14] In November local communities were warned to expect a new wave of evacuees from the pocket of Saint-Nazaire and appeals were made to their sense of "solidarity." Many towns and villages were willing to make another effort, but there were also clear signs of refugee fatigue. One mayor in the Mauges said that "we have already made a huge effort for two months for the refugees from the Calvados. We had seventy refugees, while many neighboring communes had none at all." A mayor of a village near Baugé said that the villagers had recently looked after fifty-six people fleeing from Normandy with no possessions at all. "We had to give them so much that our capacity to give is now much diminished, not to say exhausted."[15]

The displacement of populations as a result of the war was a problem that long outlasted the Liberation and was still there after the war ended. In July 1945 there were still 15,000 refugees in Indre-et-Loire and 16,000 in Maine-et-Loire, but there were 150,000 in Loire-Inférieure in May 1945 and 100,000 in October. About two-thirds of displaced persons received some kind of benefit, either as evacuees or as victims of bomb damage (*sinistrés*), but there were generally delays in payment. A spokesman for 7,000–8,000 refugees in Vertou, a suburb of Nantes, asked in September for the benefit due in July and August to be paid, especially as local traders were still charging high prices, even though German requisitions had ceased and the harvest was in.[16] Meanwhile the pressure on accommodation was extremely severe, and refugees found themselves competing for a roof with private landlords, businesses, and the army. Working-class refugees from the pocket who had been housed in a local château by the municipality of Rézé, another suburb of Nantes, were told that they had to vacate premises by 1 April 1945, as the château was needed by the army for barracks.[17] The liberation of the pocket of Saint-Nazaire in May 1945 should have eased the problem, but ruined Saint-Nazaire looked like a moonscape and pressure for food and accommodation simply shifted to La Baule and other resorts. Homeless Nazairians living in La Baule marched on the subprefecture in August 1945 to demand better supplies of milk, potatoes, and meat and back rations of sugar and tobacco, which they had not been able to enjoy while the pocket was occupied.[18] Refugees on the coast had to compete with the army, industries like SNCASO and the Chantiers de Penhouët, which were starting up again and needed to house their workforces, and the owners of vacation villas who wanted to rent them out for the season.[19] Those still bearing the scars of the war were thus pitted against those who now wanted a return to pleasure and profit. The Saint-Nazaire evacuees based in Saint-Brévin-les-Pins, a resort on the other side of the Loire estuary from the port, responded to these pressures by forming an association of 800 that met in a local cinema to defend their interests. They were still there in the spring of 1946, representing 4,500 refugees and writing to their local deputy to protest "the offensive of landlords who are using all means to try to recover their properties in time for the summer season."[20]

While the homecoming of evacuees and bomb victims was slow and difficult, the return of POWs, STO workers, and deportees happened fairly quickly in the spring of 1945, as German territory was conquered and camps were thrown open. The joy felt as they were reunited with family and friends soon gave way, however, to anger and resentment when the reality of their condition struck home.[21] On 24 June 1945 a meeting of recently returned POWs at the Apollo Theater in Nantes became a demonstration of about a thousand people in front of the prefecture. Regretting that their first meeting had not been "the great emotional ceremony we had dreamed about in the camps," they now expressed their "bitterness and disappointment." Their demands included an increase in the compensation payable for every year spent in captivity to 3,000 francs, an increase in the pay for the single month's leave they were allowed on their return from 1,650 to 4,000 francs, and clothes and shoes to help them rejoin civilian life.[22] The association of POWs of Rézé turned down an invitation from the prefect of Loire-Inférieure to attend a "Grande Kermesse de Retour" in August 1945, with music, dancing, sports, and fireworks, on the grounds that "after five years of harsh captivity, which has not generally been understood by those who have not gone through it, the POWs have returned depressed, most of them without resources, to a France where the black market is the norm and they have had enormous problems recovering their housing, jobs, and income."[23] The predicament of POWs in Nantes was contrasted not only with the wealth of the black marketeers but with the ease of German POWs in Saint-Nazaire, described by the wife of a French POW as "reclining on deck chairs on their old boats, sunbathing or fishing."[24] Another comparison made by the POWs of Tours was with the new French army. A thousand of them marched on the prefecture on 4 August 1945 with placards saying, "We want clothes" and "We want shoes," having met at the Chamber of Commerce to denounce the beautiful new uniforms of the French army and reminding the government that they, too, had been proud soldiers once.[25]

Had all those who had somehow been displaced stuck together they may have been able to defend their interests more effectively. The provisional government saw things that way and at the end of 1943 set up a Commissariat (later Ministry) for Prisoners, Deportees, and Refugees to manage the repatriation of prisoners of war, STO workers, deportees, French evacuees from combat zones, and foreign nationals. It organized a week to remember and collect funds for all those absent for Christmas between 23 December 1944 and 1 January 1945 and proposed that 14 July 1945 be dedicated to all the dead of the war and Resistance, celebrating "the equality of prisoners, deportees, and resistants." The message, as passed on by the prefect of Maine-et-Loire, was to exalt "the sense of union that exists between those who fell in the fighting and those who came back."[26]

Unfortunately, the rapprochement between the different groups did not last long. To begin with, quarrels soon broke out over the benefits allotted to each category. Returning STO workers in Touraine were incensed to receive double rations for only three months, whereas POWs and political deportees received them for six months. The political deportees of Maine-et-Loire protested that POWs were getting an additional coal ration, while they were not. "What happened to the fine promises made when we returned?" asked their spokesman. "Everything was promised to these miserable survivors of the Nazi hell, but until now they have received nothing."[27]

Competition for material benefits, important though they were, was one way of expressing a much more powerful competition for honor. Honor was accorded after the Liberation to those who were deemed to have contributed most to that liberation through participation in the Resistance.

Those with greater Resistance credentials tried to separate themselves from those whose claims were less obvious or less secure, creating a hierarchy with heroes at the top, villains at the bottom, and all sorts of gradations in between. Disappointment was therefore felt by those who, though they had suffered for France and behaved like "good Frenchmen," were told that their contribution had not been enough.

At the top of the pyramid were the political deportees. In the municipal elections of April–May 1945 political deportees like Dr. Leccia of Bléré won, even if they had not yet touched French soil or even if, like Dr. Labussière of Chinon, they were—unbeknownst to the electorate—already dead. Welcoming Dr. Leccia and others, Jean Meunier, stalwart of Libération-Nord, president of the CDL of Indre-et-Loire, and mayor of Tours, called them "among the most heroic of our absentees." He organized a meeting in the municipal theater at which Dr. Leccia talked about Dachau, General Chasles about Buchenwald, and Mme Fournier about Auschwitz, an event that was said to have "made a vivid impression on the Tours public."[28]

Heroes and heroines they may have been, but they were keen to keep their kudos to themselves. Early in 1944 a National Movement of Prisoners of War and Deportees (MNPGD) was set up to bring together POWs, STO workers, and political deportees sent to concentration camps, using the motto "They are united, do not divide them!"[29] Political deportees were organized into a National Federation of Patriotic Deportees and Internees, which was affiliated with the MNPGD, but those who had been deported for "acts of resistance" wanted to distinguish·themselves from those who had been deported simply for being communists and set up a separate National Federation of Deportees and Internees *of the Resistance* (FNDIR) to "defend the ideal and the spirit of the Resistance." This, it has to be admitted, was also basically a noncommunist and even anticommunist organization that demonstrated a deep rift that ran through the heart of the Resistance.[30]

The political deportees, communist or noncommunist, could nevertheless agree on one thing, that they were superior to those who had been conscripted for work in Germany under the Relève or the STO. The latter set up organizations of labor deportees and founded reviews with titles like *Forced Labor*, but the political deportees fought hard to deny them the right to call themselves deportees. Because some workers had gone to work voluntarily, a question mark always hung over Relève or STO workers, who were judged to have had a choice as to whether to go. The Vichy labor inspector of Indre-et-Loire, Dos, summoned before the purging commission of the CDL, argued that workers were "perfectly free to go or not" under the Relève and that the relatively high ration of STO departures in the department was explained by "the apathy of Tourangeaux." This may have been true or it may have been to rebut charges that he had conscripted labor under German authority. At any rate, the CDL seemed to appreciate his argument, and Dos got away with simply being tranferred to another department.[31] Volunteer workers, of course, were considered to be collaborators and ran the risk of being interned or lynched on their return. But the ability of Relève and STO conscripts to resist was constantly emphasized by political deportees, who repeatedly frustrated the campaign of the former to be recognized as "labor deportees."

Prisoners of war returning after an absence of nearly five years, far from being acclaimed as heroes, were virtually ignored. They had enjoyed almost a cult status under the Vichy government, which had acclaimed them as pure patriots who had paid a heavy price for the military and psychological unpreparedness of the Third Republic and for whom the civilian population must now make sacrifices. Once Vichy had gone, however, their fortunes changed. "It seems that people want to forget us, to obliterate us," complained a spokesman for a group of POWs in Tours in September 1944, pointing out that they had not been invited to the great celebrations of the Liberation. One reason, he surmised, was that many of those who had returned during the Occupation had been dragooned into the Pétainist cause and identified with Vichy.[32] Another reason, however, was that the POWs were the incarnation of the worst defeat in French history, shamed by comparison with their fathers, who had won the Great War, and a constant reminder of national inferiority.

At the bottom of the hierarchy, in 1945 at least, were the Jews. Administratively they were almost invisible, known at best as "racial deportees." The vast majority, of course, did not return from the camps. Émile Aron, who had been dismissed under the Statut des Juifs and had fled to the Free Zone early in 1942 to escape being arrested as a hostage, returned to Tours and managed to recover both his job and, after a court case, his family property of La Chauvinière, near Château-Renault.[33] As a notable in Tours society, he wielded a certain influence and could make the new law nullifying "acts of despoilment undertaken by the enemy or under his control" work for him. Others were less fortunate. Three Jews who had entrusted their furnished property to the Tours firm of Coutancin-Chatry were told that it had been sold because the firm did not expect them to come back.[34] Businesses that had been liquidated, moreover, were almost impossible to recover. The agenda of surviving Jews was rebuilding their lives as individuals and families rather than promoting the cause of the Jewish people, which did not happen for another thirty years. Anti-Semitism had not evaporated just because of the suffering of the Jews. Only a month before the liberation of Nantes, in July 1944, *Le Phare* was holding forth about "the invasion of the Yids" and concluding that "there is no place on our soil for the wandering Jew."[35]

Disappointment was felt not only by those who had been displaced and who returned to a home that did not regard them as heroes but also by communities that had doggedly lived out the Occupation and hoped for something better after the Germans had gone. The most fundamental issue was bread. Now that the Germans were no longer there to requisition foodstuffs for their own needs it was felt that there should be more than enough for the French. The Vichy system of strict price controls, requisitioning on behalf of both Germans and the urban population and distribution agencies, would cease. The free market would be restored, supplied automatically to the satisfaction of both producers and consumers, and the black market would simply wither away.

Unfortunately, all this remained a pipe dream. Within weeks of the Liberation a petition was addressed to the prefect of Maine-et-Loire by 873 blue- and white-collar workers from the iron mines, tannery, sawmill, and railway works of Segré asking why prices were still rising. Bread had gone up from 3.8 francs to 4 francs a kilo, they said; butchers were buying animals for 16 francs a kilo and selling the meat for 70 to 80 francs a kilo, and they were selling pork for 90 to 100 francs a kilo. "Is it necessary for the recovery of our country," they inquired, "that traders in general continue to accumulate fortunes?"[36] They demanded strict price controls, but strict price controls and delivery quotas made producers reluctant to supply the market. The peasantry had become used to being embattled in

a closed economy, hiding their wares from prying Germans or Ravitaillement officials and selling it on their own terms to the highest bidder. At
the end of August the new prefect in Maine-et-Loire issued an "appeal to
the peasants," pointing out that quotas were now imposed for the benefit
of French people only and calling for "patriotism" and "solidarity" with
urban consumers. Milk was in particularly short supply and urgently
required for "children, women, and old people."[37] The following month,
as the Vichy administration had done in 1942, he wrote to the bishop of
Angers, Monsignor Costes, asking him to support the campaign in his
next pastoral letter.[38] By October, when milk deliveries had still not
improved, the subprefect of Cholet switched from blandishments to
threats, using the language of French revolutionaries. "The names of the
guilty parties have already been noted," he told the mayors of the Mauges,
who as usual were particularly recalcitrant. "Those who starve the towns
(*les affameurs des villes*) will be treated like collaborators and interned with
them. Heavy fines will be imposed on bad Frenchmen who oppose a just
distribution of the country's resources."[39]

Politics, religion, and class may all have set some landowners and peasants against the new regime, but the main reason for their lack of cooperation was the beckoning of the black market, with trucks coming from
as far away as Paris to scour the countryside for supplies. As Christmas
approached, traffickers came to Touraine to buy geese, turkeys, and other
poultry at inflated prices that only the rich could pay. *La Nouvelle République* argued that a gulf was opening between workers and small employees,
who could afford very little, and "the privileged," who were now, in easier
times, openly flaunting their wealth. The problem was one of distribution
as well as of price. Very few vehicles were available for the official collection
and delivery of quotas but, observed a Tours police chief who thought the
food situation worse than it had ever been since 1940, "the trucks of the
black market pound up and down, never stopped and never checked, even
though most bridges are still down and all the traffic has to cross the few
that remain." Just to make sure, the big restaurants in Paris were using
army trucks, which the gendarmerie would not dare look into.[40]

Unless officials were simply incompetent, it is a fair assumption that
corruption was still rife. The Ravitaillement administration set up by Vichy
was carried over at the Liberation and had the dual reputation of harshness

and corruptibility. The common assumption was that small fry were dealt with mercilessly, but the bigger the crook, the easier it was for him to corrupt the administration. Intendant Rouleau, the head of Vichy's Ravitaillement administration in the region, who had a reputation for militaristic brutality, was brought before the *cour de justice* in Angers, but his patriotic conduct was vouched for by his colleagues and by former regional prefect Donati, and he was acquitted in June 1945.[41] M. Le Bonhomme, head of Ravitaillement in Indre-et-Loire, was said to be protecting a number of large black-market operators.[42] Opinion in Touraine was reassured when he was suspended in December 1944 and left his job the following January but aghast when, in February, he was brought back to run another branch of the Ravitaillement. His reputation was a factor in the troubles that broke out in Tours at the end of the year, which we shall look at shortly.

Among the instruments available to the administration to clamp down on those who had made corrupt fortunes during the Occupation and since were the aptly named Committees to Confiscate Illicit Profits set up in each department under a law of 18 October 1944. These might have done excellent work recouping some of the fortunes made on the black market, but at the highest level it seems that the Ministry of Finance did not want them to be too tough. CDLs were allowed to nominate three individuals per department, but the committees were not permitted to recruit anyone from commercial and industrial milieux, including lawyers. They were dominated by tax officials who, in the opinion of the CDL of Maine-et-Loire, did not have "the necessary repressive mentality to carry out effectively the task entrusted to them."[43] In addition, they lacked teeth, having no authority to intern suspects to prevent them from concealing their gains and no way to access bank accounts bursting with German payments. When Debré wrote to the Finance Ministry about these shortcomings, he was told sharply that no one else had complained.[44] As a result, while two millers, a grain merchant, three wine merchants, a butcher, a builder, a garagist, a painter and decorator, a shoemaker, a hotelier, a stall holder, and a rag-and-bone man went before the Indre-et-Loire committee between March and October 1945, these were relatively small-time crooks. A Vouvray producer had 334,000 francs confiscated, and someone named

Szabo had 9 million francs confiscated and a fine of 27 million francs imposed for "important black-market activities," but his was the only case in that league.[45]

If those who wanted to purge corruption at the Liberation were disappointed, so also were those who wanted to break up the autarky of the farmers by abolishing Vichy's Peasant Corporation and setting up something to make agriculture more responsive to the needs of the towns. The Peasant Corporation was duly abolished, and the new minister of agriculture who took over in September 1944, Pierre Tanguy-Prigent, was a Breton socialist who wanted to replace it with another single union, the General Confederation of Agriculture (GCA), in which working farmers rather than rentier landowners were represented. Collaborators and Pétainists were to be excluded as far as possible, and responsibility was to be given to those who had stayed clear of partisan conflicts and had proved their professional competence.[46] In each department a Departmental Committee of Agricultural Action (CDAA) was set up to prepare the new organization, but what was striking was the continuity of personnel. In Loire-Inférieure, Raymond Lefeuvre, former president of the Peasant Corporation in the department and a member of its national council, was arrested in February 1945 but then released, the administration admitting an "error."[47] The weight in the CDAA shifted from landowners to working farmers, but Olivier de Sesmaisons was still there as secretary and only three of the nineteen members, from the CDL or the Front National, had any Resistance credentials.[48] The CDAA of Maine-et-Loire decided by eight votes to two, on the proposition of a token agricultural laborer on the committee, to ban Henri Dèze, Vichy's regional syndic, who had belonged to Henri Dorgères's Parti Agraire and was suspected of collaboration, from any responsible post in agriculture for five years.[49] Eugène Forget, however, who regarded Dèze as innocent of all collaboration and who himself survived a 3–7 vote on whether he should be banned, was singled out by Tanguy-Prigent as the obvious leader of what the CGA became in March 1946, at its Paris congress—namely, the National Federation of Farmers Unions (FNSEA). Forget insisted that all parties, including the communists, be represented on its governing bureau and demanded that all representatives to the congress take an Oath of Unity, on the lines of the Tennis Court

Oath taken by the deputies to the Estates-General in 1789, to the effect that they would not adjourn until they had passed a new constitution.[50]

Agricultural leaders with a distinctly Pétainist background were thus able to put the unity demanded by Tanguy-Prigent to their own use and renew their grip on power. All this gave no advantage to the urban working and lower-middle classes, who went just as hungry as before. Indeed, it is possible to argue that during the winter of 1945–46 they were hungrier than they had been during the Occupation. Certainly they were determined to vent their anger as never before, not only through trade unions and consumer organizations but in popular violence reminiscent of the French Revolution.

Faced with the rising cost of living, referred to now, as in revolutionary times, as *la vie chère*, the labor force launched a succession of strikes to demand higher wages, protest unreasonable productivity increases, and insist on measures against the black market, the confiscation of war profits, and the nationalization of trusts—much as promised in the program of the CNR. Strikes took place not only in the industrial heartland of Nantes, where 10,000 engineering workers marched on the prefecture on 29 January 1945 to deliver their demands, but in the much less industrialized and militant Anjou. In Trélazé, the industrial suburb of Angers, the slate cutters went on strike on 17 October 1944, and 330 female match makers who refused to work more than one machine were locked out.[51] When 6,000 Trélazé workers headed the May Day procession in Angers in 1945, shouting "Death to Pétain!," "Death to Hitler!," "Death to the trusts!," the prefect realized that the CGT had parted company with the government.[52] By the end of the year civil servants were striking in Maine-et-Loire with the support of the CGT and the Catholic CFTC, and teachers went on strike in Loire-Inférieure.

Alongside the traditional labor movement, specially dedicated consumer organizations were now springing up. Consumer defense committees were set up in Tours in February 1945 and 7,000 people demonstrated peacefully on 7 April, presenting their demands to the prefecture.[53] The police were not sanguine about the peacefulness persisting, however, especially with the price of bread going up. In October 1945 the government abolished bread rationing to promote optimism in time for the elections to the Constituent Assembly. Its action was a reckless gamble that depended on supply's being adequate to meet demand. Unfortunately, it was not and in December, after the elections, bread rationing was reimposed and the daily ration cut from 350 to 300 grams.[54] This was like a spark to a gunpowder barrel. In Tours, the CGT and the Federation of Consumers called a demonstration for 29 December. Prefect Vivier met the organizers at 3:00 P.M. in an attempt to defuse the situation, but even they realized that they were losing their grip on the situation. Some wanted to burn the reissued ration cards in public. Vivier had a poor opinion of the federation's leader, Martin, whom he regarded as putty in the hands of a communist named Marchais and of people like the woman who grabbed hold of a loudspeaker and shouted, *"Tous à la préfecture!"* The prefect described what happened next in terms worthy of Zola or Taine:

> The demonstration, which was disorganized, became a howling mob. It was made up of disorderly elements, the scum of Tours . . . women, fishwives, youths foreign to the town and even to the region. The organizers were swept aside by determined agitators, prostitutes, young people seen in previous demonstrations, . . . former collaborators wanting to exploit popular discontent for political ends . . . a few Trotskyists, even anarchists. . . . The pillage and vandalism were the result of a fermentation in consumers' milieux such as the housewives' committees of *quartiers* like the *quartier* Beaujardin, which think that the Consumers Federation itself is not militant enough.

Police, gendarmes, and the recently formed CRS were in short supply because of the holiday period. The crowd of 6,000 protesters invaded the prefecture, pillaging its archives and throwing files out the window. They then proceeded to the town hall and sacked the offices in search of ration cards. Finally they went to the Ravitaillement offices, where they found more ration cards and burned them. Vivier was forced to bring in the army to guard grain and flour supplies and to issue a whole new edition of ration cards.[55]

The account of Vivier, normally a moderate and discreet man, is a reflection of how powerless he felt. He fell back on a conventional discourse to describe the mob in terms of outsiders, extremists, the rising flotsam and jetsam of the suburbs, and above all the bloodthirsty and immoral women, the heirs of the *tricotteuses* around the guillotine and the *pétroleuses* of the Paris Commune. The demonstration was frightening because it escaped the organizational channels of the trade unions and the Consumers Federation. Whatever Vivier said about Martin, however, the Communist Party in fact disowned the violence and urged the public to be calm. Other evidence shows that the agitators, far from being scum, included a lieutenant in the air force and a number of soldiers; those arrested were all from Tours and included an apprentice baker aged sixteen, a pharmacy assistant aged nineteen, a young married woman (twenty-two), a thirty-nine-year-old laborer at the railway workshops, the manager of La Paix café, and his forty-nine-year-old waitress.[56] The importance of Vivier's outburst lies in his subjective perception that the Liberation had failed to meet popular expectations, so that the dancing in the streets that had welcomed the retreat of the Germans sixteen months earlier had become a witches' Sabbath, a *danse macabre*, a world turned upside down and destroying any confidence that had been built between government and people.

The Liberation has frequently been characterized as a moment of deliverance and hope, as a time of reform and renewal, but for many ordinary French people hopes were all too soon and too often disappointed.[57] France did not suddenly become a land of freedom and plenty after the Germans left. War continued, and many restrictions that had been imposed by Vichy were simply continued, as those who wished to dance, for example, discovered. Populations displaced by bombing raids and the Allied invasion were confronted by communities that had little more to give, materially or morally. Returning POWs, labor conscripts, and deportees were welcomed with open arms but then found themselves competing for jobs, rations, benefits, and, not least, recognition of what they had suffered. Even basic foodstuffs remained in short supply, the corruption and black marketeering of occupied France continued after the Liberation, and bread riots in the winter of 1945–46 suggested a country familiar more to the revolutionary Jean-Paul Marat than to the architect of modernization Jean Monnet.

16

Memories

Paris! Paris violated! Paris broken! Paris martyrized! But Paris lib-
erated! Liberated by its own efforts, liberated by its people with the help
of the armies of France, with the help of the whole of France, of fighting
France, of the one and true France, of eternal France![1]

Thus at the Hôtel de Ville in Paris on 25 August 1944 was announced the
gospel of the Resistance according to Charles de Gaulle. As the general
had marched down the Champs-Élysées to cheering crowds, his appeal of
18 June 1940, in which he had called on the French people not to accept
defeat and armistice, was somehow made flesh. The fact that Parisian
crowds had turned out in force to cheer Marshal Pétain only a few months
before was studiously ignored; collaboration was brushed aside as the sin
of "a handful of wretches." The gospel declared that the Resistance had
been pure and heroic and the vast majority of French people had behaved
under the Occupation as "bons français." They had been inspired by the
eternal values of France, of patriotism and the rights of man, and it was

around these values that union could now be reforged. Above all it was declared that the French had liberated themselves by their own efforts. The shame of defeat and the guilt of having obeyed the orders of a foreign power were now redeemed by the act of self-liberation by which dignity and honor were recovered. De Gaulle made virtually no mention of the role played in the ongoing liberation of France by the British and Americans, apart from a mildly patronizing reference to the "help of our dear and admirable Allies." Liberation meant the recovery of freedom, national unity, and greatness under the leadership of Charles de Gaulle.

This gospel had a wonderful mythic power in the years after the Liberation. The French were only too pleased to accept their role as "bons français" and to present the smallest gestures as "acts of resistance" that had contributed to the ultimate liberation of the country. And yet the gospel according to de Gaulle never achieved the consensus for which it was designed. Other versions, putting forward different heroes and different villains, vied for an audience. Rival interpretations of what had happened under the Occupation divided the French from one another and split communities. De Gaulle preached the primacy in the Resistance of the Free French, who had been under his control in London and Algiers, over the internal Resistance—the *maquisards* and the FFIs. Communists insisted that they had been the most dynamic force in the Resistance, the Party counting 75,000 martyrs to the cause. Others argued that the Communists, by accepting the Nazi-Soviet Pact of 1939, had undermined the war effort in 1940 and subsequently made things worse in France by their strategy of violent resistance. These might be Gaullists, but they also might be Pétainists, who argued that de Gaulle had taken an easy option by escaping to London while Marshal Pétain, who had stayed in France to protect the French people, had embodied the real Resistance. Some local communities were desperate to promote their own heroes, however tenuous the connection, while ones that had suffered collective reprisals as a result of Resistance activity in the vicinity had only victims to commemorate. People who returned from deportation were also deeply divided. Those who had been deported for "acts of resistance" claimed to be more heroic than those who had been deported simply for political opinions, notably membership in the Communist Party. Both were meanwhile keen to reject the claims of labor conscripts to deportee status and to minimize the claim to special recognition of deported Jews. The fact that the persecution of the Jews and the French part in it took literally decades to come to light reflected the effectiveness with which groups speaking for the Resistance were able to impose their version of events. Once the Holocaust factor came into play, however, it swept all before it, forcing a full reconsideration of both Vichy and the Resistance.[2]

Attempts were made to fix interpretations of the Resistance by formal commemoration through the erection of monuments.[3] Commemorations were also bids to achieve orthodox status for cults that might otherwise be considered marginal, even heretical. I have traced the shaping of collective memories by the commemoration of heroes and martyrs in the Loire region, but I have also listened to individuals whose private memories may or may not have coincided with the public memory. To a large extent, as I suggest in the introduction, private accounts are shaped by dominant narratives, but they also diverge either fully or at crucial points, and these privileged moments may allow the historian to glimpse alternative interpretations that have hitherto been marginalized or suppressed.

The tension between de Gaulle's gospel and that of the internal Resistance was in part a tension between a national perspective and local views. It also, however, expressed a conflict for the leadership of the Resistance between de Gaulle's Free French, whose main aim was to prevent the establishment of an Allied military government in France, and the internal Resistance, which often had political goals of its own. De Gaulle, both in and out of power, was a frequent guest of honor at the unveiling of local monuments to the Resistance, but his gloss on events was not necessarily the same as that of local protagonists. In 1965, for example, as president of the Republic, he visited Saumur on the twenty-fifth anniversary of the valiant attempt of the cadets of the cavalry school between 19 and 21 June 1940 to hold up the German crossing of the Loire. He told a crowd of 10,000 that the heroic action of the school "prefigured . . . the Liberation and victory." This presentation of the fighting at Saumur as the first act of the drama of the Resistance was relatively recent. Not until the tenth anniversary, in 1955, was a link made explicitly between the "despairing heroism" of 19–21 June and "the date of 18 June [1940], sublime in more ways than one," as if the Saumur combats had been a direct response to de Gaulle's BBC appeal.[4] Under Vichy the bravery of the cadets had been likened to that of the forlorn heroes of 1870 or 1815. The subprefect of Saumur had compared the skirmish at the nearby farmhouse of Aunis to the fighting at the farm of La Haie Sainte on the battlefield of Waterloo 125 years earlier, "almost to the day."[5] The comparison to 1870 was also instructive, because although, as in 1940, the war had been lost, pockets of heroism in the fight against overwhelming odds had allowed French honor to be saved. The difference was that after 1870 patriots spoke of revenge against Germany whereas after 1940 the lesson drawn by Vichy was "revenge against ourselves," an internal moral revolution.[6]

De Gaulle had been appearing at local commemorations of the Resistance since his departure from office in 1946, but always to stress French unity in the Resistance under his leadership. In 1950, for example, accompanied by General Audibert, commander of the Armée Secrète in Brittany, and before a crowd of 50,000, he unveiled a huge monument in Saffré in honor of the *maquisards* who fell when they were attacked by German forces on 28 June 1944. General Audibert duly proclaimed that the *maquisards* had been replying to de Gaulle's appeal of 18 June and that though they had joined the battle at the end of the Occupation they had played as important a role in the French victory as those who fought from the beginning. In particular, he was keen to reject the idea that the thirteen Frenchmen who had died on the spot in Saffré and the twenty-seven who were shot later had made a "useless sacrifice." De Gaulle, for his part, insisted that "the action of the Saffré combatants must not be separated from that undertaken against the occupier outside France by the Free French. Everything was part of a whole and made up our national defense." He also underlined that the survivors of the battle who remembered their comrades must contribute to "national solidarity and the unity of our people."[7]

The nagging perception that the *maquisards* of Saffré had been victims rather than heroes was confronted again, on the twenty-fifth anniversary of the event, when General de Jussieu-Pontcarrel, national chief of staff of the FFIs, delighted his audience by citing Eisenhower's memoirs to the effect that the internal Resistance was worth five or six divisions to the Allies.[8] A glance at Eisenhower's memoirs, however, reveals that this reading was somewhat free. The only possible reference to such divisions is to the Sixth Army Group under the American general Devers, which drove up from the south of France. Eisenhower praised the Free French for their "inestimable value in the campaign" but in fact criticized the Maquis as "separate armed bands" that refused to be integrated into the regular army and were heavily subverted by communism.[9]

The group of survivors of the Maquis of Saffré whom I met in 1997 were certainly not subverted by communism. They exalted the fraternity of the Maquis and its ecumenical nature. "You didn't ask your mates to which religion or political party they belonged," said Pierre Hervé, president of the Comité du Souvenir. And yet, further conversation revealed that the ecumenism of the Maquis was relative: most members belonged to Catholic organizations of workers, peasants, and students and were informed by a discreet but well-founded anticommunism. "You didn't take anyone," clarified François Boudet, secretary of the Comité, "but a dozen guys you had known from school." The Maquis was reluctant to accept communists, he confessed, because they were already known to the authorities and might talk under torture. It was also evident that there was no necessary connection between joining the Maquis in June 1944 and the appeal of 18 June. François Boudet admitted to saying "*Ouf*" (Phew!) when Pétain requested an armistice. Far from being a rootless outlaw, he had been a local officer or syndic of Vichy's Peasant Corporation and on good terms with Lieutenant Laurens, the local German quartermaster; Laurens, he said, knew that he was in the Resistance but did not betray him. The official cult of the Maquis of Saffré emphasized efficacy, unity, and the response to de Gaulle, but private conversation, even with the *maquisards* themselves, paints a more complex picture.[10]

The tension between the Gaullist version and the local version was also evident twenty-five kilometers west of Saffré, in Bouvron. Every year the village celebrates the end of the Second World War in Europe—only it claims that the war in Europe actually ended right there in Bouvron with the surrender on 11 May 1945 of the German general commanding the pocket of Saint-Nazaire. The surrender was commemorated before a humble wooden cross of Lorraine until October 1949, when a magnificent stone monument was unveiled, proclaiming that the moment the Germans of the pocket surrendered "the whole of France was liberated." In his speech General Larminat, commander of the FFIs on the Atlantic, paid homage to "the agents of *réseaux*, saboteurs, *maquisards*, FFI soldiers, and regular soldiers who took over from our armies, which had been torn to pieces."[11]

An official seal of approval for the myth was given in 1951 when General de Gaulle himself attended the event. As in Saffré, however, he was quick to deflate the pretensions of the internal Resistance. While the mayor, Walsh de Serrant, repeated that the monument marked "the day of the total liberation of the whole French nation," de Gaulle replied that the surrender of the Germans of the pocket "had not only a local significance. Saint-Nazaire was only a historical episode in the war of liberation won at the cost of huge sacrifice. . . . What was done here, what was done during the last great war, is only a link in the chain on which the life and greatness of France depends."[12] This cool contextualization, however, was not permitted to undermine the local cult. In 1970, for the twenty-fifth anniversary, a new mayor of Bouvron, Hervy, misquoted de Gaulle in order to replace the surrender at the center of the stage. Neatly omitting one "only," he quoted the general as having said that the event "had not only local significance but was an episode in the history of France."[13]

Such local cults generally served to unite communities and link them to the grand narrative of the official Resistance. There were cases, however, in which discordant voices were heard, undermining the local cult and at the same time demonstrating its artificiality. This is scarcely surprising, because open resistance had not been at the forefront of most people's minds under the Occupation. Andrée Trudeau, whose father had a farm close to the château overlooking Saumur, remembered seeking shelter in the limestone caves in the hillside during the three-day German bombardment in 1940. Employed in the ration-card service of the Saumur town hall, she admitted sometimes slipping extra ration tickets into the hands of hungry-looking people, but she never became involved in the issuing of false identity cards to those who had been forced to go underground. Such activity was dangerous work, for which her section head was arrested, and it was men's work in the bargain. "It was only men who did that," she confessed. "Women didn't have the same [role] as today." Her sole patriotic gesture was of a symbolic nature, attending the funeral of British airmen whose plane had crashed near Saumur in February 1943. "There was a huge procession to the cemetery, which was covered with flowers," she recalled. "Oh, I shall always remember that, I was there along with everyone else." She never attended the commemoration of the battle of Saumur because she found the heroism fictitious. The events of 1940, she insisted, were "a complete debacle," as officers retreated and left the young cadets to their fate. "It is common knowledge," she asserted, "that they were massacred to no purpose." Her image of a real hero in the mold of local patriotism was the extraordinary nun of the Bon Pasteur who, built like a man and working with fallen women as she was, had an excellent grasp of bad language. She had access to the POWs who were housed for several months in the cavalry school, fetching and carrying laundry in a horse-drawn wagon, and used to smuggle them out with the dirty linen before sending them on their way to the demarcation line. Though Trudeau could no longer remember the woman's name, she said that the nun was "legendary. She is still talked about today."[14]

Michel Ancelin, son of the *procureur* of Saumur who in 1940 at great personal risk negotiated a peaceful outcome for the town, remained the spokesman for the burghers who resented the folly of a battle on their doorstep that would only lead to heavy civilian casualties.[15] Even more explicitly than Andrée Trudeau, he dismissed as "ridiculous" the patriotic celebrations organized each June by the military and local officials of the Souvenir Français. He handed me a report written by Dr. von Senger of the Twenty-fourth Panzer Division, which, he asserted, "completely destroys the beautiful legend" of the cadets because it says that when the Germans arrived in Aunis they found "some young men, unarmed and completely drunk," whom they didn't think were soldiers. In fact, the German report simply states that on 21 June a group of forty officers and 200 men of the cavalry school of Saumur were "taken totally by surprise and made prisoner in Chinon." Yet Michel Ancelin's irritation points to a fault line between those with a vested interest in the Resistance story and those attuned to other priorities in 1940, when the military was in full flight, leaving mayors and other notables to prevent the bombardment and massacre of their townspeople.[16]

Michel Ancelin's father, of course, later went on to join a Resistance network, as a result of which he was arrested and tortured. This brought up another issue for Ancelin, the discrepancy between the heroic status conferred on some Resistance leaders and the evidence of neglect, if not worse, which led to the deportation of their comrades. In November 1994 the grand old man of the Resistance in the Saumur area, Aristide Royer, died at the age of ninety-two. His obituary stated that, as commander of the Saumur gendarmerie, he had been responsible for clandestine military operations in Anjou and had 1,500 resistants under his command. "Aristide Royer . . . no longer counted his distinctions and medals. Commander of the Legion of Honor, he had notably been awarded the Military Cross with palm, the Resistance Medal with rosette, the Voluntary Resistance Combatant Cross, the Deportation Medal, and many others."[17] The story of a Resistance force of 1,500 went back at least to 1948, when Commandant Royer declared that in June–September 1943 his networks had twenty-two officers, thirteen NCOs, and 1,210 men. This was contradicted by one of his former colleagues, chief superintendent Éprinchard, who turned down an offer in 1949 to write the history of the Saumur Resistance, pointing out that "in 1941–43 the number of resistants could be counted on the fingers of two hands, while in 1945 the crowd of heroes was innumerable in Saumur, as elsewhere."[18] There had also been a major disaster during the night of 17–18 September 1943, when the Gestapo arrested eighteen individuals, including former *procureur* Ancelin, and on 8 October, when they arrested another twenty-five. Only ten of the forty-three, including Royer, returned alive from German concentration camps.

Questions began to be asked after the Liberation about how Royer's networks had been exposed. Another of his colleagues, René Marnot, said that Royer had been warned of his impending arrest three days earlier by a comrade in the Resistance, Daniel Durand, thanks to a tip from a German known to him, the translator at the Feldgendarmerie of Saumur, Corporal Hubert Sommer.[19] Royer did not go underground, nor did he warn any of the members in the networks for which he was responsible. This allegation was substantiated in 1998 by Michael Nerlich, a professor of Romance literature at the Technical University of Berlin, who published Sommer's 1942 Marburg thesis on French literature and uncovered the records of the Gestapo interrogations of Royer and Durand in Angers on 21 September 1943. Nerlich established that Sommer, who had taught as an assistant at the lycée of Roanne in 1937–38, knew Durand through a German family who had cared for Durand's son when Durand was working in Germany and that Sommer had dined with him three times before returning on 15 September to warn him of Royer's impending arrest. Durand sent these warnings to Royer, who nevertheless decided to say nothing and remained at his post. As a result, concluded Nerlich, Royer's network remained ignorant of the threat and was decimated. Meanwhile Sommer, whom Durand sought to protect under interrogation, was allegedly betrayed by Royer and arrested by the Gestapo on 29 September. He was sentenced to five years in prison and then, a year later, was enrolled in a disciplinary battalion on the French front, where he was killed.[20]

This well-documented catastrophe is a good example of how the Resistance story has often been elaborated in defiance of tricky contradictions. It shows how the size of networks ballooned after the Liberation, when to have resisted was what one needed to have done. It illustrates how idols of the Resistance like Royer, who were feted as local heroes for fifty years, may in fact have concealed secrets about how their comrades were arrested and deported. Michel Ancelin, who saw his father tortured at the Feldgendarmerie of Saumur, went so far as to suggest that "Royer was in cahoots with the Gestapo and an infamous traitor."[21] It demonstrates, finally, that relations between French and Germans were sometimes more complicated than a crude division between oppressors and oppressed. The relationship of Hubert Sommer and Daniel Durand, based on a common appreciation of French culture and services rendered, led to Sommer's risking his life for his French friends and eventually to his own death. These subtleties are very difficult, however, to integrate into the Resistance story. So when, in 1994, Nerlich wrote to the mayor of Saumur to propose that Sommer's name be added to the town's monument to the Resistance, he received no answer. "Do people not want to know what happened in Saumur in 1943?" he asked. "Or don't they want a German in the French Resistance?"[22]

Saumur, it seems, has been able to rebuff criticisms both of its heroism in 1940 and of its later contribution to the Resistance. The memories of other towns have been much more painful and divisive. Nantes, it is true, had a wonderful local hero in Christian de Mondragon, who, on Armistice Day 1940, at the age of sixteen, climbed the cathedral tower under cover of darkness to attach a tricolor to the lightning rod as Germans patrolled the streets below. He said that news of the exploit spread "like a powder trail," not only through the city, as crowds gathered to marvel, but throughout Brittany. This purely symbolic gesture provoked no reprisals and simply confirmed the Gallic *esprit frondeur*. De Mondragon's identity was unknown until the Liberation but thereafter, he said with pride, his exploit became the toast of Nantes. "There is not a book that comes out on the Occupation that does not mention it," he asserted. To prove his point he showed me a collection beginning with Perraud-Charmantier's *War in Brittany* (1947) and concluding with Jocelyn Gille's cartoon strip, *Nantes in Upheaval* (1993).[23]

Unfortunately, the Nantais are much more divided about how to commemorate the events that occurred less than a year later: the shooting of the Feldkommandant of Nantes by a communist commando on 20 October 1941 and the execution by the Germans of nearly fifty hostages in Nantes, Châteaubriant, and Paris two days later. Immediately after the Liberation a struggle broke out between the Communist Party, which wanted to use the communist hostages shot at Châteaubriant to develop its myth of the "75,000 *fusillés*," and the families of those (mainly war veterans and Catholics) executed in Nantes, who were opposed to any communist appropriation of the tragedy. The Pétainist bishop of Nantes portrayed the Nantes victims as Catholic martyrs, promised to light a candle every year if a second batch of hostages destined for the firing squad was spared, and at a ceremony on 22 October 1945 declared that "the Church would not forget them, any more than a mother could forget her children."[24] That same afternoon, communists swamped the commemoration at Châteaubriant, brandishing banners demanding "Avenge our dead" and power for the party secretary, Maurice Thorez, and singing the "Internationale," to the annoyance of the French officials and American officers present. The seventy-six-year-old Marcel Cachin called the French Communist Party *"le parti des fusillés"* and warned, "Much ill has been said of the communists but in future it will be prohibited to say that communists are not loyal to France. . . . Many died for her, and their tragic fate will be mourned, but their death showed France the way."[25] Nine months later, when the bodies of the twenty-one Nantes hostages were ceremonially reburied, veterans groups organized a riposte to the communist claims. They argued that Jost, Fourny, and the others who were shot at Nantes were veterans of 1914–18 who had been imprisoned for engineering the escape of 50,000 POWs in the region. Their colleague, Maître Ridel, who had escaped execution, declared of the veterans, "Resistants you were; when everyone else was keeping their heads down, you were the precursors of the Liberation."[26]

As the communists tightened their grip on the Châteaubriant ceremony, the gulf between them and the Nantes families deepened. In 1946
Thorez himself addressed the gathering, exalting the patriotism of the
communists and denouncing the pro-Munich Daladier government, which
had thrown communists into jail; the Vichy minister Pierre Pucheu (executed at the insistence of the communists in 1944), who had tried to
"decapitate the labor movement" through mass executions; and even de
Gaulle, who had tried to stop communist attacks on German personnel.[27]
For the ceremony in October 1950 the communists unveiled a heroic statue
of five nude figures with proud heads and muscular torsos, embracing one
another in front of a stake and singing—most probably the "Marseillaise"
or the "Internationale."[28] For its part, the city of Nantes launched a fund
for its own quota of martyrs in October 1944 but complained a few months
later that, although "there are plenty of traders, market gardeners, managers
of restaurants getting 500 francs a meal, and people from the wealthy
classes who could easily donate a thousand-franc note," little money had
been forthcoming.[29] It was not until 22 October 1952 that the city's memorial was unveiled, and the mayor, Henri Orrion, who had also been the
Vichy mayor in 1942–44, endeavored to associate the town as a whole with
the suffering. He spoke of those, including Mayor Rondeau, who had
offered themselves to avert a second batch of executions, of the courage of
the chaplains who had visited the condemned men, and of the dignity of
the population, and he declared that the hostages themselves belonged
"neither to a class nor to a clan." This infuriated the communist press,
which attacked him as a Pétainist, boycotted the official ceremony, and
held an alternative, popular vigil on the evening of 22 October, after the
factories closed.[30]

Controversy extended not only to the victims but also to the killer.
There were those who defended the communist militant who arrived from
Paris, pulled a gun on the local German military commander, and was
credited with launching the Resistance in the west of France, while others
had nothing but contempt for the outsider who had come unbidden into
their midst to inflict suffering and grief. The identity of the killer was soon
known to the Germans but it was not until 1950 that Gilbert Brustlein, a
communist who had since broken with the Party, announced that he had
shot Colonel Hotz.[31] There were plenty of Nantais for whom Hotz was

not the villain but a good and fair administrator whose death had been a catastrophe for the city. Edmond Duméril, who had served as interpreter at the prefecture during the Occupation, had been to the same German university as Hotz, and admired his anti-Hitlerian humanity, argued in 1959 that Hotz had been killed not by communists but by the Gestapo, because he was too Francophile.[32] This view was supported at the time of the fiftieth anniversary of the shooting in 1991 by a local historian, Étienne Gasche, who argued that although Brustlein had pulled the trigger he had in fact been arrested, gone over to the Germans, and been allowed to escape by the Gestapo.[33] Brustlein subsequently brought a libel case against Gasche and won. Meanwhile Louis Oury, a metallurgical worker turned novelist and historian, invited Brustlein himself to return to Nantes for the fiftieth anniversary. Brustlein found it difficult to convince onlookers at the spot where he had pulled the trigger that he had committed not a murder but an "act of war" and had "unleashed armed resistance in the west of France."[34] Michel Jost, son of the most illustrious hostage to be shot and president of the association of hostages' families, declared at the monument to the fifty hostages on 22 October 1991: "Gilbert Brustlein is using the blood of the dead for publicity. This anniversary has been organized not in memory of the attack on Hotz but in honor of the forty-eight dead of Nantes, Châteaubriant, and Paris."[35] The visitors' book of the exhibition marking the affair of the fifty hostages showed twenty-one entries critical of Brustlein and only three in favor. He was accused of shooting the German in the back, of failing to turn himself in in order to spare the lives of the hostages, and then of daring shamelessly to return to the scene of the crime.[36]

Controversy in Nantes then centered on whether a plaque commemorating the killing of Colonel Hotz should be unveiled in the rue du Roi-Albert, where he was shot, and how the inscription should read. The campaign for the plaque was undertaken almost solely by Louis Oury and was opposed initially not only by the families of the hostages under Michel Jost but also by the Resistance organizations headed by André Chauvel of the Nantes branch of the Fédération Nationale des Déportés et Internés de la Résistance. Oury proposed a text that honored the execution by Brustlein and his comrades, Spartaco Guisco and Marcel Bourdarias of "the Feldkommandant of the occupying forces," under orders from the communist "Organization Spéciale," as "the first offensive action in the Occupied Zone," undertaken to "launch the armed struggle in the west of France." The Resistance organizations and the families of the hostages demanded a text that baldly stated that "the Feldkommandant of Nantes was shot [*abattu*] by resisters" and then went on to list the number and place of execution of the victims shot in reprisal. For Oury this was "a scandalous text worthy of Vichy," which would simply have used the word *terrorist* instead of *resister*, and he managed to have the word *execution* to refer to the death of the Feldkommandant reinstated.[37]

A provisional version of the plaque was unveiled in the rue du Roi-Albert, in the presence of the minister of war veterans and the deputy mayor of Nantes, on the sixtieth anniversary of the events, 22 October 2001. This version aligned the "execution of the Feldkommandant by a Resistance commando of Communist youth" with the execution of the forty-eight hostages in Nantes, Châteaubriant, and Paris "by the occupying German authorities on the orders of Hitler and with the collaboration of the Vichy authorities." The ceremony was attended by Gilbert Brustlein, this time brought in an official car from Paris, but while the names of Spartaco and Bourdarias were mentioned on the plaque, his own name was not. The reason given was that "republican tradition" ruled that only the names of the dead could be publicly commemorated in this way, even though Louis Oury pointed out that a lycée and a college bore the name of the living resister Lucie Aubrac. This disappointment was redeemed, however, by the poignant act of reconciliation as Michel Jost agreed to shake Gilbert Brustlein's hand in public, saying that Brustlein had only been obeying orders and had no idea of the consequences of his actions. Consensus was still not complete. Many hostages' families and the noncommunist Resistance organizations around André Chauvel were still horrified by the presence of Brustlein and a plaque commemorating the execution of the Feldkommandant, and twelve of the fifteen local Resistance organizations boycotted the commemoration. "The wound remains deep in Nantes," reported *L'Ouest-France*, "among the families of hostages who held the commandos responsible for the death of their loved ones." Moreover, the Resistance was never a bloc, and its internal rivalries were never clearer than when an act of resistance was celebrated.[38]

The enduring conflict in Nantes over the fifty hostages is a powerful expression of a hostility to communist claims to have played a leading role in the Resistance that has been voiced not only by Gaullists but by Pétainists. Sometimes the distinction between Gaullists and Pétainists was not all that plain because Pétainists, too, claimed to have been "bons français" in the front line of the Resistance. Marquis Olivier and Marquise Yolande de Sesmaisons were members of the conservative establishment in Loire-Inférieure who were also master and mistress of the *double jeu* under the Occupation. Olivier, who was not a parliamentarian and had not voted to give full powers to Marshal Pétain in July 1940, nevertheless used his place on the CDL to defend the very Pétainist Marquis de La Ferronnays and was elected a conservative deputy of the Constituent Assembly. Yolande was a society lady who made the best use of her contacts with the Germans and was awarded the Légion d'Honneur.[39] Their sons, Marquis Donatien and General Yves de Sesmaisons, whom I met in 1997, argued that the defeat and Occupation were explained entirely by the Nazi-Soviet Pact. After that, they said, communists sabotaged the armaments industry and Thorez deserted the army, leaving conservatives to fly the patriotic flag. The politicians Daladier and Reynaud "led us into the shit," they said, and when Pétain sued for an armistice, "80 percent of French people said, '*Ouf,* at last an honest fellow.'" They agreed that "the Vichy motto Work, Family, Fatherland impressed the traditional right," but they claimed that enthusiasm for Pétain did not exclude hostility to the Germans. Indeed, they said, the French long believed in a "tacit agreement between Pétain and de Gaulle." The military nobility, including their older brother Jean, an officer in the armistice army and then, after its dissolution, in the Armée Secrète, were among the first resistants. To reinforce this point after the interview, General de Sesmaisons wrote to me to say, "It is thus false to argue, as the 'politically correct' version would now have it, that the right were all collabos and only the communists were resistants. . . . French people could be in favor of Vichy while at the same time hating the Germans."[40]

Similar anticommunist views were expressed by Vicomte Gilles de la Grandière, the son of Senator Palamède de la Grandière, who was invited to join the CDL of Maine-et-Loire in August 1944 but was no less a Pétainist for that. The senator, Gilles was clear, was an admirer of Pétain because he had been at Verdun and was president of the Union des Anciens Combattants in Anjou. He said that his father was very close to the Marquis de La Ferronnays but "was not involved in politics" under Vichy and (unlike his cousin Jacques) refused to become a member of Vichy's Conseil National. Gilles—presumably echoing his father—called de Gaulle a "deserter" who "might have unified the French" but fell under the influence of the communists. He denounced the "string of murders committed by the so-called Resistance" and pointed out that his father joined the CDL to "counterbalance the left." His wife, the vicomtesse, asserted that "it was not only the left that was involved in the Resistance" and explained that resistance was in the "military tradition" of the French nobility. They lent me a *Memorial of the French Nobility in the Fighting against the Invader, 1939–45*, which cited two members of the de la Grandière family as resistants and calculated that, though nobles formed only 0.2 percent of the population, they accounted for 4.4 percent of Compagnons de la Libération. The resistance of the young Gilles consisted in squirting German sentries with his water pistol from the battlements of the château. Unfortunately, he says, the Resistance movement in Maine-et-Loire was taken over by anti-Catholic and anti-aristocratic elements who discovered pro-German articles his father had written for an Angers paper during the Occupation and forced him off the CDL, after which he went back to his traditional Catholic and conservative politics.[41]

Two more apologists for the Resistance credentials of Marshal Pétain were Paule de Beaumont, the daughter of Vichy's second regional prefect in the Loire region, Charles Donati, and her husband, Louis. Madame de Beaumont put her cards on the table straight away, attacking the "present climate of historical disinformation that passes off Pétain as a criminal against humanity" and expressing concern that this would be reinforced by the forthcoming trial of former Vichy official Maurice Papon. Pétain, she said, was close to her father and "opened his heart to him." In return, Donati "entirely espoused the theory of Pétain that you had to stay in France to protect the French population," the only alternative being a German gauleiter. On the other hand, she insisted, he did not get on with the head of government, Laval, whose enthusiasm for collaboration was difficult to disguise and with whom "no discussion was possible." She described her father as a "man of duty" and absolute rectitude who fought every moment against German demands. On one occasion, in a meeting with a Feldkommandant who was making unreasonable demands, she remembered, he banged loudly on the table with his fist and demanded, "Is *that* what you call collaboration?" and obliged the German to give ground. He took great risks, she insisted, and was "on the list for the next deportations," following the deportation of the former prefect of Loire-Inférieure, Bonnefoy. As a veteran who had lost his left arm in the 1914–18 war, Donati enjoyed a certain prestige with the Germans, which he exploited, but he "never gave even the smallest reception" for them, neither did he invite them to dine.

For Paule and Louis de Beaumont, Donati was a Pétainist but also a genuine resistant. Louis, who made religious broadcasts and discovered that at their château 300 counterrevolutionaries were massacred by republican troops in 1795, argued that there were two Resistances, the first staffed by former army officers and engaged in military operations, the second "monstrous," full of "hooligans" [*voyous*] who "took to the Maquis to pillage and steal." Paule de Beaumont continued the analysis, saying that her father hated communists because they sabotaged the armaments factories during the war, were "practically deserters" in 1940, and had a policy of "better a civil war than a war against Germany." Fortunately, there was an orderly transfer of power between high civil servants at the Liberation, notably between her father and the new *commissaire de la République*, Michel Debré, who shook hands at the prefecture of Angers on 10 August 1944. She regretted only that de Gaulle did not hold out his hand to Pétain in the same way. Later she sent me an extract of her father's statement at the trial of Pétain, before the marshal was bundled from the courtroom, to the effect that "millions and millions of French people think that this trial is an immense political mistake."[42]

What emerges from such interviews is that there is still in some French circles a coherent and passionately held Pétainist position. According to this view, Marshal Pétain was the legitimate ruler of France, acclaimed by the National Assembly and a martyr to the protection of his people. De Gaulle is seen as a deserter who had, in any case, fallen prey to the communists. The communists proved by the Nazi-Soviet Pact of 1939 that they had no sense of patriotism, undermined the war effort in 1940, and used the Resistance for their own political ends. The real Resistance was that of Vichy officials who stayed their ground and negotiated eyeball-to-eyeball with the Germans on a daily basis; *maquisards* who called themselves resisters were often no better than bandits and terrorists.

When I repeated these stories to the Académie de Tours they told me that such Angevin *hobereaux*, or petty nobles, were in no way typical and that in Touraine a genuine left-wing Resistance held sway. As an antidote, they introduced me to Georges Audebert, an official at the prefecture of Tours during the Occupation. Although in public he told gallant stories about his Resistance activities, in private, as we saw, he adopted a different line, which was dictated by his responsibilities under Vichy. He argued that in 1940 there was no alternative to the armistice "as people were getting killed and buildings were on fire. France was abandoned by everyone except England, of course, but people said that England was finished. People argued that perhaps a man like Pétain, who had the glory of being a marshal of France and was respected by the Germans, could limit the damage and save something." Resistance, Audebert insisted, was impossible, so keen was German repression, and the Liberation was marked by "terrible abuses and mistakes." He simply waited for his moment, carrying a German pass in his pocket and one issued by the Resistance in his shoe, and managed to make the transition to the prefecture of Mayenne with special responsibility for "preventing excessive purges."[43]

This sentiment of relief at the armistice went all the way down the social order and was probably plainest among the peasantry, such as the future *maquisards* of Saffré. As André Treulier, the winegrower of Le Thoureil near Saumur, poured me a glass of wine in his cellar, he opened the conversation by announcing that, by suing for an armistice and letting him out of the army, "Pétain saved my life."[44] Max Ménard, a candle maker from Beaupréau, a pious and conservative town in the Mauges, was a former seminarist who knew all the priests in the area and had a captive market for his candles. He made no bones about his sympathy for Pétain, who he said acted as a buffer between the Germans and the French population, and argued that it was ill-considered to put him on trial. His wife, Jeanne, recalled that the Germans were well-behaved (*corrects*), and Max agreed that he was not unduly troubled by them under the Occupation. When the Germans started to requisition vehicles in the locality, Max asked a mechanic to remove a piece from his so that it would not start. "We conned them as much as we could," he said. "It was passive resistance." He resisted in his way, he continued, by not replying to letters calling on him to report for the STO. There was no question, however, of joining a Maquis. "I would have done more resistance," he apologized, "if we hadn't been going to get married."[45]

In the more educated classes Pétainism was a choice dictated as much by fervor as by self-preservation or family priorities. Abbé Henri Richer, chaplain of the Little Sisters of the Poor in Angers, was a seminarist who went to Germany on the STO in 1943. Some seminarists, he conceded, went into hiding or joined the Resistance rather than go to Germany, but in his opinion it was "better to accompany" the workers to provide religious services, and he explained how he received support in his mission from German parish priests. The conversation revealed, however, another reason for his leaving. Richer's father was a career army officer until 1925, when he became a bookseller in Angers. His father followed Pétain, and Henri followed his father. "We were always Pétainists," he confided. "We never listened to English radio. We gave ourselves over to prayer to ask for the liberation of the prisoners of war [and] the reconstruction of the country." The Occupation saw "an intense religious life, at least in Christian circles," and the restoration of state subsidies to church schools for the first time since the 1880s was "a burst of oxygen . . . a joy." He said, "We knew very little about what was going on in the Resistance" and thought de Gaulle was a "troublemaker . . . disruptive, irritating." When Richer returned to France in April 1945, he was told at the frontier to acclaim de Gaulle, but he could not, arguing that he was "still more or less illegal." That summer he followed the trial of Pétain in the press and thought the condemnation to death "unjust." In the Pétainist world of Abbé Richer, still intact after more than fifty years, the Vichy regime was the city of God, the STO the opportunity for missionary work, and the Resistance open defiance of loyalty and discipline.[46]

Another cleric who remained true to Pétainism and criticized the excesses of the Resistance was Abbé Jamonneau, who had been a POW in Germany and at the end of the Occupation was secretary to Monsignor Villepelet, the very Pétainist bishop of Nantes. He recalled that Michel Debré, when he came to Nantes in August 1944 to rally opinion to General de Gaulle, "expressed great surprise" at finding a portrait of the marshal still hanging in the bishop's office. Jamonneau insisted that those who preferred Pétain to de Gaulle were not for that reason "unpatriotic Frenchmen" and that the German Occupation was "not a gulag, anyway." He had nothing but scorn for the Resistance and the Americans. The Maquis of Saffré was in his eyes guilty of "imprudence" and "stupidity," as was his own brother, who killed two Germans only a few kilometers from the family farm and got his uncle, his uncle's daughter, and himself arrested by the Gestapo. He criticized the Americans for their artillery bombardment of churches in the pocket of Saint-Nazaire and showed me a photograph of the ruined church of Bouvron, where he became curé after the war. Although he regularly attended the Bouvron ceremonies marking the end of the war, he denounced the FFIs, recalling that while he was helping a community of nuns in Saint-Étienne-de-Montluc move away from the front, an FFI officer demanded the nuns' beds be put in his men's trenches. "I was in the war," Jamonneau roared at the officer. "You don't put beds in trenches!" For him the FFIs were not the heroic soldiers of the Year II but the republican "infernal columns" that put counterrevolutionary Brittany and the Vendée to fire and sword in 1793. Over his door there was an engraving of a secret forest mass celebrated by Vendeans, and he pointed out that his ancestors were massacred by the self-same "infernal columns." His vision of the Second World War was colored by the heritage of the French Revolution, the revolutionaries of 1944, like those of 1793, being the force for evil.[47]

Nobles and clerics, of course, are not a cross section of the French population, and Pétainist opinion, however strongly expressed, is a minority view. But one point often raised by such people—that attacks by armed resisters on German personnel inevitably provoked collective reprisals against local populations and were therefore foolhardy—merits attention. In the Loire area, there does not seem to have been the same community support for Resistance fighters as in the Midi, and the feeling of many Nantais that armed attacks were counterproductive has been echoed in other villages that experienced or nearly experienced brutal collective punishments. The massacres of Tulle, Saint-Amand, and Oradour-sur-Glane in the violent months surrounding the Liberation were the most famous but unfortunately not the only ones.[48]

Yves de Saint-Seine was appointed by Vichy mayor of the small village of Toutlemonde, near Cholet, where, following the discovery by the Germans of a van full of weapons on 8 August 1944, a tragedy was only just averted. The Breton resistant Michel Créac'h had confessed under torture that the weapons were destined for "*tout le monde*," and the linguistic confusion led to Saint-Seine, the curé, and every sixth man in the village being lined up against the schoolhouse wall to be shot, unless they revealed where the weapons had been hidden. After fifteen tense minutes, when the misunderstanding was cleared up by a German-speaking Alsatian interpreter, they were released. A monument was raised outside the village to Michel Créac'h, but following a good lunch Yves de Saint-Seine revealed his true feelings about this cult. "I am against the Resistance, which was responsible for the deaths of many decent people," he let slip. His hostility to the Resistance was of a piece with his loyalty to Pétain, who he said had prevented France from becoming totally occupied and should never have been sentenced to death. In his opinion de Gaulle was a deserter, and he argued that "the British and Americans would have liberated France just as well without the Resistance." The Liberation authorities kept him on as mayor in 1944 because of his exemplary conduct under the threat of massive reprisals, and he was duly elected in 1945 and for forty years subsequently. He might have become the father of his village but the fact that he was initially appointed by Vichy denied him the honors that would normally be bestowed. He said he did not care that he had not been awarded the Légion d'Honneur or the Ordre du Mérite National, but he clearly did.[49]

The villagers of Maillé in Touraine were not so lucky. On 25 August 1944, after *maquisards* ambushed some retreating Germans in the vicinity, a German unit covering the retreat put the village to fire and sword, massacring 124 of the 627 inhabitants. Those who survived the massacre were torn between anger and despair. The first plaque, unveiled on 25 August 1945 in the presence of the archbishop of Tours, read: "To the 124 inhabitants massacred by Nazi barbarism. Let us never forget." The monument unveiled by Raoul Dautry, minister of reconstruction, on the main road to Bordeaux in 1947 commanded: "Passerby, the Nazis have pillaged, killed, burned." In 1948 Maillé, along with Tours and Saint-Pierre-des-Corps, was awarded the Croix de Guerre for "the sacrifice, spirit of resistance, and heroism of the citizens of the village."[50] What the survivors did not want, however, was for the tragedy to be hijacked for political purposes. This almost happened in 1953 during the trial of members of the Das Reich SS division held responsible for the Oradour massacre, when Resistance groups from Chinon used the commemoration to protest against the amnesty of collaborators voted by parliament at the same time.[51] From then on, the commemoration was held in silence, without speeches, a moment to remember the dead, not to make political capital.

The villagers do not want to criticize the Resistance, because of its status and legitimacy, although their deep feeling is that it was responsible for detroying their loved ones. Henri Chedozeau, the mayor, who lost his father in the carnage, admitted that "if there had been no Resistance in France, that would have helped the Occupation." On the other hand, he revealed that on the fiftieth anniversary of the massacre he received a letter from one of the *maquisards*, now living outside Angers, saying, "I feel that I am responsible for the massacre of Maillé." He made no comment. The massacre remains unspeakable. Mme Guitton, who lost her grandparents, aunt, and cousins in the massacre, confessed that she had not been able to tell the full story to her six children. She stood in the middle of the village cemetery, head bowed, in tears. An association to establish a *"maison du souvenir"* in one of the few remaining original buildings has only recently been founded. And yet the inhabitants of Maillé are pained that they have been forgotten by others. The village is not a focus of national concern, like Oradour. Nothing is known of the German soldier who was responsible for the massacre, apart from the fact that he was condemned to death in absentia in 1952. Ministers are regularly invited to the annual commemoration but never come, because the date is the same as that of the Liberation of Paris and might cast a shadow on it. In the words of the local paper in 1994, "A little recognition would be enough for this commune of Indre-et-Loire, which fifty years on still suffers from not understanding what happened."[52]

Mayor Chedozeau and the surviving villagers of Maillé were ambivalent about the Resistance: it redeemed France, but it brought tragedy to them. Most communities in the region, of course, did not participate in the Resistance but were simply liberated by Allied forces. A survey undertaken by the Comité d'Histoire de la Deuxième Guerre Mondiale in Maine-et-Loire in 1948 indicated that only a third of communes claimed that they produced so much as one deportee or member of the FFI. Two-thirds of mayors reported that there had been no resistance at all in their communes. That of Chaudefonds-sur-Layon, for example, said that "the population in general was obliged to tolerate the Germans but had an unfavorable opinion of them." At most it was claimed that reluctance to meet German requistions was "passive resistance."[53] And yet the pressure to display Resistance credentials was such that many communities cultivated a special relationship with a resister or liberator whose glory might be reflected onto the town or village. If a local hero like Christian de Mondragon could not be found, a national or even foreign hero would do, so long as a local association could be demonstrated.

After the Liberation the little village of Grugé l'Hôpital in northern Anjou claimed that it acted as a launchpad of the Liberation, sending the great General Leclerc on his long military adventure. As Captain Philippe de Hautecloque, wounded in the fighting, he had sought refuge with his sister, Mme Yvonne de Bodard, in the local château on 26 June 1940. The Germans had set up a temporary Kommandantur at the *mairie*, and with the help of the mayor and the curé, Abbé Brossier, the captain was able to obtain a pass in the name of Leclerc, wine merchant, to cross to the Free Zone. In September 1946 he returned to the village for a thanksgiving mass celebrated by Abbé Brossier and signed a document in the *mairie* that described how the pass had allowed him to escape "providentially" from the Germans, to join General de Gaulle, and to begin the "glorious epic that from the Cameroons, Chad, and Tunisia to Normandy, Paris, and Strasbourg was to finish at Berchtesgaden, with the Liberation of occupied France."[54] Leclerc was killed in an air crash in North Africa the following year, but a plaque was unveiled on the façade of the *mairie* in 1953 announcing that "Grugé l'Hôpital wishes to preserve the pious memory of he whom it considers in some measure to be one of its children." In 1980, on the fortieth anniversary of the occasion, a statue of Leclerc was unveiled in the main square of the village in a ceremony attended by the marshal's widow, the bishop of Angers, cadets of the cavalry school of Saumur, where he had been a student, and veterans of the Second Tank Division. The secretary of state for ex-servicemen neatly rewrote history by declaring that "people often commit sins of omission when they narrate the events of history, for what the mayor and curé of Grugé l'Hôpital did in 1940, permitting him who freely chose the name of Leclerc to take the first steps toward glory, was one of the first acts of the Resistance."[55]

This invention of an "act of resistance" and appropriation of General Leclerc as one of the village's children contrasted with a real local fear of resistance under the Occupation itself, relayed by both the documents and the oral record. The subprefect of Segré said of Grugé in 1941, "I witnessed a national spirit that was most comprehensive and most committed to the country's restoration. The municipal assembly has the most complete confidence in the marshal's policies."[56] The mayor, Édouard Delanoë, son of the mayor in 1940, told me in 1997 how his father managed to avert a nasty incident in 1940, when the Germans arrived, by persuading French troops "armed to the teeth" in the forest not to fight, in return for providing them with civilian clothing to allow them to escape.[57] Francis Bossé, a local farmer, said at the beginning of his memoirs that "from my childhood I have had a horror of war, so much had I heard about it from my father and his ex-servicemen friends." Born in 1921, he escaped the initial call-up and confessed that "for us young people the armistice was a relief, as we thought we were rid of the war for good."[58] The Germans left the village in September 1940 and the community settled into a peaceable Occupation. Its war memorial bears the names of twenty-four dead in the First World War and only two in the Second, including a student teacher shot by the Germans in the affair of the *normaliens* of Angers.[59]

On Sunday, 7 August 1994, a plaque was unveiled at the Pont des Pruniers, Bouchemaine, outside Angers, to the memory of a sea-scout leader, Louis Bordier, by his brother Yann, now a rear admiral. Fifty years earlier, Louis had led the advancing American forces to a lightly defended railway bridge over the Maine downstream of Angers, which they were able to cross to attack the Germans in the rear and liberate the city.[60] The Angevins, who had weathered four years of Occupation under the same mayor, had no other local heroes to cultivate. In the absence of French liberators, they decided to raise their profile by associating their liberation with the great General Patton, who was awarded the freedom of the city. His visit almost didn't happen, for clearly Angers needed the general more than the general needed Angers. Patton was due to be feted in Angers on 5 August 1945, but the visit had to be canceled. He visited a number of towns liberated by the Third Army that October but was again unable to visit Angers. He thanked Mayor Allonneau for awarding him the freedom of the city but asked whether the mayor could come to Rennes and present it there. Allonneau went to Rennes with his deputy mayor, Germaine Canonne, who in fact prevailed on Patton to travel the 130 kilometers to Angers, where he made a grand entrance on 27 October.[61]

The significance of this moment for Angers, and indeed for Germaine Canonne, would be difficult to underestimate. Although Mme Canonne was the first female deputy mayor of Angers, the first female member of the *conseil général* of Maine-et-Loire, and the pioneer of many welfare reforms, including the closure of the city's brothels, these achievements were nothing compared with her triumph in persuading General Patton to come to Angers. The essence of her tale, which she read aloud to me from her manuscript memoirs, was that the airfield at Angers was out of action and that Patton had been warned by a clairvoyant not to travel by car. The subtext was that she spoke good English and that Patton was persuaded by her charms. In fact, Patton was killed in a car crash in Mannheim two months later, and Germaine Canonne expresses relief that no accident happened on the road to Angers. Fifty years after the Liberation, she was able to meet Patton's granddaughter, Helen, who told her that she was happy to shake hands with someone who had met her grandfather, as she had never met him.[62] For the Angevins Patton achieved the status of a hero or modern saint whom, though he was associated with them only tangentially, they could somehow claim for their own in order to privilege the liberation of their city in the history of the Second World War.

To have resisted personally or even by proxy conferred great legitimacy, but simply to claim Resistance credentials was not enough. The gateway to Resistance accreditation was policed by powerful Resistance organizations that established a hierarchy of credentials—certificates and medals—differentiating between various levels of activity and blocking the claims of rivals. The most powerful of the Resistance organizations was the Fédération Nationale des Déportés et Internés de la Résistance (FNDIR), which obtained, under a law of 6 August 1948, a special status equivalent to having served in the army for those who had been deported or interned for *acts* of resistance. They were awarded the title of Voluntary Combatant of the Resistance (CVR) and the Resistance Medal. The CVR was given only to those who could demonstrate that they had joined the Resistance at least ninety days before the landings of 6 June 1944; those who joined later, such as FFIs, qualified only as Combatants in a Resistance Capacity. The prime intention of the FNDIR was to reject the claims of the communist Fédération Nationale des Déportés et Internés de la Résistance Patriotes (FNDIRP), whose members, in their opinion, had been deported or interned simply for being in a political party. The FNDIR was also determined to reject the claims of the STO workers, who campaigned repeatedly for the title of "labor deportees." Working in a German factory, the FNDIR argued, was nothing compared with slaving in a German concentration camp. Those who had been conscripted but had refused to go—and could prove that the police were looking for them—were entitled to a *réfractaire* card, but those who went to Germany were allowed no more exalted a title than "person constrained to work in enemy territory." In defiance of this ruling many STO organizations continued to call themselves "labor deportees," and in 1985, under pressure from the FNDIR, the appeals court of Bourges ruled that enough had been said about "the heroism and martyrdom of the Resistance deportees that an incomparable title should correspond to their incomparable fate." Their monopoly on honor was thereby confirmed.[63]

The struggle for honor, heavily bureaucratized, was not free of partiality and corruption. The patronage of a Resistance chief like Jean Meunier in Tours or of a Resistance organization was indispensable. As the Cold War began to bite, the authorities became less and less willing to recognize communists as resistants. While many of the noncommunist *fusillés* of Nantes, for example, were posthumously awarded the Resistance Medal and the Legion of Honor in 1948, these were refused to the communist *fusillés* of Châteaubriant.[64] Conditions were set impossibly high for communists seeking recognition as resistants. For example, the brother-in-law, mother, and grandparents of two communist brothers from Rézé hunted by the Gestapo were arrested in their place and deported to Oranienburg. They claimed that they, too, were resistants, but the prefect of Loire-Inférieure ruled in 1951 that "they could not adduce any provable fact (act of sabotage, participation in an attack against the installations or members of the Army of Occupation)" and were "considered to be hostages rather than resistants."[65]

The FNDIR increased its profile still further through the National Day of Remembrance of the Victims and Heroes of the Deportation, an annual gala of the deportees instituted under a law of 14 April 1954 to mark the liberation of the concentration camps in 1945 and held on the last Sunday of April. The constant refrain of these gatherings was unity, and to prevent quarreling between movements and organizations of deportees, the official speech was handed down each year from the Ministry of War Veterans. The gospel to be passed on to future generations was that the barbarism of the concentration camps must never be allowed to recur and that the survivors' dream of a free and fraternal world must now be realized. The subtext was nevertheless to link deportation and resistance, highlighting the primacy of the Resistance deportees and the contribution of the deportees to the Resistance. This became explicit in 1964 when associations of resistants and deportees, under the auspices of the Education Ministry, founded an essay competition linking the themes of resistance and deportation "to develop an understanding of the civic and moral values that were at stake in the combat."[66] Each year a different topic was set, ranging from the Resistance and the principles of 1789 in 1989 to Nazi concentration camps in 1991 and women and the Resistance in 1997. In the Loire-Atlantique, one of the first departments to participate under the enthusiastic guidance of André Chauvel of the FNDIR, the annual prize giving at the prefecture is a gala where the aging representatives of associations of deportees, resistants, and veterans bestow laurels on the gilded youth of the department. In 1997 the Marquis Donatien de Sesmaisons, speaking on behalf of the sponsoring *conseil général*, paid homage to the Resistance activities of his mother and declared that the Resistance "united brothers-in-arms of all social and political conditions."[67] The winning essay, by Kristell Retière of Le Loquidy School, Nantes (of which Christian de Mondragon was a graduate), entirely fulfilled the expectations of the organizers. She explained how French women turned away from Marshal Pétain after his attacks on women's employment, contraception, and abortion and argued that "in spite of their different social situations, their opposing political opinions, and their diverse beliefs and ideologies, they overcame their particularities in order to unite for what was essential, in a struggle without quarter: they became resistants, with exactly the same credentials as men."[68]

The most striking thing about the French commemoration of the deportation, however, is that for nearly fifty years the Jewish dimension was scarcely mentioned. The text from the Ministry of War Veterans habitually referred to the "200,000 French people" who had been deported or to the "ten million victims of the most diverse nationalities." Since most Jews deported from France were immigrants, they were hidden behind the term *diverse nationalities*. In Angers, the twenty-fifth anniversary of the liberation of the camps in 1970 was commemorated by a meeting addressed by a Free French officer, a Jewish survivor of Auschwitz, and Mme Geneviève Anthonioz-de Gaulle, niece of the general and a Ravensbrück deportee. Only Mme Anthonioz-de Gaulle attracted any attention; she was presented with the visitors' book signed by Angevins on the day of her uncle's funeral.[69] For the fortieth anniversary, in 1985, young people were brought much more fully into the commemorations, and in Nantes one of them read the official message, this time penned by a survivor. Even so, reference was made only to "the degradation, the torture, and the extermination of millions of people," and the familiar summons was to "build that free and fraternal world of which we dreamed on the exhilarating day of our liberation, forty years ago."[70]

This extraordinary omission requires explanation. The Resistance gospel, as we have seen, always privileged the hero over the victim, accorded the highest honors to Resistance deportees or internees, followed by political deportees and internees. It refused to recognize that STO workers were deportees and nursed the prejudice that, far from resisting, the Jews went like lambs to the slaughter. The communists who dominated the association of Auschwitz survivors ensured that Auschwitz was regarded above all as a camp for political deportees and in June 1946 inhumed the ashes brought back from Auschwitz in the Père Lachaise cemetery in Paris next to the Mur des Fédérés dedicated to the Communards of 1871. The inscription, "To the memory of the 180,000 men, women, and children deported from France and exterminated at Auschwitz, victims of Nazi barbarism," made no specific mention of the Jews.[71] The Resistance cult also insisted that over and above social, political, religious, or ethnic differences, all individuals and movements dedicated to the struggle against Nazism shared the same fundamental values of the rights of man, liberty, equality, and fraternity, and were committed to rebuilding a "one and indivisible" France. For that reason, Deportation Day always presented a united front, a single message was proclaimed, and any attempt at separatism was vehemently discouraged. A final explanation brings in the French state. The extermination of the Jews called into question the responsibility first of the Vichy state, then of the French state in general. The fact that de Gaulle declared the Vichy state null and void and restored republican legitimacy made things easy for the Republic. When President Mitterrand, on 16 July 1992, attended the commemoration of the fiftieth anniversary of the roundup of French Jews by French police in Paris, he refused to accept the responsibility of the French state, on the grounds that Vichy was not the Republic and the Republic was not Vichy. Only with the declaration of Prime Minister Chirac, on 16 July 1995, that "the criminal folly of the occupier was, as everyone knows, assisted by the French, assisted by the French state" and that "on that day France accomplished something irreparable" was the responsibility of the French state for the first time acknowledged and the door opened to place the Holocaust at the center of the deportation debate.

The Holocaust salvo dealt a blow to the Resistance organizations, breaching their monopoly of honor. At a meeting of the Nantes FNDIR chaired by André Chauvel in 1997, twelve or fifteen white-haired resistants agreed that "too much importance" had been given to the Jews for the fiftieth anniversary of the liberation of the camps in 1995. Chauvel acknowledged that the Jews had caught the media spotlight and regretted that "the deportées [sic] were put to one side, forgotten." School students answering a recent questionnaire on who was deported, he said, cited Jews first and workers second. He was concerned that homosexuals would soon want to lay their own wreath on Deportation Day, even though, he affirmed, "no one was deported from France for homosexuality."[72]

This resentment was confirmed to me by Ernest Gluck, an Auschwitz survivor of Slovak origin and president of the Jewish community of Nantes. He was present at a ceremony on 16 July 1993 to unveil alongside the monument to the fifty hostages in Nantes a plaque recording the homage of the Republic to "the victims of racist and anti-Semitic persecution and crimes against humanity committed under the de facto Government of the French State, 1940–1944." Gluck revealed that the local organizations of deportees and resistants had been extremely reluctant to concede a separate ceremony for Jewish deportees to coincide with the *rafles du Vel d'Hiv* rather than with Deportation Day—although it had been decreed nationally—arguing that unity had to be maintained at all costs and that, if the Jews obtained their own ceremony, the next request would come from the homosexual community.[73] Once the unitary nature of the commemoration was broken by the concession of a Jewish ceremony on 16 July, the next best option was to relativize the Jews. Thus in 1993 the deputy mayor of Nantes, Jean-Marc Ayrault, attacked the "shameful, unacceptable laws and decrees" of Vichy against the Jews, but spent much time dilating on the persecution of the gypsies.[74]

In Angers, public recognition of the deportation of the Jews took place a year earlier. On 20 July 1992 a ceremony was held in the courtyard of the Grand Séminaire, where exactly fifty years earlier 824 Jews had been crammed before being loaded onto convoy 8 for Auschwitz. The initiative for the dedication of a plaque was taken by one of the three remaining survivors of the convoy, Désiré Hafner, now living in Tours. The wording that he chose, and the speech that he gave, made the gesture easier to make by the Angevins, since he blamed the whole episode on the Nazis. The recognition, moreover, was superficial. The bishop of Angers, Monsignor Orchampt, who paid for the plaque, said that he had been totally unaware of the drama until a few weeks previously and that the seminary had been requisitioned at the time by the Nazis (which was only partially correct). The mayor of Angers, Jean Monnier, simply threw up his hands, wondering innocently "how such goings-on could have taken place in our good city of Angers, without leaving any memory, except in the departmental archives."[75] The fears of Charles Toubon, then head of the Jewish community of Angers, meanwhile, were not fully assuaged. He said privately that he had not pardoned the Church and that it was "written in the Gospels that the Jews were wrong." There was still a danger, as evidenced by Poland and the likes of Monsignor Lefebvre in France, that "Catholicism misunderstood" would be anti-Semitic.[76]

The difficulty experienced by the Jewish community in promoting its own version of events alongside the received orthodoxy was most clearly illustrated in the commemoration of the camp of La Lande, near the village of Monts, outside Tours. The camp, as we saw, had been used in

1940–42 as a detention camp for foreign and displaced Jews and thereafter for communist women. The first initiative in collective remembrance came in 1983 from two communist women of Monts, Huguette Robin, whose father had been shot by the Germans in 1942, and Lucie Lancezeux, who had worked at the Ripault factory. They had an article published in *L'Humanité* and attracted a number of communist women who had once been prisoners in the camp and were willing to talk. The visitors, seeing that all signs of the camp had vanished under a housing project, suggested that a monument should mark the spot, and Mmes Robin and Lancezeux, with the help of a sympathetic communist councillor, persuaded the somewhat reluctant conservative municipal council to adopt the idea.[77]

At this point a former Jewish internee of the camp from Nancy, Jérôme Scorin, learned of the plan and contacted the Jewish community in Tours. When it discovered that the projected inscription for the monument contained no specific reference to the Jews, only to the "victims of racial and political hatred interned here from 1940 to 1944," they asked the permission of the mayor, Dr. Prunier, to place their own plaque. The mayor, ever the local politician, amiably promised to meet their request but found himself opposed by his council and therefore did nothing. As a consequence, on 16 October 1988, the unveiling ceremony was boycotted by the Jewish community of Tours, which declared itself, in the words of its leader, Marcel Messalati, "wounded and scandalized," insulted and betrayed.[78] The prefect, fearing controversy, did not come. The ceremony was attended by Serge Klarsfeld, on behalf of the Association of Sons and Daughters of Deported Jews of France, and Jérôme Scorin, but only to protest. In an angry speech, which the mayor later said "brought me down in flames," Scorin asked whether the "hatred" described on the plaque was that of the Nazis or of the French and asserted that "not only does the laconic wording of the monument fail to express the horror of the racist crime and the extent of the human catastrophe, but it seems to minimize the reality." He himself, he said, had managed to escape from the camp, but his mother, father, and brother had been among 489 Jews taken from there to Auschwitz. "Does the municipality of Monts," he asked, "want to disguise the fact that the internees of La Lande exterminated at Auschwitz were all Jews? Does it want to agree with the pseudorevisionists, the falsifiers of history, or with a certain political party that claims that the crime committed against so many innocent people was only a detail?"[79]

After this collision of memories a reconciliation was gradually negotiated. A more left-wing municipality was elected, and a more diplomatic leader of the Jewish community, François Guggenheim, emerged. A municipal commission was appointed, including two members of the Jewish community, to discuss the wording of a second plaque.[80] At the same time, André Bellegarde, a local teacher, persuaded the College of Monts to undertake research into the camp and put on an exhibition. This exhibition, which opened early in 1995, brought the Holocaust to the village and had a powerful influence on local opinion. It mediated between the Jewish community and the local community and paved the way to the unveiling of the second plaque, in honor of the deported Jews, in the presence of, among others, the prefect and Serge Klarsfeld on 3 December 1995.[81]

Unfortunately, public recognition did not completely efface private resentment. Like the noncommunist resistants of Nantes, the communists of Monts felt that they had been marginalized in the interests of political correctness. In his large office on the outskirts of Tours, François Guggenheim expressed satisfaction with developments: the Jews now occupied center stage in the deportation memory. Lucie Lancezeux's tone was somewhat different as we sat in the garage of her little house for coolness. "What annoyed me," confessed Lancezeux, "is that never, ever did a Jew thank us. They took it over for themselves. No one ever said that it's thanks to the Communist Party cell that there is a monument. We cleared the land and then they ploughed it up." Huguette Robin set the issue in the context of the Resistance's teaching on the deportation. "During the war," she said, "if you were against the Occupation, against repression and all that, people didn't ask who you were or where you came from." The Jews, however, she continued, "always want to make distinctions—Jews on one side, communists on the other." "That sort of thing didn't exist during the war." added Lancezeux. "People were striving toward a single goal." Besides, concluded Robin, in this area they don't remember any Jews who took part in the Resistance.

The public recognition of the special claim of the Jews had the effect of unseating the Resistance establishment from its pedestal and of high-lighting the actions of "bad Frenchmen," some of whom were belatedly brought to trial. In addition, the Holocaust factor reminded French people that it was no longer essential to present themselves as "good French" with a Resistance record; the role of "poor French," who had also suffered the oppression and hardships of the Occupation, was possibly even more powerful.

When I met the Amis du Vieux Chinon in the elegant Maison des États Généraux, I was introduced to "a person who took part in the Resis-tance," René Arnoult, a large and powerful man who clearly enjoyed some status. A young man at the time, he had been active in Resistance activities with his father, who had become a member of the CDL of Indre-et-Loire. The conversation that afternoon, however, was dominated by the slight and wizened Christian Beugnet, older than his years, who held forth on the day the Germans erupted into his childhood:

> Today I can still see the arrival of the German forces. For three days and three nights came first of all the tanks, then the soldiers on foot with their officers on horseback, in the direction of the Atlantic. Then, in the days that followed, columns of French prisoners moved up in the opposite direc-tion. . . . Hotels were requisitioned for the Kommandantur and the Feldgendarmerie and a number of other services answerable to the German army, and of course the swastika flew from all these buildings. . . . From the moment these organizations were set up, the curfew was imposed, one could only move around outside the authorized times with a pass, and patrols came by regularly in the town. . . . You had to take precautions: some people were arrested just for things they said. . . . If you had a disagreement with your neighbor, he just had to go and find someone at the Kommandantur and you could be arrested . . . and then there were roundups in town. The Germans came by with a truck and if by mis-fortune you didn't have your identity card, well then. . . . It was four years of fascist dictatorship.

This classic statement of the suffering of the "poor French" was listened to with great respect, but it did not command full agreement. Beugnet's wife, Léonie, interrupted to say that there had been only a few arrests in Chinon, while the jovial president of the Amis, Claude Bougreau, claimed that "the Occupation in Chinon was very mild, in fact. There were no reprisals. . . . The majority of the population adjusted fairly well to the Occupation and some people actually did well out of it, with the black market."[82]

As in Tours, memories of French people differed about the severity of the Occupation. It is perhaps significant that the "Nazi dictatorship" view is often espoused by those who might have resisted but did not, while women or those who were boys at the time are more likely to remember the Occupation as fairly mild. Many, of course, expected the Germans to repeat the atrocities of which they had been guilty in northern France in 1914–18 or even in 1870, particularly those who had family connections with the frontier area; they were pleasantly surprised when things did not turn out that way. French and Germans lived cheek by jowl for four or five years and came to see each other as real people, not just as the stereotypes of propaganda and myth. It also became clear that the Germans were as much the victims as the perpetrators of the war, far from home, suffering fear and hardship, and in this sense they had much in common with the French population.

"I heard so much about the Germans from my mother," said Andrée Trudeau of Saumur, "that I lived with the memory of the 1914 war even though, of course, I hadn't known it." Her mother came from Le Chemin des Dames, in the Aisne, which became a battlefield in 1917, and told of how they were under the Germans one day, the English another, the Scots a third. Her grandmother had been treated by a German doctor who left instructions for her care before he was obliged to retreat. Trudeau was quite clear that "there were good and bad" among the Germans. Of the Occupation in Saumur, she said, "For the first few years, here as everywhere else, they left us alone." Later in the war people were not allowed to talk on the bridge in groups of more than three; if they were caught, the punishment "wasn't nasty," usually polishing boots at the Kommandantur or watching the Loire for an hour without turning around. Her view of the

Germans in Saumur was that they, too, suffered from the war. The Kommandant was "not bad . . . humane, there because he had to be there. People make war because they are obliged to. Those who declare war don't make it, they send others."[83]

Having heard stories of atrocities committed by the Germans in 1914–18, the parents of Michel Leterme, who lived in Angers, were racked by anxiety about the grandparents, who lived in Armentières, near the Belgian border. Later it transpired that they had tried to flee with a wheelbarrow but got only as far as Hazebrouck, twenty-five kilometers down the road. Michel, ten at the time, remembers seeing his first Germans in Angers, "young and handsome, clean and polite." They were, he said, keen to "efface the image of terror that had become associated with them," and they practiced a "policy of fraternization." The French eyed them curiously and asked them for news of towns the tanks had come through, where they had friends or relations. He argued that "the presence of the German army was not disagreeable." Michel's sister married in 1942, and two "kind and peaceable" workers for the Todt Organization billeted on them for five or six months used her vacant room. Sometimes they shared coffee in the kitchen and mused in broken French about their common plight: "War, very unfortunate." The military band used to play in the Jardin du Mail on a Sunday afternoon and French and Germans rubbed up against one another in cafés, cinemas, and the opera. "It was what people now call cohabitation."[84]

When I delivered my paper to the Academy of Tours in 1997, I quoted Violette Lemasson, who grew up during the Occupation in the small Angevin village of Saint-Ellier-sur-Aubance. "We never lacked anything," she had told me, "we never went hungry." This assertion provoked a wave of disagreement in the audience, many of whom would have spent the Occupation in Tours. The academy's secretary, Marcel Girard, drove the point home. "What is striking," he wrote to me, "is the memory of food shortages. Here one must distinguish between the farmers, who had ample food and sometimes even made a good deal of money, and those who produced nothing, in the large towns and even in the small ones, who lost on average (according to the statistics) twenty kilos!"[85] Hunger was, of course, one of the main characteristics of the *années noires*, but French people are much more eloquent about the tricks they got up to in order to obtain food than about standing forlornly in bread lines.

Huguette Robin was precisely the kind of person who should have starved under the Occupation. Her parents ran a café in the place Velpeau in Tours, between the railway station and Saint-Pierre-des-Corps, the clientele of which was working-class, mainly railwaymen. When they were arrested for communist activities in 1942 she was left, at the age of eighteen, to manage the café with her younger sister. She remembered being cold and hungry and in debt to the local baker. But there were ways of getting by. They had little wine to sell but collected the wine-ration tickets to which (even at that age) they were entitled and built up a stock to which they treated their clients on market day. More importantly, they had relations in the Free Zone who were bakers, and once the demarcation line was abolished after the total Occupation of France in November 1942, these were able to come to their assistance.[86]

Another inhabitant of Tours, Lucienne Despouy, who was herself arrested along with her husband for communist activities in 1942, returned to her business making rubber stamps after three months in prison while he was executed. Bereaved like Huguette Robin, whose father was shot, she remembered the food situation more positively. She remembered people raising rabbits and chickens at home, pointed out that the villages of La Riche, Chambray, and La Ville-aux-Dames, now part of the conurbation of Tours, were then full of market gardeners, and said that the black market flourished. She also had her own country uncle, who used to arrive from the Sarthe in his gas-fired car (gasoline being almost impossible to find) with wood and potatoes. "The inhabitants of Tours," she concluded, "did not really go without."[87]

Just as memories of hunger under the Occupation are challenged by recollections of imaginative ways of getting by, of the famous "Système D," so memories of Nazi dictatorship and the moralizing prohibitions of the Vichy regime are contradicted by memories of flourishing religious, cultural, and social life. Sometimes the contradiction between obeying rules and creating friendship networks informed the same account, as if internalized orders were still in conflict with the desire to make life tolerable.

Odette Goxe, whose husband ran a textile business in Angers, began by saying that associative and social life was "dormant." There was the cinema, of course, but "no more cultural meetings. People stayed at home." Religious life, she said, was the exception. She was with a group of women who met under the supervision of the curé of Saint-Serge in Angers, listening to him read messages from Marshal Pétain, "which did not enthuse anyone," making cakes, and knitting for the parish fund-raiser. This, of course, was perfectly legal, but her son's Catholic Boy Scout camp was not. Nevertheless, he went to a clandestine camp in the Vendée, "around a little lake, with the French flag flying," and she showed me photographs of the event. She was most enthusiastic when conversation turned to the procession of the statue of Our Lady of Boulogne, which, having been taken to Lourdes in 1942, began a long and ceremonial odyssey across France in 1943–44. She remembered the "huge production, the church flooded with light" in Angers, where the statue rested after one of its stages. "People turned out in great numbers," she recalled, many walking in bare feet and throwing written prayers into the boat in which the statue was carried. For Mme Goxe and for the crowds, Our Lady "represented hope, [divine] intercession for the liberation of France."[88]

Pierre Boudet, at the time president of a student association, then a young doctor in the Sarthe, initially declared that "all meetings of students or of scouts or other demonstrations were absolutely forbidden." There was "absolutely no" social or associative life, he asserted. He then let slip that "we did all sorts of prohibited things." These included demonstrating on Joan of Arc Day on instructions from de Gaulle, walking at some distance from one another so as to evade the ban on processions, and dancing secretly in one another's houses and even in bistros. With pleasure and nostalgia he cited Roberte Marnor's charming song "Le Bal défendu."[89]

Abel Avenet, a peasant of Dierre, "the little Moscow" in the Cher valley, emphasized that what young people were interested in during the Occupation was not politics but music and dancing. "When you are young," he confided, "you think only about having fun." "We made music during the war," and his own instrument was the trombone. He remembered that in the spring of 1941, feeling "on a leash," he and others organized a clandestine ball one Sunday night in a barn. The second Sunday some youths came by train from Tours to join the fun, and the locals decided to allow the girls in but not the boys. As a result, they were denounced and fined fifteen or twenty francs by the JP. After that they restricted the balls to locals, with local musicians (including himself); he had no recollection of being bothered by the gendarmerie. Sometimes they danced in a mill at Bléré, where the thick walls muffled the sound, although they had to take care returning home after the curfew because of German patrols near the demarcation line. Asked whether to dance in defiance of the law constituted resistance, Avenet shrugged his shoulders. "The young people didn't see it like that," he assured me. "Boys and girls just wanted to have fun, to amuse themselves."[90] These sentiments were confirmed by André Roussel, the grocer's son from Bléré, who showed me the old accordion he used to play at clandestine balls and lovingly squeezed a few chords out of it. "Many things were forbidden," he recalled, "but lots of things happened anyway." At the time, he said, he was only eighteen, and "at that age it's the time to live. The only thing that interested me was going out with girls and playing the accordion. . . . Those were the good old days, weren't they?"[91]

The official memories and the stories people tell have been, and continue to be, shaped by the dominant narrative of the "good French" who resisted or who supported the Resistance. There has always, however, been conflict as to who the "good French" were and what constituted good actions. The Free French considered their role more important than that of the internal Resistance. Gaullists vied with Communists and Pétainists for recognition as the most effective resisters. Some communities sought to associate themselves with Resistance heroes while others, who had suffered the fallout of Resistance activity, were torn between praising heroism and mourning the tragedy that had befallen them. Deportees who were deported for "acts of resistance" claimed superiority over political dissidents, labor conscripts, and Jews and exercised a sort of moral police in order to defend their position.

Conflicts over memory have not remained static in the years since the Liberation. The claim of resisters to deserve most public recognition because they were bravest has been challenged by Jews, on the grounds that they suffered the most. Suggestions that resisters may not have been as pure and heroic as they once seemed have also undermined their status. Meanwhile, in private, the Pétainist account of the Occupation has been voiced and may at some time be accorded a wider audience. Finally, the concept of the "poor French" enduring the hardships of *les années noires* has enjoyed much popularity with historians but should not be allowed to silence those who have spoken of the imagination, creativity, and resourcefulness of the inhabitants of occupied France. The least that can be claimed for oral history is that sometimes the vox populi may be allowed to guide historical reflection.

Conclusion

The main purpose of this book has been to break out of the straitjacket of interpretations based on the Resistance/collaboration version of events, while also refusing to reduce the French to passive victims of the Occupation, cold, hungry, and fearful. The model of "good French," "bad French," and "poor French" is very attractive but too simple to make sense of the diverse and contradictory experiences of ordinary people. I have tried to concentrate on the strategies they adopted, the networks they created, and the institutions they subverted in order to negotiate a tricky passage through the Occupation. As often as not this involved keeping one's options open, not committing oneself irretrievably either to resistance or to collaboration, playing a number of roles at once, changing direction as the occasion demanded. This interpretation does not seek to downgrade the serious ideological and political commitments that some people had but suggests only that prudence played a significant part in determining what decisions were made and when. Such an approach has the advantage of moving beyond praise and blame, which for a historian born several years after the war ended would seem anyway to be inappropriate. It tries to understand actions and sentiments in terms of the options and values that obtained under the Occupation, the one extremely limited and the other extremely fluid.

The first conclusion is that Franco-German relations under the Occupation were not always as brutal or even as one-sided as they have often been portrayed. Recent German research points in the same direction and reinforces the call for a reassessment.[1] The Germans were content to allow the French administration a certain autonomy, to practice indirect rule, so long as that administration delivered public order and resources. Indeed, it was felt that these were more likely to be delivered by means of good relations with the French, with their tacit consent, than by means of what was called "Polonization." The French administration, isolated from Vichy, had no alternative but to do business with the German military administration and, like indigenous chiefs under indirect colonial rule, occasionally found its authority thereby reinforced. Despite the heredity enmity between French and Germans, intensified by the ideology of Nazism, there was a countercurrent of mutual respect based on a common sense of military honor shared by veterans of 1914–18, a common European civilization, and sometimes a common religion, too. These relationships made it possible to defuse crises that arose when public order was threatened by either side. Prefects and mayors instructed French citizens how unwise it was to persist in graffiti campaigns or to demonstrate too openly. The consequences of deaths on each side were minimized by negotiation, especially when they seemed like accidents. Even when the military commander of Nantes was shot in October 1941, frantic negotiations at all levels saved the lives of a second batch of fifty hostages.

Ordinary French and Germans also learned to live together. German atrocities feared by the French population in the summer of 1940 never took place: troops arriving in towns and cities declared "open" by their municipalities were more likely to distribute cigarettes and sweets. The billeting of German troops on French families could be very trying, but there were cases of disruptive lodgers being moved on after appeal to the Kommandantur, and relations between German guests and French families were not always as icy as those described in *Le Silence de la mer*. The Germans requisitioned everything that could be requisitioned at various times, but they also gave lucrative contracts to French firms, did plentiful business with French people on the black market, and employed a vast array of French domestics, with whom relations sometimes became more intimate.

This interaction suggests that the French were not just the passive victims of the Occupation. Neither, however, were they only cynical collaborators. Informal rules were devised by the French governing what was legitimate and what illegitimate in Franco-German relations. As a rule of thumb, actions that undermined the family, community, or nation were illegitimate. On the economic front, it was deemed permissible for a firm to accept a contract to supply the Wehrmacht, provided the employer did not force his employees to work with undue zeal or put pressure on them to go work in Germany. To rip off the Germans by small-scale black marketeering was just Gallic cunning, but large-scale dealing that deprived the community of scarce resources was not considered right. Socially, it was acceptable to drink with a German in a bar but not to invite him home. If a German was billeted on a family it was not thought proper that he should dine at the family table. Flirting with Germans was normal and to have sex with them for money was not a crime, particularly as the German military was very worried about its men catching VD. Exaggerated merrymaking by French women and German soldiers was frowned on, however, while affairs with Germans by married women such as the wives of POWs was beyond the pale on every count.

This is not to deny the brutality of the Occupation or the imbalance of power between French and Germans; rather, these were both intensified as the Occupation dragged on. The German invasion of the Soviet Union, nullifying the Nazi-Soviet Pact, tipped some communists in France into a campaign of assassination directed against members of the Wehrmacht. It caused the Germans to increase their demands for resources and labor as they fought a total war and to seek to eliminate "enemies within," who were seen to be sabotaging their war effort, notably communists and Jews. The Germans gradually concluded that the French authorities were not able to guarantee the public order or to deliver supplies in the quantities they required. The French authorities were steadily swept aside as indirect rule gave way to direct rule and the German military was displaced by the secret police. A style of collaboration based on negotiation was replaced by

Diktat—the imposition of terms—or rather by collaboration with those elements of the French administration and police who alone were prepared to do the Germans' bidding. Most officials found themselves squeezed in a vise between the ruthlessness and insatiable demands of the Germans and the growing fear and anger of the population. They pretended to keep faith while doing what they could to protect the population. Some made contact with Resistance organizations or were fingered for the post-Liberation administration by Gaullist 'moles like Michel Debré. Such a double game was of course extremely dangerous: the German security police were highly sensitized to any evidence of disloyalty and increasingly put pressure on Vichy to remove unreliable officials or simply arrested and deported them. A small minority deserted their positions and went into hiding. By the summer of 1944 the Germans had only limited cooperation from French officials in the regions, who were preparing to switch their allegiance either to the Allied forces when they appeared or to de Gaulle's provisional government. All this led the way to a smooth transfer of power at the Liberation and ensured the continuity of the state.

The second conclusion is that from the perspective of occupied France the Vichy regime seems neither as authoritarian nor as reactionary as it perhaps looked in the Free Zone. Isolated from Vichy and without the transmission belt of the Légion, which was banned in the Occupied Zone, the French administration there had to fall back on the notables to ensure that the local population cooperated. These notables, whose influence was based less on party than on their independent standing in the community, served as mayors, municipal councillors, and members of prefects' vestigial administrative councils. Parliament had been abolished, but all national politicians had local power bases and these could not simply be uprooted. There might be something to be said for handing local government over to reactionaries in the interest of "work, family, and fatherland," but a conservative landowner who had influence in Brittany would have no purchase in Touraine. Similarly, a large industrial town needed a socialist mayor, so long as he "rallied" to the regime, not a representative of the employers who had no authority over the workforce. Under the Occupation, trimming was thus developed into a fine art.

As the Occupation wore on, however, the Vichy regime became less and less able to maintain adequate communications with local communities. It therefore replaced the small administrative commissions invented to advise prefects with larger departmental councils that were like the *conseils généraux* of the Third Republic, abolished in 1940, but now appointed rather than elected. The need to rebuild bridges to the political class of the Third Republic was felt particularly keenly by Pierre Laval when he returned to government in April 1942. Although he favored close collaboration with the Germans in the war against communists and Jews, he also realized that local politicians would gravitate en masse to the alternative government established by de Gaulle in Algiers unless Vichy gave them more reason to stay loyal. The Napoleonic experiment that removed the check of elective assemblies on prefects thus gave way to Vichy's search for a republican base.

The key function of the notables was to mediate between the demands of the Germans and the interests of local communities. If anyone acted as a shield under the Occupation, it was they rather than the marshal. In 1940 they protected their towns by persuading the retreating military not to defend them and declaring them "open" to the advancing Germans. Regularly they negotiated with the Germans to limit the number of horses, vehicles, or food they demanded or the quota of STO workers they wanted to draft. Whether the notables protected all citizens equally, however, is open to question. The distiction between "Vichy" and the "state" breaks down when considering local notables, who essentially represented one to the other. An interesting light is nevertheless cast on the responsibility of the French for the deportation of Jews by the fact that notables who protested the requisitioning of their farmers' grain and the conscription of their local youths for STO did not protest the Aryanization of local Jewish businesses or the deportation of the Jews in their midst.

The pressure on notables to, in effect, turn against their own communities became intolerable. Like officials, they also began to look to the future. Hence the departmental councils were dogged by absenteeism, and mayors resigned in droves. Vichy was unable to consolidate a republican base, and after the Liberation these trimmers were generally happy to rally to the new republican regime. Meanwhile the Liberation authorities, who initially had even less power than Vichy, were content to confirm them in office so long as they had not violated the minimum requirements of republican legitimacy. After all, they needed to bring over communities whose Pétainism had often been tenacious and to guarantee order against the revolutionary challenge of communism. The continuity of local elites across the turbulent years from 1935 to 1945 was thus remarkable. It was not until elections were held in more peaceful circumstances in 1945 that these notables, who had sacrificed consistency to longevity, were unceremoniously dumped by a popular vote that was seeking something fresh and untarnished. Even this, however, did not mean that the country suddenly lurched from left to right. Provided that they could demonstrate some association with the Resistance, parties of the center and right were able, in parts of the region at least, to ensure the continuity of conservatism.

The third conclusion is that, however great the hardships suffered by ordinary people under the Occupation, the monolithic concept of *les années noires* needs to be nuanced. The danger of this term is that it enshrines the image of the "poor French," paralyzed by cold, hunger, and fear. In spite of the repressive policies of both the Germans and Vichy, a civil society remained, old and new networks and associations were sustained and created, and different subcultures of workers, peasants, and youth developed. This is not to deny that the French were often cold, hungry, and fearful under the Occupation but to underline that they demonstrated imagination, resourcefulness, and Gallic cunning in order to make the Occupation livable.

When it came to getting daily bread, for example, the image of food lines should be replaced by the image of bicycles and trailers scouring the countryside. A whole series of parallel markets sprang up to counter the evils of requisitioning and price controls, both local and long-distance, setting to work relations between family members, neighbors, or profiteers. Again, there were winners and losers, exploiters and exploited, but everyone took part in Système D, which was far more flexible and responsive to people's needs than the official hunger market. Economic life was neither anarchic nor was it regimented, with workers and peasants marching in step to the prescriptions of the Labor Charter and the Peasant Corporation. Trade unions did not disappear under Vichy, which for some labor leaders was supposed to reach an apotheosis as a syndicalist state. Other labor leaders, including Catholic ones, remained totally suspicious of the Labor

Charter as the tool of trusts and the state and effectively put an end to it by insisting on their autonomy. Farmers, arguably, were more subtle. They went along with the Peasant Corporation but only to convert it to a vehicle for their own interests, to challenge the traditional domination of agricultural organization by landowners, and to defend the resources of the agricultural sector from the claws of the requisitioning agencies. Lastly, a more important economic role was undertaken by women, running farms and small businesses in the absence of their husbands in POW camps, despite Vichy's sermonizing about "*la femme au foyer.*"

Associational life was not confined to satisfying basic needs. The Occupation was a flourishing moment for sport, cinema, the theater, music, and dancing, sometimes in accordance with the policies of Vichy and the Germans, sometimes against them, and often exploiting the contradictions between the two. For as we have seen, while Vichy was obsessed with moral regeneration, the Germans were interested only in the security of their armed forces. The craze for clandestine dancing in particular demonstrates that the gloom and despondency that constituted Vichy's official policy was far from successful. French people, however, did not just indulge their hedonism. There was an explosion of religious activity, which was tolerated by the Germans and encouraged by Vichy but which represented for many of the faithful the best hope of deliverance from their current ills. The Catholic hierarchy was overwhelmingly Pétainist, but institutionally it offered protection from Nazism and many of the lower clergy and Catholic laity were active resisters. Above all, there was a massive development of prayer, of saint cults, of processions and pilgrimages as people turned to heaven for salvation from the bombs of the Allies as well as the bullets of the Germans. This religious upsurge was something that the Church was able to play on after the Liberation, mobilizing Catholic opinion, which had been trained in opposing antireligious ideologies, to defend church schools against another wave of republican anticlericalism.

Of course, solidarity extended only so far. The shock of defeat and Occupation caused horizons to contract: people resorted for material and emotional support to their family, neighborhood, village, town, or *pays*. This can be seen clearly when it came to charity. The Secours National was supposed to mobilize charitable giving on a national scale, under the benevolent eye of Marshal Pétain. But local communities were far readier to provide for their own needy or their own prisoners of war than for the needy and prisoners of war of France as a whole. Likewise, inland communities were often reluctant to take in evacuees from the bombed seaports of the Atlantic or refugees from the Normandy battles of 1944, and evacuees had to set up their own pressure groups to ensure that they were properly cared for by the local authorities whose charges they had become.

Communities also divided against themselves. Old rivalries and new threatened to undermine much collective work, such as that of the prisoner-of-war committee of Saint-Brévin-les-Pins. The presence of the Germans both attracted people into their orbit and antagonized others, who thought that they were violating the conventions of the local community. But the accusation of "Boche" leveled against a French man or woman could easily set in action a mechanism of denunciation of the offender to the Germans, his or her arrest, and an inevitable settling of accounts with the denouncer by the victim (if still alive) and by the community after the Germans had left. Communities also turned on those who were not fully integrated. This was the experience of many Jewish traders, artisans, and even company directors under the Aryanization laws. The enthusiasm of the French to squeeze out Jewish partners from company boards, to present themselves as agents for the liquidation and sale of Jewish businesses, and to apply to buy up such businesses seems as good a sign as any of the extent of popular anti-Semitism.

The narrowing of horizons and community conflicts did not exclude demonstrations of patriotism. In one sense the political antennae of the French people were never more finely attuned, but under the Occupation they had to be imaginative about how to reconstruct the French nation symbolically. Every V sign scrawled on a wall, every wreath smuggled beneath a statue of Joan of Arc, every tricolor flag or boutonniere sported for an hour, every glance exchanged at the appointed moment in a procession that pretended to be a crowd served to reflect the continued existence of the French nation to the French. As demands from the Germans increased, so the French took more to a more concrete but passive resistance. Hiding farm stocks targeted for requisition or sending the oldest horse, striking against the Relève, going underground rather than turn up for the STO, singing the "Marseillaise" on the STO, or failing to report back after a period of leave from work in Germany were all ways of undermining the German war machine that did not carry too many risks. Not all *réfractaires*, or draft dodgers, were *maquisards* and not all armed bands contributed anything to the Resistance. The Loire area, which is flat and lacks forests except on the frontier with Brittany, was not a good habitat for *maquisards* in the way that the Massif Central or the Alps were. Armed attacks on retreating German units in the summer of 1944 brought the region its fair share of collective reprisals and made local communities very ambivalent toward the armed struggle. Liberation, in the end, came less from French insurgents, who in any case had difficulty acquiring weapons, than from the industrial firepower of the Allies. In this context, the steady pounding of the German military-industrial base from the air, inflicting substantial collateral damage on the French population, was a vital prelude to the land assault of June 1944.

The last observation to be made is that from the point of view of ordinary French people the Liberation was a mixture of joy and disappointment. The joy is evident on the smiling faces in myriad pictures of the French welcoming the liberating forces into their towns and villages and dancing in the streets. The disappointment, however, was also very real— not only because dancing remained formally banned until the end of the war in Europe but because hundreds of thousands of people remained homeless, shortages and the black market did not disappear overnight, and POWs, conscripted workers, and deportees did not return to a home fit for heroes. But the gospel of Resistance and Liberation was already over-laying the complexities of the Occupation and it would be a long time before all the truths were out.

ABBREVIATIONS

AD	Archives Départementales
A.Dio.	Archives Diocésaines
AM	Archives Municipales
AN	Archives Nationales
BAMA	Bundesarchiv-Militärarchiv
CDAA	Comité Départemental d'Action Agricole
CDL	Comité Départemental de Libération
CFLN	Comité Français de Libération Nationale
CFTC	Confédération Française des Travailleurs Chrétiens
CGA	Confédération Générale de l'Agriculture
CGMO	Commissariat Générale à la Main d'Oeuvre
CGPF	Confédération Générale du Patronat Français
CGQJ	Commissariat Général aux Questions Juives
CGT	Confédération Générale du Travail
CHDGM	Comité d'Histoire de la Deuxième Guerre Mondiale
CHOLF	Comité d'Histoire de l'Occupation et de la Libération de la France
CIEE	Comité Interprofessionnel d'Épuration des Entreprises

CIMT	Compagnie Industrielle de Matériel de Transport
CNR	Conseil National de la Résistance
CO	Comité d'Organisation
COSI	Comité Ouvrier de Secours Immédiat
COSR	Comité des Oeuvres Sociales de la Résistance
CVR	Combattant Volontaire de la Résistance
DGGFTO	Délégué Général du Gouvernement Français dans les Territoires Occupées
FFI	Forces Françaises de l'Intérieur
FNC	Fédération Nationale Catholique
FNDIR	Fédération Nationale des Déportés et Internés de la Résistance
FNDIRP	Fédération Nationale des Déportés et Internés de la Résistance Patriotes
FNSEA	Fédération Nationale des Syndicats d'Exploitants Agricoles
FTPF	Francs-Tireurs et Partisans Français
IHTP	Institut d'Histoire du Temps Présent
I-et-L	Indre-et-Loire
I-et-V	Ille-et-Vilaine
JAC	Jeunesse Agricole Chrétienne
JEC	Jeunesse Étudiante Chrétienne
JOC	Jeunesse Ouvrière Chrétienne
L-A	Loire-Atlantique
L-I	Loire-Inférieure
LVF	Ligue des Volontaires Français contre le Bolchévisme
M-et-L	Maine-et-Loire
MNPD	Mouvement National des Prisonniers de Guerre et des Déportés
MRP	Mouvement Républicain Populaire
ORA	Organisation de la Résistance Armée
PPF	Parti Populaire Français
PSF	Parti Social Français
SFIO	Section Française de l'Internationale Ouvrière
SNCASO	Société Nationale de Construction Aéronautique du Sud-Ouest
STO	Service du Travail Obligatoire
UNC	Union Nationale des Combattants
UNMRAC	Union Nationale des Mutilés, Réformés et Anciens Combattants

NOTES

NaN*Introduction*

1. Letter of Marcel Girard to the author, 13 Jan. 1998.
2. Interview with Georges Audebert (b. 1913), Tours, 24 June 1998.
3. *La Nouvelle République*, 20 Mar. 1998.
4. For a comparative view, see Timothy Garton Ash, "Trials, Purges, and History Lessons," in his *History of the Present: Essays, Sketches, and Dispatches from Europe in the 1990s* (London: Penguin, 2000), 294–314.
5. See, for example, Henri Michel, *Histoire de la Résistance, 1940–1944* (Paris: PUF, 1950).
6. Robert O. Paxton, *Vichy France: Old Guard and New Order, 1940–1944* (London: Barrie and Jenkins, 1972). Sarah Farmer et al., eds., *France at War: Vichy and the Historians* (Oxford and New York: Berg, 2000) is a Festschrift for Paxton.
7. The key text on this subject is Henry Rousso, *The Vichy Syndrome: History and Memory in France since 1944* (Cambridge, Mass.: Harvard UP, 1991). See also Eric Conan and Henry Rousso, *Vichy: Un passé qui ne passe pas* (Paris: Fayard, 1994), and Henry Rousso, *La Hantise du passé* (Paris: Textuel, 1998).
8. On these debates, see Thierry Wolton, *Le Grand Recrutement* (Paris: Grasset, 1993); Gérard Chauvy, *Aubrac: Lyon 1943* (Paris: Albin Michel, 1997); Pierre

Péan, *Vies et morts de Jean Moulin* (Paris: Fayard, 1998); and Daniel Cordier, *Jean Moulin: La République des catacombes* (Paris: Gallimard, 1999).

9. Michael Marrus and Robert Paxton, *Vichy France and the Jews* (New York: Basic Books, 1981); Serge Klarsfeld, *Vichy-Auschwitz: Le rôle de Vichy dans la solution finale de la question juive en France*, 2 vols. (Paris: Fayard, 1983–85). See also Paul Webster, *Petain's Crime: The Full Story of French Collaboration in the Holocaust* (London: Macmillan, 1990).

10. *Le Monde*, 18 July 1995.

11. *Le Monde*, 21 Oct. 1997. On the Papon trial, see Richard Golsan, *The Papon Affair: Memory and Justice on Trial* (New York: Routledge, 2000); Gérard Boulanger, *Maurice Papon, un technocrate français sous l'Occupation* (Paris: Seuil, 1994), and his *Papon: Un intrus dans la République* (Paris: Seuil, 1997); Jean-Jacques Gandini, *Le Procès Papon* (Paris: Librio, 1999); Arno Klarsfeld, *La Cour, les nains, et le bouffon* (Paris: Laffont, 1998); and Maurice Papon, *La Vérité n'intéressait personne* (Paris: Bergès, 1999).

12. Conan and Rousso, *Vichy: Un passé qui ne passe pas*, 268–75.

13. *Le Monde*, 28 Oct. 1997.

14. See Jean-Pierre Azéma and François Bédarida, eds., *Vichy et les français* (Paris: Fayard, 1992).

15. Dominique Veillon, *Vivre et Survivre en France, 1939–1947* (Paris: Payot, 1995), 105.

16. Jean Guéhenno, *Journal des Années noires* (Paris: Gallimard, 1947); Henry Rousso, *Les Années noires: Vivre sous l'Occupation* (Paris: Gallimard, 1992); Jean-Pierre Azéma and François Bédarida, *La France des années noires*, 2 vols. (Paris: Seuil, 1993); Julian Jackson, *The Dark Years, 1940–1944* (Oxford: Oxford UP, 2001).

17. AD M-et-L 95W63, prefect of M-et-L to subprefect of Cholet, 18 Dec. 1946; police captain of Cholet to subprefecture, 26 Dec. 1946.

18. See especially the 72AJ series in the Archives Nationales.

19. Alistair Thomson, "Unreliable Memories? The Use and Abuse of Oral History," in William Lamont, ed., *Historical Controversies and Historians* (London: UCL Press, 1998), 23–34. See also, in general, Peter Thompson, *The Voice of the Past* (Oxford: Oxford UP, 1988), and Elizabeth Tonkin, *Narrating Our Pasts* (Cambridge: Cambridge UP, 1992)

20. *Le Courrier de l'Ouest*, 3 April 1997.

21. Interviews with Andrée Trudeau, Saumur, 22 June 1998; Lucienne Despouy, Saint-Avertin, Tours, 9 June 1997; and Thérèse Boucher, Angers, 12 Dec. 1996.

22. Interview with André Chardonnnet (b. 1917), Angers, 11 April 1997.

23. Michelle Mouton and Helena Pohlandt-McCormick, "Boundary Crossings: Oral History of Nazi Germany and Apartheid South Africa—A Comparative Perspective," *History Workshop Journal* 48 (1999): 41–63.

24. Karl Figlio, "Oral History and the Unconscious," *History Workshop Journal* 26 (1988): 120–32.

25. See, for example, Marc Ferro, *Pétain* (Paris: Fayard, 1987); Nick Atkin, *Pétain* (London: Longman, 1998); Fred Kupferman, *Laval* (Paris: Balland, 1987); Hervé Coutau-Bégarie and Claude Huan, *Darlan* (Paris: Fayard, 1989); George E. Melton, *Darlan: Admiral and Statesman of France* (London: Praeger, 1998); Jean-Paul Brunet, *Jacques Doriot* (Paris: Balland, 1986); Daniel Cordier, *Jean Moulin: L'inconnu du Panthéon* (Paris: Lattès, 1989).

26. Philippe Burrin, *Living with Defeat: France under the German Occupation, 1940–1944* (London: Arnold, 1996).

27. Pierre Laborie, *L'Opinion française sous Vichy* (Paris: Seuil, 1990).

28. See Yves Durand, *Vivre au Pays au XVIIIe siècle* (Paris: PUF, 1984), and, importing the concept, Charles Pythian-Adams, ed., *Societies, Culture, and Kinship, 1580–1850* (Leicester: Leicester UP, 1993).

29. C. J. Calhoun, "Community: Towards a Variable Conceptualization for Comparative Research," *Social History* 5 (1980): 105–29. See also David Garrioch, *Neighbourhood and Community in Paris, 1740–1790* (Cambridge: Cambridge UP, 1986), 4–6.

30. Michèle Cointet, *Vichy capitale, 1940–1944* (Paris: Perrin, 1993).

31. On First World War atrocities, see Ruth Harris, "The 'Child of the Barbarian': Rape, Race and Nationalism during the First World War," *Past and Present* 141 (Nov. 1993): 170–206; Stéphane Audoin-Rouzeau, *L'Enfant de l'ennemi* (Paris: Aubier, 1995); and John Horne and Alan Kramer, *German Atrocities 1914: A History of Denial* (New Haven and London: Yale UP, 2001).

32. See the survey of the Institut d'Histoire du Temps Présent, *Les Élites local dans la tourmente du Front Populaire aux années cinquante*, ed., Gilles Le Beguec and Denis Peschanski (Paris: CNRS, 2000). For a suggestive anthropological approach, see Marc Abélès, *Quiet Days in Burgundy: A Study of Local Politics* (Paris and Cambridge: Éditions de la Maison des Sciences de l'Homme/Cambridge UP, 1991).

33. On denunciation, see L. J. Colanéri and G. Gérante, *La Dénonciation et les dénonciateurs* (Paris: PUF, 1948); André Halimi, *La Dénonciation sous l'Occupation* (Paris: Alain Moreau, 1983); and Sheila Fitzpatrick and Robert Gellately, eds., *Accusatory Practices* (Chicago and London: University of Chicago Press, 1997).

CHAPTER 1 *Encounter*

1. Charles de Gaulle, *Discours et messages I, juin 1940–janvier 1946* (Paris: Plon, 1970), 4.

2. AD L-A 75W560, prefect of L-I to DGGFTO, 23 July 1940.

3. Marinette Rameau, "Journal de Guerre," 17 June 1940.

4. Fonds Goxe, Angers, Ninette Bordereau to Camille Charpentier, president of the Angers Tribunal de Commerce, 19 July 1940.

5. See below, p. 367–68.

6. Elie Chamard, *Les Combats de Saumur* (Paris: Berger-Levrault, 1948), 8, 27–28, 127–32. Note that the reference to "little rabbits" was removed by the municipality in Michel Ancelin's account in *Saumur 1990*, 33–35.

7. Winston S. Churchill, *Their Finest Hour*, vol. 2 of *The Second World War*, (London: Cassell, 1949); 158–62; Martin Gilbert, *Winston S. Churchill VI. 1939–1941* (London: Heinemann, 1983), 526–38; Sir Edward Spears, *Assignment to Catastrophe II* (London: Heinemann, 1954), 208–31; Paul Baudouin, *Neuf Mois au gouvernement, avril–décembre 1940* (Paris: Éditions de la Table Ronde, 1948), 152–66. Paul Reynaud, *Au Coeur de la mêlée, 1930–1945* (Paris: Flammarion, 1951), 764–84, denies that he asked to be allowed to sue for an armistice.

8. Philippe Pétain, *Actes et Écrits*, ed. Jacques Isorni (Paris: Fayard, 1974), 448; Marc Ferro, *Pétain* (Paris: Fayard, 1987), 75–78.

9. Louis Chollet, *Les Heures tragiques: Tours, juin 1940* (Tours: Arrault et Cie, 1946), 38.

10. Elizabeth Prat and Jeannine Labussière, *Tours, cité meurtrie, juin 1940* (Chambray-lès-Tours, 1991)

11. AN AJ40/571, M. Collon, chief librarian and archivist of Tours, to Minister of Public Instruction, 2 Oct. 1940.

12. Chollet, *Les Heures tragiques*, 88–9; Jérôme Guillard, "Les Catholiques tourangeaux pendant la Deuxième Guerre Mondiale," master's thesis, University of Tours, 1996, 33–5; Michèle Cointet, *L'Église sous Vichy, 1940–1945* (Paris: Perrin, 1998), 14–15.

13. AM Tours, Bulletin municipal de la Ville de Tours, 8 July 1940.

14. AM Tours, Livre d'Or offert à Ferdinand Morin, maire de Tours, par ces concitoyens, 1941. Presented at council meeting, 2 July 1941.

15. AM Chinon, Registre des délibérations du conseil municipal, 4 Sept., 12 Nov. 1940.

16. Marinette Rameau, "Journal de Guerre," 18 June 1940.

17. AM Angers, Conseil municipal, 18 June 1940.

18. AD M-et-L 116J9, CHDGM, "Extrait du Journal illustré bimensuel," *Die Wehrmacht*, no. 25 (4 Dec. 1940); Michel Lemesle, *Chronique d'Angers sous l'Occupation, 1939–1945* (Angers: Philippe Petit, 1972), 44–58.

19. *Le Petit Courrier*, 20 June 1940.

20. Fonds Goxe, Marcel Moncany, wholesale hatter, to M. Charpentier, president of the Tribunal de Commerce, Angers, 24 July 1940.

21. AM Angers, Conseil municipal, 8 Aug. 1940.

22. Churchill, *Their Finest Hour*, 123, 161, 169.

23. Edmond Duméril, *Journal d'un honnête homme pendant l'Occupation, juin 1940–août 1944* (Thonon-les-Bains: L'Albaron/Société Présence du Livre, 1990), 28.

24. A. Dio. Nantes, Livre de Paroisse, Ste-Croix, entry by Abbé Jean Luneau, 19 June 1940.

25. AD L-A 13W40, police reports, 21 and 22 June 1940.

26. AN 72AJ 144, report of meeting of municipal council, Nantes, 20 June 1940.

NOTES

27. Livre de Paroisse, Ste-Croix, 26–27 June 1940.

28. AD L-A 75W551, circular of Feldkommandant, 8 July 1940.

29. AD L-A 13W40, Jean Loutrel to mayor of Nantes, 23 Sept. 1941.

30. AM Nantes 38W5, note of assistant mayor Duchemin on meeting with Feld-kommandant, 31 Aug. 1940; AD L-A 27J18, "Carnets de M. Soil, secrétaire général de la mairie de Nantes," n.d., 31 Aug., 1 Sept. 1940.

31. AN AJ40 544, Feldkommandant of Nantes to chief of Bezirk B, Angers, 12 and 16 Oct. 1940, Bezirk B to Miltärbefehlshaber, Paris, 28 Nov. 1940; AD L-A 13W26, résumé of the "affaire Pageot"; Duméril, *Journal d'un honnête homme*, 67–71.

32. Heinrich Bucheler, *Carl-Heinrich von Stülpnagel: Soldat, Philosoph, Verschwörer* (Berlin: Ullstein, 1989).

33. AD M-et-L 116J9, CHDGM, H. Godivier, "Occupation de Segré par les alle-mands" (MS, 11 pp., n.d.).

34. See, in general, on the German military administration, Hans Umbreit, *Der Militärbefehlshaber in Frankreich, 1940–1944* (Boppard-am-Rhein, 1968), and Rita Thalmann, *La Mise au pas: Idéologie et stratégie sécuritaire dans la France occupée* (Paris: Fayard, 1991).

35. Louis Oury, *Le Cours des cinquante otages/Die Strasse der fünfzig Geiseln* (Saar-brücken: Geschichts Werkstatt, 1989), 22–23; Oury, *Rue du Roi Albert* (Paris: Le Temps des Cerises, 1996), 20–21.

36. Yves de Sesmaisons, *Marquise de Sesmaisons, 1898–1977: Souvenirs de l'Occupation* (Craon, 1978).

37. Interview with Marquis Donatien de Sesmaisons and General Yves de Sesmai-sons, Nantes, 16 July 1998.

38. Duméril, *Journal d'un honnête homme*, 30–31, 101–02, 129.

39. See below, pp. 198–99.

40. A. Dio. Nantes, Mgr. Villepelet, "Le Diocèse de Nantes. 1940–1945," 18 Dec. 1941. See also Laurent Berger, "L'Episcopat Nantais de Mgr Villepelet, 1936–1966," master's thesis, University of Nantes, 1991.

41. F. D. Lugard, *The Dual Mandate in British Tropical Africa* (Edinburgh and Lon-don: William Blackwood and Sons, 1922), ch. 10.

42. AD M-et-L 24W1, Roussillon to Interior Minister, 4 Dec. 1940.

43. AD M-et-L 24W4, reports of Roussillon to Interior Minister, 9 May, 1 July, and 28 Sept. 1941.

44. Report of Jean Chaigneau, 3 Dec. 1941, cited in Claude Morin, *Les Allemands en Touraine, 1940–1944* (Chambray-lès-Tours: CLD, 1996), 30.

45. AD I-et-LXVZ27, report of Feldkommandant Marloh to chief of District B, Angers, 13 Nov. 1940.

46. Interview with Émile Aron, Tours, 24 June 1998.

47. AD L-A 75W551, posters signed by General Braemer, end of June 1940; Kom-mandantur of Nantes to town hall of Nantes, 28 June 1940.

48. AD I-et-L 10W7, circulars of General de la Laurencie, 2 Sept. and 9 Oct. 1940. On international law and occupation, see Gerhard von Glahn, *The Occupation*

of Enemy Territory (Minneapolis: University of Minnesota Press, 1957), and Karma Nabulsi, *Traditions of War: Occupation, Resistance, and the Law* (Oxford: Oxford UP, 1999).

49. Marc-Olivier Baruch, *Servir l'État français: L'administration en France de 1940 à 1944* (Paris: Fayard, 1997), 90–95.

50. AN Fla 3664, Armistice Commission, 2 Aug. and 23 Dec. 1941.

51. AD L-A 13W41, Meeting at Feldkommandantur of Nantes, 26 Feb. 1942, Feldkommandant to prefect, 27 Feb. 1941.

52. AM Nantes 9Z1, Guineaudeau to CHOLF, 9 Dec. 1948.

53. AD L-A 243W163, cases of André Lenglart, Oct.–Dec. 1940, and Arthur Martineau, Oct. 1940–July 1941; 13W21, case of Abbé Tourillon, March 1941.

54. AD M-et-L 80W40, Fernand de Brinon to prefect of M-et-L, 23 May 1941.

55. AD I-et-L 10W5, military court councillor of Tours to procureur de la République, Chinon, 14 Oct. 1941.

56. AD M-et-L 24W2, report of prefect of M-et-L, 28 Sept. 1941; 7U4 1–2, Registre des arrêtés rendus par le Tribunal spécial de la Cour d'Appel d'Angers, 2 Oct. 1941.

57. AD M-et-L 18W27, subprefect of Saumur to prefect, 30 Dec. 1940.

58. AD M-et-L 18W29, subprefect of Saumur to prefect, 1 March 1941; Kloss to Roussillon, 5 March; Roussillon to Kloss, 5 March; Kloss to Roussillon, 15 March 1941. AD I-et-L XV Z 21. Kreiskommandant of Saumur to Kloss, 4 March 1941.

59. AD M-et-L 18W29, subprefect of Cholet to prefect, 1 March 1941; prefect to Interior Minister, 4 March; AD I-et-L XV Z 21, von Trotha to Kloss, 3 and 14 March; Kloss to chief of District B, Angers, 4 March and 21 March 1941; A. Darmaillacq, *Cholet sous l'Occupation* (Cholet, 1946; rpt. 1991), 39–40.

CHAPTER 2 *Cohabitation*

1. Vercors [Jean Bruller], *Le Silence de la mer* (Paris: Éditions de Minuit, 1942).

2. Marinette Rameau, "Journal de Guerre," 21 July 1940.

3. Interview with Marinette Rameau, Charcé (M-et-L), 28 Nov. 1996.

4. Rameau, "Journal de Guerre," 5 May, 12 June, 7 July 1944.

5. AD I-et-L 52W48, survey by prefect of I-et-L, Sept.–Oct. 1940.

6. AD M-et-L 148J, CD2eGM, "Enquête de 1948 sur l'histoire de l'Occupation et de la Libération dans le département de Maine-et-Loire."

7. AD M-et-L 116J9, H. Granger [secretary of the town hall], "Une Commune d'Anjou pendant la Guerre, l'Occupation, la Libération: Nyoiseau" (MS, n.d.).

8. AD L-A 13W20, Major Graf Spee to Kommandant of Nantes and Kommandant of Nantes to prefect of L-I, both 27 July 1940.

9. AD M-et-L 95W108, duc de Blacas to subprefect of Cholet, 16 July and 14 Sept. 1940.

10. Collection Lemesle, Helmut Voss, "Truppenbelegung in Stadt und Arrondisse-

ment Angers," in documentation from the Kommandantur of Angers taken in Aug. 1944 by General de Coulange, military attaché to General Bradley.

11. Rameau, "Journal de Guerre," 18 July 1940.

12. AD M-et-L 140W94, Colonel de Sauvebeuf to Feldkommandantur of Angers, 21 Aug. 1940.

13. Interview with Odette Goxe (b. 1907), Angers, 14 April 1997.

14. Ludwig Tewes, *Frankreich in der Besatzungszeit, 1940–1943: Die Sicht deutscher Augenzeugen* (Bonn: Bouvier, 1998), 107, 140, 144, 157, 387. See also Wolfgang Geiger, *L'Image de la France dans l'Allemagne nazie* (Rennes: Presses Universitaires de Rennes, 1999), and Bertram M. Gordon, "Ist Gott französich? Germans, Tourism and Occupied France, 1940–1944," *Modern and Contemporary France*, vol. 4, no. 3 (1996): 288–98.

15. Collection Michel Lemesle, Helmut Radssat to Lemesle, 16 Feb. 1972; Helmut Voss to Lemesle, 19 July 1973.

16. Rameau, "Journal de Guerre," 17 Oct. 1942.

17. Interview with Michel Leterme, Angers, 13 May 1997.

18. Interview with Jacques Hervé, Tours, 12 June 1996.

19. Léon Mousseau, *Le Pont cassé: Souvenirs d'un médecin des bords de Loire* (Angers: J. Palussière, 1981), 35.

20. Collection Michel Lemesle, *Sturmmarch zur Loire* [history of the Sixth Infantry Division of the Thirty-eighth Army Corps in 1940] (Berlin: Verlag Die Wehrmacht KG, 1941), 142.

21. See above, pp. 23–24.

22. Collection Michel Lemesle, Helmut Voss, "Angers" [history of the Sixth Pioneer Battalion], MS, n.d.

23. Claude Morin, *Les Allemands en Touraine, 1940–1944* (Chambray-lès-Tours: CLD, 1996), 196.

24. Jean Texcier, *Conseils à l'occupé* (Paris: 1940), *conseil* 10. Richard Cobb, *French and Germans, Germans and French* (Hanover and London: UP of New England, 1983), 65–67, and Hanna Diamond, *Women and the Second World War in France, 1939–1948: Choices and Constraints* (Harlow: Pearson 1999), 82–86; also see the need to reassess the significance of sexual relations between French and Germans.

25. Interview with Marinette Rameau, 28 Oct. 1996.

26. AD I-et-L 1119W5, reports of gendarmerie of Ligueil, 31 Oct. and 7 Nov. 1944.

27. AD M-et-L 7U4/26, case of M-L Coisnault before Chambre civique of Angers, 14 March 1945.

28. AD L-A 13W19, subprefect of Saint-Nazaire to prefect of L-I, 24 March 1941.

29. AD I-et-L 1119W25, depositions for Cour de Justice of I-et-L in the case of Mme Longuépée by Mehmed Kapandji, 8 Jan. 1945, E. Ponset, 16 Nov. 1944, and Leopold Florens, 16 Nov. 1944.

30. AD I-et-L 10W84, postal inspector Pouyol to departmental director of the PTT,

Barra, 20 June 1941; report of Barra to prefect, 25 June 1941; Pouyol to Barra, 8 Aug. 1941; Barra to prefect, 21 Aug. 1941.

31. AD I-et-L 10W84, subprefect Cay to prefect, 20 Aug. 1941.

32. AD I-et-L 46W94, Captain Arlot of Tours gendarmerie to prefect, 2 Aug. 1944.

33. AD I-et-L 1119W25, trials of Simone Peltier, Madeleine Longuépée, and Adalbert Chevalier.

34. AD L-A 13W41, report of commissaire principal, Nantes, 22 Sept. 1941.

35. AD M-et-L 80W37, Kommandantur of Angers to police chief, Angers, 8 July 1940; text of poster placed in brothels forwarded by chief to prefect of M-et-L, 27 Aug. 1940; weekly statistics on prostitution in Angers, 13 July 1940–1 Aug. 1941.

36. AD M-et-L 12W20, Ernst to regional prefect of Angers, 10 July 1943; police chief Cholet to police intendant, Angers, 18 July 1943; regional prefect to Ernst, 19 July 1943.

37. AD L-A 13W41, Lieutenant Pana of Ancenis gendarmerie to prefect of L-I, 3 and 17 April 1943; letters of mayor and Dr. Chauveau also on file.

38. AD M-et-L 12W3, prefect of L-I to Interior Minister, 1 April 1942.

39. AD I-et-V 217W217, Chambre civique of L-I, La Baule police reports on Mme Deflandre, May 1945.

40. AD I-et-L 52W3, curé of Le Loroux (I-et-L) to Pétain, 4 Oct. 1940; director of agricultural services to prefect, 9 Dec. 1940.

41. AD L-A 13W40, prefect of L-I to General de La Laurencie, 4 Nov. 1940.

42. AD L-A 13W20, Mme Bar of École Normale d'Institutrices of Nantes to prefect of L-I, 19 Oct. 1940; report of Duméril on his interview with Hotz, 18 Oct. 1940.

43. AD M-et-L 7U4/95, gendarmerie report of 28 Feb. 1945. Odile Talon was sentenced to two years in prison at the Liberation for collaboration.

44. René Leprince, ed., *La Pommeraye dans la Guerre par ceux quil'ont vécue* (Bibliothèque de La Pommeraye, 1995), 75.

45. BAMA Freiburg RH36/312, Feldkommandantur of Nantes, report on food supply and agriculture, 7 Aug. 1940.

46. Collection Michel Lemesle, Angers. Helmuth Voss, "Weinachten 1940: Der Heimat einen Gruss aus Frankreich."

47. AD I-et-L III Z 1, reports of Feldkommandant Kloss, Angers, 29 July and 19 Sept. 1940.

48. AD I-et-L 52W52, Feldkommandant Witter of Tours to prefect of I-et-L Chaigneau, 5 Dec. 1940, and reply of prefect, 17 Dec. 1940; AD M-et-L 95W76, Kreiskommandant of Cholet to subprefect Hudson, 17 Nov. 1941; circular of Hudson to mayors, 19 Nov. 1941; and their replies, Nov.–Dec. 1941.

49. AD I-et-L XV Z 27, Propagandastaffel of Bezirk B, Angers, to Feldkommandant of Tours, 25 Nov. and 11 Dec. 1941.

50. AD L-A 65W11, dossier on campaigns against Colorado beetle, June 1941–June 1944.

51. AD I-et-L 10W5, Dr. Herbig to prefect of I-et-L, 14 Sept. 1940, 2 May 1941; prefect Chaigneau to mayors, 17 June 1941.

52. BAMA Freiburg RH36/312, report of Feldkommandantur of Nantes, 23 June 1943. Other Germans were aghast that French toilets were just holes in the ground. See Tewes, *Frankreich in der Besatzungszeit*, 107.

53. AD I-et-L XIV Z29, reports of Feldkommandant Marloh of Tours, 14 and 31 Oct. 1940.

54. AD M-et-L 54W11, Jaujard, director of the Musées Nationaux, to prefect of M-et-L, 3 Dec. 1940.

55. AD I-et-L XIV Z29, list of 31 Jan. 1942.

56. AD M-et-L 97W79, subprefect of Saumur to president of special delegation of Saumur, 19 Feb. 1941.

57. *Le Chinonais*, 15 and 29 Jan. 1942, 4 June 1942.

58. AN Fla 3658, list of statues for conservation and melting down, 1 March 1942.

59. BAMA Freiburg RH36/312, report of Kriegsverwaltungsrat Dr. Jung, 7 Aug. 1940.

60. AD M-et-L 95W109, report of chief engineer of bridges and roads, 7 May 1941.

61. AN Fla 3669 and AD M-et-L 12W2, Feldkommandantur of Tours to prefect of I-et-L, 22 Feb. 1942, and reply, 3 March 1942.

62. BAMA Freiburg RW24/126, orders from German army, navy, and air force, 24 Aug. 1940–20 Feb. 1941.

63. BAMA Freiburg RW24/122, war diary of Rüstungsinspektion B (southwest France), 24 Feb.–2 March 1941, 21–27 April 1941.

64. BAMA Freiburg RH36/512, orders on notepaper of Veltrup-Werke K.G., Aachen, May 1942–May 1944.

65. BAMA Freiburg RH36/511, list of 29 Sept. 1941; RH24/174, war diary of Rüstungskommando of Le Mans, 7 Sept. 1942.

66. AD M-et-L 74W2, report on Entreprises Dodin by subcommission of Comité interprofessionnel d'épuration dans les entreprises, n.d but early 1945; AD L-A 132W161, report of police chief of the Renseignements Généraux, Nantes, 8 Jan. 1945.

67. AD L-A 13W8, anonymous report to DGGFTO, May 1941.

68. AM Nantes 38W27, report of M. Helbert, Nov. 1944.

69. BAMA Freiburg RW24/176, war diary of Rüstungskommando of Le Mans, 24–30 Jan. and 21–31 March 1943.

70. A. Beltran, R. Frank, and H. Rousso, *La Vie des entreprises sous l'Occupation: Une enquête à l'échelle locale* (Paris: Belin, 1944), 22–23, 386. See also Renaud de Rochebrune and Jean-Clause Hazera, *Face aux allemands*, vol. 1 of *Les Patrons sous l'Occupation* (Paris: Odile Jacob, 1997), 573–76.

71. Jacques Delarue, *Trafics et crimes sous l'Occupation* (Paris: Fayard, 1993), concentrates on the Bureau Otto buying agency of the Abwehr and big-time crooks such as the Russian Jew Mendel Skolnikoff but examines only the tip of the iceberg.

72. AD L-A 96W13, note of officer of civil affairs, district of La Baule, 15 April 1945.

73. AD I-et-V 217W218, Chambre civique of L-I, report of gendarmerie of Pont-Rousseau, 29 Sept. 1944, and report of police inspector of the Renseignements Généraux, 6 April 1945. Couturier received twenty years' national degradation.

74. AD M-et-L 48W34, report of Renseignements Généraux, 27 Nov. 1944.

75. AD I-et-L 46W112, reports of Captain Arlot of Tours gendarmerie, 8 May and 21 Sept. 1944.

76. AD L-A 132W161, prefect of L-I to president of Comité de Confiscation des Profits Illicites, 12 Feb. 1945.

77. AD I-et-V 217W217, Chambre civique of L-I, report of gendarmerie of Coueron, 28 Dec. 1944.

78. AD I-et-V, Cour de Justice of L-I, report of gendarmerie of Le Pellerin, 8 Dec. 1944.

79. Burrin, Living with Defeat, 197.

80. Burrin, Living with Defeat, 207.

CHAPTER 3 *Separation*

1. Fonds Goxe, Ninette Bordereau to M. et Mme Camille Charpentier, 19 July 1940; handwritten account of the events of 2 July in Angers by Odette Goxe given to the author, 3 May 1997.

2. AD I-et-L 10W33, Feldkommandant Marloh of Tours to prefect, 2 July 1940.

3. AD I-et-L 52W52, Feldkommandant of Tours to prefect, 20 July, and reply, 30 July 1940.

4. AD L-A 13W8, Elizabeth Walter to secretary-general of the prefecture, 25 Nov. 1940. The prefect was told by Fernand de Brinon on 14 Dec. that the Germans had no intention of exerting pressure on Alsatians and Lorrainers.

5. AD L-A 13W15, undated report of prefecture [Oct. 1940]; AD I-et-L III Z 1, situation report of Feldkommandantur of Angers, 19 Oct. 1940.

6. La Gilette, Via Dolorosa: De Nantes à Châteaubriant (juin–juillet 1940) (Fontenay-le-Comte, 1945), 25.

7. AN 72AJ145, departmental inspector of hygiene to doctor-general in charge of the Nantes region, 30 June 1940.

8. Mgr Villepelet, "Le Diocèse de Nantes, 1940–1945," entry for 10 July 1940.

9. AD L-A 13W15, mayor of Sucé in reply to prefect's circular of 20 Feb. 1941. See also AN 72AJ147, "L'Oeuvre d'une française sous l'Occupation: Mme de Sesmaisons" (anonymous account of 21 Nov. 1944), and Yves de Sesmaisons, Marquise de Sesmaisons, 1898–1977: Souvenirs de l'Occupation (Craon, 1978), 8.

10. AN 72AJ145, "Mouvement Bouvron, Nantes—historique," from collection of CHOLF, Nantes. See also Fernand Ridel, Témoignages 1939–1945: Une Page d'histoire (La Baule: Éditions des Paludiers, 1974).

11. AN F9 3064, Commissariat Général aux Prisonniers de Guerre Rapatriés et aux Familles des Prisonniers de Guerre. Statistics 1 Nov. 1942. See Yves Durand,

La Vie quotidienne des prisonniers de guerre dans les stalags, oflags et kommandos, 1939–1945 (Paris: Hachette, 1994).

12. Sarah Fishman, *We Will Wait: Wives of French Prisoners of War, 1940–1945* (New Haven and London: Yale UP, 1991).

13. See Miranda Pollard, *Reign of Virtue: Mobilizing Gender in Vichy France* (Chicago and London: University of Chicago Press, 1998), and Francine Muel-Dreyfus, *Vichy et l'éternel féminin* (Paris: Seuil, 1996).

14. AD M-et-L 24W11, Mme Bonin of Trélazé to prefect of Maine-et-Loire, 14 Oct. 1941.

15. A. Dio Tours 1D6, Mgr Gaillard to Feldkommandantur of Tours, 15 and 22 Aug. 1940, and to Red Cross in Paris, 18 Sept. 1940.

16. AD I-et-L 10W33, Oberleutnant Brucher to prefect of I-et-L, 13 Aug. 1940; AD M-et-L 24W11, circular of prefect of Roussillon, 18 Sept. 1940, on new regulations of Feldkommandant Kloss, 12 Sept. 1940.

17. AD I-et-L 10W82, gendarmerie reports from brigades of l'Ile Bouchard, 21 Oct., Montbazon, 28 Oct., Ligueil, 1 Nov., Richelieu, 3 Dec. 1940, and Beaumont-la-Ronce, 27 Mar. 1941.

18. See above, p. 39.

19. AD M-et-L 97W38, subprefect of Saumur to prefect of M-et-L, 23 Feb. 1941.

20. AD M-et-L 24W11, subprefect of Saumur to prefect of M-et-L, 14 April 1941.

21. AD M-et-L 24W11, Marquis de Saint-Pern, deputy of M-et-L, to prefect of M-et-L, 25 March 1941.

22. AD M-et-L 80W36, press communiqué of 26 March 1941.

23. Fonds Grenouilleau (Angers), Georges Mazeaud to Gaston Grenouilleau, 5 July 1941.

24. AD M-et-L 97W38, subprefect of Saumur to mayor of Montsoreau, Gustave Tessier, 21 July 1941, and reply of Tessier, 25 July 1941.

25. AD M-et-L 97W120, *kermesse* of Meigné-sous-Doué, 20 Sept. 1942.

26. AN F9 3037, report of director of the Maison du Prisonnier of Angers, Aug. 1943, concerning Beaufort-en-Vallée.

27. AD L-A 65W2, instructions of Education Minister Jérôme Carcopino, 13 Nov. 1941.

28. AD M-et-L 41W3, Rémy René-Bazin, delegate to youth, to regional prefect, 22 and 29 Nov. 1941.

29. AD M-et-L 80W41, SS Hauptsturmführer Busch to Count Gaël de Coniac of Secrétariat d'Éducation Populaire, 30 Sept. 1942.

30. Mgr Villepelet, "Le Diocèse de Nantes, 1940–1945," entry for 29 Nov. 1941.

31. *La Semaine religieuse du Diocèse de Nantes,* 28 Nov. 1941. A thousand of the 2,546 Catholic priests in German POW camps were authorized to serve as chaplains.

32. *La Semaine religieuse du Diocèse d'Angers,* 1 Feb. 1942.

33. A. Dio Angers 9E41, letters to Mgr Costes of René Sallé of la Chapelle-sur-Oudon, 10 Jan. 1942, and Sergeant Jean Renaud, curate of La Trinité, 18 Nov. 1941.

34. A. Dio Nantes, lettres et cartes envoyés à Mgr Villepelet par les séminaristes et prêtres prisonniers, letter of Pierre Roberdel, 12 Dec. 1943.

35. *La Semaine religieuse du Diocèse de Tours*, 2 May 1941.

36. AD M-et-L 97W133, speech of Mayor Moreau forwarded to subprefect of Saumur, 2 June 1942.

37. On the working of this law, which was repealed in 1942 when labor became scarce, see Diamond, *Women and the Second World War in France*, 32–36, and Pollard, *Reign of Virtue*, 153–65.

38. AD M-et-L 95W109, rector of Rennes to Mme Talbot, 31 Jan. 1941, copied to subprefect of Cholet, 26 Sept. 1941.

39. AD L-A 13W7, M. Huteau to prefect of L-I, 1 June 1942.

40. AD L-A 51W28, prefect Dupard to prefect-delegate of Ministry of the Interior, Paris, 29 June 1942.

41. See, for example, Diamond, *Women and the Second World War in France*, 109–10, and Veillon, *Vivre et Survivre en France*, 223.

42. AD M-et-L 80W47, Mme Hubert to prefect of M-et-L, 1 May 1943.

43. AD M-et-L 24W11, mayor of Concourson-sur-Layon to prefect of M-et-L, 3 Feb. 1943; reply of prefect, 9 Feb. 1943; reply of mayor, 13 Feb. 1943. Letter of Paul Grenouilleau (b. Concourson, 1930) to the author, 28 Sept. 1999.

44. AD L-A 51W28, Paul Urien to prefect of L-I, 15 Nov. 1942.

45. AD I-et-L 52W41, card of Albert Loiseau to prefect of I-et-L, 12 July 1942; report of social worker of Saint-Pierre-des-Corps, 11 Aug. 1942; prefect of Loiseau, 17 Aug. 1942.

46. AD M-et-L 8W93, Lucien Vétaut to mayor of Jumelles, 8 Nov. 1943; mayor of Jumelles to Secours National, 9 Dec. 1943; subprefect of Saumur to prefect of M-et-L, 12 Jan. 1944; prefect to Maison du Prisonnier, 15 Jan. 1944, and their reply, 29 Mar. 1944.

47. See below, p. 273.

48. AD L-A 51W28, prefect of L-I to Laval, 11 and 17 May 1943.

49. AD M-et-L 140W39, subprefect of Saumur to prefect of M-et-L, 12 Aug. 1943.

50. AN F9 3064, census of POWs, 22 July 1942.

51. AD I-et-L 6W20, director of the Office du Travail, Tours, to prefect of I-et-L, 29 Sept. 1943.

52. AN F9 3055, A. Tijou to M. Lot, public works administrator at Tours, 25 March 1943; AN F9 3081, report of Maison du Prisonnier, Angers, Jan. 1944.

53. AN F9 3049, reports of Maison du Prisonnier, Nantes, 29 Nov. 1943 and 7 Aug. 1944.

54. AD L-A 51W28, record of meeting at prefecture of L-I to set up the Comité Départemental d'Aide aux Prisonniers de Guerre, 28 July 1940; Ridel, *Témognages 1939–1945*, 43–69.

55. AD L-A 6W1 and 6W2, files of Comité Nantais d'Aide aux Prisonniers de Guerre, 1941–46.

56. AD L-A 13W14, director of Forges de Basse-Indre, 28 Dec. 1940; mayor of Vertou, 3 Jan. 1941; and mayor of La Baule, 9 Jan. 1941.

57. AD M-et-L 140W38, secretary of Commission des Manifestations pour les Prisonniers de Guerre of M-et-L to M. Vanneyre of Angers, 17 July 1943; reply of M. Vanneyre, 23 July 1943.

58. AD L-A 51W28, summary of dossier by departmental information delegate for prefect Bonnefoy of L-I, 11 Nov. 1943; Modena to prefect Vincent of L-I, 15 Nov. 1944; 10W34, Herault to prefect Vincent, n.d., and to Modena, president of CDL, 5 and 11 May 1945.

59. AD M-et-L 24W2, report of regional prefect Roussillon to Interior Minister, 1 Dec. 1941.

60. AN F9 3037, reports from Angers of M. 'Georges, inspector of Mouvement du Prisonnier, to André Masson, leader of the Mouvement, 19 April and June 1943; report of M. de Clauzade to M. Zaepffel, director-general of Maisons du Prisonnier, 5 July 1943.

61. An F9 3055, report of Lardy, 5 July 1943; Zaeppfel to Lardy, 15 July and 26 Aug. 1943; Philipon to secretary-general of Mouvement du Prisonnier, 1 Sept. 1943; Zaeppfel to Renault, 25 Oct. 1943.

62. AD I-et-L 52W23, General de Witowski, delegate of Comité Central d'Assistance aux Prisonniers de Guerre, to prefect of I-et-L, 18 Feb. 1942; AD M-et-L 140W38, Laval circular to prefects, 27 Oct. 1942.

63. AN F9 3055, Lardy to director of Maisons du Prisonnier, Paris, 21 April 1943.

64. AD M-et-L 24W11, prefect delegate of M-et-L, Pierre Daguerre, to André Masson, commissioner-general of repatriated POWs, 6 May 1943.

65. AD M-et-L 7U4-1, register of judgments of Special Tribunal of Appeal Court of Angers, 6 May 1943, 29 July 1943, 13 Jan. 1944.

66. AD L-A 51W29, Laurent Ollivier of Stalag VIIIC to prefect of L-I, 14 Sept. 1943; Roger Jeffredo of Stalag IIIA to prefect of L-I, 13 Aug. 1943.

67. AM Nantes 38W21, Kommando 106 to mayor of Nantes, 9 Nov. 1943.

68. A. Dio. Nantes, Letters and cards sent to Mgr Villepelet, Louis Nouais to Mgr Villepelet, 12 Dec. 1943.

CHAPTER 4 *Bread*

1. Fonds Paul Grenouilleau (Angers), Georges Mazeaud to Gaston Grenouilleau, 3 Jan. 1941.

2. Ibid., letters of 13, 16, 23, and 30 Jan. 1941.

3. Ibid., Georges Mazeaud to Gaston Grenouilleau, 22 April 1942; Lucienne Mazeaud to Grenouilleau, 28 May and 17 June 1941; Paul Mazeaud to Grenouilleau, 22 Feb. and 2 Mar. 1943.

4. Ibid., Georges Mazeaud to Gaston Grenouilleau, 6 Feb., 10 April and 18 Aug. 1941, 13 Mar. 1943, 14 Jan. 1944, 24 Feb. 1945, 22 June 1946.

5. Dominique Veillon, *Vivre et survivre en France, 1939–1947* (Paris: Payot, 1995), 112–26; Jennifer Davies, *The Wartime Kitchen and Garden* (London: BBC Book, 1993), 19–20.

6. AD L-A 75W561, prefect of L-I to delegate-general, Paris, 22 Oct. 1940.

7. AD M-et-L 7U4/99, report of commissaire attached to Angers Cour de Justice, 4 May 1945.

8. Dominique Veillon and Jean-Marie Flonneau, eds., *Le Temps des restrictions en France, 1939–1949* (Paris: IHTP, 1995), contrast the "*départements ruraux nourriciers*" of the west and the "*départements affamés*" of the Mediterranean.

9. AD M-et-L 24W2, prefect of M-et-L to Interior Minister, 9 May 1941.

10. AD M-et-L 80W6, prefect of M-et-L to Interior Minister, 31 Jan. 1943.

11. AD M-et-L 12W2, prefect of L-I to Interior Minister, 4 Mar. 1942 and 4 Jan. 1943.

12. AD M-et-L 54W11, "Les Angevines" to prefect of M-et-L, 5 Nov. 1940.

13. AD M-et-L 103W34, Henri Foquereau to mayor of Anger's deputy responsible for the municipal police, 16 July 1941.

14. AD I-et-L 10W55, police chief, Tours, to central office, Tours, 21 June 1943.

15. AD I-et-L 10W55, Andrée Simonneau to prefect of I-et-L, 26 March 1941.

16. AD M-et-L 95W109, Robert Steux, accountant with Pellaumail, to prefect of M-et-L, 14 June 1941.

17. AD I-et-L 10W8, report of subprefect of Chinon, 25 Aug. 1942.

18. AM Chinon, Registre des délibérations du conseil municipal, report of finance commission, 19 Sept. 1943.

19. AD I-et-L 121W2, subprefect of Chinon to prefect, 2 June 1943; 10W53, head chief of police, Tours, to prefect, 26 June 1943.

20. Interview with Michel Leterme, Angers, 13 June 1997.

21. Interview with Christian and Léonie Beugnet, Chinon, 23 June 1997.

22. Interview with Andrée Trudeau, Saumur, 22 June 1998.

23. Interview with André Treulier, Le Thoureil, 13 May 1997.

24. Léon Mousseau, *Le Pont cassé: Souvenirs d'un médecin des bords de la Loire* (Angers: J. Palussière, 1981), 98.

25. Interview with Lucienne Cohu (b. 1907) and Jacqueline and Louis David, Trélazé, 18 April 1997.

26. See, for example, Julian Jackson, *The Popular Front in France: Defending Democracy, 1934–38* (Cambridge: Cambridge UP, 1988), 85–112; Gérard Noiriel, *Workers in French Society in the Nineteenth and Twentieth Centuries* (Oxford: Berg, 1990), ch. 5; Jacques Danos and Marcel Gibelin, *June '36: Class Struggle and the Popular Front in France* (London and Chicago: Bookmarks, 1986); Jacques Kergoat, *La France du Front populaire* (Paris: Éditions La Découverte, 1986); Georges Lefranc, *Juin '36* (Paris: Julliard, 1965).

27. Guy Bourdé, *La Défaite du Front populaire* (Paris: Maspéro, 1977); J.-P. Rioux, A. Prost, and J.-P. Azéma, *Les Communistes français de Munich à Châteaubriant* (Paris: FNSP, 1987).

28. Étienne Dejonghe, "Les Aspects économiques et sociaux du Nord pendant la première année de l'Occupation," *Revue du Nord*, Oct. 1969.

29. AD L-A 13W8, reports of chief of police, Saint-Nazaire, 30 March 1941, commissaire spécial, Saint-Nazaire, 24 May 1941, and prefect of L-I to de Brinon, 3 Sept. 1941.

30. AD L-A 13W6, reports of subprefect of Saint-Nazaire, 7, 10, and 20 Oct. 1941.

31. AD L-A 270W476, police of the Renseignements Généraux to prefect of L-I, 4 and 9 July 1942.

32. AD M-et-L 116W7, circular of Belin to prefects, 23 Dec. 1940; circular of Roussillon to mayors of Maine-et-Loire, 17 Feb. 1941.

33. AD M-et-L 12W3, report of prefect Dupard of L-I to Interior Minister, 1 Dec. 1941.

34. The best study to date is Jean-Pierre Le Crom, *Syndicats nous voilà! Vichy et le corporatisme* (Paris: Les Éditions de l'Atelier/Éditions ouvrières, 1995).

35. AD L-A 13W9, message of Pucheu to prefects forwarded by prefect Dupard to his subprefects, 24 Nov. 1941.

36. Centre d'Histoire du Travail, Nantes, Fonds Pennaneach 4, Bernard Neau of Syndicat Général des Employés d'Angers et Environs to Jean Pennaneach, 10 July 1941.

37. AD M-et-L 18W16, account of visit of regional prefect Roussillon to Saint-Nazaire, 26 Feb. 1941.

38. Centre d'Histoire du Travail, Nantes, CGT 1939–45, Jouvance to Engineers Federation, Paris, 13 Feb. 1942.

39. Centre d'Histoire du Travail, Nantes, Fonds Pennaneach 4, Déaud to directors of Chantiers de la Loire, Dubigeon, de Bretagne, Batignolles, and SNCASO, 19 April 1944.

40. AD I-et-L 6W64, secretary-general of the Bourse du Travail, Tours, to inspector of labor Terpault, 2 April 1943.

41. AD M-et-L 12W2, report of prefect Tracou of I-et-L to Interior Minister, 3 Nov. 1943.

42. AD M-et-L 136W24, report of principal commissar of Renseignements Généraux, Angers, 12 Jan. 1944.

43. AD M-et-L 21W52, regional inspector of police to principal commissar of Renseignements Généraux, 8 Jan. 1944.

44. AD M-et-L 25W61, dossiers on twenty-nine occupational families in Angers region, 1943–44.

45. AD L-A 132W64, M. Bourget to prefect of L-I, 20 April and 9 May 1944; prefect to Bourget, 27 April and 17 May 1944.

46. See, for example, Christian Faure, *Le Projet culturel de Vichy* (Paris and Lyon: CNRS, Presses Universitaires de Lyon, 1989), 105–26.

47. AD M-et-L 24W2, regional prefect Roussillon to Interior Minister, 1 July and 28 Sept. 1941; AD M-et-L 12W4, Roussillon to Interior Minister, 1 Jan. 1942.

48. AD M-et-L 12W2, prefect of I-et-L, to Interior Minister, 3 Nov. and 3 Dec. 1941.

49. AD M-et-L 12W3, report of Dupard, prefect of L-I, to Interior Minister, 1 April 1942; AN Fla 3659, press cuttings on visit of M. Charbin to Nantes, 10–12 March 1942.

50. *La Semaine religieuse du Diocèse de Nantes*, 21 March 1942; *La Semaine religieuse du Diocèse d'Angers*, 22 March 1942.

51. AD L-A 13W9, prefect delegate of M-et-L to regional prefect, 22 May 1942; prefect of L-I to regional prefect, 28 May 1942.

52. AD I-et-L 10W55, "un paysan vrai" to prefect of I-et-L, 14 Feb. 1941.

53. AD L-A 13W6, Marquis de Sesmaisons to prefect of L-I, 29 Aug. 1941.

54. AN Fla 3659, Ravitaillement minister Max Bonnafous to Interior Minister, 3 Oct. 1942.

55. AD M-et-L 97W145, mayor of Courléon to subprefect of Saumur, 3 March 1943.

56. AD M-et-L 103W26; district Ravitaillement officer of Pouancé to director of Ravitaillement, M-et-L, 24 Oct. 1942.

57. AD M-et-L 24W30, Société Maggi to prefect of M-et-L, 7 July 1941.

58. AD M-et-L 97W33, Jules Diot, mayor of Gennes, to tax collector, 22 Dec. 1943; subprefect of Saumur to prefect of M-et-L, 28 Jan. and 20 March 1944.

59. AD M-et-L 80W4, principal commissar of Renseignements Généraux to prefect of M-et-L, 27 March 1942.

60. AD M-et-L 95W111, mayor of Saint-Macaire to subprefect of Cholet, 12 Oct. 1943; AD M-et-L 8W93, departmental delegate of central committee of potato supply to intendant Ganot, departmental director of Ravitaillement, M-et-L, 4 Sept. 1943, and prefect delegate Saissier to Ganot, 28 Oct. 1943.

61. AD M-et-L 140W150, intendant Ganot to prefect of M-et-L, 17 March 1944; report of gendarmerie of Montjean, 10 March 1944; subprefect of Cholet to prefect, 24 and 31 March 1944.

62. See Isabel Boussard's standard study, *Vichy et la Corporation Paysanne* (Paris: FNSP, 1980).

63. AD M-et-L 18W16, clipping from *La Dépêche*, 11 Dec. 1943.

64. Eugène Forget, *Le Serment de l'unité paysanne* (Paris: Nouvelle Cité, 1982), 104; Robert Paxton, *French Peasant Fascism: Henri Dorgères's Greenshirts and the Crises of French Agriculture, 1929–1939* (New York and Oxford: Oxford UP, 1997), 195 nn. 122 and 127, 120–21.

65. AD M-et-L 18W112, Dèze to director of Ravitaillement Général, 18 July 1942.

66. AD M-et-L 80W40, syndic of Chanteloup-les-Bois in meeting with prefect delegate Saissier, 26 April 1944; regional syndic Dèze to regional prefect Donati, 6 and 22 May, 2 June 1944.

67. Bernard Potier, *Aspects de la vie économique en Maine-et-Loire sous l'Occupation allemande* (Angers: Université Catholique de l'Ouest, 1985), 189.

68. AD L-A 31W41, proceedings for irregular slaughter and sale of meat, Dec. 1942–July 1943.

69. AD M-et-L 12W2, report of prefect of I-et-L to Interior Minister, 3 Sept. 1943.

70. AD I-et-L 10W53, principal commissar of Renseignements Généraux, Tours, 24 April 1943.

71. AD M-et-L 80W40, prefect Saissier to district chiefs of Ravitaillement, M-et-L, 24 Sept. 1943.

72. AD M-et-L 140W150, reports of gendarmerie of Chalonnes-sur-Loire, 24 Feb. 1944.

73. AD M-et-L 12W20, report of special controller Renaud, n.d. [1943].

74. AD M-et-L 18W9, Paul Leroux, secretary of Francist Party of La Baule, to regional prefect, 2 April 1944; prefect of L-I to regional prefect, 16 May 1944.

CHAPTER 5 *Circuses*

1. Interview with André Roussel (b. 1926), Bléré (I-et-L), 25 June 1998.

2. AD I-et-L 46W88, Dr. Foussereau to prefect of I-et-L, 26 March 1941; Robert Vivier, inspector of academy of I-et-L, 28 March 1941.

3. AD I-et-L 10W7, prefect Chaigneau of I-et-L to prefect delegated by the Interior Minister to Paris, 7 Aug. 1941.

4. AD I-et-L 10W7, report on meeting of Comité des Jeunes by Marcel Bocquet, departmental delegate of La Jeunesse, 31 March 1941.

5. AD I-et-L 52W22, special inspector of police to special commissioner, Tours, 11 March 1942; prefect of I-et-L to mayor of Bléré, 7 Jan. 1943.

6. AD I-et-L 52W21, census of associations and unions for the Feldkommandantur of Tours, Nov. 1940, Amboise.

7. AD I-et-L 52W21, census of associations and unions for the Feldkommandantur of Tours, Nov. 1940, Saint-Pierre-des-Corps; AD M-et-L 97W121, associations declared Oct. 1940, Saumur; AD M-et-L 95W121, associations declared Oct. 1940, Cholet.

8. AD M-et-L 140W95, president of Club des Fêtes of École des Arts et Métiers, Angers, to prefect of M-et-L, 8 May 1942; prefect delegate Daguerre to Feldkommandantur, 19 May, SS Hauptsturmführer Busch to prefect, 8 Oct. 1942. On these schools, see Charles R. Day, *Education for the Industrial World: The Écoles d'Arts et Métiers and the Rise of French Industrial Engineering* (Cambridge, Mass.: MIT Press, 1987).

9. AD I-etL 10W43, Feldkommandantur of Tours to prefect of I-et-L, 24 May 1941; police chief of Tours to prefect, 29 May 1941.

10. AD M-et-L 54W5, librarian of Bibliothèque Saint-Michel, Angers, to prefect of M-et-L, 17 Feb. 1942.

11. AD I-et-L 10W48, note of special delegation of Saint-Pierre-des-Corps, 11

Sept. 1940; AD L-A 270W491, central commissioner, Nantes, to prefect of L-I, 23 Feb. and 1 Aug. 1942.

12. Jean-Paul Cointet, *La Légion Française des Combattants, 1940–1944; La Tentation du fascisme* (Paris: Albin Michel, 1995).

13. Bernard Briais, *Le Lochois pendant la Guerre 1939–1945* (Chambray-lès-Tours: CLD, 1988), 61–65.

14. AD I-et-L 10W43, Feldkommandantur of Tours to prefect of I-et-L, 29 Oct. 1940.

15. AD M-et-L 41W2, subprefect of Saumur to prefect of M-et-L, 6 Nov. 1940, and reply, 8 Nov. 1940.

16. AD M-et-L 18W13, Panaget to regional prefect Donati, 19 Mar. 1943; Donati to secretariat of Marshal Pétain, 29 July 1943.

17. On Vichy youth movements, see the pioneering work of W. D. Halls, *The Youth of Vichy France* (Oxford: Clarendon Press, 1981).

18. AD M-et-L 140W28, Feldkommandantur of Angers to prefect of M-et-L, 29 April 1941; AD L-A 13W25, Feldkommandant of Nantes to prefect of L-I, 29 Aug. and 10 Sept. 1941.·

19. AD M-et-L 140W28, Rémy René-Bazin, assistant regional delegate for youth in M-et-L, to prefect, 28 May 1941.

20. AD M-et-L 54W3, director of agricultural services of M-et-L to prefect of M-et-L, 6 Nov. 1940; AD L-A 13W25, departmental delegate of the Mission for Peasant Restoration to prefect of L-I, 6 Oct. 1941.

21. AD I-et-L 52W21, note of Émile Chauveau, head of section at prefecture of I-et-L, based on verbal instructions from Feldkommandantur of Tours.

22. Rozenn Corre, "Le Scoutisme Catholique à Nantes des origines au Jamborée de la Paix, 1925–1947," master's thesis, University of Nantes, 1992, 206–11; Jérôme Gaillard, "Les Catholiques Tourangeaux pendant la Deuxième Guerre Mondiale," master's thesis, University of Tours, 1996, 85–86, 106–08; AD M-et-L Bibliothèque 73O4 "Ici 3ème Angers, 1934–1944"; AD M-et-L 60W5, extract from *Le Courrier de l'Ouest*, 8 Nov. 1944; interviews with Odette Goxe, Angers, 14 April 1997; Abbé Henri Richer, Angers, 6 June 1997; and Abbé Jacques Ménard, Tours, 2 June 1997.

23. AD I-et-L 218W14, report of Colonel de Busnel of Touraine Secours National, 5 Feb. 1941; AD M-et-L 18W109, report of Colonel de Sauvebeuf of Anjou Secours National, 4 Nov. 1942.

24. AD M-et-L 41W3, René Hersen of Niort to prefect of M-et-L, 19 Feb. 1941.

25. Camille de Montergon, *Le Colonel François de Sauvebeuf* (Niort: Imprimerie Saint-Denis, n.d.), and de Montergon, *Une Victime de Flossenburg: Le Colonel François de Sauvebeuf* (Niort: Imprimerie Saint-Denis, n.d.).

26. AD M-et-L 71W2, reports of Colonel O'Kelly of Cuisines d'Entr'aide, Angers, 18 Sept. 1941 and 25 June 1942; report of Colonel Sauvebeuf, 12 June 1942.

27. AD M-et-L 18W109, report of Colonel de Sauvebeuf, 4 March 1942.

28. AD I-et-L 10W3, statement of Interior Minister, Feb. 1942; AD M-et-L 41W3, report of subprefect of Saumur, 2 April 1942.

29. *Le Petit Courrier*, 26 and 28 Nov. 1941; regional prefect Roussillon to Interior Minister, 8 Dec. 1941.

30. AD I-et-L 218W17, M. Scmitt of l'Ile-Bouchard to Secours National of Touraine, 20 April 1943; "Étude sur les modalités de secours avec l'appréciation et les suggestions des services sociaux des délégations," 1 Jan. 1944.

31. AD M-et-L 8W91, minutes of meeting at prefecture of M-et-L, 25 Aug. 1943.

32. AD M-et-L 41W3, prefect of M-et-L to Mme Vve Poirier, 22 Jan. 1942.

33. AD L-A 16W38, director of Maison du Prisonnier Roy to prefect of L-I, 5 Feb. 1943.

34. AD I-et-L, report of prefect of I-et-L, n.d. (April 1943); prefect of I-et-L to Victor Mangeant of Cangey, 11 Dec. 1943, and reply of Mangeant, 14 Jan. 1944.

35. AD I-et-L 31W1, circulars of prefect Chaigneau to mayors of Occupied Zone of I-et-L, 9 June and 16 Oct. 1941; mayor of Bléré to prefect, 17 Oct. 1941.

36. AD L-A 132W159, circulars of prefect Dupard to mayors, 18 Oct. 1941 and 20 Mar. 1942; note of Feldkommandantur of Nantes, 27 March 1942.

37. AD I-et-L 31W1, circular of prefect Tracou to mayors, 27 Aug. 1942; reply of mayor of Montlouis-sur-Loire, 4 Sept. 1942.

38. See, for example, AD M-et-L 48W34, protests of Marc Bigeard, struck from the municipal council of Pellouailles for hunting with and selling wood and charcoal to the Germans, n.d. (Sept./Oct. 1944).

39. AD M-et-L 80W36, mayor of Chênehutte-les-Tuffeaux, forwarded to Feldkommandantur with stamp of prefecture of M-et-L, 25 March 1942.

40. AD I-et-L 10W5, Dr. Herbig to Baron de Champchevrier, 13 Sept. 1940; AD I-et-L IIZ3, reports of Dr. Herbig to head of military administration of District B, 25 Sept. 1940 and 13 Jan. 1943; Claude Morin, *Les Allemands en Touraine, 1940–1944* (Chambray-lès-Tours: CLD, 1996), 182–83.

41. AD I-et-L 106W76, Louis Théret to prefect of I-et-L, 5 March, 1942, and prefect to *procureurs* of the French state in Tours and Chinon, 14 March 1942; AD I-et-L IIZ2, departmental director of Ravitaillement Général to Feldkommandantur of Tours, 10 June 1943, and Feldkommandantur to prefect of I-et-L, 19 July 1943.

42. Collection Michel Lemesle, letter of Mme Delépine, La Ferrière-de-Flée, 28 Nov. 1973.

43. René Le Prince, ed., *La Pommeraye dans la guerre par ceux qui l'ont vécue* (La Pommeraye: Bibliothèque de La Pommeraye, 1995), accounts of Serge and Joseph Plumeseau.

44. AD M-et-L 117W33, order of Roussillon, 8 May 1941; letter of Ministry of Agriculture, 13 May; second order of Roussillon, 28 May 1941.

45. AD M-et-L 80W5, Feldkommandant of Angers to prefect Roussillon, 12 and 27 Aug. 1942.

46. AD M-et-L 80W36, Clément Varambier to prefect of M-et-L, 19 Sept. 1941; prefect to Feldkommandant of Tours, 24 Oct. 1941.

47. *Le Chinonais*, 8 July 1943.

48. *Le Chinonais*, 28 May 1941.

49. AD L-A 75W560, Marcel Braud to mayor of Nantes, 23 Dec. 1940.

50. AD L-A 132W64, invitations to prefect of L-I, 1 Dec. 1941 and July 1943.

51. AD M-et-L 140W28, principal commissaire, head of Renseignements Généraux in M-et-L, to divisional commissaire, head of Renseignements Généraux in Vichy, 28 June 1943.

52. On the flourishing of sport under Vichy, see Jean-Louis Gay-Lescot, *Sport et éducation sous Vichy, 1940–1944* (Lyon: Presses Universitaires de Lyon, 1991).

53. AD I-et-L 10W9, report of departmental delegate for youth, H. Biessy, 1 May 1943. See also his reports of 3 March and 31 Dec. 1943.

54. AD I-et-L 46W88, Goupil de Bouillé to prefect of I-et-L, 27 Dec. 1941.

55. AD M-et-L 140W98, Casadeus to prefect of M-et-L, 26 Jan. and 11 Feb. 1943.

56. AD I-et-L 52W23, authorizations by Sicherheitspolizei, 1942–44.

57. AD I-et-L 10W37, file of Propagandastaffel Sud-West, Aussenstelle Tours, 1942–43. The song was "C'était Basile," by Charles Colmache.

58. AD M-et-L 140W95, prefecture note, n.d. (Aug. 1942); Gaillard, "Les Catholiques Tourangeaux pendant la Deuxième Guerre Mondiale," 153. See also Gabriel Jacobs, "The Role of Joan of Arc on the Stage of Occupied Paris," in Roderick Kedward and Roger Austin, eds., *Vichy France and the Resistance: Culture and Ideology* (London and Sydney: Croom Helm, 1985), 106–22, and Serge Addad, *Le Théâtre dans les années Vichy* (Paris, 1992).

59. In general, see Jean-Pierre Bertin-Maghit, *Le Cinéma français sous Vichy: Les Films français de 1940 à 1944* (Paris: Albatros, 1980), and Evelyn Ehrlich, *Cinema of Paradox: French Filmmaking under the German Occupation* (New York: Columbia UP, 1987).

60. AN Fla 3868, CFLN Zone Handbook no. 7, part 3, Nov. 1943.

61. AD L-A 13W41, subprefect of Saint-Nazaire to prefect of L-I, 21 Oct. 1940; AD I-et-L 10W69, Roger Morel to prefect of I-et-L, 8 Dec. 1940. Morel was in prison in Tours and asked permission to marry his girlfriend.

62. AD I-et-L 10W36, Feldkommandant of Tours to prefects of I-et-L and M-et-L, 22 Aug. 1941; AD I-et-L 52W31, police chief to central commissaire, Tours, and chief of Sicherheitspolizei to prefect of I-et-L, 8 March 1943; AD M-et-L 12W54, police intendant of Angers region to regional prefect, 8 March 1943.

63. Muriel Paquelet, "Le Cinéma paroissial en Loire-Inférieure de 1919 à 1958," master's thesis, University of Nantes, 1994, 25–31.

64. AD L-A 132W160, Jean Briand of JOC to Clément, assistant regional delegate for youth, 15 July 1941.

65. *La Famille catholique: Bulletin mensuel des chefs de famille catholique*, March 1942.

66. AD M-et-L 12W4, report of prefect Daguerre, 2 Sept. 1942.

67. Robert Gildea, "*Les Années Noires?* Clandestine Dancing in Occupied France,"

in Ceri Crossley and Martyn Cornick, eds., *Problems in French History* (Basingstoke: Palgrave, 2000), 197–212.

68. AD M-et-L 95W75, subprefect of Cholet to Kreiskommandant of Cholet, 7 July 1941.

69. AD I-et-L 52W24, petitions of 4, 6, and 10 Nov. 1940.

70. AD I-et-L 52W24, prefect of I-et-L to mayor of Sorigny, 16 April 1941, and to mayor of Reugny, 4 July 1941.

71. AD M-et-L 8W93, Mireille Gense to prefect of M-et-L, 22 Sept. 1941, and reply of prefecture, 24 Sept. 1941.

72. AD M-et-L 56W17, regional prefect's order of 30 July 1942.

73. AD M-et-L 117W32, circular of prefect Daguerre of M-et-L to mayors, 27 July 1943.

74. AD M-et-L 117W32 and 80W34, reports of gendarmerie of Vernantes, 5, 28, and 29 Dec. 1943, 2 Jan. 1944.

75. AD I-et-L 10W38, report of gendarmerie of Monnaie, 7 June 1943.

76. AD I-et-L 52W24, Pierre Renou and Maurice Rigoureau of Semblançay to prefect of I-et-L, 18 July 1941.

77. AD M-et-L 18W50, Gendarmerie Legion of Anjou, synthesis of Sept. 1943.

78. AD M-et-L 80W34, report of gendarmerie of Longué, 18 May 1944.

79. AD I-et-L 218W17, report of cantonal representative of Neuillé-Pont-Pierre, April 1943.

80. AD I-et-L 10W38, letter of Raymond Couella, curé of Nouzilly, 24 April 1944.

Chapter 6 *Demonstrators*

1. Bernard Briais, *Le Lochois pendant la Guerre 1939–1945* (Chambray-lès-Tours: CLD, 1988), 35–42; *Le Progrès de Loches*, 17 July 1940.

2. André Goupille, *Mon Village sous la botte: La Haye Descartes, juin 1940–septembre 1944* (Tours, n.d.) 29.

3. Eric Alary, *La Ligne de démarcation, 1940–1944* (Paris: PUF, 1995), 39–41.

4. AD I-et-L 10W7, prefect of I-et-L to Interior Minister, 10 Feb. 1941.

5. See above, p. 71.

6. AD I-et-L 52W40, prefect of I-et-L to prefect of Ille-et-Vilaine, 20 March 1941.

7. AD 72AJ136, manuscript account by André Goupille, p. 3.

8. AD I-et-L 42J1, Fonds Goupille, letter from family in Wingles (Pas-de-Calais), 13 Nov. 1940.

9. AD I-et-L 10W75, trainee inspector Chavenne of Loches to special commissar, Loches, 13 Nov. 1941.

10. AD I-et-L 34W4, Cour de Justice of I-et-L, testimony of Aimé Brédif, a farmer (72) and his son Marius (41), 15 Nov. 1943. Sidonie Bichet was interned by the prefect of I-et-L for intelligence with the enemy, 5 Jan. 1945.

11. AD M-et-L 12W48, subprefect of Saumur to prefect of M-et-L, 24 Oct. 1940;

prect of M-et-L to General Laure, DGGFTO, 26 Oct. 1940, and to Minister of the Interior, 30 Oct. 1940.

12. On commemoration and French identity, see Pierre Nora, ed., *Les Lieux de mémoire* (Paris: Gallimard), vol. 1: *La République* (1984), vol. 2: *La Nation* (1986), and vol. 3: *Les France* (1992). See also Rosamonde Sanson, *Les 14 juillet: Fête et conscience nationale, 1789–1975* (Paris: Flammarion, 1976); Danielle Tartakowsky, *Les Usages politiques des fêtes aux XIXe–XXe siècles* (Paris: Publications de la Sorbonne, 1994); Robert Gildea, *The Past in French History* (New Haven and London: Yale UP, 1994); Olivier Ihl, *La Fête républicaine* (Paris: Gallimard, 1996); and Tartakowsky, *Les Manifestations de la rue en France, 1918–1968* (Paris: Publications de la Sorbonne, 1997). On official Vichy commemorations from a regional perspective, see François Cochet, "Les Fêtes publiques de la période pétainiste (1940–1944)," in Sylvette Guibert, ed., *Fêtes et politique en Champagne à travers les siècles* (Nancy: Presses Universitaires de Nancy, 1992), 276–85.

13. *Le Progrès de Loches*, 17 July 1940.

14. AD L-A 75W551, prefecture of L-I to subprefects and mayors, 11 July 1940.

15. Duméril, *Journal d'un honnête homme pendant l'Occupation*, 10 Nov. 1940.

16. Halls, *The Youth of Vichy France*, 404–06, has an interesting appendix on this incident.

17. AD I-et-L 10W65, subprefect of Chinon to prefect, 22 Nov. 1940.

18. AD L-A 13W25, commissaire central, Nantes, to prefect of L-I, 9 Nov. 1940; AD L-A 51W21, prefect of L-I to Interior Minister, 17 Nov. 1940; Duméril, *Journal*, 12 Nov. 1940.

19. Gérard Le Marec, *La Bretagne dans la Résistance* (Rennes: Ouest-France, 1983), 18; Sarah Choyeau, "La Mémoire de la Résistance à Nantes," master's thesis; University of Nantes, 1994, 10; interview with Christian de Mondragon (b. 1923), Nantes, 29 April 1997. On student behavior, see André Gueslin, *Les Facs sous Vichy: Actes du Colloque des Universités de Clermont-Ferrand et de Strasbourg, novembre 1993* (Clermont-Ferrand: Publications de l'Institut d'Études du Massif Central Université Blaise-Pascal, 1994).

20. AD L-A 132W54, prefect of L-I to Interior Minister, 11 Dec. 1940.

21. AD M-et-L 80W36, appeal of prefect of M-et-L, copied to Feldkommandantur of Angers, 4 Feb. 1941.

22. AD M-et-L 97W33, Feldkommandant Kloss, communiqué, 14 March 1941, and letter to prefect Roussillon, 31 March 1941.

23. AD L-A 51W21, central commissaire of Nantes to prefect of L-I, 31 March 1941.

24. AD L-A 13W8, Feldkommandant Hotz to prefect Dupard, 30 March 1941; prefect Dupard, instructions of 31 March and circular to mayors, 4 April 1941.

25. Maurice Dommanget, *Histoire du premier mai* (Paris: Société Universitaire d'Éditions et de Librairie, 1953).

26. AD M-et-L 132W54, prefect of L-I to Interior Minister, 15 May 1941.

27. AD L-A 13W19, tract forwarded to prefect of L-I by "un Français," 6 May 1941.
28. AD M-et-L 18W119, prefect of L-I to regional prefect, Angers, and Interior Minister, 3 May 1941.
29. *La Semaine religieuse du Diocèse d'Angers*, 11 May 1941.
30. AD M-et-L 41W2, commissaire central, Angers, to prefect of M-et-L, 2 May 1941.
31. AD M-et-L 18W119, prefect of L-I to regional prefect, Angers, and Interior Minister, 7 May 1941.
32. AD M-et-L 41W2, commissaire principal, Angers, to prefect of M-et-L, 2 May 1941.
33. On the cult of Joan of Arc since the Revolution, see Gerd Krumeich, "Joan of Arc between Right and Left," in Robert Tombs, ed., *Nationhood and Nationalism in France: From Boulangism to the Great War, 1889–1918* (London: Harper-Collins Academic, 1991), 63–73; Krumeich, *Jeanne d'Arc in der Geschichte: Historiographie-Politik-Kultur* (Sigmaringen: Thorbecke, 1989); Gildea, *The Past in French History*, 154–65.
34. *La Semaine religieuse du Diocèse d'Angers*, 18 May 1941. In general on this ceremony, see Cointet, *L'Église sous Vichy*, 51.
35. *Le Chinonais*, 15 May 1941, 13 May 1943.
36. AD I-et-L XV Z 23, Feldkommandant of Tours to head of German military administration, Bezirk B, Angers, 13 May 1941; AD I-et-L 10W84, report of gendarmerie of Bléré, 11 May 1941.
37. AD M-et-L 41W2, central police superintendent, Angers, to prefect of M-et-L, 12 May 1941.
38. AD L-A 27J17, account of Les Fils de France by Luc Belliard and A. Praud (two-page typescript, n.d.).
39. AD L-A 13W21, note of Duméril for prefect of L-I, 13 May 1941; AD L-A 51W21, central commissaire of Nantes to prefect of L-I, 15 May 1941.
40. AD M-et-L 136W12, prefect of M-et-L to Feldkommandant of Angers, 8 Sept. 1941.
41. AD M-et-L 12W48, report of gendarmerie of Gennes, 18 July 1941; "an indignant French woman" to prefect of M-et-L, 3 June 1941.
42. AD I-et-L III Z 1, report of Feldkommandant of Tours, 18 March 1941.
43. AD M-et-L 24W2, central police superintendent, Angers, to prefect, 1 Nov. 1941; prefect Roussillon to Interior Minister, 1 Dec. 1941.
44. *La Semaine religieuse du Diocèse d'Angers*, 10 May 1942.
45. AD I-et-L 10W40, prefect Tracou of I-et-L to directors of Le Corozo-Darzouge, 7 May 1942, and Établissements Schmid, 16 May 1942.
46. AD M-et-L 41W2, report of gendarmerie of Trélazé, 14 July 1942; subprefect of Saumur to prefect of M-et-L, 15 July 1942.
47. AD M-et-L 18W119, report of prefect of M-et-L, 16 July 1942.
48. Gildea, *The Past in French History*, 149–50.

49. AD L-A 243W163, reports of central police superintendent of Nantes, with tracts appended, 18 and 20 Sept. 1942.

50. AD M-et-L 80W5, chief superintendent of Renseignements Généraux to prefect of M-et-L, 23 Sept. 1942.

51. AD M-et-L 18W13, rector of Academy of Rennes to regional prefect Donati, 27 Feb. 1943, and reply of Donati, 17 March 1943.

52. AD L-A 132W159, prefect of L-I to central superintendent, Nantes, 13 April 1943; reports of Nantes police, 27 April and 8 May 1943.

53. AN 72AJ145, complaint by M. Decure to Nantes police, 2 May 1943; AD M-et-L 18W13, regional prefect Donati to Laval, 27 May 1943.

54. AD I-et-L 10W40, prefect of I-et-L to Pétain's private secretariat, 1 May 1943; regional prefect of Angers to prefect of I-et-L, 18 May 1943.

55. AD M-et-L 18W119, circular of Laval to regional prefects and police intendants, 21 April 1944; Déat to regional and departmental prefects, 4 April 1944.

56. AD I-et-L 10W40, prefect of I-et-L to Laval, 2 May 1944.

57. AD M-et-L 80W7, prefect of M-et-L to Interior Minister Laval, 17 July 1943.

58. AD M-et-L 18W119, prefect of L-I to regional prefect, Angers, 17 July 1943.

59. AD I-et-L 10W40, telegram of Laval to all prefects and police intendants, 14 July 1944; police superintendent of Tours to central superintendent of Tours, 15 July 1944; head of Renseignements Généraux, I-et-L, to director of Renseignements Généraux, Vichy, 15 July 1944.

60. AD M-et-L 90W1, police superintendent, Angers, to prefect of M-et-L, 14 July 1944.

61. Jacques Maurice, *Cinquante mois sous la botte* (Tours, 1992), 30. See also Jacques Semelin, *Unarmed against Hitler: Civilian Resistance in Europe, 1939–1943* (Westport and London: Praeger, 1993).

CHAPTER 7 *Trimmers*

1. Fonds Émile Aron, Tours, petition of teachers at the École de Médecine, Tours, to prefect of I-et-L, 16 Feb. 1942.

2. See the tribute to his mentor by Émile Aron in *Figures Tourangelles* (Chambray-lès-Tours: CLD, 1986), 187–204.

3. For this distinction, see Max Weber, "Politics as a Vocation," in H. H. Gerth and C. Wright Mills, eds., *From Max Weber: Essays in Sociology* (London and Boston: Routledge and Kegan Paul, 1970), 84–86.

4. Ernest Gellner and John Waterbury, eds., *Patrons and Clients in Mediterranean Societies* (London: Duckworth, 1977), 4–5; Marc Abélès, *Quiet Days in Burgundy: A Study of Local Politics* (Paris and Cambridge: Éditions de la Maison des Sciences de l'Homme/Cambridge UP, 1991), 222–28; Mattei Dogan, "Les Filières de la carrière politique en France," *Revue française de sociologie* 8 (1967): 468–92.

5. Raymond Lavigne, *Saint-Pierre-des-Corps ou la Clarté républicaine* (Paris: Éditions Messidor, 1988), 60–75.

6. Julien Papp, "Les Pouvoirs locaux en Indre-et-Loire," paper delivered at the IHTP conference on "Les Élites locales en France, 1935–1953," 12–13 June 1996; J. Feneant, *Histoire de la Franc-Maçonnerie en Touraine* (Chambray-lès-Tours: CLD, 1981).

7. Jean Le Cour Grandmaison, *Le Marquis de La Ferronnays, 1876–1946* (Paris: Éditions Siloë, 1952), and Annik Lassus Saint-Geniès, *Jean Le Cour Grandmaison* (Paris: Beauchesne, 1980); Christian Bougeard, "Regards sur les réseaux de notables en Bretagne, des années 1930 aux années 1950," *Annales de Bretagne et des Pays de l'Ouest* 103 (1996): 31–51; René Bourrigaud, *Le Développement agricole au 19e siècle en Loire-Atlantique* (Nantes: Centre d'Histoire du Travail, 1994), 462–75; René Bourreau, *Une Utopie religieuse et sa modernisation lors des élections en Pays nantais contemporain: La logique restitutionniste de la noblesse nantaise* (Paris: EHESS, 1992), 272–317; Jean-Clément Martin, *La Vendée de la mémoire* (Paris: Seuil, 1989); AD L-A 1M473, file of Association des Chefs de Famille Catholiques du Diocèse de Nantes, 1927–30. I am grateful to Frank Liaigre for drawing my attention to this organization.

8. AD L-A 132W54, minutes of meetings at prefecture of 26 June, 2, 10, 12, and 16 July 1940; Mgr Villepelet, "Le Diocèse de Nantes, 1940–1945," entry for 18 Aug. 1940.

9. AN Fla 3630, circular of Interior Minister Adrien Marquet to prefects, 7 Aug. 1940.

10. AD L-A 132W54, prefect Dupard of L-I to Interior Minister, 12 Nov. 1940; AD M-et-L 12W20, prefect Dupard to Interior Minister, 13 Dec. 1941.

11. AD M-et-L 12W4, prefect Roussillon of M-et-L to DGGFTO, 30 Oct. 1940.

12. AD M-et-L 18W136, prefect Roussillon to Interior Minister, 22 Jan. 1941.

13. AD M-et-L 18W135, subprefect of Saumur to prefect of M-et-L, 29 Dec. 1941; AD M-et-L 18W120, article in *Le Petit Parisien*, 29 Dec. 1941, annotated by Roussillon.

14. Philippe Gabillard, "L'Extrême Droite en Maine-et-Loire, 1919–1934," master's thesis, Catholic University, Angers, 1980, 81–86.

15. AD M-et-L 60W4, regional prefect Roussillon to Interior Minister, 8 Dec. 1941; AD M-et-L 12W74, article in *Les Nouveaux Temps*, 6 Dec. 1940; Feldkommandant Kloss to Roussillon, 12 Dec. 1940.

16. AD M-et-L 136W12, prefect Roussillon to Feldkommandant of Angers, 25 June 1941; AD M-et-L 24W2, prefect Roussillon to Interior Minister, 1 July and 1 Aug. 1941; AD M-et-L 303W85, subprefect of Cholet Georges Husson to Roussillon, 4 Aug. 1941; the minutes of the municipal council in AM Cholet contain no reference to the wayward vote, only an effusive vote of confidence in Darlan, Huntziger, Barthélémy, Bouthillier, "and all the other members of the government."

17. AD M-et-L 12W74, prefect Roussillon to Interior Minister and DGGFTO, 15 Sept. 1941.

18. See above, p. 126

19. *Le Petit Courrier*, 5 Dec. 1941; AD M-et-L 12W74, Roussillon to Ministry of Industrial Production, 5 Dec., and to General Matthaei, 8 Dec. 1941; AD M-et-L 60W4, prefect Roussillon to Interior Minister, 8 Dec. 1941; AD M-et-L 116W3, Chamber of Commerce of Cholet, 15 Dec. 1941.

20. Lavigne, *Saint-Pierre-des-Corps*, 75; AD I-et-L XV Z 23, prefect Chaigneau of I-et-L to Feldkommandant of Tours, 27 June 1941.

21. AD L-A 132W157, "Notices on influential figures," 1942.

22. AD M-et-L 12W48, subprefect of Saumur to prefect Roussillon, 11 Feb. 1941.

23. AD I-et-L 10W25, circular to prefects of Interior Minister Peyrouton, 6 Jan. 1941.

24. *Tours Soir*, 7 June 1941 (clipping in AD I-et-L XIV Z 17).

25. AD I-et-L 10W25, prefect Chaigneau of I-et-L to Interior Minister, 20 Jan. 1941; see also Robert Vivier, *Touraine 39–45: Histoire de l'Indre-et-Loire durant la Deuxième Guerre Mondiale* (Chambray-lès-Tours: CLD, 1990), 135.

26. AD L-A 13W19, Lamaigre-Dubreuil, president of Fédération Départementale des Contribuables de la Loire-Inférieure, to prefect Dupard for forwarding to Pétain, 15 March 1941.

27. AD L-A 132W157, notices on influential figures, 1942.

28. AD L-A 132W159, text read to CDL of L-I, 19 Oct. 1944.

29. AD L-A 10W11, subprefect Douay of Saint-Nazaire to prefect Dupard, 5 July 1941.

30. AD L-A 13W9, "Advice to the prefectoral administration" given at a meeting of Interior Minister and regional prefects, forwarded by prefect Dupard of L-I to subprefects of Châteaubriant and Saint-Nazaire, 24 Nov. 1941.

31. AD L-A 132W85, subprefect of Châteaubriant to prefect of L-I, 10 April 1942.

32. AD M-et-L 18W107, information on regional personalities, 1942.

33. Statistic from details on individual communes in AD I-et-L 3W9 and 10W25.

34. AD M-et-L 140W8, subprefect Milliat of Saumur to prefect Roussillon, 10 and 15 Feb. 1941.

35. AD M-et-L 140W5, report of prefect delegate Daguerre, 3 Feb. 1942.

36. AD M-et-L 97W179, police chief of Saumur to subprefect, 5 Feb. 1943; Drouart to subprefect, 28 March; Captain Narcisse Clochard, second *adjoint*, to subprefect, 5 April; anonymous letter to subprefect, 24 April; subprefect to prefect of M-et-L, 21 July 1943.

37. Pierre Barral, "Idéal et pratique du régionalisme dans le régime de Vichy," *Revue française de science politique* 24 (Oct. 1974); 911–13; Gildea, *The Past in French History*, 166–85

38. Michèle Cointet, *Le Conseil National de Vichy, 1940–1944* (Paris: Aux Amateurs du Livre, 1989).

39. Mgr Villepelet, "Le Diocèse de Nantes, 1940–1945," 6 Aug. 1940.

40. AD L-A 132W157, Société Archéologique et Historique de Nantes et de la Loire-Inférieure to Marshal Pétain via prefect Dupard, 17 Dec. 1940.

41. AD L-A 243W163, central commissaire, Nantes, to prefect of L-I, 23 Jan., 21 and 28 Feb., 6 and 17 March, 8 April, and 4 May 1941. See, in general, Alain Déniel, *Le Mouvement breton* (Paris: Maspéro, 1976); Michel Nicolas, *Le Separatisme en Bretagne* (Brasparts: Éditions Beltan, 1986); Paul Serant, *La Bretagne et la France* (Paris: Fayard, 1971); Olier Mordrel, *Breiz Atao ou Histoire et actualité du nationalisme breton* (Paris: A. Moreau, 1973).

42. On the chambers of commerce, see Henri Hauser, *Le Problème du régionalisme* (Paris: PUF, 1924), 69–113.

43. AD L-A 132W157, prefect Dupard of L-I to prefect delegate of Interior Minister, Paris, summing up a paper by Durand, 18 Dec. 1940; report of Chamber of Commerce, Nantes, 23 Dec. 1940, forwarded to prefect delegate by Dupard, 2 Jan. 1941; Dupard to Darlan, 14 April 1941; Abel Durand, *Nantes dans la France de l'Ouest* (Paris: Plon, 1941), with a preface by Gaëtan Rondeau.

44. AD M-et-L 18W136, prefect Roussillon to Interior Minister, 22 Jan. 1941.

45. AD M-et-L 18W120, paper by Jacques de la Grandière and Joachim du Plessis de Grenadan, 20 May 1941.

46. AD M-et-L 116W4, Chambre de Commerce de Saumur, *Bulletin des Séances, 1940–1954.*

47. AD I-et-L 52W4, report by vice president of Chamber of Commerce of Tours, F. Martin, endorsed 14 Jan. 1941 and forwarded to prefect of I-et-L, 17 Jan. 1941.

48. AD M-et-L 12W48, draft of prefect Roussillon, n.d. (Nov.–Dec. 1941).

49. AD L-A 13W9, resolution of Chamber of Commerce of Nantes, 7 July 1941, forwarded by prefect Dupard to prefect delegate of Interior Minister, Paris, 18 July 1941; Hervé Le Boterf, *La Bretagne sous le gouvernement de Vichy* (Paris: France-Empire, 1982), 109–13.

50. AD L-A 13W6, Rondeau, Brossier, and employers' leader Bertin to Laval, 26 Aug. 1942. The prefect delegate of the Interior Minister, J.-P. Ingrand, told the regional prefect of Angers, 25 Aug. 1942, that the government had no plans to revise the regions. See also Yvonnig Gicquel, *Le Comité consultatif de Bretagne* (Rennes: Simon, 1961).

51. AD 18W135, prefect Roussillon to Interior Ministry, 25 Oct. and 20 Dec. 1940, order of appointment of Interior Ministry, 30 Jan. 1941; *Le Petit Courrier*, 9 Feb. 1941. See also Marc Bergère, "Permanences et ruptures au sein du conseil général du Maine-et-Loire (1935–1953): Étude prosopographique des élus," *Annales de Bretagne et des Pays de l'Ouest* 103 (1996): 69–77.

52. AD L-A 13W10, minutes of administrative commission of L-I, 5 March 1941.

53. Ad I-et-L 225W1 and 10W3, correspondence on the composition of the administrative commission of I-et-L, 1940–41; Vivier, *Touraine 39–45*, 127–28.

54. Émile Aron, *La Médecine en Touraine des origines à nos jours* (Chambray-lès-Tours: CLD, 1992), 240–41. See also Jack Vivier, "Le docteur Labussière: Destin d'un homme révolté," *Amis du Vieux Chinon* 10, no. 5 (2001).

55. AD I-etL 225W2/3, minutes of the administrative commission of I-et-L, 1 March 1941–14 Nov. 1942.
56. AD M-et-L 12W23, speech of Interior Minister Pucheu, 19 Feb. 1942.
57. AD M-et-L 12W4, prefect delegate Daguerre to Interior Minister, 1 Feb. 1942.
58. AD M-et-L 18W9, prefect Tracou of I-et-L to Roussillon, 9 Feb. 1942.
59. AD M-et-L 18W16, speech of Roussillon in Tours, 29 Jan. 1942; report of Roussillon to Interior Minister Pucheu, n.d. (early 1942).
60. AD M-et-L 18W13, prefect Tracou to Roussillon, 24 Aug. 1942.
61. AN F1a 3634 and AD L-A 13W10, circular of Interior Minister Pucheu, 9 Dec. 1941; prefect Dupard to Interior Minister, 11 April 1942.
62. AD I-et-L 225W1, prefect Tracou of I-et-L to Interior Minister, 23 June 1942.
63. AN F1a 3635, unsigned note of Interior Ministry, 13 May 1942.
64. AD I-et-L 10W3, minutes of meeting of regional prefects of Occupied Zone, n.d. (May 1942). On Hilaire and Bousquet, see Baruch, *Servir l'État français*, 336–37.
65. AD I-et-L 225W6, Comité d'Organisation des Pelleteries et Fourrures to prefect of I-et-L, 28 Aug. 1942
66. AD I-et-L 225W6, prefect Tracou to Laval, 16 Oct. 1942
67. AD M-et-L 18W107, notes on regional personalities, 1942.
68. AD M-et-L 2W4, prefect delegate Daguerre to Interior Minister, 3 May 1943.
69. AD M-et-L 18W138, prefect delegate Daguerre to Laval, 13 Oct. 1942.
70. AD M-et-L 7U4/98, prefect delegate Daguerre to Interior Minister, 29 Aug. 1942; Daguerre's testimony to examining magistrate in proceedings against Moreau, 17 April 1945.
71. AD L-A 13W10, *conseil départemental* of L-I, 7–8 June 1943.
72. AD M-et-L 18W138, *conseil départemental* of M-et-L, April 1943.
73. *Demain*, 30 April 1943 (clipping in AD M-et-L 140W9).
74. AD I-et-L 225W8/9, *conseil départemental* of I-et-L, 8 July 1944.
75. AD M-et-L 95W112, report of subprefect of Cholet, 26 July 1941.
76. AD M-et-L 8W87, report of subprefect of Cholet, 31 Aug. 1943.
77. AD M-et-L 90W6, circular of Laval to mayors, 4 Dec. 1942; AD I-et-L 10W25, circular of Laval to prefects, 22 June 1942. Changes to the law of 16 Nov. 1940 on municipal councils were brought in on 13 Nov. 1941 and 4 Oct. 1943.
78. AD M-et-L 80W5, circular of prefect of M-et-L to mayors, 3 June 1942; 80W6, report of prefect to Interior Minister, 2 March 1943.
79. AD I-et-L 52W4, Guillaume-Louis to prefect of I-et-L, 4 Oct. 1943; clipping from *La Dépêche du Centre*, n.d.; AD I-et-L 18W133, list of mayors from the Angers region, Oct. 1943; AD M-et-L 24W24, notes of prefect delegate of M-et-L for regional prefect Donati, 5 Oct. 1943.
80. AD I-et-L 18W134, prefect Tracou to regional prefect Roussillon, 3 April 1943, and reply, 19 April 1943. On Gounin, see AD M-et-L 18W107, notes on regional personalities, 1942.

81. AD L-A 132W157, subprefect of Châteaubriant to prefect of L-I, 9 Nov. 1942.

82. AD M-et-L 18W138, Jacques Hedouin, mayor of Vernoil, to regional prefect Donati, 26 July 1944.

83. AD I-et-L 10W25, prefect of I-et-L to Laval, 10 Jan. 1944.

CHAPTER 8 *Saints*

1. *La Semaine religieuse du Diocèse de Nantes*, 9 June 1944, 185–86. See also Mgr Villepelet, *Au Service de l'Église: Choix de discours, 1936–1966* (n.p., n.d.), 89.

2. In general, on this period, see Gérard Cholvy and Yves-Marie Hilaire, *Histoire religieuse de la France contemporaine*, vol. 3 (Toulouse: Privat, 1988).

3. *La Semaine religieuse du Diocèse de Nantes*, 25 May and 8 June 1940.

4. *Le Courrier de Saint-Nazaire*, 22 June 1940.

5. *La Semaine religieuse du Diocèse de Tours*, 4 Oct. and 1 Nov. 1940, 10 Jan. and 21 Feb. 1941; *La Semaine religieuse du Diocèse d'Angers*, 9 March 1941; Mgr Villepelet, "Le Diocèse de Nantes, 1940–1945," 4–11 Oct. 1940; Cointet, *L'Église sous Vichy*, 16–21; W. D. Halls, *Politics, Society, and Christianity in Vichy France* (Oxford and Providence: Berg, 1995), 45–53.

6. Nicholas Atkin, *Church and Schools in Vichy France, 1940–1944* (New York and London: Garland, 1991).

7. See below, pp. 213–15.

8. Mgr Villepelet, "Le Diocèse de Nantes," 8 June 1941; *La Révolution Nationale*, 6 Feb. 1943.

9. A. Dio. Tours, Mgr Gaillard, "Tournée pastorale, 1942."

10. A. Dio. Angers, Rector Vincent to Mgr Bressolles of Institut Catholique, Paris, 24 Aug. 1941.

11. AN F1a 3868, CFLN Zone handbook no. 7, part 3, Nov. 1943.

12. *Le Sou de la Presse*, July–Aug. 1939; Cholvy and Hilaire, *Histoire religieuse de la France contemporaine*, 29–36, 85–89.

13. James McMillan, "France," in Tom Buchanan and Martin Conway, eds., *Political Catholicism in Europe, 1918–1965* (Oxford: Clarendon Press, 1996), 41–43.

14. Gabillard, "L'Extrême Droite en Maine-et-Loire," 125.

15. See above, p. 135.

16. Fernand Boulard, ed., *Matériaux pour l'histoire religieuse du peuple français, XIXe–XXe siècles: Région de Paris, Haute-Normandie, Pays de Loire, Centre* (Paris: Éditions de l'École des Hautes Études en Sciences Sociales, 1982), 117, 389, 417; André Siegfried, *Tableau politique de la France de l'Ouest sous la Troisième République* (Paris: A. Colin, 1964), 4–7, 40–41; Laurence Wylie, ed., *Chanzeaux: A Village in Anjou* (Cambridge, Mass.: Harvard UP, 1966), 3–4.

17. See John S. Conway, *The Nazi Persecution of the Churches* (London: Weidenfeld and Nicolson, 1968).

18. Mgr Villepelet, "Le Diocèse de Nantes," 24 July 1940.

19. AD L-A 75W551, Kommandantur to bishop of Nantes, 19 July 1940; Mgr

Villepelet, "Le Diocèse de Nantes," 19 July, 25 and 28 Sept. 1940; Laurent Berger, "L'Épiscopat nantais de Mgr Villepelet, 1936–1966," master's thesis, University of Nantes, 1991, 192.

20. AD I-et-L 10W42, Feldkommandant of Tours to prefect of I-et-L, 15 Aug. 1940; Ad L-A 13W25, Feldkommandant of Nantes to Mgr Villepelet, 25 Oct. 1940; mayors of St Étienne-de-Corcoué and Mauves-sur-Loire to prefect of L-A, 28 Oct. and 5 Nov. 1940; AD M-et-L 5W17, Feldkommandant of Angers to prefecture of M-et-L, 23 Oct. 1940; curé of Nueil-sur-Layon to prefect of M-et-L, 6 Nov. 1940.

21. Mgr Villepelet, "Le Diocèse de Nantes," 24 Nov. 1940; Berger, "L'Épiscopat nantais," 193

22. AD M-et-L 95W75, Feldkommandant Kloss to prefect of M-et-L, 10 Oct. 1940, and report of gendarmerie of Champtoceaux, M-et-L, 3 June 1941; BAMA Freiburg RW35/1261, report of Neumann-Neurode, 22 Feb. 1941; AD I-et-L 10W43, Feldkommandant of Tours to prefect of I-et-L, 3 May 1941, and prefect to Mgr Gaillard, 17 and 26 May 1941; AD M-et-L 97W34, prefect of M-et-L to subprefect of Saumur, 24 May 1941, and latter to archpriest of Saumur, 24 May 1941.

23. *La Semaine religieuse du Diocèse d'Angers*, 11 Aug. 1940, 8 June 1941; AD M-et-L 80W36, Feldkommandant Kloss to Mgr Costes, 29 May 1941; prefect of M-et-L to Kloss, 4 June 1941; A. Dio Angers, funeral oration for Mgr Costes by Mgr Cesbron, bishop of Annecy, 28 Mar. 1950.

24. Mgr Villepelet, "Le Diocèse de Nantes," 28 June, 20 July, 24 Sept., 12, 13, 14, and 24 Dec. 1940.

25. *La Semaine religieuse du Diocèse de Nantes*, 7 and 21 June 1941.

26. See *La Famille catholique: Bulletin mensuel des Chefs de famille catholique*, 1941–43.

27. *La Semaine religieuse du Diocèse de Tours*, 16 June 1978; Guillard, "Les Catholiques tourangeaux pendant la Deuxième Guerre Mondiale," 147–48. On Catholics and the STO, see Cholvy and Hilaire, *Histoire religieuse de la France contemporaine*, 100–03, and Émile Poulat, *Naissance des Prêtres ouvriers* (Paris: Casterman, 1965).

28. See, for example, Vera Drapac, *War and Religion: Catholics in the Churches of Occupied Paris* (Washington: Catholic University of America, 1998), 278–84.

29. AN 72AJ136 and AD I-et-L 81J1, report on Canon Robin by J. M. Demezil, archivist of Loir-et-Cher, 15 March 1949; Vivier, *Touraine 39–45*, 158–60; Jack Vivier, *Prêtres de Touraine dans la Résistance* (Chambray-lès-Tours: CLD, 1993), 22–34; Canon Robert Fiot, *Un Prêtre de Touraine: L'Abbé Georges Lhermitte, 1887–1944* (Tours: Barbot et Gallon, 1945); Abbé Joseph Perret, *Le Curé de Draché: "Un Pur de la Résistance"* (n.p., n.p.: 1948). For an upbeat account of clerical resistance, see Charles Molette, *Prêtres, religieux, et religieuses dans la Résistance au Nazisme, 1940–1945* (Paris; Fayard, 1995).

30. See pp. 246–48.

31. BAMA Freiburg RH36/228, report of Cholet office to Feldkommandant of Tours, 7 May 1942.

32. Interview with Suzanne Le Chat, Ingrandes (M-et-L), 15 April 1997; Dom Guy Oury, *Dom Gabriel Sortais* (Solesmes, 1975).

33. Guillard, "Les Catholiques tourangeaux," 140.

34. Mgr Villepelet, "Le Diocèse de Nantes," 14 Sept. 1942. On the differences between the lower clergy and the hierarchy over the Resistance, see Cointet, *L'Église sous Vichy*, 308–09, 320.

35. E. R. Vaucelle, *La Collégiale de Saint Martin de Tours des origines à l'avènement des Valois, 397–1328* (Tours, 1907), 165–66. I am grateful to Professor David Ganz of King's College, London, for this reference.

36. *La Semaine religieuse du Diocèse de Tours*, 12 and 19 Dec. 1940, 19 June and 17 July 1941.

37. A. Dio Angers 2K50, Notre-Dame de Béhuard, and 2K52, Notre-Dame des Gardes; *La Semaine religieuse du Diocèse d'Angers*, 27 Sept. 1942.

38. *La Semaine religieuse du Diocèse d'Angers*, 15 Aug. 1943, 23 Jan., 26 March and 30 April 1944.

39. Mgr Villepelet, "Le Diocèse de Nantes," 23 Sept. and 14 Nov. 1943; A. Dio. Nantes, Livre de Paroisse, Ste Croix, Nantes, 23 Sept. 1943; *La Semaine religieuse du Diocèse de Nantes*, 25 Sept. and 4 Dec. 1943.

40. *La Semaine religieuse du Diocèse de Nantes*, 2 Aug. 1941; AD L-A 13W22, Feldkommandant of Nantes to prefect of L-I, 26 July 1943; report of police chief, 12 Aug. 1943.

41. *La Semaine religieuse du Diocèse de Nantes*, 20 May 1944. In general, see Louis Perouas, "Le Grand Retour de Notre Dame de Boulogne à travers la France (1943–48): Essai de reconstitution," *Annales de Bretagne et des Pays de l'Ouest*, 90 (1983): 171–83; reprinted in *Archives des Sciences sociales des Religions* 56, no. 1 (1983): 37–59.

42. *La Semaine religieuse du Diocèse de Tours*, 2 June 1944.

43. Interview with Abbé Jacques Ménard (b. 1922), Tours, 2 June 1997.

44. *La Semaine religieuse du Diocèse d'Anjou*, 19 and 26 March 1944.

45. *La Semaine religieuse du Diocèse d'Anjou*, 16 April 1944; Michel Lemesle, *1939–1945: À Travers l'Anjou* (Cholet: Les Éditions du Choletais, 1976), 164–66.

46. A. Dio. Nantes, Livre de Paroisse, Ste Croix, Nantes, 15 June 1944.

47. Mgr Villepelet, "Le Diocèse de Nantes," 12, 15, and 25 June and 27 July 1944; Mgr Villepelet, *Au Service de l'Église*, 94; *La Semaine religieuse du Diocèse de Nantes*, 24 June and 1 July 1944.

CHAPTER 9 *Sinners*

1. AD I-et-L 10W73, commissaire spécial, Tours, to prefect of I-et-L, 18 Jan. 1941.

2. AD M-et-L 116J9, "Les Camps de Montreuil-Bellay" (typescript, 30pp., n.d.);

Jacques Sigot, *Un Camp pour les Tsiganes . . . et les autres: Montreuil-Bellay, 1940–1945* (Éditions Wallada, 1983), 54–55; Sophie Paisot-Béal and Roger Prévost, *Histoire des camps d'internement en Indre-et-Loire, 1940–1944*, privately published, 1993, 46–53.

3. Renée Poznanski, *Les Juifs en France pendant la Seconde Guerre Mondiale* (Paris: Hachette, 1997), 21–22.

4. AD M-et-L 97W39, subprefect Milliat of Saumur to prefect of M-et-L, 31 May 1941.

5. Annie Lambert and Claude Toczé, *Être Juif à Nantes sous Vichy* (Nantes: Siloë, 1994), 19–23.

6. AD M-et-L 12W41, register of Jews of M-et-L, 2 Oct. 1940.

7. AD M-et-L 37W10, register of Jews of I-et-L, 1 Oct. 1940, and of L-I, 31 Oct. 1940.

8. AD I-et-L 120W7, prefect Chaigneau to inspector-general of internment camps at Interior Ministry, 22 Oct. 1941; Paisot-Béal and Prévost, *Histoire des Camps d'Internement*, 46–53, 77–78.

9. AD L-A 51W21, central commissaire, Nantes, to prefect of L-I, 30 Oct. 1940.

10. AD L-A 51W21, prefect of L-I to Interior Minister, 30 Nov. and 16 Dec. 1940, 2 Jan. and 19 Feb. 1941; central commissaire, Nantes, to prefect.

11. AD I-et-L 10W7, prefect Chaigneau of I-et-L to prefect delegate of Interior Ministry, Paris, 9 April and 4 Oct. 1941. See also Yves Durand and Robert Vivier, *Libération des Pays de Loire. Blésois, Orléanais, Touraine* (Paris: Hachette, 1974), 37–40.

12. AD I-et-L 10W7, special commissaire, Tours, to prefect of I-et-L, 1 Feb. 1941; AD M-et-L 12W20, police inspector Charpentier to principal commissaire, Tours, 5 Nov. 1942.

13. AD I-et-L 10W75, General Mouton to prefect of I-et-L, 6 and 8 Nov. 1941.

14. *La Dépêche*, 16 Aug. 1941, and *Le Petit Courrier*, 16 Aug. 1941. Clippings in AD M-et-L 12W72. The articles have identical wording.

15. AD M-et-L 140W24, circular of Interior Minister Pucheu to prefects, 13 Sept. 1941.

16. Denis Peschanski, *Vichy 1940–1944: Contrôle et exclusion* (Paris: Complexe, 1997).

17. See above, p. 166.

18. Fonds Émile Aron, minutes of municipal council of Le Boulay, 10 Nov. 1940.

19. AD M-et-L 8W93, chef de cabinet of prefect of M-et-L to subprefect of Saumur, 25 Sept. 1941; AD M-et-L 97W37, subprefect of Saumur to prefect of M-et-L, 9 Oct. 1941.

20. AD M-et-L 97W37, police commissaire Eprinchard to subprefect of Saumur, 14 and 22 March 1941; Déré to subprefect, 22 Mar. 1941; Clémence Veau to DGGFTO, 16 Sept. 1941; subprefect to prefect, 9 Oct. 1941.

21. AD M-et-L 60W2, Bousquet to regional prefect Roussillon, 18 Nov. 1942.

22. AD M-et-L 12W20, prefect Tracou to regional prefect Roussillon, 9 Dec. 1942.

23. AD I-et-L 10W75, police commissaire, Renseignements Généraux, Loches, to prefect of Indre, 26 April 1943; internment order of 2 June 1942.

24. AD L-A 132w160, director of Contributions Indirectes, Nantes, to prefect Dupard, 26 Nov. 1940; Roussillon to Dupard, 9 Oct. 1941; principal commissaire of Police Nationale (Sûreté) to prefect Dupard, 13 Oct. 1941; Dupard to de Brinon, 19 Jan. 1943.

25. AM Nantes 38W9, head of personnel, Nantes, to *adjoint* Prieur, 27 Nov. 1940.

26. Poznanski, *Les Juifs en France*, 71.

27. AD I-et-L 10W66, Feldkommandant of Tours to prefect of I-et-L, 25 Oct. 1940.

28. AD M-et-L 97W39, police commissaire of Saumur to subprefect Milliat, 13 Aug. 1941; Milliat to Kreiskommandantur of Saumur, 2 Sept. 1941, and reply, 4 Sept. 1941; prefect Roussillon to Milliat, 26 Aug. 1941, and Milliat to prefect Daguerre of M-et-L, 28 Jan. 1942.

29. AD L-A 13W46, Ross to Pétain, 21 Oct. 1940, and to Interior Minister, 14 Feb. 1941, supported by letter of prefect Dupard, 18 March 1941; Ross to Dupard, 26 Dec. 1941. AN AJ38/150 contains most of this dossier.

30. André Kaspi, *Les Juifs pendant l'Occupation* (Paris: Seuil, 1997), 116–17.

31. AD M-et-L 97W39, Feldkommandant of Angers to prefect of M-et-L, 8 Nov. 1940; AD L-A 13W44, Feldkommandant of Nantes to prefect Dupard, 18 and 19 Nov. 1940; AD L-A 75W560, prefect Dupard to mayors, 28 Oct. 1940.

32. AD L-A 13W20, prefect Dupard to Dr. Rheinfels, 17 Feb. and 6 June 1941.

33. AD M-et-L 12W42, departmental labor inspector Lehlmann to prefect Roussillon, 10 Dec. 1940.

34. AD M-et-L 97W39, Laraia to subprefect of Saumur Milliat, 5 Nov. 1940; minutes of interview of Laraia with police commissaire René Drouart and report of Drouart to Milliat, 6 Nov. 1940.

35. AD L-A 13W49, return of questionnaire to prefect of L-I by Société Parisienne de Confection, 9 Nov. 1940.

36. AD M-et-L 12W42, prefect Roussillon to presidents of chambers of commerce of Angers, Cholet, and Saumur, 10 and 19 Dec. 1940, and replies of 13 Dec. 1940 and 6 Jan. 1941 (Angers), 18 Dec. 1940 (Cholet), and 19 Dec. 1940 (Saumur).

37. AD M-et-L 61W3, Palamède de la Grandière to Xavier Vallat, 6 July 1941; table of Aryanization and administration of Jewish businesses in Angers by prefect Daguerre, 19 May 1942. See also details of provisional administrators in AN AJ 38/977.

38. AD L-A 13W50, correspondence addressed to prefect Dupard, 12 Jan. 1941–15 Sept. 1942.

39. See, for example, Poznanski, *Les Juifs en France*, 569–71; Cointet, *L'Église sous Vichy*, 197–207; and Halls, *Politics, Society, and Christianity in Vichy France*, 95–103. Lambert and Toczé, *Être Juif à Nantes*, 152, are more scathing about French complicity in the spoliation of the Jews.

40. AD M-et-L 61W4, ruling by prefect on Sainte-Radégonde, June 1941; David Sternschuss to prefect of M-et-L, 15 July 1941; Feldkommandantur of Angers to prefect, 2 Aug. 1941.

41. AD M-et-L 12W42, secretary-general Foulquié to central commissaire, Angers, 20 Aug. 1941.

42. AD M-et-L 61W4, Chené to prefect Roussillon, 14 Oct. 1941, and reply, 23 Oct. 1941; chief of police on Jewish questions to Roussillon, 7 May 1942.

43. AD L-A 270W491, subprefect Lecornu of Châteaubriant to prefect Dupard, 26 May 1941; police commissioner of Nantes to Dupard, 27 May 1941, and internment decision of Dupard, 8 July 1941.

44. Interview with Abbé François Jammoneau, Nantes, 26 May 1997.

45. AD I-et-L 120W7, statistics on population of La Lande, 18 July 1941; AD I-et-L 10W6, Feldkommandantur of Tours to prefect of I-et-L, 28 Aug. 1941.

46. CDJC CCXIII-100, Oeuvres sociales du Centre d'acceuil de Monts, près Tours, n.d.

47. AD I-et-L 120W7, prefect Chaigneau to inspector general of internment camps, Interior Ministry, 22 Oct. 1941; Jérôme Scorin, *L'Itinéraire d'un adolescent juif de 1939 à 1945* (Nancy: Christmann, 1994), 19‑34.

48. AD I-et-L 120W7, prefect of I-et-L to director of La Lande, 24 Oct. 1941, to stationmaster of Monts, 29 Oct. 1941, and to inspector general of internment camps, Interior Ministry, 9 Dec. 1941; AD I-et-L 52W13, Dr. Haueisen of Feldkommandantur of Tours to prefect of I-et-L, 5 Nov. 194; Sigot, *Un Camp de Tziganes*, 81.

49. AD I-et-L 10W75, General Mouton to prefect of I-et-L, 6 and 8 Nov. 1941.

50. AD I-et-L 10W7, prefect of I-et-L to Interior Ministry, 4 Oct. 1941.

51. AD M-et-L 7U4/1–2, register of judgments of the special tribunal of the appeals court of Angers, 14 Aug. 1941.

52. AD M-et-L 136W12, prefect Roussillon to Feldkommandant of Angers, 25 July 1941; AD M-et-L 7U4/1–2, Special Tribunal, Angers, 18 Sept. 1941

53. See above, p. 72.

54. AD L-A 270W494, reports of camp governor Captain Leclercq, May, June, July, and Aug. 1941.

Chapter 10 *Murder*

1. The fullest account of this incident is in Oury, *Rue du Roi Albert*, 13–14, 89–93.

2. *Ouest-France*, 21 Oct. 1991.

3. Duméril, *Journal d'un Honnête Homme sous l'Occupation*, 20 Oct. 1941 (p. 81).

4. AN 72AJ145 and AM-Nantes H4/116, F. Soil, secretary-general of the prefectures, "Meutre du Lieutenant Colonel Hotz, Feldkommandant de Nantes, le 20 octobre 1941." The file in the AM also includes examples of the posters.

5. AM Nantes 1134W9, letters to mayor of Nantes, 21 Oct. 1941.

6. *Le Phare*, 22 Oct. 1941. See clippings in AM Nantes 1134W12.

7. On 21 October the communist commandos sent to Bordeaux shot Commandant Reimers of the Wehrmacht general staff. See Dominique Lormier, *Bordeaux pendant l'Occupation* (Bordeaux: Éditions Sud-Ouest, 1992), 122–24.

8. BAMA Freiburg 35/543, circular of Keitel, 16 Sept. 1941, and circulars of Stülpnagel, 19 and 28 Sept. 1941; Eberhard Jäckel, *Frankreich in Hitlers Europa* (Stuttgart: Verlags-Anstalt, 1966), 191–92; Richard Cavill Fattig, "Reprisal: The German Army and the Execution of Hostages during the Second World War," (PhD dissertation, University of California at San Diego, 1980, 63–65.

9. BAMA Freiburg 35/542, "Das Geiselverfahren im Bereich des Militärbefehlshabers in Frankreich von August 1941 bis Mai 1942."

10. See above, p. 72.

11. AD L-A 243W163, notes of *procureur* on "l'Affaire Jost," n.d., and report of Duméril on execution of Poirier, n.d. The latter is also in AN Fla 3667.

12. AM Nantes H4/116, poster dated 21 Oct. 1941.

13. Bernard Lecornu, *Un Préfet sous l'Occupation allemande: Châteaubriant, Saint-Nazaire, Tulle* (Paris: France-Empire, 1997), 47–51, 85–95. See also his account in AD L-A 270W480.

14. Oury, *Rue du Roi Albert*, 114–15.

15. A. Dio. Nantes, Mgr Villepelet, "Le Diocèse de Nantes," 22 Oct. 1941.

16. AN 72AJ145 and AM Nantes H4/116, F. Soil, "Meurtre du Lieutenant Colonel Hotz."

17. AD L-A 132W54, report of Lecomte, commander of the Gendarmerie Company of Loire-Inférieure, 29 Oct. 1941.

18. Pétain *Actes et Écrits*, 603–04; Ferro, *Pétain*, 344–47.

19. AM Nantes 1134W10, Mlle Benoîte to mayor of Nantes, 6 Dec. 1941; Duméril, *Journal d'un honnête homme*, 194.

20. Mgr Villepelet, "Le Diocèse de Nantes," 23 Oct. 1941.

21. AM Nantes 1134W10, Mayor Rondeau to chef de cabinet of de Brinon, 23 Oct. 1941.

22. AM Nantes 1134W10, Mayor Rondeau to Alphonse de Châteaubriant, 23 Oct. 1941.

23. *Le Phare*, 25 Oct. 1941; *L'Ouest-Éclair*, 25 Oct. 1941. Clippings in AM Nantes 1134W12.

24. AD L-A 270W480, report of commissaire de police, Nantes, 24 Oct. 1941.

25. AD L-A 270W480, letter of M. Méroviac to prefect, 24 Oct. 1941.

26. Mgr Villepelet, "Le Diocèse de Nantes," 24, 25, and 27 Oct. and 18 Nov. 1941.

27. Ridel, *Témoignages*, 162–65; Sesmaisons, *Marquise de Sesmaisons*, 70, 93–95.

28. AD L-A 270W480, petition of families, 25 Oct. 1941, and note of Duméril for prefect, n.d.; Duméril *Journal d'un honnête homme*, 195; AM Nantes 1134W11, Mayor Rondeau to M. Glou, 27 Oct., and reply of Glou, 29 Oct. 1941.

29. BAMA Freiburg RW 35/1, von Stülpnagel to Major General Wagner, 24 Oct.

1941. See also Jäckel, *Frankreich*, 192–94, and Bücheler, *Carl-Heinrich von Stülp-nagel*, 246–47.

30. Ernst Jünger, *Premier Journal Parisien: Journal II, 1941–1943* (Paris: Christian Bourgois, 1980), 108–09.
31. Fattig, "Reprisal," 153; Anatoly Kuznetsov, *Babi Yar: A Documentary Novel* (London: MacGibbon and Kee, 1967); George St. George, *The Road to Babi Yar* (London: Neville Spearman, 1967).
32. AD L-A 270W480, report of Commissaire Divisonnaire, Chef de la Iere Brigade de la Police Judiciaire, 4 Nov. 1941.
33. AN 72AJ 145, questioning of Mme Huau, Nantes, 20 Oct. 1944.
34. AM Nantes 1134W11, address of Mayor Rondeau, 29 Oct. 1941. This was authorized by the Feldkommandantur but prohibited by the Propagandastaffel in Nantes.
35. Charles de Gaulle, *Discours et Messages I, juin 1940–janvier 1946* (Paris: Plon, 1970), 122–25. Broadcast of 25 Oct. 1941, repeated 30 Oct.
36. AD M-et-L 12W3, prefect Dupard to Interior Minister, 2 Nov. 1941.
37. AD M-et-L 12W48, report of prefect Dupard, 1 Nov. 1941.
38. AM Nantes 1134W14, decree of 11 Nov. 1941.
39. AD L-A 132W54, report of prefect Dupard, 1 Dec. 1941.
40. AD L-A 270W480, *La Bretagne ouvrière, paysanne, et maritime: Édition spéciale de la Loire-Inférieure*, n.d.
41. Duméril, *Journal d'un honnête homme*, 236.

CHAPTER II *Terror*

1. AD I-et-L 10W81, account by the young men, 15 May 1942; report of Bossy, commissaire spécial of I-et-L, to prefect, 18/20 Oct. 1944.
2. AD M-et-L 60W10, accounts of André Maurice, 24 Oct. 1944; Jean Moracchini, 1 Dec. 1944; and police commissioner Georges Gouchet, 2 Jan. 1945.
3. AD I-et-L 10W8, police commissioner Moracchini to prefect Tracou, 26 May 1942; AD M-et-L 12W2, Tracou to regional prefect, Angers, 28 May 1942.
4. Robert Guérinau and Jean-Claude Guillon, *La Touraine sous le règne des Feld-kommandants* (Tours: Centre-Loire, 1985), 47. See also Guérineau, *Les Martys du 16 mai 1942: Les premiers fusillés de la Touraine* (Tours: La Voix du Peuple, 1963). Guérineau and Guillon were communist militants who had met on 30 April 1942 to organize the campaign of tracts and graffiti.
5. AD M-et-L 12W2, report of prefect Tracou to Interior Minister, 3 Feb. 1942.
6. Interview with Émile Aron, Tours, 19 March 1997.
7. AD M-et-L 12W2, report of prefect Tracou to Interior Minister 3 March 1942.
8. BAMA Freiburg RW35/542, order of Militärbefehlshaber in Frankreich, 17 Feb. 1942.
9. AD M-et-L 12W3, report of prefect Dupard to Interior Minister, 1 May 1942;

Lecornu, *Un Préfet sous l'Occupation allemande*, 122–34; Mgr Villepelet, "Le Diocèse de Nantes," 1 May 1942.

10. AD I-et-L 10W8, Bousquet to Oberg, 29 July 1942; text of Oberg address, 8 Aug. 1942; Bousquet to prefects, 13 Aug. 1942; Maurice Rajsfus, *La Police de Vichy: Forces de l'ordre français au service de la Gestapo* (Paris: Le Cherche-Midi, 1995), 75–97.

11. AD M-et-L 12W20, Ernst to regional prefect of Angers, 3 July 1942.

12. AD M-et-L 10W18, Ernst to regional prefect of Angers, 10 July 1942; regional prefect to prefects, 16 July 1942.

13. AD I-et-L 60W6, report on the Germans in I-et-L by commissaire spécial Laforge, May 1945, based on captured archives of the Tours Gestapo; AD I-et-L 34W4, report by Brückle on Boucherie, 15 Aug. 1942; Morin, *Les Allemands en Touraine*, 71–79..

14. AD M-et-L 140W95, prefect to Feldkommandant of Angers, 25 Aug. 1942.

15. AD L-A 51W29, prefect Dupard to prefect delegate of Interior Ministry, Paris, 31 Oct. 1942.

16. AD M-et-L 18W24, Ernst to Roussillon, 29 Oct. 1942; Roussillon to Mgr Costes, 2 Nov. 1942; Costes to Roussillon, 7 Nov. 1942; AD M-et-L 18W25, Ernst to Mgr Costes, 16 Dec. 1942.

17. See above, p. 202.

18. AD M-et-L 12W54, report of regional police intendant, Angers, 30 Sept. 1942; AN 72AJ147, court of Feldkommandantur 518, Nantes, 6 Jan. 1943, charges against forty-two communist terrorists sent for trial.

19. AD L-A 132W89, report of prefect Dupard on Commissioner Fourcade, 1942; AD M-et-L 12W3, report of Yves Bayet, 1 Sept. 1942, and of prefect Dupard, 4 Nov. 1942.

20. Duméril, *Journal d'un honnête homme*, 260–72.

21. *Le Phare de Nantes*, 16 Jan. 1943, cited in Duméril, *Journal d'un honnête homme*, 264–65.

22. AD M-et-L 12W3, prefect Dupard to regional prefect, Angers, 4 March 1943.

23. AD M-et-L 60W6, meeting of regional prefects and chiefs of Sicherheitspolizei, 16 April 1943.

24. AM Nantes 38W9, Mayor Rondeau to prefect Dupard, 20 June 1942; prefect to mayor, 16 July 1942.

25. AD M-et-L 12W41, prefect delegate Daguerre to mayor of Seiches-sur-Loire, 5 June 1942.

26. AD M-et-L 61W3, Daguerre to CGQJ, 8 July 1942, and reply, 11 July 1942.

27. Michelle Audoin-Le Marec, *Le Maine-et-Loire dans la guerre, 1939–1945* (Le Coteau: Horvath, 1987), 136.

28. Among others, Asher Cohen, *Persécutions et sauvetages: Juifs et français sous l'Occupation et sous Vichy* (Paris: Éditions du Cerf, 1993); Poznanski, *Les Juifs en France*, 313–46.

29. AD L-A 13W45, reports of squadron chief Lecomte and subprefect Lecornu of Saint-Nazaire to prefect, 16 July 1942.

30. AD M-et-L 140W97, police commissioner of Angers to prefect, 16 July 1942.

31. AD M-et-L 97W40, adjutant Barreau of Gennes to captain of Saumur gendarmerie, 23 Oct. 1942.

32. Interview with Abbé Henri Richer (b. 1920), Angers, 6 June 1997.

33. AD M-et-L 140W97, police commissioner of Angers to prefect, 16 July 1942.

34. AD M-et-L 12W4, subprefect on behalf of prefect delegate of M-et-L to regional prefect, Angers, 24 July 1942.

35. AD M-et-L 140W97, subprefect of Cholet to prefect of M-et-L, 18 July 1942.

36. AD M-et-L 12W4, prefect delegate Daguerre to Interior Minister, 2 Sept. 1942.

37. AD M-et-L, 12W2, prefect Tracou to regional prefect, Angers, 24 July 1942.

38. AD I-et-L 120W8, report of director of camp of La Lande, July 1942.

39. AD M-et-L 140W97, subprefect of Saumur to prefect delegate, Angers, 16 July 1942.

40. AD M-et-L 7W1, list of children of Jews arrested in Angers since 15 July 1942.

41. AD L-A 13W44, decision of Ernst communicated to prefect of L-I, 24 Aug. 1941.

42. AD M-et-L 7W1, details of arrests of Jews, 1942–44.

43. AD M-et-L 18W25, Dr. Barrault to mayor of Les Ponts-de-Cé, 18 July 1942. SS Kommandeur Pfleider gave a favorable reply to the prefect of M-et-L, 19 Aug. 1942.

44. AD M-et-L 7W1, police commissioner of Angers to prefect, 27 July and 10 Aug. 1942.

45. Audoin-Le Marec, *Le Maine-et-Loire*, 137.

46. AD L-A 13W45, Lucien Bernheim to prefect of L-I, 7 Sept. 1942.

47. AD L-A 13W45, subprefect Lecornu to prefect of L-I, 6 Oct. 1942.

48. AD I-et-L 10W84, Maître Siecklucki to prefect of I-et-L, 29 July 1942, and reply of prefect, 4 Aug. 1942.

49. AD I-et-L 52W20, regional prefect Roussillon to prefect Tracou, 1 Sept. 1942, and reply of Tracou, 18 Sept. 1942.

50. AD M-et-L 97W40, president of Union Générale des Israéllites to prefect of M-et-L, 7 Aug. 1942, and reply of prefect Daguerre, 10 Aug. 1942; prefect Daguerre to Dr. Ernst, 10 Aug. 1942. and reply of Ernst, 18 Aug. 1942; AD M-et-L 140W97, Daguerre to Laval, 10 Aug. 1942, and reply of prefect delegate of Interior Ministry, 20 Aug. 1942.

51. See below, ch. 12.

52. AD I-et-L 120W8, reports of director of camp of La Lande, 13 Sept. and 16 Nov. 1942.

53. AD M-et-L 18W83, Lieutenant Colonel Chambon, commander of gendarmerie of M-et-L, to colonel commanding Ninth Gendarmerie Legion of Tours, 8 Oct. 1942.

54. AD M-et-L 140W97, Daguerre to Laval, 19 Oct. 1942.

55. AD M-et-L 97W40, lists of arrested Jews, Angers, Oct. 1942.

56. AD I-et-L 44W421, identity cards of deported Jews returned by prefecture of I-et-L to prefecture of M-et-L, 7 April 1943.

57. AD I-et-L 10W66, A. and D. Aron to prefect Tracou, 28 Oct. 1942, and reply of Tracou, 14 Nov. 1942.

58. AD M-et-L 12W4, Daguerre to Interior Minister, 3 Nov. 1943.

59. AD M-et-L 18W83, prefect Dupard to regional prefect, 9 Oct. 1942.

60. AD M-et-L 80W7, chief superintendent of Renseignements Généraux, Angers, 26 June 1943.

61. AD M-et-L 97W40, report of Baugé gendarmerie to prefect of M-et-L, 22 Nov. 1943.

62. AD M-et-L 18W85, report of CGQJ, Angers, 2 Nov. 1943.

63. AD L-A 13W50, regional delegate of CGQJ, Angers, to police commissioner, Nantes, May 1943; police superintendent, 5th arrondissement, Nantes, to police commissioner, 1 June 1943; Paris CGQJ to prefect of L-I, 11 Jan. 1944; prefect to CGQJ, Angers, 26 April 1944.

64. Fitzpatrick and Gellately, *Accusatory Practices* (Chicago and London: University of Chicago Press, 1997).

65. AD I-et-L 10W53, report of police commissioner, Tours, 12 Nov. and 24 Dec. 1943.

66. AN Fla 3874, weekly bulletin of Renseignements Généraux, 14 Jan. 1943.

67. AD M-et-L 12W82, Roussillon to Laval, 26 March 1943.

68. AD M-et-L 136W12, prefect to Feldkommandant of Angers, 7 Aug. 1942.

69. AN AJ40 544, military chief of Angers region to Dr. Medicus, Paris, 7 Jan. and 18 Feb. 1943.

70. Montergon, *Le Colonel François de Sauvebeuf,* 249.

71. AD I-et-L 10W84, police commissioner, Tours, to prefect of I-et-L, 3 May 1943.

72. AD M-et-L 80W6, police commissioner, Angers, to prefect, 17 and 24 April 1943.

73. AD M-et-L 12W4, prefect Daguerre of M-et-L to Interior Minister, 3 May 1943.

74. AD M-et-L 12W2, prefect Tracou of I-et-L to Interior Minister, 4 May 1943.

75. AD M-et-L 12W2, prefect Tracou to Interior Minister, 3 Sept. 1943; AN AJ40 542, German notes on Molas-Quenescourt, 14 Jan. 1944, and on Aubert, n.d; AD I-et-L 52W57, file on Molas-Quenescourt, 1944–45.

76. AD M-et-L 60W12, police commissioner, Angers, to prefect, 1 Sept. 1943; regional prefect Donati to Bousquet, 24 Sept. 1943; prefect Bonnefoy of L-I to regional prefect, 15 Sept. 1943; AD M-et-L 60W13, report by Inspector Vairé, 12 July 1945. On Wilkinson, see M. R. D. Foot, *SOE in France: An Account of the Work of the British Special Operations Executive in France, 1940–1944* (London: Her Majesty's Stationery Office, 1966), 196–97, 222, 258, 314.

77. AD M-et-L 80W7, report of Renseignements Généraux, 25 Sept. and 9 Oct. 1943.

Chapter 12 *Conscription*

1. AD L-A 132W157, Colonel Mauris, departmental delegate of Information Ministry, to general delegate of the ministry, 2 Oct. 1942; Robert Tillaut to Colonel Mauris, 2 Oct. 1942.
2. AD M-et-L 18W35, tract sent by regional prefect Roussillon to Laval, 9 Oct. 1942.
3. Jacques Evrard, *La Déportation des travailleurs français dans le Troisième Reich* (Paris: Fayard, 1972), 39–41.
4. AD M-et-L 12W3, prefect Dupard to Interior Minister, 4 Nov. 1942.
5. AD M-et-L 18W35, copy of *Le Phare*, 11 Aug. 1942, forwarded by Dupard to regional prefect Roussillon.
6. Mgr Villepelet, "Le Diocèse de Nantes," 10 and 21 Aug. 1942.
7. AD M-et-L 18W36, Rondeau to regional delegate of Information Ministry Cambier, 31 Aug. 1942, and reply of Cambier, 8 Sept., forwarded by prefect Dupard to Roussillon, 28 Sept. 1942.
8. AD L-A 13W8, Rondeau to Pétain, 19 Aug. 1942.
9. AD M-et-L 18W134, prefect Dupard to Laval, 10 Oct. 1942.
10. AD L-A 27J18, "Carnets de M. Soil, secrétaire-général de la Mairie de Nantes," 10, 13, and 20 Oct. 1942.
11. AD L-A 132W157, prefect Dupard to Laval, 20 Oct. 1942; BAMA Freiburg RW24/125, report of Wehrwirtschaftsinspektion, SW Frankreich, 29 Oct. 1942.
12. AD L-A 132157, Dupard to Laval, 21 Oct. 1942.
13. AD M-et-L 12W54, report of intendant of police, Angers, 2 Nov. 1942.
14. AD M-et-L 18W134, Dupard to Laval, 20 Oct. 1942; AD L-A 27J18, "Carnets de M. Soil," 31 Oct. 1942: *Le Phare*, 30 Nov. 1942.
15. AD L-A 132W157, prefect Dupard to prefect delegate of Interior Ministry, 8 Nov. 1942.
16. AN F1a 3869, report for CFLN, Saint-Nazaire region, 15 Nov. 1942.
17. AD M-et-L 12W3, prefect Dupard to Interior Minister, 4 Nov. 1942.
18. Evrard, *La Déportation des travailleurs*, 74–83.
19. AD I-et-L 121W1, prefect Tracou to Labor Minister, 17 Oct. 1942, and to Feldkommandant of Tours, 22 Oct. 1942.
20. AD I-et-L 121W1, Feldkommandant of Tours to prefect Tracou, 12 Dec. 1942; labor inspector Dos to Tracou, 14 Dec. 1942.
21. BAM A RH36/312, report of Kriegsverwaltungsrat, FK 518 Nantes, 23 March 1943.
22. BAMA RW24/179, war diary of Rüstungskommando, Le Mans, 1–14 Nov. 1943; Alan S. Milward, *The New Order and the French Economy* (Oxford: Oxford UP, 1984; rpt. Gregg Revivals, 1993), 157–67.
23. AD I-et-L 10W9, labor inspector to prefect of I-et-L, 1 March 1943. This form of words was taken up exactly by prefect Tracou in his report to the Interior Minister, 6 March 1943, in AD M-et-L 12W2.

24. BAM Freiburg RH36/138, reports to chief of Militärverwaltung Bezirk B from Kriegsverwaltungsrat Buchholtz, Angers, 8 Feb. 1943; Kriegsverwaltung Nantes, 13 Feb. 1943; and Feldkommandant von Trotha, Nantes, 21 Feb. 1943.

25. AD M-et-L 7U4/95, Cour de Justice file on Hupfer, who was sentenced to three years' imprisonment and confiscation of property, 22 March 1945.

26. AD M-et-L 12W3, prefect Dupard of L-I to Interior Minister, 4 Jan. 1943.

27. AD M-et-L 12W4, prefect Daguerre to Interior Minister, 5 Jan. 1943.

28. AD M-et-L 12W3, prefect Dupard to regional prefect, Angers, 4 March 1943.

29. AD M-et-L 12W2, prefect Tracou of I-et-L to Interior Minister, 6 July 1943.

30. AD M-et-L 12W4, prefect Daguerre to Interior Minister, 5 Jan. 1943.

31. AD I-et-L 10W9, subprefect of Chinon to prefect of I-et-L, 24 June 1943.

32. AD M-et-L 12W4, prefect Daguerre to Interior Minister, 2 March 1943.

33. AD M-et-L 12W2, prefect Tracou of I-et-L to Interior Minister, 3 Sept. 1943.

34. AD L-A 132W157, minutes of meeting of 8 March 1943 at Feldkommandantur of Nantes.

35. Darmaillacq, *Cholet sous l'Occupation*, 42–43, 63–64.

36. AD I-et-L 121W5, replies to labor inspector, Tours, of mayor of Saint-Roch, 3 Feb. 1943, and mayor of Saint-Laurent-en-Gâtines, 5 Feb. 1943.

37. AD I-et-LXIV Z 17, correspondence of Kriegsverwaltungsrat of Feldkommandantur of Tours and Befehlshaber SW Frankreich, Angers, 13 April–8 June 1943; Feldkommandantur to prefect of I-et-L, 8 June and 1 July 1943, and reply of prefect, 7 July 1943.

38. AD I-et-L 10W61, Brückle to prefect of I-et-L, 1 Nov. and 13 Dec. 1943; prefect to Laval, 15 Nov. 1943; prefect to Brückle, 14 Jan. 1944.

39. AD L-A 132W157, report of subprefect of Châteaubriant, 9 Nov. 1942.

40. AN AJ40/544, note on prefect Roussillon, n.d.; Befehlshaber der SP und der SD to Militärbefehlshaber in Frankreich, 4 March 1943.

41. AN F1a 3869, report of CFLN, 29 Aug. 1943.

42. See, for example, Jean Estèbe, ed., *Les Juifs à Toulouse et en Midi toulousain au temps de Vichy* (Toulouse: Presses Universitaires Le Mirail, 1996), 154–56; Halls, *Politics, Society, and Christianity in Vichy France*, 118–24.

43. Cointet, *L'Église sous Vichy*, 290.

44. Mgr Villepelet, "Le Diocèse de Nantes," 19 April 1943.

45. Mgr Villepelet, "Le Diocèse de Nantes," 29 April 1943.

46. AD M-et-L 18W35, Donati to Laval, 14 May 1943.

47. AD L-A 13W26, Obersturmführer Doescher of Nantes Sicherheitspolizei to prefect Dupard, 17 April 1943.

48. AD M-et-L 12W54, report of intendant of police, Angers, 3 May 1943.

49. AD M-et-L 80W7, report of chief superintendent, Renseignements Généraux, 26 June 1943.

50. AD M-et-L 12W2, prefect Tracou to Interior Minister, 4 May 1943; François Tauzun, "Le STO en Touraine occupé, 1942–1944," master's thesis, University of Tours, 1996, 56.

51. AD L-A 40W24, report of Secretary-General Yves Bayet for prefect of L-I, 26 June 1943; AD M-et-L 18W50, report of Lieutenant Colonel Pentel, commander of Eleventh Legion of Gendarmerie, Nantes, June and July 1943.

52. Leprince, *La Pommeraye dans la guerre*, 87–102, 146.

53. Collection Michel Lemesle, letter of Mme Delépine, La Ferrière-de-Flée (M-et-L), 28 Nov. 1973.

54. BAMA Freiburg RH 36/588, commanding captain in Cholet to Feldkommandantur of Tours, 7 May 1942.

55. AD M-et-L 80W7, report of chief superintendent Renseignements Généraux, Angers, 3 July 1943.

56. AD M-et-L 12W3, prefect Gaudard of L-I to Intendant du Maintien de l'Ordre, Angers, 3 May 1944.

57. AD M-et-L 18W47, daily reports of intendant of police, 19 and 25 May 1944. This file is a rich Vichy source for the activities of "terrorists" in the region in 1944.

58. See Fabrice Virgili, *Shorn Women: Gender and Punishment in Liberation France* (Oxford, Berg, 2002) Corran Laurens, "La Femme au turban: Les femmes tondues," in H. R. Kedward and Nancy Wood, eds., *The Liberation of France: Image and Event* (Oxford and Washington: Berg, 1995), 155–79; Diamond, *Women and the Second World War in France*, 134–42.

59. AD L-A 40W14, Viennot, director of CGMO, L-et-I, to prefect, 7 March 1944; deputy director of CGMO to prefect, 6 April 1944.

60. AD L-A 40W14, General Feldt to regional prefect Donati, 16 May 1944.

61. AD M-et-L 18W36, press clippings from *Le Petit Courrier*, 28 Feb., *Tours-Soir*, 29 Feb., and *Le Petit Parisien*, 1 March 1944; letter from Lübeck worker to Donati, 2 March 1944; Donati to Laval, 20 March 1944. This is also in AN F1a 3870.

62. AD I-et-L 10W53, police commissioner, Tours, 19 Feb. 1944.

63. AD M-et-L 136W3, G. Michelet, departmental delegate of the Ministry of Information, to prefect of M-et-L, 19 Jan. 1944.

64. Cointet, *L'Église sous Vichy*, 291. The statement is dated 17 Feb. 1944.

65. AD M-et-L 12W54, intendant of police, Angers, to regional prefect, 15 June, 28 Aug., and 14 Sept. 1943.

66. AD L-A 40W15, departmental director of CGMO, L-I, to regional director, Angers, 26 May 1944.

67. AD L-A 40W15, police commissioner, Nantes, to prefect, 13 and 20 June 1944.

CHAPTER 13 *Disintegration*

1. *Le Courrier de Saint-Nazaire*, 20 Feb. 1942.

2. AD L-A 75W553, Kreiskommandant Major von Hasselbach to prefect Dupard, 16 May 1942.

3. BAMA Freiburg RW24/125, war diary of Wehrwirtschaftsinspektion, SW

Frankreich, 23 Nov., 16 Dec. 1942; AN F1a 3871, report for CFLN, 11 March 1943.

4. AN 72AJ 146, statistics on bombings of Saint-Nazaire, 1939–44.

5. AD M-et-L 12W3, prefect Dupard of L-I to regional prefect, Angers, 4 March, and to Interior Minister, 1 May 1943.

6. See above, pp. 101, 104.

7. *La Semaine religieuse du diocèse de Nantes*, 28 Feb. 1942.

8. Anne Curet, "Quelques Souvenirs de 1941 à 1945," communicated to the author, 14 April 1997.

9. AD M-et-L 18W39, president of COSI in Angers to regional prefect, 5 May 1943.

10. AD M-et-L 18W38, report of regional head of Refugees Service, 29 March 1943.

11. AD M-et-L 95W91, replies to subprefect of Cholet from mayor of Tilliers, 15 May 1943, and mayor of Jallais, 17 May 1943.

12. AD M-et-L 140W108, reports of chief superintendent, Renseignments Généraux, Angers, 31 Aug. 1943, and of inspector of regional police, Angers, 20 Sept. 1943.

13. Duméril, *Journal d'un honnête homme*, 293 (entry for 27 March 1943).

14. AD L-A 54W14, Abel Durand of Secours National to prefect Dupard, 8 and 24 July 1943; Pompes Funèbres Générales, Nantes, to Orrion, president of special delegation, Nantes, 12 Aug. 1943; hospices civiles, Nantes, to Dupard, 22 Oct. 1943.

15. AN F1a 3871 and AD M-et-L 18W24, M. Gon of SNCSO to prefect Dupard, 19 July 1943.

16. AM Nantes 38W17, police officer Morillon to commander of Nantes police, 14 Sept. 1943.

17. BAMA Freiburg RW24/155, war diary of Rüstungskommando of Nantes, July–Sept. 1943; AN F1a 3872, report of prefect Bonnefoy of L-I, 8 Nov. 1943.

18. BAMA Freiburg RH36/525, report by Feldkommandantur of Nantes on effect of Nantes bombings of food sector, n.d. (Oct. 1943).

19. AD M-et-L 12W3, prefect Bonnefoy of L-I to Interior Minister, 5 Nov. 1943.

20. BAMA Freiburg RH36/146, report of Arbeitseinsatzstab, Nantes, 22 Oct. 1943.

21. AD M-et-L 136W2, subprefect of Cholet to prefect of M-et-L, 20 Dec. 1943.

22. AD M-et-L 18W38, evacuee statistics for 1 Oct. 1943.

23. AD I-et-L 218W14, Secours National director of propaganda to Indre-et-Loire delegate, 18 May 1943.

24. AD I-et-L 218W17, reports from Ligueil and L'Ile Bouchard, April 1943.

25. AD I-et-L 18W50, report of commander of Ninth Legion of Gendarmerie, Tours, 3 April 1943.

26. AD I-et-L 10W63, report of inspector of police, Renseignements Généraux, Tours, 25 March 1943.

27. AD I-et-L 108W8, prefect Tracou to prefect of Morbihan, 7 April 1943.

28. BAMA Freiburg RW24/179–180, war diaries of Rüstungskommando, Le Mans, 17–23 Oct. 1943, 31 Jan.–5 Feb. 1944; AN F1a 3874, interview with engineer of Le Ripault, 15 Nov. 1943; AN F1a 3869, report on Le Ripault, 20 Feb. 1944.

29. AN F1a 3874, eyewitness account of air raid on Saint-Pierre-des-Corps, 13 April 1944.

30. AN F1a 3874, record of Vichy radio broadcast, 25 May 1944; diverse information, 26 May 1944. Claude Morin, *La Touraine sous les bombes* (Chambray-lès-Tours: CLD, 2000), 112–13, 140–41, 158–61.

31. BAMA Freiburg RW24/141, war diary of Rüstungskommando, Angers, 9–15 April, 14–20 May, 28 May–3 June 1944.

32. AD M-et-L 18W25, prefect of I-et-L to regional prefect, 21 Feb. 1944; regional prefect to secretary of state for industrial production, 2 and 18 March 1944.

33. AD M-et-L 136W4, subprefect of Saumur to prefect of M-et-L, 20 April 1944.

34. AN F1a 3874, report from Tours, 5 April 1944.

35. But see Alain Beltran, "Le Cas des entreprises d'électricité," in Beltran, Frank, and Rousso, *La Vie des entreprises sous l'Occupation*, 69–89; P. Perraud, "Électricité et défense: Rôle et importance de l'électricité dans l'exploitation des potentiels industriels durant l'Occupation par la Wehrmacht," master's thesis, Université de Paul-Valéry, Montpellier II, 1987.

36. BAMA Freiburg RW24/180, war diary of Rüstungskommando, Le Mans, 9–15 Jan., 16–22 Jan., 30 Jan.–5 Feb., 12–18 March 1944.

37. BAMA Freiburg RW24/141, report of Oberst Keil, Rüstungskommando Angers, 1 April–30 June 1944; RW24/159, report of Rüstungskommando Nantes, 30 June 1944.

38. AD M-et-L 12W16, "Réception des personnalités du département du Maine-et-Loire et de la Ville d'Angers à l'occasion de l'installation du nouveau préfet régional, M. Donati, lundi 9 août 1943."

39. AD M-et-L 12W17, *Bulletin mensuel de la Chambre de Commerce d'Angers et de Maine-et-Loire*, no. 9 (Oct. 1943): 227–30. The meeting was on 7 Oct.

40. AN AJ40/542, German assessment of Charles Donati, n.d.

41. AD M-et-L 18W25, Donati to Feldt, 5 Dec. 1943, and reply, 18 Dec. 1943.

42. BAMA Freiburg RH36/131, report of Feldkommandantur of Nantes, 4 Jan. 1944.

43. Duméril, *Journal d'un honnête homme*, 347 (23 Sept. 1943).

44. AD M-et-L 12W3, prefect Bonnefoy to Interior Minister, 3 Sept. 1943.

45. AD L-A 13W22, Bonnefoy to Lieutenant Doescher, head of Sicherheitspolizei, Nantes, 2 Sept. 1943.

46. AD L-A 13W22, police commissioner to director of Renseignements Généraux, Vichy, 29 Dec. 1943; AN 72AJ/144, information on General Reinhardt by E. Duméril, 25 Jan. 1950.

47. AN AJ40/542, report of Feldkommandantur of Tours on prefect Musso, 12 May 1944.

48. AD I-et-L 52W57, Gestapo report to Feldkommandantur of Tours, 8 March 1944; subprefect Cay to prefect Musso, 16 and 19 May 1944; prefect Musso to regional prefect Donati, 20 March 1944, and Donati's reply, 29 March 1944. See also declaration of Cay after the Liberation, n.d..

49. AM Tours, *Bulletin municipal de la Ville de Tours*, 28 Dec. 1943.

50. AN AJ 40/542, German note on Paul Cay, n.d.

51. AD I-et-L 10W8, subprefect Cay to prefect, 23 Dec. 1942.

52. AN AJ40/542, report of Feldkommandant of Angers on Saissier, n.d. (Feb. 1944); AD M-et-L 136W3, departmental delegate of Ministry of Information to Donati, 28 Feb. 1944; AD M-et-L 18W13, Donati to Laval, 17 March 1944.

53. AN AJ40/542, report of Feldkommandantur and Propagandastaffel of Nantes, 7 Nov. 1943; AN AJ40/544, Befehlshaber SW Frankreich to Militärbefehlshaber in Frankreich, 1 Jan. 1944; Lecornu, *Un Préfet sous l'Occupation allemande*, 164–65; Mgr Villepelet, "Le Diocèse de Nantes," 14 Feb. 1944.

54. BAMA Freiburg RH36/142, report of Feldkommandantur of Nantes, 28 Feb. 1944.

55. AN F1a 3869, report of Mission Militaire de Liaison Administrative on Gaudard, n.d.

56. AD L-A 13W22, prefect Gaudard to Dr. Baessler, 13 May 1944.

57. Mgr Villepelet, "Le Diocèse de Nantes," 14 May 1944.

58. See below, p. 318.

59. AD M-et-L 12W2, prefect Tracou to Interior Minister, 3 Sept. 1943; AD I-et-L XIV Z 17, internal circular of Feldkommandantur of Tours, 4 Sept. 1943; Feldkommandantur to Sicherheitspolizei, Tours, 14 Sept. 1943.

60. AD M-et-L 12W2, prefect Musso of I-et-L to Interior Minister, 2 March 1944.

61. AD M-et-L 18W134, Donati to Laval, 8 Feb. 1944; Donati to Bernier, 4 March, and reply of Bernier, 6 March 1944.

62. See above, pp. 185–86.

63. AD L-A 13W18, report of Renseignements Généraux, Nantes, 22 and 28 Feb. 1944.

64. AD M-et-L 140W9, subprefect Tremeaud to prefect Daguerre, 21 May 1943.

65. AN AJ40/542, German information on subprefect Tremeaud, 11 March 1944.

66. AD I-et-L 10W25, figures for resignation of mayors, 1942–43.

67. AD M-et-L 12W2, prefect Musso of I-et-L to Interior Minister, 2 March 1944.

68. AD I-et-L 10W9, report of prefect Musso, 13 May 1944.

69. Collection Michel Lemesle, Angers, Renaud de Razilly, "La Résistance dans le Maine-et-Loire," typescript, n.d.

70. AD M-et-L 19W13, prefect Fourré-Cormeray to Interior Minister, 3 Sept. 1944.

71. Michel Debré, *Combattre*, vol. 1 of *Trois Républiques pour une France* (Paris: Albin Michel, 1984), 308.

72. Pierre Laborie, *L'Opinion française sous Vichy*, 262–70.

73. AD M-et-L 80W4, chief superintendent, Renseignements Généraux, Angers, to prefect of M-et-L, 27 March 1942.

74. AD M-et-L 24W27, letters to Marshal Pétain from Angevins, Jan. 1943–July 1944. These letters were generally referred back to departmental prefects for handling.

75. AD M-et-L 24W30, Mme Legouic of Saumur to Pétain, 8 Feb. 1944.

76. AN 72AJ145, report of police superintendent, Nantes, 9 May 1943.

77. AD M-et-L 18W50, report of commander of Ninth Legion of Gendarmerie, Tours, 3 July 1943.

78. See above.

79. AD M-et-L 12W2, prefect Tracou to Interior Minister, 3 Jan. 1944.

80. AD L-A 13W7, prefect Gaudard of L-I to Interior Minister, 11 April 1944.

81. AD M-et-L 136W4, Renseignements Généraux, Angers, to Interior Minister, 11 March and 15 April 1944.

82. BAMA Freiburg RW35/1252, final report of military administration of southwest France region for July, Aug., and Sept. 1944, 17–18.

83. AD M-et-L 21W58, Feldkommandant of Angers to prefect of M-et-L, 26 July 1943; Michel Lemesle, *L'Anjou des années 40: Chroniques* (Angers: Les Éditions du Choletais, 1984), 123–26.

84. Account of Lieutenant Blée of Forces Françaises Libres and Bréhémont, cited in Maurice, *Cinquante mois sous la botte*, 40–41.

85. AN 72AJ136, account of Jean Meunier, 22 May 1947; AD I-et-L 66W1, proceedings of interrogation of resistants arrested by the Gestapo, Oct–Nov. 1943; Durand and Vivier, *Libération des pays*, 57–59.

86. Marcel Baudot, *Libération de la Bretagne* (Paris: Hachette, 1973), 99. See also AN 72AJ144, account of Bernier, 9 March 1950.

87. AN 72AJ146, account of Abbé Ploquin, 1965.

88. AD L-A 96W138, reports of Lieutenant Broustal of gendarmerie of Châteaubriant, 6 July; divisional commissioner (Renseignements Généraux of Nantes, 8 July; and subprefect of Châteaubriant, 22 July 1944; statement of Saint-Herblain farmer Joseph Lucas to gendarmerie of Indre, 24 Oct. 1944; Mgr Villepelet, "Le Diocèse de Nantes," 3 and 25 July 1944. Villepelet took credit for the reprieve of Abbé Ploquin.

89. BAMA Freiburg RW24/159, diary of Rüstungskommando, Nantes, by Captain Zimmermann, dated Dresden, 11 Oct. 1944.

90. AD M-et-L 18W46, information note, 7 Aug. 1944.

91. P.-A. Fouet [subprefect of Segré], *Angoisses et espoirs: Segré, août 1944* (Maine Libre, 1945), in AD M-et-L 116J9.

92. Darmaillacq, *Cholet sous l'Occupation*, 55–59; *Toutlemonde, 1944–1994. 50ème anniversaire du 8 août 1944* (Toutlemonde, 1994).

93. AD M-et-L 30W219, report of Meunier to *commissaire de la République* Debré, 28 Aug. 1944.

94. AD I-et-L 46W124 and AD M-et-L 30W219, account of massacre of Maillé,

25 Aug. 1944. BAMA Freiburg RW 35/1253, "Experience and Final Reports of a Few Feldkommandants of Bezirk B, Aug. 1944–Jan. 1945." See also the account by the local curé, Abbé André Payan, *Maillé martyr* (Tours: Arnault et Cie, 1945).

CHAPTER 14 *Liberation*

1. Interview with Paule and Louis de Beaumont, Daumeray (M-et-L), 20 May 1997.
2. Debré, *Combattre*, 295. See also AD M-et-L 30W193, Debré to Commissaire à l'Intérieur Astier de la Vigerie, n.d.
3. Boulanger, *Papon*, 233, 235.
4. BAMA Freiburg RW35/1252, final report of German military authority in southwest France, July, Aug., and Sept. 1944, p. 18. Emphasis in original.
5. Jacqueline Sainclivier, "Le Pouvoir résistant (été 1944)," in Philippe Buton and Jean-Marie Guillon, eds., *Les Pouvoirs en France à la Libération* (Paris: Belin, 1944), 28. In this category Sainclivier cites eight departments out of thirty-three studied: Côtes-du-Nord, Mayenne, Sarthe, Oise, Haute-Garonne, Basses-Pyrénées, Haute-Saône, Vaucluse.
6. AD I-et-L 46W94, file on administration of I-et-L, July–Aug. 1944; Vivier, *Touraine 39–45*, 274–89.
7. Jacques Feneant, *Francs-Maçons et sociétés secrètes en Val de Loire* (Chambray-lès-Tours: CLD, 1986), 321–22.
8. Interview with Jack Vivier, Tours, 16 June 1997. See also Jack Vivier, *Les Instituteurs de Touraine dans la République* (Chambray-lès-Tours: CLD, 1997), 97.
9. Debré, *Combattre*, 298–303; AD L-A 10W2, proceedings of CDL, 23, 25, and 26 Aug. 1944; Mgr Villepelet, "Le Diocèse de Nantes," 17 Aug. and 22 Sept. 1944.
10. Sainclivier, "Le Pouvoir résistant," proposes five models of prefect/commissioner–CDL relations: subjection of the CDL, close collaboration, the CDL as pressure group, conflict provoked by the CDL, and conflict provoked by the prefect.
11. AD I-et-L 66W7, meetings of CDL, 13 and 20 Feb. 1945; congress of CLLs in Tours, 24 March 1945; 66W7, CDL subcommission for purging of firms, 6 and 13 April 1944.
12. Guy Haudebourg, "Le Parti Communiste Français en Loire-Inférieure à la Libération, 1944–1947," master's thesis, University of Nantes, 1987, 46–52.
13. See above, pp. 105–06.
14. Bougeard, "Regards sur les réseaux de notables en Bretagne," 33; Sesmaisons, *Marquise de Sesmaisons*, 135–38, 207–09, 216.
15. Baudot, *La Libération de la Bretagne*, 191.
16. Membership of CDLs in AN Fla 4020 and AD M-et-L 30W193.
17. AD M-et-L 30W197, CDL meetings, 17 and 26 Aug. 1944.

18. Interview with René Le Bault de la Morinière, Landemont (M-et-L), 7 May 1997.

19. Oury, *Dom Gabriel Sortais*, 162. See also Elie Chamard, *Vingt siècles d'histoire à Cholet* (Cholet: Farré et Fils, 1981), 323–25, 340.

20. Marc Bergère, "Tensions et rivalités entre les pouvoirs issus de la Résistance en Maine-et-Loire," in Jacqueline Sainclivier, ed., *La Résistance et les français: Enjeux stratégiques et environnement social* (Rennes: Presses Universitaires de Rennes, 1995), 297–304.

21. AD M-et-L 30W197, CLD meetings, 30 Nov. and 4 Dec. 1944, 25 Jan. 1945.

22. Bergère, "Tensions et rivalités," 304–05.

23. Roderick Kedward, "The Maquis and the Culture of the Outlaw," in Kedward and Roger Austin, eds., *Vichy France and the Resistance: Culture and Ideology* (London and Sydney: Croom Helm), 1985, 232–51.

24. Luc Capdevila, *Les Bretons au lendemain de l'Occupation: Imaginaire et comportement d'une sortie de guerre, 1944–1945* (Rennes: Presses Universitaires de France, 1999), 128, 146–49; Jean-Marie Guillon, "Parti du mouvement et parti de l'ordre," in Philippe Buton and Jean-Marie Guillon, eds., *Les Pouvoirs en France à la Libération* (Paris: Belin, 1994), 39. See also Richard Cobb, *Les Armees révolutionnaires: Instrument de la Terreur dans les départements, avril 1793–floréal an II* (Paris: Mouton, 1961–63), trans. Marianne Elliott as *The People's Armies* (New Haven and London: Yale UP, 1987).

25. AD M-et-L 30W197, CLD meetings, 20 and 21 Sept., 6 Oct. 1944.

26. AD I-et-L 66W6, prefect Vincent to Debré, 27 Sept. 1944; 66W7, CDL meetings, 26 Sept., 3 and 7 Oct. 1944.

27. AN 72AJ136, account by Robert Vivier on "Les lendemains de la Libération en Touraine."

28. AD I-et-L 81J1, Vivier to *commissaire de la République*, Angers, 16 and 22 Sept, 4 Oct. 1944.

29. On the Le Coz affair, see also Durand and Vivier, *Libération des Pays de la Loire*, 227–29; Briais, *Le Lochois pendant la guerre*, 124–65; and Alfred Hangouët, *L'Affaire Le Coz* (CLD, Normand et Cie, 1978).

30. See, for example, AD L-A 270W510, complaints of mayor of Plessé, 7 Nov., and municipal council of Fégreac, 24 Dec. 1944; AD M-et-L 19W13, prefect Vincent to Debré, 7 Oct. 1944; AD L-A 132W159, prefecture memos, 12 and 14 Dec. 1944.

31. Interview with Pierre and Yolande (née Fitzgerald) de Montalembert, Neuilly, 9 Jan. 1999.

32. AD L-A 10W2, meetings of CDL of L-I, 26 Aug. and 2 Sept. 1944.

33. AD L-A 132W167, prefect Vincent to Colonel Félix, 8 and 19 Sept. 1944; AD L-A 270W510, mayor of Le Gâvre to prefect, 25 Sept., who forwarded it to Colonel Félix, 5 Oct. 1944.

34. Mgr Villepelet, "Le Diocèse de Nantes," 16 and 25 Aug. 1944.

35. AD L-A 10W18 & 27J16, General Hary to colonel commanding Military Region of Rennes, 18 Oct. 1944.

36. AD M-et-L 22W67, General Hary to *commissaire de la République*, Angers, 31 Dec. 1945.

37. For instance, Philippe Bourdrel, *L'Épuration sauvage, 1944–1945* (Paris: Perrin, 1988). Other good accounts include Marcel Baudot, "La Résistance française face aux problèmes de répression et d'épuration," *RHDGM* 81 (Jan. 1971): 23–47; Peter Novick, *The Resistance versus Vichy: The Purge of Collaborators in Liberated France* (London: Chatto and Windus, 1968); and Herbert Lottman, *The People's Anger: Justice and Revenge in Post-Liberation France* (London: Hutchinson, 1986).

38. Debré, *Trois Républiques pour la France*, 332.

39. To compare, see Megan Koreman, *The Expectation of Justice: France, 1944–1946* (Durham and London: Duke UP, 1999), 98–100.

40. The trial dossier is in AD I-et-V 217W109. See especially note of CDL, 13 Aug. 1944; Captain Saint-Roch to *procureur de la République*, Nantes, 10 Oct. 1944; Amicale of 170th and 174th Infantry Regiment, 22 Dec. 1944; statements of Jean Lucas, retired teacher of CLL of Ancenis, 25 Jan. 1945; former teacher Anne-Marie Turbau, 30 Jan. 1945; and insurance agent/municipal councillor Prosper Baudoin, 31 Jan. 1945. See also AD L-A 10W2, CDL debate, 16 Sept. 1944, and 132W167, prefect Vincent to Debré, 9 Oct. 1944.

41. AD L-A 10W7, CLL congress, 24–25 Feb. 1945; AD M-et-L 19W13, prefect Vincent to Debré, 1 March 1945.

42. Cited in Le Cour Grandmaison, *Le Marquis de La Ferronnays*, 121–22.

43. AD M-et-L 22W76, trial dossier, including letters of Cholet's CLL, 8 Jan.; Chamber of Commerce, 22 Feb. and 29 June; and Jean Soulard, 7 July 1945. See also Manceau's own *La Spoliation du "Petit Courrier"* (Cholet, 1948), 7–9, 33–34, 54–56, 70–74.

44. AD I-et-L 60W10, divisional superintendent, Angers, to secretary-general of police, Angers, 16 Dec., and latter to Debré, 28 Dec. 1944. *La Voix du Peuple*, 2 and 9 Dec. 1944, 6 and 13 Jan., 10 and 24 Feb., 7 April 1945.

45. AD I-et-L 34W6, prefect Vivier to Interior Minister, 17 Feb. 1945; 52W57, Feld to president of CDL, Tours, 24 Aug. 1944, and to president of Palais de Justice, Tours, 10 Oct. 1944.

46. AD M-et-L 7U4/104, trial dossier of Musso. See especially submissions of Cay, 21 Feb. and 17 April 1945, and of Donati, 6 April 1945.

47. *Le Procès du Maréchal Pétain* (Paris: Albin Michel, [1945]), 814.

48. See above, p. 254.

49. AN 72AJ160, report of police commissioner, Tours, 20 June 1945; AD I-et-L 34W7, report of police commissioner, Tours, 29 June 1945; Durand and Vivier, *Libération des Pays de la Loire*, 246.

50. AD L-A 132W90, dossier on tramways of Nantes, Dec. 1944–March 1945; AD

M-et-L 74W4, meetings of Comité Interprofessionnel d'Épuration dans les Entreprises (CIEE), 22 Dec. 1944, 8 and 22 Jan. 1945.

51. AD L-A 132W90, dossier on Batignolles locomotive works, Nantes, Jan.–Feb. 1945; AD M-et-L 74W4, meeting of CIEE, 19 Feb. 1945.

52. AD L-A 132W90, dossier on Chantiers de Bretagne, Nantes, Dec. 1944–March 1945.

53. Mgr Villepelet, "Le Diocèse de Nantes," 17 Aug. and 11 Nov. 1944; AD L-A 210W508, note of chief superintendent, Renseignements Généraux, Nantes, 7 Oct., forwarded by prefect Vincent to Debré, 12 Oct. 1944.

54. AD M-et-L 30W146, Debré to archbishop of Rennes, 25 Aug., and reply, 4 Sept. 1944; Mgr Villepelet, "Le Diocèse de Nantes," 14–15 Nov. 1944; Debré, *Trois Républiques pour une France*, 313. On the very limited nature of the purge of the clergy, see Cointet, *L'Église sous Vichy*, 352–57, and Halls, *Politics, Society, and Christianity in Vichy France*, 361–79.

55. A. Dio. Angers 4K42, "Fédération Nationale d'Action Catholique. L'Union des Catholiques de l'Anjou," brochure dated 8 May 1945; Lassus Saint-Geniès, *Jean Le Cour Grandmaison*, 196–205.

56. AD M-et-L 140W27, subprefect of Cholet to prefect of M-et-L, 7 Sept. and 3 Sept. 1945; *L'Avenir de l'Ouest*, 8 Oct. 1945. In general, see Étienne Fouilloux, "Les Forces religieuses," in Philippe Buton and Jean-Marie Guillon, *Les Pouvoirs en France à la Libération* (Paris: Belin, 1994), 116–139.

57. AD L-A 10W13, dossier on Guémené-Penfao, Aug.–Sept. 1944; L-A 27J23, report of André Laurens, n.d; L-A 10W6, Mlle Rolland to CDL, 19 Oct. 1944. I am also grateful to the *mairie* of Guémené-Penfao for documentation communicated on 2 Jan. 2000.

58. AD I-et-L 46W116, report of police commissioner, Tours, 29 Jan. 1945; AM Tours, dossier Ferdinand Morin.

59. AM Angers, minutes of municipal council of Angers, 7 Sept. 1944; Am Angers 1I141, speech of Bernier, 14 Jan. 1945; AD M-et-L 19W13, prefect of M-et-L to Debré, 8 Feb. 1945; Lemesle, *Chronique d'Angers sous l'Occupation*, 241–43.

60. AD L-A 10W2, proceedings of CDL, Nantes, 19 Oct. 1944; AD M-et-L 30W222, dossier on rehabilitation of Blancho, 1944–45.

61. AD L-A 10W13, reorganization of municipality of Nantes, Aug. 1944.

62. AM Nantes 1134W14 and AD M-et-L 30W49, visit of de Gaulle to Nantes, 14 Jan. 1945.

63. AD L-A 10W12, report of CLL, Ancenis, n.d.; prefect Vincent to president of CDL, 5 Sept. 1944; 132W167, prefect to Debré, 26 Sept. 1944.

64. AD M-et-L 303W85, Darmaillacq to prefect of M-et-L, 26 Jan., 13 and 25 Feb. 1945. Darmaillacq wrote his *Cholet sous l'Occupation* in 1946, essentially to clear his name. On 14 March 1946 he was acquitted by the Chambre Civique of Angers.

65. AD I-et-L 46W116, police commissioner, Tours, to prefect, 29 Jan. 1945.

66. AD I-et-L 52W54, prefect Vivier to Debré, 31 Oct. 1944.

67. Statistics calculated from returns for individual communes in AD I-et-L 3W9 and 10W25, AD L-A 10W11-13 and 132W85, and AD M-et-L 140W 8 and 11.

68. AD M-et-L 97W154, subprefect of Saumur to Tardif, 31 Oct. 1944.

69. AD M-et-L 95W41, note of G. Cohn, 28 Sept. 1944.

70. AD L-A 10W2, CDL meeting of 31 Aug. 1944.

71. AD L-A 10W6, report of CDL emissary Thévenon, n.d.; report of Dr. Capel, 28 and 29 Nov. 1944.

72. AD I-et-L 46W117, prefect Vivier to Interior Minister, 28 Jan. 1945.

73. AD M-et-L 30W196.

74. AD M-et-L 30W196 (L-I), 140W10 (M-et-L), and AD I-et-L 46W117 give full details of the remodeling of *conseils généraux*. See also AD I-et-L 46W116 for personal comments on candidates in Touraine.

75. AD I-et-L 66W4, report of *cabinet du préfet*, 23 Aug. 1945.

76. AD L-A 132W159, Durtertre de la Coudre and municipal council of Machecoul to prefect, 21 April and 19 May 1945.

77. AM Chinon, Registre des délibérations du conseil municipal, 18 Sept. 1944.

78. Ibid., 27 Sept. 1944.

79. Auguste Correch, *L'Activité du Docteur Henri Mattraits avant la guerre et pendant l'Occupation* (Chinon, n.d. but end 1944)

80. AM Chinon, Registre des Délibérations du Conseil municipal, 12 July 1945.

81. *Le Courrier de l'Ouest*, 27 Oct. 1948; *La Nouvelle République*, 27 Oct. 1948.

82. Interview with Jean Sauvage, Angers, 25 April 1997.

83. Cantonal election results in *conseil général* of L-I, 1945; AD M-et-L 30W153, AD I-et-L 3W326. See also AD M-et-L 19W14, report of prefect Vivier, 4 Oct. 1944.

84. *Le Courrier de l'Ouest*, 23 Oct. 1945.

85. *La Résistance de l'Ouest*, 19 Oct. 1945. On Audibert's PSF background, see Jacques Nobécourt, *Le Colonel de La Rocque, 1885–1946: Ou les pièges du nationalisme chrétien* (Paris: Fayard, 1996), 884.

86. *L'Avenir de l'Ouest*, 15, 17, 18, 20–21 Oct. 1945.

CHAPTER 15 *Disappointment*

1. See, for example, Antony Beevor and Artemis Cooper, *Paris after the Liberation, 1944–1949* (London: Penguin, 1995).

2. AD M-et-L 97W123, Albert Chevalier to subprefect of Saumur, 31 Jan. 1945.

3. AD M-et-L 117W2, report of gendarmerie of Saumur, 7 Jan. 1945.

4. AD M-et-L 117W32, report of gendarmerie of Saumur on dances at Chacé, 18 and 19 Feb. 1945.

5. AD I-et-L 46W83, report of gendarmerie of Preuilly-sur-Claise, 5 April 1945.

6. AD M-et-L 97W123, anonymous letter from inhabitant of Charcé to subprefect of Saumur, 28 Dec. 1944.

7. AD M-et-L 97W123, subprefect of Saumur to Captain Viala of Saumur gendarmerie, 30 Dec. 1944.

8. Hervé Tremblay, *À Quédillac dans la poche: Neuf mois dans la vie quotidienne des Bouvronnais, août 1944–11 mai 1945* (Bouvron, 1995), 11–13.

9. ADL-A 27J18, "Journal de guerre de M. l'abbé Verger, curé de Guenrouet" (typescript, 1947), 2.

10. Ibid., 4–6, 19–22; Jean-Anne Chalet, *Peau-de-Grenouille: Histoire d'un petit village dans la "Poche" de Saint-Nazaire, août 1944–mai 1945* (Paris: Serge Godin, 1980).

11. AD L-A 270W503, prefecture memo, 24 Oct. 1944; 270W504, report of subprefect of Saint-Nazaire Benedetti, 2 Dec. 1944; 270W502, report of Charles Mabit of Red Cross, 5 Jan. 1945, and gendarmerie of Ancenis, 13 Jan. 1945.

12. AN 72AJ146, "Après la reddition," n.d.

13. AD L-A 270W504, note of prefecture of L-I, 15 June 1945.

14. AD M-et-L 97W99, mayors of Baugé and Noyant to prefect of M-et-L, 1 Aug. 1944.

15. AD M-et-L 95W93, mayor of Sainte-Christine to subprefect of Cholet, 27 Nov. 1944; 97W99, mayor of Cheviré-le-Rouge to subprefect of Saumur, 24 Nov. 1944.

16. AD L-A 132W72, former municipal councillor Étienne Louerat to prefect of L-I, 5 Sept. 1944.

17. AD L-A 80W8, postman Legault on behalf of Rézé refugees to prefect of L-I, 28 March 1945.

18. AD L-A 270W502, subprefect of Saint-Nazaire to prefect of L-I, 7 Aug. 1945.

19. AD L-A 80W64, correspondence of SNCASO and Chantiers de Penhouët with local authorities in Saint-Nazaire, Sept. 1944–June 1945.

20. AD L-A 132W72, Association des Réfugiés et Sinistrés de Saint-Nazaire/Section de Saint-Brévin to deputy Moisan, 14 March 1946.

21. In general, see Christophe Lewin, *Le Retour des prisonniers de guerre français: Naissance et développement de la FNPG, 1944–1952* (Paris: Publications de la Sorbone, 1986), and François Cochet, *Les Exclus de la victoire: Histoire des prisonniers de guerre, déportés, et STO, 1945–1985* (Paris: SPM, 1992).

22. AD L-A 51W29, police commissioner, Nantes, to prefect, 25 June 1945.

23. AD L-A 52W29, motion of Association Communale des Prisonniers de Guerre of Rézé, 20 Sept. 1945.

24. AD I-et-L 46W97, unsigned letter from wife of POW in Semblançay to prefect of I-et-L, 25 June 1945.

25. AD I-et-L 46W122, extraordinary general meeting of Association Départementale des Prisonniers de Guerre d'Indre-et-Loire, 2 Aug. 1945; memo of prefecture, 7 Aug. 1945.

26. AD M-et-L 90W1, telegram of Frenay, minister of prisoners and deportees, to *commissaires de la République* and prefects, n.d.; prefect of Maine-et-Loire to subprefects and mayors, 9 July 1945.

27. AD I-et-L 46W122, note d'information, 8 June 1945; AD M-et-L 140W50, Albert Charleux, president of the Association Départementale des Déportés et Internés Politiques, to prefect, 12 Oct. 1945.

28. AD L-A 10W8, Jean Meunier to Liberation Committee of Loire-Inférieure, 27 April 1945; AD I-et-L 46W122, memo of 22 June 1945.

29. Annette Wieviorka, *Déportation ou Génocide* (Paris: Plon, 1992), 121–23.

30. AD L-A 165J3, meeting of Fédération Nationale des Déportés et Internés de la Résistance, Oct. 1948; Olivier Lalieu, "La Crétation des Associations d'Anciens Déportés," in Christiane Franck, ed., *La France de 1945; Résistances, retours, renaissances. Actes du Colloque de Caen, 17–19 mai 1995* (Presses Universitaires de Caen, 1996), 193–203.

31. AD I-et-L 66W8, purging commission of CDL of I-et-L, 19 Oct. 1944.

32. AD I-et-L 46W122, Bernard Montigaud for "a group of ex-POWs" to secretary-general of the prefecture, 22 Sept. 1944.

33. Fonds Émile Aron, decision of civil tribunal, Tours, 10 Jan. 1945.

34. AD I-et-L 46W102, CDL to prefect of I-et-L, 30 May 1945.

35. *Le Phare*, 13–14 July 1944.

36. AD M-et-L 103W26, petition of Segré workers to prefect of M-et-L, 31 Aug. 1944.

37. AD M-et-L 140W92, "Appel aux paysans" of prefect Fourré-Cormeray, 25 Aug. 1944.

38. AD M-et-L 103W23, Fourré-Cormeray to Mgr Costes, 20 Sept. 1944.

39. AD M-et-L 97W100, subprefect Coiffard to mayors of arrondissement of Cholet, 10 Oct. 1944.

40. AD I-et-L 52W54, clippings from *La Nouvelle République*, 20 and 27 Dec. 1944; reports of police commissioner, Tours, 2 and 16 Jan. 1945.

41. AD M-et-L 7U4/99, dossier on Rouleau trial, Dec. 1944–June 1945.

42. *La Voix du Peuple*, 8 Nov. 1944.

43. AD M-et-L 22W100, motion of CDL of M-et-L, 25 Nov. 1944.

44. AD M-et-L 22W99, Debré to Finance Minister, 14 Dec. 1944, and reply, 22 Jan. 1945; Debré to Finance Minister, 2 Feb. 1945.

45. AD I-et-L 1305W54, Comité de Confiscation des Profits Illicites, I-et-L, Mar.–Oct. 1945.

46. AD M-et-L 140W30, circular of Agriculture Minister to prefects, 25 Oct. 1944; Isabel Boussard, "Résistance et syndicalisme agricole: Unité paysanne et liberté syndicale," in Franck, ed., *Résistances, retours, renaissances*, 27–48.

47. AD L-A 132W167, prefect Vincent to Interior Minister, 22 March 1945.

48. Hervé Camus, "La FDSEA de Loire-Inférieure, 1945–1957," master's thesis, University of Nantes, 1988, 45–47.

49. AD M-et-L 140W30, meeting of CDAA of M-et-L, 27 Nov. 1944.

50. Forget, *Le Serment de l'Unité paysanne*, 113–28.

51. AD M-et-L 21W55, report of commander of Trélazé gendarmerie brigade, 20 Oct. 1944.

52. AD M-et-L 30W215, prefect of L-I to Interior Minister, 1 May 1945.

53. AD I-et-L 52W54, reports of police commissioner, Tours, 20 Feb. and 10 April 1945.

54. Koreman, *The Expectation of Justice*, 251–57.

55. AD M-et-L 30W218, prefect Vivier to *commissaire de la République*, 29 and 30 Dec. 1945; Vivier to Interior Minister, 7 Jan. 1946.

56. AD M-et-L 302W218, chief superintendent, Renseignements Généraux, Angers, to director of Renseignements Généraux, Paris, 1 Jan. 1946; *La Nouvelle République*, 3 Jan. 1946.

57. For the Liberation as renewal, see, for example, Andrew Shennan, *Rethinking France: Plans for Renewal, 1940–1946* (Oxford: Clarendon Press, 1989).

CHAPTER 16 *Memories*

1. De Gaulle, *Discours et messages*, 439–40.

2. Marrus and Paxton, *Vichy France and the Jews*; Klarsfeld, *Vichy-Auschwitz*; and Webster, *Pétain's Crime*.

3. Serge Barcellini and Annette Wieviorka, *Passant, Souviens-toi: Les lieux de souvenir de la Seconde Guerre mondiale* (Paris: Plon, 1995). The authors use the term *lieux de souvenir* rather than Pierre Nora's *lieux de mémoire* because they take the view that many sites simply commemorate the dead rather than "structure the political field." This interpretation is unduly modest. See also *La Mémoire des Français: Quarante ans de commémoration de la Seconde Guerre Mondiale* (Paris: CNRS, 1986).

4. *La Nouvelle République*, 20 June 1955, 21 May 1965.

5. Robert Milliat, *Le Dernier Carousel: Défense de Saumur, 1940* (Grenoble and Paris: B. Arthaud, 1943), 97.

6. Antoine Redier, *Les Cadets de Saumur* (Lyon and Paris: Emmanuel Vitte, 1940), 210, and Gildea, *The Past in French History*, 119–20.

7. *Ouest-France*, 12 June 1950.

8. *Presse-Océan*, 30 June 1969.

9. Dwight D. Eisenhower, *Crusade in Europe* (London: Heinemann, 1948), 322, 325, 349–50.

10. Interviews with Pierre Hervé, Félix Boudet, Xavier Garçon, and Louis David in Saffré, 30 May 1997.

11. *La Résistance de l'Ouest*, 10 Oct. 1949.

12. Ibid., 21 May 1951.

13. *Presse-Océan*, 11 May 1970.

14. Interview with Andrée Trudeau (b. 1923), Saumur, 22 June 1998.

15. See above, p. 23.

16. Interview with Michel Ancelin (b. 1933), Saumur, 22 June 1998. Ancelin's account is taken up in "Mes souvenirs d'enfant" in *Saumur 1990*, 33–35.

17. *La Nouvelle République*, 8 Nov. 1994.

18. AD M-et-L 116J9, reports of Commandant Royer, 25 June 1948, and chief superintendent Éprinchard, 4 Nov. 1940.

19. René Marnot, *Ma Ville sous la botte* (Saumur: Éditions Roland, 1947).

20. Hubert Sommer, *Génie: Zur Bedeutungsgeschichte des Wortes von der Renaissance zur Aufklärung*, ed. Michael Nerlich (Frankfurt am Main: Peter Lang, 1998), ix–xlvi.

21. Michel Ancelin, "Miettes—18 septembre 1943," 26 July 1996; interview of 22 June 1998.

22. Sommer, *Génie*, xli; letter of Nerlich to the author, 16 July 1998.

23. Interview with Christian de Mondragon, Nantes, 29 April 1997. See above, pp. 146–47.

24. Mgr Villepelet, "Le Diocèse de Nantes," 22 Oct. 1945.

25. AD M-et-L 90W4, inspectors of Renseignements Généraux, Angers, 23 Oct. 1945.

26. AM Nantes, 1205W1, speech of Maître Ridel, 9 June 1945.

27. Maurice Thorez, *Oeuvres*, book 5, vol. 22 (Paris: Éditions Sociales, 1964), 231–34.

28. Barcellini and Wieviorka, *Passant, Souviens-toi*, 331–32.

29. AM Nantes 1205W2, report of secretary-general of Nantes, 9 Feb. 1945.

30. AM Nantes 1205WI, speech of Mayor Orrion, 22 Oct. 1952; clipping from *Ouest-Matin*, n.d.

31. *Humanité Dimanche*, 20 Aug. 1950. See file in AM Nantes, 1134W12.

32. Duméril, "Un Témoignage capital: Les cinquante otages de Nantes," *Historia* 154 (Sept. 1959): 254–62.

33. Étienne Gasche, *50 Otages: Mémoire sensible* (Nantes: Éditions du Petit Véhicule, 1991), 102–31.

34. *Ouest-France*, 21 Oct. 1991.

35. *Presse-Océan*, 23 Oct. 1991.

36. Livre d'Or. Exposition des 50 Otages, Nantes, 16 Oct.–24 Nov. 1991. I am indebted to Frank Liaigre for lending me a photocopy of these entries.

37. Oury, *Rue du Roi-Albert*, 308; Oury, *Au Soleil de la victoire* (Pantin: Le Temps des Cerises, 1999), 197–212; letters of Oury to the author, 17 Nov. 1999, 18 May, and 24 Oct. 2000.

38. *Ouest-France* and *Presse-Océan*, 23 Oct. 2001; letter of Oury to the author, 18 Nov. 2001.

39. See above, pp. 321–22.

40. Interview with Marquis Donatien and General Yves de Sesmaisons, Nantes, 16 July 1997; letter from General de Sesmaisons to the author, 21 July 1997.

41. Interview with Vicomte and Vicomtesse de la Grandière, La Jumellière (M-et-L), 5 May 1997.

42. Interview with Paule and Louis de Beaumont, Daumeray (M-et-L), 20 May

1997; letter of Paule de Beaumont to the author, 5 June 1997, enclosing extract from *Procès du Maréchal Pétain: Compte-rendu sténographique* (Paris: Albin Michel, 1945), 245.

43. Interview with Georges Audebert, Tours, 24 June 1998. See above, pp. 2–3.

44. Interview with André Treulier, Le Thoureil, 13 May 1997.

45. Interview with Max (b. 1916) and Jeanne (b. 1921) Ménard, Jallais (M-et-L), 22 April 1997. Interview with Suzanne Le Chat, Ingrandes, 15 April 1997.

46. Interview with Abbé Henri Richer (b. 1920), Angers, 6 June 1997.

47. Interviews with Abbé François Jamonneau, Nantes, 26 May and 5 June 1997.

48. Farmer, *Martyred Village*; Tzvetan Todorov, *A French Tragedy: Scenes of a Civil War, Summer 1944* (Hanover: Dartmouth College, 1996).

49. Interview with Yves de Saint-Seine, Toutlemonde (M-et-L), 22 April 1997; *Toutlemonde: 50e anniversaire du 8 août 1944* (Toutlemonde, 1994).

50. AD I-et-L 33W13, prefect to mayor of Maillé, 18 Aug. 1948.

51. AD I-et-L 46W124, press clippings of 13 and 18 May 1953.

52. *La Nouvelle République*, 23 Aug. 1994; interview with Henri Chedozeau, Mme Guitton, and Serge Martin, 6 June 1997.

53. AD M-et-L 148J, Comité d'Histoire de la Deuxième Guerre Mondiale, survey of 1948.

54. AD M-et-L 116J9, documents on visit of General Leclerc to Grugé l'Hôpital, 17 Sept. 1946.

55. *Le Courrier de l'Ouest*, 13 Oct. 1980.

56. AD M-et-L 140W6, subprefect of Segré to prefect, 9 May 1941.

57. Interview with Édouard Delanoë, Grugé l'Hôpital, 14 April 1997.

58. Francis Bossé, memoirs (typescript, 1997), 1, 10.

59. See above, p. 311.

60. *Le Courrier de l'Ouest*, 8 Aug. 1994. See above, pp. 123–24.

61. AM Angers 11227, visit of General Patton to Angers.

62. *Le Courrier de l'Ouest*, 24 Oct. 1995; interview with Germaine Canonne, Angers, 28 April 1997; Germaine Canonne, "Souvenirs de la première femme élue en Maine-et-Loire" (typescript, n.d.).

63. Ruling of Cour d'Appel, Bourges, 23 July 1985; letter of FNDIR to president of the Republic, 25 June 1986. Documents kindly communicated by André Chauvel, president of the FNDIR, Nantes.

64. AM Nantes 1134W13, mayor of Nantes to Interior Minister Jules Moch, 4 Aug. 1948, and reply, 15 Sept. 1948; AD L-A 270W480, prefecture of L-I to parents of Frédéric Creusé, 30 April 1948; Comité National des Héros de Châteaubriant to prefect of L-I, 10 Aug. 1949.

65. AD L-A 161W350, prefect to secretary of state for armed forces, 23 June 1951.

66. Choyeau, "La Mémoire de la Résistance à Nantes," 110.

67. Remise des Prix du Concours Départemental de la Résistance et de la Libération, Nantes, 18 June 1997.

68. Essay kindly communicated by André Chauvel.

69. AM Angers 11265, *Courrier de l'Ouest* and *Nouvelle République*, 24 Nov. 1970.

70. *Presse Océan*, 29 April 1985.

71. Wieviorka, *Déportation ou Génocide*, 136–39. This figure, accepted until the 1960s, was calculated on the basis of 120,000 Jews and 60,000 non-Jews.

72. Meeting of FNDIR, Nantes, 6 May 1997.

73. Interview with Ernest Gluck, Nantes, 22 June 1997.

74. *Ouest-France*, 19 July 1993.

75. Ibid., 18 and 21 July 1992.

76. Interview with Charles Toubon, Angers, 22 June 1997.

77. Interview with Lucie Lancezeux and Huguette Robin, Monts, 23 June 1998.

78. *La Nouvelle République*, 15 Oct. 1988.

79. Collège de Monts, Jérôme Scorin, speech of 16 Oct. 1988.

80. Interview with François Guggenheim, Tours, 30 June 1997.

81. *La Nouvelle République*, 4 Dec. 1995; interviews with André Bellegarde of the Lycée Jean-Monnet, Joué-lès-Tours, and Marie-Paule Fresneau of the Collège de Monts, 30 June 1997.

82. Interview with Christian and Léonie Beugnet (both b. 1929), Claude Bougreau (b. 1936), and René Arnoult (b. 1921), Chinon, 23 June 1998.

83. Interview with Andrée Trudeau, Saumur, 22 June 1998.

84. Interview with Michel Leterme (b. 1930), Angers, 13 May 1997.

85. Letter of Marcel Girard to the author, 13 Jan. 1998.

86. Interview with Huguette Robin, Monts, 23 June 1998.

87. Interview with Lucienne Despouy, Saint-Avertin, Tours, 9 June 1997.

88. Interview with Odette Goxe, Angers, 14 April 1997.

89. Interview with Pierre Boudet (b. 1915), Angers, 11 Oct. 1997.

90. Interview with Abel and Claudine Avenet, Dierre, 25 June 1998.

91. Interview with André Roussel (b. 1926), Bléré, 25 June 1998. See above, pp. 116–17.

Conclusion

1. Tewes, *Frankreich in der Besatzungszeit.*

BIBLIOGRAPHY

1. *Manuscript Sources*

Bundesarchiv-Militärarchiv, Freiburg

Three series were used:

(i) those of the Militärbefehlshaber in Frankreich/Military Administration in France (RW35), notably on hostages (RW35/536, 542–43), and of the Military Administration of Bezirk B, based in Angers, notably reports from 1940–42 (RW35/1254, 1260–64) and reports relating to the end of the Occupation (RW35/1252–53);

(ii) those of the Kommandanturen within the Bezirk B, notably Nantes (RH36/131, 133, 142, 146, 148, 312, 511, 512, 525) and Tours (RH36/26, 228);

(iii) those of the Rüstungsdienstellen in France (RW24): the Rüstungsinspektion of SW France based in Angers (RW24/122–26, 129, 131, 132), and the Rüstungkommandos based in Angers, Le Mans (RW24/174–80), Nantes (RW24/153–60).

Archives Nationales, Paris

Five series were used:

(i) Fla: Ministry of the Interior: personnel of prefectures (3630), administrative commissions (3634), and departmental councils (3635), questions of production and supply (3658–59), detailed reports on the situation within France by the Free French Mission Militaire de Liaison Administrative, 1943–44 (3868–69), and reports of the Service Central des Commissariats de la République (4020);

(ii) F9: General Commissariat for repatriated POWs and their families (3037, 3049, 3055, 3064);

(iii) AJ 38: General Commissariat for Jewish Questions, notably personal questions (150) and Aryanization (977).

(iv) AJ 40: German Archives of the Second World War, dealing notably with French officials (542–44) and the Liberation (571);

(v) 72 AJ: Archives of the Comité d'Histoire de la Deuxième Guerre Mondiale, which includes numerous firsthand accounts collected in the years after the war (136, 144–47, 160).

Departmental Archives

The Departmental Archives of Loire-Atlantique (L-A), Maine-et-Loire (M-et-L), and Indre-et-Loire (I-et-L) provided the greatest mass of documentation. Since Angers was a regional capital, some material relating to the other two departments is found under Maine-et-Loire. Series W relates to the Second World War. There are also judicial files in Series U. The following grid gives a guide to the main subseries within Series W; references to individual files are found in the notes.

	Loire-Atlantique	Maine-et-Loire	Indre-et-Loire
prefecture	12, 13, 22, 43 (Châteaubriant), 51, 75, 132 W	8, 12, 18, 24, 60, 80, 95 (Cholet), 97 (Saumur), 136, 140W	10, 46, 52, 121W
Franco-German relations	13, 18, 43, 51, 65, 75, 118, 132, 161, 243, 270W	5, 18, 60, 80, 95, 97, 80, 136, 140W	10, 52, 66, 108W
Vichy regime: departmental assemblies municipalities	13, 132, 157W 10, 13, 132W	18, 140W 2, 12, 24, 80, 90 140W	10, 52, 225W 3, 10, 18, 52W

courts police	243W 13, 51, 132, 243W	7U4 12, 18, 24, 41, 60, 75, 80, 90, 136, 140W	10, 44, 52, 120W
propaganda/ public opinion	1, 13W	18, 56, 136, 140W	10W
Church		140W	10W
Secours National	13, 54, 132W	8, 18, 41, 71W	46, 218W
refugees/ evacuees	8, 54, 80, 132W	18, 54, 93, 136, 140W	10, 18, 52, 108W
POWs	6, 16, 38, 43, 51, 52, 75W	8, 24, 90, 140W	10, 46, 218W
bombings	13, 43, 54, 75, 253W	18W	10W
food supply	31, 46, 56, 75, 80, 161, 253W	21, 24, 30, 32, 54, 103, 117, 140W	10, 46, 52, 63, 106, 135W
Peasant Corporation	13W	18, 69, 95, 140W	63, 106W
labor	13, 18, 42, 132W	12, 21, 25, 30, 33, 69W	6, 52W
Relève, STO	16, 18, 40, 75, 132,	18, 140W	6, 10, 63, 121W
Jews	13, 65, 270W	7, 12, 18, 24, 37, 61, 97W	10, 44, 46, 52, 120W
associations	75, 82, 132, 270W	18, 41, 54, 80, 97, 116, 140W	10, 28, 30, 31, 46, 52, 106W
clandestine dancing		8, 18, 56, 80, 117W	10, 46, 52, 218W

Liberation	10, 96, 270W	18, 30, 60, 140W	33, 46, 60, 66, 121, 124W
purges	96, 132, 243, 270W	22, 30, 46, 48, 60, 74, 140, 303W	34, 46, 52, 1305W
courts	*Archives of Ille-et-Vilaine* 217W	7U4, 2, 22W	7, 34, 46, 217, 1119W
commissaire de la République	132W	19, 30W	46W
Liberation Committees	10, 96, 132, 270W	30, 48, 140W	46, 66W
local councils	30W	19, 30, 56, 140W	3, 46, 66W
FFIs	270W	22W	52W
pocket of Saint-Nazaire	26, 270W		

The AD I-et-L also have a useful collection of documents recovered from the German authorities at the end of the Occupation:

II Z 3 (hunting)
III Z 1, situation reports from Feldkommandantur of Angers, 1940–41
XIV Z 17 (mayors), 27, 29 (art conservation), 32 (French officials)
XV Z 21 (Maine-et-Loire), 23 (enemy propaganda), 27 (French officials, Indre-et-Loire)

The departmental archives also contain private collections (Series J) such as:

AD L-A 27J16–18, various contemporary accounts
165J, archives of the FNDIR
AD M-et-L 116J9 and 148J, archives of the Comité d'Histoire de la Deuxième Guerre Mondiale
AD I-et-L 42J1, archives of Dr. Goupille, veterinary surgeon near the demarcation line
81J1, archives of Robert Vivier, Liberation prefect

Municipal Archives

(i) Nantes
H4 116, diary of F. Soil, secretary-general of the municipality
38W5, 9, 17, 27 municipal administration

134W9–12 Hotz/hostages affair, W14 visit of de Gaulle
1205W1–2 commemoration of hostages

(ii) Angers
1 I commemoration of visits of de Gaulle, 1944–5 (141), of General Patton (227), of liberation of Angers (253–4), of deportees (265)
1 D register of proceedings of municipal council, 1938–45

(iii) Tours
Municipal bulletin 1940
Golden Book presented to Ferdinand Morin by the citizens of Tours, 1941

(iv) Chinon
register of proceedings of municipal council, 1940–45

Diocesan Archives

Nantes: Monsignor Villepelet, "Le Diocèse de Nantes, 1940–1945." This diary is an indispensable source.
Register of the parish of Sainte-Croix, Nantes, 1940–44
Letters and cards sent by Monsignor Villepelet to seminarists and priests in POW camps and letters and cards sent to him.

Angers: 1D12, file on Monsignor Costes
9E41, letters of Monsignor Costes to seminarists and priests in POW camps
4K42, Union des Catholiques de l'Anjou
6J4 Université Catholique d'Angers

Tours: 1D6, correspondence of Monsignor Gaillard and Feldkommandantur of Tours, 1940
"Prêtres de 1939 à 1945"
Pastoral visit, 1942

To these must be added the printed *Semaine religieuse* for each diocese, 1940–44

Labor Archives

Centre d'Histoire du Travail, Nantes:
CGT, 1939–45
Pennaneach papers

Bourse du Travail, Angers:
Papers of Raymond Déaud

Private Memoirs and Diaries

Collection Lemesle: private collection of Michel Lemesle, local historian in Angers

Marinette Rameau, "Journal de Guerre"

Francis Bossé, "Mémoires"

Suzanne Le Chat, "En Souvenir de l'époque tourmentée vécue dans les années 1939 à 1945"

Papers of Émile Aron, Tours

Papers of Odette Goxe, Angers

Papers of Paul Grenouilleau, Angers

2. Selected Printed Sources

Abélès, Marc. *Quiet Days in Burgundy: A Study of Local Politics* (Paris and Cambridge: Éditions de la Maison des Sciences de l'Homme/Cambridge UP, 1991).

Addad, Serge. *Le Théâtre dans les années Vichy* (Paris, 1992).

Alary, Eric. *La Ligne de démarcation, 1940–1944* (Paris: PUF, 1995).

Amouroux, Henri. *Quarante millions de Pétainistes, juin 1940–juin 1941* (Paris: R. Laffont, 1977).

Aron, Émile. *Figures Tourangelles* (Chambray-lès-Tours: CLD, 1986).

———.*La Médecine en Touraine des origines à nos jours* (Chambray-lès-Tours: CLD, 1992).

Atkin, Nicholas. *Church and Schools in Vichy France, 1940–1944* (New York and London: Garland, 1991).

———.*Pétain* (London: Longman, 1998).

Audoin-Le Marec, Michelle. *Le Maine-et-Loire dans la guerre, 1939–1945* (Le Coteau: Horvath, 1987).

Audoin-Rouzeau, Stéphane. *L'Enfant de l'ennemi, 1914–1918* (Paris: Aubier, 1995).

Aulton, Margaret. *Fair Touraine* (London: John Lane/Bodley Head, 1925).

Azéma, Jean-Pierre, François Bédarida, and Robert Frank, eds. *Jean Moulin et la Résistance en 1943* (Paris: IHTP, 1994).

Bakhtin, Mikhail. *Rabelais and His World* (Bloomington: Indiana UP, 1984).

Barcellini, Serge, and Annette Wieviorka. *Passant, Souviens-toi: Les lieux de souvenir de la Seconde Guerre Mondiale* (Paris: Plon, 1995).

Barral, Pierre. "Idéal et pratique du régionalisme dans le régime de Vichy." *Revue française de science politique* 24 (Oct. 1974): 911–13.

Baruch, Marc-Olivier. *Servir L'État français: L'administration en France de 1940 à 1944* (Paris: Fayard, 1997).

Baudot, Michel. "La Résistance française face aux problèmes de répression et d'épuration," *RHDGM* 81 (Jan. 1971): 23–47.

———. *Libération de la Bretagne* (Paris: Hachette, 1973).

Baudouin, Paul. *Neuf Mois au gouvernement, avril–décembre 1940* (Paris: Éditions de la Table Ronde, 1948).

Beevor, Antony, and Artemis Cooper. *Paris after the Liberation, 1944–1949* (London: Penguin, 1995).

Beltran, A., R. Frank, and H. Rousso. *La Vie des enterprises sous l'Occupation: Une enquête à l'échelle locale* (Paris: Belin, 1994).

Berger, Laurent. "L'Épiscopat nantais de Mgr Villepelet, 1936–1966." Master's thesis, University of Nantes, 1991.

Bergère, Marc. "Permanences et ruptures au sein du conseil général du Maine-et-Loire (1935–1953): Étude prosopographique des élus." *Annales de Bretagne et des Pays de l'Ouest* 103 (1996): 69–77.

———. "Tensions et rivalités entre les pouvoirs issus de la Résistance en Maine-et-Loire." In Jacqueline Sainclivier, *La Résistance et les français: Enjeux stratégiques et environnement social* (Rennes: Presses Universitaires de Rennes, 1995).

Bertin-Maghit, Jean-Pierre. *Le Cinéma français sous Vichy: Les Films français de 1940 à 1944* (Paris: Albatros, 1980).

Bougeard, Christian. "Regards sur les réseaux de notables en Bretagne, des années 1930 aux années 1950." *Annales de Bretagne et des Pays de l'Ouest* 103 (1996): 31–51.

Boulanger, Gérard, *Papon: Un intrus dans la République* (Paris: Seuil, 1997).

Boulard, Fernand, ed. *Matériaux pour l'histoire religieuse du peuple français, XIXe–XXe siècles: Région de Paris, Haute-Normandie, Pays de Loire, Centre* (Paris: Éditions de l'École des Hautes Études en Sciences Sociales, 1982).

Bourdé, Guy. *La Défaite du Front populaire* (Paris: Maspero, 1977).

Bourdrel, Philippe. *L' Épuration sauvage, 1944–1945* (Paris: Perrin, 1988).

Bourreau, René. *Une Utopie religieuse et sa modernisation lors des élections en pays nantais contemporain: La logique restitutionniste de la noblesse nantaise* (Paris: EHESS, 1992).

Bourrigaud, René. *Le Développement agricole au 19e siècle en Loire-Atlantique* (Nantes: Centre d'Histoire du Travail, 1994).

Boussard, Isabel. "Résistance et syndicalisme agricole: Unité paysanne et liberté syndicale." *La France de 1945: Résistances, retours, renaissances. Actes du Colloque de Caen, 17–19 mai 1995*. Ed. Christiane Franck (Presses Universitaires de Caen, 1996).

———. *Vichy et la Corporation Paysanne* (Paris: FNSP, 1980).

Boylesve, René. *La Jeune Fille bien élévée* (Paris: Calmann-Lévy, 1924).

Briais, Bernard. *Le Lochois pendant la Guerre 1939–1945* (Chambray-lès-Tours: CLD, 1988).

Brunet, Jean-Paul. *Jacques Doriot* (Paris: Balland, 1986).

Bücheler, Heinrich. *Carl-Heinrich von Stülpnagel: Soldat, Philosoph, Verschwörer* (Berlin: Ullstein, 1989).

Burrin, Philippe. *Living with Defeat: France under the German Occupation, 1940–1944* (London: Arnold, 1996).

Camus, Hervé. "La FDSEA de Loire-Inférieure, 1945–1957." Master's thesis, University of Nantes, 1988.

Capdevila, Luc. *Les Bretons au lendemain de l'Occupation: Imaginaire et comportement d'une sortie de guerre, 1944–1945* (Rennes: Presses Univesitaires de Rennes, 1999).

Chalet, Jean-Anne. *Peau-de-Grenouille: Histoire d'un petit village dans la "Poche" de Saint-Nazaire, août 1944–mai 1945* (Paris: Serge Godin, 1980).

Chamard, Elie, *Les Combats de Saumur* (Paris: Berger-Levrault, 1948).

———. *Vingt Siècles d'histoire à Cholet* (Cholet: Farré et Fils, 1981).

Chauvy, Gérard. *Aubrac: Lyon 1943* (Paris: Albin Michel, 1997).

Chollet, Louis. *Les Heures tragiques: Tours, juin 1940* (Tours: Arrault et Cie, 1946).

Cholvy, Gérard, and Yves-Marie Hilaire. *Histoire religieuse de la France contemporaine.* Vol. 3 (Toulouse: Privat, 1988).

Choyeau, Sarah. "La Mémoire de la Résistance à Nantes." Master's thesis, University of Nantes, 1994.

Churchill, Winston S. *Their Finest Hour.* Vol. 2 of *The Second World War* (London: Cassell, 1949).

Cobb, Richard. *French and Germans, Germans and French* (Hanover and London: UP of New England, 1983).

———. *Les Armées révolutionnaires: Instrument de la Terreur dans les départements, avril 1793–floréal an II* (Paris: Mouton, 1961–63). Translated by Marianne Elliott as *The People's Armies* (New Haven and London: Yale UP, 1987).

Cochet, François. *Les Exclus de la victoire: Histoire des prisonniers de guerre, déportés, et STO, 1945–1985* (Paris: SPM, 1992).

Cohen, Asher. *Persécutions et sauvetages: Juifs et français sous l'Occupation et sous Vichy* (Paris: Éditions du Cerf, 1993).

Cointet, Jean-Paul. *La Légion française des combattants, 1940–1944: La Tentation du fascisme* (Paris: Albin Michel, 1995).

Cointet, Michèle, *Le Conseil National de Vichy, 1940–1944* (Paris: Aux Amateurs du Livre, 1989).

———. *L'Église sous Vichy, 1940–1945* (Paris: Perrin, 1998).

Colanéri, L.-J., and G. Gérante. *La Dénonciation et les dénonciateurs* (Paris: PUF, 1948).

Conway, John S. *The Nazi Persecution of the Churches* (London: Weidenfeld and Nicholson, 1968).

Cordier, Daniel. *Jean Moulin: L'inconnu du Panthéon* (Paris: Lattès, 1989).

Corre, Rozenn. "Le Scoutisme Catholique à Nantes des origines au Jamborée de la Paix, 1925–1947." Master's thesis, University of Nantes, 1992.

Correch, Auguste. *L'Activité du Docteur Henri Mattraits avant la guerre et pendant l'Occupation* (Chinon, 1944).

Danos, Jacques, and Marcel Gibelin. *June '36: Class Struggle and the Popular Front in France* (London and Chicago: Bookmarks, 1986).

Darmaillacq, A. *Cholet sous l'Occupation* (Cholet, 1946; rpt. 1991).

Davies, Jennifer. *The Wartime Kitchen and Garden* (London: BBC Book, 1993).

Day, Charles R. *Education for the Industrial World: The Écoles d'Arts et Métiers and the Rise of French Industrial Engineering* (Cambridge, Mass.: MIT Press, 1987).

Debré, Michel. *Combattre*. Vol. 1 of *Trois Républiques pour une France* (Paris: Albin Michel, 1984).

Dejonghe, Étienne. "Les Aspects économiques et sociaux du Nord pendant la première année de l'Occupation." *Revue du Nord*, Oct. 1969.

Delarue, Jacques. *Trafics et crimes sous L'Occupation* (Paris: Fayard, 1993).

Delpla, François. *Aubrac: Les faits et la calomnie* (Pantin: Le Temps des Cerises, 1997).

Déniel, Alain. *Le Mouvement breton* (Paris: Maspéro, 1976).

Diamond, Hanna. *Women and the Second World War in France, 1939–1948: Choices and Constraints* (Harlow, Pearson, 1999).

Dogan, Mattei. "Les Filières de la carrière politique en France." *Revue française de sociologie* 8 (1967): 468–92.

Dommanget, Maurice. *Histoire du premier mai* (Paris: Société Universitaire d'Éditions et de Librairie, 1953).

Duméril, Edmond. *Journal d'un honnête homme pendant l'Occupation, juin 1940–août 1944* (Thonon-les-Bains: L'Albaron/Société Présence du Livre, 1990).

———. "Un Témoignage capital: Les cinquante otages de Nantes." *Historia* 154 (Sept. 1959): 254–62.

Durand, Abel. *Nantes dans la France de l'Ouest* (Paris: Plon, 1941).

Durand, Yves. *La Vie quotidienne des prisonniers de guerre dans les stalags, oflags et kommandos, 1939–1945* (Paris: Hachette, 1994).

Durand, Yves, and Robert Vivier. *Libération des Pays de Loire, Blésois, Orléanais, Touraine* (Paris: Hachette, 1974).

Ehrlich, Evelyn. *Cinema of a Paradox: French Filmmaking under the German Occupation* (New York: Columbia UP, 1987).

Eisenhower, Dwight D. *Crusade in Europe* (London: Heinemann, 1948).

Estèbe, Jean, ed. *Les Juifs à Toulouse et en Midi toulousain au temps de Vichy* (Toulouse: Presses Universitaires Le Mirail, 1996).

Evrard, Jacques. *La Déportation des travailleurs français dans le Troisième Reich* (Paris: Fayard, 1972).

Farmer, Sarah. *Martyred Village: Commemorating the 1944 Massacre at Oradour-sur-Glane* (Berkeley: University of California Press, 1999).

Faure, Christian. *Le Projet culturel de Vichy* (Paris and Lyon: CNRS, Presses Universitaires de Lyon, 1989).

Feneant, Jacques. *Francs-Maçons et sociétés secrètes en Val de Loire* (Chambray-lès-Tours: CLD, 1986).

———. *Histoire de la Franc-Maçonnerie en Touraine* (Chambray-lès-Tours: CLD, 1981).

Ferro, Marc. *Pétain* (Paris: Fayard, 1987).

Figlio, Karl. "Oral History and the Unconscious." *History Workshop Journal* 26 (1988): 120–32.

Fiot, Canon Robert. *Un Prêtre de Touraine: L'Abbé Georges Lhermitte, 1887–1944* (Tours: Barbot et Gallon, 1945).

Fishman, Sarah. *We Will Wait: Wives of French Prisoners of War, 1940–1945* (New Haven and London: Yale UP, 1991).

Fitzpatrick, Sheila, and Robert Gellately. *Accusatory Practices* (Chicago and London: University of Chicago Press, 1997).

Forget, Eugène. *Le Serment de l'unité paysanne* (Paris: Nouvelle Cité, 1982).

Fouet, P.-A. *Angoisses et espoirs: Segré, août 1944* (Maine Libre, 1945).

Fouilloux, Étienne. "Les Forces religieuses." *Les Pouvoirs en France à la Libération.* Ed. Philippe Buton and Jean-Marie Guillon (Paris: Belin, 1994).

Gabillard, Philippe. "L'Extrême Droite en Maine-et-Loire, 1919–1934." Master's thesis, Catholic University, Angers, 1980.

Gasche. Etienne, *Cinquante Otages: Mémoire sensible* (Nantes: Éditions du Petit Véhicule, 1991).

Gay-Lescot, Jean-Louis. *Sport et éducation sous Vichy, 1940–1944* (Lyon: Presses Universitaires de Lyon, 1991).

Gaulle, Charles de. *Discours et Messages I, juin 1940–janvier 1946* (Paris: Plon, 1970).

Gellner, Ernest, and John Waterbury, eds. *Patrons and Clients in Mediterranean Societies* (London: Duckworth, 1977).

Gicquel, Yvonnig. *Le Comité consultatif de Bretagne* (Rennes: Simon, 1961).

Gilbert, Martin. *Winston Churchill VI. 1939–1941* (London: Heinemann, 1983).

Gildea, Robert, "Les Années Noires? Clandestine dancing in Occupied France" in Ceri Crossley and Martyn Cornick (eds.), *Problems in French History* (Basingstoke: Palgrave, 2000), 197–212

———. *The Past in French History* (New Haven and London: Yale UP, 1994).

Golsan, Richard. *The Papon Affair: Memory and Justice on Trial* (New York: Routledge, 2000).

Goupille, André. *Mon Village sous la botte: La Haye Descartes, juin 1940–septembre 1944* (Tours, n.d.).

Guérinau, Robert. *Les Martyrs du 16 mai 1942: Les premiers fusillés de la Touraine* (Tours: La Voix du Peuple, 1963).

Guérinau, Robert, and Jean-Claude Guillon. *La Touraine sous le règne des Feldkommandants* (Tours: Centre-Loire, 1985).

Gueslin, André. *Les Facs sous Vichy: Actes du Colloque des Universités de Clermont-Ferrand et de Strasbourg, novembre 1993* (Clermont-Ferrand: Publications de l'Institut d' Études du Massif Central Université Blaise-Pascal, 1994).

Guillard, Jérôme. "Les Catholiques tourangeaux pendant la Deuxième Guerre Mondiale." Master's thesis, University of Tours, 1996.

Guillon, Jean-Marie. "L'Affaire Aubrac ou la dérive d'une certaine façon de faire l'histoire." *Modern and Contemporary France* 7, no. 1 (1999): 89–108.

————. "Parti du mouvement et parti de l'order." *Les Pouvoirs en France à la Libération.* Ed. Philippe Buton and Jean-Marie Guillon (Paris: Belin, 1994).

Halimi, André. *La Dénonciation sous l'Occupation* (Paris: Alain Moreau, 1983).

Halls, W. D. *Politics, Society, and Christianity in Vichy France* (Oxford and Providence: Berg, 1995).

————. *The Youth of Vichy France* (Oxford: Clarendon Press, 1981).

Hangouët, Alfred. *L'Affaire Le Coz* (CLD, Normand et Cie, 1978).

Harris, Ruth. "The 'Child of the Barbarian': Rape, Race and Nationalism in France during the First World War," *Past and Present* 141 (Nov. 1993): 170–206.

Haudebourg, Guy. "Le Parti Communiste Français en Loire-Inférieure à la Libération, 1944–1947." Master's thesis, University of Nantes, 1987.

Hauser, Henri. *Le Problème du régionalisme* (Paris: PUF, 1924).

Horne, John and Alan Kramer. *German Atrocities 1914: A History of Denial* (New Haven and London: Yale University Press, 2001)

Jäckel, Eberhard. *Frankreich in Hitlers Europa* (Stuttgart: Deutsche Verlags-Anstalt, 1966).

Jackson, Julian. *The Popular Front in France: Defending Democracy, 1934–1938* (Cambridge: Cambridge UP, 1988).

Jacobs, Gabriel. "The Role of Joan of Arc on the Stage of Occupied Paris." *Vichy France and the Resistance: Culture and Ideology.* Ed. Roderick Kedward and Roger Austin (London and Sydney: Croom Helm, 1985).

Jünger, Ernst. *Premier Journal Parisien: Journal II, 1941–1943* (Paris: Christian Bourgois, 1980).

Kaspi, André. *Les Juifs pendant l'Occupation* (Paris: Seuil, 1997).

Kedward, Roderick. "The Maquis and the Culture of the Outlaw." *Vichy France and the Resistance: Culture and Ideology.* Ed. Kedward and Roger Austin (London and Sydney: Croom Helm, 1985).

Kergoat, Jacques. *La France du Front Populaire* (Paris: Éditions La Découverte, 1986).

Klarsfield, Serge. *Vichy-Auschwitz: Le rôle de Vichy dans la solution finale de la question juive en France,* 2 vols. (Paris: Fayard, 1983–85).

Koureman, Megan. *The Expectations of Justice: France 1944–1946* (Durham and London: Duke UP, 1999).

Krumeich, Gerd. *Jeanne d'Arc in der Geschichte: Historiographie-Politik-Kultur* (Sigmaringen: Thorbecke, 1989).

————. "Joan of Arc between Right and Left." *Nationhood and Nationalism in France: From Boulangism to the Great War, 1889–1918.* Ed. Robert Tombs (London: HarperCollins Academic, 1991).

Kupferman, Fred. *Laval* (Paris: Balland, 1987).

Laborie, Pierre. *L'Opinion française sous Vichy* (Paris: Seuil, 1990).

Lalieu, Olivier. "La Création des Associations d'Anciens Déportés." *La France de 1945: Résistances, retours, renaissances. Actes du Colloque de Caen, 17–19 mai 1995.* Ed. Christiane Franck (Presses Universitaires de Caen, 1996).

Lambert, Annie, and Claude Toczé. *Être Juif à Nantes sous Vichy* (Nantes: Siloë, 1994).

Lassus Saint-Geniès, Annik de. *Jean Le Cour Grandmaison* (Paris: Beauchesne, 1980).

Laurens, Corran. "La Femme au turban: Les femmes tondues." *The Liberation of France: Image and Event.* Ed. Roderick Kedward and Nancy Wood (Oxford and Washington: Berg, 1995).

Lavigne, Raymond. *Saint-Pierre-des-Corps ou la Clarté républicaine* (Paris: Éditions Messidor, 1998).

Le Boterf, Hervé. *La Bretagne sous le Gouvernement de Vichy* (Paris: France-Empire, 1982).

Lecornu, Bernard. *Un Préfet sous l'Occupation allemande: Châteaubriant, Saint-Nazaire, Tulle* (Paris: France-Empire, 1997).

Le Cour Grandmaison, Jean. *Le Marquis de La Ferronnays, 1876–1946* (Paris: Éditions Siloë, 1952).

Le Crom, Jean-Pierre. *Syndicats nous voilà! Vichy et le corporatisme* (Paris: Les Éditions de l'Atelier/Éditions ouvrières, 1995).

Lefranc, Georges. *Juin '36* (Paris: Julliard, 1965).

Le Marec, Gérard. *La Bretagne dans la Résistance* (Rennes: Ouest-France, 1983).

Lemesle, Michel. *1939–1945: À Travers l'Anjou* (Cholet: Les Éditions du Choletais, 1976).

———. *Chronique d'Angers sous l'Occupation, 1939–1945* (Angers: Philippe Petit, 1972).

———. *L'Anjou des années 40: Chroniques* (Angers: Les Éditions du Choletais, 1984).

Leprince, René, ed. *La Pommeraye dans la guerre par ceux qui l'ont vécue* (La Pommeraye: Bibliothèque de La Pommeraye, 1995).

Lewin, Christophe. *Le Retour des prisonniers de guerre français: Naissance et développement de la FNPG, 1944–1952* (Paris: Publications de la Sorbonne, 1986).

Lottmann, Herbert. *The People's Anger: Justice and Revenge in Post-Liberation France* (London: Hutchinson, 1986).

Lugard, F. D. *The Dual Mandate in British Tropical Africa* (Edinburgh and London: William Blackwood and Sons, 1922).

Marnot, René. *Ma Ville sous la botte* (Saumur: Éditions Roland, 1947).

Marrus, Michael, and Robert Paxton. *Vichy France and the Jews* (New York: Basic Books, 1981).

Martin, Jean-Clément. *La Vendée de la mémoire* (Paris: Seuil, 1989).

Maurice, Jacques. *Cinquante mois sous la botte* (Tours, 1992).

McMillan, James. "France." *Political Catholicism in Europe.* Ed. Tom Buchanan and Martin Conway (Oxford: Clarendon Press, 1996).

Melton, George F. *Darlan: Admiral and Statesman of France* (London: Praeger, 1998).

Milliat, Robert. *Le Dernier Carousel: Défense de Saumur, 1940* (Grenoble and Paris: B. Arthaud, 1943).

Milward, Alan S. *The New Order and the French Economy* (Oxford: Oxford UP, 1984; rpt. Gregg Revivals, 1993).

Molette, Charles. *Prêtres, religieux, et religieuses dans la Résistance au Nazisme, 1940–1945* (Paris: Fayard, 1995).

Montergon, Camille de. *Le Colonel François de Sauvebeuf* (Niort: Imprimerie de Saint-Denis, n.d.).

————. *Une Victime de Flossenburg: Le Colonel François de Sauvebeuf* (Niort: Imprimerie de Saint-Denis, n.d.).

Mordrel, Olier. *Breiz Atao ou Histoire et actualité du nationalisme breton* (Paris: A. Moreau, 1973).

Morin, Claude. *La Touraine sous les bombes* (Chambray-lès-Tours: CLD, 2000).

————. *Les Allemands en Touraine, 1940–1944* (Chambray-lès-Tours: CLD, 1996).

Mousseau, Léon. *Le Pont cassé: Souvenirs d'un médecin des bords de Loire* (Angers: J. Palussière, 1981).

Muel-Dreyfus, Francine. *Vichy et l'éternel féminin* (Paris: Seuil, 1996).

Nabulsi, Karma. *Traditions of War: Occupation, Resistance, and the Law* (Oxford: Oxford UP, 1999).

Nicolas, Michel. *Le Separatisme en Bretagne* (Brasparts: Éditions Beltan, 1986).

Nobécourt, Jacques. *Le Colonel de La Rocque, 1885–1946: Ou les pièges du nationalisme chrétien* (Paris: Fayard, 1996).

Noiriel, Gérard. *Workers in French Society in the Nineteenth and Twentieth Centuries* (Oxford: Berg, 1990).

Novick, Peter. *The Resistance versus Vichy: The Purge of Collaborators in Liberated France* (London: Chatto and Windus, 1968).

Oury, Dom Guy. *Dom Gabriel Sortais* (Solesmes, 1975).

Oury, Louis. *Au Soleil de la Victoire* (Pantin: Le Temps des Cerises, 1999).

————. *Le Cours des cinquante otages/Die Strasse der fünfzig Geiseln* (Saarbrücken: Geschichts Werkstatt, 1989).

————. *Rue du Roi Albert: Les otages de Nantes, Châteaubriant, et Bordeaux* (Paris: Le Temps des Cerises, 1996).

Pacquelet, Muriel. "Le Cinéma paroissial en Loire-Inférieure de 1919 à 1958." Master's thesis, University of Nantes, 1994.

Paisot-Béal, Sophie, and Roger Prévost. *Histoire des camps d'internement en Indre-et-Loire, 1940–1944*. Privately published, 1993.

Papp, Julien. "Les Pouvoirs locaux en Indre-et-Loire." Paper delivered at the IHTP conference on "Les Élites locales en France, 1935–1953," 12–13 June 1996.

Paxton, Robert. *French Peasant Fascism: Henri Dorgères's Greenshirts and the Crises of French Agriculture, 1929–1939* (New York and Oxford: Oxford UP, 1997).

Payan, Abbé André. *Maillé martyr* (Tours: Arnault et Cie, 1945).

Perouas, Louis. "Le Grand Retour de Notre Dame de Boulogne à travers la France (1943–48): Essai de renconstitution." *Annales de Bretagne et des Pays de l'Ouest* 90 (1983): 171–83. Rpt. in *Archives des Sciences Sociales des Religions* 56, no. 1 (1983): 37–59.

Perraud, P. "Électricité et défense: Rôle et importance de l'électricité dans l'exploitation des potentiels industriels durant l'Occupation par la Wehrmacht." Master's thesis, Université de Paul-Valéry, Montpellier II, 1987.

Perraud-Charmantier, André. *Le Drame du Maquis de Saffré* (Nantes: Éditions du Fleuve, 1946).

Peschanski, Denis. *Vichy 1940–1944: Contrôle et exclusion* (Paris: Complexe, 1997).

Pétain, Philippe. *Actes et Écrits*. Ed. Jacques Isorni (Paris: Fayard, 1974).

———. *Haute Cour de Justice: Le Procès du Maréchal Pétain* (Paris: Albin Michel, 1945).

Pollard, Miranda. *Reign of Virtue: Mobilizing Gender in Vichy France* (Chicago and London: University of Chicago Press, 1998).

Potier, Bernard. *Aspects de la vie économique en Maine-et-Loire sous l'Occupation allemande* (Angers: Université Catholique de l'Ouest, 1985).

Poulat, Émile. *Naissance des Prêtres ouvriers* (Paris: Casterman, 1965).

Poznanski, Renée. *Les Juifs en France pendant la Seconde Guerre Mondiale* (Paris: Hachette, 1997).

Prat, Elizabeth, and Jeannine Labussière. *Tours, cité meurtrie, juin 1940* (Chambray-lès-Tours, 1991).

Rabelais, François. *Gargantua*. Ed. Abel Lefranc. Vol. 1 of *Oeuvres* (Paris: Champion, 1913).

Rajsfus, Maurice. *La Police de Vichy: Forces de l'ordre français au service de la Gestapo* (Paris: Le Cherche-Midi, 1995).

Redier, Antoine. *Les Cadets de Saumur* (Lyon and Paris: Emmanuel Vitte, 1940).

Reynaud, Paul. *Au Coeur de la mêlée, 1930–1945* (Paris: Flammarion, 1951).

Ridel, Fernand. *Témoignages 1939–1945: Une Page d'histoire* (La Baule: Éditions des Paludiers, 1974).

Rioux, J.-P., A. Prost, and J.-P. Azéma. *Les Communistes français de Munich à Châteaubriant* (Paris: FNSP, 1987).

Rochebrune, Renaud de, and Jean-Claude Hazera. *Face aux allemands*. Vol. 1 of *Les Patrons sous l'Occupation* (Paris: Odile Jacob, 1997).

Roper, Lyndal. *Oedipus and the Devil: Witchcraft, Sexuality, and Religion in Early Modern Europe* (London and New York: Routledge, 1994).

Sainclivier, Jacqueline. "Le Pouvoir résistant (été 1944)." *Les Pouvoirs en France à la Libération*. Ed. Philippe Buton and Jean-Marie Guillon (Paris: Belin, 1944).

Scorin, Jérôme. *L'Itinéraire d'un adolescent juif de 1939 à 1945* (Nancy: Christmann, 1994).

Semelin, Jacques. *Unarmed against Hitler: Civilian Resistance in Europe, 1939–1943* (Westport and London: Praeger, 1993).

Serant, Paul. *La Bretagne et la France* (Paris: Fayard, 1971).

Sesmaisons, Yves de. *Marquise de Sesmaisons, 1898–1977: Souvenirs de l'Occupation* (Craon, 1978).

Shennan, Andrew. *Rethinking France: Plans for Renewal 1940–1946* (Oxford: Clarendon Press, 1989).

Siegried, André. *Tableau politique de la France de l'Ouest sous la Troisième République* (Paris: Armand Colin, 1964).

Sigot, Jacques. *Un Camp pour les Tsiganes . . . et les autres. Montreuil-Bellay, 1940–1945* (Éditions Wallada, 1983).

Sommer, Hubert. *Génie: Zur Bedeutungsgeschichte des Wortes von der Renaissance zur Aufklärung.* Ed. Michael Nerlich (Frankfurt am Main: Peter Lang, 1998).

Spears, Sir Edward. *Assignment to Catastrophe II* (London: Heinemann, 1954).

Tauzan, François. *Le STO en Touraine occupé, 1942–1944.* Master's thesis, University of Tours, 1996.

Tewes, Ludwig. *Frankreich in der Besatzungszeit, 1940–1943: Die Sicht deutscher Augenzeugen* (Bonn: Bouvier, 1998).

Texcier, Jean. *Conseils à l'occupé* (Paris, 1940).

Thalmann, Rita. *La Mise au pas: Idéologie et stratégie sécuritaire dans la France occupée* (Paris: Fayard, 1991).

Thorez, Maurice. *Oeuvres.* Book 5. Vol. 22 (Paris: Éditions Sociales, 1964).

Todorov, Tzvetan. *A French Tragedy: Scenes of a Civil War, Summer 1944* (Hanover: Dartmouth College, 1996).

Tourlet, E. H. *La Statue de Rabelais d'Émile Hébert: Relation des fêtes données à Chinon les premier, 2, et 3 juillet 1882 à l'occasion de l'inauguration du monument* (Chinon, 1894).

Tremblay, Hervé. *A Quédillac dans la poche: Neuf mois dans la vie quotidienne des Bouvronnais, août 1944–11 mai 1945* (Bouvron, 1995).

Umbreit, Hans. *Der Militärbefehlshaber in Frankreich, 1940–1944* (Boppard-am-Rhein, 1968).

Veillon, Dominique. *Vivre et Survivre en France, 1939–1947* (Paris: Payot, 1995).

Veillon, Dominique, and Jean-Marie Flonneau, eds. *Le Temps des restrictions en France, 1939–1949* (Paris: IHTP, 1995).

Vercors, Jean Bruller. *Le Silence de la mer* (Paris: Éditions de Minuit, 1942).

Vidal-Naquet, Pierre. *Le Trait empoisonné: Réflexions sur l'affaire Jean Moulin* (Paris: Éditions de la Decouverte, 1993).

Virgili, Fabrice, *Shorn Women: Gender and Punishment in Liberation France* (Oxford, Berg, 2002).

Vivier, Jack. *Les Instituteurs de Touraine dans la République* (Chambray-lès-Tours: CLD, 1986).

———. *Prêtres en Touraine dans la Résistance* (Chambray-lès-Tours: CLD, 1993).

Vivier, Robert. *Touraine 39–45: Histoire de l'Indre-et-Loire durant la Deuxième Guerre Mondiale* (Chambray-lès-Tours: CLD, 1990).

von Glahn, Gerhard. *The Occupation of Enemy Territory* (Minneapolis: University of Minnesota, Press, 1957).

Weber, Max. "Politics as a Vocation." *From Max Weber: Essays in Sociology.* Ed. H. H.

Werth and C. Wright Mills (London and Boston: Routledge and Kegan Paul, 1970).

Webster, Paul. *Pétain's Crime: The Full Story of French Collaboration in the Holocaust* (London: Macmillan, 1990).

Wieviorka, Annette. *Déportation ou Génocide* (Paris: Plon, 1992).

Wolton, Thierry. *Le Grand Recrutement* (Paris: Grasset, 1993).

Wylie, Laurence, ed. *Chanzeaux: A Village in Anjou* (Cambridge, Mass.: Harvard UP, 1966).

3. *Interviews*

Ancelin, Michel (Saumur), 22 June 1998

Arnoult, René (Chinon), 23 June 1998

Aron, Émile (Tours), 19 March 1997 and 24 June 1998

Audebert, Georges (Tours), 24 June 1998

Avenet, Abel and Claudine (Dierre, I-et-L), 25 June 1998

Beaumont, Paule and Louis (Daumeray, M-et-L), 20 May 1997

Bellier, Madeleine (Angers), 30 April 1997

Beugnet, Christian and Léonie (Chinon), 23 June 1998

Bossé, Francis (Grugé l'Hôpital, M-et-L), 14 April 1997

Bouche, Thérèse (Angers), 13 Dec. 1996

Boudet, Pierre (Angers), 11 Oct. 1996

Bougreau, Claude (Chinon), 23 June 1998

Canonne, Germaine (Angers), 28 April 1997

Cavigneaux, André (Avrillé, Angers), 30 April 1997

Chardonnet, André (Angers), 11 April 1997

Chauvel, André, and meeting of FNDIR (Nantes), 6 May 1997

Chedozeau, Gilbert, Mme Guitton, and Serge Martin (Maillé, I-et-L), 6 June 1997

Cohu, Lucienne (Trélazé, M-et-L), 18 April 1997

Delanoë, Édouard (Grugé l'Hôpital, M-et-L), 14 April 1997

Denis, Jacqueline and Louis (Trélazé), 18 April 1997

Despouy, Lucienne (Saint-Avertin, Tours), 9 June 1997

Geindreau, Jeanne (Saint-Pierre-Montlimart, M-et-L), 11 Nov. 1996

Gluck, Ernest (Nantes), 22 June 1997

Goxe, Odette (Angers), 14 April 1997

Grandière, Vicomte Gilles et Vicomtesse de la (La Jumellière, M-et-L), 5 May 1997

Grenouilleau, Paul (Angers), 17 April 1997

Gros, Colonel Pierre (Avrillé, Angers) 23 April 1997

Guggenheim, François (Tours), 30 June 1997

Hervé, Jacques (Joué-lès-Tours), 12 June 1997

Hervé, Pierre, Félix Boudet, Louis David, and Xavier Garçon (Saffré, L-A), 30 May 1997

Idier, Marguerite and Jeanne (Angers), 6 Nov. 1996

Jamonneau, Abbé François (Nantes), 26 May and 5 June 1997

Lallemand, Georgette (La Genevraie, M-et-L), 13 May 1997

Lancezeux, Lucie, and Huguette Robin, (Monts, l-et-L), 23 June 1998

Le Bault de la Morinière, René (Landemont, M-et-L), 7 May 1997

Le Chat, Suzanne (Ingrandes, M-et-L), 15 April 1997

Lemasson, Violette and Rémi (Belle-Beille, Angbers), 16 April 1997

Leterme, Michel (Angers), 13 May 1997

Ménard, Abbé Jacques (Tours), 2 June 1997

Ménard, Max and Jeanne (Jallais, M-et-L), 22 April 1997

Mondragon, Christian de (Nantes), 29 April 1997

Montalembert, Pierre and Yolande de (Neuilly), 9 Jan. 1999

Peltier, Robert (Le Poissonnière, M-et-L), 16 April 1997

Perruchaud, Aline (Angers), 12 Sept. 1996

Prévost, Roger (Chambray-lès-Tours), 9 June 1997

Rameau, Marinette (Charcé, M-et-L), 28 Oct. 1996

Richer, Abbé Henri (Angers), 6 June 1997

Roussel, André (Bléré, I-et-L), 25 June 1998

Saint-Seine, Yves de (Toutlemonde, M-et-L), 22 April 1997

Sauvage, Jean (Angers), 25 April 1997

Sesmaisons, Marquis Donatien and General Yves de (Nantes), 16 July 1997

Toubon, Charles (Angers), 2 June 1997

Treulier, André (Le Thoureil, M-et-L), 13 May 1997

Trudeau, Andrée (Saumur), 22 June 1998

Vivier, Jack (Tours), 16 June 1997

ACKNOWLEDGMENTS

First of all I would like to thank my family—Lucy-Jean, Rachel, Georgia, and William—who agreed to be uprooted and live in France for a year in 1996–97, to make research on this book possible. The birth of our youngest, Adam, during the stay in France meant that we all returned home the richer. Many friends made our French stay enjoyable: in particular I would like to mention Pierre-André and Monique Vincent, who were always ready to welcome and look after us in Angers.

I am grateful to the British Academy, the Leverhulme Trust, the Modern History faculty, Oxford, and Merton College, Oxford, for their generous support in funding this project.

I am indebted to my research assistant, Isabelle Goldsztejn, who labored in the Paris archives while I explored the provinces, and with whom I had a valuable exchange of ideas. The local correspondents of the Institut d'Histoire du Temps Présent—Julien Papp in Tours, Franck Liaigre in Nantes, and Marc Bergère in Angers—gave me excellent guidance in the early stages of my research. Among the numerous archivists who helped me, not least in my dealings with the French administration, I would like to thank Jacques Mourier, Elizabeth Verry, and Vivienne Miguet, Departmental Archivists respectively of Indre-et-Loire, Maine-et-Loire, and Loire-Atlantique. I would also like to thank Abbé Gérard Lefeuvre, the Diocesan Archivist of Nantes, for his wisdom and unstinting generosity.

Among local historians who advised me and supplied me with documentation I must thank above all Michel Lemesle in Angers and Louis Oury in Nantes. Others who offered me assistance and advice, and to whom I owe so much, include Émile Aron, Marcel Girard, André Bellegarde, and Marie-Paule Fresneau in and around Tours, Claude Bougreau in Chinon, Michel Ancelin in Saumur, Paul Grenouilleau, Violette Lemasson, Marinette Rameau, Aymar de Sauvebeuf, and Jean-Paul Vincent in Angers, M. Gilabet at Doué, Pierre Hervé at Saffré, Isabelle de Paysac in Versailles, and Jérôme Scorin in Nancy.

A number of colleagues and friends read and commented with great insight on various drafts of the book, and gave much encouragement. I would like to register my thanks to Philippe Burrin, Ruth Harris, Sudhir Hazareesingh, and Karma Nabulsi. Felicity Bryan, my agent, prevailed on me to write in a more accessible style and supplied constant enthusiasm and encouragement. At Macmillan Tanya Stobbs saw the possibilities of the project and Georgina Morley at Macmillan improved the manuscript and sustained me with good humor. At Metropolitan Books Sara Bershtel helped me with modifications for the American reader and Riva Hocherman oversaw the editorial process. Lastly, I would like to thank my research student Jessica Irons for her dedication and high standards in compiling the bibliography and checking the proofs.

INDEX

Made in the USA
Lexington, KY
08 March 2016